Professional
IIS 7.0

Professional
IIS 7.0

Ken Schaefer, Jeff Cochran, Scott Forsyth,
Rob Baugh, Mike Everest & Dennis Glendenning

WILEY

Wiley Publishing, Inc.

Professional IIS 7.0

Published by
Wiley Publishing, Inc.
10475 Crosspoint Boulevard
Indianapolis, IN 46256
www.wiley.com

Copyright © 2008 by Wiley Publishing, Inc., Indianapolis, Indiana

Published simultaneously in Canada

ISBN: 978-0-470-09782-3

Manufactured in the United States of America

10 9 8 7 6 5 4 3 2 1

Library of Congress Cataloging-in-Publication Data

Professional IIS 7 / Ken Schaefer ... [et al.].
    p. cm.
Includes index.
 ISBN 978-0-470-09782-3 (paper/website)
 1. Microsoft Internet information server. 2. Web servers. I. Schaefer, Ken. II. Title: Professional Internet
Information Server 7.
 TK5105.875.I57P755 2008
 005.7'1376--dc22
                         2008001369

About the Authors

Ken Schaefer is a systems engineer consultant for global systems integrator Avanade. Avanade is a joint partnership between Microsoft and Accenture and focuses on enterprise projects across the Microsoft product stack. Ken has worked with IIS for around 10 years and has been a Microsoft MVP for IIS since 2003. He has presented at numerous Microsoft Tech.Ed events across the United States, Australia, and Asia; written articles for Microsoft TechNet; and spent countless hours talking about IIS at other events, user group meetings, and road shows. He is currently an MCSE, MCDBA, MCTS, and holds a Masters in Business and Technology from UNSW. When he isn't thinking about IIS, Ken can usually be found tinkering with Active Directory, Operations Manager, SQL Server, Windows Media Center, Virtual PC…

Thank you, Julia, Sebastien, and Theo for putting up with the trials, tribulations, and late nights involved in writing a book, again. This would not have been possible without your love and support.

As the lead author, on behalf of all the authors, I'd like to thank Bob Elliot and John Sleeva and the rest of the team from Wiley for their never-ending patience whilst we put this book together.

Jeff Cochran is a Senior Network Specialist for the City of Naples, Florida, and has been employed in the computer networking industry for nearly two decades. Beginning with computer bulletin boards on a Commodore 64 in the early 1980s, he has worked with nearly every method of communication via computer since. In the early 1990s, he started the first commercial ISP in Southwest Florida, using Windows NT 3.51 systems for mail, web, and FTP servers.

Jeff is married to Zina, a self-employed graphic designer, and spends his free time remodeling a 1950s home in Naples. Although most of his personal hobbies revolve around computers, he enjoys Geocaching and collecting pinball machines, and is still addicted to Age of Empires.

Writing for this book, I must thank members of the IIS team, especially Chris, Carlos, Alexis, Mai-lan, Faith, Robert, Anil, Bilal, Eric, and Thomas. I also thank my coauthors for their suggestions and insight.

To Zina, without whom there would be no reason to write.

Scott Forsyth works for ORCS Web, Inc. as the Director of IT. ORCS Web is a Microsoft Certified Partner offering web hosting services utilizing the IIS platform for hosting of ASP.NET, SharePoint, SQL Server, Exchange and other technologies. He is a Microsoft MVP for ASP.NET, an ASP Insider and has multiple MCP certifications.

Scott is married and has two kids, Joel and Alisha, who don't work with IIS yet but do spend countless hours on the computer. When he's not in front of a computer, Scott leads a youth group at his local church, plays the drums and enjoys playing table tennis.

For my wife, Melissa, and my children, Joel and Alisha, who patiently support me in work and writing.

Rob Baugh is the VP of IT for Anres Technologies. He has been in the IT field since 1999 and has worked with IIS the entire time. He has multiple Microsoft Certified Professional certifications.

Rob is married to Stacy and they have one daughter, Emily. His passion (when away from computers) is scuba diving, so he recently relocated to Merida, Mexico to be closer to the blue waters of the Caribbean.

Thanks to my ever faithful bride, Stacy, for supporting me throughout the many late nights spent writing.

Mike Everest has had an interest in computing from the time he first laid eyes on a PC at high school in 1978. He operated a series of Bulletin Board Systems throughout the 1980s while completing his undergraduate studies and experimenting with early Internet technologies.

Mike began working with web servers in the early 1990s and established the first commercial web hosting platform in his regional hometown of Geelong, Australia. Since then, specializing in Internet infrastructure, hosting services, and ISP systems, he has participated in establishing and developing no fewer than seven technology companies, sold two, and maintains an ongoing interest in three.

Mike is delighted to have had the opportunity to contribute to this book and is more than happy to receive comments, questions, and criticisms from readers.

Special thanks to all of the IIS 7.0 team at Microsoft, for without such an excellent product we would have nothing to write about.

Dennis Glendenning (MA, MBA, MCSA+Msg, MCSE, PMP) is a Principal Systems Engineer with Avanade, where he provides design and delivery leadership for large-scale technology integration projects. Dennis's background includes graduate training, professional certifications, and a blend of technical and project management experience that spans more than 15 years. In addition to delivering technology architectures for Fortune 500 companies, Dennis has led several eCommerce infrastructure teams to leverage IIS in the public safety, insurance, and financial industries. Although he travels the United States for work, Dennis lives in Cleveland, Ohio with his wife and two children, and he revels in hiking, history, great speeches, and epic FPS PC games. Dennis can be reached at dglendenni@hotmail.com.

I would like to thank Ken Schaefer for offering the opportunity to contribute and for coordinating many tasks among the authors. John Sleeva has my thanks for doing a fantastic job editing, with much of the quality of my contributions due to John's terrific advice. Finally, Greg Molnar also has my gratitude, for giving support and accommodations, advice, and friendship during this project.

To my lovely wife and new mother, Melissa Jean, and to our amazing children, Jessica and Nicolas: May you see, do, and love all that life promises.

Credits

Executive Editor
Robert Elliott

Development Editor
John Sleeva

Technical Editor
Pierre Greborio

Production Editor
Daniel Scribner

Copy Editor
Catherine Caffrey

Editorial Manager
Mary Beth Wakefield

Production Manager
Tim Tate

Vice President and Executive Group Publisher
Richard Swadley

Vice President and Executive Publisher
Joseph B. Wikert

Project Coordinator, Cover
Lynsey Stanford

Proofreaders
Christopher M. Jones, Kate Reilly,
Corina Copp, Jeremy Bagai

Indexer
Robert Swanson

Compositors
Craig Thomas, Craig Woods
Happenstance Type-O-Rama

Contents

Contents

Contents

Contents

Contents

Contents

Contents

Introduction

Windows Server 2008 is the first update to Microsoft's server operating system in nearly five years, and among the major changes is the new Internet Information Services 7.0, which probably marks the biggest departure from previous IIS versions that we have ever seen.

Previous recent releases of IIS have concentrated on improving security and reliability and thus have mostly involved changes "under the hood." For administrators and developers, adaptation to the new products had been relatively simple.

With IIS 7.0, however, Microsoft has fundamentally changed the way the product works, with new configuration, delegated administration, and extensibility options designed to address perceived feature weakness compared to competing products. At the same time, IIS 7.0 now has new, real-time diagnostic and troubleshooting features and absorbs functionality from ASP.NET (such as caching and forms-based authentication), making this available across all requests.

With the addition of a brand-new FTP server and FastCGI support, IIS 7.0 leapfrogs its major competitors in feature and flexibility options and indicates a clear effort by Microsoft to capture more of the public-facing web server market, in addition to its existing strong presence in the corporate sphere.

For administrators and developers, the fundamental changes in the way that IIS 7.0 works, is administered, and can be extended mean that the knowledge required to fully take advantage of IIS 7.0's new features is substantially greater than in previous versions.

The authors have focused on capturing the very best of the new features in IIS 7.0 and how you can take advantage of them. The writing styles vary from chapter to chapter because some of the foremost experts on IIS 7.0 have contributed to this book. Drawing on our expertise in deployment, hosting, development, and enterprise operations, we believe that this book captures much of what today's IIS administrators need in their day-to-day work.

Who This Book Is For

This book is aimed at IIS administrators (or those who need to ramp up quickly in anticipation of having to administer IIS). What differentiates this book is that it doesn't just focus on features and how to configure them using a GUI administrative tool. Instead, we explain how features work (for example, how Kerberos authentication actually works under the covers) so that you can better troubleshoot issues when something goes wrong.

Additionally, since most administrators need to be able to automate common procedures, we have included specific chapters on programmatic administration and command-line tools as well as code snippets (using AppCmd.exe, WMI, and .NET) throughout the book.

This book covers features that many other IIS books don't touch (such as high availability and web farm scenarios, or extending IIS) and has a dedicated chapter on troubleshooting and diagnostics.

Real-life IIS administration is about people, processes, and technology. Although a technical book can't teach you much about hiring the right people, this book doesn't focus solely on technology. Operations management and monitoring (key components of good processes) are also addressed.

Overall, we think that this book provides comprehensive coverage of the real-life challenges facing IIS administrators: getting up to speed on the new features of a product, understanding how the product works under the covers, and being able to operate and manage the product effectively over the long term.

How This Book Is Structured

The book is divided into four major parts. Part I covers the new features and architecture of IIS 7.0, as well as deployment and installation considerations.

Part II discusses the basics of the new administration tools (both GUI and command-line) as well as basic administrative tasks for web sites, delegated administration, and supporting services (such as FTP, SMTP, and publishing options).

Part III introduces more advanced topics, such as extending IIS 7.0, programmatic administration, web farms and high availability, and security.

Finally, Part IV covers topics that go beyond the initial understanding of the new feature set. We cover topics that administrators will need on an ongoing basis, such as operations management, performance monitoring and tuning, and diagnostics and troubleshooting.

What You Need to Use This Book

Although IIS 7.0 ships in both Vista and Windows Server 2008, certain functionality (such as load balancing) is available only in the server edition. Because the full functionality of IIS 7.0 is available in Windows Server 2008, the authors have focused on that product for this book.

For IIS 7.0 extensibility, Microsoft Visual Studio 2008 has been used throughout the book; however, any IDE suitable for .NET development can be used for implementing the code samples presented.

Conventions

To help you get the most from the text and keep track of what's happening, we've used several conventions throughout the book.

Sidebar

> **Boxes like this one hold important, not-to-be forgotten information that is directly relevant to the surrounding text.**

Tips, hints, tricks, and asides to the current discussion are offset and placed in italics like this.

As for styles in the text:

❑ We *highlight* new terms and important words when we introduce them.

❑ We show keyboard strokes like this: *Ctrl+A.*

❑ We show file names, URLs, and code within the text like so: `persistence.properties`.

❑ We present code in two different ways:

```
In code examples we highlight new and important code with a gray background.
```

```
The gray highlighting is not used for code that's less important in the present
context, or has been shown before.
```

Source Code

As you work through the examples in this book, you may choose either to type in all the code manually or to use the source code files that accompany the book. All the source code used in this book is available for download at `www.wrox.com`. Once at the site, simply locate the book's title (either by using the Search box or by using one of the title lists), and click the Download Code link on the book's detail page to obtain all the source code for the book.

Because many books have similar titles, you may find it easiest to search by ISBN; this book's ISBN is 978-0-470-09782-3.

Once you download the code, just decompress it with your favorite compression tool. Alternately, you can go to the main Wrox code download page at `www.wrox.com/dynamic/books/download.aspx` to see the code available for this book and all other Wrox books.

Errata

We make every effort to ensure that there are no errors in the text or in the code. However, no one is perfect, and mistakes do occur. If you find an error in one of our books, like a spelling mistake or a faulty piece of code, we would be very grateful for your feedback. By sending in errata you may save another reader hours of frustration, and at the same time you will be helping us provide even higher quality information.

To find the errata page for this book, go to `www.wrox.com`, and locate the title using the Search box or one of the title lists. Then, on the book details page, click the Book Errata link. On this page, you can view all errata that have been submitted for this book and posted by Wrox editors. A complete book list including links to each book's errata is also available at `www.wrox.com/misc-pages/booklist.shtml`.

If you don't spot "your" error on the Book Errata page, go to `www.wrox.com/contact/techsupport.shtml` and complete the form there to send us the error you have found. We'll check the information and, if appropriate, post a message to the book's errata page and fix the problem in subsequent editions of the book.

p2p.wrox.com

For author and peer discussion, join the P2P forums at p2p.wrox.com. The forums are a Web-based system for you to post messages relating to Wrox books and related technologies and interact with other readers and technology users. The forums offer a subscription feature to e-mail you topics of interest of your choosing when new posts are made to the forums. Wrox authors, editors, other industry experts, and your fellow readers are present on these forums.

At http://p2p.wrox.com, you will find several different forums that will help you not only as you read this book, but also as you develop your own applications. To join the forums, just follow these steps:

1. Go to p2p.wrox.com and click the Register link.
2. Read the terms of use and click Agree.
3. Complete the required information to join as well as any optional information you wish to provide and click Submit.
4. You will receive an e-mail with information describing how to verify your account and complete the joining process.

> *You can read messages in the forums without joining P2P, but in order to post your own messages, you must join.*

Once you join, you can post new messages and respond to messages other users post. You can read messages at any time on the Web. If you would like to have new messages from a particular forum e-mailed to you, click the "Subscribe to this Forum" icon by the forum name in the forum listing.

For more information about how to use the Wrox P2P, be sure to read the P2P FAQs for answers to questions about how the forum software works as well as many common questions specific to P2P and Wrox books. To read the FAQs, click the FAQ link on any P2P page.

Part I: Introduction and Deployment

Background on IIS and New Features in IIS 7.0

Microsoft's Internet Information Services (IIS) has been around for more than a decade, from its first incarnation in Windows NT 3.51 to the current release of IIS 7.0 on the Windows Server 2008 and Vista platforms. It has evolved from providing basic service as an HTTP server, as well as additional Internet services such as Gopher and WAIS, to a fully configurable application services platform integrated with the operating system.

IIS 7.0 is a dramatic change in the way IIS is configured and managed. Modularity, granularity, and interoperability are the guiding factors across the entire product, from setup to security, management to automation. Integrated heavily into the operating system, IIS 7.0 benefits from the improvements in the Windows Server 2008 operating system but IIS has been re-engineered to meet the demands of a true application platform.

This chapter will provide you with an overview of the changes in IIS 7.0 as well as a sampling of some of the new technologies. If you are familiar with IIS 6.0, you will want to skim through this chapter for changes before digging into future chapters for specifics. If you are new to IIS, this chapter will provide an introduction to the features in IIS 7.0 and provide you with a basis for understanding future chapters. And if you're the kind of reader who just wants to skip to the part that applies to your immediate needs, this chapter can help you figure out in what area those needs will lie.

IIS Versions 1.0 to 4.0

IIS was released with Service Pack 3 for Windows NT 3.51, as a set of services providing HTTP, Gopher, and WAIS functionality. Although the functions were there, most users chose alternates from third-party vendors such as O'Reilly's Website or Netscape's server. Although these services had been available for years with the various flavors of UNIX operating systems, native Internet services for Windows were mostly an afterthought, with little integration with the Windows operating system.

With the advent of Windows NT 4.0, IIS also matured in version 2.0. The most notable improvement in IIS version 2.0 was closer integration with the Windows NT operating system, taking advantage of Windows security accounts and providing integrated administration through a management console similar to many other Windows services. IIS 2.0 introduced support for HTTP Host headers, which allowed multiple sites to run on a single IP address, and aligned Microsoft's IIS development with NCSA standards, providing for NCSA common log formats and NCSA-style map files. IIS 2.0 also introduced a web browser interface for management, and content indexing through Microsoft's Index Server.

IIS version 3.0 was introduced with Windows NT Service Pack 3 and introduced the world to ASP (Active Server Pages) and Microsoft's concept of an *application server*. A precursor to the ASP.NET environment, ASP (now referred to as *classic ASP*) is a server-side scripting environment for the creation of dynamic web pages. Using VBScript, JScript or any other active scripting engine, programmers finally had a viable competitor to CGI and scripting technologies available on non-Microsoft platforms, such as Perl.

IIS 4.0, available in the NT Option Pack, introduced ASP 2.0, an object-based version of ASP that included six built-in objects to provide standardized functionality in ASP pages. IIS 4.0 was the last version of IIS that could be downloaded and installed outside of the operating system.

IIS 5.0 and 5.1

With the release of Windows 2000, IIS became integrated with the operating system. Version numbers reflected the operating system, and there were no upgrades to IIS available without upgrading the operating system. IIS 5.0 shipped with Windows 2000 Server versions and Windows 2000 Professional, and IIS version 5.1 shipped with Windows XP Professional, but not Windows XP Home Edition. For all essential functions, IIS 5.0 and IIS 5.1 are identical, differing only slightly as needed by the changes to the operating system.

With Windows 2000 and IIS 5.0, IIS became a service of the operating system, meant to be the base for other applications, especially for ASP applications. The IIS 5.0 architecture served static content, ISAPI functions, or ASP scripts, with ASP script processing handed off to a script engine based on the file extension. Using file extensions to determine the program that handles the file has always been a common part of Windows functionality, and in the case of ASP processing, the speed of serving pages was increased by the automatic handoff of ASP scripts directly to the ASP engine, bypassing the static content handler. This architecture has endured in IIS to the current version.

IIS 6.0

IIS 6.0 shipped with Windows Server 2003 editions and Windows XP Professional 64bit edition, which was built on the Windows Server 2003 Service Pack 1 code base. IIS 6.0 was identical among operating system versions, but there were restrictions or expansions depending on the version of Server 2003 under which IIS was running. For example, Server 2003 Web Edition would only run IIS and a few ancillary services; it could not be used to run Microsoft SQL Server. On the other end of the spectrum, only the Enterprise and Data Center versions of Server 2003 included clustering technology.

Operating system changes also expanded the capabilities of IIS as an application server. Native XML Web Services appeared in Server 2003. Process-independent session states made web farms easier to configure and manage, allowing session states to be stored outside the application for redundancy and failover. Web farms also became easier with Server 2003's improved Network Load-Balancing features, such as the NLB Manager, which provided a single management point for NLB functions.

Secure by Default

Windows Server 2003 and IIS 6.0 shipped in a secure state, with IIS no longer installed by default. Even when IIS was installed, the default installation would serve only static HTML pages; all dynamic content was locked down. Managed through Web Service Extensions, applications such as ASP and ASP.NET had to be specifically enabled, minimizing default security holes with unknown services open to the world.

IIS 6.0 also ran user code under a low privilege account, Network Service, which had few privileges on the server outside of the IIS processes and the web-site hierarchy. Designed to reduce the damage exposure from rogue code, access to virtual directories and other resources had to be specifically enabled by the administrator for the Network Service account.

IIS 6.0 also allowed delegation for the authentication process; thus administrators and programmers could further restrict account access. Passport authentication was also included with IIS 6.0, although in real-world use, it never found widespread favor among administrators. Kerberos authentication, on the other hand, allowed secure communication within an Active Directory domain and solved many remote resource permission issues.

IIS 6.0 also would serve only specific file requests, by default not allowing execution of command-line code or even the transfer of executable files. Unless the administrator assigned a specific MIME type to be served, IIS would return a 404 error to the request, reporting the file not found. Earlier versions of IIS included a wildcard mapping and would serve any file type.

Request Processing

IIS 6.0 changed the way IIS processed requests, eliminating what had been a major performance hurdle in scaling prior IIS versions to serve multiple sites. IIS 6.0 used the Http.sys listener to receive requests, and then handed them off to worker processes to be addressed. These worker processes were isolated to application pools, and the administrator could assign application pools to specific sites and applications. This meant that many more requests could be handled simultaneously, and it also provided for an isolated architecture in cases of error. If a worker process failed, the effects would not be seen outside the application pool, providing stability across the server's sites. In addition, worker processes could be assigned a processor affinity, allowing multiprocessor systems to split the workload.

Additional Features

As did its predecessors, IIS 6.0 included additional features and functionality. Some internal features, such as HTTP compression and kernel mode caching, increased performance of the web server and applications served from it. Other features affected configuration, such as the move to an XML metabase, or stability, such as being able to configure individual application pools and isolate potential application failures. Still others added or expanded utility and ancillary functions, such as the improved FTP services or the addition of POP services to the existing SMTP service.

HTTP Compression

IIS 6.0 extended HTTP compression over the minimal compression allowed in previous versions. The HTTP 1.1 specification includes HTTP compression, and IIS 6.0 supported it for both static and dynamic content. Available in IIS 5.0 as an ISAPI add-on for the entire site, HTTP compression in IIS 6.0 became an integrated feature granularly controllable down to the specific file.

Kernel Mode and Persistent Caching

IIS 6.0 added a kernel mode cache to increase performance for dynamic content. In previous versions, static content was cached and served from cache whenever possible, but in IIS 6.0 caching was expanded to include dynamic content. In addition, whereas ASP templates were formerly cached in memory when allocated, IIS 6.0 added a persistent cache so that de-allocated templates were written to disk for future reallocation, as needed. Caching heuristics were also used to determine what to cache and when.

XML Metabase

The metabase, where IIS configuration settings are stored, was a binary file prior to IIS 6.0. Changed to an XML file, the metabase in IIS 6.0 could be edited while the site was active, and, although many functions wouldn't change until IIS was recycled, changes were in plain text. The XML metabase in IIS 6.0 was unstructured and not well documented though, and several functions still resided in registry settings, all of which gets changed in IIS 7.0.

Application Pools

IIS 6.0 changed the way applications behaved in memory, isolating applications into memory pools. Administrators could configure separate memory pools for separate applications, thus preventing a faulty application from crashing other applications outside its memory pool. This is particularly important in any shared web server environment, especially with ASP.NET applications.

FTP Service

The FTP service grew up in IIS 6.0, providing for greater security and separation of accounts through a new isolation mode using either Active Directory or local Windows accounts. Using Windows accounts or Active Directory accounts, users could be restricted to their own available FTP locations without resorting to naming the home directories the same as the FTP accounts. In addition, users were prevented from traversing above their home directories and seeing what other accounts may exist on the server. Even without NTFS permissions to the content, security in FTP before IIS 6.0 was still compromised because a user could discover other valid user accounts on the system.

The FTP service that ships with Windows Server 2008 is exactly the same as shipped in Server 2003. However, the Microsoft IIS development team is also shipping a new FTP server that includes many of the enhancements requested over the years. This server ships as a free download from www.iis.net, *as will many supported and unsupported tools. For more about configuring FTP, see Chapter 10, "Configuring Other Services."*

SMTP and POP Services

The SMTP service in Windows Server 2003 didn't change much from previous versions, allowing for greater flexibility and security but not altering the core SMTP functions. Most administrators would not use the SMTP service in IIS for anything other than outbound mail, instead relying on third-party servers or Microsoft's Exchange Server for receiving and distributing mail. But the addition of a POP3 service in Server 2003 allowed a rudimentary mail server configuration, useful for testing or small mail domains. Although SMTP can be used to transfer mail, most mail clients such as Microsoft Outlook rely on the POP3 or IMAP protocols to retrieve mail, which was unavailable without additional products until Windows Server 2003 and IIS 6.0.

IIS 7.0 Versions

Although there is really only a single version of IIS 7.0, the availability and capabilities vary with the choice of operating system. Because IIS 7.0 is tied to the operating system, as were all versions of IIS since IIS 4.0, it is not available on operating systems prior to Vista or Windows Server 2008. As in Windows XP, the workstation operating systems have limited IIS functionality or no functionality at all. Unlike in Windows XP, Vista versions have no concurrent HTTP connection limitations but instead use concurrent request processing limitations. In XP, reaching a maximum concurrent HTTP connection limit would result in IIS returning a 403.9 result code (too many users), while a request limitation merely queues requests in the order received. The end result is slower response, but no errors.

Some Windows Server 2008 versions also have limitations that affect IIS 7.0. Although IIS 7.0 is included with no limitations in all server versions, the server version itself may have limitations in use. For example, if you install Windows Server 2008 Core Edition, IIS 7.0 can be installed, but there is no GUI configuration application. This version of Windows does not have the .NET Framework available; thus, no managed code can be run on the server.

Windows Server 2008 Web Edition has no functional limits to IIS, but only supports three role services: Web Server, Windows Media Server and Sharepoint Services – it cannot be used to host a Domain Controller, or other types of roles. The following table shows which versions of Windows Vista and Windows Server 2008 have IIS 7.0 and what the limitations are.

Windows Version	IIS 7.0 Included	Limitations
Vista Starter Edition	No	No IIS functions available.
Vista Home Basic Edition	No	Contains some IIS functions, such as HTTP processing, but cannot be used as a web server.

Continued

Windows Version	IIS 7.0 Included	Limitations
Vista Home Premium Edition	Yes	Limited to three concurrent requests; no FTP server.
Vista Business Edition	Yes	Limited to 10 concurrent requests.
Vista Enterprise Edition	Yes	Limited to 10 concurrent requests.
Vista Ultimate Edition	Yes	Limited to 10 concurrent requests.
Vista Home Basic N Edition[1]	No	Contains some IIS functions, such as HTTP processing, but cannot be used as a web server.
Vista Business N Edition	Yes	Limited to 10 concurrent requests.
Server 2008 Core	Yes	No GUI management interface and no .NET Framework.
Server 2008 Web Edition	Yes	Supports Web Server, SharePoint, and Windows Media Server roles.
Server 2008 Standard Edition	Yes	None

1 The N editions of Windows Vista are for release in the European Union and do not include an embedded Windows Media Player.

IIS 7.0 Features

IIS 7.0 is a ground-up rewrite of IIS 6.0, designed as an integrated web application platform. Integration with the ASP.NET framework combined with fully exposed APIs for complete extensibility of the platform and management interfaces make IIS 7.0 a programmer's dream. Security that includes delegation of configuration and a complete diagnostic suite with request tracing and advanced logging satisfies the administrator's desires.

While the most substantial change in IIS 7.0 may be the integration of ASP.NET into the request pipeline, the extensibility of IIS 7.0, configuration delegation and the use of XML configuration files, request tracing and diagnostics, and the new administration tools are all welcome changes from previous versions of IIS.

Unlike previous versions of IIS, the modular design of IIS 7.0 allows for easy implementation of custom modules and additional functionality. This increased functionality can come from in-house development, third-party sources, or even Microsoft. Since these modules and additional programs can be plugged into IIS at any time, without changing core operating system functions, the Microsoft IIS development team can ship additional supported and unsupported modules outside of Microsoft's standard service pack process. The bottom line is that you get what you need faster. Microsoft's web site at www.iis.net is the source for these additional downloads.

Integrated Request Pipeline

One of the most radical changes in IIS 7.0 is its close integration with ASP.NET and the ASP.NET processes. There is a unified event pipeline in IIS 7.0. This pipeline merges the existing two separate IIS and ASP.NET pipelines that existed in IIS 6.0 and earlier. ASP.NET HTTP modules that previously only listened for events within the ASP.NET pipeline can now be used for any request. For backwards compatibility, a Classic pipeline mode exists, which emulates the separate IIS and ASP.NET pipeline model from IIS 6.0

In the IIS 6.0 model, an HTTP request first would be checked for the required authentication and then passed on through the pipeline. The request would be evaluated for any ISAPI filters that had been installed, such as processing by URLScan; the cache was checked to see if the request already existed; and if the request could not be served from the cache, the file extension was evaluated to determine the appropriate handler for the request. For example, if the extension was .SHTM, the server-side includes process was invoked, additional code was inserted in the page being served, and then that page was processed as an HTML request and sent along the pipeline, the response was logged, and eventually the requested page was returned to the browser.

If that requested file was an ASP.NET file with an .ASPX extension, then the process grew even more complicated, as shown in Figure 1-1. The request was shunted to the ASPNET_ISAPI.DLL and began a process through the ASP.NET pipeline. The request was again evaluated for authentication and processed for ASP.NET caching; the appropriate ASP.NET handler was determined; and the request was processed, cached, logged, and handed back to the Http.sys pipeline for completion and serving to the requesting browser.

This process occurred because the architecture consisted of a single, monolithic DLL with all the components loaded. ISAPI extensions were also single DLLs, as were any CGI processes, and each had to be loaded in memory and each request processed through the same DLL. IIS 6.0 allowed application pools and separate implementations of the Http.sys process, which increased overall performance, but there was no way to tune the core server operations themselves.

In IIS 7.0, there is a single, unified pipeline, as shown in Figure 1-2. Forms authentication and role management from ASP.NET are part of the authentication and authorization process; thus a request is authenticated a single time. In IIS 7.0, all requests can be processed through the ASP.NET Forms authentication module, not just those requests for files ending in an .ASPX extension. A request for www.domain1.com/images/myimage.gif will pass through the ASP.NET Forms authentication process, and if an authentication constraint in the web.config prevents serving that file or folder, unauthorized users will be unable to view or download the image. Requests now pass through the pipeline and exit, served to the requesting browser, without having to branch into ISAPI processes like ASP.NET. Although the ISAPI handlers exist for compatibility with existing code, the request doesn't need to be processed through ISAPI, and you don't even need to load the handlers if you don't need the compatibility for legacy code. Programmers may find themselves moving away from ISAPI now that the more familiar managed code of ASP.NET is available to meet the same needs.

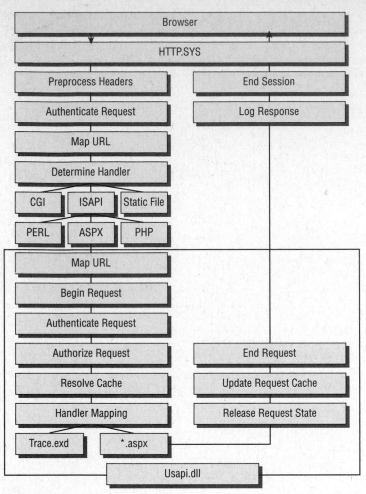

Figure 1-1

Within the IIS 7.0 pipeline, each process is handled by an individual component. These components can be specifically loaded for those sites that need them, and left out of the pipeline for sites and applications that do not. The components are configurable at the application, site, and server levels, and the ability to configure components can be delegated at any of those levels. In addition, custom components can be inserted into the pipeline, and even the order of components in the pipeline can be rearranged — for example, triggering a log trace at the start of the request and writing that log trace to a file as the request finishes processing. The order of execution is simply the order of the components in the configuration file. Components and their functions, as well as programming your own components, are covered in later chapters.

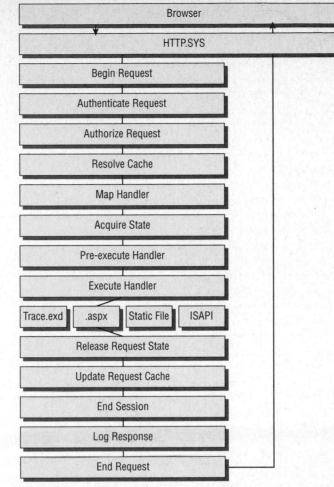

Figure 1-2

Configurability

Another and more visible change is the integration of IIS configuration into the same process used for configuring ASP.NET applications. Gone are the IIS registry settings, and the metabase that has been the repository of IIS configurations in previous versions has been replaced by XML-based configuration files that store both IIS and ASP.NET settings. This integration not only erases the line between ASP.NET applications and the application server on which they run, but it also allows for better configurability and easier deployment of both sites and applications. It also makes deployment across multiple systems in web farms more straightforward and allows for extensibility of the configurations. IIS 7.0 introduces the concept of shared configuration, wherein multiple web servers can point to the same physical file for configuration, making deploying configuration changes to web farms nearly instantaneous.

IIS 7.0 now stores settings in a new applicationHost.config file. Additionally, IIS 7.0 configuration options for individual websites or web applications can be stored in web.config files alongside ASP.NET settings, in a new system.webServer section.

Using applicationHost.config

The `applicationHost.config` file, new in IIS 7.0, stores IIS configurations for both the web server and the process model. Global configurations are now stored in the `%windir%\system32\inetsrv` folder in `applicationHost.config`. This file has two primary sections:

- ❏ `system.applicationHost` — Contains the configurations for the site, application, virtual directory, and application pools.
- ❏ `system.webServer` — Contains the rest of the settings and the global defaults.

Configurations by URL location can also be in `applicationHost.config` or in the `web.config` files for those locations. This allows administrators to set location defaults on the server, while developers can be allowed to override those settings as needed. These settings are inherited by the `web.config` files at both the root and application levels. This becomes important in the delegation of settings, since the IIS administrator can allow developers control over settings in a very granular manner at the application level, while retaining control for the site level.

The `applicationHost.config` file can be used to change the characteristics of an IIS server or site after IIS has been installed. For example, if you choose to use Windows authentication in an IIS site, you can use the IIS Manager to add Windows authentication, similar to the manner required with previous versions of IIS. Or you can use the following code within the `applicationHost.config` file to accomplish the same task for the site named *MyWebSite*:

```
<location path="MyWebSite">
    <system.webServer>
        <security>
            <authentication>
                <windowsAuthentication/>
            </authentication>
        </security>
    </system.webServer>
</location>
```

Similarly, adding ASP to a site is as simple as

```
<system.webServer>
    <asp/>
</system.webServer>
```

Configuring application pools is as easy as

```
<system.applicationHost>
    <applicationPools>
        <applicationPoolDefaults>
            <processModel
                userName="Site1AppPoolUser"
                password="Passw0rd"
            />
        </applicationPoolDefaults>
        <add name="Site1AppPool"/>
    </applicationPools>
</system.applicationHost>
```

There are two great benefits to this new configuration style in IIS 7.0. The first is that by not using the registry for configuration, deploying a site and applications can be done by using XCopy to transfer both content and configuration settings. This makes deployment across web farms far easier than trying to export/import metabase settings. It also speeds deployment to remote servers and provides for simplified customer installations of custom web-site applications that include specific web-site configurations.

The second benefit to this process is that developers can be allowed to modify the configuration files for their applications, determining the IIS configuration requirements necessary. This modification can be delegated so that required settings cannot be changed, and the settings are hierarchical, thus server settings cascade to the site and on to the application level, pending modifications allowed at lower levels. Developers accustomed to using configuration files for their applications need not learn IIS administration, and administrators can allow developers the flexibility they need while still maintaining overall control.

Extensible Configuration Schemas

IIS 7.0 configurations can be extended quite easily with the new configuration model. Suppose you want to create a new module for IIS. You would need to point to the module's DLL in the `<globalModules>` section of the `applicationHost.config` file and declare the module in either the `applicationHost.config` or the appropriate `web.config` file. Extending the configuration schema for your new module is as simple as creating the schema file in the `inetsrv\config\schema` folder on the system. Getting IIS to recognize and use the schema is done by adding a section for the module under the `<configSections>` section of `applicationHost.config`.

For example, you might add the following to the `<globalModules>` section:

```
<globalModules>
  <add name="MyNewModule" image="c:\modules\MyNewModule.dll" />
  ....
</global Modules>
```

The following would need to be added to the `<modules>` section of the `applicationHost.config` file or to the `web.config` file for the individual site in which the module would be used:

```
<modules>
  <add name="MyNewModule" />
  ....
</modules>
```

Then you would need to create a new schema file, `MyNewModule.xml`, in the `inetsrv\config\schema` folder for your new module:

```
<configSchema>
  <sectionSchema name="MyNewModule">
    <attribute name="enabled" type="bool" defaultValue="false" />
    <attribute name="message" type="string" defaultValue="Hello World!" />
  </sectionSchema>
</configSchema>
```

Finally, you need to register the section on the system in `applicationHost.config`, as follows:

```
<configSections>
```

```
      <section name="MyNewModule" />
      ....
</configSections>
```

With these simple changes to the configuration files, you've added the custom module MyNewModule to IIS, with its own custom schema.

Componentization

Extensibility doesn't only apply to configurations. Because of the changes to the request processing pipeline, the core server itself is extensible, using both native and managed code. This extensibility comes from the componentization of the core IIS functions. Instead of having to work with ISAPI filters to modify the request process, you can now inject your own components directly into the processing pipeline. These components can be your own code, third-party utilities and components, and existing Microsoft core components. This means that if you don't like Microsoft's Windows authentication process, you can not only choose to use forms authentication on all files, but also you can choose to bypass all built-in authentication and roll your own. This also means that if you don't need to process classic ASP files, you can simply not load that component. Unlike in previous versions, where components were loaded into memory in a single DLL, you can reduce the memory footprint of IIS 7.0 by not loading what you don't need.

Security

Componentization also increases the already strong security that existed in IIS 6.0. A perennial complaint against Microsoft had always been that IIS installed by default and that all services were active by default. IIS 6.0 and Server 2003 reversed that course — almost nothing was installed by default, and even when you did install it, the majority of components were disabled by default. To enable ASP.NET, you had to choose to allow ASP.NET as a web service extension. Classic ASP had to be enabled separately, as did third-party CGI application processors such as Perl or PHP.

With the exception of third-party software, though, IIS 6.0 still loaded all the services into memory — it just loaded them as disabled. For example, if you didn't want to use Windows authentication, as would be the case if you were using your own authentication scheme, you could choose not to enable it, but the code still resided in memory. Similarly, default IIS 6.0 installations were locked down to processing static HTML files, a good choice from a security standpoint. But what if you were never going to use static HTML files in your application or site? In IIS 7.0, you have the option of never loading the code in the first place.

> *This book devotes three chapters to security-related issues. In Chapter 13, securing your server is discussed. In Chapter 14, authentication and authorization are covered. Finally, in Chapter 15, SSL, and TLS are discussed. General Windows and network security precautions are not a major part of this book, but remember that IIS doesn't operate in a vacuum. Security risks need to be mitigated in all areas of your network infrastructure as well as all applications on your servers. A SQL Server breach won't technically be a compromise of your IIS security, but if the server is compromised, it really doesn't matter that it wasn't an IIS configuration, does it?*

Minimal Installation

IIS 7.0 continues the tradition of its predecessor with minimal installation the default. IIS is not installed with the default operating system install, and a basic install only selects those options needed for serving static HTML files. The installation GUI for IIS 6.0 allowed a choice of eight different options, including installing FTP, whereas IIS 7.0's setup allows for more than 40 options. This granularity of setup reduces the memory footprint of IIS 7.0, but more importantly, it reduces the security footprint as well. In IIS 6.0, a component such as CGI might never be used, but the code was still present in the core DLL. That means that a security exploit discovered in the CGI code will affect all IIS 6.0 installations, regardless of whether they use CGI. It also means that patches for the CGI code would need to be applied, even if you didn't run CGI.

The default installation of IIS 7.0 installs components needed for static HTML content, along with default documents, directory browsing, HTTP errors, and redirection. It also adds .NET extensibility for module extensions, as well as basic logging and tracing functions and request filtering (similar to the functionality provided by URLScan in previous versions), HTTP compression for static content, and the administration console. This means that, similar to IIS 6.0, a default installation can serve static content, with little other functionality.

Figure 1-3 shows the default installation options, enabling static content and very little else. Additional services, such as ASP.NET, can be installed either at installation or through configuration files. By leaving out services you don't need, the reduced amount of code provides for a reduced attack footprint for the overall installation. Installation options are covered in Chapter 4.

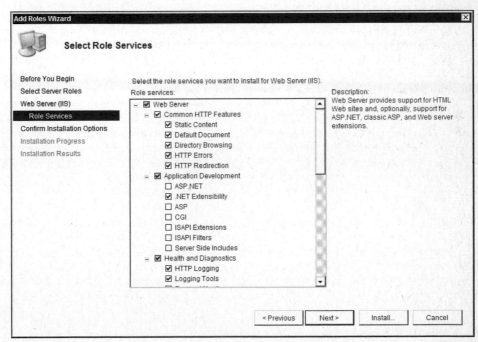

Figure 1-3

Management Delegation

Management of IIS in previous versions meant either granting local administrator privileges to the user or working through WMI and ADSI options to directly manage the site configurations. The only other option was for developers to work through the IIS administrators to change configurations — an option that could often be frustrating for both administrators and programmers. IIS 7.0 changes this through delegation of administration permissions at the server, site, and application levels.

In IIS 7.0, configuration options can be delegated in a very granular fashion. By default, most IIS settings are locked down and cannot be configured below the `applicationHost.config` file. You will see settings similar to this in the default file:

```
<sectionGroup name="system.applicationHost" type="…">
    <section name="applicationPools" overrideModeDefault="Deny" />
</sectionGroup>
```

To allow configuration delegation for a specific site, you would add a `<location>` element for that site, allowing the configuration files for the site to override the default settings in the `applicationHost.config` file. The code would be similar to

```
<location path="MyWebSite" overrideMode="Allow">
    <system.webServer>
        <asp />
    </system.webServer>
</location>
```

In a default installation, all IIS features are locked down except for HTTP, HTTP redirects, default documents, and directory browsing. All ASP.NET configurations are unlocked by default. In addition to delegations allowed within the configuration files, the configuration files themselves can be controlled through NTFS permissions. By setting ACLs on the files, an administrator can prevent unauthorized access to the files.

For an even more granular locking of specific elements in IIS, you can use attribute locking. Using `overrideMode`, an administrator can allow specific sites to be managed through configuration files by a developer. Attribute locking can be used to lock a specific attribute or element of the configuration while using `overrideMode="Allow"` on a web site. Developers can still override configurations at a local level, but the administrator maintains control of attributes they don't want changed. For example, to allow a developer to configure IIS options except for Windows authentication for the site MySite, you could use the following code in your `applicationHost.config` file to force the values required for Windows authentication:

```
<location path="MySite" overrideMode="Allow">
    <system.webServer>
      <security>
        <authentication>
          <windowsAuthentication enabled="true" lockAttributes="enabled">
            <providers>
              <add value="Negotiate" />
              <add value="NTLM" />
            </providers>
          </windowsAuthentication>
        </authentication>
```

```
      </security>
    </system.webServer>
  </location>
```

To allow the same developer on the same site to enable or disable Windows authentication but not to change the `providers` element, you could use

```
<location path="MySite" overrideMode="Allow">
  <system.webServer>
    <security>
      <authentication>
        <windowsAuthentication enabled="true" lockElements="providers">
          <providers>
            <add value="Negotiate" />
            <add value="NTLM" />
          </providers>
        </windowsAuthentication>
      </authentication>
    </security>
  </system.webServer>
</location>
```

Feature delegation extends to the GUI administration tool as well. At the server level, for example, you can configure which features can be changed by lower-level administrators using the Administration tool. You can configure administrators for any level in the Administration tool, and those administrators have access to features at or below their level. For example, server administrators can configure any site, whereas a site administrator can configure only features within that site.

Delegation of management functions is something administrators should consider carefully when planning an IIS 7.0 deployment in their organization. In Chapter 3, we discuss planning deployments. Chapter 6 covers using the `applicationHost.config` *file. Chapter 9 describes administration delegation.*

Unified Authentication and Authorization

In IIS 7.0, the authentication and authorization process merges the traditional IIS authentication options with ASP.NET options. This allows administrators and developers to use ASP.NET authentication across all files, folders, and applications in a site.

In IIS 6.0 and previous versions, controlling access to an Adobe Acrobat (PDF) file was difficult through ASP.NET authentication schemes. You would need to enable Windows authentication or basic authentication on the web site, folder, or file and create a Windows account to have access to the file. Then you would need to require the user to provide valid credentials for that Windows account, even if he or she already had logged into your ASP.NET application, to be able to access that PDF file. The alternative was to use impersonation in ASP.NET to access the file using the ASP.NET process account — all to prevent someone from opening the PDF file by pasting the direct URL into their browser. Options involving streaming the content from a protected location were just as cumbersome, and redirecting files to be processed by the ASP.NET DLL was even more problematic.

In IIS 7.0, using ASP.NET authentication no longer requires the file to be processed as an ASPX extension; thus file extensions of all types can be secured with Forms authentication or any other ASP.NET method. This reduces the requirement for Windows Client Access Licenses (CALs) to provide access control, which was prohibitive in an Internet environment. It also allows, with the extensibility of the pipeline components, developers to create their own authentication schemes and easily apply them to any file or folder on the server.

Using ASP.NET Forms authentication for content other than ASP.NET is covered in Chapter 14, "Authentication and Authorization."

Request Filtering

IIS 7.0 includes request filtering as a standard function. While some of this ability was included in the unsupported URLScan tool released for IIS 5.0, request filtering takes this concept even further with hidden namespaces, where a particular section of a URL can be hidden and not served. Making the transition from using URLScan to request filtering is easy.

For example, in URLScan you could control serving specific file extensions using the `AllowExtension` or `DenyExtension` configurations. Request filtering uses the same allow or deny concept. For example, to allow all files to be served except for Microsoft Word files with a .DOC extension, you could use

```
<configuration>
    <system.webServer>
        <security>
            <requestFiltering>
                <fileExtensions allowUnlisted="true" >
                    <add fileExtension=".doc" allowed="false" />
                </fileExtensions>
            </requestFiltering>
        </security>
    </system.webServer>
</configuration>
```

To allow only .ASPX files in a request, you could use

```
<configuration>
    <system.webServer>
        <security>
            <requestFiltering>
                <fileExtensions allowUnlisted="false" >
                    <add fileExtension=".aspx" allowed="true" />
                </fileExtensions>
            </requestFiltering>
        </security>
    </system.webServer>
</configuration>
```

Denying access to a folder such as the BIN folder so that your DLLs could not be directly requested is handled by a new option called `hiddenNamespaces`. In URLScan, you could deny a URL sequence, so "BIN" could not appear in a URL, but that would affect requests for both `www.domain1.com/bin` and `www.domain1.com/binder/legalfiles`. With request filtering, you can hide the BIN folder by using

```
<configuration>
    <system.webServer>
        <security>
```

```
        <requestFiltering>
          <hiddenNamespaces>
            <add hiddenDirectory="BIN" />
          </hiddenNamespaces>
        </requestFiltering>
      </security>
    </system.webServer>
  </configuration>
```

Using `allow` or `deny` in request filtering doesn't override any MIME-type settings or other security; it simply evaluates the HTTP request and allows it to be processed or rejects it based on filtering rules. If your Word documents were protected from being served by ACLs, they would be denied even without using request filtering, except the request would have to be processed to the step where access is denied instead of returning a failed result code immediately. The IIS result codes have been modified to indicate whether a request has been denied by request filtering.

Remote Management

Whilst IIS could be remotely managed in previous versions using the IIS Manager over RPC, this wasn't firewall friendly. A HTML based management option also existed, however this didn't allow management of all IIS features. In both cases, users were required to be in the local Administrators group on the machine.

IIS 7.0 introduces a new remote Management Service that permits the IIS Manager tool to administer remote IIS 7.0 installations over HTTPS. By utilizing the new delegation features in IIS 7.0, remote users can be given access to the entire server, a single website or even just a single web application. Additionally, features that have not been delegated will not be visible to the end user when connecting remotely.

Lastly, the Remote Management service introduces the concept of IIS Users. These user accounts do not exist outside of IIS. An administrator can choose to permit either Windows users, or IIS users, access to administer IIS remotely. IIS Users do not consume Windows client access licenses (CALs), nor do they have any permissions outside IIS itself, so are a cheaper and more secure option for permitting external IIS administration.

Although many security administrators will wisely insist on using a VPN for access from a public network, the remote Management Service is useful in hosting scenarios where a company has many external customers that you do not wish to allow access to the internal network. The remote Management Service is covered in Chapter 6, "Web-Site Administration."

IIS Administration Tools

IIS 7.0 uses a new IIS Manager that brings all the IIS and ASP.NET configurations into one management location. IIS 7.0 also has a full-functioned command-line tool for configuration, `AppCmd.exe`, as well as an ASP.NET namespace, `Microsoft.Web.Administration`, for management of all IIS functions through ASP.NET managed code. In addition, not only is there still WMI management functionality, but the management API has also been extended to allow complete control of all IIS features.

IIS Manager

The new IIS Manager for IIS 7.0, shown in Figure 1-4, combines all management functions for both IIS and ASP.NET in one location. Administrators will find the tool much easier to navigate than the MMC from previous IIS versions. Developers will find that they can manage individual sites and applications without needing local administrator access to the server. The IIS Manager is also extensible through the addition of modules.

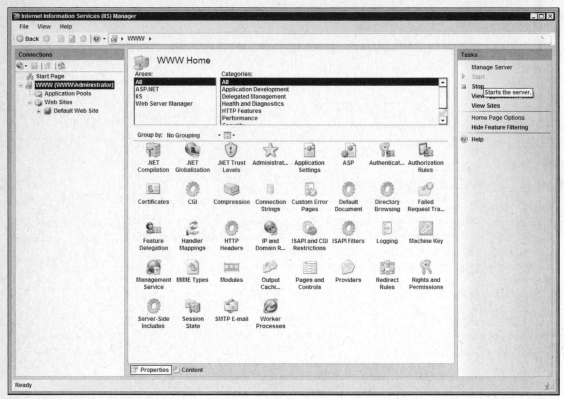

Figure 1-4

When you first open the IIS Manager, you will find that the interface is based on navigation and task. Each task that appears in the task pane is related to the point where you are in the navigation pane. Tasks that are not available at a specific navigation level are not displayed, and the task affects that navigation level and below. Additional sorting and selection options enable you to display only relevant tasks for the job at hand.

Administrators will also enjoy the delegation capabilities of the IIS Manager. You can have different administrators for specific applications within a site, as well as a site administrator, and each can configure functionality at or below their delegation level. The capability to delegate administration tasks allows non-administrators to administer web sites and/or applications, maintaining Windows security levels on the server itself. As shown in Figure 1-5, administration can be delegated to Windows accounts or IIS accounts, at any level.

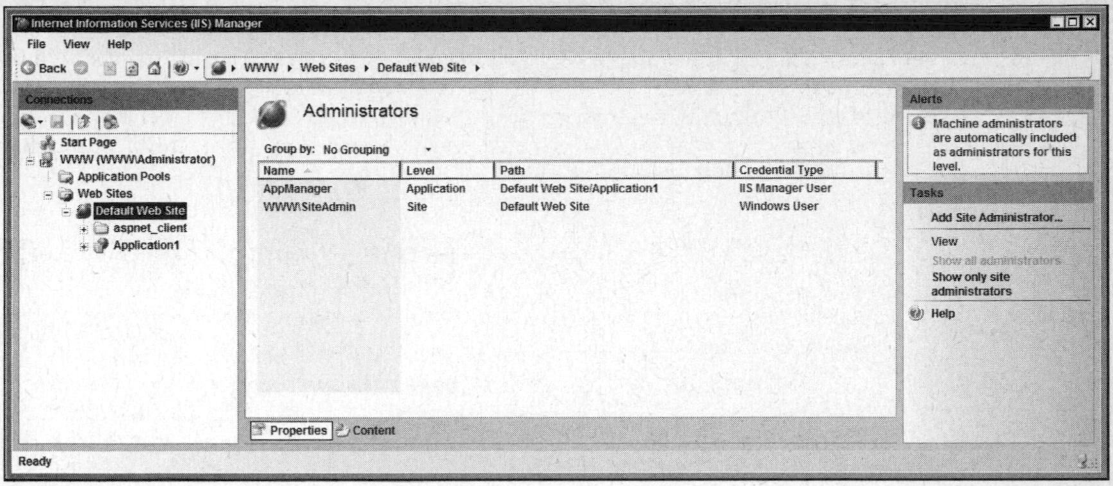

Figure 1-5

AppCmd.exe Command-Line Utility

IIS 7.0 introduces a new command-line utility, AppCmd.exe, which replaces the functionality provided by the various VBScript command-line utilities included with previous versions. AppCmd.exe also expands command-line control to all IIS configuration functions.

Creating a new web site from the command line is as easy as

```
appcmd.exe add site /name:MyNewSite /id:999 /bindings:"http/*:80:"
/physicalPath:"C:\inetpub\MyNewSite"
```

This single command line is shorter than the code involved in using the ASP.NET management namespace or WMI (each of which is described in the following two sections, respectively). The command line is even quicker than using an editor to enter the new web site directly into the applicationHost.config file.

One troublesome function in previous versions of IIS was obtaining a valid backup of the configuration of a single site. Exporting values from the registry or metabase, using Metabase Explorer or other tools, was possible but messy. And importing that backup into another server was all but impossible. AppCmd.exe makes a configuration backup a simple command line:

```
appcmd.exe add backup MyWebSiteBackup
```

Restoring that backup is as easy as

```
appcmd.exe restore backup MyWebSiteBackup
```

Before you make any configuration changes, you should run a quick backup using AppCmd.exe. Every administrator has at least one horror story about a long weekend spent restoring a configuration just because a simple change turned out to be not so simple.

ASP.NET Management Namespace

IIS 7.0 may be configured through the new ASP.NET namespace, `Microsoft.Web.Administration`, which is used for administration of IIS web sites and servers. This namespace is an addition to the ASP.NET framework that is installed with IIS 7.0.

An example of using the `Microsoft.Web.Administration` namespace would be the creation of a new web site. The following C# code sample creates a new site named *My New Site* with the root at c:\inetpub\MyNewSite, running HTTP on port 80:

```
using System;
using System.Collections.Generic;
using System.Text;
using Microsoft.Web.Administration;
namespace MSWebAdmin_Application
{
    class Program
    {
        static void Main(string[] args)
        {
            ServerManager serverManager = new ServerManager();
            serverManager.Sites.Add("MyNewSite", "http", ":80:",
                "c:\\inetpub\\MyNewSite");
            serverManager.Sites["My New Site"].ServerAutoStart = true;
            serverManager.Update();
        }
    }
}
```

This would be the same as editing the `applicationHost.config` file with

```
<site name="My New Site" id="999" serverAutoStart="true">
   <application path="/">
      <virtualDirectory path="/" physicalPath="c:\inetpub\MyNewSite" />
   </application>
   <bindings>
      <binding protocol="http" bindingInformation=":80:" />
   </bindings>
</site>
```

More details and examples of using the `Microsoft.Web.Administration` namespace appear throughout the book. You can find the full documentation of the class at `http://msdn2.microsoft.com/en-us/library/microsoft.web.administration.aspx`.

Windows Management Instrumentation

The classic Windows Management Instrumentation (WMI) is still available in IIS 7.0. All your previous WMI scripts will work out of the box, and the API has been extended to include all features in IIS 7.0.

The example used in configuring a new web site through the `Microsoft.Web.Administration` namespace would look something like this using WMI:

```
Set oService = GetObject("winmgmts:root\WebAdministration")
```

```
Set oBinding = oService.Get("BindingElement").SpawnInstance_
    oBinding.BindingInformation = "*:80:"
    oBinding.Protocol = "http"
oService.Get("Site").Create
    "MyNewSite", array(oBinding), "C:\inetpub\MyNewSite"
oService.Get("Application").Create _
    "/", "MyNewSite", "C:\inetpub\MyNewSite"
```

The WMI provider for IIS 7.0 must be specifically installed, and Microsoft provides a set of WMI tools that can be downloaded from Microsoft.com.

Diagnostics

IIS 7.0 makes diagnostic tracing and server state management easy. Okay, it really makes it possible, since the diagnostic functions in IIS 7.0 didn't exist in previous versions. Run-time status can now be determined through a new set of APIs that expose the run-time state of sites, applications, and application pools, as well as allow for control of those states, through both WMI and managed code. The new Request Tracing module allows for tracing any request through the pipeline to the point of exit or failure, and provides a logging function for those traces.

Run-Time State and Control API

The Run-Time State and Control API allows for the determination of a point-in-time status of the server, site, or application, and the requests being processed. The API exposes the HttpRequest object in the worker process, as well as the application domain, and allows better tracing of a hung process and its cause. Within the HttpRequest, you can pull the pipeline state and current module the request is in, as well as details about the request such as the host name and IP address, client IP address, and URL requested. Runtime state information about running application pools, currently processing requests, and other exposed information is available from within the IIS Manager GUI, through the command line appcmd.exe tool and also programmatically through WMI and .NET management classes.

Request Tracing

Using the request tracing module, you can configure logging and tracing of any type of content or result code. Like most IIS settings, request tracing can be configured at the server, site, or application level.

Configuring request tracing is a simple task. First, you define a trace condition, such as File Not Found (result code 404) errors. Conditions can be based on result codes or the time taken for the request, or both. For example, a result code of 200 would only log a trace for a successful request. Once the trace condition is defined, you choose which trace provider to use and then begin logging traces that meet these conditions. Traces show in the log, where each step of the request is time stamped and you can see exactly what happened at each point in the request pipeline, as shown in Figure 1-6. Chapter 20, "Diagnostics and Troubleshooting," contains more information on request tracing.

Compatibility

IIS 7.0 has maintained compatibility with IIS 6.0 for easy migration of existing web sites. All existing ISAPI filters, classic ASP and ASP.NET applications, and ADSI or WMI scripts will work in exactly the same way they did with IIS 6.0. This is handled through two primary means. Firstly, IIS 7.0 has a Classic mode application pool setting that allows an application pool to function in the same way that it did in

IIS 6.0, in case your application is not able to run in the new IIS 7.0 integrated pipeline mode. Secondly, an optional IIS 6.0 Metabase Compatibility module can be installed for those applications or scripts that query the IIS metabase. Installing this module installs an ABO mapper that transparently redirects calls to metabase properties to the corresponding section in the new applicationHost.config file. All existing scripts and code (whether they read or write to the metabase) should continue to workThis mapper does not allow any new IIS 7.0 functionality to be configured, and scripts using it are limited to IIS 6.0 features. For example, an existing script could create a new web site but could not configure failed request tracing for that site, because there are no metabase properties related to request tracing. ASP.NET configurations are also unavailable through this wrapper.

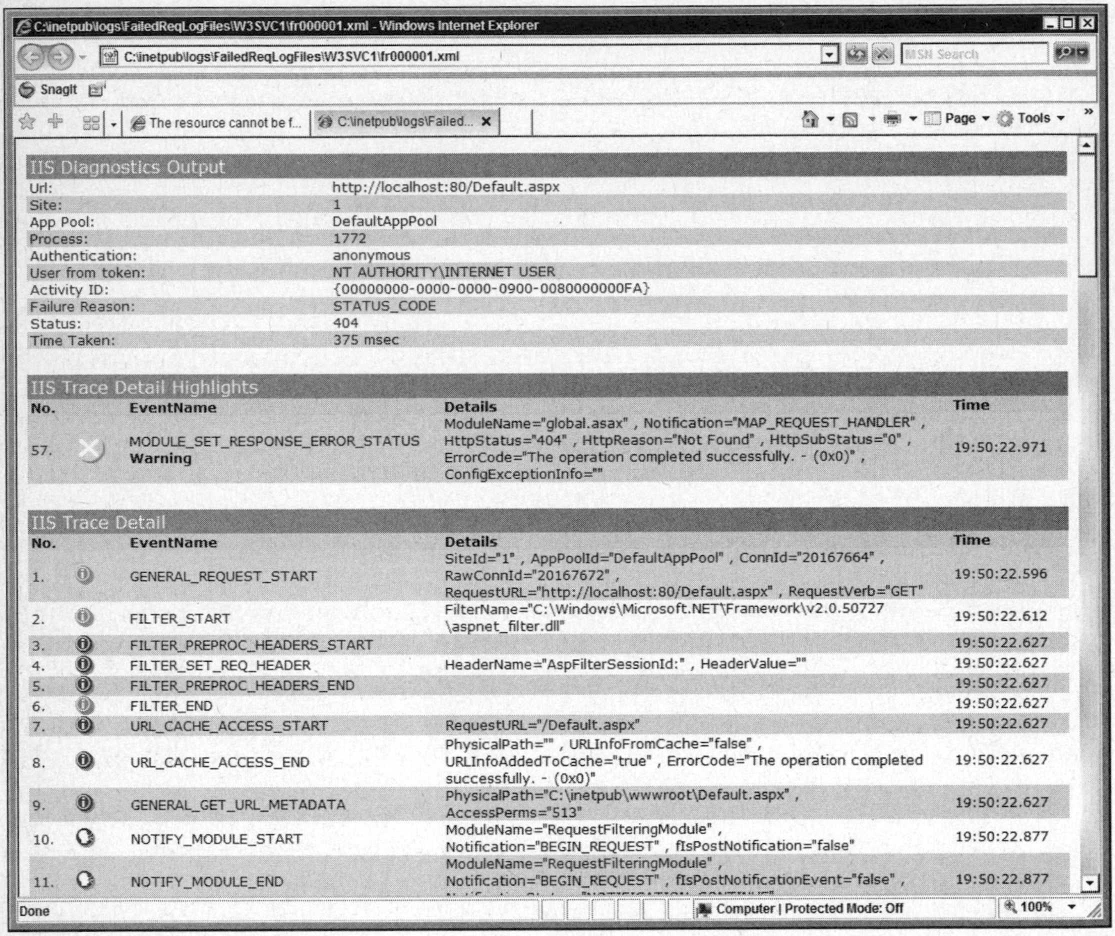

Figure 1-6

There are two possible compatibility issues you may face in migrating sites from IIS 6.0. The first has to do with the new security model for Vista/Longhorn. Because the security model is one of least privileges, if you have altered the default settings or accounts for IIS 6.0 on Windows Server 2003, you may need to correct permission errors that show up in IIS 7.0. Depending on whether the site and/or application are on a server that was upgraded to Longhorn or have been migrated to a new installation of Longhorn, you may need to create new accounts and assign the correct permissions.

The second caveat that will catch you on transfers to a new IIS installation is the modularity of IIS 7.0. On a default install of IIS 7.0, components such as classic ASP, ASP.NET, and ISAPI filters and extensions are not installed; thus these functions will not work if you simply copy the site contents and code over to a new default IIS 7.0 installation. You must install components in IIS 7.0 that were used in your site under IIS 6.0 for the transfer to work seamlessly. Upgrades of existing IIS 6.0 setups will retain all their previous functionality but will not receive any new functionality unless specifically configured.

Additional Features

As in previous versions, IIS 7.0 includes FTP and SMTP services. SMTP remains unchanged from Windows Server 2003 and IIS 6.0, as does the version of FTP that ships with Windows Server 2008. A new FTP server is available as a free download from Microsoft's web site at www.iis.net, and this version incorporates many of the requested changes from customers as well as tight integration with web sites to simplify publishing through FT. Windows Server 2008 drops the POP3 service that was introduced in Windows Server 2003. Both FTP and SMTP are covered in detail in Chapter 10.

FTP

Windows Vista shipped with exactly the same FTP code and functions found in Windows Server 2003 and IIS 6.0, and Windows Server 2008 ships with the same code as well. A new FTP server, shipped as a free download from www.iis.net, includes secure FTP using SSL certificates. This has been one of the primary reasons for using third-party FTP servers. In addition, the new version of FTP for Windows Server 2008 is integrated with the IIS 7.0 management functions, including extensibility of the authentication process. This means that FTP can use ASP.NET authentication, including membership and roles features, and will not require Windows CALs. Both versions of FTP are covered in detail in Chapter 10.

SMTP

SMTP is still available on Windows Server 2008, as it was on Windows Server 2003, without the need to purchase Microsoft Exchange Server. Unchanged from the Windows Server 2003 implementation, SMTP code is actually developed and owned by the Windows Exchange Server development team. The SMTP service in Windows Server 2008 is not meant to be a full-featured implementation, but rather a simplified service that provides minimum functionality without the need for additional services. Most professional users of IIS will want to install another mail server product, such as Microsoft's Exchange Server.

That doesn't mean that SMTP in Windows Server 2008 is a lightweight product. It is still functional for sending mail from applications on IIS 7.0, and it is a fully compliant implementation of SMTP that functions well in an Internet environment. While not having the configurability of Microsoft's Exchange Server, it will still function with multiple virtual servers and serve multiple SMTP domains while providing for security through relay permissions and IP restrictions as well as Windows login account access.

Windows Server 2008 no longer provides a POP3 server, and no IMAP functionality is available without additional products installed. Chapter 10 goes into more detail on SMTP installation and configuration.

Summary

IIS 7.0 is an evolution of previous IIS versions, building on their strengths while overcoming their weaknesses. Microsoft has listened to user comments on previous versions and responded positively, to make IIS 7.0 the most robust, configurable, and secure version of their web server. In addition, Microsoft has further enhanced the tie between IIS and ASP.NET, making IIS 7.0 a fully functional application server with entirely integrated processing and configuration of both sides.

Programmers will see the improvements in IIS 7.0 as making their job easier and more manageable. They will no longer need to justify web server changes that might affect numerous sites just to adapt to their application. True XCopy deployment of applications and configurations will allow them to spend less time on deployment schemes that need to work around server configurations. Senior programmers on a site will be able to delegate appropriate permissions for configuration changes to junior programmers, just as administrators will delegate permission to developers.

Administrators will find that the delegation in IIS 7.0 greatly assists in lowering the administrative effort required to maintain an IIS server. Administrators will be able to granularly control their servers and site administration functions while allowing developers to control the areas they need to. Security concerns about opening servers to development staff are a thing of the past, and auditors will be pleased with the control available. The reduction in security exposure provided by the modular installation, as well as the ability to provide unified authentication across an entire site, will further help to lock down an already secure system. Administrators will also enjoy the simplified and unified management tools.

Both administrators and developers will appreciate IIS 7.0's tracing and diagnostic capabilities. The ability to see into a request will ease troubleshooting failed requests as well as allow better tuning for performance even in completed requests. The modularity of IIS will also appeal to both camps, especially the ability to write custom modules that sit in the request pipeline and affect all requests, whether for a custom authentication system or simply to add a copyright notice to all images or content served.

After reviewing this chapter, you should have a good idea of the changes and new features in IIS 7.0. The following chapters will take you through installing and configuring the web server and environment. If you have a particular interest, feel free to skip to the chapter or chapters covering it. Otherwise, let's take an in-depth look at the architecture of IIS 7.0, followed by planning your installation and installing IIS 7.0.

2

IIS 7.0 Architecture

The origins of IIS as a service to deliver data via HTTP and Gopher requests determined the architecture of IIS for six generations. Over the years, IIS architecture has evolved from serving simple requests and providing a Common Gateway Interface (CGI), to include interpreted scripting languages for active server pages, or ASP, now referred to as *ASP Classic*. Newer versions added the ability to include the ASP.NET framework for server-processed programs, as well as brand-new technologies such as AJAX and SilverLight.

Understanding the basic architecture of IIS through previous versions will help you understand the changes in IIS 7.0, as well as help you understand problems in converting applications and sites from previous versions. IIS has often been compared to the Apache open source server, and often derided as not providing the configurability of Apache. Many organizations have chosen Apache as their web platform, often because of misinformation, and in some cases have regretted the decision. While most organizations can work with either web server technology as a base, the choice of web server technology determines many future choices as well, such as the ability to leverage ASP.NET for web applications. In many ways, IIS 7.0 architecture changes void the reasons for choosing Apache as a web platform. IIS 7.0 still supports previous architectures for those who need to reuse applications and sites.

IIS 4.0 and Previous Versions

IIS 4.0, first introduced in an option pack for Windows NT 4, was the first major change in IIS since its inclusion in Windows NT as the Internet Information Service, now referred to as IIS 1. IIS originally was a single-process application, where all requests were executed in process by `inetinfo.exe`. This included the WWW service as well as any DLLs written using Microsoft's Internet Service Application Programming Interface (ISAPI). ISAPI had been developed as an alternative to the CGI process used by UNIX-style systems, which would need to spawn a new CGI process for each request, even to the same CGI application. ISAPI was far more scalable than CGI because it could respond to multiple requests in the same process, but it also had the disadvantage of running within the single process, meaning that any failing ISAPI DLL could also crash the entire web service.

In IIS 3.0, Microsoft introduced active server pages, or ASP. This was an interpreted scripting language, meant to compete with the ease of development of Perl. Since the implementation of ASP was an ISAPI extension, using ASP.DLL, it benefited from the in-process scalability and also suffered from the same issues of a single DLL being able to take down the service. IIS 4.0 changed this with the concept of process isolation, where each DLL could be isolated to a process, and if the DLL failed, only that process would crash, not the other processes running on the server.

IIS 4.0 also moved configuration of the web server, except for configuration options needed at startup, to a new storage area called the *metabase*. This kept most configuration information out of the registry and made it easier to monitor and back up if needed. Using a metabase instead of the registry also improved access time to configurations and meant that the registry could be secured better since most IIS processes did not need to access it directly.

Inetinfo.exe

Throughout the early versions of IIS — indeed, virtually unchanged between IIS 1.0, 2.0, and 3.0 — the IIS web server process, `inetinfo.exe`, handled all of the functions of servicing a web request. The client request came in, and whether it needed processing by ISAPI applications or just the web server process, `inetinfo.exe` handled the entire process. Figure 2-1 shows a request processing through `inetinfo.exe` and serving content back to the browser, as occurred in IIS versions 1.0, 2.0, and 3.0. The request passes through any ISAPI filters, then through the WWW service and any ISAPI applications, retrieving the requested content, which is then served back to the client.

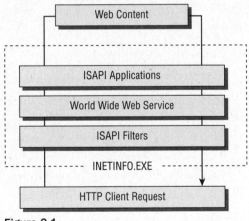

Figure 2-1

IIS 4.0 changed this architecture by adding process isolation to the mix. ISAPI applications could be run in a separate process, meaning that a crash in that application would not bring down the entire WWW service. These out-of-process applications could also be stopped and restarted without affecting other applications, and could be configured to auto-restart the process if it stopped. Applications that still ran in-process would not be affected, but could not be restarted without restarting `inetinfo.exe`, or often the entire server.

This was accomplished by the *Microsoft transaction server, or MTS*, part of the architecture of IIS 4.0. An MTS component, the Web Application Manager (WAM), was a wrapper for the ISAPI applications and allowed them to run out-of-process. The MTS executive, `mtxex.exe`, hosted all IIS applications, and a component called the WAM director would spawn separate proxy processes, using `mtx.exe` and running under the IWAM_{ComputerName} account, for each out-of-process application. As shown in Figure 2-2, a request coming into the MTS executive would be directed to the out-of-process application by the WAM director, bypassing the in-process applications in `inetinfo.exe`.

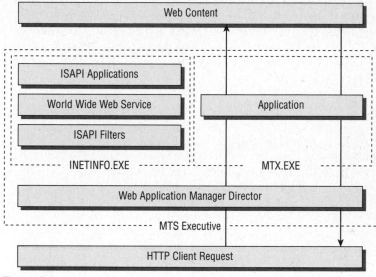

Figure 2-2

ISAPI versus CGI

Early in the development of IIS, Microsoft recognized that the inherent problem with the traditional UNIX-style use of the Common Gateway Interface (CGI) to run applications responding to web requests was that the method did not scale well. Each CGI application request would start a new copy of the CGI application; thus multiple requests would launch multiple instances, quickly running out of resources and slowing down the web server. Their solution to this was the Internet Service Application Programming Interface (ISAPI). An ISAPI application could respond to multiple requests, conserving resources and scaling far better than a CGI application.

But ISAPI had a drawback. Responding to all requests with a single application places a lot of faith in that single application. In essence, ISAPI applications became a single egg basket holding all your eggs. And like the "eggs in the basket" adage, the crash of a single application request will cause the entire server to fail.

ISAPI programs came in two flavors, filters and applications. Filters acted on requests and "filtered" them before they were processed by the WWW service. ISAPI applications, such as ASP, which acted on requests after the WWW service had processed the request, were often referred to as extensions, since they "extended" the web server's processing. This ISAPI technology allowed IIS to do more than just serve static content, or HTML, and competed well with the CGI model that was used by UNIX-style web servers at the time. But IIS also included the CGI model.

CGI applications, commonly written in Perl, were available and working in many web servers based on the UNIX-style of web server, even those running under Windows. ISAPI applications required programming in C, and programming Windows Dynamic Link Libraries (DLLs) required better than average skills in C. Debugging C applications was made even more difficult since IIS processed all ISAPI applications in-process, until IIS 4.0 introduced out-of-process applications. A DLL that crashed would bring down the entire web server, ending any chance of isolating the offending application. CGI acted out-of-process by nature, and CGI programming languages like Perl were often easier to learn because they are interpreted and not compiled. These issues meant that many organizations continued to use CGI, often with Perl, on IIS web servers. Until third-party developers introduced Perl as an ISAPI application, CGI was still a very popular method for writing web applications.

Active Server Pages

IIS 3.0 introduced *active server pages*, or ASP, often called *ASP Classic* now. *ASP* was Microsoft's answer to Perl, an interpreted scripting language that was both easy to learn and easy to implement in IIS. Using either Visual Basic Scripting Language (VBScript) or Jscript, a server-side version of JavaScript, most beginning programmers could master server-side scripting in a much shorter time than it would take to learn C and develop DLLs to run as ISAPI applications.

ASP runs as an ISAPI application itself, lending itself to improved scalability over a Perl script using a CGI executable. Through additional technology, such as ADO and OLEDB access to databases, ASP became the predominant dynamic web-site development technology for IIS servers in a very short time. Today, four IIS generations after ASP was introduced, many organizations still rely on ASP scripting for running web applications. IIS 7.0 includes full native support of ASP, just needing the user to have the ASP Classic module installed.

IIS 5.0

IIS 5.0 changed the architecture of IIS again, although the changes were more evolutionary than revolutionary. Part of the change was due to Windows 2000 using a new COM+ architecture, which means that the `mtx.exe` proxy is no longer used for running out-of-process applications. The other change in architecture is that IIS 5.0 allowed three types of application protection compared to the two — in-process or out-of-process — allowed in IIS 4.0.

Application Protection

Application protection in IIS 5.0 takes the form of three possible choices: in-process, pooled process, or out-of-process. These application protection levels were termed *low*, *medium*, and *high*. In *low protection mode*, applications run in-process as they did in IIS 3.0. The process runs within the `inetinfo.exe` web process, and just as in previous versions, a crash of a low isolation process can bring down the entire web server.

Medium protection mode, or pooled process mode, runs multiple applications within a single out-of-process pool. This pool runs in a COM+ process named `dllhost.exe`, and applications running in this pooled process gain the advantage of being able to communicate with each other. Prior to this new pooling of the applications running out-of-process, all out-of-process applications ran in their own restricted memory space and could not communicate directly.

High protection mode, or isolated mode, runs each application out-of-process in its own `dllhost.exe`. Applications run in high isolation mode are unaffected by the crashes of each other since each application is entirely isolated from others. A common recommendation was that mission-critical applications as well as applications being developed that might still contain flaws be run in high isolation mode.

IIS 5.0 was restricted in the number of isolated mode applications that could be run on a single Windows 2000 server because of limited memory resources. The default application mode then was for applications to run in pooled mode. While this helped protect the core web server from application problems, there was a performance hit for running out-of-process applications. A common setup was to run `inetinfo.exe` in its own process, protecting it, most applications in pooled mode, and those that were mission-critical in high isolation. IIS could run many applications in pooled mode, but few in high isolation because of memory use.

IIS 6.0

IIS 6.0 further extended the architecture of IIS, with the addition of a *worker process isolation mode* and the ability to run multiple application pools. In addition, the HTTP request portion of `inetinfo.exe` was moved into the kernel to further improve performance. IIS 6.0 also introduced recycling of worker processes, an XML metabase, and rapid fail protection.

Http.sys

`Http.sys` was the new HTTP listener for IIS 6.0. Prior to IIS 6.0, `inetinfo.exe` listened for HTTP requests as well as routed them to the appropriate handler. Beginning with IIS 6.0, the listener function was broken out of `inetinfo.exe`, which ran in user mode, and `Http.sys` became the listener, running in kernel mode.

Kernel Mode versus User Mode

Kernel mode and *user mode* are the two modes that a process can run in under Windows Server 2003. *Kernel mode* has full access to all hardware and system data, whereas *user mode* processes cannot access hardware directly and have only limited access to system data. In the Intel processor architecture, kernel mode runs in ring 0, while user mode runs in ring 3. By running Http.sys in kernel mode, the listener has access to the TCP/IP stack directly, and sits outside of the WWW service, unaffected by faulty code or crashes in applications.

By running in kernel mode, Http.sys enjoys a higher priority and can respond to HTTP requests faster than in previous versions of IIS. Http.sys not only improves IIS performance by its priority response, it also can queue requests while waiting for application responses, even if the application has stopped responding. Each application pool in IIS 6.0 has a kernel mode queue, and Http.sys routes requests to the appropriate queue. This is why performance tuning includes separating intensive applications into individual application pools, allowing other, less intensive applications to benefit by not having to share the same queue. Queue size is configurable for each application pool.

Http.sys also caches requests and will serve requests from this kernel mode cache whenever possible. A cached response will eliminate all processing by IIS, as Http.sys will simply return the response from the cache and bypass any IIS functions for heavily requested material. This cache is memory cache and cannot be paged, thus maximizing RAM in a system is a simple way to increase IIS performance.

Maximizing RAM also reduces paging of `inetinfo.exe`, which, running in user mode, can be paged to disk as needed. Too little RAM for an IIS system will dramatically slow performance.

Other Http.sys Functions

Http.sys also handles TCP/IP connections for HTTP requests and responses, including creating and breaking down the connection itself. Because Http.sys sits directly on top of the TCP/IP stack, it also handles connections and timeouts, as well as the limit for number of connections and bandwidth throttling. Logs are also handled by Http.sys.

Http.sys performs two important functions that improve performance in IIS 6.0. It caches requests in kernel mode, meaning requests for recently served content, both static and dynamic, can be served from kernel mode without needing to switch to user mode and the `inetinfo.exe` process.

Http.sys also queues requests until they can be serviced by the appropriate worker process. Each application pool has its own queue, and the size of the queue is configurable to tune performance of specific pools. This queuing also has an advantage for applications that might fail, since requests for a failed application are still queued to the limit of the queue size. These requests can be processed when the application begins responding again and, combined with the ability to auto-restart failed application pools, can keep applications responding with no more indication to the client than a slight delay.

IIS Admin Service

IIS 6.0 broke out everything unrelated to web service and placed it into a separate service, the *IIS Admin service*. This service handles FTP, SMTP, and non-web services other than HTTP. This changed how web applications can run, and no application will now run in-process within `inetinfo.exe`. This further stabilizes the web server and means that all applications run in either a pooled process or an isolated process. The IIS Admin service handles the copy of the metabase resident in memory.

Web Administration Service

The *Web Administration Service (WAS)* handles all the web site functions in IIS 6.0. There are two components to WAS: the Configuration Manager and the Application Pool Manager. The *Configuration Manager* handles all the web-site configuration details in the metabase, reading or writing configuration changes. The *Application Pool Manager* manages the worker processes. Each application pool will spin up its own worker process, and the Application Pool Manager is the process that creates the worker process, as well as restarts it if needed.

WAS runs in user mode, as do the applications in the worker process, but WAS does not run any applications inside it. WAS runs within its own `svchost.exe`, as does each application pool. `svchost.exe` exists to host services on a Windows machine, and many applications may use `svchost.exe` to run specific services. Services that run under `svchost.exe` act as DLLs and not executables, and you may find several instances of `svchost.exe` if you look at the Processes tab in the Task Manager.

> *The Web Administration Service (WAS) in IIS 6.0 and Windows Server 2003 should not be confused with the Windows Process Activation Service, also abbreviated "WAS," in IIS 7.0 and Windows Server 2008.*

Worker Process

IIS 6.0 runs any applications inside a *host worker process*, a user-mode process specifically designed for this task. IIS 6.0 will normally have several worker processes running at any one time, each one accepting requests from the Http.sys queue and passing them to the applications it hosts. A worker process can host ISAPI applications, such as ASP and ASP.NET applications, as well as CGI applications or just static content. The `w3wp.exe` executable loads ISAPI filters and starts a worker process, handling authentication and authorization for that worker process.

Worker processes are managed by WAS and can be recycled or even restarted by WAS if they fail to respond. A worker process is begun by WAS when the first request from Http.sys hits an application within the pool that is serviced by that worker process. This process, called a *demand start*, keeps IIS 6.0 from using large amounts of memory to instantiate worker processes that don't even have a request yet. Resources such as memory and disk space are allocated on demand, allowing IIS 6.0 to host a larger number of web sites on a server.

IIS 6.0 also introduced *rapid fail protection*, a means of keeping WAS from recycling or restarting an application pool and worker process that is repeatedly failing. If an application pool is configured for rapid fail protection, a threshold of failures being met will cause WAS to take that application pool offline, so that it responds with a 503 Service Unavailable error when a request is made to it.

Process Isolation

IIS 6.0 improved application protection yet again by changing to a *process isolation mode*. There is an IIS 5.0 isolation mode that allows applications developed in IIS 5.0 to be run in IIS 6.0 without changes, but the real change is in a worker process isolation mode. In IIS 6.0, unless the server was upgraded from Windows 2000 and IIS 5.0, worker processes are isolated from each other. Since each worker process handles an application pool, single or multiple applications may be running within a worker process. Crashes of applications may take down the applications in the pool and the associated worker process, but they do not affect other application pools or the `inetinfo.exe`. The application pool manager in WAS will also attempt to recover the application pool by recycling the worker process or spinning up a new one to service requests to applications in the pool. This all combines to make IIS 6.0 a very robust web server.

Application Pools

IIS 6.0 was the first version of IIS in which you could assign applications to an *application pool*. Multiple applications could be assigned to an application pool, and each application pool could be assigned an ASP.NET process account and identity. The version of ASP.NET framework was also set for each application pool. IIS 6.0 also allowed multiple application pools, something unavailable in IIS 5.0.

By default in IIS 6.0, there was one application pool with one worker process running multiple applications, the equivalent of IIS 5.0's medium application protection. You could also run a single application pool per web site, hosting a single worker process and a single application, the equivalent of IIS 5.0's high isolation mode. Both of these are natural extensions of IIS 5.0 and carry the same recommendation of running mission-critical or development applications in their own application pools and pooling all other applications under one or more multiple application pools. But IIS 6.0 included a third, brand-new worker process configuration for application pools, termed a *web garden*.

Web gardens in IIS 6.0 consisted of multiple worker processes for a single application pool, with one or more applications in the application pool. A web garden thus becomes an application pool that is serviced by multiple worker processes, in effect a web farm, but all on a single machine. IIS 6.0 also has the ability to support processor affinity, meaning that a worker process in a web garden can be assigned to a specific processor in a multiple processor system, potentially improving performance. In Chapter 8, "Web Application Pool Administration," we discuss web gardens in more depth and cover the pros and cons of using them in your environment.

Application pools are a great improvement on the IIS architecture because separate web sites and web applications can be assigned to combinations of application pools. On a server hosting multiple web sites, separating sites into separate application pools can protect one site when the applications in another misbehave. Figure 2-3 shows these three application pool configurations available in IIS 6.0.

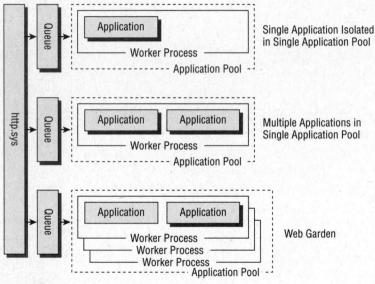

Figure 2-3

IIS 7.0 Architecture

Although the architecture in IIS 7.0 is quite different from that of IIS 6.0, and even though the code base has been entirely rewritten, many of the concepts and most of the architecture of the IIS family live on. ISAPI still exists, even though pipeline modules can be written to replace most ISAPI applications. The worker process and application pools are still in place, process isolation still works in a similar fashion, and `inetinfo.exe` and Http.sys still perform similar functions. In IIS 7.0, however, the web server has become the application server, an integral part of the operating system included in all versions of Windows Server 2008, including the core version.

Whereas IIS 6.0 was the supporting platform for many applications, from ASP and ASP.NET to SharePoint, IIS 7.0 has become part of the application itself. In many ways, IIS 7.0 is the application framework, supporting the application code and function. The architecture of IIS 7.0 has been designed around this concept, allowing developers great freedom to alter, tune, and improve not only their applications, but also now the web server itself. The modularity and extensibility of IIS 7.0 goes far beyond the capability of ISAPI extensions, which in IIS 6.0 were tacked on as handlers for specific file types. Developers can now modify the server functionality to meet the needs of the application.

Integrated Pipeline Mode

A major factor in the growth and development of IIS has been its use as a platform for applications, especially ASP.NET. IIS 7.0 advances the platform further by integrating ASP.NET directly into IIS 7.0, for everything from management to authentication and the request processing pipeline itself. Pipeline integration provides two advantages for IIS 7.0 — better performance and control for ASP.NET web applications and IIS 7.0 extensibility through managed code.

ASP.NET performance has been improved because ASP.NET applications no longer need to exit the pipeline and load the ISAPI process to handle ASP.NET code, then return to the pipeline for response to the client. IIS 7.0 still supports the classic pipeline mode for application compatibility, but wherever possible you should use the new integrated pipeline.

Classic Mode

In IIS 6.0, ASP.NET was enacted as an ISAPI filter, that is, requests exited the pipeline to be processed by aspnet.dll and then returned to the pipeline for further processing of the response to the client. As shown in Figure 2-4, a client's HTTP request in IIS 6.0 would move through the pipeline until a handler was determined, and if the file was an ASP.NET file, it would be shunted to the ASP.NET ISAPI filter, move through the ISAPI process, and return to the pipeline before a HTTP response was eventually sent back to the client. In IIS 7.0, this mode is still available, as the *Classic Mode*. Setting pipeline modes is covered in detail in Chapter 4, "Installing IIS 7.0."

Integrated Pipeline Mode

The integrated pipeline in IIS 7.0 allows developers to integrate their own managed code as a module in the pipeline. In prior versions of IIS, this required development of ISAPI filters or applications, not a trivial task for most developers. In IIS 7.0, modules can be developed with managed code and act as part of the request pipeline. In the *integrated pipeline mode* in IIS 7.0, shown in Figure 2-5, ASP.NET files are processed within the pipeline, allowing ASP.NET code at any step in the process. Since ASP.NET is integrated into the pipeline, ASP.NET functions such as authentication can be used even for non-ASP.NET content. Every request, regardless of type, is processed by IIS and ASP.NET.

ASP.NET integration also means that ASP.NET authentication can be used across the board for any files, folders, or functions of IIS 7.0. Prior to IIS 7.0, since ASP.NET exited the pipeline for processing, any files not served by ASP.NET — such as HTML, Perl, or even content such as graphic images — were unaffected by any ASP.NET code and couldn't be secured with ASP.NET authentication schemes. This meant that Windows integrated authentication or a custom authentication scheme had to be used for securing non-ASP.NET content. With the integrated pipeline, development of authentication methods is greatly simplified.

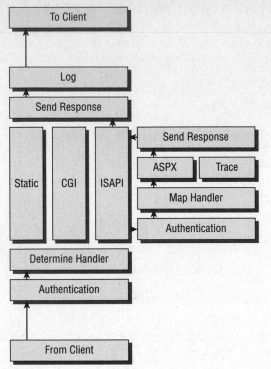

Figure 2-4

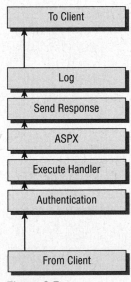

Figure 2-5

Moving an Application to the Integrated Pipeline

IIS 7.0 maintains the classic pipeline mode for compatibility, and you can run ASP.NET applications in the classic pipeline if they have compatibility issues with the integrated pipeline mode. Because the `web.config` configuration file has a different structure in the integrated pipeline mode, if you have `httpModules` or `httpHandlers`, they must be migrated to the new mode. Moving most ASP.NET applications to the new pipeline is relatively straightforward, and IIS 7.0 commands can be used for the migration.

IIS 7.0 configures ASP.NET applications in the integrated pipeline by default. Most applications will run as written, and those that won't will generate configuration errors to tell you what is going on. Using `AppCmd.exe`, IIS 7.0 provides a command-line method to migrate application configurations to the integrated pipeline, which will correct most errors with incompatible configuration files. From the command line, use the following command:

```
appcmd.exe migrate config {Application Path}
```

Replace `{Application Path}` with the site name and application, similar to `default web site/application1`. Chapter 8, "Web Application Pool Administration," covers this in depth.

Application Pools and the Pipeline

The pipeline mode is set for the application pool in which the application runs. To configure an ASP.NET application to run in the classic pipeline instead of the default integrated pipeline, create an application pool for the classic pipeline, and assign the application to that application pool. You may want to configure an application pool for the classic pipeline and assign applications to it until those applications can be migrated, then simply move the application to an application pool that runs under the integrated pipeline after you have finished your migration.

Extensibility and Modularity

IIS 7.0's modular architecture differs from the monolithic `inetinfo.exe` in previous IIS versions. More than 40 components are available with IIS 7.0, and custom-written or third-party modules can be added as well. For an example of a custom module, take a look at the Image-copyright module sample on MSDN (`http://msdn2.microsoft.com/en-us/library/bb332050.aspx`). Creating custom modules to extend the core server is also covered in detail in Chapter 12.

The modularity of IIS 7.0 accomplishes two tasks. The first is that you only need to load those modules required for your application or configuration. This reduces the attack surface of IIS, but it also reduces the amount of useless code loaded into memory. The guiding principle of server management should always be "If you don't need it, don't load it," and IIS 7.0 meshes with that principle completely.

The second task accomplished by modularity is the ability to insert custom modules into the pipeline. This extensibility allows developers to add integrated modules as well as for Microsoft to further extend IIS functions after Windows Server 2008 has shipped.

Modules

IIS 7.0 ships with more than 40 modules, handling everything from authentication token caching to the ability to process ISAPI Filters to URL Mapping, all of which can be installed or left out of an installation, according to the web-site and application requirements. Many of these modules will commonly be installed, such as HTTP Caching and HTTP Logging, which enable kernel mode caching of HTTP requests and standard IIS logging, respectively. Others, such as Digest Authentication or the CGI module, which allow for the use of digest authentication and the ability to use CGI applications, are normally not installed unless you need to support those functions.

The following is a very brief recap of the modules that ship with Windows Server 2008. See Appendix A, "Module Reference," for the complete listing. In Chapter 12, "Core Server Extensibility," we discuss how to extend IIS 7.0 by adding custom modules.

- ❑ **Utility Modules** — Utility modules are those that handle internal server operations, not directly acting on any requests. These modules provide caching functions — for files, authentication tokens, and server state — relative to the URI request. Without these modules installed, performance can degrade because caching is reduced.

- ❑ **Managed Engine: ASP.NET** — This is essentially a single, specialized module, ManagedEngine, that allows for the integration of ASP.NET into the request pipeline. Without this, the IIS request pipeline essentially only runs in classic mode.

- ❑ **IIS 7.0 Native Modules** — Native modules are those written in native code, not dependent on the ASP.NET framework. This includes the majority of the functions from IIS 6.0 that have been moved to modules; code remains in native mode to aid in backward compatibility. These modules also do not require the ASP.NET framework, and can thus be run in the core server implementation of IIS 7.0, which does not have an implementation of the ASP.NET framework available.

- ❑ **Managed Modules** — Managed modules run in managed code, written using ASP.NET. These modules naturally include those functions that rely on the ASP.NET framework, such as Forms authentication, as well as modules that handle profiles, roles, and the ASP.NET session state.

IIS Manager Extensibility

In IIS 7.0, IIS Manager is a Windows Forms application and is fully extensible, as any other Windows Forms application would be. Extending the administration user interface begins with a module provider, a basic server-side ASP.NET class that contains configuration information for the IIS Manager module. There is a `moduleProviders` section of the `administration.config` file, described below in this chapter, which defines the modules available to IIS Manager. The modules section of the same file lists which modules are actually implemented in the web server.

The corresponding client-side module ("client" as in the IIS Manager, even if it is run on the server) is the Windows Forms Application that is used to manage the module in the provider. To aid in programming this form, Microsoft has added the `Microsoft.Web.Management.Client` and `Microsoft.Web.Management.Client.Win32` namespaces that developers can inherit from to ensure consistency and compatibility. More on extending the IIS Manager can be found in Chapter 12.

Metabase — Going, Going, Gone!

IIS 7.0 loses the metabase — well, not completely, since the metabase is still available for IIS 6.0 compatibility. IIS 7.0 removes configurations from the metabase, which was a proprietary and unfriendly format, and stores them in XML configuration files, which are industry standard ASCII text files. Almost all IIS 7.0 configurations are in these plain text XML files that can be edited directly or managed through IIS Manager — "almost all" because some IIS configuration information is still stored in the registry. Since

IIS can read configuration files only after IIS is running, those configuration items that must be available as IIS starts must be in the registry.

There are also legacy applications that require the metabase. FTP, SMTP, and NNTP configurations remain in the metabase as in IIS 6.0, since they are unchanged from IIS 6.0. This is only true for NNTP if the server was upgraded from Windows Server 2003 and IIS 6.0 and already had NNTP installed. IIS 7.0 does not support NNTP, and it is not available in Windows Server 2008.

FTP is a different story. The FTP server that ships with Windows Server 2008, along with the SMTP server, is the same that shipped with Windows Server 2008. SMTP has no replacement, but an IIS 7.0 version of FTP is available from www.iis.net. Both FTP and SMTP installation and management are covered in Chapter 10.

applicationHost.config and web.config

The two XML files that control IIS 7.0 configuration are applicationHost.config and web.config. The web.config file can control configurations at the site and application levels, while applicationHost.config controls the server itself. Since configurations are inherited, web.config settings can override settings at higher levels. With configuration locking and delegation of administration, covered in more detail in Chapter 9, administrators can allow developers and lower-level administrators control over specific configuration sections while locking others to prevent changes.

The applicationHost.config file, located in the %windir%\system32\inetsrv\config folder, follows a standard XML format, <attribute-name>="<default-value>" [<metadata>] [<description>]. A typical section might look like this:

```
<system.webserver>
    <defaultDocument enabled="true">
        <files>
            <add value=Default.aspx" />
        </files>
    </defaultDocument>
</system.webserver>
```

This section is fairly self-explanatory. It enables the default document for the server, setting it to Default.aspx and only Default.aspx. This can be modified at the site level in the web.config using the same syntax in the same section, as in the snippet below, which changes the default document from Default.aspx to Home.asx for the site containing the web.config file. Other sites will still inherit from the applicationHost.config.

```
<system.webserver>
    <defaultDocument enabled="true">
        <files>
            <remove value=Default.aspx" />
            <add value=Home.aspx" />
        </files>
    </defaultDocument>
</system.webserver>
```

In the default installation, IIS 7.0 does not create a web.config file in the root of a site; all settings are contained in applicationHost.config. Modifying settings, such as the default document, in IIS

Manager for a specific site will create a `web.config` file in the root folder of the site, with configuration information for the site itself. This same `web.config` may also hold ASP.NET application configuration information, but even without ASP.NET, the `web.config` will hold all IIS settings that modify the defaults contained in `applicationHost.config`.

Why Is applicationHost.config Not Called webServer.config?

In previous versions of IIS, the metabase held the configuration information for IIS. In moving to the new configuration file in IIS 7.0, why didn't the Product Group name it `webServer.config`? In IIS 7.0, it is now possible for additional application platforms to leverage some of the functionality that IIS 7.0 provides. This includes both storing configuration in `applicationHost.config` and leveraging the Windows Process Activation Service. One such platform is the Windows Communication Foundation (WCF), discussed in Appendix B.

Other XML Configuration Files

There are other XML configuration files that affect IIS 7.0 and web-site configurations. These are also found in the `%windir%\system32\inetsrv\config` folder and include `administration.config`, where configurations for IIS Manager are stored, and `redirection.config`, which holds information for centralized configuration files.

The `redirection.config` file simply holds the information needed to direct the web server to the correct centralized configuration file, along with credentials for accessing that file. It might look something like this:

```
<configuration>
    <configSections>
        <section name="configurationRedirection" />
    </configSections>
    <configurationRedirection enabled="true"
        path="\\server1\centralconfig$\" userName="domain1.local\config"
        password="Passw0rd1" />
</configuration>
```

The `administration.config` file holds much more information, such as which modules are available to IIS Manager. A configuration entry similar to the one below will add the default document module to IIS Manager for all sites.

```
<location path=".">
    <modules>
        <add name="defaultDocument" />
    </modules>
</location>
```

The `administration.config` file becomes important when you add custom modules, since they need to be added to the `administration.config` file to be able to use the GUI management interface. Extending IIS core modules with a custom module is covered in more detail in Chapter 12.

Metabase Compatibility

Legacy management interfaces pose a problem for the IIS 7.0 management system with XML configuration files, and some changes made to IIS 7.0 would cause applications and utilities compatible with IIS 6.0 to fail if IIS 7.0 could not support these legacy interfaces. *Metabase compatibility* provides this support. Not installed by default in IIS 7.0, because it isn't needed, you install metabase compatibility by installing the IIS 6.0 manager.

Scripts and applications running with metabase compatibility are unable to be delegated in IIS Manager and do not have access to IIS 7.0 management functions. For this reason, porting these applications to the IIS 7.0 model will likely be a part of any migration, and new versions of these applications will probably be shipping within a short time frame after the release of Windows Server 2008.

Metabase compatibility works at the API level with legacy functions, as well as with the ADSI and WMI interfaces to those functions. It remaps calls to the administration functions to the appropriate function in IIS 7.0 and also persists these mappings through entries in `applicationHost.config`.

WAS and the Worker Process

IIS 7.0 maintains all of the familiar IIS 6.0 components, such as listener processes, worker processes, and application managers, but moves them from the w3svc to the Windows Process Activation Service (WAS). In IIS 6.0 and Windows Server 2003, requests retrieved by Http.sys were sent to a HTTP listener process, which handed them off to the appropriate worker process in w3svc, where the application manager would direct them to the specific application. A similar process still exists in IIS 7.0, but WAS will respond to requests other than HTTP, such as TCP, named pipes, and MSMQ. HTTP requests are retrieved by Http.sys and passed to the HTTP manager in w3svc before being passed to WAS, but other requests are directed through the WAS listener adapter interface to the configuration manager and process manager without passing through w3svc.

As shown in Figure 2-6, both Http.sys and `SMSsvchost.exe`, which hosts the non-HTTP listeners, reside outside of IIS 7.0. This means that requests received by these listeners can be processed outside of IIS 7.0, and Windows communication foundation services can be hosted as services, Windows applications, or other processes outside of IIS 7.0. For the adventurous programmer, WAS is extensible, although you will need to write your own listener handler and the accompanying application domain protocol handler.

Windows Server 2008 Architecture

Windows Server 2008 architecture has changed from that of Windows Server 2003, and many of these changes affect IIS 7.0. A new, stripped-down installation option for Windows Server 2008, the *Server Core* provides a minimum footprint server capable of running on minimal hardware, ideal for server farms. Windows Server 2008 virtualization allows for consolidation of physical systems as well as simplified re-purposing of systems as the organization's needs change. Enhanced clustering options can especially benefit the back-end database servers that web applications often depend on. And the new Windows Communication Foundation (WCF) allows for richer web experiences and expanded content delivery.

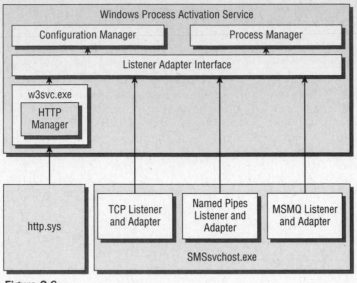

Figure 2-6

Server Core

A *Server Core* installation provides a server with the minimum footprint possible. There is no shell, thus no GUI functions such as IIS Manager will run, and ASP.NET support is not in the shipping version. For developers of applications using PHP or ASP Classic, Server Core means fewer other applications on the system that can be hacked or lock the system, and a reduced hardware configuration, as low as 512 MB of RAM. For large-scale web farms running legacy applications, Server Core is an ideal operating system installation.

Installing Windows Server 2008 Server Core is simply a choice during the installation process. Choosing to install Server Core means that you will need to configure IIS and your applications via the command line, although shared configuration files work with IIS 7.0 on Server Core. Unfortunately, modules that depend on ASP.NET functions cannot be installed on Server Core because of the lack of the ASP.NET framework in Server Core.

Virtualization

Data center rack space is at a premium in many organizations, with power consumption and cooling requirements hitting critical levels as well. Efforts at "going green" are also mandating reduced power consumption and hardware requirements. The ability to adapt servers to specific shorter-term needs, especially for development and testing, is also changing data center requirements. All of these are excellent reasons to look at server virtualization.

Virtual servers have been available for a long time and hark back to the mainframe era when shared systems were the norm. Products such as Microsoft Virtual Server or VMWare have been adopted in many organizations. Windows Server 2008 has virtualization baked into the foundation of the operating system, creating a de facto dynamic data center capable of handling many virtualization scenarios.

Windows Server 2008 virtualization requires hardware-assisted virtualization technology, Intel VT or AMD-V, as well as a 64-bit environment. Both 32-bit and 64-bit operating systems can be run as guests in Windows Server 2008, with up to 64 guest machines, depending on memory and drive space available. The Windows Server 2008 presents a minimal attack surface and has strong isolation between virtual partitions with inherently strong security. Virtualization in Windows Server 2008 is hypervisor-based, unlike Microsoft Virtual Server, which is a hosted virtualization platform. Hypervisor virtualization does not require a host platform, where virtual machines, such as in Virtual PC and Virtual Server, require a host operating system that supports other operating systems as guests. In hosted virtualization, access to hardware occurs through the hosting operating system. To be totally correct, Microsoft's Virtual PC and Virtual Server do use some hypervisor technology instead of being a pure hosted system, and Microsoft often refers to them as "hybrid" technology.

Two primary uses for virtualization exist for IIS 7.0 administrators: development and testing, and disaster recovery. Consolidating server hardware is a benefit for IIS servers as well, as is the ability to run a legacy IIS 6.0 site on Windows Server 2003 on new hardware until the site can be migrated to IIS 7.0. Disaster recovery is especially easy with virtual servers, as the server can be exported as a VHD and imported into new hardware, even in a new location, quite rapidly. But development and testing present the greatest advantage to IIS administrators and developers.

A virtual server environment can be configured for development and testing, matching a production server, or even being a copy of a virtualized production server. Once the application has been developed, tested, and deployed to production, the virtual server can be archived, and a new one created for the next development project. Isolation of development servers is assured, and the virtual server can even run on the same physical hardware as the production server.

Failover Clustering

Windows Server 2008 has expanded *failover clustering* abilities, making it easier to add clusters to a network topology and easier to initially configure clusters, and providing the ability for shadow copy services to back up and restore cluster configurations. Cluster disk sizes have grown from a 2-TB (terabyte, or 10^{12} bytes) limit up to 16 exabytes (EB, one quintillion, or 10^{18}, bytes). Okay, so nobody has exabyte storage capacity yet, but a 100-TB cluster is possible with current storage technology and is supported under Windows Server 2008.

For IIS 7.0 installations, failover clusters can be used on both the front and back ends, although they would be primarily used for content or SQL Server clusters. Clusters are not a direct substitute for disaster recovery options but can play a part of your disaster recovery plan. Because clustering requires more expensive Windows Server 2008 licenses, it makes sense to use a web farm, possibly using Windows Server 2008 Web Edition, as a front end to a content cluster, providing the fastest response times and, with shared configuration, the easiest management.

WCF

Windows Communication Foundation (WCF) is a technology that allows ASP.NET applications to communicate among themselves, even between disparate systems over a network. Introduced as part of the ASP.NET 3.0 framework, along with Windows Presentation Foundation (WPF), which spawned Silverlight, WCF unifies communications among web services.

WCF does not require IIS 7.0, but IIS 7.0 can host WCF services. ASP.NET 3.0 must be installed on the server. If IIS 7.0 is already installed, ASP.NET 3.0 will register itself automatically. If IIS 7.0 is installed after ASP.NET 3.0, you need to install the Windows Communication Foundation activation components.

WCF requires an application in IIS 7.0, either an existing or a new application set for the ASP.NET 2.0 framework. This application will hold the service information, an .svc file, and the WCF configuration in the web.config file for the application.

> For more information on WCF and how it interfaces with IIS 7.0, the Windows Process Activation Service, and applicationHost.config, see Appendix C, "WCF Primer."

In IIS 7.0, it is now possible for additional application platforms to leverage some of the functionality that IIS 7.0 provides. This includes both storing configuration in applicationHost.config and leveraging the Windows Process Activation Service. One such platform is Windows Communication Foundation.

BitLocker Encryption

Windows *BitLocker drive encryption* is primarily designed to protect data on laptops that may be lost or stolen, but it is also available on Windows Server 2008. In relation to IIS 7.0, data drive encryption can be used to protect sensitive data stored on servers, adding protection in case the server may be physically accessed in an attempt to bypass authentication within an application or the server operating system itself. This is particularly important on remote servers that may have content covered by data regulations such as the Health Information Portability and Accountability Act (HIPAA) or the Sarbanes-Oxley Act (SBA), among other statutory regulations that may apply in your jurisdiction.

Network Access Protection

Windows *Network Access Protection (NAP)* is designed to prevent clients that do not meet specific health requirements from connecting to the network. "Health," in NAP terms, is the level of protection that the client has installed, such as required service packs or updates, anti-virus protection with current signatures, or other requirements defined by the administrator.

NAP is important to keep in mind for IIS 7.0 for two reasons. First, an IIS 7.0 server should likely not be configured for NAP, since a missed anti-virus update could take a server off the network. While NAP could be used to ensure compliance of IIS 7.0 servers with health requirements, there are better options available, such as Windows updates or Microsoft Operations Manager (MOM). The second reason IIS administrators may need to keep NAP in mind is that it can cause network clients to lose access to the web or application server. When you're trying to debug a server issue, always remember that client connectivity may be part, or all, of the problem.

Summary

The architecture of IIS 7.0 is both substantially different from that of IIS 6.0 in execution and amazing similar in concept. While modularity and the integration of the ASP.NET framework into the IIS 7.0 pipeline provide significant architectural benefits, the overall concept of application pools and application processing is quite similar to that in IIS 6.0, with a different implementation. Most applications and sites will move easily from IIS 6.0 to IIS 7.0, even with the new architecture, because of the similarity in process goals.

IIS 7.0 architecture caters greatly to the developer, with the ability to write modules that are loaded into the pipeline and the integration that allows ASP.NET applications to cover all content types on the host. With the ability to run a functionally identical IIS 7.0 installation in Windows Vista, combined with the ability to run virtual servers for development and testing, development of ASP.NET applications for deployment on IIS 7.0 web sites should be a much more satisfying experience.

In the next chapter, we cover planning for IIS 7.0 installation, followed by the actual installation process in Chapter 4. You may want to look at Chapter 10 for information on installing other services, as well as Chapter 11 for details of the core IIS 7.0 server and Chapter 12 for information on extending the core server.

Planning Your Deployment

Deploying Windows Server 2008 and IIS 7.0 is a journey, and as in all journeys, you need to know three things: your starting point, your ending point, and the path between. The starting and ending points seem to be the most obvious, but the failure to determine them accurately is why the path in many deployments seems to wander astray. There are also many paths in between — all of which lead to the same point, and all of which have different terrain to be negotiated.

In many deployment scenarios, there are two landscapes to be traversed. The first is technical and is often the easiest. Which piece of hardware or which software setting to use for a specific task is often straightforward. But combining that with the second landscape, which is organizational, will determine which technical choices can be made. Many times the best technical choice is not the best organizational choice, and it is often hard for administrators to accept, or even see, the organizational hills and valleys that must be traversed.

In this chapter, you will learn what technical choices are available and some options for applying those choices in the organizational landscape. If your organization has no limits to resources like cash and manpower, you will find your choices unlimited. But, if your organization is like most, resources will dictate your range of choices. You may find that your choices are further limited by management choices, developer needs, and other constraints placed by network access or security concerns. Your choices may even be limited by the skill of in-house staff and, as you read through this chapter, you should honestly assess whether the planning and deployment could be handled by an outside contractor more effectively and efficiently. Even if you will not be responsible for the planning or deployment, this chapter will provide valuable background material that will help you understand why some choices were made.

Windows 2008 Server Deployment Planning

Deploying IIS 7.0 begins with deploying the operating system and platform that IIS 7.0 runs on, and decisions made concerning the operating system will affect IIS 7.0. Most of the decisions for deploying IIS 7.0 are really decisions on deploying the server itself — the operating system, the network topology, backup and recovery, replication, and even whether to upgrade existing systems or install the server from scratch. IIS 7.0 is less often installed to run on its own, serving only static content. It is normally installed to support an application, such as SharePoint or ASP.NET, even if the intent is simply to serve content.

Deploying IIS 7.0 also includes deploying the mechanisms for production of applications and content. The planning stage must encompass the development, testing, and deployment of applications and content, such as whether a development server is used, if a staging server exists for code testing, or if a web farm will be needed for the production system. To a certain extent, planning some deployment features is a guessing game. How many users will you have? How much traffic will be on the network? Where will the bottlenecks be? What if your site or service catches on and you have to expand? These are all scenarios you should plan for, although some may simply be an educated guess. And the scenarios will depend greatly on what your IIS 7.0 deployment is for.

Windows Server 2008 Requirements

Windows Server 2008 requires the following minimum and recommended hardware:

Hardware Component	Minimum Requirement	Recommended Minimum
Processor	x86 — 1.0 GHz x64 — 1.4 GHz	2 GHz or faster Itanium systems require an Intel Itanium 2 processor. Windows Server 2008 Standard and Windows Web Server 2008 support up to four processors. Enterprise Edition supports up to eight processors, and Datacenter Edition supports up to 32 for x86 systems, 64 for x64 systems.
Memory	512 MB	2 GB Maximum (x86) — 4 GB (Enterprise and Datacenter versions support 64 GB). Maximum (x64) — 32 GB (Enterprise, Datacenter, and Itanium systems support 2 TB, terabytes).
Drive space	10 GB	40 GB

Itanium or x64 systems and any system with greater than 16 GB of RAM will require more hard drive space for paging and hibernation. Windows Server 2008 also requires a DVD drive to install from the media.

All multiprocessor support for Windows Server 2008 Editions is for physical processors. Multi-core processors still count as a single physical processor, no matter how many cores they have. This means that multi-core processors are always a good investment, since they provide the advantages of multiple processors without the licensing and operating system requirements.

32 Bit or 64 Bit?

Windows Server 2008 is the last Microsoft server operating system that will be shipped in both 32-bit and 64-bit versions, referred to as x86 and x64, respectively. Only about 10 percent of servers currently shipping have 32-bit processors, and by the time the next server operating system is developed, it's likely that 32-bit systems will no longer be available. The question, therefore, becomes, should you run the 64-bit version of Windows Server 2008 on your server?

Other than the obvious choices, such as you are repurposing an existing server with 32-bit hardware or you have the need for 64 physical processors and require a 64-bit operating system, you will usually have the choice of running the x86 or x64 version of Windows Server 2008. Microsoft Exchange 2007 and Windows Server Virtualization will only run on the x64 version, which may determine your choice.

The major advantage to a 64-bit operating system, other than the ability to take advantage of 64-bit hardware, is the ability to use up to 32 GB of memory, or up to 2 TB (terabytes) of memory in Enterprise and Datacenter versions. The main disadvantage, other than licensing cost, is that some 32-bit applications will have trouble using the Windows on the Windows 64 (WoW64) subsystem. If you have legacy 32-bit applications that are critical or cannot be replaced, check with the vendor for WoW64 compatibility. For shared hosting, you can run 64-bit Windows Server 2008 to take advantage of the memory sizes but run 32-bit worker processes, which reduces the memory footprint of the worker process. This can be done by setting the W3SVC/AppPools/Enable32bitAppOnWin64 metabase property to 1. If this either doesn't exist or is set to 0, then IIS spins up the worker process in 64-bit mode.

Which Server Edition?

IIS 7.0, like IIS 4.0, 5.0, and 6.0, is tied to the operating system version. Although IIS 7.0 is available on versions of Vista, limitations of a workstation operating system make Vista unsuitable as a professional IIS 7.0 production platform. Developers can use the Vista version to test code, but even this is less than satisfactory since program development and testing should always be done in an environment as close to the final deployment environment as possible. The assumption of this book is that you will be using a version of Windows Server 2008 for your IIS 7.0 deployment, although most of the book applies to Vista installations with few changes.

Windows Server 2008 Standard Edition

The most common version of Windows Server 2008, if the pattern for Windows Server 2003 holds true, is Windows Server 2008 Standard Edition. The Standard Edition lacks features of the Enterprise and Datacenter Editions of Windows but is fully functional for all IIS functions as well as ASP.NET. The primary difference is that Windows Server 2008 Standard Edition lacks server clustering features that appear in the Enterprise and Datacenter Editions. In x86 versions of Windows Server 2008, the Standard Edition also lacks the large memory support, up to 64 GB in the Enterprise and Datacenter Editions, being limited to just 4 GB of RAM. 64-bit versions of Windows Server 2008 support up to 32 GB in Standard Edition and 2 TB in Enterprise or Datacenter Editions.

Windows Server 2008 Web Edition

As with Windows Server 2003, Windows Server 2008 has a web edition, specifically designed to run web applications to the exclusion of other functions. Windows Web Server 2008 will run IIS 7.0 and ASP.NET applications and it will run SQL Server for local web applications, but will not run applications such as Microsoft Exchange Server. Windows Web Server 2008 is less expensive to license, but it also provides a smaller footprint and attack surface since features that are not related to Web serving have been removed.

Windows Web Server 2008 supports four processors and 4 GB of RAM, 32 GB on the x64 version. Windows Web Server 2008 supports three server roles — IIS 7.0 and Windows SharePoint Services, which both can be installed from the operating system media; and Windows Media Services, which can be downloaded and installed separately.

Windows Server 2008 Enterprise and Datacenter Editions

Both the Enterprise and Datacenter Editions of Windows Server 2008 support clustering, and they both support large memory sizes — 64 GB for x86 versions and 2 TB for x64 and Itanium versions. Both clustering and large memory support can be useful in IIS 7.0 scenarios, particularly in virtualized servers or hosting environments. These editions also support more processors, up to 32 in the x86 Datacenter Edition and 64 in the x64, which can be useful if your application is developed to support them. The Datacenter Edition is especially designed for large-capacity SQL Server installations and may be a valid choice for back-end database servers for your IIS 7.0 deployment.

Server Core

Windows Server 2008 introduces a new installation option called the *Server Core*. This installs Windows Server 2008 without the Windows Explorer shell, leaving only a command-line interface for management. Unfortunately for many IIS 7.0 deployments, although a Server Core installation will run IIS 7.0, it does not run the ASP.NET framework; therefore, the web server cannot use managed code. A Server Core installation is designed to run networking services such as DNS, Active Directory services, or DHCP functions, and can run IIS 7.0 applications that do not use managed code. IIS 7.0 on Server Core can be managed remotely with Remote Desktop or IIS Manager, as well as controlled through the command-line interface at the server itself. Server Core optionally supports Network Load Balancing and Microsoft Failover Clustering, making it ideal for back-end web content storage.

Server Virtualization

Windows *server virtualization*, running multiple Windows Server 2008 installations on a single physical server using a hypervisor technology, is an additional component for Windows Server 2008 Enterprise Edition. Windows Server 2008 was developed with virtualization as a key feature, and virtualization has become a major trend in many organizations. Reduction of hardware, including the power and cooling needs, as well as reducing physical server space, can yield important savings in many IT departments. Even more important is the security of the virtualized systems from failure due to other resource uses for the hardware. For many organizations, a DNS server, for example, uses very little in the way of CPU, disk space, or memory. Therefore, a single-use system running DNS doesn't make sense. Adding DHCP, making the system a domain controller, and having it serve as a VPN host would allow better use of the available resources, but now each use is at risk if another task has problems and crashes the server. It's also hard to manage peak use of the resources; if all services need the same resource at the same time, it may be unavailable.

Server virtualization solves these issues. It's not a new concept; time sharing on mainframes provided each account with a similar setup, a system that appeared to be only used by that account. Sharing CPU cycles was important from a cost standpoint on those systems, where on PC-based servers the use of CPU cycles is fairly inexpensive. But the concept, extended for today's needs, is still relevant. An example would be a web hosting company selling virtual servers to clients. Instead of needing a physical system for each client, the host can use virtual servers, vastly reducing hardware as dozens of client systems can exist on one physical system.

Windows Server Virtualization is an add-on for Windows Server 2008 Enterprise Edition and is available for download from Microsoft's web site. Windows Server Virtualization requires an x64-based processor, hardware-assisted virtualization, and hardware data execution protection; thus you must select the correct hardware if you intend to use this technology. Windows Server Virtualization will only run on Windows Server 2008 Enterprise Edition but will allow any version of Windows Server 2008 as a guest operating system.

A lower performance option is to install Microsoft's Virtual Server product, a free download from Microsoft's web site, which will run on any version of Windows Server 2008 or Windows Vista. Virtual Server allows running multiple guest operating systems, although without the hypervisor technology that provides the increased performance in Windows Server Virtualization.

Windows Server 2008 for Itanium-Based Systems

Windows Server 2008 for Itanium-Based Systems is designed to run highly scalable databases and other custom applications. Applications for Windows Server 2008 for Itanium-Based Systems would normally be designed using Windows APIs and not the ASP.NET framework. IIS and ASP.NET are supported on Windows Server 2008 for Itanium-Based Systems, but the intended use is for applications that are not performance-sensitive. This means that although you can install IIS and ASP.NET applications for access and monitoring, you would not normally want to run Windows Server 2008 for Itanium-Based Systems for a production IIS 7.0 or application server.

Licensing

Microsoft has many licensing options for its software, from individual server licenses to enterprise agreements with maintenance on a range of operating systems. As far as IIS 7.0 is concerned, if the server is licensed, IIS 7.0 is licensed. There are no additional licenses for IIS 7.0, with a minor exception.

A Windows Server license only licenses the operation of the server itself. It does not license clients to connect to it. For a client to connect to a server, the client requires a client access license, or CAL. Each server version is licensed with a minimum of five CALs, which may or may not be enough for using IIS 7.0, depending on how the clients are accessing the server. If a client accesses the web server and does not authenticate via a Windows account, as in an anonymous user or when using Forms authentication in ASP.NET, then no additional CALs are required. However, if a user accesses the web server as a Windows user, as with Windows integrated authentication, a CAL is required for that user.

The area in which this most often comes into play is in an intranet setup. Most intranets will have Windows integrated authentication, so that users can be identified by their login accounts in the Active Directory. Each of those users must have a CAL to use the web server in this case. Fortunately, on an intranet, most clients will already have CALs since CAL is required for the workstation to use other network resources such as file and print services.

For Windows Server hosting companies, Microsoft has a Service Provider license agreement program that allows commercial hosting of Microsoft products. For web hosters, the program provides for licensing based on usage, thus hosting companies pay only for the licensing their clients use in a given month. This allows hosters to have almost no start-up costs and to pay only for software they are already reselling access to. More on the program can be found online at Microsoft's licensing web site, `www.microsoft.com/licensing/programs/spla/default.mspx`.

Hosting services using IIS versions prior to IIS 7.0 often used a control panel to provide control over IIS settings, since granting access to use the IIS management console would require a CAL. This access also required local administrator access, which might be granted in a virtual server, and could provoke security concerns. In IIS 7.0, hosting customers can be given IIS user accounts for management, which do not require either local administrator access or client access licenses. Delegating management and IIS users is covered in Chapter 9.

Upgrade or New Installation?

Choosing to upgrade existing web servers, to migrate to new hardware, or to set up a new server from scratch depends on several factors, not the least of which are the suitability and availability of new hardware resources. If you have existing hardware that meets the minimum requirements for Windows Server 2008, then you have a choice of doing an in-place upgrade. If your hardware is unsuitable for running the new operating system, you can install new hardware and a new operating system and migrate only the applications and content. There are pros and cons to each choice, and the proper choice for one organization may not be the perfect choice for another.

New Installations

A new installation to new hardware, or existing hardware that has had the operating system wiped clean, has the advantage of being a known quantity. You are starting from base, with nothing strange that may get in the way later. It's surprising how many small settings become big problems when an operating system is upgraded. A clean install also ensures that drivers, utilities, and other parts of the operating system are at the most recent level, so that updates begin at a known step as well. If you are deploying multiple servers, a clean install ensures that all are identical, which makes life simpler when managing replication and configuration. If you have existing installations you upgrade, you don't get the opportunity to rearrange disk partitions as you do with a new install. Many installations of Windows Server 2003 have already been upgraded from Windows Server 2000, further increasing the chances for out-of-date drivers that can lower performance. A new installation is usually the best of all worlds. But you may still have a valid reason to upgrade an existing installation.

Upgrades

Upgrades can be a viable option in several instances — for example, if you have an existing application that you do not want to have to reinstall and reconfigure, or if the time for the upgrade is critically short. An upgrade doesn't take time for reinstalling applications, reconfiguring them, altering security, testing new configurations, and redeploying. In most cases, you can simply upgrade the system and be on your way … with a few caveats.

The first caveat is that you must already be running on hardware sufficient to run the new operating system and applications. Most hardware purchased in the last few years is capable of handling Windows Server 2008, although you may want to upgrade RAM. Drive space requirements also need to be taken into consideration, since during an upgrade you will not have the ability to resize the system partition. If you're short on drive space, a clean install, even on the same hardware, is often the best choice.

A second caveat is that you will carry settings with you to the new operating system and IIS configuration. In the case of the operating system, Windows Server 2008 provides improved security options that may not be configured in an upgrade. In the case of IIS 7.0, many of the new and more desirable features will not be configured or even available as you upgrade IIS 6.0 to IIS 7.0. You will usually find yourself having to migrate your applications and IIS settings to IIS 7.0 or be forced to run in IIS 6.0 mode to handle your setup. There's no guarantee that a new installation will help with this, and your applications may still need converting, but at least IIS can be installed cleanly with all the new features you need activated.

Another IIS caveat is that IIS 7.0 is modular; you need to install only the modules you will be using. An upgrade from IIS 6.0 will install modules that you may not need because those features could be disabled in IIS 6.0 but not left uninstalled. If you intend to install Windows Server 2008 and IIS as an upgrade to an existing Windows Server 2003 system with IIS 6.0, you should test your upgrade first to make sure that you don't have any trouble with applications and settings.

Upgrades from Windows Server 2003 and IIS 6.0 with ASP.NET installed will leave IIS 7.0 in classic pipeline mode, which can be changed after the upgrade for any application pool to the integrated pipeline Your web site will need to meet the requirements of the integrated pipeline, which was discussed in Chapter 2, most notably that third-party or custom ISAPI applications may not work. Upgrades will also not change the ASP.NET identity, by default the NETWORK SERVICE account in Windows Server 2003. Security accounts are discussed in more detail in Chapter 14.

Upgrade Paths

Windows Server 2008 has an upgrade path that may limit your choice for upgrading. Any version of Windows Server 2003 can be upgraded to Windows Server 2008, but previous versions of Windows must be upgraded to Windows Server 2003 first. In other words, if you are running IIS 5.0 on Windows Server 2000, you must upgrade to Windows Server 2003 and IIS 6.0 before you can upgrade to Windows Server 2008 and IIS 7.0, even if your hardware supports Windows Server 2008. In most cases, you will want to perform a fresh installation of Windows Server 2008 to new hardware and then migrate the sites and applications from your Windows 2000 server.

Planning Your Hardware

Hardware planning consists primarily of inventorying existing hardware and determining whether a hardware upgrade is in order, or even hardware replacement. If the hardware will run Windows Server 2008, then it will run IIS, but, depending on applications and configuration, the minimum hardware specifications for Windows Server 2008 may be suboptimal for IIS in a given environment. For example, a system with 1 GB of RAM will run Windows Server 2008, but if you intend to run multiple IIS servers in a virtualized environment, you will be extremely limited in performance as the memory is swapped out. Virtual servers require the same resources as a physical server, thus memory, drive space, and processor capacity requirements increase in proportion. Shared hosting systems should be 64 bit to accommodate the additional memory needed.

Hardware planning for IIS deployments should also take into account the entire development and deployment environment. A development server, staging server, and production server can be on separate physical hardware boxes, virtual installations on a single box, or even clusters of physical boxes for each function. Deployment of large numbers of servers could take place using Windows Deployment Services, discussed below in this chapter, and require physical systems for that function as well.

Hardware planning also must include communications hardware, including network schemas as well as the physical components of the network. File storage may include planning for a Storage Area Network (SAN) or Network Attached Storage (NAS), and back-end database hardware adds even more planning.

Hardware Compatibility

Microsoft has always stressed the Hardware Compatibility List (HCL) for its operating systems. This list contains all the hardware tested for Windows Server 2008, but as all administrators know, hardware not on this list will usually function. In Windows Server 2008, there are several areas where you need to pay attention to whether hardware is on the list, and where you should only use hardware on the compatibility list.

The most important area for ensuring that hardware is on the compatibility list is when you are using clusters. Many issues with clustering, and even Network Load Balancing, can be traced to unsupported or untested network interface cards and drivers. Making sure that your choice of NIC has been vetted for use in a clustering setup is the best way to reduce your intake of antacids, antidepressants, and alcohol.

Fortunately, the new cluster validation tool in Windows Server 2008 will help you verify that hardware, as well as your network configuration, meets the needs of clustering.

Hardware Requirements and Recommendations

As indicated in the following table, Windows Server 2008 requires a minimum of 512 MB of RAM and a minimum of 8 GB of hard drive space. Since every administrator knows that running a system on bare minimum hardware results in a barely usable system, the optimal requirement in the chart should usually be considered as the minimum, especially in RAM. For RAM, you should use the maximum amount supported by your hardware and operating system choice. With IIS 7.0, the more RAM you have, the less paging the system will do, and the more performance you can gain from caching.

Component	Requirement
Processor[1]	Minimum: 1 GHz Recommended: 2 GHz Optimal: 3 GHz or faster
Memory	Minimum: 512 MB of RAM Recommended: 1 GB of RAM Optimal: 2 GB of RAM (Full installation) or 1 GB of RAM (Server Core installation) or more Maximum (32-bit systems): 4 GB (Standard) or 64 GB (Enterprise and Datacenter) Maximum (64-bit systems): 32 GB (Standard) or 2 TB (Enterprise, Datacenter, and Itanium-Based systems)
Available disk space[2]	Minimum: 8 GB Recommended: 40 GB (Full installation) or 10 GB (Server Core installation) Optimal: 80 GB (Full installation) or 40 GB (Server Core installation) or more
Drive	DVD-ROM drive
Display and peripherals	Super VGA (800×600) or higher resolution monitor Keyboard Microsoft Mouse or compatible pointing device

1 An Intel Itanium 2 processor is required for Windows Server 2008 for Itanium-Based Systems.

2 Computers with more than 16 GB of RAM will require more disk space for paging, hibernation, and dump files.

Planning Your Network

No IIS server is very useful without a network connection, and while there are often limitations imposed on what can be configured, configuring a network to support IIS 7.0 is crucial. Simple choices such as whether to locate a web server inside or outside a firewall can have enormous influence on other deployment choices. For example, a server inside a firewall would require ports opened in the firewall, quite commonly for HTTP, HTTPS, SMTP, FTP, and DNS. Failure to plan for the firewall security required by a choice of server location can result in security holes to other servers inside the network.

Active Directory or Stand-Alone?

In small networks, often with a single server, a workgroup may be used for network connections, but most commonly a domain would be used. You might choose to make your server a part of your domain, separate it into its own domain, or even make it a stand-alone server outside a domain. In most professional IIS 7.0 installations, the use of an Active Directory domain is generally a given, if the server will be in a domain.

There are several advantages to using a domain for your IIS servers, and a few disadvantages as well. For one, you should not run IIS 7.0 applications on a domain controller, mostly because of security concerns. A domain controller has no local accounts, thus all process accounts, even the anonymous user account, run as domain accounts with the associated domain access. You must carefully lock down these accounts to prevent them from being used on unintended servers in your network. Additionally, when IIS 7.0 is on a domain controller, compromise of the system through an IIS application can allow full domain access.

The advantages to using a domain primarily come in the administration category. An intranet server, for example, within the same domain as your administrative accounts, can be managed by those same administrative accounts. Domain accounts can be easily delegated access to IIS 7.0 administration tasks without the need for additional accounts within IIS 7.0. If you are managing a web farm, the ability to use domain policies can make server management far easier. Replication and backup become simplified when using domain accounts, and even SQL Server access can be centrally managed in a domain.

A stand-alone server is a choice made by many organizations, most often when a single IIS server will serve a limited number of sites and applications available to the public. It eliminates the security issues with domains, becoming an island with few connections to other servers or domains for security breaches. A few local accounts, an FTP connection, and the applications in IIS become the only potential targets, and it's far harder to forget to secure an account when there are few to begin with.

The best recommendation for choosing a domain membership option is that if a web server is internal, such as a SharePoint or intranet server, make it a member of the internal domain. If you have one or two dedicated Internet servers with public access, firewalled from your internal domain, consider a stand-alone server that is not a domain member. If you have multiple public-facing servers, such as a web farm, outside the firewall from your internal network, consider placing them in their own domain with a separate domain controller. Carefully examine the security implications of making this domain a part of your internal domain tree, even with restricted trust relationships. Security changes such as opening domain replication ports in the firewall are risks that you may not be able to balance with the reward of easier management and internal connections.

You will find more on security in Chapters 13, 14, and 15, and you should read those chapters as part of planning your deployment. You will find sample diagrams for typical deployments below in this chapter.

Server Location

Server location isn't a choice of whether to locate the server in the top of the rack or the bottom of the rack, or even whether to locate it in Kansas City or the Cayman Islands. You should already know that rack location will depend on cooling and power availability and that, while having fewer hurricanes, Kansas City isn't as fun a place to make onsite inspections as the Cayman Islands. No, this is a choice of placing your server inside your network, in a DMZ, or outside the firewall, or even co-locating it at an ISP or purchasing server space at a hosting company.

Server location depends on two factors. The first factor is the function of the server and who needs access. For example, if your server will be for an intranet, locating it inside firewalls will help with accessibility since you can use network accounts to control access. Security is enhanced because access is restricted to those inside your organization. If a server must be accessed over the Internet, whether as a public server or an extranet server sharing information with partners, you should always place it outside a firewall from your internal network. This maintains the security of your internal network. Placing the firewall in a DMZ — in essence firewalling it from both the internal LAN and external WAN — is even more secure and should be common practice in most organizations.

When locating servers, you must also address the location of companion servers. For example, if you locate your web servers in a DMZ, you probably want to locate any domain controllers for a web server domain and DNS servers for the web domains in the same DMZ. Alternatively, you can use a product such as Microsoft's Internet Security and Acceleration server (ISA) to proxy these services to an internal server. This simplifies management and restricts any breach of security to the DMZ and not across to the internal network. A little different approach may be more appropriate with database servers. If the server must be accessed by both internal and external accounts, then a location within the internal network may be more feasible. Ports may be opened for SQL communication, although it is wise to run SQL servers on nonstandard ports for further security.

Server Farms

A traditional trend in large-scale IIS implementations is the use of a *server farm* — dozens or even hundreds of systems behaving as a single web server. A primary reason for this is redundancy, in which multiple servers are available at any time should one or more fail. A second function is load balancing, in which each server receives a portion of the requests, and no server becomes overloaded with requests and slow in response time. Redundancy must be planned for in any server farm since at any one time there may be one or more servers offline, either for maintenance or repair.

Working with IIS in a server farm also requires maintaining state in the server farm, so that an application's state is maintained whether or not the next request from the client hits the same server. Load-balancing solutions often involve hardware that will maintain a "sticky IP" and direct a client to the same server for each request. In other cases, a developer may choose to use a SQL server for maintaining state in an ASP.NET application. There are no session state changes between the way IIS 6.0 and IIS 7.0 work, thus an application that already manages system state should not need changes to upgrade to IIS 7.0. Working with web farms is covered in more detail in Chapter 16, "Clustering and Load Balancing Web Farms."

Network Load Balancing

Network Load Balancing (NLB) is Microsoft's default load-balancing process for all versions of Windows Server 2008, as it was for Windows Server 2003. IIS uses server cookies by default to preserve session state, and since NLB does not assign requests to servers based on cookies or session state, sessions will often get lost in a standard NLB configuration. If you are planning on using NLB to cluster several IIS 7.0 servers, you should consider the following options for maintaining session state.

❑ **Use client-side cookies** — Read the cookie on each request for session information. The advantage is that the information in a cookie persists even if a connection is dropped, until the cookie is set to expire. A major disadvantage is the limited size of a cookie, that is, you would be unlikely to be able to use cookies for large amounts of session information.

❑ **Use a state server or SQL server to maintain session information** — ASP.NET applications can use a state server to maintain session state across NLB servers, provided that the machine keys in each server's `machine.config` file are identical. You can also write information to a central location such as a SQL server that can be read by all servers.

❑ **Enable client affinity for the NLB cluster** — In the NLB manager, under Port Rules, choose "single affinity" so that a client is always serviced by the same server. The disadvantage to this is that session redundancy is lost because if that server fails, the session is lost.

Clustering

Clustering, as opposed to network load balancing, is a function available only in the Enterprise Edition and Datacenter Edition of Windows Server 2008. *Clustering* is the combination of two or more separate physical servers, or nodes, into a single server cluster, appearing as a single server. In Windows Server 2008, a cluster can consist of up to eight nodes. Applications on a cluster, as well as other resources, can be designated as running in an active/passive mode, where one node serves the request and the others act as a failover; or active/active, where all nodes can service requests for applications or resources.

In most situations, you will not want to run IIS on a cluster. IIS is not designed to act on a cluster, and the only reason to use it on a cluster is for failover redundancy. Using a cluster in this way is an expensive failover option for just an IIS server. What is often used is a cluster for a back-end SQL server, with IIS in a NLB configuration as a front-end. Figure 3-1 shows a common IIS configuration with a SQL server cluster.

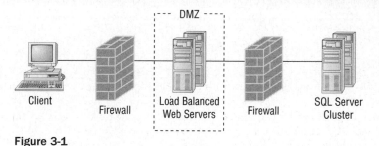

Figure 3-1

Virtualization

Virtualization is a major feature in Windows Server 2008. The architecture behind virtualization is covered in Chapter 2; the end result is the ability to run multiple servers within one physical system. Many organizations will run DNS, DHCP, and Active Directory servers as virtualized servers on a single host, and, with Windows Server 2008, application servers running IIS 7.0 will likely be virtualized for many organizations. A major area in which to plan virtual servers is for development purposes. Individual development servers can be set up for each developer, or each application, and images of these servers saved. If development crashes a server, it can be restarted without affecting any other system or application, and, if needed, a server can be wiped out and reinstalled in a short time from the image. No longer do administrators need to worry that developers will cause problems for other network resources. Developers can even run Microsoft's Virtual Server product in a workstation under Windows Vista and have a server and workstation available for development. Configured on a laptop, this provides a portable and safe environment for developers to work in.

Common Scenarios

To visualize your IIS deployment, it is helpful to create network diagrams of your proposed environment. You can use a product such as Microsoft's Visio, a Microsoft Office product, to draw professional diagrams, but even a pencil and a napkin can save you a lot of grief when it comes time to deploy hardware and configurations. It is suggested that you make these diagrams as explicit as possible, indicating existing servers in the network, routers and switches, IP addresses or network ranges, even access rules and routing information. Below are some typical configurations and diagrams that represent them. These are less detailed than you should have, lacking IP addressing and routing, but the generic layouts here should help you prepare your own.

Intranet

An *intranet* situation, as shown in Figure 3-2, calls for access to your IIS server by internal clients and the exclusion of external clients from access. A firewall is the main means for restricting access, but routers with access rules can be used as well. Documenting these rules in a diagram is important for tracing future access-related issues.

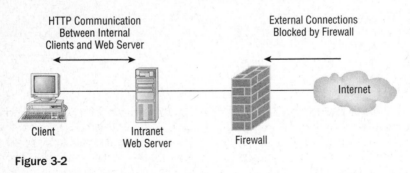

Figure 3-2

Extranet

An *extranet* allows business partners access to your systems but restricts access from outside sources. In many cases, an IIS 7.0 server can sit outside the firewall in a DMZ and provide access for only the business partner, as shown in Figure 3-3, and retrieve data from a database inside the network. In others, an organization may wish to allow business partners through the firewall to an internal IIS server, as shown in Figure 3-4.

Web Farm

In a *web farm* situation, as shown in Figure 3-5, the servers in the web farm will often sit outside the firewall in a DMZ, whereas the back-end database servers sit inside the network. You may want a domain controller for these servers as well, providing a domain for management purposes, and you may wish to segregate it from the internal network to provide security if it is compromised. In this scenario, the domain controller can be in the LAN, with appropriate firewall settings to allow the domain controller to authenticate logons through a firewall or, as shown in Figure 3-5, in the DMZ.

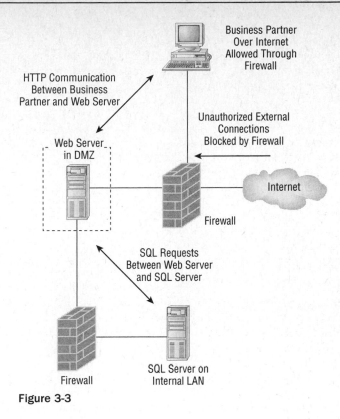

Figure 3-3

Planning Your Security

Security is an important part of any network, and this is especially true of a network that provides access to resources from unknown or outside sources, as is the case with a web server exposed to the Internet. Internal IIS applications, such as an intranet, may be easier to define security for, but security should be no less a concern. There are multiple levels where security can be enforced and addressed, from the network level with firewalls and router access lists, to the application level with security for applications themselves. Physical security, hardware security, and operating system security options should also be considered.

While this section of this chapter covers security planning, security is covered at various points throughout the book, as well as specifically in Chapters 13, 14, and 15. Chapter 13 covers server security in more detail, but a responsible administrator would be wise to consult multiple sources for all facets of security. Many organizations will have dedicated security administration, and an IIS administrator should consult with them, if available, in planning any deployment.

Network Security

Network security for an IIS server consists of three parts: authorization, access, and auditing. Authorization comes from network user accounts, access comes from firewall and NTFS security settings, and auditing comes from log files. Network security is covered in more depth in Chapter 13, but entire books have been written covering nothing but small portions of network security. The few paragraphs here will give you an idea of what to plan for, but do not consider this to be a treatise on everything you need to do to secure your IIS 7.0 system.

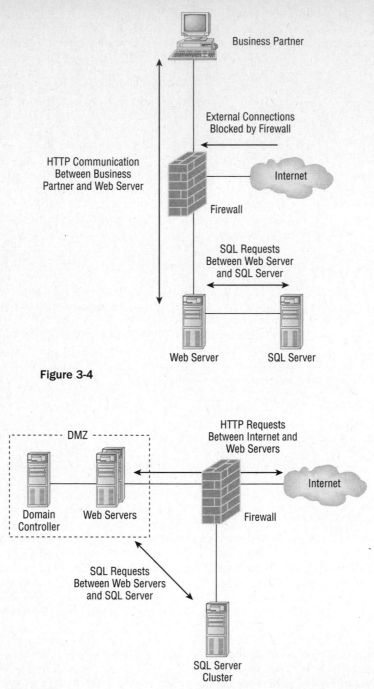

Business Partner

External Connections
Blocked by Firewall

HTTP Communication
Between Business
Partner and Web Server

Internet

Firewall

SQL Requests
Between Web Server
and SQL Server

Web Server   SQL Server

Figure 3-4

HTTP Requests
Between Internet and
Web Servers

DMZ

Internet

Domain   Web Servers
Controller

Firewall

SQL Requests
Between Web Servers
and SQL Server

SQL Server
Cluster

Figure 3-5

Network User Accounts

Network user accounts are what provide authorization to access resources on the network as well as on the server itself. Windows Server 2008 will try to force you to use strong passwords, although you can bypass this if you want to. A password of eight or more characters with a mix of uppercase letters, lowercase letters, numbers, and non-alphanumeric characters is recommended. A password like *Mix3dP!ckL3$* is far harder to crack than *mixedpickles*, and isn't much harder to remember since the characters look similar. Okay, not that similar, but you get the idea.

The default IIS 7.0 anonymous user account is the IUSR account created during installation. In IIS 7.0, the application pool identity account can be used for anonymous access instead of the default anonymous user account, providing better demarcation between applications and sites on a shared server. This account can be a network user account, making accounts easier to manage and allowing for better access to content on a remote resource. Remote content, such as content located on a network share on a different server, would have access granted for the application pool identity account. More information on access to remote content can be found in Chapter 14, "Authentication and Authorization."

Firewalls and Proxy Servers

Firewalls and *proxy servers* are important in your network planning since they either allow or block access to your web servers. There are common ports that will normally be open to web servers, such as HTTP on port 80 or HTTPS on port 443, but you will often need other ports opened for access to ancillary services such as DNS and FTP and even ports for passing Active Directory, LDAP, SQL, and other connections. The Internet Assigned Numbers Authority assigns service ports, and a list of current port number assignments is maintained online at the IANA web site, at `www.iana.org/assignments/port-numbers`.

Firewalls can normally be locked down further than just opening or closing ports, and in most cases should be. For example, if all your development servers are in a specific IP address range, it would be prudent to lock FTP access for uploading code and pages to the web server to just that IP range. That way, FTP attempts on your web server are not only stopped by the login and password check, but also, if the attempt is from outside the restricted IP address range, the attempt is blocked before it even hits your web server.

Network Access Protection

Windows Server 2008 introduces *Network Access Protection (NAP)*, which ensures that systems connecting to the network meet specific minimum health standards in terms of patches, virus protection, and even registry settings. Although NAP doesn't directly affect deploying a web server, you should be aware of any policies in effect in your organization that might cause a test laptop or workstation to be unable to connect to the web server.

IPv6

Windows Server 2008 supports IPv6, and as with NAP, improper settings can cause network connections to fail. The primary issue with IPv6 as it relates to IIS 7.0 is when troubleshooting, and you should know whether your organization has deployed IPv6 when you choose network options for deploying IIS 7.0. One example is that Windows Deployment Services, discussed below in this chapter, will not deploy IPv6 networking.

Logging and Auditing

IIS 7.0 has logging functions, which are covered in other chapters in detail, but Windows Server 2008 also has both logging and auditing functions that you need to consider when planning a deployment. Especially critical are *Windows event logs*, which will show many application and system errors related to IIS. Planning a monitoring system for these logs is important, and many organizations already have management software, such as Microsoft's Systems Center Operations Manager, which will monitor event logs and provide auditing functions.

Operations management tools are discussed in Chapter 18, but you will need to understand which options are available for planning your deployment. If you do not have a tool already in use, you can use Microsoft's LogParser, discussed briefly in Chapter 10 and available from www.iis.net, to analyze event and other logs. If you need auditing, you can configure Microsoft's auditing functions so that audit information appears in the security event log. One common tactic is to configure successful and unsuccessful login attempts for auditing and use LogParser to track attempts to log in as administrator or other privileged accounts. If you rename the administrator account and then create a new account named *Administrator* with a complicated password and no access to anything, you can easily report on attacks against the Administrator account, a common target for hackers.

Windows Server Security

Windows server security is covered in Chapter 13, but for planning purposes you should consider the folder structure and the security assigned to it. In the case of web servers, there are some areas of server security that need more specific planning. The most crucial of these is remote access. Whether by remote desktop, remote administration interfaces, or Windows terminal services, remote access to a server, especially a Windows Server 2008 Server Core installation, is a necessary evil. And with that remote access come security risks. Remote access to your web servers should always be secured by a VPN or by firewalls limiting access from all but specific IP ranges.

Windows file and folder security is also important to planning your deployment. It is important that the folders your web code and content are in have only the security needed to access them for the needs of your applications. One mistake many administrators make is using a subfolder other than the default Inetpub folder for web-site home directories. You should use Inetpub or create a new folder off the root to put the home directories of web sites in; you should not use a subfolder of the Program Files folder or any other folder. This is because those folders will have permissions for other accounts, and you may run into problems managing security effectively. A bad example of production servers is the default virtual directory configurations used by Microsoft's Visual Studio. The physical folder that the virtual directory points to normally defaults to a folder within a user's profile, making security management a nightmare. In deploying an IIS 7.0 server with ASP.NET applications, a folder structure should be planned that allows for proper security and organization.

Administrators are often concerned about the default administrative shares on Windows servers, with a share name like \\servername\c$. These shares are useful for administrative connections, but you can disable the shares if you are concerned about the security risk they may expose. The risk is simply that they are a known attack point, and if you have secured your server well and the administrative accounts use strong passwords, these administrative shares should not be of undue concern for most administrators. If you are unfamiliar with Windows file and folder permissions, or Windows share-level permissions, you should find a good book or online resource to boost your skills. While this is not a Windows administration or security book, you will find that Windows server security is covered in more detail in Chapter 13.

Application Security

The security of any Windows server is a function of the security of all the applications on it. An insecure application that allows a server to be compromised is as bad as a server with no password protection. Your planning for Windows server deployments should always include planning for what applications will be running on a server.

In a perfect world, every server would serve a single function — web server, SQL server, Exchange server, and so on. In the real world, however, servers often have to handle multiple applications, and the licensing and hardware costs for additional servers, even virtual servers, don't make financial sense. But some simple planning can provide additional security when servers must share duties. For example, planning to have a web server and SQL server on the same physical hardware is often not the securest of choices. Never mind that SQL is a performance hog; it also uses different ports for the SQL service, a separate account structure, and separate management tools. This means multiple accounts added to the server, each of which is a potential source of attack; additional ports opened in the firewall; and additional services that may hang and consume resources.

But a DNS server installed on a web server may be a natural fit. The extra ports opened in a firewall present little or no additional attack surface because the DNS service has no known attacks that can be used to gain control of the system. Both DNS and web services are often needed by the same end users, and DNS presents very little in the way of resource use. FTP is another service that is often enabled on web servers for the purpose of transferring content and, in the case of IIS 7.0, does not need to use Windows accounts. FTP on an IIS 7.0 server, covered in Chapter 10, presents very little additional security risk.

ASP.NET and other developed applications can, and usually do, incorporate their own security. This book does not cover this type of application security; programmers should reference other materials for help in this topic. Keep in mind that all security is a trade-off between security and functionality. As long as you understand the risks of applications running on your web server, and accept those risks in return for the added functionality, planning to accommodate those risks is a simple task.

Physical Security

Physical security is sometimes overlooked in IIS servers, especially where a web server may be managed by a specific group for intranet or SharePoint use. Sometimes these department servers end up stuck in broom closets, under the manager's desk, or on a table next to a printer, open to public access. This type of location is a poor choice for many reasons, but the most persuasive one is that the server that your department depends on might be turned off by anyone passing by. It could be unplugged to plug in a vacuum cleaner, knocked off a desk, or damaged in a coffee/soda/water incident.

More important in physical security is preventing access to the system by those with more nefarious intent. Any system that can be physically accessed is more easily hacked, especially when other security tenets are not enforced. Leaving a system logged in with a local administrator account and with physical access from unauthorized individuals is like handing out the administrator password. This is basic security, but for some reason departmental web servers seem to suffer from lapses in security. Always plan to physically restrict access to all deployed systems with at least a lock and key.

Planning Backup and Recovery

Backing up and restoring web sites is covered in detail in Chapter 6, but backing up and restoring file systems and entire services is an important part of administering IIS 7.0 and Windows Server 2008. Many organizations use a third-party product for backing up enterprise systems, but for those systems where the enterprise backup isn't available or isn't feasible, Microsoft has included a Windows backup function in all server versions. This function also gets a makeover and improvements in Windows Server 2008.

Volume Shadow Copy Services

In many organizations, Microsoft's Volume Shadow Copy service, introduced in Windows Server 2003, is the first line of defense against lost data. Taking a snapshot of the file system and storing changed files on a scheduled basis, Shadow Copies can be restored to provide previous versions of data, including restoring data that has been changed or deleted. Shadow Copies can be restored by end users who have the Volume Shadow Copy client installed, but they are especially handy for administrators who may need to back out changes or restore accidentally deleted files quickly.

One tip for administrators is to install the Volume Shadow Copy client on the server, and then use Windows Explorer to browse to the administrative share (if you haven't disabled it) to use the client on the same server you are trying to restore previous file versions from. The client cannot be used locally, but by connecting to the administrative share you have connected to the server from the server by way of the network, not the file system directly.

Volume Shadow Copy files are found in the \System Volume Information folder and consist of two files with a unique GUID and a large file named tracking.log. The amount of space allowed to Shadow Copies can be configured by the administrator, as can the location. The size of these files, as well as the overhead of creating Shadow Copies should be considered when choosing whether or not to activate Shadow Copies on a server. A good choice is to enable Shadow Copies on development servers, which have a greater chance of accidental file deletions, and not enable them on production servers, since deleted files can be restored by redeploying from a staging or development server. Keep in mind that Shadow Copy services are not a substitute for regular system backups. Owing to the size and performance impact, you should only enable Shadow Copies on data volumes. Planning your server configuration with data stored on a separate volume eases the use of Shadow Copies.

Windows Server 2008 Backup

Windows Server 2008, as with previous Windows versions, includes its own backup utility, Windows Server 2008 Backup. The new version is faster, partly because of its use of the Volume Shadow Copy service, and does block-level backups, allowing more granular restorations than previous versions. You can restore individual items in a backup, or, with applications that support Volume Shadow Copies such as Microsoft SQL Server and SharePoint, you can restore applications. Also, owing to the use of the Volume Shadow Copy service, you can restore an incremental backup from a chosen date without having to restore all incremental backups from the last full backup. Naturally, Windows Server 2008 Backup supports a graphical management interface, as shown in Figure 3-6, but it also supports an extensive command-line backup and remote administration. The command line is especially important when using Windows Server 2008 in a Server Core installation. Because a Server Core installation does not offer a graphic shell, you must either use a command line or administer the backups remotely.

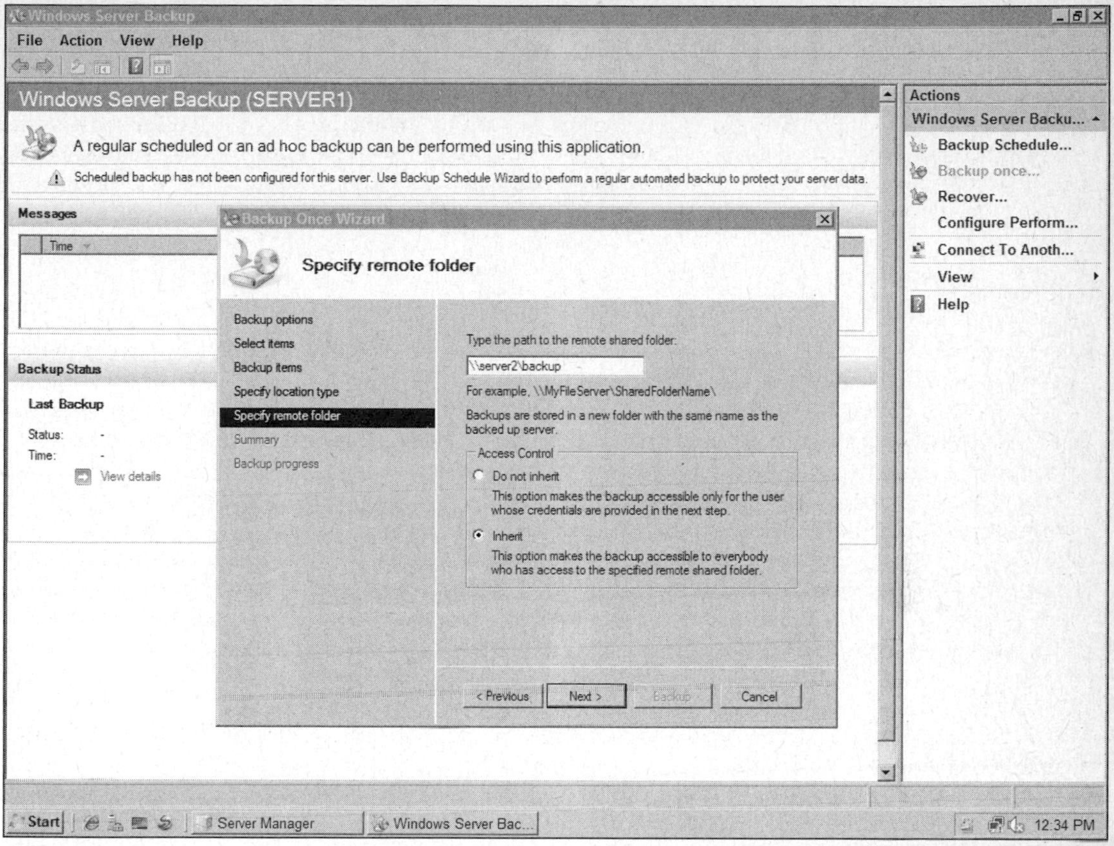

Figure 3-6

The new backup tool also supports newer disk technologies, including backups direct to DVD media. Support for off-site storage is improved; you can configure a backup rotation to removable drives, and if one is taken off-site, the next in rotation is used. Windows Server 2008 also manages backup storage space, reusing space from older backups as needed. If you will be using Windows Server 2008 Backup, you will need to plan for backup storage space; in most cases, a separate drive array or volume would be most practical. You will also need to plan for backup security by limiting the number of users in the administrator or backup users group. Securing the backup media, especially when transporting off-site, is also critical for a secure environment. Windows Server 2008 no longer supports backup to tape, although third-party backup options do.

IIS 7.0 Deployment Planning

Planning your IIS 7.0 deployment becomes easier after you've considered the issues in deploying the Windows Server 2008 operating system, but there are still decisions to be made. You need to ensure that your system and the operating system configuration meet the requirements of your IIS 7.0 deployment. You have some installation decisions to make, such as installing with the operating system, after the operating system is configured, or even installing as part of an upgrade from Windows Server 2003 and IIS 6.0. You will need to plan IIS 7.0 security, such as whether you'll use IIS accounts for managing users and IIS 7.0 installations. You'll need to plan for shared configurations if you're using a web farm and choose to use shared configurations. And you'll need to plan for replication among sites. There are also some IIS-specific planning decisions related to development environments and production environments. The installation of IIS 7.0 is covered in the next chapter, and some of these topics are discussed in more depth throughout the book; therefore, part of your planning should include reading relevant sections of this book for specific information.

IIS 7.0 Requirements

IIS 7.0 requires a Windows Vista operating system or a Windows Server 2008 operating system. Since the version of IIS is tied to the version of the operating system, there is no "IIS 7.0 upgrade" without upgrading the operating system as well. As noted in Chapter 1, not all versions of Windows Vista will run IIS 7.0 and some have limitations, while all versions of Windows Server 2008 will run IIS 7.0. IIS 7.0 is a part of the operating system, and not a separate download, thus you will need the operating system media at some point for the installation. You can install from the physical media, from a network install point, or use several varieties of automated and unattended installs.

Beyond having the correct operating system, the only other requirement for an IIS 7.0 installation is a network interface with an IP address. It could be a local loopback adapter, with no physical connection to other systems, or any other network interface, but since IIS 7.0 answers requests over TCP/IP, some form of network connection must be available.

Installation Decisions

Naturally, many decisions on how you're going to install IIS 7.0 depend on your installation choices for Windows Server 2008. If you are going to be upgrading your operating system from Windows Server 2003, for example, you have a choice of upgrading IIS 6.0 to IIS 7.0 as part of the process, or of removing IIS 6.0 before the upgrade, then upgrading the operating system and reinstalling IIS 7.0.

Planning for IIS-Specific Security

IIS 7.0 has security that is independent, at least to a certain extent, from Windows Server 2008 security. IIS 7.0, unlike previous versions, has its own security accounts that can be used for access and delegation; plus there are security accounts for application pools to run in, shared configuration shares, and FTP or SMTP access. Planning for this security depends greatly on the end function of your IIS 7.0 server.

For example, on an intranet server, maybe running SharePoint, you're likely to use Windows accounts for all access. You may only have a single application pool and a single site, requiring very little in the way of security management beyond the default installation. Or you may run a web host, with hundreds of sites on a server, configured in multiple application pools with separate accounts for each. You may use IIS accounts to delegate management of the sites to the hosting clients, and more IIS accounts for FTP access. A back-end SQL Server may be configured with SQL accounts for these sites, or you may be running SQL Express and using the application pool account for access, with each site in a separate application pool.

Security Changes from IIS 6.0

IIS 7.0's unified pipeline architecture, a primary change from that of IIS 6.0, provides for some significant security changes as well. The first change is that Forms authentication is no longer restricted to ASP.NET files. Developers may want to choose to drop Windows-integrated authentication from their applications since any content can be protected through ASP.NET security schemes.

The second major change in IIS 7.0 is the ability of the anonymous user account to run as the ASP.NET process account, used for the application pool. The default account for anonymous authentication is the IUSR account, which is changed from the IUSR_{MachineName} account that is used with previous versions of IIS, and is a low privilege account with limited access. The IUSR account is a member of the IIS_IUSRS group, which replaces the IIS_WPG group in IIS 6.0. You can configure your anonymous user account to the application pool identity through IIS Manager or by editing the `applicationHost.config` file. To change to using the application pool account as the anonymous user account, edit your `applicationHost.config` file to remove the anonymous authentication user name. The line in the `applicationHost.config` file should look like this:

```
<anonymousAuthentication enabled="true" userName="" defaultLogonDomain="" />
```

This changes IIS to run anonymous requests under the worker process identity, which can be used when configuring ACLs for your file system and assigned network access rights if needed. Refer to Chapter 14 for more information on authentication and authorization. Both administrators and developers will want to review this chapter for information on planning deployments as well as planning application security development.

Management Accounts and Delegation

IIS 7.0 accounts, as well as Windows accounts, can be used for delegating management of web sites, and administrators, developers, or users can be allowed access to IIS Manager to manage specific sections of the server. Having management accounts in IIS that are separate from the Windows account system is new in IIS 7.0. IIS 7.0 also includes delegation, both for access to the management interface and for locking configuration sections to restrict specific users from making specific changes to the configuration. These two changes in IIS 7.0 give the administrator more options for security and more granular control over management of IIS.

Using IIS 7.0 accounts has several advantages, depending on your use of IIS 7.0. For web hosters, or for any use where managing the server is not going to be done by users who already have Windows accounts with access to the server, IIS 7.0 accounts do not require Windows client access licenses. IIS 7.0 accounts can also be managed by administrators who have access to the web server but do not have access to accounts in the Active Directory. For intranet use, where Windows accounts already exist, there are few advantages to a separate IIS account system, although administrators may choose to deploy IIS accounts for centralizing web access management.

Delegation, on the other hand, is useful for any organization that needs to restrict IIS management from requiring local administrator access to the system itself, and for allowing developers to make changes to the configurations of their sites and applications while restricting them from any further access. There are actually two parts to delegation: the configuration section locking mode, or `overrideMode`, and delegation of IIS Manager for managing sections to which the user has access.

Delegating access to configuration sections can be done in IIS Manager or by using the command line with `AppCmd.exe`. For example, to lock the configuration to prevent custom HTTP errors from being added to a web site, you would run the following command, which will lock the configuration of HTTP errors on `WebSite1`, leaving other sites unlocked:

```
appcmd.exe lock config "WebSite1" -section:httpErrors
```

IIS 7 Access Policies

IIS 7.0 has the ability to restrict access to web sites, and even folders, by limiting the IP addresses allowed access. A new security feature for IIS 7.0, *Request Filtering*, replaces the use of URLScan from previous IIS versions, making possible the restriction of specific requests from being executed. Using these tools, you can lock access to your site from a specific IP address range and serve only a limited set of requests.

One example of restricting IP address access is if you are creating an extranet, allowing access from a specific business partner and denying access from all other sources. If that business partner has a specific IP address range that will access your extranet, you can reject any request coming from other IP addresses. This process shouldn't be used instead of locking down firewall rules, but it does provide an extra layer of security.

Restricting access based on the request can be more flexible. For example, if you do not use MP3 files on your site, you can create a filtering rule that will drop requests for the .MP3 extension. This prevents the server from expending resources to process a request for a file that should not exist on the server and also enforces a policy of not serving MP3 files.

Determining the policy for access and filtering that meets the needs of your organization and your applications should begin with any corporate policy restrictions. Determine what content will be served and to whom, then deny all other requests through IP restrictions or Request Filtering as appropriate. Whenever you implement changes, use the IIS log files to analyze any requests that behaved in an unexpected manner. You may find a developer using a file extension you haven't allowed and need to adjust either the policy or the developer as appropriate.

Implementing access policies using IP address restrictions or Request Filtering is discussed more completely in Chapter 13. You may wish to review the process as you develop your policies to ensure that you understand how to implement your policies.

Planning Development Environments

Most professional IIS 7.0 installations will include a development environment and a production environment, and often a staging server will be used for code testing before deployment. For maximum efficiency, it is important that development environments be configured as close to the production environment as possible. Microsoft has made this both simpler and more complex by including IIS 7.0 on Windows Vista — simpler because this is the first version of IIS since version 4.0 where the workstation and server versions are identical — or at least mostly identical. Vista Service Pack 1 updates IIS 7.0 to match the newer Windows Server 2008 version, maintaining the very close similarity between client and server versions.

For developers using Visual Studio, there are some significant differences between the development server in Visual Studio and that in IIS 7.0 that affect the deployment of applications. The Visual Studio development server runs under the logged-in user account, most often a local administrator account, whereas by default, IIS runs under the less privileged anonymous user account or the ASP.NET process account. Applications that function perfectly well during development often run into problems when deployed because of the lower security access accorded them under IIS 7.0.

Another issue with the development server is its use of nonstandard ports. Ports are randomly selected for each service, and the ports are not standardized between sessions. This means that URLs will have a port appended to them, looking something like `http://localhost:2058/myapp/index.aspx`. Using that URL in a link within your application will undoubtedly break when the application is transferred to a production server, where IIS 7.0 will be using HTTP on port 80, not to mention a fully qualified domain name instead of localhost.

For most developers, using IIS 7.0 for development is the best solution. Either a development server or a virtual server environment solves issues between the Visual Studio development server settings and the settings for the IIS 7.0 production server. Visual Studio can be changed to use IIS for web projects, attaching a debugger to the IIS process, providing a development environment well matched to the final deployment environment.

Whichever option is used in your organization, planning for differences between development servers and deployment servers is essential. Making the ASP.NET process account a local administrator on the production server is not a valid choice to cure security woes generated by using a less than optimum development environment.

Planning Production Environments

Production environments, while being as close as possible to those used for development, must by nature be more secure and robust. You should plan any production environment to contain the bare minimum of installed IIS 7.0 modules needed to run the deployed applications, and you should minimize any additional programs running on the system. While development servers may need programs such as Visual Studio installed, production servers would rarely benefit from having such software running on them. In fact, production servers often don't require Internet Explorer or an FTP client, or any other standard client software. In Windows Server 2008, many client components are not installed, such as Windows Media Player, the Photo Gallery, and so on. While these can be installed using the Desktop Experience feature, unless the server will be used as a desktop client, you should not install them. Your production environment can have these removed and still meet the needs of any applications you choose to deploy.

Shared Configuration

IIS 7.0's *Shared Configuration* option allows multiple servers to share the same configuration files, making it easier to keep configurations synced across a web farm, as well as easier to deploy configuration changes. Using shared configurations, deployments to all servers of any configuration changes are almost instantaneous. If you will be using shared configurations, you need to plan a location for the configuration files. This location must be on a Windows share that is accessible to all systems running the shared configuration. Since the shared configuration needs a user account to access this share, you should create a domain user specifically for this shared configuration and assign it read rights to the share, then use this domain user for the shared configuration connection. It is possible to create identical, mirrored, local accounts on each server, but the passwords must be synched for this type of access to work, making this choice more prone to disconnects than using a single domain account.

Content Replication

Microsoft has retired the Content Management Server and does not, at the time of this writing, have a similar product available. That leaves you to work out a method of *content replication* when dealing with either development and staging servers or web farms. One solution is to use a distributed file system setup with replication, or DFS Replication. There are a few limitations to be aware of when planning for DFS replication in your environment.

DFS is not supported on clusters, thus you can't use a replicated folder on a cluster. DFS also does not work with encrypting file system files. DFS replication requires ports opened in firewalls, specifically port 135 and a port you may configure using a port number above 1024. Most important, DFS replication should not be used when there is a chance that files may be modified by two different users. DFS may try to replicate dissimilar files, which can cause serious problems. If you face this situation, use a staging server that files are copied to for replication to other servers, and be sure to use some sort of check-in/check-out control software, such as Visual Source Safe for programming or SharePoint for Office documents.

Other content replication options are available, from third-party tools to custom scripts to even a scheduled Robocopy event. Robocopy is a free utility that can copy changed files and ships in the Windows Server Resource Kit. When scheduled through the Task Scheduler Service, it makes a handy, although awkward to manage, replication utility.

Application Deployment Planning

Rarely is an IIS 7.0 web server going to be deployed to serve just static content. Applications will need to be deployed as well, both the application code and the configuration changes necessary to run the application in IIS 7.0. IIS 7.0 simplifies application deployment, at least as far as the IIS settings go, with a true XCopy deployment scenario. Because all the IIS 7.0 configurations are maintained in XML-formatted configuration files, these can easily be copied to new servers and sites as needed — with the caveat that the new server must have the proper modules installed.

Planning your application deployment should begin with an inventory of what is required by your application in terms of ASP.NET framework version, IIS 7.0 modules, NTFS file and folder permissions, and ancillary programs and connections, such as Microsoft SQL Server locations and connection strings. These existing requirements must be mapped to the new installation so that code can be deployed, then tested, on the new server. A list of required items for your application might include:

- ❏ ISAPI Filters.
- ❏ COM components.
- ❏ ASP.NET assemblies installed in the global assembly cache (GAC).
- ❏ SSL certificates.
- ❏ Database DSNs (or migrate to a DSN-less connection).
- ❏ Machine Keys (normally copied with ASP.NET configuration files).
- ❏ Custom registry settings.

This list is not comprehensive, but covers most common application requirements. Each specific application may have its own requirements, and each should be thoroughly tested after migration before deployment for live use.

Upgrading existing IIS 6.0 applications adds a twist to the deployment of applications since the new integrated pipeline doesn't directly support applications configured for IIS 6.0's ISAPI pipeline. There are two paths you can take to an upgrade deployment: you can run the application using the classic pipeline mode, complete with ISAPI and CGI applications, or you can modify the configuration, and sometimes the application code, to run under the new IIS 7.0 integrated pipeline model. These modifications may also include upgrading authentication schemes from Windows integrated, Basic authentication, or even Passport authentication, to ASP.NET Forms authentication in IIS 7.0.

Automation and Deployment Tools

In the next chapter, you will find instructions for a single-instance installation of IIS 7.0 on Windows Server 2008. However, most professional IIS 7.0 installations won't be manually installing a single instance of IIS on a single server. Automating deployment is important in most organizations, whether it is workstations, applications, servers, or IIS installations. Even when manual installations are feasible in terms of time and location, automated deployments are preferable since exact configurations can easily be achieved.

Over the various versions of Windows and IIS, automated deployment has improved steadily. WMI scripting for configurations, remote installation service (RIS), deployment and unattended installs, and even third-party cloning tools have all been used effectively and made deployment much easier for administrators. Windows Server 2008 extends automated deployments yet again with Windows Deployment Services.

Windows Deployment Services

The updated version of RIS from Windows Server 2003 is Windows Deployment Services in Windows Server 2008. Windows Deployment Services was available for Windows Server 2003 but has been expanded and enhanced for Windows Server 2008. *Windows Deployment Services* handles full installation of Windows Server 2008 from a network connection, with no physical media required at the system.

Windows Deployment Services can deploy both the Vista client and Windows Server 2008, making deployments more efficient and less expensive in terms of organization resources. It also works in a mixed environment of Windows Server 2003 and Windows XP. Installing IIS 7.0 using Windows Deployment Services is discussed in Chapter 4.

Windows Deployment Services in Windows Server 2008 has evolved from the Windows Server 2003 version and from RIS in several key areas. Most significant is the ability to do a multicast deployment, scaling out to about 75 systems per Windows Deployment Services server. Windows Deployment Services also uses an enhanced TFTP service to transfer images and data more efficiently. The new version also includes a graphical interface and advanced reporting functions. The Windows automated installation kit still exists for Vista workstation deployment as an option to using Windows Deployment Services, and many organizations will have workstation and server deployments split between different teams.

Volume Activation

Most professional IIS 7.0 installations are likely using some sort of volume licensing agreement to license Windows Server 2008. Unlike single-server installations, volume licensing options also come with volume activation options. In Windows Server 2008, you have both multiple activation keys, similar to Windows Server 2003 licensing, and key management service. With multiple activation keys, each server connects to Microsoft and is authorized, either individually or through a proxy server. Once activated, servers are eligible for Microsoft updates and will function beyond the 30-day activation period.

If you have 10 or more server licenses, or 25 or more Vista licenses, you are able to run a key management service on your network, activating licenses without connection to Microsoft. Systems activated this way must reconnect to the key management service every six months or less to maintain activation. More information on volume activation is available from Microsoft's web site.

Capacity Planning

In many ways, capacity planning for IIS 7.0 is a guessing game. Benchmarking, testing a configuration and saving the results, then making a change and testing again so that the results can be compared, is crucial. However, it's sometimes impossible to test an application on IIS 7.0 if the application is still under development. There are load testing tools available that can test IIS 7.0 response, and they may or may not make sense in your capacity planning.

IIS 7.0 itself is capable of handling tens of thousands of requests per second. In real-life situations, this number is impossible to meet. Bottlenecks can occur at many points in the serving of a request — accessing a back-end database, retrieving data from a mainframe, or an ERP or CRM application, even hardware and network layer delays can reduce the number of serviceable requests.

A common question is, "How many web sites can I host on my server?" That question simply cannot be answered with a definitive number. The type of site, data contained on it, popularity, connection speed, and hardware it runs on are all factors. But a general rule of thumb that works for many hosting companies is that only 15 percent of the sites on a server will be active at a time. That means that you can exceed the estimated capacity of a server by about eight times and be safe. Naturally, for a low-cost web host, maximizing the number of clients on a single server is the way to maximize profits.

Traffic

Traffic is one of the first capacity planning issues you must answer and plan for. How many requests to your servers will come in on average, and what will the peak be? Then you need to test your estimates against your servers to plan for future performance. But estimating traffic before an application or server is deployed is simply an educated guess, and traffic patterns are rarely stable. Just as in street traffic, network traffic comes in bursts, with somewhat predictable peak times. Rush hour on your intranet will be when workers are arriving in the morning, probably after lunch, and right before leaving for home. Nighttime traffic, unless you run night shifts, will likely be minimal.

You can begin to estimate the load on a network connection with some simple math. For each HTTP request, the protocol overhead is about 1,800 bytes. A letter-sized page of text, without graphics, runs about 5K, or 5,120 bytes. A T-1 Internet connection can transfer 1.536 MBPS, or about 26 of those 5K pages, each second. If your average page size is more like 50K, which is small for many of today's graphically rich sites, you'll transmit about 2.6 of those pages per second. Obviously, a good start for increasing capacity would be reducing the total page size returned on a request. The table below shows estimated bandwidth saturation points for various outbound connection speeds and page content sizes. These numbers should not be relied on in a production environment, since many factors can affect the actual bandwidth consumption.

	T-1 Line (1.536 MBps)	2 Bonded T-1 Lines (3.72 MBps)	DS-3 Line (44.736 MBps)	OC-3 Optical (155.52 MBps)
5K File	26 per second	53 per second	760 per second	2,640 per second
50K File	3 per second	6 per second	90 per second	400 per second
500K File	3 seconds each	1.5 seconds each	12 per second	50 per second
5-MB File	5 minutes each	2.5 minutes each	2 seconds each	19 per second
660 MB (CD)	8 hours each	4 hours each	4 minutes each	8 seconds

On the requesting side, your clients may have high-capacity pipelines such as DSL or broadband connections. A typical T-1 line can be saturated by less than a dozen DSL lines with simultaneous requests, which is another reason to ensure that data sent in response to a request are as small as possible. Fortunately, IIS 7.0 includes HTTP compression, which will improve this performance model, as well as rich caching mechanisms to make the end result to the user seem much quicker. Finding the actual response times and overhead on your network and servers will require the use of a tool that can test the web capacity of your specific configuration. Fortunately, Microsoft has such a tool.

WCAT

Microsoft's *Web Capacity Analysis Tool (WCAT)* is designed to simulate a load on your network and web server, allowing you to benchmark your system and apply changes to improve performance. Available as a free download, WCAT comes with pre-configured tests for your site, including HTTP as well as ISAPI and CGI testing. For testing a web server and network, a simple HTML file will work, or you can test application response with WCAT as well. WCAT will also test multiprocessor scalability.

IIS 7.0 Request Tracing

IIS 7.0's *Request Tracing* utility can be used for testing performance as well. Configure a test for a valid response code, 200, and hit your web site and application with a browser. The request tracing log will show each stage of the request, as well as the time for the stage. You can use this to determine any bottlenecks in your site or application. If the longest time is in authenticating, you might want to look at the SQL Server connection for your authentication database, or possibly optimizing indexes on that database. Request tracing won't tell you what is wrong and how to fix it, but it can provide both a clue to areas that may need work and a valid baseline for testing improvements.

Scalability

Improving *scalability* in web sites and servers is a concern for most organizations. IIS 7.0 scales well, having tested with thousands of web sites on a single server, and the only limitations are hardware-based — the maximum drive space available, maximum RAM in a system, and maximum bandwidth available. But there are still hardware choices and configurations that can help scalability.

Network load balancing, either through Windows NLB or a third-party load balancer, is essential for multisystem configurations. Memory paging in Windows Server 2008 can be improved by locating the paging file on a disk array that does not contain web site data or log files, and maximizing RAM can limit the amount of paging the system will do. Choosing a processor with a large L2 cache improves performance for applications like IIS 7.0. Adding or upgrading network adapters, provided you haven't already saturated bandwidth, can improve performance. Setting longer content expiration times for content that rarely changes will mean that proxy servers won't need to refresh content from the server as frequently.

Windows Server 2008 has added networking functionality to support scalability in the network linking IIS 7.0 servers. A redesigned TCP/IP stack (tcpip.sys) supports IPv6 and expanded IPsec for integrated security. The new networking in Windows Server 2008 better handles intermittent connectivity and recovers quicker from lost packets, making wireless communications faster and providing better transmission across WAN links. Windows Server 2008 can automatically scale the TCP/IP receive window size, and combined, the networking improvements result in up to a 350 percent improvement in throughput.

Windows Server 2008 can also make use of new hardware technologies that offload network processing from the CPU, both removing the CPU as a bottleneck and freeing CPU cycles for processing application requests. Web servers can also benefit from dynamic network connection balancing, which queues network traffic for multiple processors or processor cores, also limiting the need for higher-end servers. More on hardware scalability and networking in Windows Server 2008 can be found on Technet or through Microsoft's communities.

Scalability has no single solution for all administrators. Each site's design will contribute to scalability, and the needs for scalability will vary by organization. For more information about performance optimization settings and monitoring IIS 7.0 performance, see Chapter 19, "Monitoring and Performance Tuning."

Application Capacity Planning

Capacity planning for ASP.NET applications is outside this book's scope, but there is a new setting for IIS 7.0 that may help you. ASP.NET 2.0 introduced the `processModel/autoConfig` configuration, which would automate many of the performance configurations such as `MaxIoThreads`, `MaxWorkerThreads`, and so on, setting them at run time for your application. One problem is that this configuration has a 12-request-per-CPU limit, meaning that applications with high latency will not perform as well as they could. IIS 7.0 introduces a new registry key, `MaxConcurrentRequestsPerCpu`, which can overcome this limitation. To use this key, add a `DWORD` key of `MaxConcurrentRequestsPerCpu` to `HKEY_LOCAL_MACHINE\SOFTWARE\Microsoft\ASP.NET\2.0.50727.0`, and set it to the number of requests desired. The default if this key does not exist is 12 requests per CPU. The upper limit is still set by the `processModel/requestQueueLimit` configuration, which defaults to 5,000 ASP.NET requests maximum. A setting of 0 will force each request to be immediately processed, and, in cases where static content is served, this may improve performance. Normally, this is not the setting you want, though. Keep in mind that this process means editing the registry. If you are not comfortable with this, do not perform this modification. Errors in registry settings may cause unforeseen problems, up to and including a non-working server.

Summary

Ensuring an orderly and complete deployment of IIS 7.0 web servers and sites requires significant planning. Whether your organization uses a formal deployment planning checklist and guide or you simply plan a deployment to meet a specific application need, the more thought and research you put into the planning stage, the greater your chances for a successful, and uneventful, deployment.

You should recognize the resources available in your deployment and ensure that your planning takes those resources — both equipment and human — into account. Leveraging your resources is part of planning, and, since there are varied reasons for deploying IIS 7.0, each deployment will be unique. Encouraging participation of all parties affected by the deployment, including developers, managers, and even end-users, will ensure that your deployment planning meets the needs and goals of the deployment. Since IIS 7.0 deployments will often involve networking staff, security staff, and developer staff, getting those individuals in on the planning stage will help ensure that your planning covers their requirements as well.

Because there is more to deployment planning than just what is presented in this chapter, you should review any other chapters relevant to your deployment to get the understanding you will need in your planning. In particular, you will want to review Chapter 4, "Installing IIS 7.0," and know your options for installation and migration of existing servers. If you skipped over Chapter 2, "IIS 7.0 Architecture," you might want also to review differences between IIS 7.0 and previous versions for potential deployment concerns.

4

Installing IIS 7.0

There are many ways to install IIS 7.0, from installing it as part of the Windows Server 2008 installation or adding IIS 7.0 to an existing server to upgrading a Windows Server 2003 and IIS 6.0 installation — not to mention automated or unattended installations.

In this chapter, we assume that you've read and understood the deployment planning issues discussed in Chapter 3, "Planning Your Deployment." You might also want to scan several of the upcoming chapters so that you understand which additional features you might want to install. Chapter 5, "Administration Tools," as well as Chapter 10, "Configuring Other Services," may help you.

After reading this chapter, you should be able to:

❑ Install IIS 7.0 along with Windows Server 2008.

❑ Install IIS 7.0 into an existing Windows Server 2008 system.

❑ Upgrade a Windows Server 2003 IIS 6.0 system to Windows Server 2008 and IIS 7.0.

❑ Install new features in an existing IIS 7.0 installation.

❑ Install IIS 7.0 from the command line.

❑ Configure IIS 7.0 for shared hosting recommendations.

❑ Install IIS 7.0 on Windows Vista.

Future chapters will cover advanced configuration options for IIS 7.0. While this chapter covers adding features to an existing IIS 7.0 installation, you may wish to also look at Chapter 11, "Core Server," and Chapter 18, "Programmatic Configuration and Management," as companions to this chapter.

Clean Installation

The most basic installation of IIS 7.0 is a clean installation, either at the time the operating system is installed or into an existing operating system. The default installation of Windows Server 2008 does not install IIS 7.0, and the default installation of IIS 7.0 does not enable most functions of IIS. In fact, the default installation does little more than enable serving of static content — basic HTML pages and images.

With Windows Server 2008 Installation

If you know that IIS 7.0 will be a function required on your new Windows Server 2008 server, then you might as well install IIS 7.0 at the same time you install the operating system. Naturally, you wouldn't want to install IIS 7.0 if you don't need it, but the number of applications that require IIS and ASP.NET is growing continually, so even if you're not configuring a "web server," you may very well need IIS 7.0 on the server just for the applications you intend to run. This is especially true if you intend to run many Microsoft products, such as Microsoft Exchange, Windows Server Update Services, or some Microsoft SQL Server installations, especially those using Microsoft SQL Server Reporting Services support.

Default Installation with Operating System

For this example, you'll install Windows Server 2008 to a new server with IIS 7.0 installed at the default options along with the operating system. If you are building a new server that will need to have IIS installed, such as an application server, it is often more efficient to install IIS 7.0 along with the operating system. When you boot the server from the DVD, the Windows Server 2008 installation will begin, as shown in Figure 4-1.

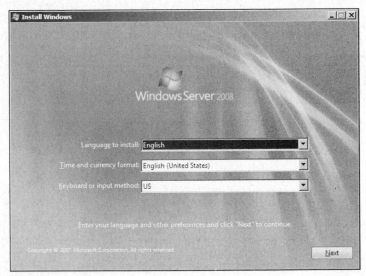

Figure 4-1

Once you have started the installation, entered the license key, and agreed to the terms of use, make sure that you do not install the Server Core version. Installing IIS 7.0 on the Server Core using the command line is covered below in this chapter. When prompted, select the custom installation choice. On a new server, this is the only option you can choose. On a server with an existing compatible operating system, you can choose to upgrade the operating system. The upgrade choice will be covered below in this chapter as well. Once you select the drive on which to install Windows Server 2008, installation will begin.

Once the server installs, you'll be presented with the initial configuration tasks, as shown in Figure 4-2. You may choose to rename the server, change the time, and make other settings at this point, including choosing roles to install. Choosing the "Add roles" option under "Customize This Server" brings up the Add Roles Wizard. After clicking Next from the first screen, which can be bypassed by checking the box labeled "Skip This Page by Default," you arrive at the Select Server Roles screen, as shown in Figure 4-3.

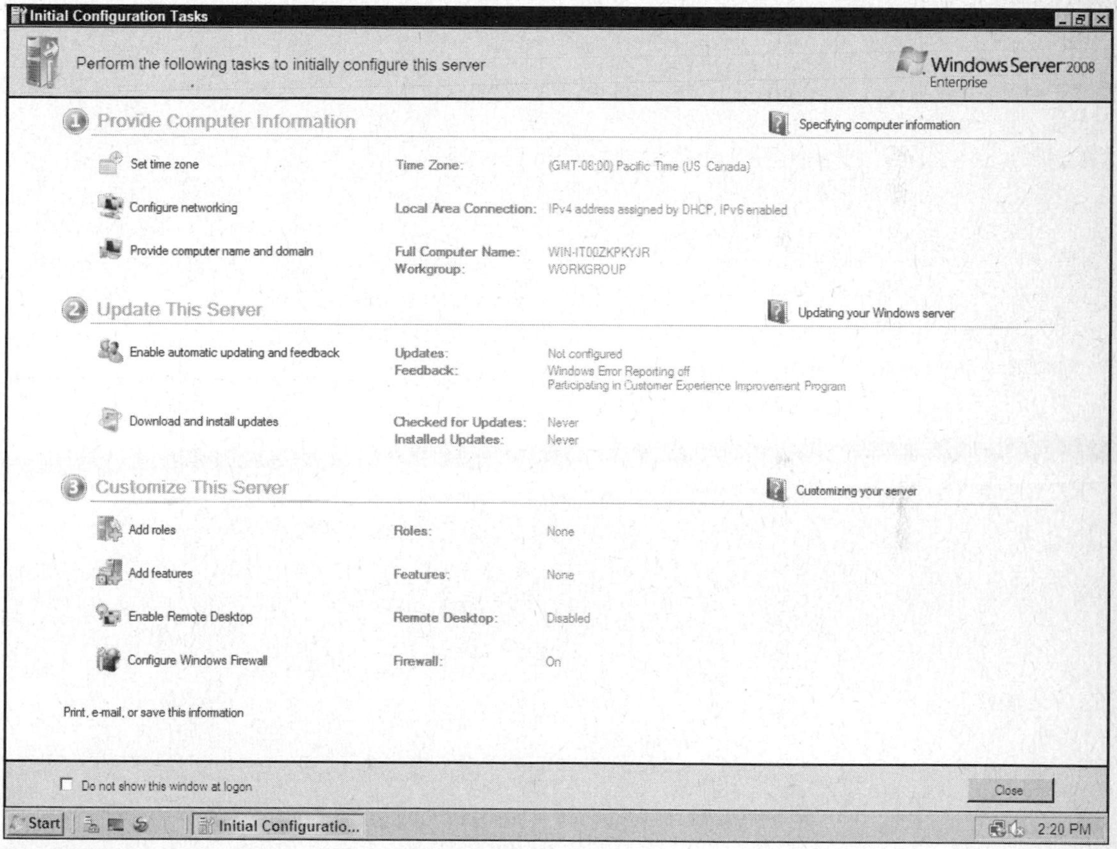

Figure 4-2

Choosing "Web Server (IIS)" will pop up a required features dialog box, as shown in Figure 4-4. You must install the required features for a role to be added, so choose Add Required Features (in this case, the Windows Process Activation Service), and then click Next.

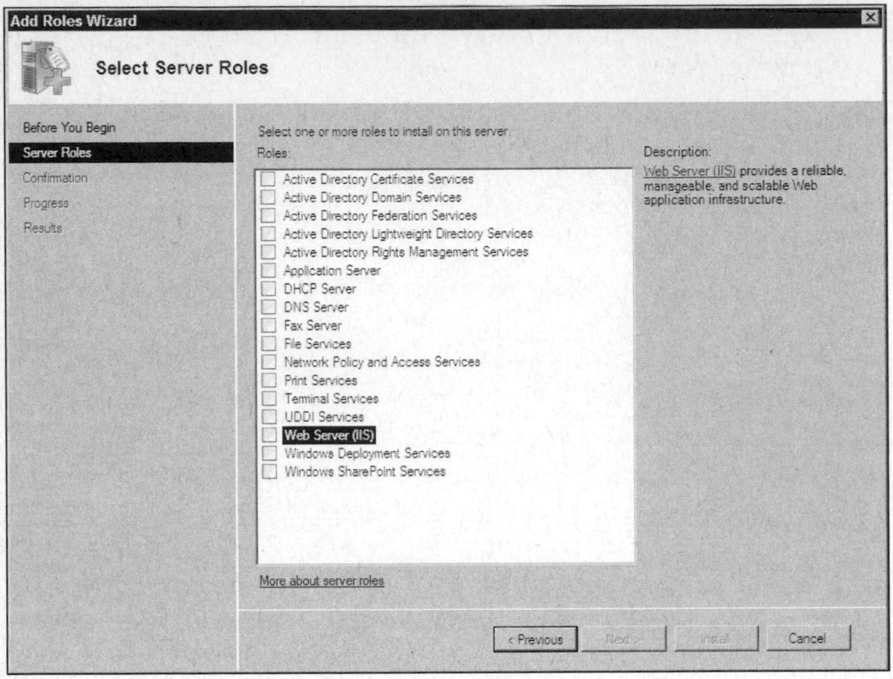

Figure 4-3

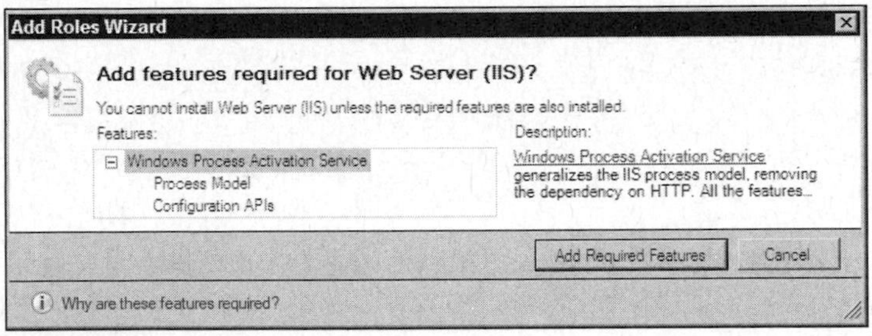

Figure 4-4

The Wizard displays information and help about IIS 7.0, and clicking to the next step will show the Select Role Services dialog box, as shown in Figure 4-5. Notice that IIS 7.0 in a default installation will serve only static content. Logging, request monitoring, request filtering, and compression are also installed by default, as is the IIS Management Console.

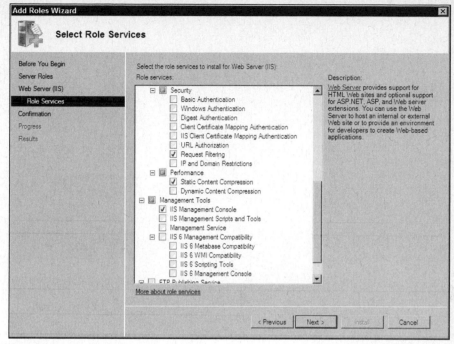

Figure 4-5

After you confirm your selections and choose to install, IIS 7.0 will install, along with the Windows Process Activation Service. If you are prompted, insert the DVD and finish the installation (by default, installation files are cached on the hard disk, so the installation DVD is not needed). The server may need to be restarted to complete the installation (by default, a restart is not required however). When the installation completes, IIS 7.0 should be able to serve static content, but not much more.

Testing Your Installation

Naturally, the first thing you'll want to do with your new web server is see if it works. If you open IIS Manager from Administrative Tools and then expand the server to reveal the Default Web Site, you should see the administrative functions shown in Figure 4-6.

Right-click the Default Web Site and choose Content View, and you'll see the content being served by this web site, as shown in Figure 4-7. Notice that two files exist, iisstart.htm and welcome.png.

If you return to the Features view, by right-clicking the web site and choosing Features View, and then double-click the default document feature, you'll see the list of documents that IIS 7.0 will serve (see Figure 4-8). These documents appear in the order IIS will choose to serve them, if they are available, with iisstart.htm at the bottom. This means that any of the other documents, if they exist in the root of the web site, will be served before iisstart.htm. For now, an easy check of the web server is to simply browse to it and see if the iisstart.htm file is displayed. Opening Internet Explorer and browsing to the server name should display the iisstart.htm file, as shown in Figure 4-9.

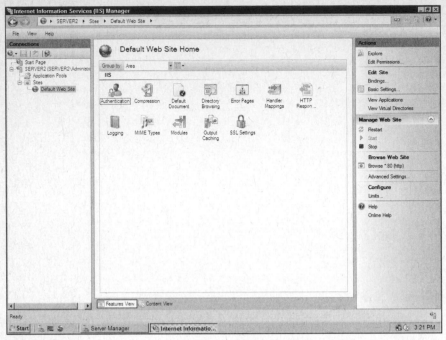

Figure 4-6

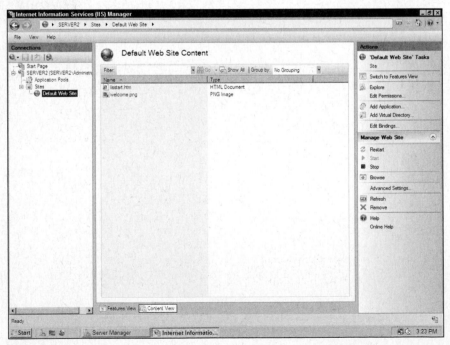

Figure 4-7

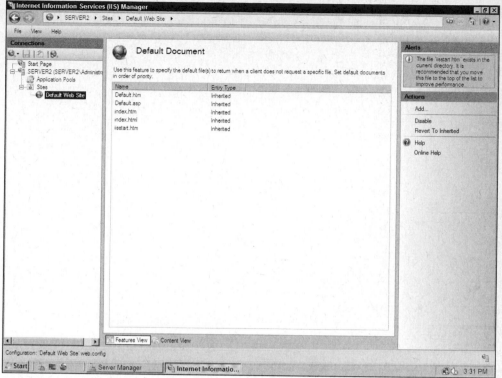

Figure 4-8

Figure 4-9

Okay, so your installation works. But since nobody wants to serve the `iisstart.htm` file to their client systems, you naturally want to test the server with your own files. The conventional means of testing a web server is through the use of a "Hello World!" test page. This is true whether you're testing static content or applications such as ASP and ASP.NET. A basic file, the Hello World! application is designed to be the simplest application you can create that will test the features of your web site. For a static HTML file, simply create the following text in a basic text editor such as Notepad, and save it as `hello.htm` in the web site's root folder. The Default Web Site installed with IIS 7.0 has its root at `c:\inetpub\WWWRoot\`. If you use Notepad, watch out for Notepad adding the .txt extension to your filename.

```html
<html>
  <head>
    <title>Hello World!</title>
  </head>
  <body>
    <h1>Hello World!</h1>
    <p>This is a Hello World! HTML file.</p>
  </body>
</html>
```

Once you have saved this file, you can again browse to your web server to view it. Because the file name `hello.htm` is not in the default document list, you must specify the file on the URL; otherwise, a default document will be served. The URL `http:\\{ServerName}\hello.htm`, with your server's name replacing `{ServerName}`, should display in your browser, similar to Figure 4-10.

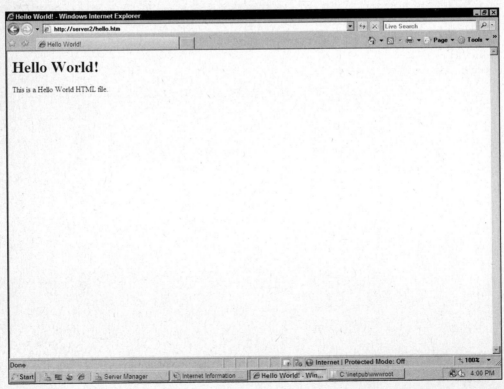

Figure 4-10

From DVD to an Existing Server

Installing IIS 7.0 from physical media, normally a DVD, is similar to installing along with the operating system. In these examples, the first installation is the bare default with no additional features. The second installation will include popular additional features and roles that are commonly installed but would not be installed in a default IIS 7.0 installation.

Default IIS 7.0 Installation

The default IIS 7.0 installation discussed in this section is the most basic installation of IIS 7.0 possible. At the end of this installation, your server will be able to serve static content. That's enough for some uses, but this is probably the least common installation. It's not uncommon to receive a server from a vendor who has pre-installed the operating system with the default IIS 7.0 installation you'll see here. Adding features during the IIS 7.0 installation is a more common installation, as is adding features to an existing IIS 7.0 installation, but this installation example will familiarize you with what to expect from a basic IIS 7.0 installation.

The installation of IIS 7.0 to a server that already has Windows Server 2008 installed begins in Server Manager, as shown in Figure 4-11. Open Server Manager by clicking the Start button and opening Administrative Tools, then choosing Server Manager. Scroll down to the Roles Summary section, and choose Add Roles to launch the Add Roles Wizard. Accept the Before You Begin prompt if it comes up, and you'll see the Select Server Roles dialog box, as shown in Figure 4-12. Select Web Server (IIS), and click Next.

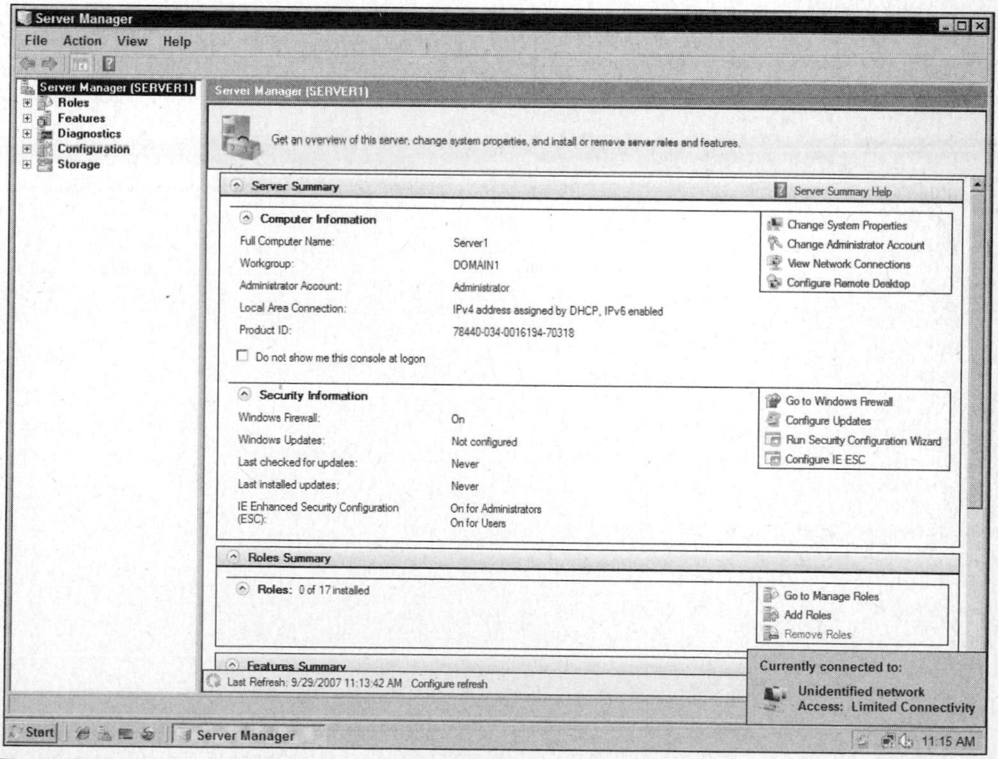

Figure 4-11

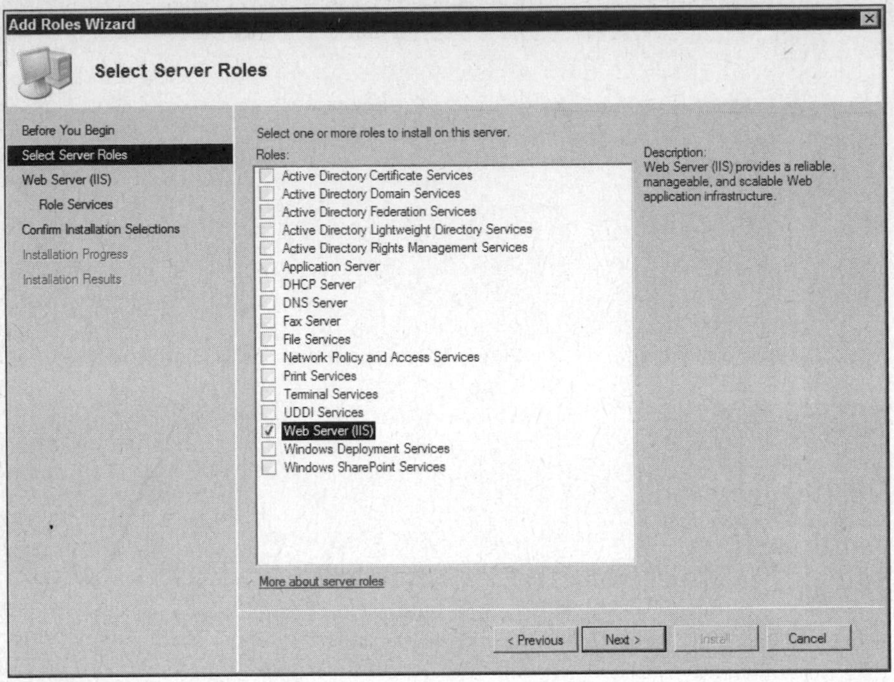

Figure 4-12

After clicking Next on the information screen, you'll see the Select Role Services dialog box, as shown in Figure 4-13. Note that, by default, IIS 7.0 serves only static content in the form of HTML web pages. HTTP logging, the request monitor, and request filters, as well as compression for static content, are also installed by default. Naturally, the IIS management console is installed; otherwise, you would have no easy way to manage your web server.

After clicking Next and confirming your selections, click Install to begin the installation. Insert the DVD if prompted, and your installation should complete successfully, as shown in Figure 4-14.

Once IIS 7.0 is installed as a role, you can click that role in Server Manager and you'll see the Role Summary and Services installed, as shown in Figure 4-15. From this summary, you will see the last 24 hours of events as well as the system services that are running. You can also manage the services from here. For example, you should see the World Wide Web Publishing Service (w3svc) running. With a right-click, you can choose to stop or restart this service, just as you could from the Services dialog in Windows Server 2003.

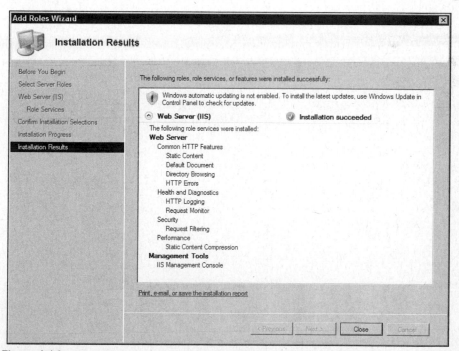

Figure 4-13

Figure 4-14

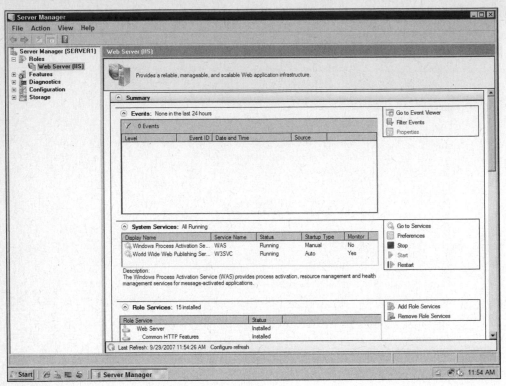

Figure 4-15

If you scroll down, you'll see the Role Services installed, as well as a list of those that are not installed. Highlighting each will present a description of the service. At the bottom of the web server role details, you'll find the Resources and Support section, as shown in Figure 4-16. This has a list of best practices, common configurations, and links to online support for your web server. An example of these suggestions is to "Provide a better user experience by configuring custom HTTP settings." The description for this gives some suggestions for you to look at, and clicking the "More about this recommendation" information link takes you to the corresponding section of the Windows Server 2008 Help files, as shown in Figure 4-17. This integration of the Help system runs throughout Windows Server 2008 and can be updated through service packs and Windows updates.

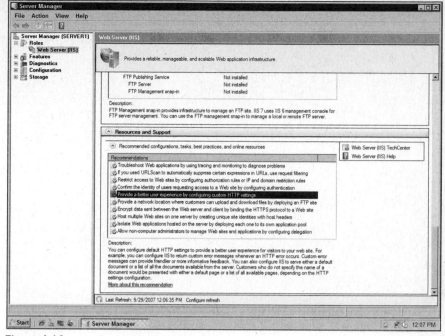

Figure 4-16

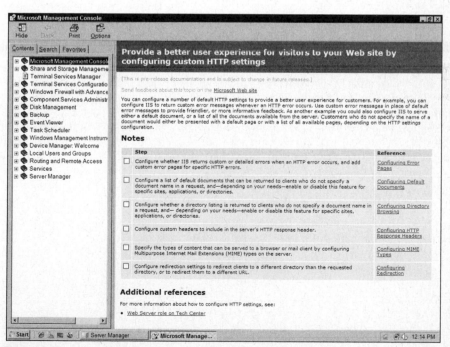

Figure 4-17

Upgrade Installation

Upgrading existing IIS 6.0 web servers to IIS 7.0, which includes updating Windows Server 2003 to Windows Server 2008, is a common scenario. There are limitations to this process, most notably that the new site will run in classic pipeline mode, essentially running as an IIS 6.0 web server. Many organizations need this capability, though, and will then migrate the web sites from IIS 6.0 to IIS 7.0 features. The downside to this is that the hardware currently running Windows Server 2003 and IIS 6.0 must already be capable of running Windows Server 2008 and IIS 7.0.

Another typical upgrade path for IIS servers is a *migration upgrade*. In this upgrade you would begin with the old Windows Server 2003 and IIS 6.0 server and end with a new Windows Server 2008 and IIS 7.0 server. You would migrate the IIS 6.0 sites to the new server and new settings, and then retire the old hardware. The advantage to this method is you don't need to have your Windows Server 2003 operating system already running on Windows Server 2008 compatible hardware.

In-Place Upgrade

If you have a current Windows Server 2003 and IIS 6.0 web server that is running on hardware compatible with Windows Server 2008 and IIS 7.0, an in-place upgrade makes sense. This section will upgrade an existing Windows Server 2003 system running IIS 6.0 with a DotNetNuke web installation.

Current Server

The current server for this demonstration is Windows Server 2003 Enterprise R2 x86 SP2, with a DotNetNuke installation on IIS 6.0, running the ASP.NET 2.0 Framework. IIS 6.0 hosts a single site, with the default ASP.NET 2.0 application pool assigned to the application DotNetNuke. Accessing this server at `http://localhost/dotnetnuke/` produces a browser view as shown in Figure 4-18. The properties for the DotNetNuke application are shown in Figure 4-19.

This server has 2 GB of RAM and plenty of hard drive space, and the hardware is compatible with Windows Server 2008, making this server a prime candidate for an in-place upgrade. IIS 6.0 on this machine has only a single web site, even though the SharePoint Administration Site has been installed in the default IIS 6.0 installation, along with FrontPage Server Extensions. Since this Windows Server 2003 system has FrontPage Server Extensions installed, we must remove them before upgrading. Windows Server 2008 will not allow an upgrade of a system with FrontPage Server Extensions installed. Removal is accomplished through Add and Remove Programs in the Control Panel, selecting the Add/Remove Windows Components. FrontPage Server Extensions is part of the Internet Information Services (IIS) category under Application Server, and unchecking the FrontPage 2002 Server Extensions checkbox, then choosing OK, will remove them from the server.

Upgrading Windows Server 2003 to Windows Server 2008

Preparing for an upgrade involves making any needed updates to the server, making a complete backup in case something goes wrong, and defragmenting the server. If the server is part of a domain, make sure that the domain controller is working and connected.

Inserting the Windows Server 2008 DVD while Windows Server 2003 is running brings up the installation splash screen. Click Install Now to begin the installation process. You can either go online for updates or skip the updates and go directly to the installation. After selecting the full installation instead of Server Core and providing the registration key, you will be presented with the option of upgrading the current server. A compatibility report will provide you with warnings about the upgrade, and a list of remedies, if needed.

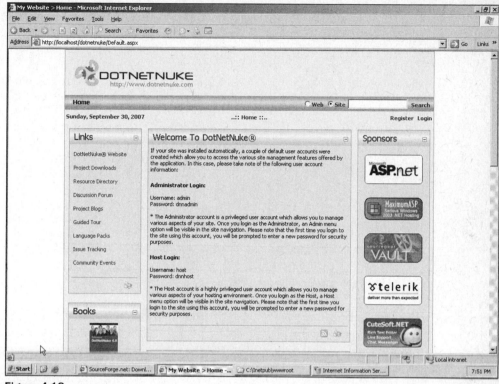

Figure 4-18

Once the upgrade launches, go out for lunch. Upgrading a Windows Server 2003 system to Windows Server 2008 takes a while, quite a while for a server that has been in use for any significant time. Once the upgrade has completed and you've logged into your Windows Server 2008 system, navigate to Administrative Tools and notice that there is both an Internet Information Services (IIS) Manager that you would expect to see for IIS 7.0 and an Internet Information Services (IIS) 6.0 Manager. The latter is for managing web-site functions that cannot be directly upgraded to IIS 7.0, such as SMTP and FTP.

Opening IIS Manager and displaying the default web site that was upgraded to IIS 7.0, as shown in Figure 4-20, reveals some components installed that are not normally installed in IIS 7.0 by default. For example, the CGI module, SSL Settings module, and IPv4 Address and Domain Restrictions module are installed as part of the upgrade. This is because with the monolithic architecture of IIS 6.0, all these modules existed on the Windows Server 2003 and IIS 6.0 configuration. Even though all three of these modules were not used in the demonstration IIS 6.0 setup, IIS 6.0 loaded them all. In IIS 7.0, with its integrated pipeline and modularity, you can remove these modules rather than simply disabling their functions.

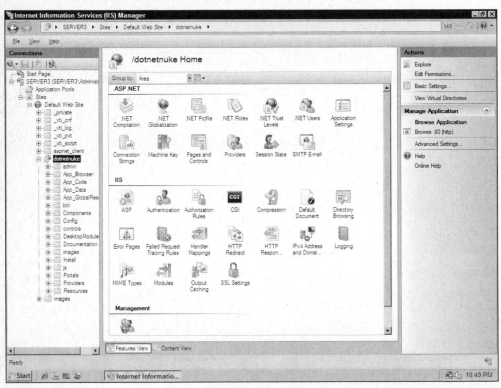

Figure 4-19

Figure 4-20

Browsing to the DotNetNuke application that was installed on Windows Server 2003 will show the same results as when it ran under IIS 6.0, as shown in Figure 4-21. IIS 7.0 accepted all the settings from IIS 6.0, migrated the necessary settings from the metabase to the XML configuration files in IIS 7.0, and maintained the existing security settings for the application pool and NTFS file and folder permissions.

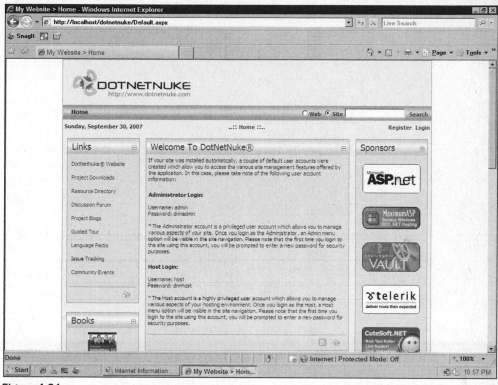

Figure 4-21

Upgrading Applications and Settings

Upgrading specific applications and settings from IIS 6.0 to IIS 7.0 may not be as easy as the simple demonstration just covered. There are several changes in IIS 7.0 that will cause some applications and utilities designed for IIS 6.0 not to function. Among these changes are the lack of a metabase, changes between the ASP.NET ISAPI mode in IIS 6.0 and the integrated pipeline mode in IIS 7.0, and changes in the management consoles. Some of these changes have workarounds available, such as metabase compatibility, whereas others, such as management console changes, will require you to update applications and utilities.

Metabase Compatibility

IIS 7.0 web-site has moved settings from the metabase to XML configuration files, and they can even appear in `web.config` files in each application. Applications or sites developed in IIS 6.0 that use metabase settings will not directly transfer to this new configuration system, thus Microsoft provides a *metabase compatibility mode* to enable many of these applications and sites to run. Metabase compatibility primarily applies either to IIS 6.0 features that are unchanged in IIS 7.0, such as SMTP and FTP, or to features that are no longer available in IIS 7.0, such as NNTP. FTP and SMTP installation is covered in Chapter 10.

Metabase compatibility is not installed by default, but can be installed through the normal set-up process and installing the IIS 6.0 Management Compatibility feature. Metabase compatibility is installed during an in-place upgrade from IIS 6.0, even if no compatibility features are needed. Metabase compatibility intercepts requests to the metabase and remaps those requests to the proper IIS 7.0 configuration file. This mapping takes place only with `applicationHost.config` and does not support settings in `web.config` files. Custom site configuration information is mapped properly, and metabase APIs are still available for applications developed to use them. In most cases, you will want to migrate these types of applications to IIS 7.0 and remove metabase compatibility, but using metabase compatibility can allow you to upgrade to IIS 7.0 before you must upgrade the application.

Integrated Pipeline Mode versus Classic Pipeline Mode

IIS 7.0 installs by default with the new integrated pipeline mode, with ASP.NET fully integrated into the process. This differs from the IIS 6.0 method of ASP.NET being an ISAPI application and processed outside the pipeline. During an upgrade from IIS 6.0, applications are automatically configured in classic pipeline mode, as is the default application pool. This differs from a standard IIS 7.0 installation, where the default application pool is configured in integrated pipeline mode. The pipeline mode is assigned by the application pool, thus moving an application into a different application pool may change the pipeline mode, which could possibly stop the application from functioning correctly. Pipeline mode changes are covered in more detail on Microsoft's web site at `www.iis.net/`.

You can configure an application pool for the pipeline mode by opening IIS Manager and navigating to the Application Pool, as shown in Figure 4-22. To change the application pool, choose Basic Settings under the Edit Application Pool section of the Actions pane, as shown in Figure 4-23.

By default, new application pools are created in the Integrated Pipeline mode in IIS 7.0. Installing an ASP.NET 2.0 application which previously worked in IIS 6.0 into a new application pool in IIS 7.0 may require changes to the application. You may elect to change the application pool to classic mode to avoid upgrading the application. Microsoft's Mike Volodarsky, a Program Manager on the IIS 7.0 development team, posted a list of breaking changes for ASP.NET 2.0 applications running on IIS 7.0 in integrated pipeline mode. These can be found online at `http://mvolo.com/blogs/serverside/archive/2007/12/08/IIS-7.0-Breaking-Changes-ASP.NET-2.0-applications-Integrated-mode.aspx`.

Migration Upgrade

A *migration upgrade* is one in which a new server is installed in your network and configured with Windows Server 2008 and IIS 7.0, then sites and applications are migrated from an existing Windows Server 2003 and IIS 6.0 installation to the new server and IIS 7.0. Microsoft is developing a set of migration tools to assist with this type of migration and expects them to be available at about the time Windows Server 2008 ships. Check the Wrox.com web site for updates to this section of the book.

Adding Features to an Existing Installation

If you have an installation of IIS 7.0 already on your server, as is the case in many servers shipped with Windows Server 2008 installed, you may need to add additional features to that installation. It's a very simple process, and probably common even when a server has been in place for a while. The installation shown in this section will add features required for running an ASP.NET application server, a common function for IIS 7.0 on Windows Server 2008.

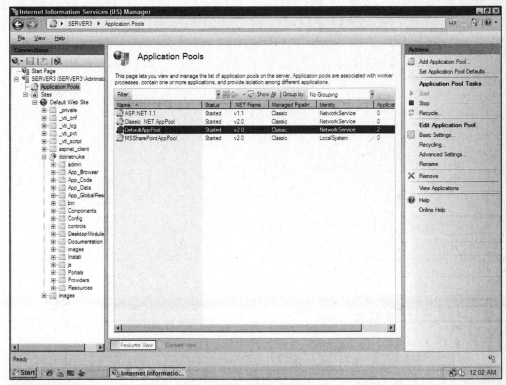

Figure 4-22

Figure 4-23

Installing New Features

Running a web server with a default IIS 7.0 installation, which will only serve static content, is rarely the desire of any organization today. Most commonly you will need to run at least an application, often ASP.NET, as well as some other features. So you have your default installation, and you want to add the following functions to your server:

❑ ASP.NET.

❑ Basic authentication.

❑ Windows authentication.

❑ Dynamic content compression.

Installing ASP.NET allows ASP.NET applications to run in IIS 7.0, both for web applications and extending the IIS 7.0 management interface, and the installation will configure additional features needed to run ASP.NET applications on your system. ASP.NET is a role service in IIS 7.0.

Open Server Manager, expand Roles, right-click Web Server (IIS), and choose Add Role Services, as shown in Figure 4-24. You should see the Role Services Selection dialog box. When you check the ASP.NET service under Application Development, you will see the Required Role Services information dialog box. Notice that ASP.NET requires ISAPI extensions and ISAPI filters, as well as .NET extensibility. The .NET environment will also be added to the Windows Process Activation Service.

Once you have accepted the required role services, continue and select "Basic Authentication," "Windows Authentication," and "Dynamic Content Compression." Basic Authentication and Windows Authentication allow for user authentication in your applications and on your site, while Dynamic Content Compression will deliver the final request to the client browser in a smaller package, decreasing the response time for the request and speeding up your site. Compression for static content, HTML files, has already been enabled. Confirm your selections, and continue the installation. The installation may ask for the DVD and may require a reboot.

Configuring and Testing New Features

Once the installation is finished, you can open IIS Manager and expand the web server, then click the default web site. You should see the ASP.NET area in the IIS Manager now that ASP.NET has been installed, as shown in Figure 4-25.

To test an ASP.NET application on your web site, create a "Hello World!" ASP.NET application using the following code. Name it hello.aspx, and place it in the root of your web site, and then browse to it using the URL `http:\\{ServerName}\hello.aspx`, with your server's name replacing `{ServerName}`. You should see a page similar to that in Figure 4-26.

```
<%@ Page Language="VB" %>
<% HelloWorld.Text = "Hello World!" %>
<html>
  <head>
    <title>Hello World! - ASP.NET version</title>
  </head>
  <body>
```

```
    <p>
        <asp:label id="HelloWorld" runat="Server" />
    </p>
    </body>
</html>
```

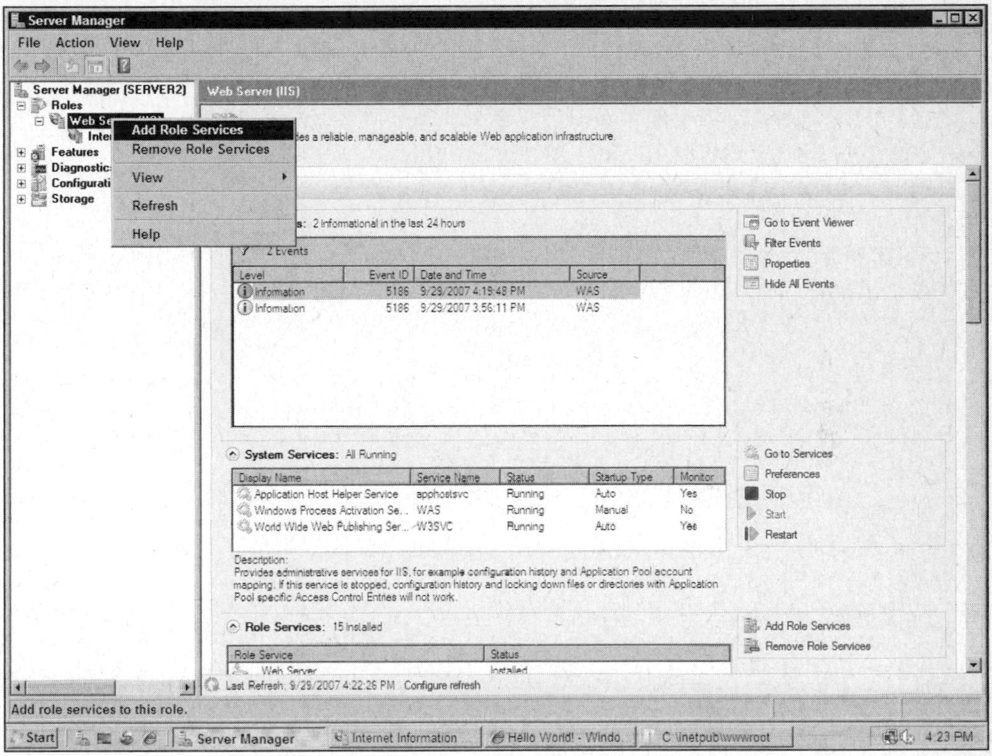

Figure 4-24

ASP.NET 1.1 on IIS 7.0

If you need to run ASP.NET 1.1 applications on IIS 7.0, there are a few other configuration changes you must make. You need to install ASP.NET 1.1, of course, but you'll also need to install IIS 6.0 metabase compatibility. You also will need to configure the ASP.NET 1.1 ISAPI extension and an application pool for your ASP.NET 1.1 applications. There are also changes to configuration files.

IIS 6.0 Metabase Compatibility

To get started, install IIS 6.0 metabase compatibility by opening the Server Manager, expanding Roles, and selecting the Web Server (IIS) role. Right-click and choose Add Role Services, or select the Add Role Services link in the right pane in the Role Services section. Under Management Tools, in the IIS 6.0 Management Compatibility section, select IIS 6.0 Metabase Compatibility. Confirm your installation choice, and continue the installation.

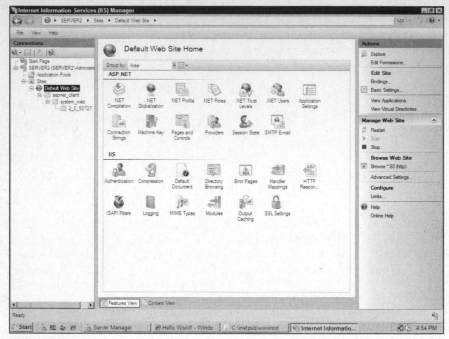

Figure 4-25

Figure 4-26

Installing ASP.NET 1.1 Framework and Updates

You will need to install the ASP.NET 1.1 Framework, as well as service packs and updates, to your server. These can be found on Microsoft's web site in the downloads section. ASP.NET 1.1 Service Pack 1 is required for ASP.NET version 1.1 to work in IIS 7.0. There is nothing special to the installations. Just complete them by accepting all the default prompts.

Enabling ASP.NET 1.1 ISAPI Extensions

To enable ISAPI extensions in IIS 7.0, whether for ASP.NET 1.1 or anything else, perform the following steps:

1. Open the IIS Manager. (Choose Start, Run, enter **inetmgr**, and then press Enter.)

2. Navigate to the web site or other level you want to configure.

3. In the Features pane, shown in Figure 4-27, double-click ISAPI Filters. In the ISAPI Filters list, either click Add in the right pane or right-click and choose Add, and then enter the name of the filter and the path to the executable or DLL, as shown in Figure 4-28. The default path for the ASP.NET 1.1 framework is `c:\Windows\Microsoft.NET\Framework\v1.1 4322\aspnet_isapi.dll`.

Configuring ASP.NET 1.1 `Machine.config` File

Because IIS 7.0 allows configuration of the web server through the `web.config` file and ASP.NET 1.1 doesn't understand this configuration section, you need to edit the `machine.config` file for the ASP.NET 1.1 Framework. Open the `machine.config` file, located by default at `c:\Windows\Microsoft.NET\Framework\v1.1 4322\config\machine.config`, in a text editor or Visual Studio, and add the following section above the final `</configSections>` tag:

```
<configSections>
  <section name="system.webServer" type="System.Configuration.IgnoreSectionHandler,
  System,  Version=1.0.5000.0, Culture=neutral, PublicKeyToken=b77a5c561934e089" />
</configSections>
```

This code tells the ASP.NET 1.1 Framework to ignore the `system.webServer` section when it reads the `web.config` file. This allows the section to remain in the `web.config` for IIS to use, but not cause errors when the ASP.NET 1.1 Framework sees a section it doesn't understand.

Configuring ASP.NET 1.1 Application Pool

Installing the ASP.NET 1.1 Framework in Windows Server 2008 creates a default ASP.NET 1.1 application pool, as shown in Figure 4-29. You can use this application pool or create your own. To use this application pool for an ASP.NET 1.1 application, open IIS Manager and navigate to the site where you'll be creating the application. Right-click the site and choose Add Application, as shown in Figure 4-30.

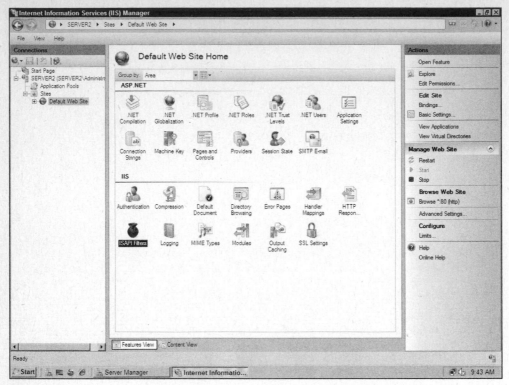

Figure 4-27

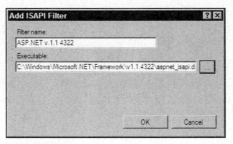

Figure 4-28

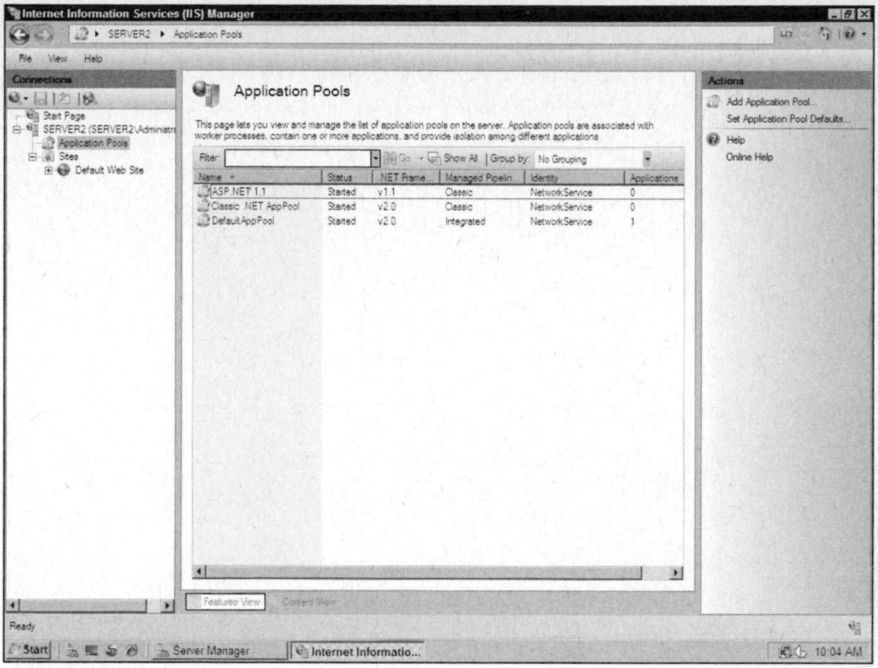

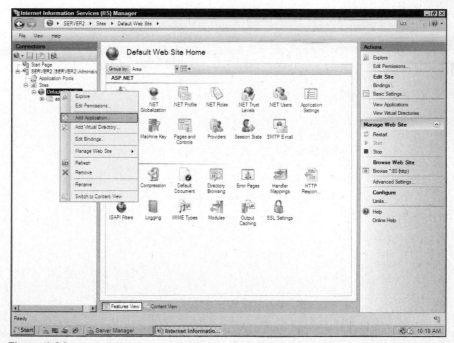

Figure 4-29

Figure 4-30

Enter your application alias and the physical path to the application, and select the ASP.NET 1.1 Application pool, as shown in Figure 4-31. You can test the application by clicking Test Settings. The most common issue is authentication for the application pool identity to access the application folder. You can find more about configuring authentication in Chapter 14, "Authentication and Authorization."

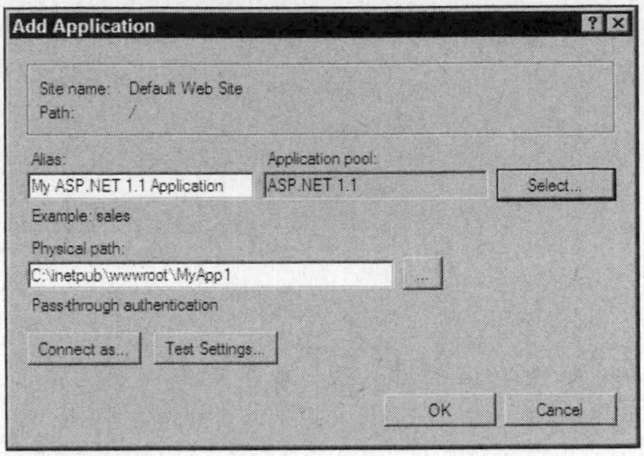

Figure 4-31

If you like, you can create your own application pool to run your ASP.NET 1.1 application in. Using the command line, you can create the application pool as follows:

```
appcmd.exe add apppool /name:"MyApplicationPool"  /managedRuntimeVersion:"v1.1"
```

You can also set the application pool for the site from the command line, as follows:

```
appcmd.exe set app "Default Web Site/" /applicationPool:"MyApplicationPool"
```

Automated Installation and Configuration

Many organizations need to install a large number of IIS 7.0 servers in diverse locations, a task not well suited for a single technician with a DVD, or even a herd of technicians. At some point, automated deployment becomes the only feasible method for creating and deploying these servers.

Previous Windows versions used Remote Installation Services, which has been updated to Windows Deployment Services (WDS). WDS is available as an update for Windows Server 2003 and is included in Windows Server 2008 as a preferred deployment technology for both server and workstation operating systems.

Server Core Command-Line Installation

IIS 7.0 can be installed entirely from the command line, lending itself quite well to scripted installations. Command-line installation is also required on the Server Core version of Windows Server 2008, as there is no GUI shell to install from. In Windows Server 2003, this same task would be accomplished with sysocmgr.exe. In Windows Server 2008, however, this is done using pkgmgr.exe, the replacement for sysocmgr.exe.

Pkgmgr.exe

Pkgmgr.exe has command-line options for installing Windows optional features and is used to install IIS 7.0 from the command line. The syntax for pkgmgr.exe is listed below; simply entering pkgmgr.exe at a command line will list these options as well.

```
Start /w pkgmgr.exe /iu:update1;update2…
```

- ❑ /iu:{update name}; — Specifies updates to install by update name. Takes a semicolon-separated name of updates to install.

- ❑ /uu:{update name}; — Specifies the updates to uninstall. Takes a semicolon-separated list of selectable updates to be uninstalled from the system. At least one update name must be specified.

- ❑ /n:{unattend XML} — Specifies the file name of the unattend XML file.

If you run pkgmgr.exe without start /w, the command line will return immediately, and you will not know when IIS 7.0 installation has finished. Since installations with pkgmgr.exe can take time, this is an important prefix. A basic installation of IIS 7.0 with default settings will take a few minutes on most systems; a full installation can take far longer.

To install IIS 7.0 using pkgmgr.exe, open a command prompt and enter the following code. You must run the code as an administrator. If you are not installing on Server Core, you can open a command prompt using the Run As Administrator option if you are logged in with a less privileged account. The code to install IIS 7.0 in a default configuration is as follows (all on one line without line breaks):

```
start /w pkgmgr /iu:IIS-WebServerRole;WAS-WindowsActivationService;WAS-Process
Model;WAS-NetFxEnvironment;WAS-ConfigurationAPI
```

This installs the web server role, along with the required Windows Activation Service options, just as if you had selected the web server role in Server Manager and selected no additional IIS options. In Server Core, you cannot use Server Manager; thus, this command line accomplishes the same task without the need of the graphical interface.

Installing IIS 7.0 with all options would use this command line (one single line without line breaks):

```
start /w pkgmgr
/iu:IIS-WebServerRole;IIS-WebServer;IIS-CommonHttpFeatures;IIS-StaticContent;IIS-De
faultDocument;IIS-DirectoryBrowsing;IIS-HttpErrors;IIS-HttpRedirect;
IIS-ApplicationDevelopment;IIS-ASPNET;IIS-NetFxExtensibility;IIS-ASP;IIS-CGI;IIS-IS
APIExtensions;IIS-ISAPIFilter;IIS-ServerSideIncludes;IIS-HealthAndDiagnostics;IIS-H
ttpLogging;IIS-LoggingLibraries;IIS-RequestMonitor;IIS-HttpTracing;IIS-CustomLoggin
g;IIS-ODBCLogging;IIS-Security;IIS-BasicAuthentication;IIS-WindowsAuthentication;II
S-DigestAuthentication;IIS-ClientCertificateMappingAuthentication;IIS-IISCertificat
eMappingAuthentication;IIS-URLAuthorization;IIS-RequestFiltering;IIS-IPSecurity;IIS
-Performance;IIS-HttpCompressionStatic;IIS-HttpCompressionDynamic;IIS-WebServerMana
gementTools;IIS-ManagementConsole;IIS-ManagementScriptingTools;IIS-ManagementServic
e;IIS-IIS6ManagementCompatibility;IIS-Metabase;IIS-WMICompatibility;IIS-LegacyScrip
ts;IIS-LegacySnapIn;IIS-FTPPublishingService;IIS-FTPServer;IIS-FTPManagement;WAS-Wi
ndowsActivationService;WAS-ProcessModel;WAS-NetFxEnvironment;WAS-ConfigurationAPI
```

This command line is the equivalent of installing the web server role from Server Manager and selecting all possible options for IIS 7.0. Again, using Server Core, you have no option other than the command line for installation. If you wish to install fewer options, such as not installing CGI support or support for server-side include files, simply remove those sections from the command line above. This would be the IIS-CGI and IIS-ServerSideIncludes options in the example.

After installation, you can check for errors using the following command:

```
echo %errorlevel%
```

Pkgmgr.exe commands can be used in a batch file to simplify entering the command-line options.

Testing IIS Installations on Server Core

Normally, to test an IIS 7.0 installation, you would simply open a browser and browse to the local host. Since Server Core has no browser, you can either test from a client system, or you can use the Wfetch utility from the IIS 6.0 Resource Kit tools to test your installation. Simply run Wfetch.exe from the command line, then click Go! in the Wfetch console window to connect to your web site. You will see the HTML output of the default site in the Log output pane of the Wfetch console.

Unattended Installations Using Pkgmgr.exe

Microsoft recommends unattended installations for organizations with multiple IIS 7 servers, since each server is guaranteed to be identical when following the same installation parameters. Pkgmgr.exe can be used for an unattended installation of IIS 7.0, using the /n: command of pkgmgr.exe to specify an XML file containing the installation parameters. The command line for this installation is

```
start /w pkgmgr /n:{unattend XML}
```

where {unattend XML} is the name of the XML file. Of course, first you need the XML file. For a basic IIS 7.0 installation, you can use the following XML code, saved in a file named unattend.xml.

```xml
<?xml version="1.0" ?>
<unattend xmlns="urn:schemas-microsoft-com:unattend"
    xmlns:wcm="http://schemas.microsoft.com/WMIConfig/2002/State">
<servicing>
    <!-- Install a selectable update in a package that is in the Windows Foundation
namespace -->
    <package action="configure">
        <assemblyIdentity
            name="Microsoft-Windows-Foundation-Package"
            version="6.0.5308.6"  <!-- Replace with your Windows version -->
            language="neutral"
            processorArchitecture="x86"
            publicKeyToken="31bf3856ad364e35"
            versionScope="nonSxS"
        />
        <selection name="IIS-WebServerRole" state="true"/>
        <selection name="WAS-WindowsActivationService" state="true"/>
        <selection name="WAS-ProcessModel" state="true"/>
        <selection name="WAS-NetFxEnvironment" state="true"/>
        <selection name="WAS-ConfigurationAPI" state="true"/>
    </package>
```

```
    </servicing>
  </unattend>
</pre>
```

To find the Windows version for this XML, open Windows Explorer and navigate to the Windows folder, and then find the `regedit.exe` file. Right-click it and choose Properties, and then select the Details tab. The number listed as product version is the number you need in your XML file. Each of the selection statements in the file contains an IIS 7.0 option to install, in this case the web server role and required Windows Activation Service options for the default IIS 7.0 installation. This is the equivalent of selecting the web server role in Server Manager and selecting no additional IIS 7.0 options.

Launch this with the following command (specify the path to the `unattend.xml` file if it is located outside the folder you run the command prompt from):

```
start /w pkgmgr /n:unattend.xml
```

On a 64-bit system, you will also need to change the `processorArchitecture` to be

```
processorArchitecture="amd64"
```

A complete installation of all IIS 7.0 features would use an `unattend.xml` file of

```
<?xml version="1.0" ?>
<unattend xmlns="urn:schemas-microsoft-com:unattend"
    xmlns:wcm="http://schemas.microsoft.com/WMIConfig/2002/State">
<servicing>
   <!-- Install a selectable update in a package that is in the Windows Foundation
namespace -->
   <package action="configure">
      <assemblyIdentity
          name="Microsoft-Windows-Foundation-Package"
          version="6.0.5303.0"
          language="neutral"
          processorArchitecture="x86"
          publicKeyToken="31bf3856ad364e35"
          versionScope="nonSxS"
      />
   <selection name="IIS-WebServerRole" state="true"/>
   <selection name="IIS-WebServer" state="true"/>
   <selection name="IIS-CommonHttpFeatures" state="true"/>
   <selection name="IIS-StaticContent" state="true"/>
   <selection name="IIS-DefaultDocument" state="true"/>
   <selection name="IIS-DirectoryBrowsing" state="true"/>
   <selection name="IIS-HttpErrors" state="true"/>
   <selection name="IIS-HttpRedirect" state="true"/>
   <selection name="IIS-ApplicationDevelopment" state="true"/>
   <selection name="IIS-ASPNET" state="true"/>
   <selection name="IIS-NetFxExtensibility" state="true"/>
   <selection name="IIS-ASP" state="true"/>
   <selection name="IIS-CGI" state="true"/>
   <selection name="IIS-ISAPIExtensions" state="true"/>
   <selection name="IIS-ISAPIFilter" state="true"/>
```

```
        <selection name="IIS-ServerSideIncludes" state="true"/>
        <selection name="IIS-HealthAndDiagnostics" state="true"/>
        <selection name="IIS-HttpLogging" state="true"/>
        <selection name="IIS-LoggingLibraries" state="true"/>
        <selection name="IIS-RequestMonitor" state="true"/>
        <selection name="IIS-HttpTracing" state="true"/>
        <selection name="IIS-CustomLogging" state="true"/>
        <selection name="IIS-ODBCLogging" state="true"/>
        <selection name="IIS-Security" state="true"/>
        <selection name="IIS-BasicAuthentication" state="true"/>
        <selection name="IIS-URLAuthorization" state="true"/>
        <selection name="IIS-RequestFiltering" state="true"/>
        <selection name="IIS-IPSecurity" state="true"/>
        <selection name="IIS-Performance" state="true"/>
        <selection name="IIS-HttpCompressionStatic" state="true"/>
        <selection name="IIS-HttpCompressionDynamic" state="true"/>
        <selection name="IIS-WebServerManagementTools" state="true"/>
        <selection name="IIS-ManagementConsole" state="true"/>
        <selection name="IIS-ManagementScriptingTools" state="true"/>
        <selection name="IIS-ManagementService" state="true"/>
        <selection name="IIS-IIS6ManagementCompatibility" state="true"/>
        <selection name="IIS-Metabase" state="true"/>
        <selection name="IIS-WMICompatibility" state="true"/>
        <selection name="IIS-LegacyScripts" state="true"/>
        <selection name="IIS-LegacySnapIn" state="true"/>
        <selection name="WAS-WindowsActivationService" state="true"/>
        <selection name="WAS-ProcessModel" state="true"/>
        <selection name="WAS-NetFxEnvironment" state="true"/>
        <selection name="WAS-ConfigurationAPI" state="true"/>
      </package>
    </servicing>
    </unattend>
  </pre>
```

This unattend XML code is the equivalent of installing the web server role from Server Manager, and selecting all possible options for IIS 7.0. If you want to install fewer options, such as not installing CGI support or support for server side include files, simply remove those sections from the XML above, in this case the following two lines:

```
        <selection name="IIS-CGI" state="true"/>
        <selection name="IIS-ServerSideIncludes" state="true"/>
```

After installing IIS 7.0 using `pkgmgr.exe` and an unattend XML file, you can check for errors using the following command line:

```
echo %errorlevel%
```

Installation Using Windows Deployment Services

Windows Deployment Services (WDS) for Windows Server 2008 is the update to Remote Installation Services (RIS). WDS is designed to deploy Windows Server 2008 and Windows Vista across the enterprise, without the need to physically touch the system and without using the DVD at the new system. Using a network PXE boot, WDS can install a preconfigured Windows Server 2008 operating system with specific IIS 7.0 features and roles.

On the server side, WDS uses a pre-boot execution environment (PXE) and trivial file transfer (TFTP) to install an operating system on a client system with no functioning operating system. Boot images are created from an existing client, configured for your needs, and the resulting WDS installation has identical settings and configurations as the system that the image was created from.

Windows Deployment Services are installed to a system which will act as a WDS server, and that server will store the image files to be supplied to clients. A boot menu is configured for network boots, with client images to be installed, so a user at a new system with no operating system can simply turn the system on andthen select the appropriate installation image from the boot menu, which is then installed to the client.

A limitation of the older RIS was the inability to do a true image capture of a drive or partition. This precluded a fully operational server from having a "snapshot" taken and applied to a second server. This also meant that third party products would need to be installed to a server which was deployed by RIS. WDS adds the capability to image a partition or drive directly and install that to a new system. The limitation is that the system must have been prepared with Sysprep and be offline when the image is captured, normally by booting from a separate CD or DVD.

There are no IIS 7.0 specific settings or changes needed for using WDS to deploy IIS 7.0 servers, but there are settings which must be unique between systems. Sysprep will handle many functions, such as security identifiers, but after installation an administrator may need to reconfigure IP address settings in IIS 7.0 or connection strings in ASP.NET applications. Naturally these can be scripted as well, using WMI or PowerShell for many changes, to automate complete installations.

For more information on using Windows Deployment Services, you can download the Step-by-Step Guide for Windows Deployment Services in Windows Server 2008 document from Microsoft's web site or see the MSDN documentation for WDS at `http://technet2.microsoft.com/windowsserver 2008/en/library/14b32ca9-0070-487d-89cc-e09585867c6a1033.mspx?mfr=true`.

Hosting Service Recommendations

Microsoft has dedicated resources for hosting services using IIS, but these recommendations may apply to any organization running larger numbers of web sites on its servers. IIS 7.0 has been tested with thousands of web sites per server and scales out well, assuming adequate hardware resources are available. In general, most hosting companies have a target percentage of sites that will receive requests at any point in time. Microsoft assumes a 90% idle factor. This means that only 10% of sites will be receiving requests during normal operations. You will probably want to monitor your site activity to balance the ratio for your specific circumstances.

Hosting operations have normally developed a strategy for managing application pools, account access, storage locations, and management environments, but if you are looking for a starting point, Microsoft recommends the following:

❑   Every site gets its own application pool.

❑ Windows domain accounts are used.

❑ No need for multiple accounts — Application pool account, anonymous user account, and the account connecting to the remote share use the same access account.

❑ Content is stored on a remote (UNC) share on a SAN or other storage device.

This means you will have at least three pieces of equipment:

❑ **Domain Controller** — Active Directory domain accounts are used to ensure security across machines, such as when the content is requested from the remote content server. Using domain accounts also eases management for administrators as the number of sites and servers expands.

❑ **Web Server** — Application pools run under domain accounts, and the same account is used for anonymous access. Content and configuration files are stored on a SAN, NAS. or other UNC-accessible device. Because web-site content and Microsoft SQL Server functions will exist on a different server, this hardware can run Windows Server 2008 Web Edition.

❑ **Content Hardware** — Web content and configuration files are stored on this equipment, preferably a replicated or clustered system, especially if it is running Microsoft SQL Server. DFS with replication can be used to mirror content between systems.

Directory Structure

Microsoft recommends a specific directory structure and security access to those directories, as shown in the following table. Each site will have a content directory, a log directory, and a directory for request tracing logs.

Directory	Security	Notes
`<content root>\<sitename>` (e.g. `e:\content\Site1`)	Administrators — full control System — full control <AppPool ID> — list folder contents	This is the site root folder. The AppPool ID has to be able to read this folder but does not need write access.
`<content root>\<sitename>\wwwroot` (e.g. `e:\content\site1\wwwroot`)	Administrators — full control System — full control <AppPool ID> — full control	This is the root of a web site belonging to the site owner. The application pool that runs the site needs access to this directory.

Directory	Security	Notes
`<content root>\<sitename>\logs\logfiles` (e.g., `e:\content\site1\logs\logfiles`)	Administrators — full control System — full control {DomainName}\{MachineIdentity} — full control	This folder is used for web logs. It is parallel to the content directory of the site so that it is not accessible by a visitor browsing the site. Because HTTP.SYS is writing log files, you need to give access to the identity HTTP.SYS runs under on the web server. HTTP.SYS is running as the machine identity when it writes log files to another machine.
`<content root>\<sitename>\logs\failedReqLogFiles` (e.g., `e:\content\site1\logs\failedReqLogFiles`)	Administrators — full control System — full control <AppPool ID> — full control	This is the folder used to store Failed Request log files, which allow site owners to diagnose problems with their web sites. These logs are written by the AppPool identity, which runs as the Site Owner's identity.

Using the `xcacls.exe` utility available in several Microsoft resource kits, you can create this structure and assign the NTFS permissions using the following batch file:

```
SETLOCAL
REM Save command-line arguments passed as parameters:
SET SITE_ID=%1%
SET CONTENT_ROOT=%2

md %CONTENT_ROOT%\site%SITE_ID%
md %CONTENT_ROOT%\site%SITE_ID%\logs
REM ACL SITE DIRECTORY FOR ADMINS AND the APPPOOL ACCOUNT
xcacls %CONTENT_ROOT%\site%SITE_ID% /G {DomainName}\PoolId%1:R /y
xcacls %CONTENT_ROOT%\site%SITE_ID% /E /G Administrators:F

REM CREATING FAILED REQUEST LOG DIRECTORY
md %CONTENT_ROOT%\site%SITE_ID%\logs\failedReqLogfiles
xcacls %CONTENT_ROOT%\site%SITE_ID%\logs\failedReqLogfiles /G
{DomainName}\PoolId%1:F /y
```

```
xcacls %CONTENT_ROOT%\site%SITE_ID%\logs\failedReqLogfiles /E /G Administrators:F

REM CREATING WEBLOG DIRECTORY. HTTP.SYS LOGS AS MACHINE IDENTITY
md %CONTENT_ROOT%\site%SITE_ID%\logs\logfiles
xcacls %CONTENT_ROOT%\site%SITE_ID%\logs\logfiles /G
{DomainName}\{MachineIdentity}:F /y
xcacls %CONTENT_ROOT%\site%SITE_ID%\logs\logfiles /E /G Administrators:F

REM CREATING WEB CONTENT DIRECTORY
md %CONTENT_ROOT%\site%SITE_ID%\wwwroot
xcacls %CONTENT_ROOT%\site%SITE_ID%\wwwroot /G {DomainName}\PoolId%1:F /y
xcacls %CONTENT_ROOT%\site%SITE_ID%\wwwroot /E /G Administrators:F
```

Replace {DomainName} with your domain's name, and {MachineIdentity} with your server's machine identity under which Http.sys will run. Launch this batch file on the content server with the parameters of site ID and content root folder.

Web Server Accounts and Application Pools

On your web server, you will need to set the application pools and the accounts they run under, as well as the account used for anonymous access. Because you will run all application pools in isolation, you do not need the generic anonymous user account. You can remove the anonymous user account with the following command line:

```
appcmd.exe set config -section:anonymousAuthentication -userName:"" --password
```

You can create the site and matching application pool with the following batch file code. Run this file with the parameter of the site name, which will also be used in creating the application pool. Replace {DomainName} with your domain name, {ServerName} with the name of the web content server, and {ContentShare} with the UNC share name of the content share on the content server.

```
REM Create Application Pool
Appcmd add AppPool -name:Pool_Site%1 -processModel.username:{DomainName}\PoolId%1
-processModel.password:PoolIDPwd%1 -processModel.identityType:SpecificUser

REM Creating a site with the content, freb and log
REM configuration entries set to the directories we created and
REM secured before.
AppCmd add site -name:Site%1 -bindings:http/*:80:Site%1 -physicalPath:\\
{ServerName}\{ContentShare}\Site%1\wwwroot -logfile.directory:\\
{ServerName}\{ContentShare}\Site%1\logs\logfiles -traceFailedRequestsLogging.
directory:\\{ServerName}\{--}\Site%1\logs\failedReqLogfiles

REM Now assign the root application of the newly created web-site
REM to its Application Pool
Appcmd set app -app.name:"Site%1/" -applicationPool:Pool_Site%1
```

Configuring Shared Hosting with Managed Code

Using ADSI, you can configure web server user accounts and application pools for shared hosting through managed code. The following code snippets will manage the same tasks as the batch files above.

Creating Users

The following code will create a new Windows domain user account to be used for the application pool identity:

```
using System;
using System.DirectoryServices;
class Program{
static void Main(string[] args)          {
DirectoryEntry AD = new DirectoryEntry("WinNT://" + Environment.MachineName +
",computer");
                DirectoryEntry NewUser = AD.Children.Add("PoolID1", "user");
NewUser.Invoke("SetPassword", new object[] { "PoolIDPwd1" });
NewUser.Invoke("Put", new object[] { "Description", "AppPool Account" });
    NewUser.CommitChanges();
  }
}
```

This code creates a new user in Active Directory named PoolID1 with a password of PoolIDPwd1, and a description of AppPool Account.

Setting Directory Permissions

The following code sets access for the administrator account, assuming content is in the e:\content folder.

```
using System;
using System.IO;
using System.DirectoryServices;
using System.Security.AccessControl;
using System.Security.Principal;

class Program
{
    static void Main(string[] args)
    {
        String dir = @"e:\content";
        DirectorySecurity dirsec = Directory.GetAccessControl(dir);
        dirsec.SetAccessRuleProtection(true, false);

        foreach (AuthorizationRule rule in dirsec.GetAccessRules(true, true,
typeof(NTAccount)))
        {
            dirsec.RemoveAccessRuleAll
            (
                new FileSystemAccessRule
                (
                    rule.IdentityReference,
                    FileSystemRights.FullControl,
                    AccessControlType.Allow
                )
            );
        }
```

```
                dirsec.AddAccessRule
                (
                    new FileSystemAccessRule
                    (
                        @"BUILTIN\Administrators",
                        FileSystemRights.FullControl,
                        AccessControlType.Allow
                    )
                );
                dirsec.AddAccessRule
                (
                    new FileSystemAccessRule
                    (
                        @"BUILTIN\Administrators",
                        FileSystemRights.FullControl,
                        InheritanceFlags.ObjectInherit,
                        PropagationFlags.InheritOnly,
                        AccessControlType.Allow
                    )
                );

                dirsec.AddAccessRule
                (
                    new FileSystemAccessRule
                    (
                        @"BUILTIN\Administrators",
                        FileSystemRights.FullControl,
                        InheritanceFlags.ContainerInherit,
                        PropagationFlags.InheritOnly,
                        AccessControlType.Allow
                    )
                );

                Directory.SetAccessControl(dir, dirsec);
            }
        }
```

This code first removes all security from the e:\content folder, then adds specific security settings to allow administrator accounts full control and to allow that access to be inherited by subfolders.

Creating Application Pools

This code will create 100 application pools, consecutively numbered. Depending on your organization, you might want to create generic site and application pools and assign them to users, as needed.

```
using System;
using System.Collections.Generic;
using System.Text;
using Microsoft.Web.Administration;
using System.Diagnostics;

namespace IIS7Demos
{
    class CreateAppPools
    {
```

```csharp
        const int NUMBEROFPOOLS     = 100;
        const int APPPOOLBASENUMBER = 1000;
        const string POOLPREFIX     = "Pool_Site";
        const string USERNAMEPREFIX = "PoolId";
        const string PASSWORDPREFIX = "PoolIDPwd";
        const bool ENCRYPTPASSWORD  = true;
        static void Main(string[] args)
        {

            ServerManager mgr = new ServerManager();
            ApplicationPoolCollection pools = mgr.ApplicationPools;
            for (int i = 0; i < NUMBEROFPOOLS; i++)
            {
                CreateAppPool(pools, i + APPPOOLBASENUMBER, POOLPREFIX,
USERNAMEPREFIX, PASSWORDPREFIX, ENCRYPTPASSWORD);
            }
            mgr.CommitChanges();
        }

        static bool CreateAppPool(ApplicationPoolCollection pools, int i, string
appPoolPrefix, string userNamePrefix, string passwordPrefix, bool bEncryptPassword)
        {
            try
            {
                ApplicationPool newPool = pools.Add(appPoolPrefix + i);
                newPool.ProcessModel.UserName = userNamePrefix + i;
                // the SetMetadata call will remove the encryptionprovider in the
schema. This results in clear-text passwords!!!
                if (!bEncryptPassword)

newPool.ProcessModel.Attributes["password"].SetMetadata("encryptionProvider", "");

                newPool.ProcessModel.Password = passwordPrefix + i;
                newPool.ProcessModel.IdentityType =
ProcessModelIdentityType.SpecificUser;
            }
            catch (Exception ex)
            {
                Console.WriteLine("Adding AppPool {0} failed. Reason: {1}",
appPoolPrefix+i, ex.Message);
                return false;
            }

            return true;
        }
    }
}
```

This code loops through 100 times, each time creating an application pool, identifying that pool by the APPPOOLBASENUMBER variable incremented by one in each loop. Note that the call to the SetMetadata class removes the encryption provider from the application pool identity, meaning passwords would be in clear text. This is required to set the password in this example.

Creating Sites

This code will create 100 matching sites for the application pools above. It uses the new
`microsoft.web.administration` namespace for IIS 7.0.

```csharp
using System;
using System.Collections.Generic;
using System.Text;
using System.Diagnostics;
using Microsoft.Web.Administration;

namespace IIS7Demos
{
    class CreateSites
    {
        const int NUMBEROFSITES    = 100;
        const int SITEBASENUMBER   = 1000;
        const string POOLPREFIX     = "POOL_";
        const string SITENAMEPREFIX = "SITE";
        const string ROOTDIR        = "e:\\content";

        static void Main(string[] args)
        {
            ServerManager mgr = new ServerManager();
            SiteCollection sites = mgr.Sites;

            for (int i = SITEBASENUMBER; i < NUMBEROFSITES + SITEBASENUMBER; i++)
            {
                if (!CreateSitesInIIS(sites, SITENAMEPREFIX, i, ROOTDIR))
                {
                    Console.WriteLine("Creating site {0} failed", i);
                }
            }

            mgr.CommitChanges();
        }

        static bool CreateSitesInIIS(SiteCollection sites, string sitePrefix, int
siteId, string dirRoot)
        {

            string siteName = sitePrefix + siteId;
            // site gets set to Poolname using the following format. Example:
'Site_POOL10'
            string poolName = POOLPREFIX + sitePrefix +  siteId;

            try
            {
                Site site = sites.CreateElement();
                site.Id = siteId;
                site.SetAttributeValue("name", siteName);
                sites.Add(site);

                Application app = site.Applications.CreateElement();
```

```
            app.SetAttributeValue("path", "/");
            app.SetAttributeValue("applicationPool", poolName);
            site.Applications.Add(app);

            VirtualDirectory vdir = app.VirtualDirectories.CreateElement();
            vdir.SetAttributeValue("path", "/");
            vdir.SetAttributeValue("physicalPath", dirRoot + @"\" + siteName);

            app.VirtualDirectories.Add(vdir);

            Binding b = site.Bindings.CreateElement();
            b.SetAttributeValue("protocol", "http");
            b.SetAttributeValue("bindingInformation", ":80:" + siteName);
            site.Bindings.Add(b);
        }
        catch (Exception ex)
        {
            Console.WriteLine("Create site {0} failed. Reason: {1}", siteName,
ex.Message);
            return false;
        }

        return true;
    }
  }
}
```

IIS 7.0 and Windows Server 2008 introduce a new namespace for ASP.NET, `microsoft.web.administration`, that allows control over web sites using managed code. This code loops through and creates 100 web sites, again incrementing from a base site number for identification. The code sets the site name, site path, and application pool for the site, and creates a virtual directory within that site. The code also configures site binding for HTTP requests, on port 80.

Setting IIS Properties

This code will set the IIS properties to remove the anonymous user:

```
using System;
using Microsoft.Web.Administration;

static void SetAnonymousUserToProcessId()
{
    ServerManager mgr = new ServerManager();
    try
    {
        Configuration config = mgr.GetApplicationHostConfiguration();
        ConfigurationSection section = config.GetSection(
"system.webServer/security/authentication/anonymousAuthentication");
        section.SetAttributeValue("userName", (object)"");
        // if we don't remove the attribute we end up with an encrypted empty
string
        section.RawAttributes.Remove("password");
    }
```

```
    catch (Exception ex)
    {
        Console.WriteLine("Removing anonymous user entry failed. Reason: {0}",
ex.Message);
    }

    mgr.CommitChanges();
    return;
}
```

This code also uses the `microsoft.web.administration` namespace and sets IIS properties for the site such that the anonymous user account for the site is the same as the account used for the application pool identity. This makes each site operate under its own user account for anonymous access, segregating site access accounts.

Setting the ASP.NET Compilation Directory

This code sets the compilation directory for ASP.NET and locks the `tempDirectory` attribute so that end users cannot change this in their `web.config` files.

```
using System;
using Microsoft.Web.Administration;

public class setASPNETCompilationDirectory
{
    static void Main()
    {
    ServerManager manager = new ServerManager();
    Configuration rootConfig = manager.GetWebConfiguration(new
WebConfigurationMap(), null);

    ConfigurationSection section = rootConfig.GetSection("system.web/compilation");
    section.Attributes["tempDirectory"].Value = @"e:\inetpub\temp\temporary asp.net
files\site1";
    section.SetMetadata("lockAttributes", "tempDirectory");

    manager.CommitChanges();
    }
}
```

Again using the `microsoft.web.administration` namespace, this code sets the ASP.NET compilation directory, used when an ASP.NET application is accessed for the first time or after it has expired from the cache, to a temporary folder within the site's folder structure. The code then locks this attribute at the server level, preventing users from overriding this setting in the individual `web.config` file for their site. This segregates the compilation folder from other sites and provides for all files related to a site to remain in that site's folder structure.

Further Information for Shared Hosting

The sample code in the preceding section comes from Microsoft's shared hosting recommendations. You can read the full document on Microsoft's IIS.net web site at `www.iis.net/articles/view.aspx /IIS7/Deploy-an-IIS7-Server/Deployment-for-Web-Hosters/Shared-Hosting-on-IIS7`.

More information for shared hosting and Microsoft hosting solutions can be found online at Microsoft's service providers web site, www.microsoft.com/serviceproviders/default.mspx. Programmatic management of IIS 7.0 is covered in more detail in Chapter 18.

Shared Configuration

One of the changes to IIS 7.0 that improves the experience for administrators of large-scale web farms is the ability to use shared configuration files. These configuration files are located on a Windows file share accessible to all web servers, and changes to the configurations take place across all servers almost instantaneously. Setting up shared configuration requires exporting a current configuration and then pointing the server to the exported configuration file.

To configure shared configuration options, open IIS Manager and navigate to the server level, as shown in Figure 4-32. Double-click Shared Configuration, enable shared configuration, click Export Configuration in the Actions pane, and supply a location and encryption key, as shown in Figure 4-33. Remember this key, as you'll need it to connect the server to the configuration files.

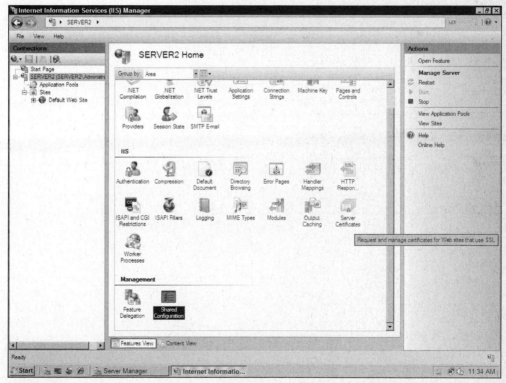

Figure 4-32

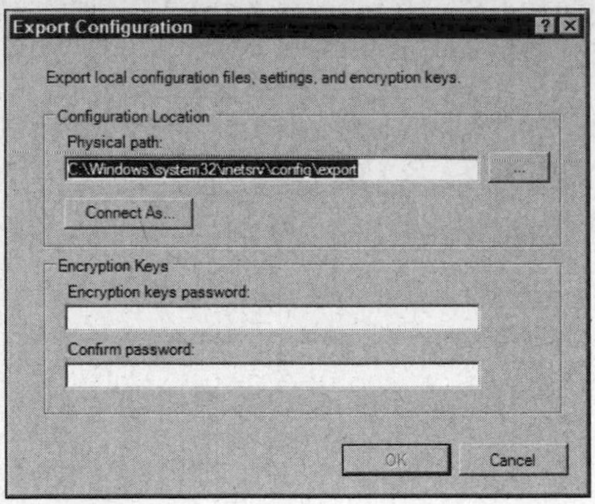

Figure 4-33

After exporting the configuration files, you will need to provide the location, as well as a User name and Password, to access this location, as shown in Figure 4-34. After you enter the path and credentials, click Apply in the Actions pane. IIS 7.0 will check that the configuration files actually exist and are accessible, and ask for the encryption key. Repeat this process on any other systems that will be using shared configurations, pointing each to the same location with the same credentials and encryption password. Shared Configuration is covered in detail in Chapter 16 "Configuring and Load Balancing Web Farms."

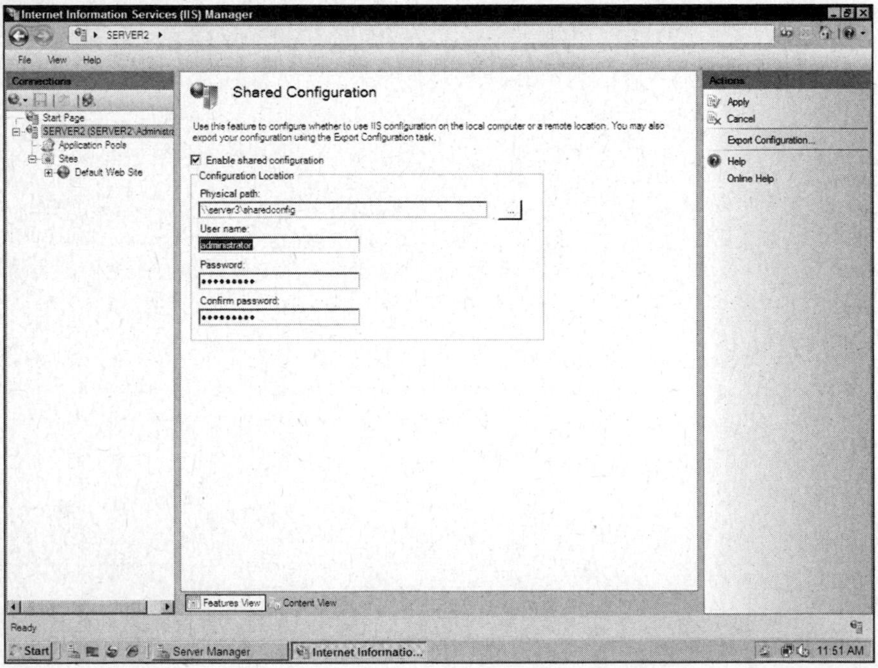

Figure 4-34

Installing IIS 7.0 on Windows Vista

The scope of this book is IIS 7.0 for professional use, which would normally cover using IIS 7.0 on Windows Server 2008, since a workstation operating system like Vista is unsuitable for deploying professional web sites. But there are a few instances where a Windows Vista environment is required, or even desirable, for IIS 7.0. Most prominent is a developer's system with a local installation of IIS 7.0 for testing and development. That is the scenario covered in this installation.

Installing IIS 7.0 on Windows Vista, in this case Windows Vista Ultimate, is not much different from installing IIS 7.0 on Windows Server 2008. Some functions are not available on workstation installations, such as the ability to create a web farm, but the base IIS installation is nearly identical. Windows Vista Service Pack 1 includes updates for IIS 7.0 to bring IIS on Vista up to the newer version of IIS 7.0 included in Windows Server 2008.

This installation assumes a fresh installation of Windows Vista, not an upgrade from Windows XP. There are issues with upgrades from XP with security functions, and many users have found that web sites upgraded from Windows XP and IIS 5.1 to Windows Vista and IIS 7.0 have been nonfunctional after the upgrade. If you must upgrade a Windows XP system, the best process is to back up your web sites on Windows XP, completely remove IIS, and then upgrade the operating system. You can then install IIS 7.0 fresh and configure your sites with the restored content.

IIS 7.0 Support

IIS 7.0 is supported on the following Vista versions:

- ❑ Windows Vista Home Premium.
- ❑ Windows Vista Business.
- ❑ Windows Vista Professional.
- ❑ Windows Vista Ultimate.

IIS 7.0 on Vista has a few limitations compared to IIS 7.0 on Windows Server 2008, most notably a limited request queue. Unlike IIS 5.1 on Windows XP, IIS 7.0 does not have a connection limit; instead, the queue is throttled to only handle a limited number of requests at a time, and the rest will queue up. While not useful as a production web server, this limitation allows IIS 7.0 on Vista to be used for development without errors. If too many requests are received, the requests will simply queue up, making response times slower.

IIS 7.0 Installation

IIS 7.0 is not a part of the Vista default installation. Installing IIS 7.0 to a Vista system results in a web server that will serve static content with anonymous access, but not much more. For developers, you will want to install IIS 7.0 with a configuration as close to the final deployment server as possible, normally with ASP.NET and authentication enabled. In many cases, a developer will turn off User Access Control, but if it is still active on the system, the installation must be done running as an administrator account.

To install IIS 7.0 on Windows Vista, open the Windows Features dialog box shown in Figure 4-35 by navigating to the Control Panel, clicking Programs, and then clicking "Turn Windows features on or off." Select "Internet Information Services" in the dialog box, and you'll notice that portions of the Web Management Tools and World Wide Web Services are also selected, as shown in Figure 4-35. These are required features and include the IIS Management Console, Management Service, and Scripts and Tools, as well as several World Wide Web services.

Figure 4-35

To install additional features, expand each option and choose the features you require. For development purposes, you should install those features that you will find installed on the production server on which your applications will be deployed. When you are satisfied with your choices, click OK, and your installation will begin. You may be asked for the operating system DVD, and you may need to restart the system. Once IIS 7.0 is installed, management on Vista is the same as management in Windows Server 2008.

Summary

IIS 7.0 is a vital part of many Windows Server 2008 installations and, as shown in this chapter, can be installed and configured to meet the needs of the organization. Whether for an intranet server running SharePoint or a web host running hundreds of sites, IIS 7.0 is scalable to the needs of your environment. In many cases, IIS 7.0 may be required for applications on your server, if only to provide a management interface for those applications.

After reading this chapter you should be able to install IIS 7.0 with a new Windows Server 2008 installation or into an existing Windows Server 2008 system. You should be able to use automated installs, and configure IIS 7.0 for a hosting environment. You should also be able to install IIS 7.0 in a Server Core installation of Windows Server 2008.

Now that IIS 7.0 has been installed, there are numerous administrative tasks that may need to be completed as well. The next chapter covers the administration tools needed for managing IIS 7.0, followed by administration of web applications and application pools. You may also want to read Chapter 10 for information on installing SMTP, FTP, and FrontPage Server Extensions.

Part II: Administration

5

Administration Tools

In this chapter, we examine the various tools Microsoft has included to administer IIS 7.0. In building IIS 7.0, Microsoft had to completely revamp the toolset used to manage IIS. They replaced the old IIS Manager MMC with a completely new IIS Manager application that provides greater functionality for its expanded role. This new admin tool allows developers and administrators to add their own extensions and tweaks to it through its extensibility features. In addition to these major changes to the administrative tools, they added the ability to set web server configuration through files in the web site. They added to the functionality of the `web.config` file and introduced the `applicationHost.config` file. Through these files, the developer can completely set up and adjust the web site. They also took the venerable command-line interface (CLI) and added to it with the `AppCmd.exe` tool, which allows complete control over every aspect of IIS.

In this chapter, you will learn about the IIS Manager, configuration settings, and command-line management using `AppCmd.exe`.

Key Characteristics

IIS 7.0 was built with the following characteristics in mind:

❑ **Simple to use** — As previously mentioned, IIS 7.0 does not use the same metabase scheme as previous versions of IIS, but rather uses a series of plain-text XML files for configuration. With IIS 7.0, the state is in the files, thus a change to the files results in an immediate change to the server, site, or application configuration.

❑ **Securely built** — The default configuration is set to allow only the system administrator to configure the server, sites, and applications. By using Feature Delegation, system administrators can securely make site and application administration available to down-level administrators without giving more permissions on the server than necessary. The system by default does not store sensitive information like passwords. However, if there is a need to store sensitive information, it is encrypted on the hard disk. In addition to these security features, applications can be isolated to prevent other applications from sharing or reading the settings.

❏ **Extensible** — Just as the IIS Manager is extensible, so is the IIS configuration. This is made easy because the schema of IIS is contained in XML files. To extend the schema, just place an XML file in the schemas folder. You'll see below how the settings are arranged in "sections" within the configuration files.

❏ **Low TCO** — By changing to the XML file-based schema, IIS 7.0 is easier to deploy and manage. The file-based schema allows for web settings to be published in the same files as the web-site content. With this used in conjunction with Feature Delegation, the system administrator doesn't have to be as involved with every site change made on the server. The web.config file can contain both the IIS settings and the ASP.NET settings for a web site permitting centralized control over the site settings. The file-based structure also makes it possible to use standard file system-based tools for maintenance (backup and restore) and security.

❏ **Compatible with previous versions** — Applications created for IIS 6.0 will continue to run on IIS 7.0 by calling interfaces such as Admin Base Objects (ABO), the ADSI provider, and the IIS 6.0 WMI provider. Because .NET Framework 2.0 was built into IIS 7.0 from the ground up, current .NET applications will continue to work by calling System.Configuration and System.Web.Configuration. The config files will continue to follow the structure of the web.config and machine.config files from IIS 6.0, as well as add IIS configuration settings to the files.

IIS Manager

Microsoft had to completely revamp IIS Manager in IIS 7.0 for a few different reasons. ASP.NET has been built into IIS 7.0 from the ground up, and the previous version of the admin tool didn't have the capability to take on the additional features that ASP.NET brought to the table while displaying them in a user-friendly way. With IIS 7.0's move from a metabase configuration to a .NET configuration, administrators can delegate configuration control to the developers through the web.config and applicationHost.config files. The new interface is able to control what modifications are allowed through the configuration files and show where the configuration is being written. The new interface permits an administrator to create extensions with an easier integration of feature pages, treeview nodes, and menu items. These new extensions are automatically downloaded by remote IIS Manager clients. The new admin tool also makes it possible to remotely administer the server over HTTPS by using the Web Management Service (WMSVC). This new look more closely resembles the Windows Control Panel and presents a more scalable approach to displaying the information needed to control the web server.

Appearance

IIS Manager has a new look and feel, with features you would find in a browser, such as the address bar and forward and back buttons. It also has the option to group items by area, category, or "no grouping," which places all the objects together in a manner similar to the Windows Control Panel.

The default page used to manage the server is the Home Page. There are two views for IIS Manager: the Features View and the Content View. Both views display a treeview in the left-hand "Connections" column, the feature list in the center column, and a tasks pane in the right-hand "Actions" column. Figure 5-1 shows the Home Page with the three columns and the Features View.

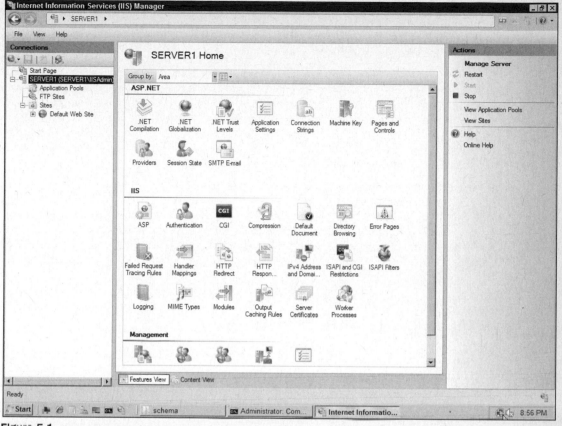

Figure 5-1

Feature Scopes

IIS 7.0 has five types of nodes in its treeview: server, site, application, virtual directory, and folder. Each node has its own Home Page, and each Home Page has a feature list.

Although many of the Home Pages share common features, the server Home Page has the following features that are not available in any other Home Page. These features appear only at the server level because they perform server-wide configuration or hold server-wide data and information.

- ❑ **ISAPI and CGI Restrictions** — Enables or restricts ISAPI or CGI extensions on the web server.

- ❑ **Server Certificates** (doesn't appear in remote connections) — Requests and manages SSL certificates for web sites.

- ❑ **Worker Processes** — Views information about currently executing requests inside the worker processes.

- ❑ **Feature Delegation** — Configures default delegation state for lower levels.

❑ **IIS Manager Users** — Configure who can administer sites and application.

❑ **Management Service** (doesn't appear in remote connections) — Configures IIS Manager for delegation and remote access.

There are also features that appear elsewhere but do not appear at the server level because they are used specifically by other levels or work better in other locations:

❑ **.NET Profile** — Configure options that track user-selected preferences in ASP.NET applications.

❑ **.NET Roles** — Configure user groups for use with .NET Users and Forms authentication.

❑ **.NET Users** — Manage users who belong to roles and who use Forms authentication.

❑ **SSL Settings** — Specify requirements for SSL and client certificates.

There are special rules for where the features associated with delegation appear:

❑ Feature Delegation appears only at the root node of a connection.

❑ IIS Manager Permissions appears only on the server, site, and application nodes.

The tasks pane of the Home Page enables you to access a variety of management tasks, including these tool selections: basic settings, restarting (IIS or Web Site), starting, stopping, advanced settings, and configuring failed request tracing.

Features View

IIS Manager's Features View uses three types of page layouts in addition to the Home Pages, depending on the type of information being displayed:

❑ List pages.

❑ Property grids.

❑ Dialog pages.

List Pages

List pages show lists of objects. Application pools and sites are two examples of list pages. Within these list pages, you can filter or group the objects. Filtering objects enables you to search for a string in the name column in order to exclude all objects that do not include that string. You also can group objects by categories such as Status or Port, depending on the list page. In Figure 5-2, the grouping options are No Grouping, Status, .NET Framework Version, Managed Pipeline Mode, and Identity.

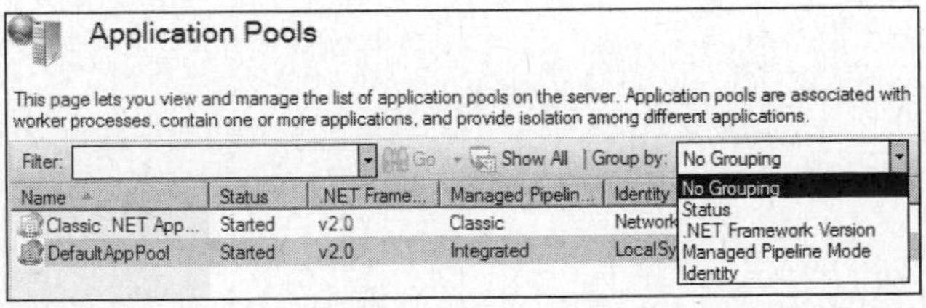

Figure 5-2

In the task pane, you can modify the contents of the list by adding, editing, or removing items. The task pane also allows you to edit the feature settings that aren't specific to a list item.

Property Grid Pages

Property grid pages, as you can imagine, show grids of properties that relate to one another. By using the Display dropdown list, you can view the properties' Friendly Names, Configuration Names, or Both.

Property grid pages allow you to choose from a selection of variables in a dropdown list or allow you to directly edit the value. In Figure 5-3, the Enable Chunked Encoding property is a dropdown list of True or False, and the Locale ID is a directly editable property.

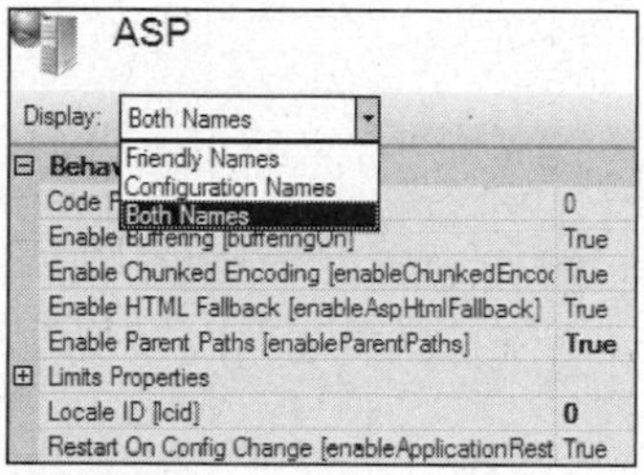

Figure 5-3

Dialog Pages

Dialog pages have a similar interface to the old IIS Manager, with textboxes, checkboxes, and radio buttons. Apply and Cancel can be selected in the task pane to save or discard changes, respectively. Figure 5-4 shows the Machine Key dialog page with dropdown menus for encryption and decryption methods, as well as checkboxes for other options.

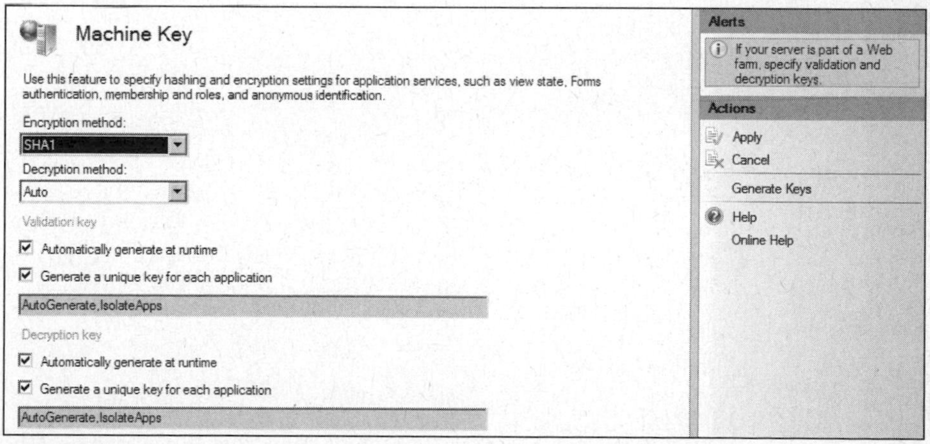

Figure 5-4

Web-Site- and Application-Specific Settings

The *web-site-* and *application-level nodes* have basic and advanced settings associated with them. Both the basic and the advanced settings tools can be found in the Actions pane when the site or application has been selected. The basic settings for both types of nodes include web-site name or alias, application pool, physical path, and connect as selections, as shown in Figure 5-5.

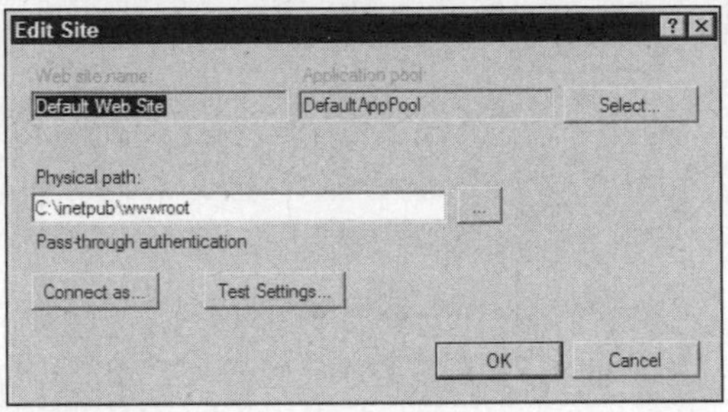

Figure 5-5

Figure 5-6 shows the advanced settings, which include the basic settings and additional settings such as connection limits and failed request tracing.

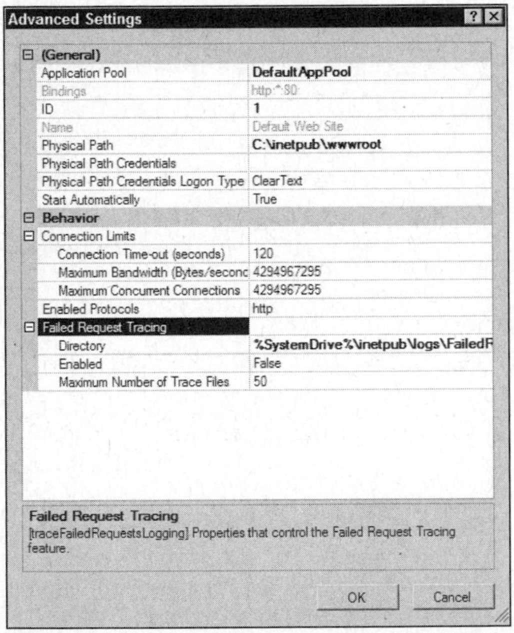

Figure 5-6

Content View

Content View is a read-only list page. Actions such as moving, copying, deleting, or creating files or folders are not allowed in this view. You can access Content View by clicking the Content View button at the bottom of the feature (see Figure 5-7), list pane, or by right-clicking a treeview node and choosing Switch to Content View. The Content View is used to set the configuration on a file. To set the configuration, switch to Content View, select the file, and click Switch to Features View. This is the only method that allows a file's configuration to be adjusted in the IIS Manager.

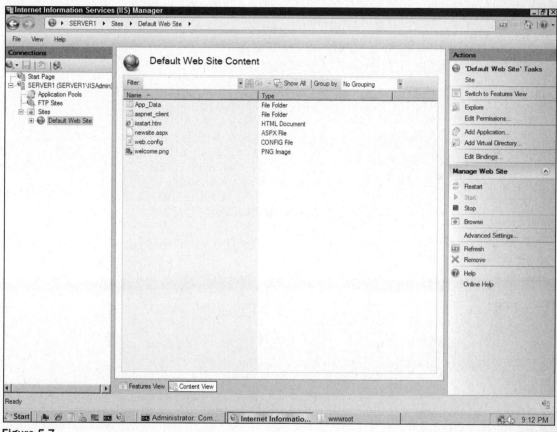

Figure 5-7

Feature Delegation

Feature Delegation gives the server administrator the ability to delegate control of web sites and applications to other administrators or developers. By default, only users in the local Administrators group (including Domain Admins) can manage an IIS 7.0 server. With Feature Delegation, the server administrator can allow non-administrators to manage either web sites or applications. These become "site administrators" or "application administrators," respectively. Remember that the hierarchy is server administrators, site administrators, and then application administrators. Chapter 9 goes into greater detail about how to set up and use Feature Delegation.

IIS Manager Extensibility

Along with the tools that are already built into the IIS Manager, there is also the ability to create your own tools and extend the capabilities of the manager. This feature, known as *IIS Manager extensibility*, allows third-party vendors, developers, or systems administrators to create their own custom tools to work with IIS 7.0.

The `Microsoft.Web.Management.dll` makes extensibility possible by providing access to the entire IIS subsystem. We go into more detail about IIS Manager extensibility and give examples and code in Chapter 12.

Configuration Settings

IIS 6.0 and ASP.NET provided the ability to control certain functions of the web site through the `web.config` file, but all IIS-specific settings were housed in the metabase. With IIS 7.0, Microsoft has changed the configuration storage from the metabase to a series of cleartext XML files. These files provide for a distributed hierarchy in which the configuration is shared among the machine-level configuration files and may optionally be set at the directory level along with the web content. This allows the system administrator to delegate control to the site or application administrators. By default, IIS 7.0 is locked down to allow only the system administrator access to modify the server, site, or application settings. The configuration settings are fully backward compatible at both the API and XML levels with previous versions of IIS and the .NET Framework.

Configuration File Hierarchy

As with most systems, the configuration files in IIS 7.0 are read and applied in a hierarchical order. The following three files are at the heart of the system:

- ❑ The `applicationHost.config` file.
- ❑ The `machine.config` file.
- ❑ The root `web.config` file.

The `applicationHost.config` file is located at `%systemroot%\system32\inetsrv\config`. The `machine.config` and root `web.config` files are both currently located in the `%systemroot%\Microsoft.NET\Framework\v2.0.50727\CONFIG` folder. When Microsoft releases the next version of the .NET Framework, this path will change.

The `applicationHost.config` file contains the IIS server settings. The `machine.config` and root `web.config` files contain the global default values for the .NET Framework settings. These two separate structures are necessary because IIS and the .NET Framework do not follow the same versioning schedule. IIS uses the Windows Server schedule, whereas the .NET Framework uses the Visual Studio schedule.

Along with the three primary files, additional `web.config` files may be located in the content directories of individual web sites or applications to control their behavior and the behavior of the hierarchical levels below them. These `web.config` files can contain settings for IIS, ASP.NET, or any other .NET Framework that can be controlled at that level. The configuration file inheritance hierarchy begins with the `machine.config` file, then the root `web.config`, the `applicationHost.config` file, and then the `web.config` files that may be in the web-site or application levels.

Configuration Levels

Owing to the hierarchical nature of the configuration, each level of the URL namespace will have a configuration associated with it. The configuration will begin at the server level and then inherit down throughout the child nodes, unless there is an override in place on a child node. These child nodes can include not only folders, but also files. As mentioned above, the best method to set per URL configuration is by using `web.config` files at the root of each individual web site.

Occasionally, you will not want to allow `web.config` files to be deployed at levels below the server level. Some of the reasons include

❑ **Security** — There are times when server administrators need to control the server configuration and cannot allow access by developers through the use of `web.config` files. An example of this could be a production server in an organization that has a policy restricting access only to administrators.

❑ **Administration Consolidation** — Consolidating the configuration of all sites on a server to the three main server configuration files presents the administrator with an easy to manage, known location for making all the changes needed for the server and sites.

❑ **Remote Change Notification** — A `web.config` file located on a remote (UNC) share can present problems with usability, scalability, or other issues. A prime example of a potential problem with remote change notification can come when the `web.config` file is located on a non-Windows system that doesn't support the file change notifications in a manner that Windows expects it to.

❑ **Shared Configuration** — If many web sites all point to the same central `web.config` for their configuration, by default the `web.config` cannot be isolated in individual `web.config` files at the lower levels.

❑ **File-Specific Configuration** — When a `web.config` file is applied at a specific level, the file is applied to every file in that folder. If a different configuration for a specific file is needed, a different method has to be used. This is usually accomplished by using location tags.

Location Tags

Location tags present another method to set configuration for lower levels in the configuration hierarchy. The location tags are set at a parent level and then applied to a specific lower level and the hierarchy of configuration below it. These lower levels can be either subfolders or a file in a subfolder. This allows a lower level to have a different configuration from that of the parent level without having to use a separate `web.config` file. Generally, location tags are set at the global level. Location tags use the `path` attribute to set the location for the configuration to be applied. The `path` attribute can be

❑ `"."` or `" "` — This designates the current level.

❑ `sitename` — This designates the root application of a specific site.

❑ `sitename/application` — This designates a specific application within a specific site.

❑ `sitename/application/vdir` — This designates a specific virtual directory within a application in a site.

❏　　`sitename/application/vdir/physicaldir` — This designates a specific physical directory.

❏　　`sitename/application/vdir/file.ext` — This designates a specific file. The file can be located anywhere in the folder structure, but the path must specify the location to the file — such as `sitename/application/vdir/folder1/file1.ext`, or, if the file is at the root of the site, `sitename/file1.ext`.

Because location tags generally are located in the `applicationHost.config` file, multiple location tags are allowed in one file. Although the location tags cannot reference the exact same path, they can reference child paths. For example, the global path for `httpLogging` can be set to log only errors by setting the location path to `"."` in the `httpLogging` tag.

```
<location path= ".">
  <system.webServer>
    <httpLogging selectiveLogging= "LogError" />
  </system.webServer>
</location>
```

The logging for the default web site can then be set to log every request by setting the location path to the default web site in the tag.

```
<location path= "Default Web Site">
  <system.webServer>
    <httpLogging selectiveLogging= "LogAll" />
  </system.webServer>
</location>
```

Finally, you can set file `1.htm` to only log errors by setting the location path to point to file `1.htm` in the tag.

```
<location path= "Default Web Site/file1.htm">
  <system.webServer>
    <httpLogging selectiveLogging= "LogError" />
  </system.webServer>
</location>
```

These examples show that by using location tags, different levels of the configuration can have different settings specified without having to use a `web.config` file at lower levels.

Configuration File Structure

Like other XML files, the configuration files are based on sections. *Sections* are groups of related settings that can be deployed as a group and are normally consumed by a single server module. Configuration sections are also the base unit for extensibility. To extend the schema, add a new section with the desired settings.

Sections belong to a section group, to create a logically related group. Sections can be nested inside section groups, but they cannot be nested inside other sections.

Section groups don't have settings in them. Section groups contain one or more sections. They provide a method of organizing the sections into the configuration. Section groups can contain other section groups. This nesting of section groups is used to build the configuration hierarchy within the settings.

Sections have both short and long names. Short names consist of the section itself, whereas long names consist of all the containing section groups and the section name. In this example, `httpLogging` is the short section name, and `system.webServer/httpLogging` is the long section name. The long section name is derived by pre-pending the short section name, in this case `httpLogging`, with the name of its parent section group(s), `system.webServer`.

```
<system.webServer>
  <httpLogging selectiveLogging= "LogError" />
</system.webServer>
```

This *hierarchical naming structure* provides the method for specifying the correct section to modify when changes are made via any of the IIS 7.0 tools. It also allows multiple sections to be named the same, as long as they are under different section groups. In the example below, `<system.webServer>` and `<httpProtocol>` are both section groups, while `<customHeaders>` and `<redirectHeaders>` are both sections within those groups.

```
<system.webServer>

...

  <httpProtocol>
    <customHeaders>
      <clear />
      <add name="X-Powerd-By" value="ASP.NET" />
    </customHeaders>
    <redirectHeaders>
      <clear />
    </redirectHeaders>
  </httpProtocol>

...

</system.webServer>
```

Configuration Schema

The configuration uses a *declarative schema*, which is housed in multiple files located at `%systemroot%\system32\inetsrv\config\schema`. You can add new schema files to the configuration by adding them to the `schema` folder. Once the configuration system has restarted, it will grab the additions to the schema. The new changes will not be used until the configuration system has restarted.

The schema is housed in the following files:

❑ **IIS_schema.xml** — Provides the schema for the IIS web server settings and the Windows Activation System.

❑ **ASPNET_schema.xml** — Provides the schema for the ASP.NET settings.

❑ **FX_schema.xml** — Provides the schema for the other .NET Framework settings.

It is highly recommended that these default files not be edited, as that may result in a corrupted schema that will not allow the server to start. If you need to edit a schema file, make a back-up copy first. Editing of these files can only be done through file access API and XML parsing\editing. The recommended method of adding configuration sections to the schema is to create a new .xml file in the schema folder.

Schema Organization

As mentioned previously, the configuration consists of a series of sections and section groups. The sections get their layout in the schema. Looking at the IIS_schema.xml file, it is possible to see that the *schema* is a collection of sections. Each of these sections is initiated with sectionSchema. Here the section system.webServer/defaultDocument is detailed in the IIS_schema.xml file. (Notice that the long name is used, showing the section group system.webServer within which the section is contained.) The schema shows an attribute of enabled with a default value of true and an element named "files". In addition to those items, it also defines a collection as a subelement of the files element and the collection's properties.

```
<sectionSchema name="system.webServer/defaultDocument">
    <attribute name="enabled" type="bool" defaultValue="true" />
    <element name="files">
      <collection addElement="add" clearElement="clear" removeElement="remove"
mergeAppend="false">
        <attribute name="value" type="string" isUniqueKey="true"/>
      </collection>
    </element>
</sectionSchema>
```

The schema for system.webServer/defaultDocument is then used in the applicationHost.config file with this result:

```
<system.webServer>
  <defaultDocument enabled="true">
      <files>
          <add value="Default.htm" />
          <add value="Default.asp" />
          <add value="index.htm" />
          <add value="index.html" />
          <add value="iisstart.htm" />
          <add value="default.aspx" />
      </files>
  </defaultDocument>
</system.webServer>
```

The enabled attribute listed in the schema is shown as being set to true. The files element is listed with no attributes; however, it is shown to have a collection of elements below it. The collection in the schema becomes a series of elements below files. Each of these elements specifies a file name that the web site can use as a default file type. The schema files provide the structure for the configuration files.

configSections

Although the schema files provide the backbone for the configuration files, there is also a section in the configuration files named configSections. configSections is in both machine.config and applicationHost.config by default. This part of the configuration may also be added to any web.config for additional structure. The purpose of configSections is to register the sections it lists with the system, including any custom configuration sections. In addition, it establishes the hierarchy of the section groups. Its purpose is not to define properties of the sections.

`configSections` uses three pieces of metadata to register a section with the system:

❑ `type` — Used to specify the managed-code section handler for the .NET Framework.

❑ `overrideModeDefault` — Determines whether the section can be overridden at lower levels or if it locked down to prevent changes at lower levels. The default is to allow override if it is not specified.

❑ `allowDefinition` — Specifies the level in the hierarchy at which the section can be set. The options include

  ❑ `MachineOnly` — Where the section can only be set in the `applicationHost.config` or `machine.config` files.

  ❑ `MachineToRootWeb` — Where the section can be set in the `applicationHost.config`, `machine.config` or the root `web.config` files.

  ❑ `MachineToApplication` — Where the section can be set in the `applicationHost.config`, `machine.config`, the root `web.config`, or the application-level `web.config` files.

  ❑ `AppHostOnly` — Where the section can be set only in the `applicationHost.config` file.

  ❑ `Everywhere` — Where the section can be set in any configuration file.

This example of the `applicationHost.config` file shows a small portion of `configSections`:

```
<configSections>
        <sectionGroup name="system.applicationHost">
                <section name="applicationPools" allowDefinition="AppHostOnly"
overrideModeDefault="Deny" />
                <section name="configHistory" allowDefinition="AppHostOnly"
overrideModeDefault="Deny" />
                <section name="customMetadata" allowDefinition="AppHostOnly"
overrideModeDefault="Deny" />
                <section name="listenerAdapters" allowDefinition="AppHostOnly"
overrideModeDefault="Deny" />
                <section name="log" allowDefinition="AppHostOnly"
overrideModeDefault="Deny" />
                <section name="sites" allowDefinition="AppHostOnly"
overrideModeDefault="Deny" />
                <section name="webLimits" allowDefinition="AppHostOnly"
overrideModeDefault="Deny" />
        </sectionGroup>

        <sectionGroup name="system.webServer">
                <section name="asp" overrideModeDefault="Deny" />
                <section name="caching" overrideModeDefault="Allow" />
                <section name="cgi" overrideModeDefault="Deny" />
                <section name="defaultDocument" overrideModeDefault="Allow" />
                <section name="directoryBrowse" overrideModeDefault="Allow" />
                <section name="fastCgi" allowDefinition="AppHostOnly"
overrideModeDefault="Deny" />
```

The first section group is the `system.applicationHost` group and specifies that the sections can only be set in the `applicationHost.config` file. The second section group is the `system.webServer` group, and the sections don't use the `allowDefinition` metadata to set which files they can be set in. The `overrideModeDefault` metadata can also be seen in each of the sections.

Locking and Unlocking Sections

Feature Delegation is one of the new features of IIS 7.0. It enables you to lock or unlock sections, preventing administrators or developers with fewer permissions than a standard system administrator from editing configuration settings. The primary method to lock or unlock a section is by using location tags. The location tags can only be used to unlock a section at the level in which it was locked. Child-level configuration files can never unlock parent-level configuration files. The following section is not locked by default, but can be locked in the `applicationHost.config` file by using the `overrideMode` attribute.

```
<location path="Default Web Site" overrideMode= "Deny">
       <system.webServer>
             <httpLogging selectiveLogging="LogError" />
       </system.webServer>
</location>
```

The previous section set the default web site to log only errors in the `applicationHost.config` file, while not allowing `web.config` files at sublevels to change the setting. It is also possible to set the configuration in lower-level files, such as website-level `web.config` files.

In IIS 7.0, locking and unlocking are done with the `overrideMode` attribute, which has the following values:

❑   `Allow` — Unlocks the specified section.

❑   `Deny` — Locks the specified section.

❑   `Inherit` — This is the default value if one isn't specified. The configuration system will determine the lockdown status based on the inheritance hierarchy of the parent files.

IIS 7.0 also supports the legacy attribute `allowOverride`. This is a carryover from the .NET framework prior to `overrideMode`. It has the following values:

❑   `true` — Equivalent to `Allow`. Unlocks the specified section.

❑   `false` — Equivalent to `Deny`. Locks the specified section.

❑   [not set] — Equivalent to `Inherit`.

The newer `overrideMode` is the preferred method to establish locking and unlocking of sections. The two locking methods cannot be used in the same location tag. Doing so will cause a failure at run time due to the illegal configuration.

It is possible when `overrideMode` is used at multiple levels for the same section to have conflicting settings, which can lead to unexpected results or errors. The best policy is to always lock and unlock sections in the `applicationHost.config` file.

Additional information on using `AppCmd.exe` to configure locking and unlocking is covered below in this chapter in the section, "Locking and Unlocking the Configuration."

Command-Line Management

Command-line management in IIS 7.0 is done with the new `AppCmd.exe` tool. Microsoft decided to name it `AppCmd.exe` rather than `IISCmd.exe` because, although we primarily use it for administering IIS 7.0, it is also used to manage the Windows Process Activation Service (WAS). This one tool consolidates complete control of the web server, providing a method to control the server with either the command prompt or through scripts. A few examples of what you can do include

- Add, delete, and modify web sites and application pools.
- Stop and start web sites and application pools.
- View information about worker processes and requests.
- List and modify the configurations of IIS and ASP.NET.

`AppCmd.exe` provides a consistent set of supported commands for performing queries and tasks against a set of supported object types. You can run these commands individually or in combination with other commands to perform complex tasks or queries.

Object Name	Description
`site`	To administer virtual sites
`app`	To administer applications
`vdir`	To administer virtual directories
`apppool`	To administer application pools
`config`	To administer general configuration sections
`wp`	To administer worker processes
`request`	To administer HTTP requests
`module`	To administer server modules
`backup`	To administer server configuration backups
`trace`	To administer failed request trace logs

Supported commands include

- `add.`
- `clear.`
- `configure.`
- `delete.`

- ❏ inspect.
- ❏ install.
- ❏ list.
- ❏ lock.
- ❏ migrate.
- ❏ recycle.
- ❏ reset.
- ❏ restore.
- ❏ search.
- ❏ set.
- ❏ start.
- ❏ stop.
- ❏ uninstall.
- ❏ unlock.

AppCmd.exe is located in the %systemroot%\system32\inetsrv directory, which is available only to members of the administrators group. Additionally, if applicationhost.config, machine.config, or web.config will be modified, you will need to start the tool with elevated permissions. We recommend placing AppCmd.exe in the system path to make it more convenient to use. To place it in the path, open PowerShell using elevated permissions, and use set-itemproperty to permanently add the path to the system variables. Run Path first to determine what folders are currently in the path and then append "%systemroot%\system32\inetsrv" to the current path string.

```
set-itemproperty -path "HKLM:\SYSTEM\CurrentControlSet\Control\Session Manager\
Environment" -name path -value "%systemroot%;%systemroot%\system32;%systemroot%\
system32\WindowsPowerShell\v1.0\;%systemroot%\system32\inetsrv"
```

Using AppCmd.exe

AppCmd.exe interacts with server management objects to expose methods in order to perform a variety of actions on those objects as well as exposing attributes that can be inspected and manipulated. For example, the app object provides methods to list, set, add, and delete applications. These objects contain attributes that can be searched for, inspected, and set.

Getting Help

To determine the objects supported for use with AppCmd.exe, use this command:

```
appcmd.exe /?
```

This returns

```
General purpose IIS command line administration tool.

APPCMD (command) (object-type) <identifier> </parameter1:value1 ...>

Supported object types:

  SITE       Administration of virtual sites
  APP        Administration of applications
  VDIR       Administration of virtual directories
  APPPOOL    Administration of application pools
  CONFIG     Administration of general configuration sections
  WP         Administration of worker processes
  REQUEST    Administration of HTTP requests
  MODULE     Administration of server modules
  BACKUP     Administration of server configuration backups
  TRACE      Working with failed request trace logs

(To list commands supported by each object use /?, e.g. 'appcmd.exe site /?')

General parameters:

/?              Display context-sensitive help message.

/text<:value>   Generate output in text format (default).
                /text:* shows all object properties in detail view.
                /text:<attr> shows the value of the specified
                attribute for each object.
/xml            Generate output in XML format.
                Use this to produce output that can be sent to another
                command running in /in mode.
/in or -        Read and operate on XML input from standard input.
                Use this to operate on input produced by another
                command running in /xml mode.
/config<:*>     Show configuration for displayed objects.
                /config:* also includes inherited configuration.
/metadata       Show configuration metadata when displaying configuration.

/commit         Set config path where configuration changes are saved.
                Can specify either a specific configuration path, "site",
                "app", or "url" to save to the appropriate portion of the
                path being edited by the command, or "apphost", "webroot",
                or "machine" for the corresponding configuration level.
/debug          Show debugging information for command execution.

Use "!" to escape parameters that have same names as the general parameters,
like "/!debug:value" to set a config property named "debug".
```

To determine the supported commands for a specific object, type **AppCmd.exe** followed by the object you want more information about and **/?**, in this case, **app** (application).

```
appcmd.exe app /?
```

This returns

```
Administration of applications

APPCMD (command) APP <identifier> <-parameter1:value1 ...>

Supported commands:

  list      List applications
  set       Configure application
  add       Add new application
  delete    Delete application

(To get help for each command use /?, e.g. 'appcmd.exe add site /?'.)
```

Once you know the command to use against the object, you can learn the attributes that you can configure with the command. Here the object is app, and the command is list.

```
appcmd.exe list app /?
```

This returns

```
Administration of applications

APPCMD (command) APP <identifier> <-parameter1:value1 ...>

Supported commands:

  list      List applications
  set       Configure application
  add       Add new application
  delete    Delete application

(To get help for each command use /?, e.g. 'appcmd.exe add site /?'.)

c:\Windows\System32\inetsrv>appcmd list app /?
List applications

APPCMD list APP <identifier> <-parameter1:value1 ...>

List the applications on the machine.  This command can be used to find a
specific application by using its identifier or url, find all applications
belonging to a specified site or application pool, or match zero or more
applications based on the specified application attributes.

Supported parameters:

 identifier

    Application path or url of the application to find

 /app.name
```

```
        Application path or url of the application to find (same as identifier)

    /?

        Display the dynamic properties that can be used to find one or more
        application objects


Examples:

    appcmd list apps

        List all applications on the machine.

    appcmd list app "Default Web Site/"

        Find the application "Default Web Site/" (root application of the site
        "Default Web Site").

    appcmd list app http://localhost/app1

        Find the application associated with the specified url.

    appcmd list apps /site.name:"Default Web Site".

        Find all applications belonging to the site "Default Web Site".

    appcmd list apps /apppool.name:"DefaultAppPool".

        Find all applications belonging to the application pool "DefaultAppPool".

    appcmd list apps /path:/app1

        Find all applications that have the "path" configuration property set to
        "/app1".
```

Using the list Command

The list command is used by every object to find the instances or attributes of the object. You can modify the results of the query by changing the criteria being searched for. The results can then be inspected, exported, or used with another command to perform actions.

Listing All Object Instances

To list all instances of an object, use AppCmd.exe with list and the object.

```
appcmd.exe list app
```

This would return a list of all web applications running on the server. A server with only the default setup would return this result:

```
APP "Default Web Site/" (applicationPool:DefaultAppPool)
```

Listing Unique Object Instances

If you are searching for a specific instance of an object, you can fine-tune `list` by adding an attribute of the object. For example, to list an application named *Default Web Site/*, use the following:

```
appcmd.exe list app "Default Web Site/"
```

This will list the Default Web Site application as well as attributes associated with it.

```
APP "Default Web Site/" (applicationPool:DefaultAppPool)
```

Listing Object Instances by Criteria

You can also use the `list` command with object attributes to return all the object instances that meet specified criteria.

```
appcmd.exe list app /apppool.name:"defaultapppool"
```

This returns a list of all applications that use the application pool `DefaultAppPool`.

```
app "Default Web Site/" (applicationPool:DefaultAppPool)
```

Remember that the command is placed before the object, and the attributes to be used are placed after the object. This creates a structure similar to a sentence or statement telling the object to do something — in this case, telling the `app` object to list all the applications that belong to the application pool `DefaultAppPool`.

AppCmd.exe Output

When you list objects, `AppCmd.exe` provides a method to return varied amounts of detail based on the parameters given. If you use only the default `list` command against an object, the data returned are short, usually consisting of one line of text that provides basic information about the object. Here we are using the `app` object Default Web Site.

```
appcmd.exe list app "Default Web Site/"
```

This returns the application name and the application pool that the Default Web Site uses.

```
APP "Default Web Site/" (applicationPool:DefaultAppPool)
```

Listing Detailed Information

To return much more data from the `list` command, append `/text:*` to it, as follows:

```
appcmd.exe list app "default web site/" /text:*
```

This returns the path, application name, and site name, as well as application information, default virtual directory settings, and current virtual directory information.

```
APP
  path:"/"
  APP.NAME:"Default Web Site/"
```

```
APPPOOL.NAME:"DefaultAppPool"
SITE.NAME:"Default Web Site"
[application]
  path:"/"
  applicationPool:"DefaultAppPool"
  enabledProtocols:"http"
  [virtualDirectoryDefaults]
    path:""
    physicalPath:""
    userName:""
    password:""
    logonMethod:"ClearText"
    allowSubDirConfig:"true"
  [virtualDirectory]
    path:"/"
    physicalPath:"%SystemDrive%\inetpub\wwwroot"
    userName:""
    password:""
    logonMethod:"ClearText"
    allowSubDirConfig:"true"
```

Listing by Property

AppCmd.exe also enables you to return only data that meet a specific property. To do this, add /text:<property> to the command. For example, to list all applications that use the default application pool as their application pool, use

```
appcmd.exe list app /text: /apppool.name:DefaultAppPool
```

The query returns

```
APP "Default Web Site/" (applicationPool:DefaultAppPool)
```

This shows that the default web site is the only site using the default application pool.

You may also want to use the data that are output by AppCmd.exe with other command-line tools or shell commands. You can take the AppCmd.exe string and insert it into another command. The following command lists the files in the logfile directory used by the default web site:

```
FOR /F %f IN ('AppCmd.exe list site "default web site" /text:logfile.directory') DO
DIR %f
```

Listing Configuration Objects

AppCmd.exe uses a series of objects to manipulate IIS 7.0. Each of these objects maps to a section in a configuration file — for example, the default web site. You can query the configuration for the default web site using this command:

```
appcmd.exe list site "default web site" /config
```

This returns

```
<site name="Default Web Site" id="1">
```

```
    <bindings>
      <binding protocol="http" bindingInformation="*:80:" />
    </bindings>
    <limits />
    <logFile />
    <traceFailedRequestsLogging />
    <applicationDefaults />
    <virtualDirectoryDefaults />
    <application path="/">
      <virtualDirectoryDefaults />
      <virtualDirectory path="/" physicalPath="C:\inetpub\wwwroot" />
    </application>
  </site>
```

The returned data are a list of the sections that can be configured for the object being queried.

AppCmd.exe Attributes and Values

The *attributes* of an object provide a method to limit the results of a list or modify the values of the object. The previous example showed how the attribute `apppool.name` could limit the results of a query of the applications on the server. In this case, the limit was to return only objects that had the attribute value of `DefaultAppPool`. It is possible then to take the object that was returned by the query and modify it by changing the value of the attribute. In this instance, assume that you have an `app` object named `WebSite1` that uses the `DefaultAppPool` and an application pool named `WebAppPool1`.

```
    appcmd.exe set app "WebSite1/" /applicationpool:"WebAppPool1"
```

This then changes the application pool of `WebSite1` from `DefaultAppPool` to `WebAppPool1`.

How did we know to use the `applicationpool` attribute? We'll show you that one shortly.

Managing Objects with add, delete, and set

We've already shown you about `list` and used `set` in one example, but we can also create and delete instances of objects by using `add` and `delete`.

Adding New Objects

By using the `add` command, we are able to create new instances of an object.

```
    appcmd.exe add apppool /name:"WebAppPool2"
```

This command created a new application pool object named `WebAppPool2`. The only attribute needed by this command was "name"; however, other objects may need additional attributes when creating a new object. This command would have been used to create the application pool that was used in the previous example.

Deleting Existing Objects

Deleting an object is exactly what it appears to be, removing it completely from the server.

```
    appcmd.exe delete apppool /apppool.name:"WebAppPool2"
```

When deleting objects, object-specific identifiers are required. Here the identifier was the app pool name WebAppPool2.

Modifying Existing Objects

The set command has two modes of use. The first mode combines set with the help syntax to determine what attributes an object has that can be modified.

```
appcmd.exe set site "WebSite1" /?
```

The second mode modifies the attributes of the object. As seen above with: AppCmd.exe set app "WebSite1/" /applicationpool:"WebAppPool1", WebSite1 was set to use WebAppPool1. Similar to the Delete command, object-specific identifiers are required with the Set command.

As a side note, when updating live web sites, we prefer to make a copy of the existing web folder, apply the updates to the new folder and then point the web site to the web folder. Following is a script that uses user-defined variables for the source "src" and destination "dest" folders. Xcopy.exe then copies the data in the src folder into the dest folder, and AppCmd.exe points the web virtual directory to the new folder.

```
echo off

Set /P Src=[old folder date]
Set /P Dest=[new folder date]

xcopy c:\inetpub\wwwroot\WebSite1\%src% c:\inetpub\wwwroot\WebSite1\%dest% /c /e /i
/o /y

AppCmd.exe set vdir WebSite1/ -physicalpath:"c:\inetpub\wwwroot\WebSite1\%dest%"
```

Determining Which Attributes Are Associated with an Object

AppCmd.exe makes it possible to control every aspect of IIS through the command line, including managing sites, applications, virtual directories, and application pools. We've already shown a few examples in which sites, applications and application pools have either been modified or listed. In order to make some of the changes to the objects, you have to know which attribute needs to be modified to achieve the desired result.

Above we changed the application pool for WebSite1 from the DefaultAppPool to the WebAppPool1 application pool and used an attribute named applicationpool. How did we know about the attribute named applicationpool? Using the list command with /text:* on the object WebSite1/ allows us to see every attribute associated with the WebSite1 application.

```
appcmd list app "WebSite1/" /text:*
```

The command returns the following:

```
APP
  path:"/"
  APP.NAME:"WebSite1/"
  APPPOOL.NAME:"WebAppPool1"
```

```
SITE.NAME:"WebSite1"
[application]
  path:"/"
  applicationPool:"WebAppPool1"
  enabledProtocols:"http"
  [virtualDirectoryDefaults]
    path:""
    physicalPath:""
    userName:""
    password:""
    logonMethod:"ClearText"
    allowSubDirConfig:"true"
  [virtualDirectory]
    path:"/"
    physicalPath:"C:\inetpub\wwwroot"
    userName:""
    password:""
    logonMethod:"ClearText"
    allowSubDirConfig:"true"
```

In this case, `applicationPool` is one of a few attributes available to be modified. Some object types will have only a few attributes, and some objects will have many. In this example, the `applicationPool` attribute is directly under the application element. However, some attributes fall under subelements. If you want to modify the virtual directory default path, you would need to use element path notation. Here `virtualdirectorydefault` is the subelement, and `path` is the attribute we are changing.

```
appcmd.exe set app "WebSite1/" /virtualdirectorydefaults.path:"/"
```

This command makes the virtual directory default path `"/"`.

Controlling Object State

In addition to the tasks already shown, you can also use `AppCmd.exe` to gather state information for sites, application pools, worker processes, and currently executing requests. For some objects, the state can also be changed. Examples include starting/stopping a site and starting/stopping/recycling an application pool.

> *To gather the state information AppCmd.exe is using the RSCA (Runtime Status and Control API). The IIS Manager and WMI also use the RSCA to gather information. Additional information on using new functionality in IIS 7.0 to analyze running processes and problems can be found in Chapter 21 "Diagnostics and Troubleshooting."*

Determining Site and Application Pool State

It is possible to determine the state of a site or application pool and then, based on the current state of the object, start, stop, or recycle it. Here we will use the `list` command on the `apppool` object:

```
appcmd.exe list apppool
```

The result of the query on a default system is

```
APPPOOL "DefaultAppPool" (MgdVersion:v2.0,MgdMode:Integrated,state:Started)
APPPOOL "Classic .NET AppPool" (MgdVersion:v2.0,MgdMode:Classic,state:Started)
```

At the end of the string state is the list for both application pools as "Started." You can also use a query to return all of the objects that meet specific criteria. This example returns all the application pools whose state is set to started:

```
appcmd.exe list apppools /state:started
```

As before, the result of this query on a default system is

```
APPPOOL "DefaultAppPool" (MgdVersion:v2.0,MgdMode:Integrated,state:Started)
APPPOOL "Classic .NET AppPool" (MgdVersion:v2.0,MgdMode:Classic,state:Started)
```

Once you know the state of the object, you can change it to meet your needs. In this case, we will stop the DefaultAppPool:

```
appcmd.exe stop apppool /apppool.name:"DefaultAppPool"
```

This returns

```
"DefaultAppPool" successfully stopped
```

Determining Worker Process State

By finding the worker process state, the Process ID (PID) number is given and can be used along with Task Manager to determine the health of an application pool process. As with other objects, the worker process object can be queried either with a list query with no attributes to narrow the search or with a specific query that returns only objects that match the attributes listed in the query. The nonspecific query uses the list command against the wp object. Prior to running this example, restart the DefaultAppPool and navigate to http://localhost/ on your server.

```
appcmd.exe list wp
```

If your DefaultAppPool was started and you navigated to http://localhost/, the query should return a result similar to this:

```
WP "1044" (applicationPool:DefaultAppPool)
```

In this example "1044" is the PID number for the DefaultAppPool application pool. If you know either the PID number or the name of the application pool that you want to query, it is possible to fine-tune the query to return only the result needed, rather than all active worker processes:

```
appcmd.exe list wp /apppool.name:"DefaultAppPool"
```

or

```
appcmd.exe list wp /wp.name:"1044"
```

Both of these queries will return only the DefaultAppPool worker process status.

Monitoring Currently Executing Requests

Requests that are currently being executed can be determined by using the `request` object:

```
appcmd.exe list request
```

Like other objects used with `AppCmd.exe`, the `request` object can use attributes to focus the information it returns. The attributes can be used to return information on a specific site, application pool, worker process, URL, or requests that have been executing for longer than a specified time (in milliseconds). Examples of attributes used with request include

❑ Requesting based on site ID.

```
appcmd.exe list request /site.id:1
```

❑ Requesting based on application pool.

```
appcmd.exe list request /apppool.exe:DefaultAppPool
```

❑ Requesting based on worker process.

```
appcmd.exe list request /wp.name:"1044"
```

❑ Requesting based on site name.

```
appcmd.exe list request /site.name:"Default Web Site"
```

❑ Requesting based on the time for which the process has been running.

```
appcmd.exe list request /elapsed:"1000"
```

Here is an example of the information returned by a request:

```
REQUEST "3d0000018000a2f1" (url:GET /default.aspx, time:324 msec,
client:192.168.0.132)
```

The information returned includes the request ID, URL, time the request has taken, and the client IP address. This provides a useful tool to look at requests that are taking longer to execute than desired.

Backing Up and Restoring

`AppCmd.exe` is also used to back up, list, and restore the global server configuration. We recommend making a backup prior to installing any component or making any modification that changes the global server configuration. When the backup is made, it contains the `applicationhost.config`, `administration.config`, `redirection.config`, `metabase.xml`, and `mbschema.xml`. (The last two contain metabase data that are still used by SMTP and FTP.)

To create a backup, use

```
appcmd.exe add backup
```

Once the backup has been created, the command prompt will return. The backups consist of folders named automatically based on the date and time of the backup and placed in the `%systemroot%\system32\`

`inetsrv\backup` directory. It is also possible to name the backups by appending the backup name at the end of the string.

```
appcmd.exe add backup test1
```

To list a backup, use

```
appcmd.exe list backup
```

The result is a list of all backups stored in the backup folder:

```
BACKUP "20070709T221615"
BACKUP "20070709T223557"
BACKUP "20070709T223601"
BACKUP "test1"
```

To restore a backup, use

```
appcmd.exe restore backup /backup.name:"20070709T221615"
```

When restoring a backup, IIS stops and performs an overwrite of the server's state. Once the configuration files have been overwritten, IIS restarts. If you prefer not to have IIS stop and restart, you can also use `/stop:false`. This allows you to stop and restart the services manually at a time that you desire.

```
appcmd.exe restore backup /backup.name:"20070709T221615" /stop:false
```

To remove a backup, use

```
appcmd.exe delete backup test1
```

Remember that 30 seconds spent backing up can save hours spent rebuilding your server.

Setting the Configuration

The configuration of IIS 7.0, as mentioned above in this chapter, is set in a series of XML files. The specifics of these files are covered below in this chapter, but for now, know that `AppCmd.exe` can also be used to manage the configuration. Tasks included in managing the configuration consist of: listing, editing, and clearing the configuration; locking and unlocking sections; and searching through the configuration.

Listing the Configuration

`AppCmd.exe` views the configuration as a series of sections and subsections. Starting at the top with no modifiers, it is possible to list the configuration of the server. You can narrow the focus of the list by adding site or application names or URLs. Beyond that, by using specific section identifiers in relation to a site or URL, you can gather the exact information that you need. Each level is seen as a section or subsection and inherits the settings from the level above it, unless explicitly overwritten.

To list the entire configuration for a server, use

```
appcmd.exe list config
```

Listing the configuration for the default web site is just as simple:

```
appcmd.exe list config "Default Web Site/"
```

To narrow the focus down to a specific section in the default web site, use

```
appcmd.exe list config "Default Web Site/" /section:system.net/settings
```

This would return the following result:

```
<system.net>
  <settings>
    <httpWebRequest />
    <ipv6 />
    <performanceCounters />
    <servicePointManager />
    <socket />
    <webProxyScript />
  </settings>
</system.net>
```

AppCmd.exe will show only sections of the configuration that are explicitly set. To display inherited or default values, append /config:* to the string.

```
appcmd.exe list config "Default Web Site/" /section:system.net/settings /config:*
```

By adding the /config:* to the string, the results that are returned contain all the information, even if it wasn't specifically set at that section level.

```
<system.net>
  <settings>
    <httpWebRequest maximumErrorResponseLength="64"
maximumResponseHeadersLength="64" maximumUnauthorizedUploadLength="-1"
 useUnsafeHeaderParsing="false" />
    <ipv6 enabled="false" />
    <performanceCounters enabled="false" />
    <servicePointManager checkCertificateName="true"
checkCertificateRevocationList="false" dnsRefreshTimeout="120000"
enableDnsRoundRobin="false" expect100Continue="true" useNagleAlgorithm="true" />
    <socket alwaysUseCompletionPortsForAccept="false"
alwaysUseCompletionPortsForConnect="false" />
    <webProxyScript downloadTimeout="00:02:00" />
  </settings>
</system.net>
```

How do you discover what the available sections are? Use this command:

```
appcmd.exe list config -section:?
```

Here is a portion of what the previous command returns:

```
system.net/authenticationModules
system.web/deployment
```

```
system.web/httpModules
system.webServer/directoryBrowse
system.webServer/cgi
configPaths
system.web/compilation
system.webServer/security/access
system.web/deviceFilters
system.transactions/defaultSettings
system.webServer/management/authorization
system.applicationHost/customMetadata
system.web/authorization
system.web/globalization
system.webServer/handlers
configurationRedirection
configProtectedData
system.web/browserCaps
system.net/mailSettings/smtp
system.web/xhtmlConformance
system.xml.serialization/dateTimeSerialization
system.webServer/urlCompression
system.web/pages
system.web/trace
appSettings
system.web/profile
system.webServer/isapiFilters
system.web/customErrors
system.net/webRequestModules
system.web/caching/outputCacheSettings
```

Editing Configuration Properties

When `AppCmd.exe` is used to edit the configuration, the section being edited consists of an object or series of objects and the attributes associated with the object. In the previous example, the section was `system.net/settings`, the object being "settings" with a series of properties listed below it that can be edited. To differentiate whether the change you are setting will be at a global level or site-specific, you must add the URL if the change is to be at site level. You can take the previous example and use the information gathered by using `list` with `/config:*` to determine what property we need to adjust. The `set` command is then used to make a global configuration change to enable IPv6 and then a site-specific change to disable IPv6 that will override the global configuration only for the one site.

```
appcmd.exe set config /section:system.net/settings -ipv6.enabled:"true"
```

The global configuration has been set to enable IPv6, and now it will be disabled on the default web site.

```
appcmd.exe set config "http://localhost" /section:system.net/settings
-ipv6.enabled:"false"
```

In this case, `http://localhost` had to be used as the site name for the default web-site, as it had no other site name.

151

Editing Configuration Collections

Sections can contain elements that are known as *collections*. Collections can, in turn, contain more elements. An example of a section that contains a collection is `httpErrors`. It contains both standard elements and a collection.

```
appcmd.exe list config /section:httpErrors
```

The result of this is

```
<system.webServer>
  <httpErrors>
    <error statusCode="401" prefixLanguageFilePath="%SystemDrive%\inetpub\custerr"
path="401.htm" />

    <error statusCode="403" prefixLanguageFilePath="%SystemDrive%\inetpub\custerr"
path="403.htm" />

    <error statusCode="404" prefixLanguageFilePath="%SystemDrive%\inetpub\custerr"
path="404.htm" />

    <error statusCode="405" prefixLanguageFilePath="%SystemDrive%\inetpub\custerr"
path="405.htm" />

    <error statusCode="406" prefixLanguageFilePath="%SystemDrive%\inetpub\custerr"
path="406.htm" />

    <error statusCode="412" prefixLanguageFilePath="%SystemDrive%\inetpub\custerr"
path="412.htm" />

    <error statusCode="500" prefixLanguageFilePath="%SystemDrive%\inetpub\custerr"
path="500.htm" />

    <error statusCode="501" prefixLanguageFilePath="%SystemDrive%\inetpub\custerr"
path="501.htm" />

    <error statusCode="502" prefixLanguageFilePath="%SystemDrive%\inetpub\custerr"
path="502.htm" />

  </httpErrors>
</system.webServer>
```

In this example, each error status code is an element in the `error` collection. Refer to `IIS_schema` at `%systemroot%\system32\inetsrv\config\schema` to see the schema for httpErrors.

```
<sectionSchema name="system.webServer/httpErrors">
    <attribute name="errorMode" type="enum" defaultValue="DetailedLocalOnly">
      <enum name="DetailedLocalOnly" value="0" />
      <enum name="Custom" value="1" />
      <enum name="Detailed" value="2" />
    </attribute>
    <attribute name="existingResponse" type="enum" defaultValue="Auto">
      <enum name="Auto" value="0" />
      <enum name="Replace" value="1" />
```

```
      <enum name="PassThrough" value="2" />
    </attribute>
    <attribute name="defaultPath" type="string" expanded="true" />
    <attribute name="defaultResponseMode" type="enum" defaultValue="File">
      <enum name="File" value="0" />
      <enum name="ExecuteURL" value="1" />
      <enum name="Redirect" value="2" />
    </attribute>
    <attribute name="detailedMoreInformationLink" type="string"
defaultValue="http://go.microsoft.com/fwlink/?LinkID=62293" required="false" />
    <collection addElement="error" clearElement="clear" removeElement="remove">
      <attribute name="statusCode" type="uint" required="true" isCombinedKey="true"
validationType="integerRange" validationParameter="400,999" />
      <attribute name="subStatusCode" type="int" defaultValue="-1"
isCombinedKey="true" validationType="integerRange" validationParameter="-1,999" />
      <attribute name="prefixLanguageFilePath" type="string" expanded="true"
defaultValue="" required="false" />
      <attribute name="path" type="string" expanded="true" required="true"
validationType="nonEmptyString" />
      <attribute name="responseMode" type="enum" defaultValue="File">
        <enum name="File" value="0" />
        <enum name="ExecuteURL" value="1" />
        <enum name="Redirect" value="2" />
      </attribute>
    </collection>
  </sectionSchema>
```

Notice that there are a series of attributes and that, toward the bottom, is the collection error. You can add, edit, or delete any of these elements in the collection by using the set command against the config object. Here we will be changing the 401 error page from "401.htm" to "defaulterror.htm". /[statusCode='401'] determines which element will be edited, and .path:defaulterror.htm states that the new path should be to the defaulterror.htm file.

```
appcmd.exe set config /section:httpErrors /[statusCode='401'].path:defaulterror.htm
```

The new result for the 401 status code is

```
<error statusCode="401" prefixLanguageFilePath="%SystemDrive%\inetpub\custerr"
path="defaulterror.htm" />
```

You can also add or remove elements from a collection by using a plus sign (+) or a minus sign (–). For example, the following adds a status code of 503 and points to the file 503.htm in the SystemDrive%\inetpub\custerr folder:

```
appcmd.exe set config /section:httpErrors
/+[statusCode='503',prefixLanguageFilePath='%SystemDrive%\inetpub\custerr',path='50
3.htm']
```

And the following removes the 503 status code:

```
appcmd.exe set config /section:httpErrors /-[statusCode='503']
```

When adding an element to a collection, you must specify every attribute. When deleting an element, however, you only need to specify the name of the element.

Configuration Location

Because the configuration of IIS 7.0 is a hierarchical system of layered levels, starting at the server level and working down to the application, you can set the configuration at any of these levels and it will be inherited by the levels below it. However, you can also set a configuration property at a higher level and have it apply only to a specific lower level. This is done by using the `commit` parameter. For example, with the `commit` parameter, it is possible to have HTTP logging log only errors by default at the server level, but force a specified URL to have HTTP logging log everything.

You can set the `commit` parameter at the following levels:

- ❏ (omitted) — The default; writes configuration at the level for which it is set.
- ❏ `url` — Same as default; writes configuration at the level for which it is set.
- ❏ `site` — Writes configuration in `web.config` at the site root of the URL for which it is set.
- ❏ `app` — Writes configuration in `web.config` at the application root of the URL for which it is set.
- ❏ `apphost` — Writes configuration at the server level, in the `applicationHost.config` file.
- ❏ `<PATH>` — Writes configurations at the specified configuration path.

To set logging to log everything for the default web site, you would use

```
appcmd.exe set config "http://localhost" /section:system.webServer/httpLogging
-selectiveLogging:LogAll -commit:apphost
```

In this example, the `commit` was executed against the `apphost` level, thus the configuration change will be made to the `applicationHost.config` file rather than the `web.config` file of the default web site.

Locating Configuration Settings

Because of the layered hierarchical structure of the configuration, a system is needed to determine the location(s) where a setting is being applied. Above in this chapter, `list` was used to find the configuration objects that needed to be edited. Here, this is reversed, and `search` is used to find every location where a setting has been applied. This is needed because a setting for the same object might be applied in multiple places.

To return all locations where configuration is set on a server, use `search` with no arguments:

```
appcmd.exe search config
```

This returns the following results on the server:

```
CONFIGSEARCH "MACHINE/WEBROOT/APPHOST"
CONFIGSEARCH "MACHINE/WEBROOT/APPHOST/Default Web Site"
CONFIGSEARCH "MACHINE/WEBROOT/APPHOST/WebSite1"
```

You can determine where the configuration for a specific site is set by including the site name in the command:

```
appcmd.exe search config "default web site"
```

The results show that the default web site has configuration set at both the apphost level and in the default web site's web.config file.

```
CONFIGSEARCH "MACHINE/WEBROOT/APPHOST"
CONFIGSEARCH "MACHINE/WEBROOT/APPHOST/Default Web Site"
```

To determine all of the locations where a specific configuration is being set, add the section to the search:

```
appcmd.exe search config /section:system.webServer/httplogging
```

This search shows that only the apphost level is being used to configure the httplogging section.

```
CONFIGSEARCH "MACHINE/WEBROOT/APPHOST"
```

To determine all of the locations where a specific property is being set, add the section and the property to the search:

```
appcmd.exe search config /section:system.webServer/httpLogging /selectiveLogging
```

This can be further refined to return only the locations where the property is set to a specific value. To determine all of the locations where a specific property is being set, add the section and the property value to the search:

```
appcmd.exe search config /section:system.webServer/httpLogging
/selectiveLogging:LogError
```

Locking and Unlocking the Configuration

As discussed above in the "Configuration Settings" section of this chapter, sections of the configuration can be locked to prevent them from being set at lower levels, or unlocked to allow delegation of authority to other users. Most IIS settings are locked by default. To allow delegation of authority, you need to unlock these sections. This is done with the unlock and lock commands. The command is given, followed by the section that needs to be locked or unlocked. The following command unlocks the authentication section in the default web site:

```
appcmd.exe unlock config "default web site" /section:system.web/authentication
```

To lock the section, use

```
appcmd.exe lock config "default web site" /section:system.web/authentication
```

Piping with XML

You can use the /xml modifier with the appcmd list command to create complex tasks or perform large batch functions. The /xml modifier enables you to export the results of a query into a standard XML format that can be used by other command-line tools or shell commands. For example, to list all the application pools that are started and export the information to an XML format, issue the following command:

```
appcmd.exe list apppool /state:Started /xml
```

which results in

```
<?xml version="1.0" encoding="UTF-8"?>
<appcmd>
    <APPPOOL APPPOOL.NAME="DefaultAppPool" PipelineMode="Integrated"
RuntimeVersion="v2.0" state="Started" />
    <APPPOOL APPPOOL.NAME="Classic .NET AppPool" PipelineMode="Classic"
RuntimeVersion="v2.0" state="Started" />
    <APPPOOL APPPOOL.NAME="WebSite1" PipelineMode="Integrated"
RuntimeVersion="v2.0" state="Started" />
</appcmd>
```

The results returned show that there are three application pools started and their names, the mode of each application pool, and the runtime version of each pool.

We can also take those XML data and pipe them directly into another AppCmd.exe command to cause an action to happen to the objects that were returned in the first query. Here we will recycle all the application pools that were returned in the first query:

```
appcmd.exe list apppool /state:Started /xml | appcmd.exe recycle apppool /in
```

This piping function gives great flexibility in creating scripts to administer sites and servers.

Web Management Service and Remote Administration

IIS 7.0 uses the new IIS Manager rather than the previous MMC that was used with IIS 6.0. With this change in the manager, there was also a change in the method of remotely managing IIS 7.0. The new IIS Manager uses web services over HTTPS rather than RPC as was used in IIS 6.0. This allows for more firewall friendly management. The new service also allows system administrators to delegate management of web sites and web applications to other administrators or developers, limiting them only to the sites or applications they need to access. Additionally, IIS 7.0 Remote Administration supports the creation of non-Windows user accounts (that are managed entirely by IIS 7.0) for managing IIS 7.0. This may be of interest to hosting companies, as there would no longer be a need to create Windows users (or to buy Windows Server CALs) to permit remote administration using IIS Manager. Unlike in IIS 6.0, remote management with the management service needs to be installed and configured prior to use. Chapter 9, "Delegating Remote Administration," covers this in more detail.

Summary

The goal of this chapter has been to introduce the variety of administration options available when working with IIS 7.0. Microsoft has developed a wonderful set of tools for managing IIS 7.0, especially AppCmd.exe and the new, easily extensible IIS Manager. Throughout the sections, we have attempted to provide step-by-step instructions when necessary and detailed explanations when appropriate. At this point, you should have a good understanding of the options available to manage IIS 7.0 with a focus on IIS Manager and AppCmd.exe. In the next chapter, we use the tools presented in this chapter to manage a web site.

Web-Site Administration

The daily challenges that you face as a web server administrator are wide and varied — from managing web-site content or ensuring that the company's web site is available for the crucial product release to figuring out why the developer's code that's just been deployed keeps crashing the web site. To manage such demands successfully and still be able to sleep at night depends on how well the server is administered and your ability to troubleshoot issues effectively and concisely. To develop these skills, you first need to accustom yourself with the core functionality of IIS and the best practices for managing it.

In this chapter, we look at the basic administration tasks required to manage an IIS 7.0 web server. We will investigate and look at the best practices of

- ❑ An overview of web sites, applications, and virtual directories.
- ❑ Creating and modifying a web site.
- ❑ Configuring logging.
- ❑ Configuring and managing host headers.
- ❑ Administering applications.
- ❑ Administering virtual directories.
- ❑ Configuring compression.
- ❑ Configuring MIME settings.
- ❑ Basic tasks to hit the ground running.

This chapter will also demonstrate the use of the latest tools for managing IIS 7.0, including IIS Manager, AppCmd.exe, Windows Management Instrumentation (WMI), and managed .NET management classes.

Web Sites, Applications, and Virtual Directories

IIS 7.0 has taken the concept of sites, applications, and virtual directories and given them a little more structure than in IIS 6.0. They now form a hierarchy of individual objects in the IIS 7.0 schema. Sites are the root object and contain applications. Applications then, in turn, contain virtual directories. Every site has at least one application, called the *root application* and signified by (/). Every application also has at least one virtual directory, the *root virtual directory*, also signified by (/), as shown in Figure 6-1. IIS 7.0 has also taken the application object and extended its functionality to have meaning for both IIS and the technologies that extend IIS, such as ASP.NET.

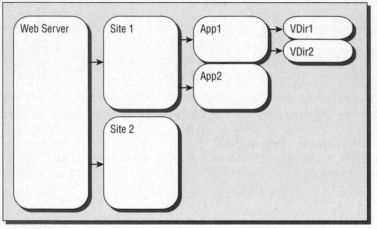

Figure 6-1

Web Sites

A *web site* is a collection of pages, images, video, or other digital content that is available via HTTP. The pages are usually in HTML, ASP, ASPX, or PHP format. These pages can be simple static pages, they can work together to access backend databases to deliver data through a web browser, or they can be a combination of the two. Web sites that serve data from a database are generally called *web applications*. Web sites have been around since 1991. The first web site was by Tim Berners-Lee, a copy of which is located at www.w3.org/History/19921103-hypertext/hypertext/WWW/TheProject.html.

Web sites are hosted on *web servers*. IIS 7.0 is Microsoft's latest web server and is a role that is available on Windows Server 2008 and Windows Vista. Web servers take HTTP requests that are sent from web browsers and then return data in the form of a web site. This chapter will explain the process of administering a web site on IIS 7.0.

As mentioned previously, sites are *root objects*. They are the containers for applications and virtual directories. Sites provide the unique bindings through which the applications are accessed. The bindings comprise two attributes: the binding protocol and the binding information. The binding protocol determines which protocol the server and the client use to exchange data — for example, HTTP or

HTTPS. The binding information determines how the server is accessed by the client. The binding information consists of the IP address, the port number, and the host header, if it is used. Multiple binding protocols can be used for the same site — for example, if the site uses HTTP to serve standard content but needs HTTPS for the sign-on page.

Applications

An *application* in IIS 7.0 is a collection of files and folders that serves content or provides services over protocols such as HTTP or HTTPS. In IIS 7.0, every site has at least one application, the *root application*, but sites can have many applications if needed. Applications in IIS 7.0 support not only HTTP and HTTPS protocols, but other protocols as well. To support a protocol, a listener adapter must be specified in the `<listenerAdapters>` section in the configuration, and the protocol must be enabled in the `<enabledProtocols>` section of the configuration. As an example, the FTP protocol can be added to an application to create an FTP binding. For more information on creating an FTP binding, see Chapter 10, "Configuring Other Services." Additional information on configuring other bindings such as Windows Communication Foundation (WCF) can be found in Appendix B.

Virtual Directories

A *virtual directory* is the directory, or path, that maps to the physical location of the files on the local or remote server. Virtual directories can use local folders, UNC paths, mapped drives, and distributed file system shares. Like sites, applications always have at least one root virtual directory, although applications can have additional virtual directories as well. Virtual directories are useful for making files available to the application without adding them to the actual folder structure that houses the application files.

We use virtual directories to allow clients to upload images via FTP to their sites without having to give them access to the code base of their web sites. The physical folder that they FTP into is isolated in a separate directory structure from their web-site files, and the virtual directory makes them available to the web site. This allows us to maintain an application-level service level agreement (SLA), although allowing the clients to update images on their web site whenever they need to.

Creating a New Web Site

Creating a web site is the most fundamental step in hosting your web site. However, you should ensure that you follow good practices for the creation of the site to ensure consistency of the platform. You can create web sites using IIS Manager, the command line, or via scripting. The following steps will show how to create a basic site to serve contents using all these methods.

Creating a Web Site Using IIS Manager

IIS Manager presents the administrator with a GUI interface that allows the creation of a web site by following these steps:

1. Start IIS Manager by clicking Start ➪ Run, entering **inetmgr**, and then pressing Enter.

2. Select the server to administer, click the Sites icon, and then select Add Web Site from the Actions pane or by right-clicking the Sites icon. This will present the Add Web Site dialog, as shown in Figure 6-2.

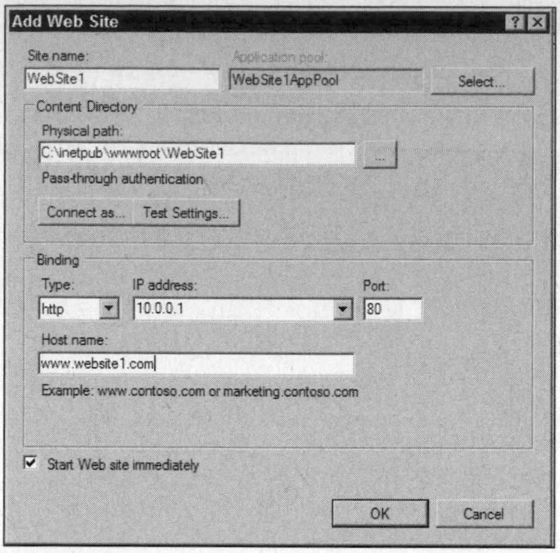

Figure 6-2

3. Enter a web-site name that is easily recognized by those who will administer the server (for example, *WebSite1*). A good tip for creating web-site names when you are doing high-volume hosting is to use a numbering system, or use the domain name without the domain prefix. This can speed up manual administration because it enables you find the site by typing the name in the web-site view list.

4. Select the application pool for your site. By default, this is set to "DefaultAppPool," which has the NetworkService identity. Normally when creating a new web site, depending on the applications context, one also creates a separate application pool. Application pools are discussed below in this chapter and in more detail in Chapter 8, "Web Application Pool Administration."

5. Set the path to the web-site files. Note that a local or network UNC path can be accepted in the console — the path must be accessible by IIS Manager or else it will error. The "Connect as…" button allows for a distinct user account to be entered for UNC paths only. This is a new feature in IIS7.0 and allows content to be published from remote paths, enabling the administrator to specify the user account in the form of servername\username. In the case of high availability or distributed hosting, where the same content is published by several servers, a domain user with rights to read the directories is needed to access the content.

6. Enter binding details. Note that the type can be set to HTTP or, if a certificate has been assigned to the site, to HTTPS. In this example, we'll set it to HTTP. Next, select the IP address to bind the site to. This will be the IP address that the web-site's domain name will resolve to.

7. A host header entry is required if you are going to host multiple web-site domains on the same IP address. When first creating the site, enter your domain to get started, and you can later add additional domains as required. There are some requirements when using host headers that are inherent to the HTTP v1.1 specification (which defined host headers). These requirements are discussed below in this chapter.

8. To start your site immediately, leave Start Web Site Immediately checked and click OK.

You can now browse to your site by its domain name, provided the DNS is correctly configured. Figure 6-3 shows WebSite1 in the Sites menu.

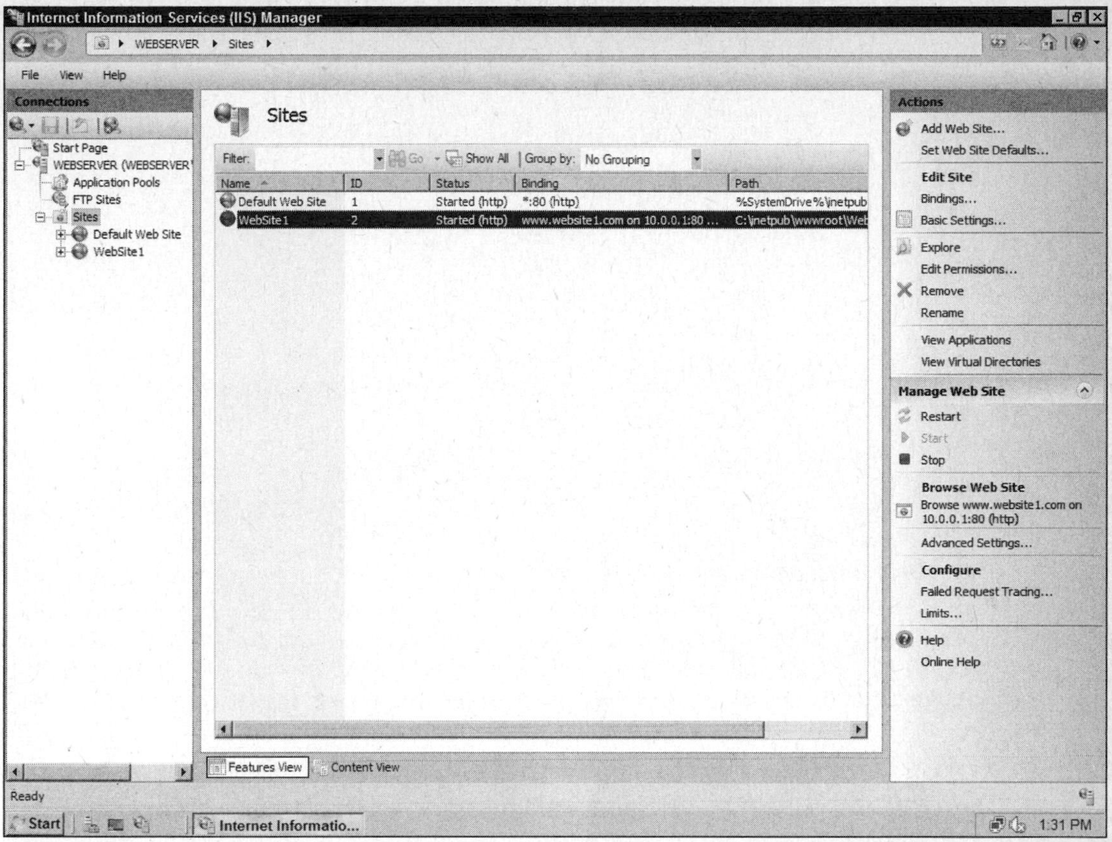

Figure 6-3

To start modifying the site configuration, simply click the site's name under the Sites list, and you will be presented with the Features view, which gives you access to alter the configuration. The Content view shows the web-site files that are in the root directory of the site.

Creating a New Application Pool for Your Site

It is a good practice to create a new application pool for each site, especially when you are hosting more than one web site on the same server. This will ensure that each web application runs inside its own process such that if an application causes a failure, it does not affect any other sites. Further information on application pools is available in Chapter 8, "Web Application Pool Administration." The Add Web Site tool in IIS Manager will automatically create a new application pool and map the site to it. If you chose not to create a new application pool when you created the site, or if you imported the site through a different method, you may need to manually create an application pool.

To create the new application pool, follow these steps:

1. Open IIS Manager, if it is not already open. (Start ⇨ Run, enter **inetmgr**, and press Enter.)

2. Select Application Pools under the server name from the Connections pane, and then select Add Application Pool from the Actions pane or right-click the Application Pools icon. This will present the Add Application Pools dialog. Figure 6-4 shows the Add Application Pool tool.

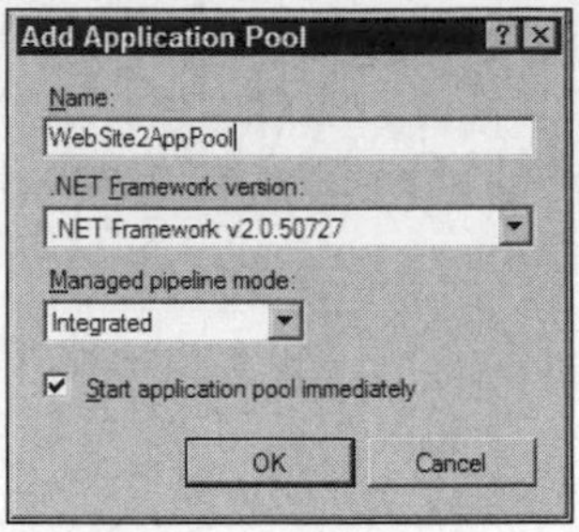

Figure 6-4

3. Set the name to something that is relevant — in this case, WebSite2AppPool. (It might seem redundant to add AppPool to the end of the name; however, it does help for easing confusion with novice or other administrators.)

4. Select the .NET Framework version for the application pool to default to, and then select the Managed Pipeline Mode. For this site, we are going to use Integrated, the default not the "classic" mode; for more information on the Managed Pipeline, see Chapter 8, "Web Application Pool Administration." By default, the application pool will be created to run with the NetworkService identity.

5. Now you can assign the new application pool to your site. To do this, select your web site under the server pane, then right-click or select Advanced Settings from the Actions pane.

6. The Advanced Settings window gives you access to configure other options such as log locations, and so forth. For this instance, select Application Pool and set it to WebSite2AppPool (see Figure 6-5).

7. As soon as you click OK, the application is moved to the new application pool, which is then recycled. Be wary of this in production environment, lest you receive any unexpected results.

Application pools need to be recycled from time to time to resolve hung applications or to reload a site if new files have been added that IIS is not seeing. For more information, see Chapter 8, "Web Application Pool Administration."

Creating a Web Site Using AppCmd

AppCmd.exe is one of the single greatest administration tool improvements that shipped with IIS 7.0. It allows for a great amount of flexibility in the creation and configuration of web sites, usually quicker and easier than using the GUI interface. In the following example, we create the site exactly as above.

AppCmd.exe is found under %systemroot%\system32\inetsrv\appcmd.exe. Running the tool directly returns the options that are available. More information on this tool can be found in Chapter 5, "Administration Tools." It is important to remember that you must open the command line with elevated permissions; otherwise, AppCmd.exe will not make changes to the configuration.

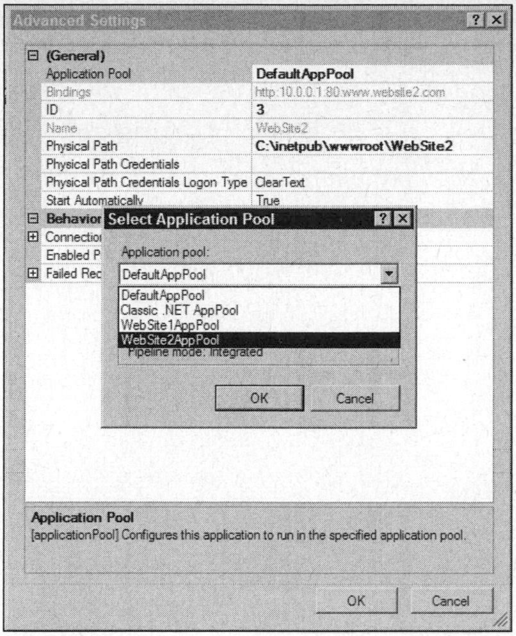

Figure 6-5

In order to create an application pool using `AppCmd.exe`, use `add` with the `apppool` object. Here you create a new application pool for WebSite2. For more information on using `AppCmd.exe`, refer to Chapter 5, "Administration Tools."

```
appcmd.exe add apppool /name:WebSite2AppPool
```

Running this code returns

```
APPPOOL object "WebSite2AppPool" added
```

Once the application pool is created, you can create the web site. `Add` is used against the site object here to create a new web site named `www.website2.com`. The line of code also details the bindings for the site, port 80, and the physical path to the files for the site, `c:\inetpub\wwwroot\website2`.

```
appcmd.exe add site /name:"www.website2.com" /bindings:http://www.website2.com:80 /
physicalpath:"c:\inetpub\wwwroot\website2"
```

When the site is created, the following lines are returned:

```
SITE object "www.website2.com" added
APP object "www.website2.com/" added
VDIR object "www.website2.com/" added
```

AppCmd.exe is great for creating multiple sites quickly. Suppose, for instance, that you need to bulk create simple sites. Just stick AppCmd.exe inside a FOR loop, as follows:

```
for /l %1 IN (4,1,50) do mkdir c:\inetpub\wwwroot\website%1 |
c:\windows\system32\inetsrv\appcmd.exe add site /name:www.website%1.com /id:%1
/bindings:http://www.website%1.com:80 /physicalpath:c:\inetpub\wwwroot\website%1
```

This code uses the for command to create 46 web sites. The first site will be www.website4.com. The for command will then increment by 1 to create the next site until it has created www.website50.com, at which point it will stop. During the process, it creates not only the site, but also a folder to house the site's files.

One additional tip when using AppCmd.exe is to issue a /? after the site command to find out which configuration items can be modified on the site.

```
appcmd.exe set site "website1/" /?
```

Running AppCmd.exe with /? shows the following list of items that can be configured for the site.

```
ERROR ( message:-name
-id
-serverAutoStart
-bindings.[protocol='string',bindingInformation='string'].protocol
-bindings.[protocol='string',bindingInformation='string'].bindingInformation
-limits.maxBandwidth
-limits.maxConnections
-limits.connectionTimeout
-logFile.logExtFileFlags
-logFile.customLogPluginClsid
-logFile.logFormat
-logFile.directory
-logFile.period
-logFile.truncateSize
-logFile.localTimeRollover
-logFile.enabled
-traceFailedRequestsLogging.enabled
-traceFailedRequestsLogging.directory
-traceFailedRequestsLogging.maxLogFiles
-applicationDefaults.path
-applicationDefaults.applicationPool
-applicationDefaults.enabledProtocols
-virtualDirectoryDefaults.path
-virtualDirectoryDefaults.physicalPath
-virtualDirectoryDefaults.userName
-virtualDirectoryDefaults.password
-virtualDirectoryDefaults.logonMethod
-virtualDirectoryDefaults.allowSubDirConfig
-[path='string'].path
-[path='string'].applicationPool
-[path='string'].enabledProtocols
-[path='string'].virtualDirectoryDefaults.path
-[path='string'].virtualDirectoryDefaults.physicalPath
-[path='string'].virtualDirectoryDefaults.userName
-[path='string'].virtualDirectoryDefaults.password
-[path='string'].virtualDirectoryDefaults.logonMethod
```

```
-[path='string'].virtualDirectoryDefaults.allowSubDirConfig
-[path='string'].[path='string'].path
-[path='string'].[path='string'].physicalPath
-[path='string'].[path='string'].userName
-[path='string'].[path='string'].password
-[path='string'].[path='string'].logonMethod
-[path='string'].[path='string'].allowSubDirConfig
 )
```

Creating a Web Site Using Microsoft.Web.Administration

To create the same basic site in C#, you must consume the `Microsoft.Web.Administration` namespace. The `Microsoft.Web.Administration` assembly can be found under `%systemroot%\system32\inetsrv` and will need to be referenced in your application to be compiled. If you are using Visual Studio, it is required for IntelliSense to work. A web site can be created using `Microsoft.Web.Administration` in partial trust, but the FileIOPermission and SecurityPermission need to be given substantially more access than the medium template provides. Generally, it's best to run the web site in full trust, because it is a trusted web site if it's creating web sites on the server, and make changes that will update `applicationHost.config`. If you are using the API with PowerShell, no changes are needed, as long as PowerShell is run with an administrative account.

```csharp
using System;
using System.Collections.Generic;
using System.Text;
using Microsoft.Web.Administration;

namespace ProfessionalIIS7
{
    class IIS7
    {
        static void Main(string[] args)
        {
            // create the server management object
            ServerManager managerServer = new ServerManager();

            //create site object off the server management object
            managerServer.Sites.Add("WebSite1", "http", "*:80:www.website1.com",
"c:\\inetpub\\wwwroot\\website1");

            //create application pool
            managerServer.ApplicationPools.Add("WebSite1AppPool");

            //assign application pool to site.
            managerServer.Sites["WebSite1"].Applications[0].ApplicationPoolName =
"WebSite1AppPool";

            //create apppool object
            ApplicationPool appPool =
managerServer.ApplicationPools["WebSite1AppPool"];

            //set app pool options
            appPool.ManagedPipelineMode = ManagedPipelineMode.Integrated;
            appPool.AutoStart = true;
```

```
            appPool.Failure.RapidFailProtection = true;

            //write the changes
            managerServer.CommitChanges();
        }
    }
}
```

The previous example was used to create a new ServerManager and then create a web site, WebSite1. The web site was assigned port 80 and pointed to the c:\inetpub\wwwroot\website1 folder. After the web site was created, the application pool WebSite1AppPool was created, and the web site was assigned to the application pool. The next step was creating the application pool object and assigning the options for it. The final step was to write the changes to the configuration files.

Changes to the applicationHost.config File

If you open the core IIS site configuration file %systemroot%\System32\inetsrv\config\applicationHost.config, you will see that all changes to application pools, web sites, and virtual directories create entries in the IIS configuration.

All changes we have made happen under the element <system.applicationHost>.

The creation of the application pools is defined under the <applicationPools> tag:

```
<applicationPools>
    <add name="DefaultAppPool" />
    <add name="WebSite1AppPool" />
    <add name="WebSite2AppPool" />
    <applicationPoolDefaults>
        <processModel identityType="NetworkService" />
    </applicationPoolDefaults>
</applicationPools>
```

The configuration of the site itself is found under the <sites> tags:

```
<site name="WebSite1" id="2" serverAutoStart="true">
   <application path="/" applicationPool="WebSite1AppPool">
                  <virtualDirectory path="/"
physicalPath="C:\inetpub\wwwroot\webSite1" />
   </application>
   <bindings>
      <binding protocol="http" bindingInformation="*:80:www.website1.com" />
   </binding>
</site>
<site name="WebSite2" id="3" serverAutoStart="true">
   <application path="/" applicationPool="WebSite2AppPool">
                  <virtualDirectory path="/"
physicalPath="C:\inetpub\wwwroot\webSite2" />
   </application>
   <bindings>
      <binding protocol="http" bindingInformation="*:80:www.website2.com" />
    </bindings>
</site>
```

From these entries, you can see that it is very simple to create your own site by simply editing the `applicationHost.config` file. Note that this is not recommended as a best practice, because there is no configuration check on the direct editing of the file, and errors could result in an invalid IIS configuration, causing your server to fail. It is strongly recommended that if you are going to edit the file directly, make a back-up copy or enable Shadow Copy built into Windows Server 2008 to manage your file versioning.

Configuring Logging

Windows Server 2008 ships with several modules that add a great deal of richness to the logging ability of IIS 7.0. The following table describes the default logging modules:

Module Name	Module Code	Description
HttpLoggingModule	`%windir%\System32\inetsrv\loghttp.dll`	Processes requests status and passes these to Http.sys. This module is required for any conventional web server logs to be generated for processing.
FailedRequestsTracingModule	`%windir%\System32\inetsrv\iisfreb.dll`	Logs failed requests as specified in filter.
RequestMonitorModule	`%windir%\System32\inetsrv\iisreqs.dll`	Watches executing worker processes.
TracingModule	`%windir%\System32\inetsrv\iisetw.dll`	Dumps events for tracing with Event Tracing for Windows.
CustomLoggingModule	`%windir%\System32\inetsrv\logcust.dll`	Loads custom log modules.

In this chapter, we look at logging from HTTP requests that are passed to the web server core for processing. Logging for diagnostics will only be touched as to where logs are configured to be stored. Further details on analyzing these logs are in Chapter 20, "Diagnostics and Troubleshooting."

IIS 7.0 introduced the options of logging only failed requests, successful requests, or all requests that are processed. On a global configuration level for the server, logging can be configured on a per-site basis or centralized, with two types of centralized logging available: Binary and W3C. First, we will discuss the types of standard logging available under IIS7.0 and the situations in which they are best used.

Enabling Logging

Before you can enable logging, you need to install the Http Logging module in the server roles.

To install the Http Logging module, follow these steps:

1. Open Server Manager, if it is not already open. (Start ⇨ Run, enter **CompMgmtLauncher.exe**, and press Enter.)

2. Click Roles, and look at the Web Server Role Services. Check to see if HTTP Logging is installed. If it is not, click Add Role Services.

3. Check the HTTP Logging box, click Next, then click Install.

4. Click Close to finish the dialog, and then close the Server Manager.

Once HTTP Logging is enabled, `<log>` tags are automatically created for the central binary log file and the central W3C log file in the `applicationHost.config` file.

```
<log>
    <centralBinaryLogFile enabled="true"
directory="%SystemDrive%\inetpub\logs\LogFiles" />
    <centralW3CLogFile enabled="true"
directory="%SystemDrive%\inetpub\logs\LogFiles" />
</log
```

Here you can see that the `centralBinaryLogFile` and the `centralW3LogFiles` are both set to `enabled="true"`.

Note the `<siteDefaults>` tag, as it shows the log file format and the location of the log files. This tag shows the settings applied in the previous steps.

```
<siteDefaults>
    <logFile logFormat="W3C" directory="%SystemDrive%\inetpub\logs\LogFiles" />
    <traceFailedRequestsLogging directory="%SystemDrive%\inetpub\logs\
FailedReqLogFiles" />
</siteDefaults>
```

It is good practice to place your web-site log files on a separate drive on your system to prevent the primary disk from being consumed.

After you have enabled logging for your site, logs will be generated as per the request policy that has been set. The following is an example of the W3C logs generated for `website1.com` on a per-site basis:

```
#Software: Microsoft Internet Information Services 7.0
#Version: 1.0
#Date: 2007-07-01 07:16:33
#Fields: date time s-ip cs-method cs-uri-stem cs-uri-query s-port cs-username c-ip
cs(User-Agent) sc-status sc-substatus sc-win32-status
2006-11-20 07:16:33 192.168.254.1 GET / - 80 - 192.168.254.1 Mozilla/
4.0+(compatible;+MSIE+7.0;+Windows+NT+6.0;+SLCC1;+.NET+CLR+2.0.50727;
+Media+Center+PC+5.0;+.NET+CLR+3.0.04506;+.NET+CLR+1.1.4322;+.NET+CLR+3.0.04320;+In
foPath.2) 200 0 0
2006-11-20 07:16:33 192.168.254.1 GET /welcome.png - 80 - 192.168.254.1 Mozilla/
4.0+(compatible;+MSIE+7.0;+Windows+NT+6.0;+SLCC1;+.NET+CLR+2.0.50727;
+Media+Center+PC+5.0;+.NET+CLR+3.0.04506;+.NET+CLR+1.1.4322;+.NET+CLR+3.0.04320;
+InfoPath.2) 200 0 0
2006-11-20 07:16:35 192.168.254.1 GET / - 80 - 192.168.254.1 Mozilla/
4.0+(compatible;+MSIE+7.0;+Windows+NT+6.0;+SLCC1;+.NET+CLR+2.0.50727;
+Media+Center+PC+5.0;+.NET+CLR+3.0.04506;+.NET+CLR+1.1.4322;+.NET+CLR+3.0.04320;+In
foPath.2) 200 0 0
```

Failed Request Tracing Logs

Failed request tracing logs are used as a logging tool and a diagnostic utility. In this chapter, you will learn how to enable the trace logs and change the directory to which they are written. Chapter 20, "Diagnostics and Troubleshooting," will go into greater detail about the use of the trace logs.

Enabling Failed Request Tracing Logs Using IIS Manager

To enable the failed request tracing logs at the web-site level using IIS Manager, perform the following steps:

1. Open IIS Manager if it is not already open. (Start ⇨ Run, enter **inetmgr**, and then press Enter.)

2. In the Connections pane, click the web site you want to enable failed request tracing on.

3. In the Actions pane, click Failed Request Tracing.

4. In the dialog box, check the Enable box.

5. You can now select where you want the log files to go and the maximum number of trace files.

6. Click OK to finish the dialog.

7. Close IIS Manager.

You have now enabled failed request tracing on a web site. Refer to Chapter 20, "Diagnostics and Troubleshooting," for more information about configuring the logging.

Enabling Failed Request Tracing Logs Using AppCmd

Enabling the failed request tracing logs via the command line is done by using `AppCmd.exe`. There are two properties that need to be set: the `enabled` element needs to be set to `true`, and the `directory` needs to be set to the location you want the logs to be written to.

```
appcmd.exe set site www.WebSite1.com /tracefailedrequestslogging.enabled:true
/tracefailedrequestslogging.directory:c:\logs\failedrequests
```

With the previous command you have enabled trace logging on `www.website1.com`. There is another command, with its own benefits and shortcomings, that you can use to enable the failed trace logging. It does provide more options for configuring the trace logging; however, it does not provide a method to change the logging directory. The command is

```
appcmd.exe configure trace "www.website1.com" /enablesite
```

This commend has more options, which are covered in Chapter 20, "Diagnostic and Troubleshooting."

W3C Logging

World Wide Web Consortium (W3C) logging writes log entries using a text-based, customizable ASCII format and is the default log format configured under IIS.

W3C logging is enabled initially on a per-site basis with a default location of `%systemdrive%\inetpub\logs\logfiles\W3SVC1`. The number after W3SVC designates the site ID of the web site.

Logging can be set to log one file per site or one file for the entire server. This example keeps the log file set to log at the site level.

1. Open IIS Manager and navigate to the server, site, or application you want to configure logging for. Under the Features view, the Logging feature will be available if the module has been installed on the site/server/application.

2. Double-click Logging or select Logging and click Open Feature under the Actions pane, opening the Logging pane. This allows the administrator to enable the logging features.

3. As with previous versions of IIS, you have the option to select the format of your logging or define your own custom log handler. This is only available when configured for logging on a per-site basis, and you have the choice of

   ❑ **IIS** — This is a fixed ASCII text-based format, and thus is not customizable on what can be logged.

   ❑ **W3C** — The World Wide Web Consortium log format is discussed in more detail below in this chapter. This is the most widely utilized log format on web servers today.

   ❑ **NCSA** — NCSA (National Center for SuperComputing Applications) generally is the default log format for Apache and other web servers. This is similar to the IIS format as it is fixed ASCII text that is noncustomizable.

4. After determining the log format, select the fields for IIS to record. This example will use the W3C format with the default fields selected. Figure 6-6 shows the W3C Logging Fields dialog box.

5. The default location specified for logging is `%systemdrive%\inetpub\logs\LogFiles\w3svc<siteID>`, with the `siteID` value updating to the site ID for each site. Again, for this example, keep the default location for the logs.

6. Encoding can be set to either UTF-8 or ANSI. Use UTF-8 for this example.

7. The log file rollover can be set to create a new log file on a scheduled basis, when the file reaches a set size, or to not create a new log file at all. If the scheduled basis is selected, the time periods are hourly, daily, weekly, or monthly. Additionally, you can set the files to use local time for naming and rollover rather than GMT time. Note that all log times are GMT times. Set the log file to roll over on a daily schedule, and use local time for naming and rollover.

8. Click Apply in the Actions pane.

You can enable the HTTP Logging module at the web server, site, or application level. This allows maximum granularity in logging control.

Enabling W3C Logs using AppCmd

Enabling W3C logging via the command line is done in a similar manner as enabling the failed trace logging. Use `AppCmd.exe` to set the `enabled` property to `true`, and then set the log file location to the desired logging folder. The one additional property is to set the format for the log to use. The available formats are IIS, NCSA, W3C, and custom.

```
appcmd.exe set site www.website1.com /logfile.enabled:true
/logfile.directory:c:\logs\site1_com /logfile.logformat:W3C
```

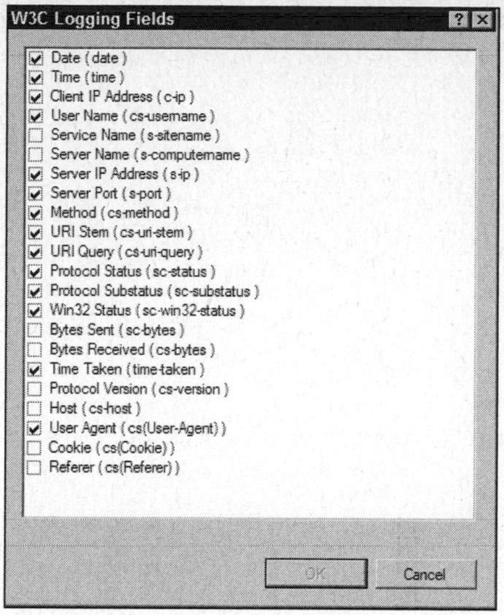

Figure 6-6

Enabling W3C Logs Using Microsoft.Web.Administration

As with all other aspects of IIS 7.0, it is possible to manage the W3C logs with `Microsoft.Web` `.Administration` as well as with IIS Manager and `AppCmd.exe`. Here is a small snippet of code using `Microsoft.Web.Administration` to enable the logging component on an already created site. You can use this code in your own scripts to manage the W3C logs.

```
using System;
using System.Collections.Generic;
using System.Text;
using Microsoft.Web.Administration;

namespace ProfessionalIIS7
{
    class IIS7
    {
        static void Main(string[] args)
        {
            // create the server management object
            ServerManager managerServer = new ServerManager();


            managerServer.Sites["WebSite1"].LogFile.Enabled = true;
            managerServer.Sites["WebSite1"].LogFile.LogFormat = LogFormat.W3c;
            managerServer.Sites["WebSite1"].LogFile.LocalTimeRollover = true;
            managerServer.Sites["WebSite1"].LogFile.Directory = "c:\\logs\\" +
managerServer.Sites["WebSite1"].Id.ToString();

            managerServer.CommitChanges();
        }
    }
}
```

This section of code creates the server management object and then uses it to enable the log file, select the W3C format, set the time rollover, and choose the location for the log files.

Centralized Logging

Centralized logging is a global server configuration that writes all HTTP-generated logs to a single log file. Centralized Binary and W3C logging has been available since IIS 6.0 with Windows 2003 Service Pack 1.

Centralized Binary Logging

Centralized binary logging was available under IIS 6.0 with Windows 2003 Service Pack 1. However, there was no interface for configuration, and the only access available was through modification of the metabase. IIS 7.0 now provides full configuration support for this function.

This type of logging is extremely useful in high-capacity hosting situations where a web server may be configured with several thousand web sites. Centralized binary logging reduces the requirement on system resources and with no cost on the detail of the log data.

Effectively, when logging takes place in centralized binary logging, raw data are written to the log file for all the web sites on the server. Note that the data are in a raw format and thus cannot be read as would W3C logs. A tool is required to interpret these logs. A good tool for analyzing these logs is LogParser (available from Microsoft Downloads); otherwise, a custom tool can be developed.

The following is an example `LogParser` command to query the binary logs for the URI requested order by most requested:

```
LogParser -i:BIN "SELECT cs-uri-stem, COUNT(*) AS Total, MAX(time-taken) AS MaxTime,
AVG(time-taken) AS AvgTime, AVG(sc-bytes) AS AvgBytesSent FROM ex*.log GROUP BY
cs-uri-stem ORDER BY Total DESC"
```

Enabling Centralized Binary Logging Using IIS Manager

All requests for all sites on a Web server are written to a single central log file. This logging format is also available for FTP sites. By default, the log file directory is `%systemdrive%\inetpub\logs\logfiles`. To enable binary centralized logging on the server, follow these steps:

1. Select the server home page in IIS Manager, and then double-click the Logging icon.

2. On the Logging page, the top dropdown allows a choice between one log file per site (default) and one log file per server. Change this to per server.

3. In the Log File format dropdown, select Binary.

4. On the directory selection, type the path to a log file directory in the Directory textbox, or click the Browse button to select a directory.

5. For Log File Rollover, select a method that IIS 7.0 uses to create a new log file. If you select MaxSize, type a maximum log file size, in bytes, in the Maximum File Size textbox. Check Use Local Time to use your local time rather than Greenwich Mean Time (GMT).

6. Click Apply in the Actions pane.

Enabling Centralized Binary Logging Using AppCmd

The following command configures centralized binary logging to be enabled on the server, with daily rotation and writing the log files to `c:\logs\inetpub\logs\LogFiles`.

```
appcmd.exe set config /section:system.applicationHost/log /centrallogfilemode:
CentralBinary /centralbinarylogfile.enabled:true /centralbinarylogfile.directory:
c:\logs\inetpub\logs\logfiles /centralbinarylogfile.period:Daily
```

Centralized W3C Logging

Enabling centralized logging to use the W3C format has many of the same advantages as centralized logging using the binary format, the primary difference being that the logs are readable as they are written. Because the log files are in a readable format, the files are larger than binary files.

Enabling Centralized W3C Logging Using IIS Manager

Setting W3C centralized logging in IIS Manager is done using the same steps as centralized binary logging, except that the log file format should be W3C rather than binary.

1. Select the server home page in IIS Manager. Double-click the Logging icon.

2. On the Logging page, the top dropdown allows a choice between one log file per site (default) and one log file per server. Change this to per server.

3. In the Log File format dropdown, select W3C.

4. In the Select Fields list, expand the list categories to select the information you want to log, and click OK. This can be changed at a later date by simply editing the web-site properties under logging.

5. On the directory selection, type the path to a log file directory in the Directory textbox, or click the Browse button to select a directory.

6. For Log File Rollover, select a method that IIS 7.0 uses to create a new log file. If you select MaxSize, type a maximum log file size, in bytes, in the Maximum File Size textbox. Check Use Local Time to use your local time rather than Greenwich Mean Time (GMT).

7. Click Apply in the Actions pane.

Enabling Centralized W3C Logging Using AppCmd

The following command is very similar to enabling centralized binary logging. This will enable centralized logging on the server, with daily rotation and writing the log files to `c:\logs\inetpub\logs\logfiles`.

```
appcmd.exe set config /section:system.applicationHost/log /centrallogfilemode:
CentralW3C /centralw3clogfile.enabled:true /centralw3clogfile.directory:
c:\logs\inetpub\logs\logfiles /centralw3clogfile.period:Daily
```

Configuring Host Headers

Host headers enable you to publish multiple domain names or web sites to a single IP address. This allows a web administrator to run several sites on a single IP. It also allows a single web site to have multiple names resolve for it, such as website1.com and www.website1.com.

Host headers are an optional configuration item on site bindings. Bindings are used to configure Http.sys to listen on ports and IP addresses. The properties of a binding are

- ❏ Type — HTTP/HTTPS — HTTPS to enable Secure Socket Layers (SSL).
- ❏ IP address.
- ❏ Port.
- ❏ Host header.

When a client sends a HTTP Host request to IIS, the HTTP header is first decoded by the server, allowing the requested location to be extracted from the GET request and checked against the IIS server's metabase for matching host header entries. In the example host header below, you can see that a GET request was made to IP 10.0.0.1 on port 80 to see if there is a site with a host header of website1.com. A message was returned to the client with a code of 200 to tell the client that the site is there and was found.

```
2007-10-07 18:01:46 W3SVC1 WEBSERVER1 10.0.0.1 GET / - 80 - 10.0.0.1 HTTP/1.1
Mozilla/4.0+(compatible;+MSIE+7.0;+Windows+NT+6.0;+SLCC1;+.NET+CLR+2.0.50727) - -
website1.com 200 0 0 934 260 220
```

If a matching entry is found, the request is forwarded to the virtual site. If there is no host header matching the entry, IIS then looks for the IP address and port with a virtual server that has a blank host header entry. If there are no virtual servers with blank host header entries, the request is then discarded.

The table below shows four web sites running on the same IIS 7.0 server. Notice that website1.com, www.website1.com, and extranet.website1.com all use the same IP address. The last site, support.website1.com, uses a different IP address from the first three.

DNS Name	IP Address
website1.com	10.0.0.1
www.website1.com	10.0.0.1
extranet.website1.com	10.0.0.1
support.website1.com	10.0.0.2

As mentioned above, both 10.0.0.1 and 10.0.0.2 are assigned to the same IIS server. The web sites that share the same IP address have to use either a host header or a port other than port 80. As port 80 is the default for HTTP, you should keep port 80 and use a host header if the web site is to be publicly accessible. The following table shows the address, port, and host header configurations for the three sites that use 10.0.0.1. If a request came in for intranet.website1.com, it would fail as there is no web site with a host header for that URL.

Site ID Number	IP Address	Port	Host Header
1	10.0.0.1	80	website1.com
			www.website1.com
2	10.0.0.2	80	extranet.website1.com

You will notice that site ID number 1 has two host headers, website1.com and www.website1.com. Having the two host headers apply to the same web site allows either URL to resolve to the same web site. Extranet.website1.com will resolve to a separate web site from the other two even though it uses the same IP and port because its host header is bound to site ID number 2.

Adding/Removing Host Headers Using IIS Manager

If a web site is not given a host header when it is initially set up, you might need to add a host header at a later date. We'll describe the process to add (and remove) a host header via IIS Manager here.

To add a host header, follow these instructions:

1. Open IIS Manager, if it is not already open. (Start ➪ Run, enter **inetmgr**, and press Enter.)
2. Right-click the site, or click the site and from the Actions pane select Bindings under Edit Site. The Site Bindings dialog will appear.
3. Select Add for a new binding, or click an existing binding and click Edit to change the configuration of an existing binding. Figure 6-7 shows the Add Site Binding dialog box.
4. Set the Type to either HTTP or HTTPS, enter the IP address or select it from a list, and then set the port for the web site to listen on.
5. Enter the domain name for the host header, and then select OK.
6. Click Close on the Site Bindings dialog box.

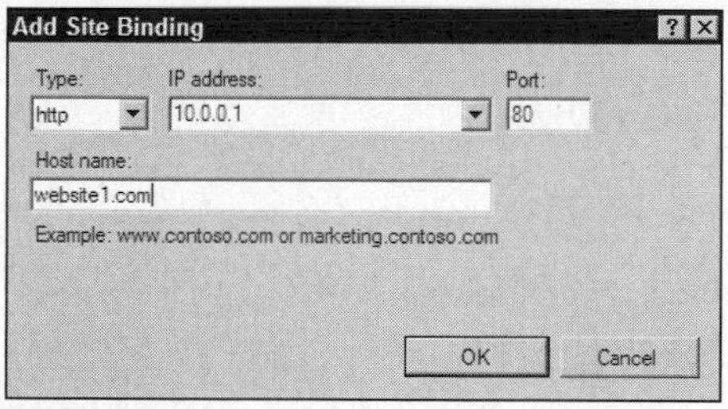

Figure 6-7

This will bind the domain to the site. Note that if you already have bound the name to another site, this will be detected, and you will be given the option to still assign it to the site. If a binding is duplicated across sites, only one site will be able to start.

Removing a host header follows the same initial steps:

1. Open IIS Manager, if it is not already open.

2. Right-click the site, or click the site and from the Actions pane select Bindings under Edit Site. The Site Bindings dialog will appear.

3. Click the binding you want to delete, and then click Remove. Click Yes in the verification dialog box.

4. Click Close on the Site Bindings dialog.

Setting Host Headers Using AppCmd

When setting the binding parameter to add the host header, list the bindings in "protocol: domain name: port" format. When adding multiple host headers, use one command and separate the bindings by a comma. Removing bindings with AppCmd.exe is done in a similar fashion. If there are two bindings and you want to remove one, run the add command with only the binding you want to keep. This will clear all bindings and then re-add the one you want to keep. To remove all bindings, you will need to use the subtraction (–) modifier on the bindings property.

The syntax to add a host header is as follows:

```
appcmd.exe set site < "site name"> /bindings:"<http/https>:<domain name>:<port>"
```

For example, to add the host header for http://website1.com, run the following:

```
appcmd.exe set site "website1" /bindings:"http://website1.com:80"
```

To add multiple host headers, use a comma to separate them in the bindings section:

```
appcmd.exe set site "website1" /bindings:"http://website1.com:80,
http://www.website1.com:80"
```

To remove all the bindings, use the following syntax:

```
appcmd.exe set site "website1" /-bindings
```

To remove only one of the two bindings you set earlier, use

```
appcmd.exe set site "website1" /bindings:http://website1.com:80
```

This results in the web site having only the website1.com host header bound to port 80, and the www.website1.com host header has been removed.

If you want to implement *Secure Sockets Layer (SSL)* on your site, you need to add a binding for the HTTPS protocol and the TCP port (443 being standard). The following command sets the web site to listen for all requests to the server over HTTPS:

```
appcmd.exe set site "website1" /bindings:"https://website1.com:443
```

Setting Host Headers Using Microsoft.Web.Administration

You can also use the `Microsoft.Web.Administration` API to add host headers to a site. The following code example uses the same `WebSite1` that was created in an earlier example. Note the `managerServer.Sites.Add` line near the top of the example. While it is creating the site, it also sets the bindings to use HTTP, port 80, and the host header `www.website1.com`.

```
using System;
using System.Collections.Generic;
using System.Text;
using Microsoft.Web.Administration;

namespace ProfessionalIIS7
{
    class IIS7
    {
        static void Main(string[] args)
        {
            // create the server management object
            ServerManager managerServer = new ServerManager();

            //create site object off the server management object
            managerServer.Sites.Add("WebSite1", "http", "*:80:www.website1.com",
"c:\\inetpub\\wwwroot\\website1");

            //create application pool
            managerServer.ApplicationPools.Add("WebSite1AppPool");

            //assign application pool to site.
            managerServer.Sites["WebSite1"].Applications[0].ApplicationPoolName =
"WebSite1AppPool";

            //create apppool object
            ApplicationPool appPool =
managerServer.ApplicationPools["WebSite1AppPool"];

            //set app pool options
            appPool.ManagedPipelineMode = ManagedPipelineMode.Integrated;
            appPool.AutoStart = true;
            appPool.Failure.RapidFailProtection = true;

            //write the changes
            managerServer.CommitChanges();
        }
    }
}
```

If a site already exists, you can use `Bindings.Add` to add additional bindings to the web site, as shown in this example, where `www.website1.com` and `website1.com` are both being added as host headers for `WebSite1`.

```
using System;
using System.Collections.Generic;
using System.Text;
```

```
using Microsoft.Web.Administration;

namespace ProfessionalIIS7
{
    class IIS7
    {
        static void Main(string[] args)
        {

            //add the bindings for www.website1.com and website1.com
            managerServer.Sites["WebSite1"].Bindings.Add("www.website1.com:80",
"http");

            managerServer.Sites["WebSite1"].Bindings.Add("website1.com:80",
"http");

            //write the changes
            managerServer.CommitChanges();
        }
    }
}
```

SSL and Host Headers

Until updates in Windows 2003 Service Pack 1, it was not possible to use host headers in conjunction with Secure Sockets Layer (SSL) on your web site. This was mainly because of complications with the protocol and limitations to the Common Name (CN) properties on certificates applied to a site. Effectively, the CN on the certificate (i.e., www.website1.com) needs to match the name request by the browser client. If these values did not match, an error would be thrown stating that the certificate was not valid for the domain and could not be trusted. Once Service Pack 1 had been applied to an IIS 6.0 server and also with IIS 7.0, it is possible to use host headers with wildcard SSL certificates. For this to work, a wildcard certificate must be available on the server (i.e., *.website1.com), and the host header must match the wildcard location (e.g., www.website1.com or marketing.website1.com). Creating SSL host headers is done using the same method as with standard HTTP host headers. You can find additional information about configuring SSL and its limitations with host headers in Chapter 15.

Administering Applications

In this section, we'll discuss adding and removing applications with IIS Manager, via the command line, and using the Microsoft.Web.Administration API.

Adding Applications Using IIS Manager

To add an application with IIS Manager, follow these steps.

1. Select the web site to create the application for and right-click Add Application, or select View Applications from the Actions pane (see Figure 6-8).

2. Enter the alias for the application; this will be the path off the web-site root. Select the application pool for the application to reside in.

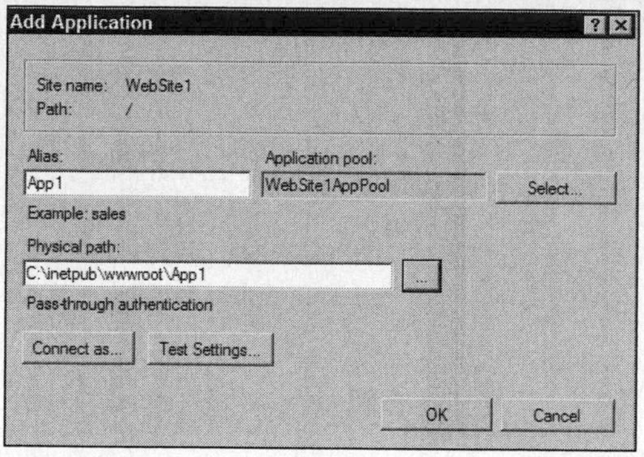

Figure 6-8

3. Note that if your application is not required to be in the same application pool as your web site, you should place it into a separate application pool to ensure that any application failures do not affect the site.

4. Enter the physical path of the application, and then select OK.

5. Refresh the Web Sites list, and alias will be listed under the site. By selecting the alias, you will have full configuration of the application as a separate application site; thus everything that can be configured on the parent site can be configured in the application.

6. Selecting Advanced settings from the Actions pane allows further configuration of the application, with the option to

  ❑ Set path credentials (that is, select a particular user for the application to run under).

  ❑ Set the credential logon type (Interactive/Batch/Network/Clear Text).

  ❑ Change the application pool.

For more information on configuring application pools, see Chapter 8, "Web Application Pool Administration."

Adding Applications Using AppCmd

To create an application under the `www.website1.com` web site with the application name App1 that maps to App1 to a location outside of the website1 physical path, you need to define the path and location for the application.

```
appcmd.exe add app /site.name:website1 /path:/App1 /physicalPath:c:\wwwroot\App1
/applicationpool:Site1AppPool
```

This returns the following:

```
APP object "www.website1.com/App1" added
VDIR object "www.website1.com/App1/" added
```

Adding Applications Using Microsoft.Web.Administration

You can use the `Microsoft.Web.Administration` API to create an application inside of an existing web site. In the following example, the `defaultSite.Applications.Add` line adds `/App1` to `WebSite1`. The physical path to the application is `c:\inetpub\wwwroot\app1`.

```
using System;
using System.Collections.Generic;
using System.Text;
using Microsoft.Web.Administration;
using Microsoft.Web.Management;

namespace ProfessionalIIS7
{
    public class IIS7
    {
        // Creates an application under WebSite1.
        public void CreateApplication()
        {
            ServerManager manager = new ServerManager();
            Site defaultSite = manager.Sites["WebSite1"];
            defaultSite.Applications.Add("/app1", @"C:\inetpub\wwwroot\app1");
            manager.CommitChanges();
        }
    }
}
```

Deleting Applications Using IIS Manager

In most cases, deleting an application is very similar to creating an application. To delete an application with IIS Manager, use the following steps:

1. Right-click on the application you want to delete.

2. Select Remove, and confirm that you want to remove it.

The application has now been deleted.

Deleting Applications Using AppCmd

`AppCmd.exe` can also be used to delete an application. In conjunction with the `app` object, use the `delete` command, and specify the application that needs to be removed.

```
appcmd.exe delete app /app.name:<name of app>
```

Replace `name of app` with the name of the application. In this example, you are deleting the `app1/` application.

```
appcmd.exe delete app /app.name:website1/app1
```

Deleting Applications Using Microsoft.Web.Administration

Removing an application from a web site using `Microsoft.Web.Administration` uses almost the exact same code as adding the application. The difference between the two is the verbs `add` and `remove`.

```
using System;
using System.Collections.Generic;
using System.Text;
using Microsoft.Web.Administration;
using Microsoft.Web.Management;

namespace ProfessionalIIS7
{
    public class IIS7
    {
        // Deletes an application under WebSite1.
        public void CreateApplication()
        {
            ServerManager manager = new ServerManager();
            Application App1 = new Application();
            defaultSite.Applications.Remove("/app1");
            manager.CommitChanges();
        }
    }
}
```

Administering Virtual Directories

Virtual directories are managed using the same tools as sites and applications. The IIS manager, `AppCmd.exe`, and the `Microsoft.Web.Administration` API all provide full administration of virtual directories in IIS 7.0.

Creating Virtual Directories Using IIS Manager

To create a virtual directory for a web site using IIS Manager, perform the following steps:

1. Open IIS Manager and right-click on the web site under which you want to create the virtual directory.

2. Select Add Virtual Directory.

3. In the Add Virtual Directory dialog box, type the alias to be used (see Figure 6-9). This will be the URL from which content is to be accessed.

4. Select the physical location of the directory. The physical path is the location of the content that is to be accessed. This can be a local location or a UNC path to the files. UNC locations can be accessed by specifying remote credentials or by using pass-through authentication of the user accessing the site.

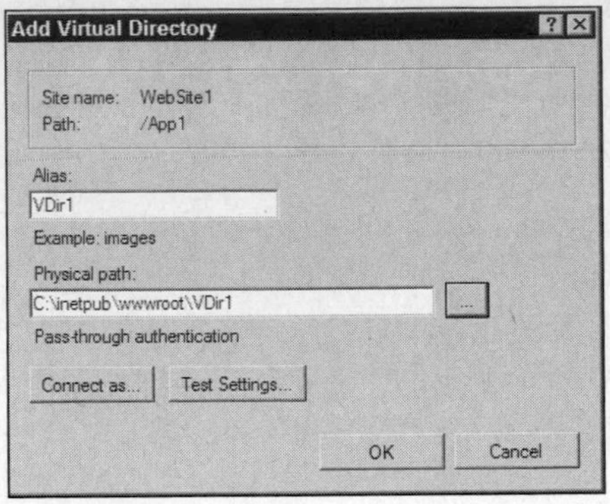

Figure 6-9

When creating a virtual directory to another location on your server or remotely, ensure that the accounts of the site anonymous user (IUSR) and the worker process identity (can be found by looking at the properties of the application pool) have the required permissions to read and execute as required. This is discussed in greater detail in Chapter 14, "Authentication and Authorization."

5. Click OK. The virtual directory will be created on the site. By expanding the site under IIS Manager, you can see the virtual directory indicated with a shortcut symbol. Figure 6-10 shows the virtual directory for WebSite1.

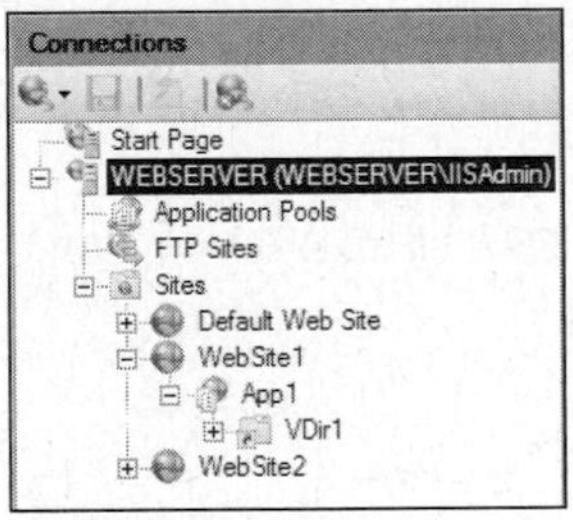

Figure 6-10

If you look at the `applicationHost.config` file under the site config, you will see that there is now an additional line for virtual directory `VDir1`.

```
<site name="www.website1.com" id="2">
   <application path="/">
      <virtualDirectory path="/" physicalPath="c:\inetpub\wwwroot\website1" />
      <virtualDirectory path="/VDir1" physicalPath="c:\inetpub\wwwroot\vdir1" />
   </application>
   <bindings>
      <binding protocol="http" bindingInformation="10.0.0.1:80:www.website1.com" />
   </bindings>
</site>
```

Creating Virtual Directories Using AppCmd

Again, command-line implementation is made simple with the use of `AppCmd.exe`. To create a virtual directory into the root of the web site, use the `vdir` object and the `add` command.

```
appcmd.exe add vdir /app.name:<website name>/ /path:<virtual directory name>
/physicalPath:<location of content>
```

The `app.name` parameter in the command corresponds to the web-site name and the path that it will refer to, thus leaving just a trailing slash after the web-site name creates the virtual directory into the root of the site. To create the virtual directory in another place other than the root, the directory name needs to be specified after the root (for example, `/app.name:www.website1.com/vdir1` to create the virtual directory under the `vdir1` folder).

`path` refers to the alias of the site name — in the example, this is `/vdir1` — and `physicalPath` is the location of the contents that is to be served from the file system.

To create a virtual directory named vdir1 under the WebSite1 web site, issue the following:

```
appcmd.exe add vdir /app.name:www.website1.com/ /path:/vdir1 /physicalPath:c:\
inetpub\wwwroot\vdir1
```

Adding Virtual Directories Using Microsoft.Web.Administration

As with most other management tasks in IIS 7.0, the `Microsoft.Web.Administration` API can be used to add a virtual directory to an application. In the following example, you will see that the web site `Website1` is the target site and `App1` is the target application. You will be adding `VDir1` to `App1` with the `VirtualDirectories.Add` line.

```csharp
using System;
using System.Collections.Generic;
using System.Text;
using Microsoft.Web.Administration;
using Microsoft.Web.Management;

namespace Professional IIS7
{
    public class IIS7
    {
        // Creates a Virtual Directory under App1.
        {
            ServerManager manager = new ServerManager();
            Application targetApp = sm.Sites["WebSite1"].Applications["/App1"];
            targetApp.VirtualDirectories.Add("/VDir1", "c:\inetpub\wwwroot\vdir1");
            manager.CommitChanges();
        }
    }
}
```

This example creates a new virtual directory named VDir1 pointing to `c:\inetpub\wwwroot\vdir1`.

Removing Virtual Directories

Removing virtual directories is almost the same action as adding a virtual directory and can be performed under IIS Manager by right-clicking on the virtual directory and clicking Remove or under the Actions pane by selecting Remove.

To use the command line to delete a virtual directory from the root of the web site, run the following command:

```
appcmd.exe delete vdir /vdir.name:www.website1.com/vdir1
```

To delete a virtual directory from an application under the Site1 web site, run the following command:

```
appcmd.exe delete vdir /vdir.name:www.website1.com/Application1/vdir1
```

Removing a virtual directory with the `Microsoft.Web.Administration` API is very similar to adding the directory. The difference comes in the `VirtualDirectory.Remove` line, where `Add` has been replaced by `Remove`, and the path to the folder is not needed for the removal of the virtual directory.

```
using System;
using System.Collections.Generic;
using System.Text;
using Microsoft.Web.Administration;
using Microsoft.Web.Management;

namespace Professional IIS7
{
    public class IIS7
    {
        // Removes a Virtual Directory from under App1.
        {
            ServerManager manager = new ServerManager();
            Application targetApp = sm.Sites["WebSite1"].Applications["/App1"];
            targetApp.VirtualDirectories.Remove("/VDir1");
            manager.CommitChanges();
        }
    }
}
```

After running this, `VDir1` has been removed from beneath `App1`.

Authentication

Authentication is the mechanism that allows determining the identity of who is making requests to your web application and then the delegation of rights to access your site. Generally authentication requests require the entering of a username/password combination or other information such as an access token.

Upon installation, IIS 7.0 allows you to determine which authentication methods will be installed on the server. The authentication options that can be installed are Basic, Windows Integrated, Digest, Client Certificate Mapping, and IIS Client Certificate Mapping. Again, all these options are installed by modules and handlers, allowing you to select which modules are used by the application. If no authentication will be needed on the server, the default Anonymous authentication is always loaded and allows the site to be used without clients having to sign on to the site.

Chapter 14, "Authentication and Authorization," goes into greater detail about authentication methods and setup.

Configuring Compression

In previous versions of IIS, compression seemed to be more of an afterthought than an integral part of the server. IIS 7.0 completely corrects this, as compression can be completely configured through the various administration tools. Why would you want to use compression? Compression enables you to use less bandwidth in delivering content, and users have a faster response time when downloading pages. Less bandwidth means less expense in running your site, and faster response time means happier users.

By default, the static compression module is installed when IIS 7.0 is set up. The dynamic compression module can be installed during setup or at any point afterward. IIS 7.0 also allows compression to be set at all levels, from server down to virtual directory. The server level allows the most configuration options; all other levels allow only the ability to enable or disable compression.

Enabling both static and dynamic compression is highly recommended. One item to keep in mind is that compression causes the server to work harder and use more processing power. If you choose to enable dynamic compression, you should monitor your server performance to ensure that it is responding within the performance window that your organization has set.

Configuring Compression with IIS Manager

In IIS 6.0, it wasn't possible to configure compression through IIS Manager. With IIS 7.0, however, you can enable compression simply by checking boxes in the Compression section of IIS Manager. We'll walk through configuring compression at the server level because it has the most options.

1. Open IIS Manager.

2. Double-click on the server name to get to the home page. In the IIS area, double-click the Compression icon. As shown in Figure 6-11, you are given two options: to enable dynamic compression and to enable static compression. In addition to the two selections, there are options to configure how static compression is configured.

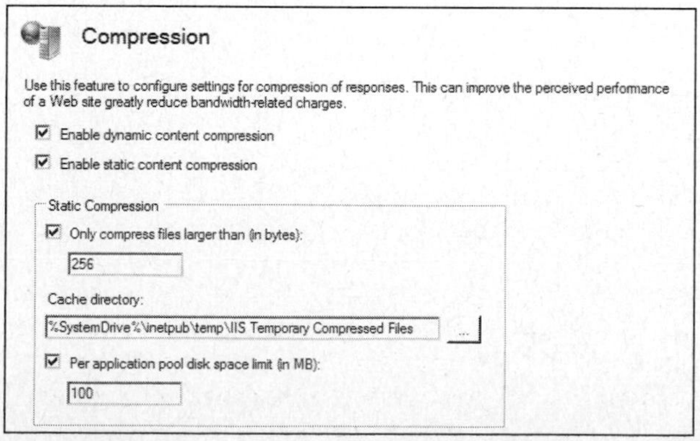

Figure 6-11

3. Check the Enable Dynamic Content Compression box. The Enable Static Content Compression box should be checked by default.

4. Optionally, you can adjust the size of the files that static compression will compress. By unchecking the "Only Compress Files Larger Than (In Bytes)" checkbox, all files will be compressed. Otherwise, you may determine the minimum size of file that IIS will compress. Here you can also set the cache directory and the disk space limit per application pool.

5. Click Apply in the Actions pane to complete the configuration change.

Configuring Compression with AppCmd.exe

To configure compression with AppCmd.exe, you will need to work with two separate sections of the configuration: system.webServer/urlCompression and system.webServer/httpCompression. The urlCompression section is where you will enable or disable compression, and the httpCompression section gives access to many adjustable properties that are not seen in IIS Manager.

Although static compression is enabled by default, you might need to enable it at some point. Enabling static compression is done with this command:

```
appcmd.exe set config /section:system.webServer/urlCompression
-doStaticCompression:true
```

Enabling dynamic compression is done with this command:

```
appcmd.exe set config /section:system.webServer/urlCompression
-doDynamicCompression:true
```

In addition to enabling and disabling compression, AppCmd.exe exposes the following additional properties for configuration through system.webServer/httpCompression:

```
-sendCacheHeaders
-expiresHeader
-cacheControlHeader
-directory
-doDiskSpaceLimiting
-maxDiskSpaceUsage
-minFileSizeForComp
-noCompressionForHttp10
-noCompressionForProxies
-noCompressionForRange
-staticCompressionDisableCpuUsage
-staticCompressionEnableCpuUsage
-dynamicCompressionDisableCpuUsage
-dynamicCompressionEnableCpuUsage
-staticTypes.[mimeType='string'].mimeType
-staticTypes.[mimeType='string'].enabled
-dynamicTypes.[mimeType='string'].mimeType
-dynamicTypes.[mimeType='string'].enabled
-[name='string'].name
-[name='string'].doStaticCompression
-[name='string'].doDynamicCompression
-[name='string'].dll
```

```
-[name='string'].staticCompressionLevel
-[name='string'].dynamicCompressionLevel
```

system.webServer/httpCompression is where the cache directory is set. In the following example, the directory is set to the %systemdrive%\temp\compression folder (systemdrive is usually c:\):

```
appcmd.exe set config /section:system.webServer/httpCompression
-directory:%systemdrive%\Temp\Compression
```

Configuring Default Document Settings

IIS uses default documents to determine which file to serve when a site is requested. The following default documents are set up automatically by IIS 7.0:

❑ Default.htm

❑ Default.asp

❑ Index.htm

❑ Index.html

❑ Iisstart.htm

❑ Default.aspx

IIS serves the files in order from top down. If you have both a default.aspx and a default.htm, you will need to place the default.aspx higher in the order if that is the file you want served automatically when the web site is accessed.

Reordering a Document

If the desired document is not at the top of the default list, you will need to move it. To move the document, click on the desired document, and then click Move Up in the Actions pane until the document is at the top of the list.

Adding a Default Document

There may be times when you will need to use a document name that is not in the pre-populated list. To add a new document to the default document settings, follow these steps:

1. Open IIS Manager.

2. Double-click the Default Document icon to navigate to the default document page.

3. Click Add in the Actions pane. The Add Default Document dialog box will pop up.

4. Type in the name of the document you want to add. In this instance, type testdoc.htm.

5. Click OK. The testdoc.htm page is now at the top of the document order.

6. Close IIS Manager.

Configuring MIME Settings

MIME (Multipurpose Internet Mail Extensions) is an Internet standard that defines the content types delivered by IIS 7.0. Although originating with e-mail, MIME has carried over to be used by other communication protocols, including HTTP. HTTP uses MIME to establish which type of content is being requested by a browser. A browser requests not only content from a web server, but also information that specifies what the content type is. This information is returned from the server as a Content_Type field in the HTTP header. When the browser gets the Content_Type field, it knows how to handle the following content.

In IIS 7.0, there is a master list of MIME types that are understood by the server. You can modify this list by adding, editing, or removing MIME types. If a MIME type is requested that is not in the master list, a 404.3 error is returned to the browser. Additionally, a wildcard (*, application/octet-stream) MIME type can be added that will allow extensions to be served, although this results in increasing the attack surface of the server and is not recommended.

Although there is a master list of MIME types in IIS 7.0, MIME types can also be set at the server, site, application, virtual directory, and file levels.

Adding MIME Types

Adding MIME types will be the most common activity you will do with MIME types. This section covers the methods to add a MIME type in IIS 7.0.

Adding MIME Types Using IIS Manager

Perform the following steps to add MIME types with IIS Manager:

1. Open IIS Manager.

2. Select the level and location that you want to set the MIME type for. Double-clicking the MIME Types icon takes you to the MIME Types page.

3. Click Add in the Actions pane. The Add MIME Type dialog box appears, as shown in Figure 6-12.

4. Add the file extension and MIME type, and then click OK. This example adds the .flv extension to allow IIS 7.0 to serve Flash videos.

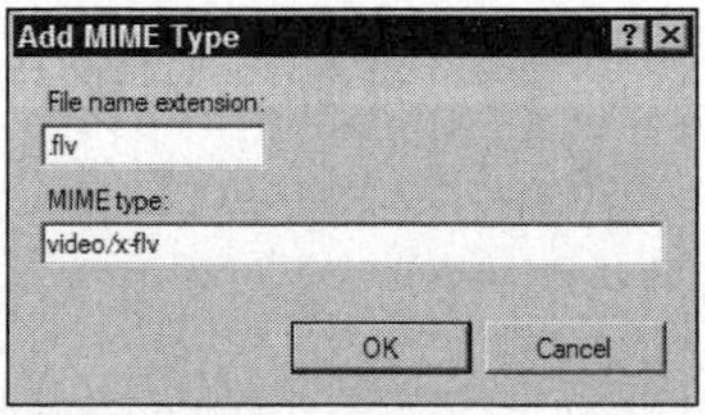

Figure 6-12

Adding MIME Types Using AppCmd

You can also use AppCmd to add MIME types. AppCmd uses the `config` object with the `set` command to modify the `staticContent` section, adding the file extension and mime type to `applicationHost` `.config`. The key to adding the MIME type is using the `/+` in the command.

```
appcmd.exe set config /section"staticContent /+"[fileExtension='<mime
extention>',mimeType='<mime type>']"
```

For example, to add the file extension .flv and the MIME type video/x-flv, run the following command:

```
appcmd.exe set config /section:staticContent
/+"[fileExtension='.flv',mimeType='video/x-flv']"
```

Editing MIME Types

You can edit MIME types using the same tools you used to add MIME types.

Editing MIME Types Using IIS Manager

To edit MIME types with IIS Manager:

1. Open IIS Manager (Click Start ➪ Run, enter **inetmgr**, and then press Enter.)
2. Select the level and location for which you want to edit the MIME type. Double-click the MIME Types icon to open it.
3. Double-click the MIME type you want to edit. The "Edit MIME type" tool will open, and you can modify the data in the MIME type section.
4. Click OK when you have completed making changes.

Editing MIME Types Using AppCmd

`AppCmd.exe` is used here to edit the .txt MIME type from text/plain to text/rich text:

```
appcmd.exe set config /section:staticContent
/[fileExtension='.txt',mimeType='text/plain'].mimeType:text/richtext
```

Removing MIME Types

When it is determined that a MIME type is no longer needed, it is possible to remove it in order to reduce the attack surface of a server.

Removing MIME Types Using IIS Manager

IIS Manager can be used to remove a MIME type with these steps:

1. Open IIS Manager (Click Start ➪ Run, enter **inetmgr**, and then press Enter.)
2. Select the level and location for which you want to remove the MIME types. Double-click the MIME Types icon to open it.
3. Right-click on the MIME type to be removed, and click Remove. Select Yes on the verification pop-up.

Removing MIME Types Using AppCmd

To remove a MIME type with `AppCmd.exe`, make sure to specify the extension and the MIME type string — in this case, `video/x-flv`. The key to removing the MIME type is to use `/-` in the command.

```
appcmd.exe set config /section:staticContent
/-"[fileExtension='.flv',mimeType='video/x-flv']"
```

The previous example removed the .flv extension and video/x-flv MIME type from the server.

Basic Administration Tasks

This section will provide you with a brief overview of common administration tasks and the quick answers to get your IIS server running with as little pain and time as possible.

Configuring Default Options for IIS

The easiest way to administer an IIS server is to ensure that all your configured sites conform to a standard configuration layout by default and that other requirements are configured as exceptions.

To configure the default options for all web sites to inherit, perform the following steps:

1. Open IIS Manager.
2. Click Sites in the Connections pane.
3. Click Set Web Site Defaults in the Actions pane (see Figure 6-13). The Web Site Defaults dialog box will pop up.
4. With this dialog box, you can set a few of the basic behaviors of a web site. Under the Behavior section, expand Failed Request Tracing, click Enabled, and then select True from the dropdown menu.
5. Click OK to close the dialog.

Changes to the fields in the Web Sites Default dialog box will apply only to sites created after the change, *not* to sites already created.

Configuring the default web site properties with `AppCmd.exe` can be accomplished by using the `config` object and the `set` command. To enable Failed Request Tracing in the default site settings, you need to edit the `siteDefaults.traceFailedRequestslogging.enabled` object to set its value to `true`.

```
appcmd set config /section:sites -siteDefaults.traceFailedRequestsLogging.
enabled:true
```

Starting and Stopping Services and Web Sites

From time to time, services and sites will need to be manually stopped, started, or restarted to resolve issues on a server.

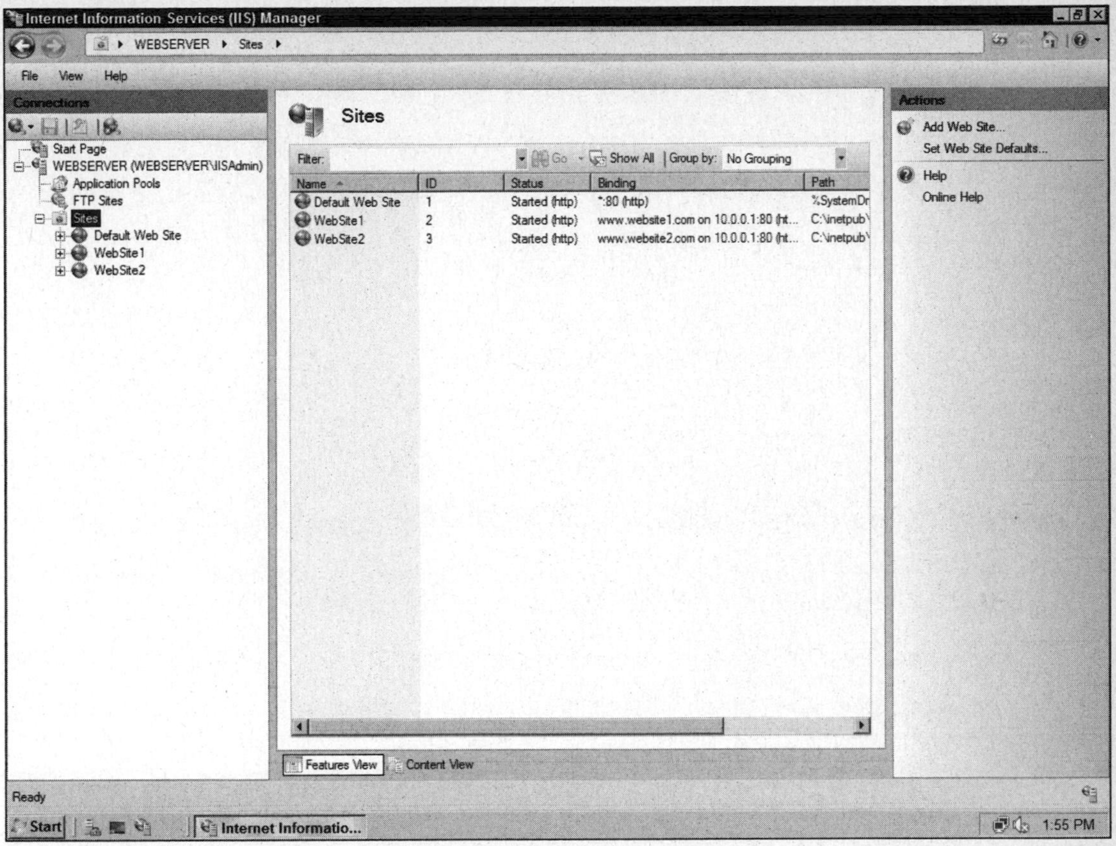

Figure 6-13

Stopping and Starting Web Services

Controlling the services that run IIS has not changed from previous versions of IIS. To stop all IIS-related services, issue a `net` command on the IIS Admin Service by its service name:

```
net stop iisadmin /y
```

You can stop individual services as follows:

- ❑ World Wide Web Publishing Service — `net stop w3svc`.
- ❑ SMTP Service — `net stop smtpsvc`.
- ❑ FTP Publishing Service — `net stop msftpsvc`.

Starting the web services follows the same process as stopping them:

```
Net start iisadmin /y
```

You can start the individual services as follows:

❑ World Wide Web Publishing Service — `net start w3svc`.

❑ SMTP Service — `net start smtpsvc`.

❑ FTP Publishing Service — `net start msftpsvc`.

Stopping and Starting Web Sites

To stop a web site with AppCmd, run the following command:

```
appcmd.exe stop site site1/
```

To start a web site, run the following command:

```
appcmd.exe start site site1/
```

Enabling Dynamic Content — ASP.NET and Classic ASP

In Chapter 7, "Web Application Administration," we'll look into the configuration of web applications in detail. To quickly enable the processing of dynamic content such as ASP:

1. Open IIS Manager.

2. Click on the site to manage, and then click Handler Mappings to navigate to the Handler Mappings page.

3. To enable Classic ASP, select the ASPClassic handler and enable it. If ASPClassic is not listed as an option, you can add the handler, as follows:

   a. Select Add Script Map from the Actions pane.

   b. Set *.asp as the request path, with "%systemroot%\system32\inetsrv\asp.dll" as the executable, and a name that refers to the mapping.

   c. You also can place request restrictions on the mapping to restrict it to particular HTTP request types.

   Note that if you are using Classic ASP code for maximum compatibility, you should ensure that your application pool is enabled for Classic ASP.

4. Close IIS Manager.

Isolating Applications

The concept of application isolation ensures that applications are separate from other applications and the IIS process, to achieve higher security, to reduce the impact of failure, and to separate management. You can achieve complete application isolation by performing the following steps:

1. Create a new application folder off the folder root.

2. Create a new application pool, or select an appropriate application pool for the user.

3. Create a separate user account for the application, and assign it to the web-site application.

Once these actions have been completed, the application can be configured as its own entity to prevent any adverse affects of failure of the application.

Summary

As the web site administrator's role has a huge variety of tasks and issues to address, effective administration of a web server is key to ensuring success.

With the introduction of new administration interfaces such as IIS Manager, the command-line `AppCmd.exe`, and the `Microsoft.Web.Administration` API, configuration tasks are simpler and easier to script to ensure low maintenance and high levels of consistency across all web servers.

This chapter has briefly touched on the fundamental configuration items that all web administrators need to address when configuring their web sites. These subjects are covered in more detail in subsequent chapters. However, by reviewing this chapter, web administrators will be able to make the management of their environments much simpler, allowing them to increase the quality of their service across their organization.

In the next chapter, "Web Application Administration," you'll learn about the various types of application technologies supported by IIS 7.0. You will be provided with information about ASP.NET, PHP, FastCGI, and other technologies, and you will be able to set up your web server to run them.

Web Application Administration

When you look at most web sites today, you are seeing some type of dynamic content. This dynamic content could be an online auction, webmail, forums, blogs, online games, or any type of nonstatic content that is on a web site. The content is delivered by a web application. Normally, a web application is a three-tiered system, where the browser is the first tier, a dynamic web content technology is the second tier, and a database is the third tier. For our purposes, the dynamic content technology will be referred to as the "web application." The web application can be based on a variety of technologies, including ASP, ASP.NET, ISAPI, CGI, and FastCGI. IIS 7.0 natively supports these technologies as well as the Windows Communication Foundation (WCF). These technologies all plug into IIS 7.0 via modules that can be added or removed based on the purpose of the server. In this chapter, we shall discuss these technologies and their administration as they relate to IIS 7.0.

Application Administration

The configuration store used by IIS 7.0 is based on the .NET Framework, allowing the server or site to have a tighter integration between IIS 7.0 and ASP.NET. As mentioned in Chapter 5, "Administration Tools," the configuration is kept in the `applicationHost.config`, `machine.config`, and various `web.config` files. Owing to the tighter integration between IIS 7.0 and ASP.NET, the other content types now have access to the features of ASP.NET. An example of this is the ASP.NET Forms authentication. For example, a PHP application can now use ASP.NET Forms authentication to secure the site. The "ASP.NET" section covers some of the shared aspects of ASP.NET. The next section covers ASP as a quick overview to show where ASP.NET came from.

ASP

ASP (Active Server Pages) is a server-side scripting engine used to create dynamic, interactive web pages. It debuted with IIS 3.0 in December 1996 and has continued to evolve to its current state of ASP.NET 2.0. ASP is also referred to as *Classic ASP*.

When a server receives a GET request for an ASP page, it runs the server-side code and generates an HTML page, which is then sent to the client's browser. ASP pages can contain standard HTML and COM components for connecting to databases or processing business logic in addition to the server-side code.

To edit the ASP settings with IIS Manager, follow these steps:

1. Start IIS Manager by clicking Start ⇨ Run, entering **inetmgr**, and then pressing Enter.

2. Double-click the ASP icon in the IIS section, and the ASP page will appear (see Figure 7-1).

3. On the ASP page, you can modify the behavior settings, such as enabling parent paths. You can modify how ASP is compiled — for example, setting the scripting language.

4. After making the changes, click Apply in the Actions pane.

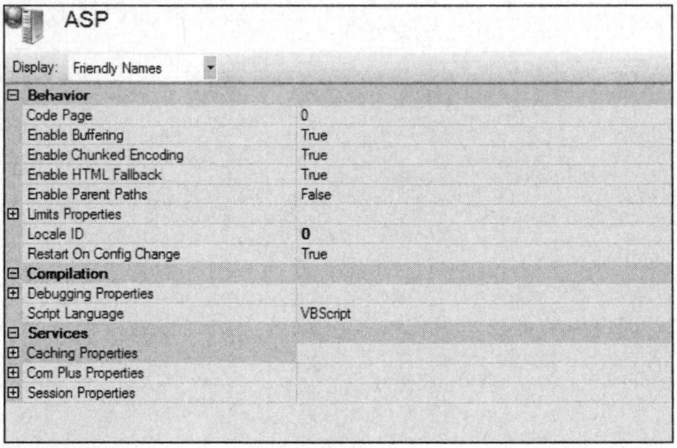

Figure 7-1

ASP.NET

As mentioned above, ASP.NET is more tightly integrated into IIS 7.0 than it was in previous versions of IIS. ASP.NET services can now be used to provide functionality to all content types, including PHP, static files, and Classic ASP pages. IIS can be extended using ASP.NET modules, rather than relying on ISAPI filters and extensions. These ASP.NET modules integrate directly into the server pipeline, thus they can run at any point in the processing pipeline. Additionally, they can be run in any order with native IIS modules. With the integration of ASP.NET and IIS comes the added benefit of a unified server run time. Many features, including configuration, error handling, and tracing, have been unified into the same interfaces for the two systems.

IIS 6.0 and Previous Architecture

Prior to IIS 7.0, ASP.NET was implemented with the `aspnet_isapi.dll`. The route an ASP.NET request would take required IIS first to process the request to determine what needed to be done with the request. If it was determined that it was an ASP.NET request, IIS then passed it off to the `aspnet_isapi.dll` to process the actual request. The `.dll` would then pass the completed request back to IIS to return the results to the client's web browser. This process worked fine for ASP.NET file types; however, other file types couldn't take advantage of the features offered in the ASP.NET architecture; nor could IIS use these features outside of the period before or after the ASP.NET execution path.

Figure 7-2 shows the processing path for an ASP.NET request, where a request comes in to IIS and goes through the Authentication handler and to the Determine handler. At the Determine handler, IIS learns that the request needs to be routed to the `aspnet_isapi.dll`. The request is sent to the ISAPI subsystem and then on to the `aspnet_isapi.dll`. The `aspnet_isapi.dll` then processes the request and sends the result back to the ISAPI subsystem in IIS and then on to the Determine handler. The Determine handler sends the processed results out to the client after logging the request.

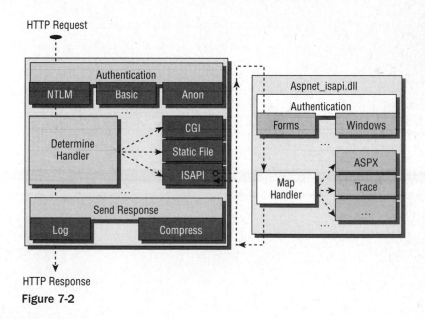

Figure 7-2

IIS 7.0 Architecture

The integration between IIS 7.0 and ASP.NET provides for a much tighter pipeline. In this latest version of IIS, the ASP.NET processing pipeline overlays the IIS pipeline. ASP.NET now acts more like a wrapper than as a plug-in. Figure 7-3 shows the new pipeline and how ASP.NET can be called at any point in a request. IIS is able to call ASP.NET from the Authentication phase to use ASP.NET Basic, Forms, Anonymous, or Windows authentication. The ExecuteHandler phase can call ASP.NET to run ASPX files, static files such as htm, ASP.NET traces, or other files such as PHP and ASP. The SendResponse phase can use ASP.NET for compression and logging prior to sending the response to the client web browser. In addition, ASP.NET modules can be used instead of the built-in IIS modules to replace or add on to IIS functionality, and the ASP.NET APIs can be used to create new modules and handlers.

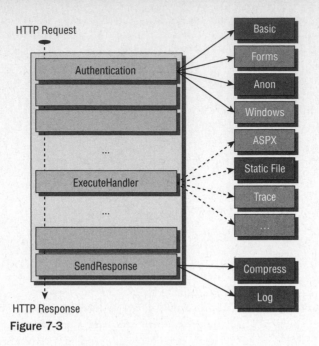

HTTP Request

HTTP Response

Figure 7-3

IIS 7.0 and ASP.NET Modules

The tighter integration between the two technologies enables you to control ASP.NET through IIS Manager.

IIS Manager has configuration options for the following ASP.NET modules:

❑ .NET Compilation

❑ .NET Globalization

❑ .NET Trust Levels

❑ Application Settings

❑ Connection Strings

❑ Machine Key

❑ Pages and Controls

❑ Providers

❑ Session State

❑ SMTP Email

.NET Compilation

Prior to ASP.NET serving a request, it first has to compile the code into the appropriate assembly(ies). These assembly files have the .dll extension. With the .NET Compilation module in IIS 7.0, you can control how the ASP.NET code is compiled on the server.

Looking at Figure 7-4, you can see that the page is divided into three sections.

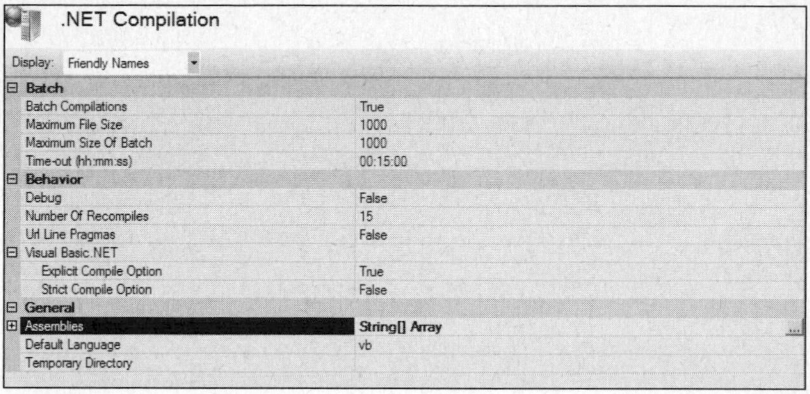

Figure 7-4

The first section, Batch, allows control of the file and batch size as well as the time-out period for batches. Setting batch compilation to True tells ASP.NET to compile all of the files in a folder into a single assembly the first time a file in the folder is accessed. This incurs a performance penalty when the first page is accessed but results in faster load times for the other files in the folder. The other settings in the Batch section relate to the maximum size of the files to put in the batch file, the maximum size of the batch, and the time-out period of the Batch file process.

The second section, Behavior, provides limits to the compiling assemblies. The section sets whether the debug mode is off or on, the number of recompiles before the application is restarted, whether URL line pragmas are set to enabled or not, and whether VB.NET uses explicit compiles and strict compiles or not. *Explicit compiles* are equivalent to specifying "Option Explicit" in VB.NET. Any variable must be explicitly declared in order for it to be used when the code is compiled. The *strict compile option* enables notification when the value of one data type is converted to another data type that has less precision or capacity.

The final section, General, lists the current assemblies, the default coding language, C# or VB, and the temporary directory to be used during the compiles.

.NET Globalization

Globalization is a process in which the developer designs the application to work in multiple cultures and locations around the world. Localization then takes the globalized application and customizes the application to the specific culture and location. This process provides for using one code base to deliver application content in any locale. The locale consists of both language and cultural information.

As shown in Figure 7-5, the IIS 7.0 settings for globalization include two sections, Culture and Encoding. The Culture section is used to set the culture-dependant properties, such as time, date, and currency. The UICulture value determines which text resources are loaded from the database. By using the Encoding settings, you can set how a page encodes its response, which enables a browser to determine the encoding without a meta tag.

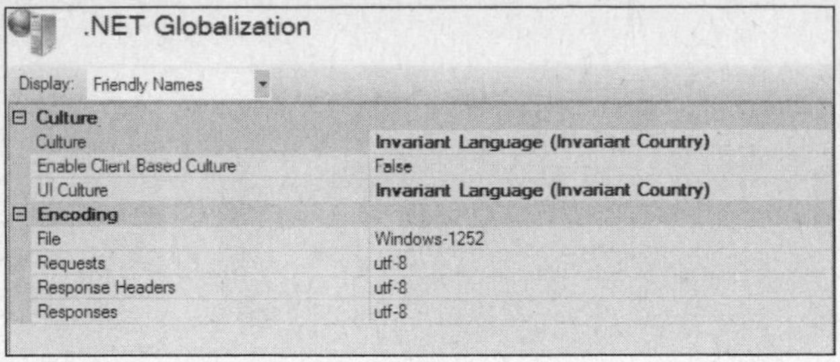

Figure 7-5

.NET Trust Levels

The ASP.NET code access security (CAS) policy is set by the trust level of an application. This CAS determines the permissions that are granted to the application on the server. Setting the CAS can be important when deploying code that gives elevated access to the server. You may need to tighten the CAS if you are deploying code that modifies the file system on the server, to prevent undesired access.

CAS has two categories of trust: full trust and partial trust. An application with *full trust* permissions can access all resources on the server and perform privileged operations. This application is then only restricted by the operating system's security settings.

The second level of trust is partial trust. This is defined as any level of trust less than full trust. When an application runs with *partial trust*, it can have different levels of resource access and server permissions from those of another application running with a partial trust. A great example is code that is running locally on a server versus code that is running from a shared network location. The local code would generally have a higher level of trust than the code located on the network location.

Applications that use the 1.0 .NET Framework always use full trust. Applications that use 1.1 or 2.0 .NET Frameworks use full trust by default but can be set to use more restrictive permissions. Windows Communication Foundation (WCF) always uses full trust.

You can set the trust level for an application in IIS Manager, by using `AppCmd.exe` directly in the configuration, and by using the WMI classes.

In the default settings, there are five different levels of trust: Full, High, Medium, Low, and Minimal. It is also possible to take one of these configurations and use it as a template to create a custom trust level.

The trust configuration files are located in the `C:\%system root%\Microsoft.NET\Framework\v2.0.50727\CONFIG` folder. To create a custom trust configuration, copy the configuration level that most closely resembles the settings you need and then rename it with a defining name. For example, take the `web_minimaltrust.config` file, copy it, and name the copy `web_customtrust.config`. At this point, you would want to modify the new configuration to make the trust changes needed for the site. After making the changes to the configuration file, save and close it. Open the `web.config` file located in the same folder, and find the `<securityPolicy>` section. You will need to add a line to designate the new trust level in the file. Here you see that the last trust level of "Custom" has been added.

```
<location allowOverride="true">
    <system.web>
```

```
    <securityPolicy>
        <trustLevel name="Full" policyFile="internal" />
        <trustLevel name="High" policyFile="web_hightrust.config" />
        <trustLevel name="Medium" policyFile="web_mediumtrust.config" />
        <trustLevel name="Low" policyFile="web_lowtrust.config" />
        <trustLevel name="Minimal" policyFile="web_minimaltrust.config" />
        <trustLevel name="Custom" policyFile="web_customtrust.config" />
    </securityPolicy>
    <trust level="Full" originUrl="" />
    </system.web>
</location>
```

When IIS Manager is opened, the Custom trust level will now be shown in the dropdown selections, as shown in Figure 7-6.

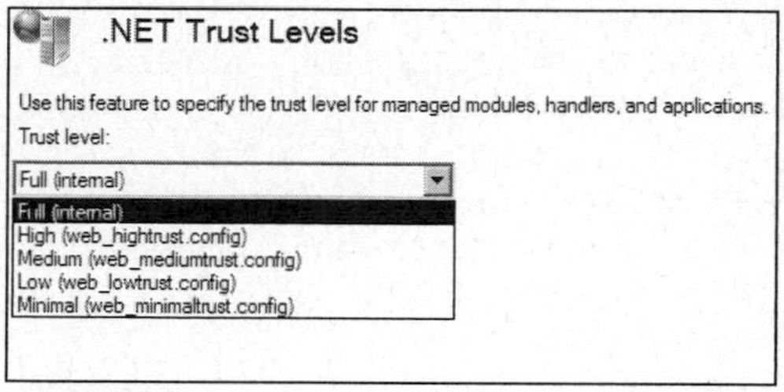

Figure 7-6

Application Settings

Application settings allow you to store configuration data in the web.config files in the form of key/value pairs. The settings create application-wide values that can be applied at any point in the web application. Configuration changes are made easily because of the centralized nature of the files. Application settings can be set in IIS Manager by using the following process:

1. Start IIS Manager by clicking Start ⇨ Run, entering **inetmgr**, and then pressing Enter.

2. At the level (web server, web site, application) where you want to apply the application settings, double-click the Application Settings icon in the ASP.NET section.

3. Click Add in the Tasks pane. The Add Application Setting dialog box appears, as shown in Figure 7-7.

4. Type in the name of the application setting and the value you want to use.

5. Click OK. The application setting is now in place.

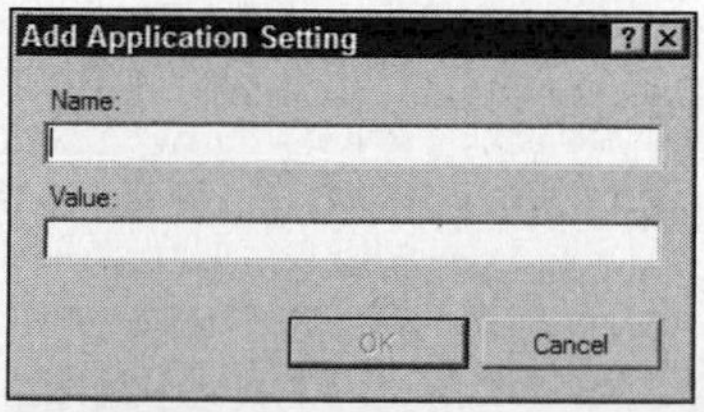

Figure 7-7

201

You can edit or remove application settings through the same section in IIS Manager. In addition to using IIS Manager, you can configure the settings using AppCmd.exe. To add an application setting, use the following syntax:

```
appcmd.exe set config /commit:MACHINE /section:appSettings
/+"[key='string',value='string']"
```

where key is the attribute you want to set and value is the desired value of the attribute. An example of setting the Async attribute to True would look like this:

```
appcmd.exe set config /commit:Machine -section:appSettings
/+[key='Buffer',value='false']
```

Editing the value follows a similar syntax. Watch where the close bracket moves to and how the value syntax changes:

```
appcmd.exe set config /commit:Machine -section:appSettings
/[key='Buffer'].value:true
```

Removing the application setting follows the same syntax as adding the settings, except you will need to substitute a − for the +.

```
appcmd.exe set config /commit:Machine -section:appSettings
/-[key='Buffer',value='false']
```

It is important to remember that any changes to the .NET settings result in an appDomain recycle, which will affect the entire server.

Connection Strings

Connection strings are used to establish communication between an application and a database. The connection string provides the server, database name, user, and password needed for the application to communicate with the database. In this example, you will add a connection named *DB1* to database DB1 on server SQL1 with user "User1" and password "PW1."

1. From the IIS Manager home page, open the Connection Strings module and select Add. The Add Connection String dialog box will appear, as shown in Figure 7-8.

2. Enter the name of the connection in the Name box, the server name in the Server line, and the database name in the Database line.
   You will need to determine whether you need to use Windows integrated security or SQL security.

3. If you use SQL security, select the Set button and add the username and password.

4. If you have a custom connection string, you can enter it by selecting the Custom option.

Machine Keys

ASP.NET uses machine keys to protect Forms authentication cookie data and page-view state data. Machine keys are hashed values that are generated to encrypt the data from the cookies and page-view states. The keys are also used to run sessions out of process. Although you can set these machine keys at any level, from server level down to file level, by default they are locked at the server and web-site levels only. These keys can be shared between servers when a site is run on multiple web servers.

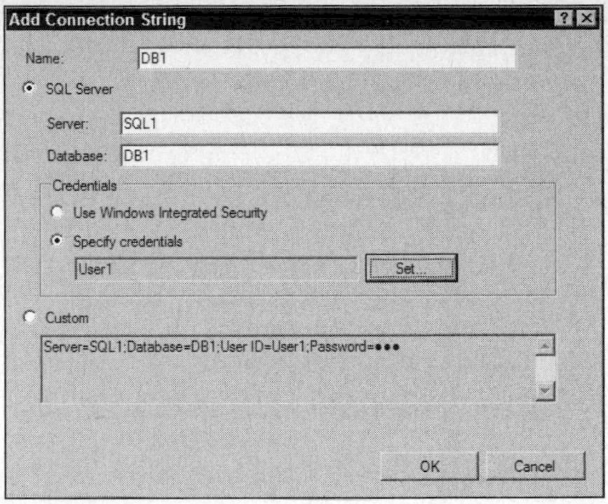

Figure 7-8

ASP.NET uses two types of machine keys: validation keys and decryption keys. The validation key is used to create a Message Authentication Code (MAC) to verify the integrity of the data. The validation key is then appended to the Forms authentication cookie or the view-state data. The decryption key is used to encrypt and decrypt the Forms authentication tickets and view-state data.

Setting machine keys in IIS Manager is done by choosing the level at which you want to apply the machine key. Figure 7-9 shows the Machine Key page.

1. Once you have determined what level to apply the machine key to, double-click the Machine Key icon in the ASP.NET group on the home page.

2. Select an encryption method.

   The default encryption method is SHA1 and should probably be used for most situations. The other options are AES, MD5, and TripleDES. AES is lightweight and easy to use. It can use 128-, 192-, or 256-bit keys and uses the same private key to encrypt and decrypt the data. MD5 creates a 128-bit message digest of the original data. It is generally used for signing applications or e-mail. SHA1 is considered to be more secure than MD5, as it uses a 160-bit message digest. TripleDES is three times slower than Data Encryption Standard (DES) but can be more secure. It creates a key of 192 bits. Use TripleDES if security is more important than speed of the site.

3. Select a decryption method. The default decryption method is Auto and should be used, as it works with whichever encryption method is used.

4. Determine whether you need to have a single validation key or if you will automatically generate one at run time each time. If you will be using the key on multiple servers, you will need to create a single validation key and share it among the servers.

5. Determine whether you need to have a single decryption key or if you will automatically generate one at run time each time. If you will be using the key on multiple servers, you will need to create a single decryption key and share it among the servers.

6. Click Apply in the Tasks panel.

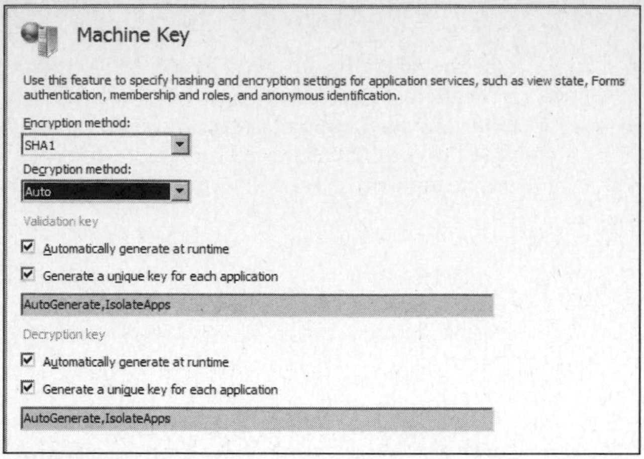

Figure 7-9

Pages and Controls

ASP.NET provides for the use of elements that can be recognized and processed when a page is run. It also supports the use of custom controls that are reusable and processed on the server. This allows server code to be used to configure ASP.NET web page properties. Figure 7-10 shows the Pages and Controls module, which includes four sections.

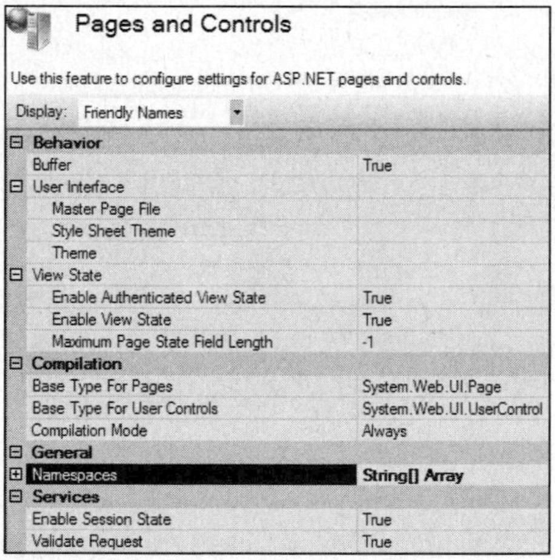

Figure 7-10

The first section, Behavior, controls the view state and authenticated view state, as well as the setting the maximum page state field length. The second section, Compilation, sets the base type for pages and user controls and determines whether pages are compiled or interpreted. The General section deals with namespaces for the pages. The Services section allows enabling or disabling the session state and request validation.

Providers

ASP.NET and applications that are created with the .NET Framework can use databases to store information. In order to map the applications to the structure of the database, a software module called a Provider is used. *Providers* are the equivalent of the hardware abstraction layer for applications and databases. IIS 7.0 allows the use of the Provider module for installing custom providers or modifying the standard ASP.NET providers. There are three different provider roles: .NET Roles, .NET Users, and .NET Profile.

The .NET Roles provider has options for creating the authorization store, SQL role, and Windows token provider types. The .NET Users provider can be used to create Active Directory membership or SQL membership provider types. The .NET Profile is used to create SQL profile providers. Figure 7-11 shows the Add Provider dialog box.

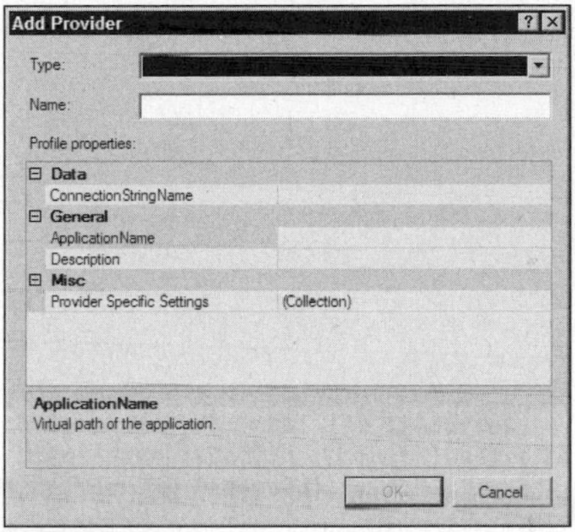

Figure 7-11

Adding a provider requires that you select the provider role first and then select .NET Role, .NET User, or .NET Profile. Once the provider role has been selected, you can then click Add to begin the Add Provider dialog. Choose the type of provider you need, name it, and then choose one of the existing connection strings. It is optional to include an application name, description, and provider-specific settings.

Session State

IIS 7.0 uses *session state* to track the pages that users browse during a single visit to a web site. Those users are differentiated by IIS creating a session ID for each user. HTTP is a stateless protocol; thus, the server keeps no information about the variables the server has already served during previous requests. IIS 7.0 can use the ASP.NET session state to store and retrieve data for users as they navigate around the web site.

Modes

Session state can be set in one of the following five modes:

❑   Not Enabled

❑   In Process

❑   Custom

❑   State Server

❑   SQL Server

Not Enabled

Not Enabled, as the name implies, means that the session state is not used on the web site.

In Process

In Process keeps the session state stored in the memory bound to the application worker process. This is the default mode in IIS 7.0. This method provides the fastest response to the session state data. However, the downside to using the In Process session state is that the more data in the session, the more memory is used. This can result in slower server performance.

Another thing to remember about storing the session state In Process is that when the worker process recycles, the data that were stored in memory are lost. If the application needs to retain the session state data, using another session state mode is recommended.

IIS 7.0 differs from previous versions of IIS, installing the `Aspnet_state.exe` service. By default, this service does not run and is set to manual. The service is required to be running for the session state to be stored In Process, thus it is recommended that the service be set to start automatically.

Custom

Storing the session state using the Custom mode provides for an out-of-process session using a custom handler to create a connection to a database. Using the custom handler allows the session state to be stored in databases other than MS SQL, such as Oracle or Access. It also provides a method to manage the session state using a database schema other than what the .NET Framework provides. To use a custom handler, you must implement a full session state provider in the `<sessionState>` `/<providers>` collection.

State Server

A second method of storing session state out of process is by using a State Server. The State Server can be either on the same server as the web site or on an external server. This State Server mode maintains the data by running a separate worker process from the worker process being run by the ASP.NET application.

If the State Server is being run on the same server as the web site, the web site can then support running as a web garden. If the web site is being run on multiple servers, then one server should be designated as the State Server to share the state among all of the web servers.

As with the In Process method above, the State Server mode also uses the `Aspnet_state.exe` service. Remember to set the service to start automatically on server start.

SQL Server

The final mode to keep the session state is to store the state in a SQL Server database. Similar to the State Server mode, the SQL Server can be run on the same server to support a web garden or on a separate server to support a web farm. The advantage of using SQL to store the session state is that the session data are maintained despite worker processes being recycled.

The SQL Server mode also uses the `Aspnet_state.exe` service that needs to be set to start automatically. In addition to the `Aspnet_state.exe` service, the SQL Server mode also needs the InstallSqlState.sql script run to configure it for the session state. The script is located at `%systemroot%\Microsoft.Net\Framework\V2.0.50727`.

Cookie Settings

Cookies are text files that contain data used for maintaining information about a user, such as authentication information or site preferences. One method of tracking session state is by using cookies. The cookies are placed on the client's machine and are then referenced by the web server. The cookie is passed back to the web server with every client request in the HTTP header.

Cookies can be set to use one of four modes:

- ❑ Auto Detect
- ❑ Use Cookie
- ❑ Use Device Profile
- ❑ Use URI

Auto Detect

The Auto Detect mode uses cookies if the browser supports cookies. If a mobile device is connecting to the web server and cookies are disabled, no cookies are used. If a desktop or laptop is connecting to the web server and cookies are disabled, the session state is stored in the URL.

When using the Auto Detect mode, session IDs should be set to regenerate. This allows attackers less time to acquire and exploit cookies to penetrate web servers, getting access to server content. The default time limit of 20 minutes should also be reduced to a level you determine as safe.

Use Cookies

When the Use Cookies mode is set, the session cookie associates session information with user information during the duration of the session.

Use Device Profile

The Use Device Profile mode uses cookies for the session state if the client browser supports cookies. If the browser does not support cookies, then no cookies will be used. If the device profile supports cookies, the session state will use cookies despite the user's cookie settings.

Session IDs should be set to regenerate for the same reasons as the Auto Detect mode.

Use URI

By Using the URI (Uniform Resource Identifier) for the session state, the session ID is embedded in the URI as a query string. The URI then is redirected to the original URL. This URI is used for the duration of the session.

Although the Use URI mode removes the disadvantages of cookies, it does have its own issues. Web pages cannot be bookmarked, and absolute URLs cannot be used without losing the session state.

Configuring Session State

You can set the session state using any of the management methods — IIS Manager, `AppCmd.exe`, editing the configuration files, or using WMI. This section describes how to configure the session state by using `AppCmd.exe`.

Open a command prompt using administrative permissions, and type

```
appcmd.exe set config /commit:WEBROOT /section:sessionState /mode:InProc
```

This sets the session state to the In Process mode and commits the change to the web-root level of the server.

In addition to setting the session state, you can also set the cookie mode by appending the cookie information to the session state configuration:

```
appcmd.exe set config /commit:WEBROOT /section:sessionState /cookieless:AutoDetect
/cookieName:website1 /timeout:5 /regenerateExpiredSessionId:True
```

This sets the cookie mode to auto detect with the cookie name of website1, a time-out value of 5 minutes, and the regeneration value to True.

SMTP e-Mail

SMTP (Simple Mail Transport Protocol) is the protocol used by IIS to send e-mail. ASP.NET has the `System.Net.Mail` API, which uses SMTP as a means to send mail for web applications. The SMTP e-Mail module allows configuration of SMTP for a web application. Figure 7-12 shows the SMTP e-Mail module.

The SMTP e-Mail module can be set to deliver mail to an SMTP server, or it can store the e-mail in a pickup directory for other use. The e-mail address test block should have the address you wish to be in the "from:" line of the e-mail. If you will be sending the e-mail to an SMTP server, determine if the server will be local or a separate server. If separate, give the server name or IP address in the SMTP Server text block. If SMTP is running locally on the server, then check the "localhost" box. Port 25 is the default port for SMTP and should be kept unless your SMTP server uses a nonstandard port. Indicate the Authentication settings that are needed to connect to the SMTP server. If storing the e-mail in a pickup directory, browse to and select the location for the mail to be saved. For more information on installing and configuring SMTP, see Chapter 10, "Configuring Other Services."

ISAPI

ISAPI (Internet Server Application Programming Interface) is a low-level programming interface that is used for running applications, such as ASP.NET, PHP, and Perl. Rather than being a server-side scripting technology, ISAPI is actually a true executable part of IIS. ISAPI applications run as .dlls and can be either extensions or filters. Extensions are applications that have access to the full functionality of IIS. Filters modify or augment the functionality of IIS. Filters check every request until one is found that needs to be processed. This check can be configured to examine either incoming or outgoing traffic. Some examples of ISAPI filters include authenticating and authorizing users, rewriting URLs, and modifying a response back to a client.

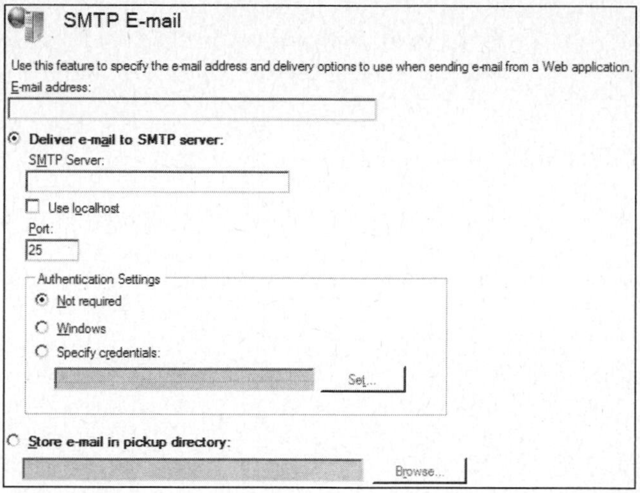

Figure 7-12

In IIS 7.0, ISAPI is being superseded by modules. Because of the integration of IIS 7.0 and ASP.NET, modules can now be written in either C++ or managed code and provide the same speed and security that only ISAPI applications once provided. ISAPI extensions and filters can still be used to provide for backward compatibility.

In order to run ISAPI applications on the server, two modules need to have the ISAPI information added. The ISAPI and CGI Restrictions module and the ISAPI Filters module both need to have the application information added in order for ISAPI to work. The ISAPI and CGI Restrictions module, shown in Figure 7-13, manages the ISAPI and CGI applications, adding descriptions and enabling or disabling the extensions.

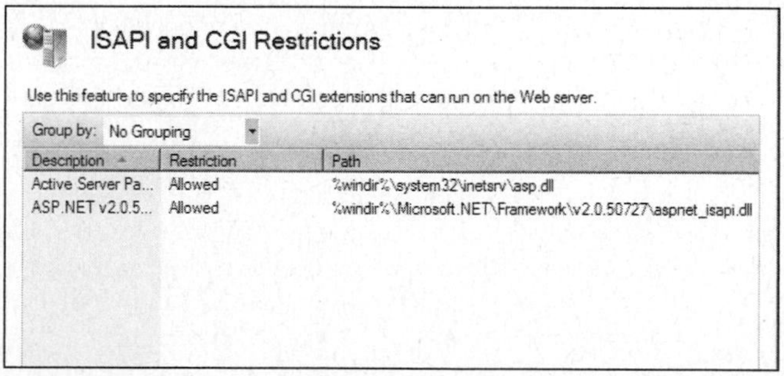

Figure 7-13

The ISAPI Filters module, shown in Figure 7-14, provides the filter name and path to the ISAPI filters.

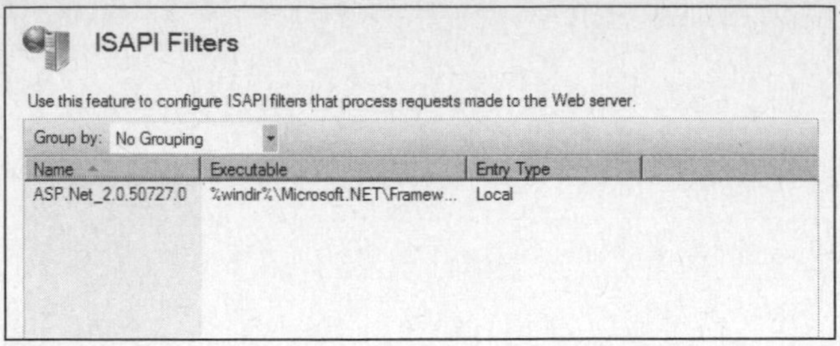

Figure 7-14

CGI

CGI (Common Gateway Interface) is a standard protocol that provides for communication between an application and a web browser. CGI was invented in 1993, and every version of IIS has supported it. The problem with CGI running on IIS is in the way it handles requests. With each new request for a CGI application, IIS has to create a new process, do the work, and then shut down the process. IIS can handle requests very quickly; however, the overhead of starting and stopping processes can become a bottleneck when running CGI on IIS. This is where FastCGI steps in. The creation of FastCGI resolves part of the bottleneck of using CGI on IIS. The next section details more about FastCGI.

FastCGI

FastCGI is a newer version of CGI that adheres to most of the original specifications. However, rather than shutting down a process at the end of a request, the process is allowed to stay running and process other requests. FastCGI, like CGI, is single-threaded, but a server can process more requests than with CGI because the processes stay open. On IIS 7.0, FastCGI is implemented as a native module using the built-in APIs.

Why would you need to run FastCGI? Well, there are many applications out there that are PHP applications. Although these applications usually work with either CGI or the ISAPI version of PHP, FastCGI provides much better performance.

Because FastCGI is a single-threaded application, it has to start multiple processes to handle multiple requests. The processes can be pooled together into groups, and the groups can then be managed together. The properties of a process group can be managed — for example, the number of processes in the group and the number of requests a process can handle before being recycled are each properties that can be managed. In addition to the multiple processes in a process group, FastCGI can have multiple process groups running. Each of these process groups can have its own settings.

Included here is a step-by-step process to install the QDig PHP application using FastCGI on your server. You will need the following prerequisites:

❑ IIS 7.0 installed.

❑ The Default Web Site that was installed by IIS.

❏   PHP 5.2.1 (www.php.net/downloads.php#v5).

❏   QDig (http://qdig.sourceforge.net/).

Installing PHP

You will need first to install PHP 5.2.1:

1.   Extract the PHP download to c:\program files\PHP.

2.   Copy PHP.INI-Recommended to PHP.INI.

3.   Open the PHP.INI file with Notepad.exe.

4.   Edit these configuration items:

```
register_long_arrays should be register_long_arrays = On
extension_dir should be extension_dir = "c:\program files\php"
add extension=php_gd.dll
```

5.   Save PHP.INI, and close it.

Installing QDig

Next, install QDig:

1.   Copy the index.php from the QDig download, and place it in c:\inetpub\wwwroot.

2.   Copy images into the c:\inetpub\wwwroot directory.

Installing FastCGI Module

Up to this point, you should have installed PHP and copied the index.php from QDig into the root of the default web site. Now you will install the FastCGI module in IIS 7.0:

1.   Open the Server Manager.

2.   Click on Web Server (IIS) under the Roles Summary.

3.   Click on Add Role Services under Role Services.

4.   Select the CGI item.

5.   Click Next.

6.   Click Install.

CGI and FastCGI are now installed on your server, but they are not yet enabled.

Enabling FastCGI for Use with PHP

After installing FastCGI on your server, you will need to create a handler mapping to associate .PHP requests to the PHP scripting engine via the FastCGI module. This can be done via any of the IIS 7.0

management interfaces, but this walkthrough will use the `AppCmd.exe` tool. Remember to open the command prompt with administrator privileges.

```
appcmd.exe set config /section:system.webServer/fastCGI /+[fullPath='c:\program
files\php\php-cgi.exe']
```

This command adds the PHP executable to FastCGI settings and should generate the following response:

```
Applied configuration changes to section "system.webServer/fastCgi" for
"MACHINE/WEBROOT/APPHOST" at configuration commit path "MACHINE/WEBROOT/APPHOST"
```

Next, you will need to add the PHP handlers to the FastCGI settings.

```
appcmd.exe set config /section:system.webServer/handlers /+[name='PHP-FastCGI',
path='*.php',verb='*',modules='FastCgiModule',scriptProcessor='c:\program
files\php\php-cgi.exe',resourceType='Either']
```

This should generate the response:

```
Applied configuration changes to section "system.webServer/handlers" for
"MACHINE/WEBROOT/APPHOST" at configuration commit path "MACHINE/WEBROOT/APPHOST"
```

Your PHP and FastCGI are now set up for use. Open your browser to `http://localhost/index.php`. QDig should now be available to view the photos in your root directory.

Windows Process Activation Service

Windows Server 2008 adds a new tool called the *Windows Process Activation Service (WAS)*. This service replaces the WWW service in managing application pool configuration and worker processes. The functionality that existed with the WWW service that ran only HTTP sites now allows WAS to run non-HTTP sites in addition to the HTTP sites. WAS is not part of IIS 7.0, but rather an external service that works in conjunction with IIS to manage the application pools and processes.

WAS can be run either with the WWW service or without it if HTTP functionality is not needed. The Windows Communication Foundation (WCF) is an example of a situation in which the HTTP protocol may not be needed. WCF is discussed in more detail in Appendix C. WCF uses a listener adapter to take the requests from WAS and route them to the WCF application, rather than using the HTTP protocol.

WAS is a prerequisite for IIS 7.0 and is automatically installed when you install IIS 7.0 on Windows Server 2008. WAS uses the same `applicationHost.config` file for its configuration as IIS uses. When the server is started, WAS reads the configuration and then shares that information with the listener adapters. The listener adapter then takes the configuration information and creates a communication link between WAS and a protocol listener. At this point, the protocol listeners just sit and listen. When they receive a request, WAS is used to determine if there is a worker process. If there is one, the request is passed to the worker process; if not, a worker process is started to handle the request.

Summary

The majority of today's web sites are actually web applications developed using a multitiered system consisting of the web browser, web server, and a database server. These web applications are generally written using ASP, ASP.NET, or PHP technologies. IIS 7.0 embraces these technologies, bringing ASP.NET integration into the IIS pipeline and using FastCGI to greatly improve the performance of PHP.

This chapter has provided detail for configuring these modules in IIS 7.0 through IIS Manager and the command line using `AppCmd.exe`. The next chapter, "Web Application Pool Administration," describes the differences between a virtual directory and an application, as well as provides in-depth information on the configuration and administration of application pools in IIS 7.0.

Web Application Pool Administration

Web sites and applications can be divided into pools of sites that make the most sense to the administrator. These pools create complete sandbox isolation between the other application pools on the server, offering strong performance and security benefits.

This chapter covers the various aspects of application pools, from overlapping worker processes during a recycle to the new Integrated Pipeline mode. A background and comparison between IIS 5.0 and IIS 6.0 are covered to set the stage for understanding why application pools are necessary and the advantages that they bring.

Effective management of application pools requires an understanding of

❑ Application pools, including what virtual directories and applications are in IIS.

❑ The w3wp.exe worker process.

❑ The two pipeline modes.

❑ Multiple methods of creating and managing application pools.

A Background of Web-Site Separation

Back in the days of IIS 5.0, applications could be placed in one of three isolation modes: low, medium, or high. Low and medium isolation placed all web sites in a large shared pool that utilized a shared user identity. Failures that affected one site often would break other sites that were set in low or medium isolation, requiring a reset of IIS to fix the sites again. Sites in high isolation did better by partially protecting some sites from each other, but each high-isolation application had an extra memory footprint, and the user identities were not unique from each other. This usually meant that a shared Windows user needed to be given Read permissions to all sites on the server, opening up a potential security hole between sites.

IIS 6.0 introduced an excellent solution for this by implementing *application pools*. This allowed the system administrator to create pools of applications bundled together into groups as the administrator saw fit. With this enhancement, it was possible to completely separate sites from each other so that a serious failure in one application wouldn't have any effect on sites or applications in other pools. In addition, each application pool defined the Windows user identity under which the applications ran, allowing complete user separation between application pools.

IIS 7.0 builds on the strong foundation of application pools. The core features and concepts implemented in IIS 6.0 remain the same, while further features and enhancements have been added on that foundation. In the remainder of this chapter, we discuss features that existed in IIS 6.0, plus enhancements that are new to IIS 7.0.

Defining Applications

An *application* is a logical grouping of resource files and components. This allows IIS to share data within the application and to have user and worker process isolation between applications. By default, the root of each web site is already an application, and subfolders and virtual directories can also be made into applications.

Classic ASP and ASP.NET are application-aware and use the application boundaries to share data and settings. InProcess session state in ASP.NET, for example, lives within the scope of the application boundaries so that all ASP.NET pages within the application have access to the same session state.

Many pre-existing web sites expect their site to be installed in an application root. Developers creating a new project in Visual Studio often expect their project to be placed in an application when it is deployed to the production server.

ASP.NET 2.0 has several resources that depend on the application boundaries. There are eight folders, plus a couple of files.

The folders are

- ❑ `Bin`
- ❑ `App_Browsers`
- ❑ `App_Code`
- ❑ `App_Data`
- ❑ `App_LocalResources`
- ❑ `App_GlobalResources`
- ❑ `App_Themes`
- ❑ `App_WebReferences`

The files include

- ❑ `web.config`
- ❑ `global.asax`

In addition, there are some common default filenames for various ASP.NET features:

❑ `masterpage.master`

❑ `web.sitemap`

`Bin`, `web.config`, and `global.asax` are the three files and folders that ASP.NET 1.1 is aware of.

Details on these folders are beyond the scope of this book, but it's important to understand their existence and their usage within an application. Each of these files and folders is referenced from the root of the application. Consider the file structure shown in the `Connections` pane in Figure 8-1.

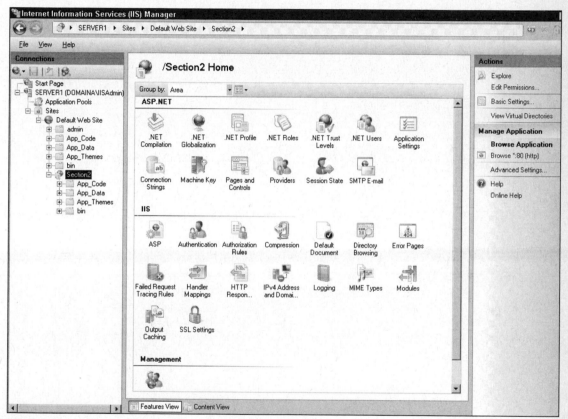

Figure 8-1

Notice that the Default Web Site folder has several subfolders. The `Section2` subfolder has a different icon, which shows that it is a separate application. An ASP.NET page in the root or `/admin` folder will use the root `App_*` folders and `bin` folder from the root. But an ASP.NET page in `/Section2` will use the `App_*` folders and `bin` folder within the `Section2` subfolder. The fact that `Section2` is marked as an application sets it as the application root for all files and folders under it.

web.config can live outside of application roots, but only a limited number of settings will work without throwing an error. ASP.NET allows you to set the scope of each configuration section. For example, the processModel *section can only be set in* machine.config, *and when trying to update a* processModel *setting at the web-site level, it will throw an error. The following four choices are available in the* allowDefinition *attribute of each configuration section:*

❑ Everywhere — Allows the section to be configured in any configuration file, even in a regular physical folder.

❑ MachineToApplication — Allows the section to be configured in any configuration file that is in an application root.

❑ MachineOnly — Allows the section to be configured only in the machine.config file that is in the config folder of the framework version.

❑ MachineToWebRoot — Allows the section to be configured only in the machine.config or root web.config files that are in the config folder of the framework version.

To find out what each section allows, check the machine.config *file and notice the* allowDefinition *attribute of the various* sectionGroup *elements. If the* allowDefinition *is not set, the default is* Everywhere.

Most commonly, an application coincides with a web site, but it can also be a subfolder under a web site that is marked as an application. Throughout this chapter, the term *application* will be used frequently. Keep in mind that this is often also a web-site root, although that is not always the case.

Comparing Virtual Directories to Applications

It is easy to get *virtual directories* and *applications* confused. In IIS 7.0, there is a clearer line of separation between them. This chapter is about applications and application pools, not virtual directories, but before moving on, it's important to understand the differences between them.

An *application* is a logical boundary to separate data and subsections of a site. A *virtual directory* is the actual pointer to a local or remote physical path. A virtual directory must always exist inside an application, but an application can contain multiple virtual directories.

Consider the following section from applicationHost.config:

```
<site name="Default Web Site" id="1">
    <application path="/">
        <virtualDirectory path="/"
            physicalPath="D:\websites\wwwroot" />
    </application>
    <application path="/Section2">
        <virtualDirectory path="/"
            physicalPath="D:\websites\wwwroot\Section2" />
    </application>

    <bindings>
        <binding protocol="http" bindingInformation="*:80:" />
```

```
      </bindings>
   </site>
```

This section shows applications and virtual directories. One application is the Root Application /, and the other is /Section2. Each of these contains a virtualDirectory: one points to D:\websites\wwwroot, which is the site root, and the other points to D:\websites\wwwroot\Section2, which is a second part of the same site. Because these folders are in two different applications, they will not share the application files and folders.

Notice in Figure 8-2 that the DefaultAppPool has both applications listed separately.

It is not required that these applications be in the same application pool. Because they are two separate applications, they don't share InProc session state or the application files or folders. For the sake of making it easier to visualize in this example, they are kept in the same application pool.

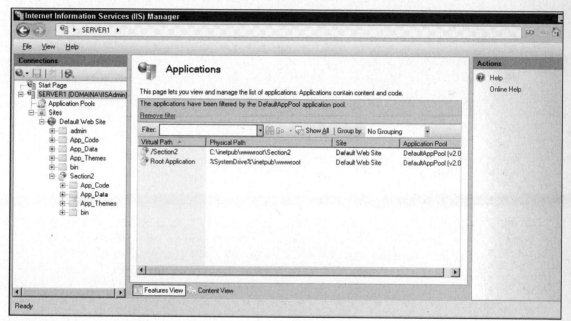

Figure 8-2

The following example further illustrates the difference between an application and a virtual directory:

```
<site name="Default Web Site" id="1">
   <application path="/">
      <virtualDirectory path="/"
         physicalPath="D:\websites\wwwroot" />
      <virtualDirectory path="/Section2"
         physicalPath="D:\elsewhere\Section2" />
   </application>

   <bindings>
      <binding protocol="http" bindingInformation="*:80:" />
```

```
    </bindings>
  </site>
```

Here, there is only one application, but two virtual directories. This means that there is no application boundary between the root of the site and /Section2. A page called /Section2/default.aspx will use the application folders in the root of the site and will ignore the application folders in the /Section2 folder.

There is only one application in the DefaultAppPool now. Notice in Figure 8-3 that the icon in the Connections pane on the Section2 folder is different than the one in Figure 8-1. This is the virtual directory icon and means that it is a virtual directory pointing to a separate physical path, but it inherits the application settings from its parent. Even InProc session state and caching will be shared between the two virtual directories since they are part of the same application.

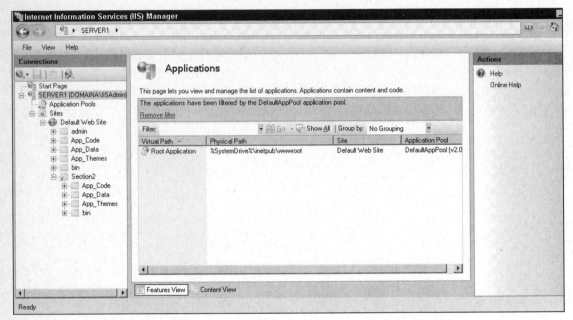

Figure 8-3

Understanding the w3wp.exe Process

Each application pool runs in its own worker process within the operating system so that there is complete separation between application pools. This also allows a specific user identity to be assigned to each worker process for security reasons.

The w3wp.exe worker process runs in user-mode and processes requests, such as static or dynamic content, for each application pool.

There are no hard limits on the amount of application pools that can run on a single server. IIS can handle hundreds of running application pools and thousands of application pools, assuming that not all of them will be running at once. Each application pool has some memory and potentially CPU overhead that together will eventually tax the server beyond a comfortable level. Mileage will vary depending on hardware and the types of sites on the server. An application pool running a static webpage has about 3 MB of memory overhead, while one running a simple ASP.NET page has a base of 10 MB of memory overhead (give or take a couple megabytes). You can use these general numbers to determine how much additional overhead is generated by separating sites into their own application pools. RAM is cheap so, when in doubt, separate them out.

Figure 8-4 shows two w3wp.exe worker processes, one for each of two application pools. The web pages are executed within these processes.

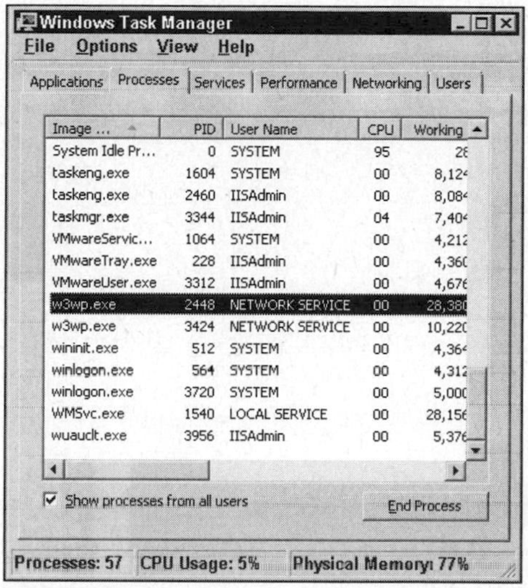

Figure 8-4

A detailed description of the IIS core architecture is outlined in Chapter 2. This section covers how IIS handles recycling application pools.

Recycling Application Pools

Back in the days if IIS 5.0, if there was a failure in a low- or medium-isolation web site, one of the only ways to reset the site was to do a complete reset of IIS. This caused an abrupt stop of IIS, and any page requests that came in during the restart would fail.

IIS 6.0 introduced a revolutionary concept of overlapping processes that allows all incoming requests to continue to be served even when an application pool is recycled. This is still true in IIS 7.0. When an application pool is recycled, the existing w3wp.exe worker process is not immediately killed. Instead, a second worker process is started, and once it is ready, Http.sys will send all new requests to the new worker process. Once the old worker process has completed all requests that it has already received, it will shut down. Because Http.sys handles and queues the incoming requests before handing off to the w3wp.exe process, there is never a page request that is lost during a recycle.

Figure 8-5 illustrates the DefaultAppPool during a recycle. Notice that the old process ID 3920 remains running while the new process ID 3168 is started. It is only when PID 3168 is in the Running state that new requests are sent to it. It's possible for a brief moment to refresh IIS Manager and see process ID 3168 in a Running state and process ID 3920 in a Stopping state.

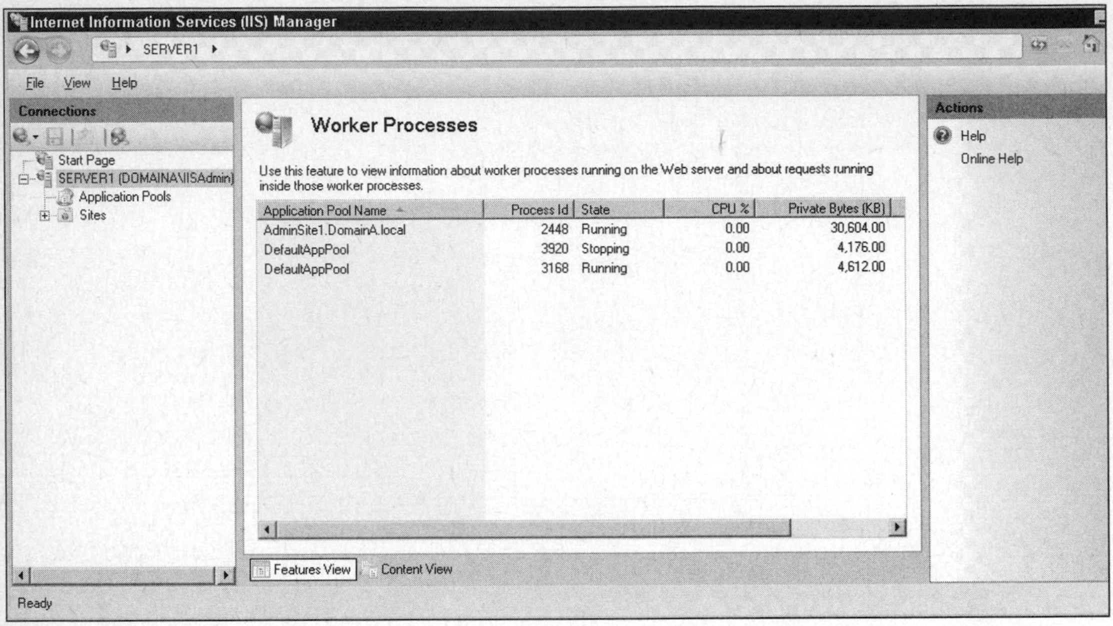

Figure 8-5

Although no page requests are lost or fail during an application pool recycle, there are some possible adverse affects to a recycle. All data that is stored in the worker process will be lost. By default, ASP.NET stores session state and caching data In Process (called InProc). This data lives only as long as the worker process is alive and needs to be created fresh after a recycle. For this reason, it may be worth considering storing the session state out of process in StateServer, SqlServer, or some other external session state store. Additionally, there is a first load performance hit when a new worker process is started. Various aspects of IIS and ASP.NET are pre-loaded into the worker process, which takes a noticeable amount of time to load. This can often take several seconds. The first page that is run after an application recycle will generally take longer to run than after the application pool has already been running.

This overlapping of processes makes administration of IIS so much more powerful than in versions prior to IIS 6.0. This means that an application pool can be recycled with minimal adverse effects, especially if the session state is not used or is stored out of process.

Web Gardens

A web garden is another concept that was introduced in IIS 6.0 and is still in effect in IIS 7.0. This allows multiple worker processes to handle the same application pool.

Figure 8-6 shows three worker processes for DefaultAppPool when the Maximum Worker Processes is set to 3 for this application pool. Recycling the application pool will recycle all three processes.

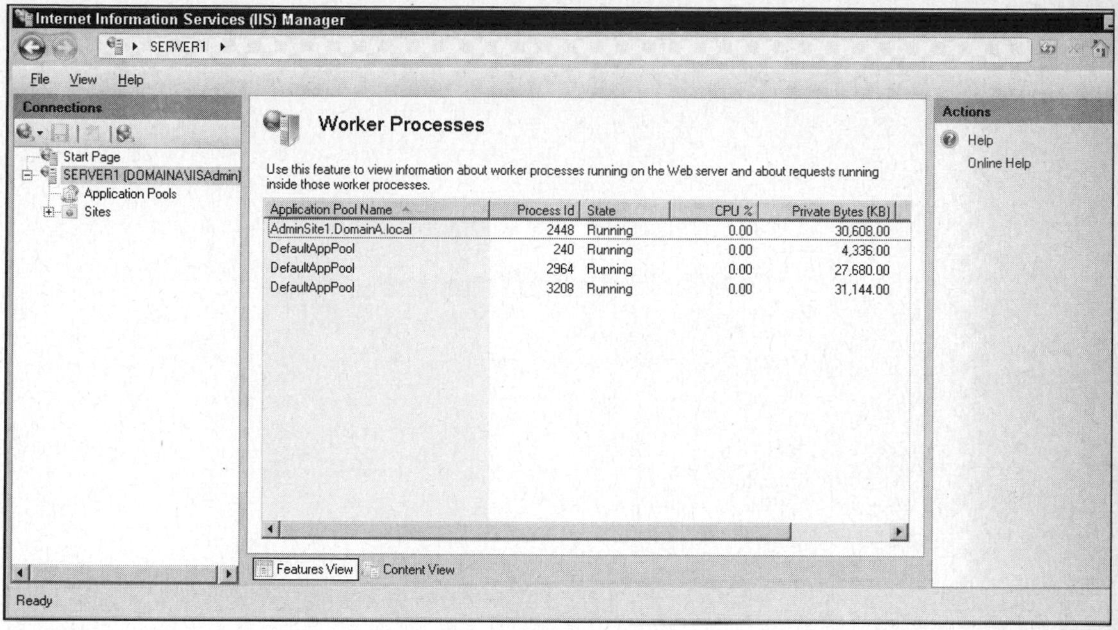

Figure 8-6

A web garden can enhance performance and has the following benefits:

❑ When one worker process is tied up (for example, if it's processing a number of long-running tasks or if it fails), other worker processes can still handle new requests.

❑ It reduces contention for resources. During normal operation, each new page request is assigned to the work processes in a round-robin fashion. This helps smooth out the workloads of the worker processes.

Because a single application is divided across multiple processes, everything that is shared has to be stored out of process. Session state, for example, will not work InProc in a web garden, because there will be multiple copies of the session state, with each process reading and writing to a different session state store.

Some web applications are a better fit for a web garden than others. The following are best-practice guidelines for web gardens:

❑ **The web application should not be CPU-intensive** — Having new CPU-intensive page requests fighting for the CPU with the first page request will cause both to suffer.

❑ **If the application is subject to synchronous high latency, it is a good candidate for a web garden** — For example, if the application calls a web service or a remote database and the response is slow, then a web garden will allow other requests to be processed while waiting for the long-running applications to complete.

❑ **Each process has memory overhead and takes extra time to start** — Having too many can quickly use up resources on a server.

Web gardens and web farms are completely different concepts, although they share some common characteristics. A web garden is composed of multiple processes on a single server handling the same application pool, whereas a web farm is composed of multiple servers working together to provide high availability or better scalability.

To set the web garden settings, modify the Maximum Worker Processes attribute in the application's Advanced Settings window (see Figure 8-7). Changing the advanced settings of an application pool is covered in depth below in this chapter.

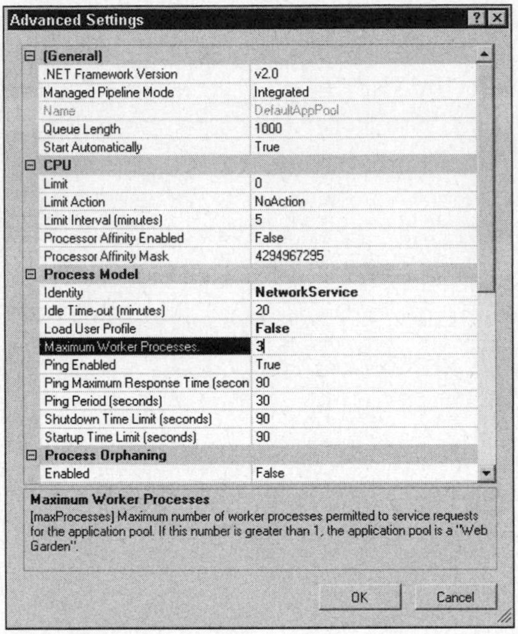

Figure 8-7

Working with Application Pools

Effectively creating and managing an application pool generally involves four steps.

1. Create the application pool.

2. Configure any advanced settings that are required.

3. Assign a web site or application to the newly created application pool.

4. Manage active application pools.

Creating Application Pools

You can create an application pool in IIS Manager by completing the following steps:

1. Open IIS Manager: click Start, enter **inetmgr** in the dialog, and then press OK.

2. Select the Application Pools section from the Connections pane.

3. Click "Add Application Pool…" in the Actions pane. Alternately, right-click the Application Pools heading or a blank area in the main pane (see Figure 8-8) and select Add Application Pool.

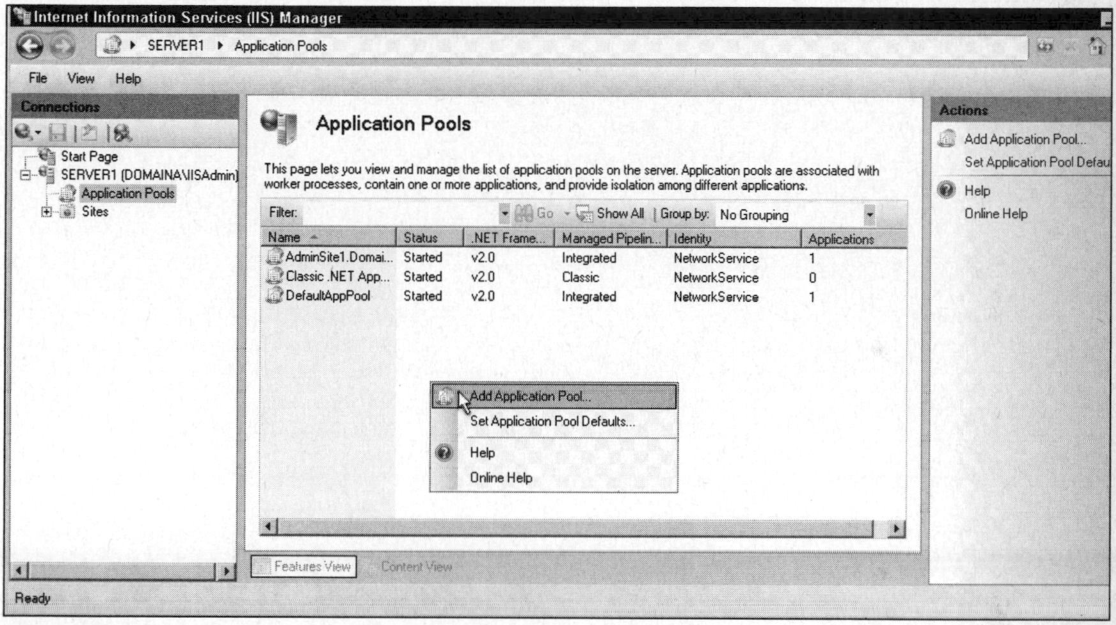

Figure 8-8

4. Enter the name of the new application pool into the Name field (see Figure 8-9).

5. Select the .NET Framework version, or select No Managed Code.

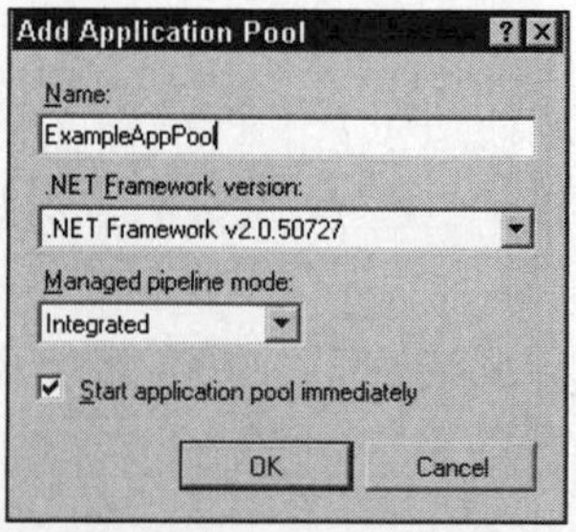

Figure 8-9

6. Set the Managed pipeline mode to Integrated or Classic. The Integrated mode is the default. Further discussion of these two modes is covered in Chapter 2.

7. Click OK.

There are additional advanced settings that may be required, but these are set later and detailed in the following section.

Alternately, you can also create an applications pool by using `AppCmd.exe`. The following example creates a new application pool, sets the managed runtime version to ASP.NET v1.1, and sets the pipeline mode to Classic. The last two properties are optional; `AppCmd.exe` can create a new application pool with just the `/name` property (this must be run on one line as a single command).

```
appcmd.exe add apppool /name:"ExampleAppPool" -managedRuntimeVersion:v1.1
-managedPipelineMode:Classic
```

Additional code examples are provided in the next section.

Managing Settings

Simply creating an application pool may not be enough. Changing the application pool user, for example, may be required to properly configure a server. IIS 6.0 had a single dialog box that enabled you to configure all application pool settings. This has changed in IIS 7.0 such that there are three configuration boxes used in IIS Manager to manage additional features: Basic Settings, Recycling, and Advanced Settings. You can access all three tools from either the Links in the Actions section or by right-clicking on the application pool and selecting the appropriate link (see Figure 8-10).

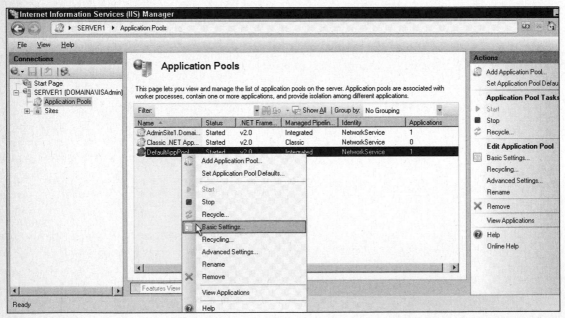

Figure 8-10

1. **Basic Settings** — The Basic Settings configuration box is the same as the one used to create the application pool. This allows editing of the framework version, pipeline mode, and whether or not the application pool should start automatically. Note that the name cannot be edited after it is created; it is in read-only mode here. Both the framework version and the pipeline mode can be edited at any time for any application pool.

2. **Recycling** — This tool is a two-step wizard (see Figure 8-11). Step one enables you to change settings like the automatic recycling intervals or times. After you have made the appropriate changes to this step, click Next, which brings you to step two of the wizard.

   The second step of the wizard enables you to configure Event Viewer logging. Here you have the ability to turn on logging for settings like on-demand recycling or when the application pool notices an unhealthy ISAPI program.

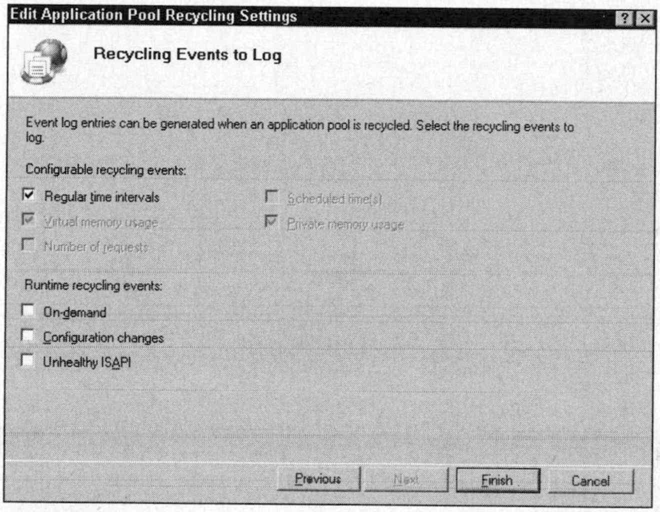

Figure 8-11

3. **Advanced Settings** — The third tool to manage the application pool settings is the Advanced Settings tool (see Figure 8-12). Here you can set many of the more advanced properties for the application pool. Everything that can be done in the other two tools can be done here as well. In fact, this tool allows you to set multiple times of the day to recycle the application tool while the Recycle tool itself only allows one.

Be sure to take note of the + and – icons beside each section, as some default to expanded and some default to collapsed.

One handy feature is a brief description of each property in the bottom of the box when a property is selected. This saves you from calling the Help file separately for a summary of each property.

There are a limited number of properties that cannot be set from IIS Manager that can be set from the command line, but almost everything you need to manage an application pool can be done from here.

Most noteworthy is the Process Model ⇨ Identity settings. Here you can change the identity under which the application pool runs. This is discussed at length below in this chapter. The identity field is not a simple property box like most of the others. Instead, it has an ellipsis button to allow you to set the identity of the application pool.

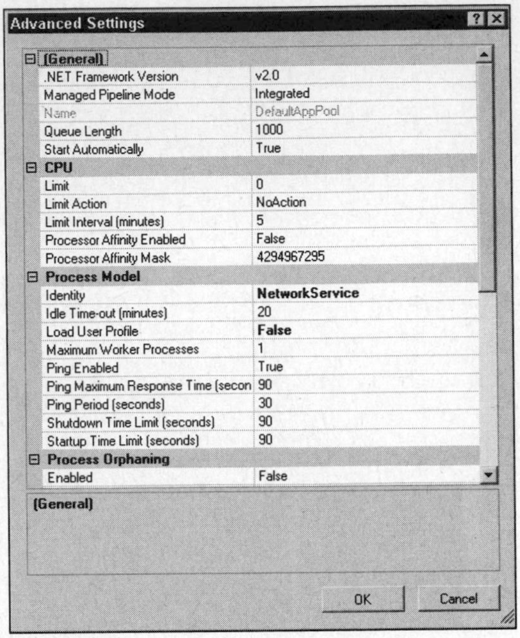

Figure 8-12

Like most everything else, changing the application pool settings can be done from the command line or code. Here it's helpful to be able to see a complete list of properties available in AppCmd.exe.

> IIS 7.0 has been well planned, and everything that is done in the IIS Manager tool uses the same back-end APIs as AppCmd.exe and Microsoft.Web.Administration use. In addition, the schema files in %windir%\system32\inetsrv\config\schema are used by all of these tools; thus, IntelliSense and the /?help in AppCmd.exe are guaranteed to give the complete list of properties. Thanks, IIS 7.0 team!

To get a complete list of additional properties that are available using the AppCmd.exe tool, use the following command. The full list of properties will not show up unless you enter the application pool name.

```
appcmd.exe set AppPool "DefaultAppPool" /?
```

Here is a sample of the properties available:

❑   -queueLength

❑   -autoStart

❑   -enable32BitAppOnWin64

❑   -managedRuntimeVersion

- ❑   -managedPipelineMode
- ❑   -passAnonymousToken
- ❑   -processModel.identityType
- ❑   -processModel.userName
- ❑   -processModel.password
- ❑   -processModel.loadUserProfile
- ❑   -processModel.manualGroupMembership
- ❑   -processModel.idleTimeout
- ❑   -processModel.maxProcesses

Notice that there are primary application pool properties and there are properties of elements delimited by a dot (.). You can enter as many properties as you want in a single command. For example, to turn off the IdleTimeout setting and enable logging of manual application pool recycles, run the following:

```
appcmd.exe set apppool "DefaultAppPool"
-processModel.idleTimeout:"00:00:00"
-recycling.logEventOnRecycle:"PrivateMemory, OnDemand, Memory, Time"
```

Sometimes it's difficult to know the format of a particular parameter. Neither parameter in this example is straightforward. An easy way to find out the syntax is to make the change using IIS Manager and then open applicationHost.config *in Notepad or your favorite editor and view the result. This will often give an easy answer to the formatting of the parameter and value.*

Following is how you can use Microsoft.Web.Administration to create an application pool and set a couple of properties:

```
Dim appPool As String = "ExampleAppPool"
Dim sm As ServerManager = New ServerManager
sm.ApplicationPools.Add(appPool)

sm.ApplicationPools(appPool).ManagedRuntimeVersion = "v2.0"
sm.ApplicationPools(appPool).ProcessModel.PingingEnabled = False

sm.CommitChanges()
```

Using WMI, after you have created an application pool, you can set additional properties, as follows:

```
strAppPool = "ExampleAppPool"

Set oService = GetObject("winmgmts:root\WebAdministration")

'create the app pool
oService.Get("ApplicationPool").Create strAppPool, True

'get the app pool instance
Set oAppPool = oService.Get("ApplicationPool.Name='" & strAppPool & "'")

'set a property
oAppPool.Enable32BitAppOnWin64 = True
```

```
'commit them
oAppPool.Put_
```

Creating an application pool in `applicationHost.config` is quite straightforward. It gets more complex when you need to create virtual directories. Within the `applicationPools` section, add an element with at least the `name` attribute set. All other settings are optional.

```
<system.applicationHost>

    <applicationPools>
        ...
        <add name="ExampleAppPool"
            enable32BitAppOnWin64="true">
            <processModel identityType="SpecificUser"
                userName="IISAdminUser" password="..." />
            <recycling disallowOverlappingRotation="true" />
        </add>
        <applicationPoolDefaults>
            <processModel identityType="NetworkService" />
        </applicationPoolDefaults>
    </applicationPools>
        ...
</system.applicationHost>
```

Assigning Applications and Sites to Application Pools

After you have created an application pool, you can assign any number of web sites or applications to it. Remember that the application pool sets the .NET Framework version that will be used; therefore, all applications in the same pool must be running the same version of .NET.

Applications are assigned to the application pool at the site or application level. This is done from either the Basic Settings or Advanced Settings tool in IIS Manager. Figure 8-13 shows the application pool setting from the Advanced Settings tool. Because the application pool is central to specifying the framework version and pipeline mode, IIS 7.0 allows the administrator to see these current settings while selecting the application pool.

Three Folder Right-Click Choices

In IIS Manager, if you right-click on a folder, you are given three choices that can be somewhat confusing. Figure 8-14 shows the three choices: Convert to Application, Add Application, and Add Virtual Directory. With these three options, you can mark an existing folder as an application or create a new virtual directory, which is either a simple virtual directory or one that is marked as an application.

It's worth reviewing the differences among these three choices.

❑ **Convert to Application** — This option will convert the folder that you right-clicked into an application. It does not allow you to set the alias name or the physical path, as these are derived from the folder you chose. Figure 8-15 shows the dialog box. Within the Add Application dialog box, you can select the "Application pool," set the "Connect as" user credentials, and click the Test Settings button to have IIS Manager run a test against the folder. This process is commonly called "Marking a folder as an application" and creates a new application boundary for your

.NET application. It's important to note that the application pool will default to the one set in the `<applicationDefaults />` tag, not the one used by the site. This confuses a lot of people because it doesn't default to what you may assume.

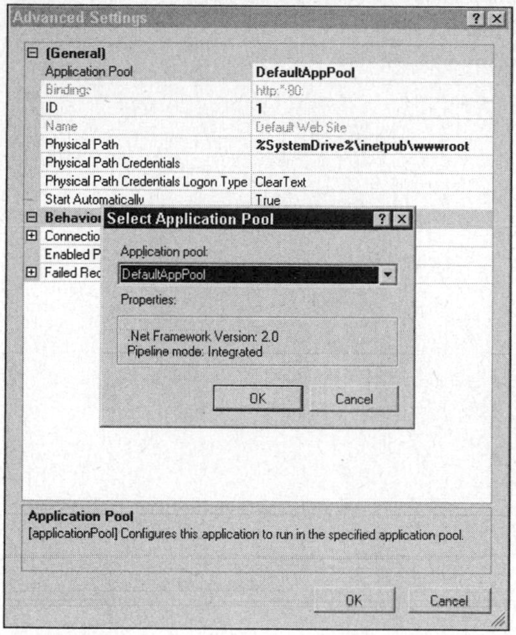

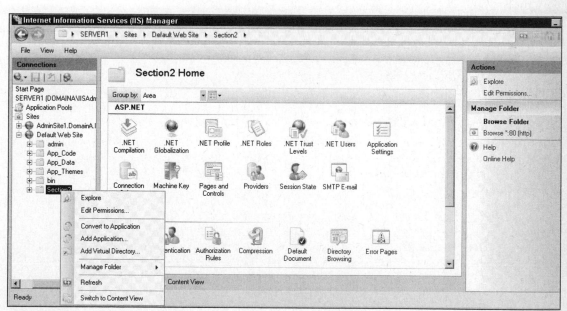

Figure 8-13

Figure 8-14

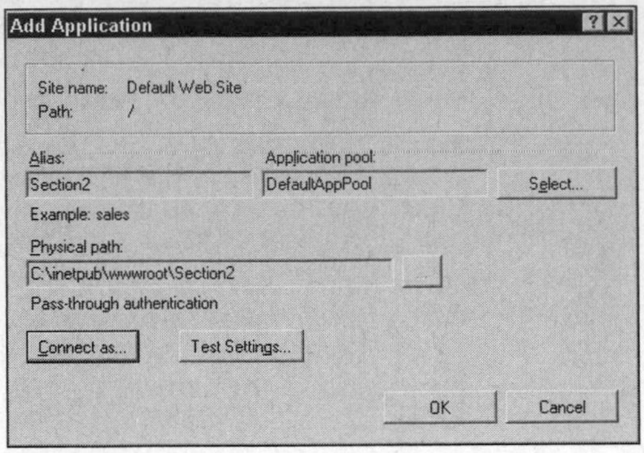

Figure 8-15

❑ **Add Application** — The second option allows you to create a new application, but unlike the Convert to Application option, it requires you to enter the alias and physical path fields. This is essentially the Convert to Application option plus the Add Virtual Directory option combined. It will create a virtual directory and mark it as an application. Figure 8-16 shows this Add Application dialog box. Notice that Convert to Application (Figure 8-15) and Add Application (Figure 8-16) share the same Add Application dialog box, but they use it differently.

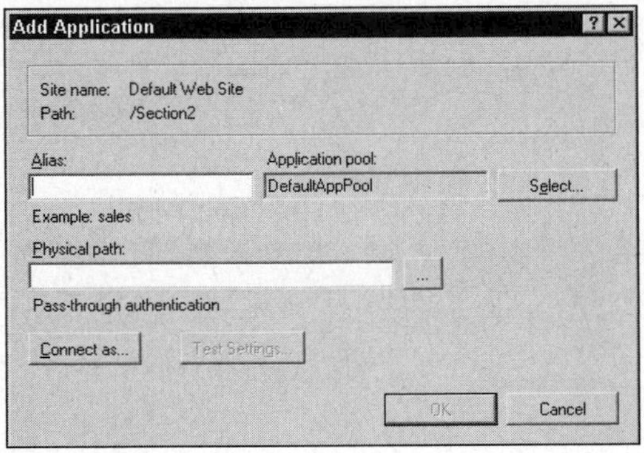

Figure 8-16

❑ **Add Virtual Directory** — The third option will create a virtual directory, but it will not set it as an application. Figure 8-17 shows the Add Virtual Directory dialog box. Notice that it does not have the option to select the application pool. This is because the virtual directory will be in the same application and share the same code folders and application boundaries as its parent folder.

It's interesting to note that the Convert to Application option will affect the folder that you right-clicked on, but the other two options will create a new virtual directory *under* the folder that you right-clicked on. This is because the latter two options create a new object instead of affecting an existing one.

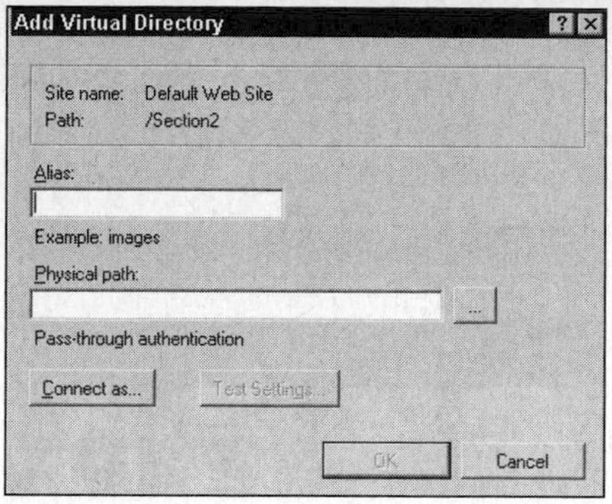

Figure 8-17

AppCmd Method

Changing the application pool with AppCmd.exe differs from what you might expect. If the application already exists, it is simply a matter of using the set site command to update the applicationPool property.

```
appcmd.exe set site "Default Web Site"
-[path='/'].applicationPool:"Classic .NET AppPool"
```

It gets more complex when the application doesn't already exist. A web-site root is already an application, but a subfolder that hasn't been touched yet is not an application or a virtual directory. Before setting the subfolder's application pool, you must first set the subfolder as an application. This is done using the add app command in AppCmd.exe:

```
appcmd.exe add app /site.name:"Default Web Site" /path:/ExampleSubDir
/physicalPath:c:\inetpub\wwwroot\defaultroot\examplesubdir
-applicationPool:DefaultAppPool
```

This will create an application and a virtual directory.

applicationHost.config

Take a look at the XML created in the applicationHost.config file:

```
<sites>
    <site name="Default Web Site" id="1">
        <application path="/ExampleSubDir"
            applicationPool="DefaultAppPool">
            <virtualDirectory path="/"
physicalPath="c:\inetpub\wwwroot\defaultroot\examplesubdir" />
        </application>
    </site>
    ...
    <applicationDefaults applicationPool="DefaultAppPool" />
    ...
</sites>
```

An `application` element is added to the `site` element. The `path` attribute of the `application` element is the relative path from the root of the site. In this case, it is `/ExampleSubDir`. The `applicationPool` attribute is optional; if left out, it will inherit from the `<applicationDefaults />` tag, not from its parent's settings as you may assume. The `<applicationDefaults />` tag is also in the `<sites />` section.

Next, you need to create a virtual directory. Without it, the configuration is invalid. The virtualDirectory path is relative to the application path, thus in this case it should be set to /. The physical path is also required, which adds some complexity when setting a folder as an application.

The `physicalPath` must be a physical path on disk, or a UNC path. A relative path will not work. You can obtain the physical path using `AppCmd.exe` or code by getting the path to the root of the site and appending the subfolder name to it. In `AppCmd.exe` you can get the physical path to a folder using the following command:

```
appcmd.exe list vdir "Site1/"
```

This will list all of the virtual directories for the Site1 site, as seen in the following output:

```
VDIR "Site1/" (physicalPath:C:\inetpub\Site1)
```

VDIR "Site1/App1" (physicalPath:C:\inetpub\Site1\App1). With this path, you can piece it together to mark the folder as an application. Notice with this example that the site requires the trailing "/"; otherwise, it will not return anything, not even an error message.

Microsoft.Web.Administration

The same concept applies to managed code as it does to `AppCmd.exe`. If the folder has not had a unique setting applied to it yet, then it must be created before the application pool can be set. Then the application can be assigned an application pool.

```
Dim subdir As String = "/ExampleSubDir"
Dim path As String = "c:\inetpub\wwwroot\defaultroot\examplesubdir"

Dim sm As ServerManager = New ServerManager

'Create the application
sm.Sites("Default Web Site").Applications.Add(subdir, path)
'Assign the application to an application pool
sm.Sites("Default Web Site").Applications( _
    subdir.ApplicationPoolName = "DefaultAppPool"
sm.CommitChanges()
```

Specifying the .NET Framework Version

If the web server hosts ASP.NET web sites, key parts of the .NET run time are loaded into the worker process when the w3wp.exe process is started. They include all the assemblies specific to that particular application, an `HttpRuntime` object, and a cache object, among other things. Because these are specific to a particular version of the framework, only one version can exist in each application pool.

This wasn't an issue in IIS 5.0 because ASP.NET lived in a separate process called `aspnet_wp.exe`. This shared process had a different set of disadvantages, but it happened to be easier to maintain.

It was in IIS 6.0 that the concept of pre-loading the .NET runtime into the `w3wp.exe` worker process began. An issue arises if you have multiple web sites or applications that have different versions of .NET assigned to them. If these are placed in the same application pool, there would be failures with one or both versions of the framework.

The solution in IIS 6.0 was to ensure that each application pool had applications that used one, and only one, version of the .NET Framework. IIS 6.0 did not have a good way to manage this or warn the administrator of this issue. Event Viewer would give a helpful recommendation after the failure, but for the average administrator, it was easy to miss and difficult to understand what was happening.

In IIS 7.0, it is now IIS itself that manages which version of the framework is loaded into the application pool worker process. When you are setting up or editing an application pool, the dialog box shown in Figure 8-18 enables you to select which version of the .NET Framework is set for that application pool. All installed versions of the framework are listed, as well as No Managed Code, which ensures that ASP.NET is not loaded at all.

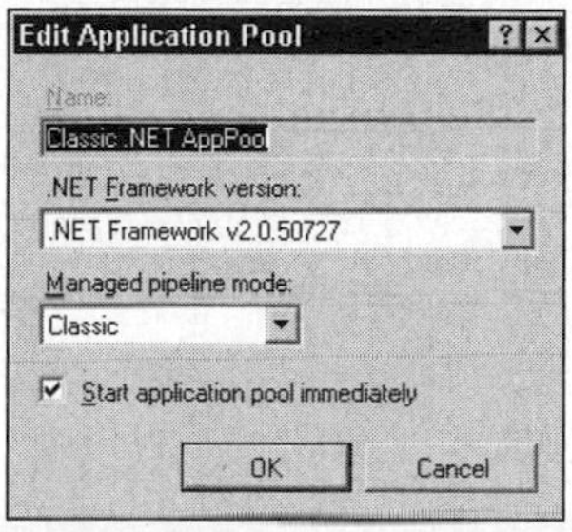

Figure 8-18

You can change the framework version for an application pool from `AppCmd.exe` as follows:

```
appcmd.exe set apppool "AppPool1"
-managedRuntimeVersion:v2.0
```

This will change the application pool AppPool1 to use ASP.NET version 2.0.

Using `Microsoft.Web.Administration` in Visual Basic .NET, it can be done as

```
Dim appPool As String = "ExampleAppPool"
Dim runtimeVersion as String = "v2.0"

Dim sm As ServerManager = New ServerManager
sm.ApplicationPools(appPool).ManagedRuntimeVersion = _
    runtimeVersion
sm.CommitChanges()
```

This accomplishes the same as the AppCmd.exe example but uses the managed API instead. The example is straightforward, essentially declaring and setting the appPool and runtimeVersion; setting the runtime version for the application pool; and then committing the changes.

Here is an example of how to accomplish the same using WMI:

```
' set values for the application pool and runtime version
strAppPool = "DefaultAppPool"
strRuntimeVersion = "v2.0"

' Set oIIS and oAppPool
Set oIIS = GetObject("winmgmts:root\WebAdministration")
Set oAppPool = oIIS.Get("ApplicationPool.Name='" _
    & strAppPool & "'")

' Set the ManagedRuntimeVersion and commit the changes
oAppPool.ManagedRuntimeVersion = strRuntimeVersion
oAppPool.Put_
```

The .config XML method can be done by modifying the managedRuntimeVersion attribute in the add element of applicationPools:

```
<applicationPools>
    ...
    <add name="ExampleAppPool" managedRuntimeVersion="v2.0" >
    ...
    </add>
    ...
</applicationPools>
```

Specifying the Managed Pipeline Mode

IIS 7.0 supports two pipeline modes: the Integrated mode, which is new in IIS 7.0, and the Classic mode, which models previous versions of IIS. This choice is made at the application pool level, which is great for an IIS administrator because it allows one or both modes to run on the same server. In Chapter 2, "IIS 7.0 Architecture," the two modes are explained in more depth.

There are significant web.config differences between the two modes, and many web.config files that work in Classic mode will not work in Integrated mode. AppCmd.exe offers an automated method to migrate configuration files from Classic mode to Integrated mode format. This will be covered below.

First, it is worthwhile to see the structure of each mode and the differences between them.

Classic Mode

The Classic mode models the IIS 6.0 model in which ASP.NET is an ISAPI add-on to IIS. This mode is available for backward compatibility but lacks many of the features in the new Integrated mode. In Classic mode, IIS has its own pipeline that can only be extended by creating an ISAPI extension, which has a well-deserved reputation for being difficult to develop. ASP.NET is run as an ISAPI extension that is just one part of the IIS pipeline.

This is best visualized by looking at Figure 8-19. Notice that ASP.NET appears to be an afterthought and doesn't come into play until IIS processes the ISAPI extensions.

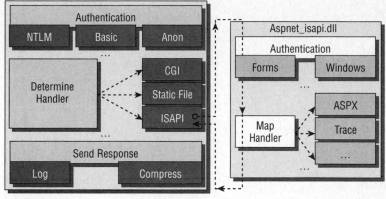

Figure 8-19

The file extension determines which ISAPI handler to use. For example, .aspx and .ascx are two of the file extensions mapped to aspnet_isapi.dll. The .asp extension is mapped to asp.dll to handle classic ASP pages, and if installed, the .php extension is mapped to php.dll to handle PHP pages.

Additionally, in IIS 6.0 and IIS 7.0 Classic mode, several features are duplicated. For example, error handling is a duplicate feature where IIS handles non-ASP.NET pages and ASP.NET handles all pages mapped to aspnet_isapi.dll.

> *It's possible to map all file extensions to ASP.NET in IIS 6.0, but there are some limitations. The most noticeable is that default documents are not processed unless they are specifically handled in* `global.asax` *or an HTTP module. There is a reasonable amount of custom configuration required to have aspnet_isapi.dll successfully handle all file types. IIS 7.0 handles this without any additional effort.*

Classic mode will run existing web sites without requiring changes to `web.config`. So if you have a web farm with mixed IIS 6.0 and IIS 7.0 servers, or if you have others reasons why you can't migrate the web.config file to the new syntax, then Classic mode may be a valid option for you.

Integrated Mode

Integrated mode makes ASP.NET an integral part of IIS. Now the IIS server functionality is split into more than 40 modules that break the IIS and ASP.NET functionality into pieces. Modules such as StaticFileModule, BasicAuthenticationModule, FormsAuthentication, Session, Profile, and RoleManager are part of the IIS pipeline. Notice that FormsAuthentication, Session, Profile, and RoleManager were previously part of ASP.NET and didn't have anything to do with IIS.

Figure 8-20 shows the IIS pipeline with modules that were previously part of ASP.NET but are now directly part of the IIS pipeline.

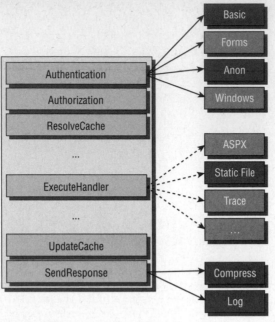

Figure 8-20

The IIS pipeline has more than twenty events that developers can easily tap into to extend the functionality of the web server. In fact, the modules that are included with IIS 7.0 can be replaced simply by creating custom modules and updating `applicationHost.config` to use the custom module instead of the ones provided by Microsoft.

Configuration Differences between Modes

IIS 7.0 brings with it several configuration file changes that are applicable to the web developer. The `<system.webServer>` is a new section that is recognized in either Classic mode or Integrated mode and can be set in `applicationHost.config` or in a `web.config` file. This section controls static pages as well as dynamic pages. Even in Classic mode, this section is honored and gives the ability for the web developer to set various IIS configuration settings in the `web.config` file.

In Integrated mode, the HTTP modules and HTTP handlers are moved from `<system.web>` to `<system.webServer>`. If you run a `web.config` file that contains HTTP modules or HTTP handlers in Integrated mode, it will fail. Fortunately, Microsoft has created a detailed 500.22 error message that will give steps to migrate the `web.config` file (see Figure 8-21).

`AppCmd.exe` is the tool that Microsoft provides to make this migration painless. To migrate the `web.config` file on the Default Web Site, run the following `AppCmd.exe` command:

```
AppCmd.exe migrate config "Default Web Site/"
```

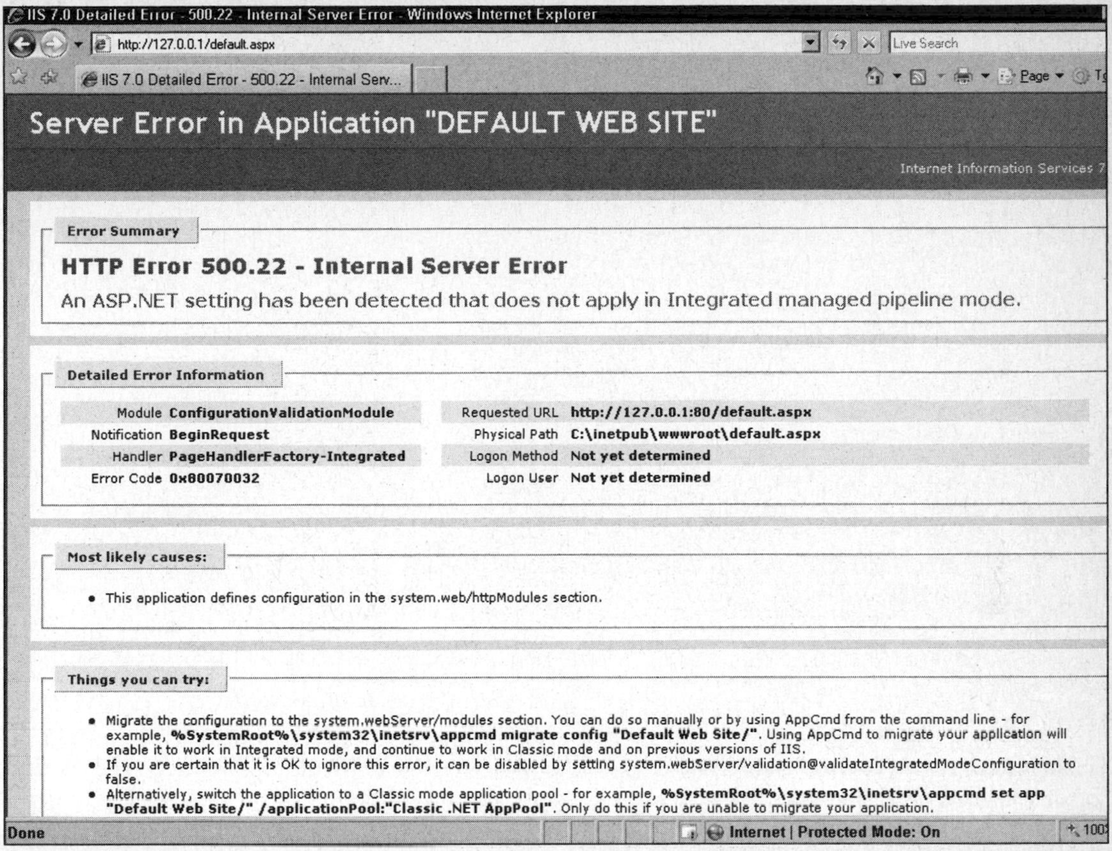

Figure 8-21

Here is an example of a web.config file that works in Classic mode and IIS 6.0:

```
<?xml version="1.0" encoding="utf-8" ?>
<configuration>

    <system.web>
        <httpModules>
            <add type="classname, assemblyname"
            name="modulename" />
        </httpModules>
    </system.web>

</configuration>
```

After you run the AppCmd.exe migrate config command, the web.config file is updated to look like the following:

```
<?xml version="1.0" encoding="utf-8" ?>
<configuration>
```

```
    <system.web>
      <httpModules>
        <add type="classname,
          assemblyname" name="modulename" />
      </httpModules>
    </system.web>
    <system.webServer>
        <modules>
            <add name="modulename"
                type="classname, assemblyname"
                preCondition="managedHandler" />
        </modules>
        <validation
            validateIntegratedModeConfiguration="false" />
    </system.webServer>

  </configuration>
```

Notice that the `httpModules` section was left in place for backward compatibility, but it is the `modules` section in `system.webServer` that will take precedence. The `validateIntegratedMode Configuration` attribute ensures that IIS doesn't complain about the legacy `<httpModules>` section.

Integrated mode is the default mode and has several significant advantages. Just be sure to migrate any existing `web.config` files that have HTTP handlers and HTTP modules so that they run correctly under IIS 7.0.

Managing Active Application Pools

Creating and updating the settings of application pools is only the start. Managing active application pools is essential to effectively managing an IIS server. As mentioned above, each running application pool starts at least one new and separate `w3wp.exe` worker process. If web gardens are enabled, more than one worker process can exist per application pool. IIS and the Windows operating system allow the administrator to view and manage these processes.

More about this is covered in Chapter 20, "Diagnostics and Troubleshooting," but common ways to view running worker processes are covered here.

Viewing Running Processes in IIS 7.0

New in IIS 7.0, the running worker processes can be viewed within IIS Manager (see Figure 8-22).

Once an application pool stops because of a reboot, restart of the IIS service, or the idle time-out reached, a new worker process is not started again until the first page request. When the first page request is made, a worker process is started. This means that there isn't always a worker process for every application pool.

To view the worker processes, in IIS Manager, click the server name and double-click Worker Processes in the IIS section.

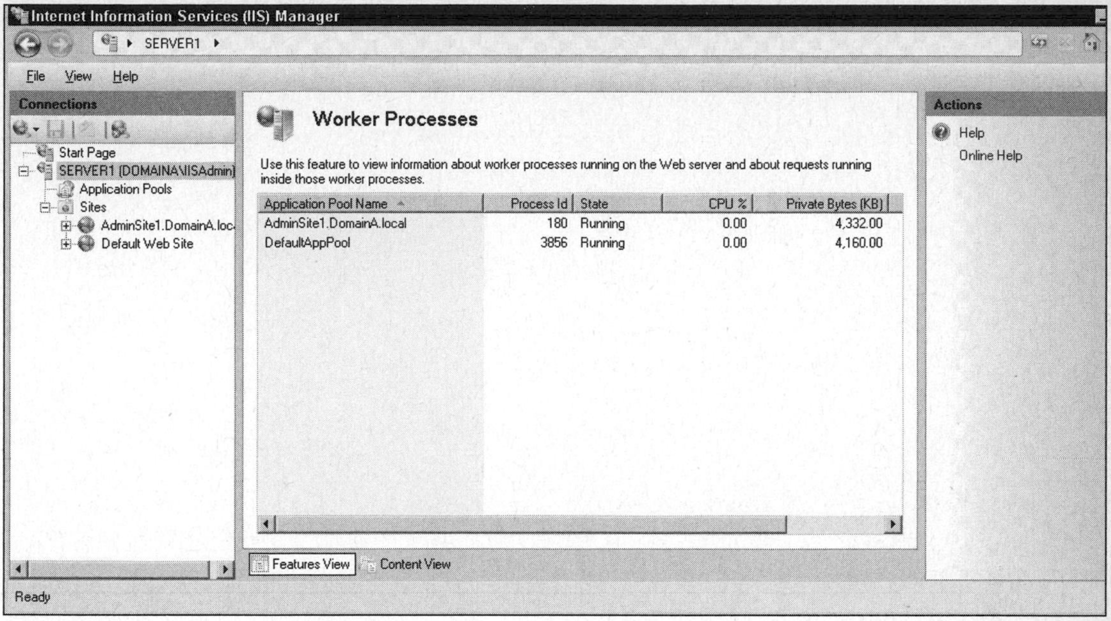

Figure 8-22

The following values are worth noting:

❑ **Process ID** — This is the Process ID (PID) of the worker process on the server. Task Manager will show this same number if the PID column is enabled.

❑ **State** — This shows the current status of the worker process (Stopping, Stopped, Starting, Started, or Unknown).

❑ **CPU %** — This is the CPU % at that instant in time. You can press F5 to refresh the display.

❑ **Private Bytes (KB)** — It's important to understand what this is. This is the allocated physical bytes that the operating system has reserved for that worker process. This is the current size of memory that this process has allocated that cannot be shared with other processes. This corresponds to the "Commit Size" column in Task Manager. Note that the Commit Size column is not shown by default. The application pool can be set to recycle if this value is exceeded.

❑ **Virtual Bytes (KB)** — The current size of the virtual address space that the process is using. There is no equivalent column in Task Manager in Windows Server 2008, although Performance Monitor will expose this information by selecting the Process object, the appropriate w3wp worker process, and the Virtual Bytes counter. The value in IIS Manager is in kilobytes, whereas the one in Performance Monitor is in bytes, so make sure to multiply or divide by 1024 so that you are comparing apples to apples. The application pool can be set to recycle if this value is exceeded.

Viewing Running Processes in Task Manager

Task Manager is a powerful tool to quickly find key information about a computer. To open it, right-click on an open place in the taskbar, and click Task Manager. The Processes tab shows a list of all running processes (see Figure 8-23). IIS will usually be running under a different user than the currently logged-in user, so click "Show processes from all users" in the bottom left-hand side of the window. Now find all w3wp.exe processes. These are the worker process for each application pool which correspond to IIS Manager values.

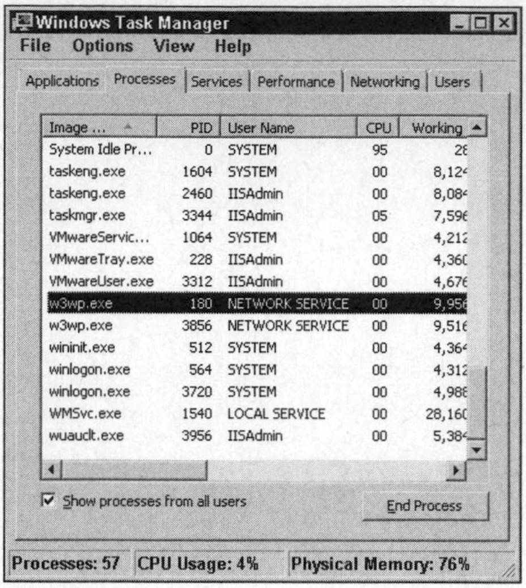

Figure 8-23

By default, the PID column is not displayed. That is worth enabling the first time Task Manager is opened on a computer. This change will remain in effect until it is purposely disabled. To do this:

1. Click View ➪ Columns.

2. Check the checkbox beside PID.

3. Click OK.

Now the PID column is visible. If each application pool runs under a different user, the User Name column gives a good clue as to which process belongs to which application pool.

> In IIS 6.0, there was a tool called IISApp.vbs that could help match PIDs with application pool names. IISApp.vbs is no longer available as it has been replaced with AppCmd.exe.

Viewing Running Processes using AppCmd.exe

AppCmd.exe will display actively running processes on the computer, along with the PID and application pool name (see Figure 8-24).

```
appcmd.exe list wp
```

It is helpful to use either IIS Manager or AppCmd.exe along with Task Manager to get a good idea of the running state of the application pool worker processes on a system. Using two or three of the tools together will allow you to match up the PID with the application pool name, then view various performance counters available in each tool.

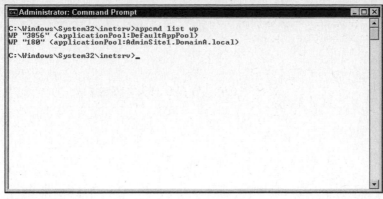

Figure 8-24

Performance Monitor is another valuable tool to troubleshoot worker process information and is covered in Chapter 20, "Diagnostics and Troubleshooting."

Viewing Running Page Requests

Not only can you view the active worker processes, something that you could do in IIS 6.0 using Task Manager, but in IIS 7.0, you can see the currently running page requests. This is a welcome new feature in IIS 7.0, something that was very difficult to gain access to in previous versions of IIS. Chapter 20, "Diagnostics and Troubleshooting," covers this in more depth, but a short walkthrough is given here.

To view the currently running page requests:

1. Start at the server level, and double-click the Worker Processes icon. This will show all currently running worker processes, as described in the "Viewing Running Processes in IIS 7.0" section above.

2. Double-click on the worker process for the application pool that you want to see the currently running page requests for. This will bring you to the Requests page, which will show all currently running pages (see Figure 8-25).

The Requests page is a list of all currently running processes. If the page completes in subsecond times, it is hard to catch it unless there are many running at a time, but for slow-running pages, this is a great tool to see what is running at any given time.

Starting, Stopping, and Recycling Application Pools

Application pools can be started, stopped, or recycled. There are several reasons that an application pool should be stopped or recycled. Reasons include requiring a fresh start because of a memory leak, a runaway site that is affecting performance on other sites, wanting to restart an application after a significant configuration change, or a multitude of other factors.

As mentioned above, recycling an application pool doesn't immediately kill an existing process unless all running pages have been completed or the shutdown time limit period has elapsed. In the case of a long running page that is consuming excessive CPU, it may be necessary to kill the w3wp.exe *worker process directly to have an immediate impact. This is a last resort measure but it will not hurt other worker processes and, depending on the situation, may be for the better good of the server. As explained in the last section, you can check the currently running page requests to see what is causing a worker process to stay alive after a recycle.*

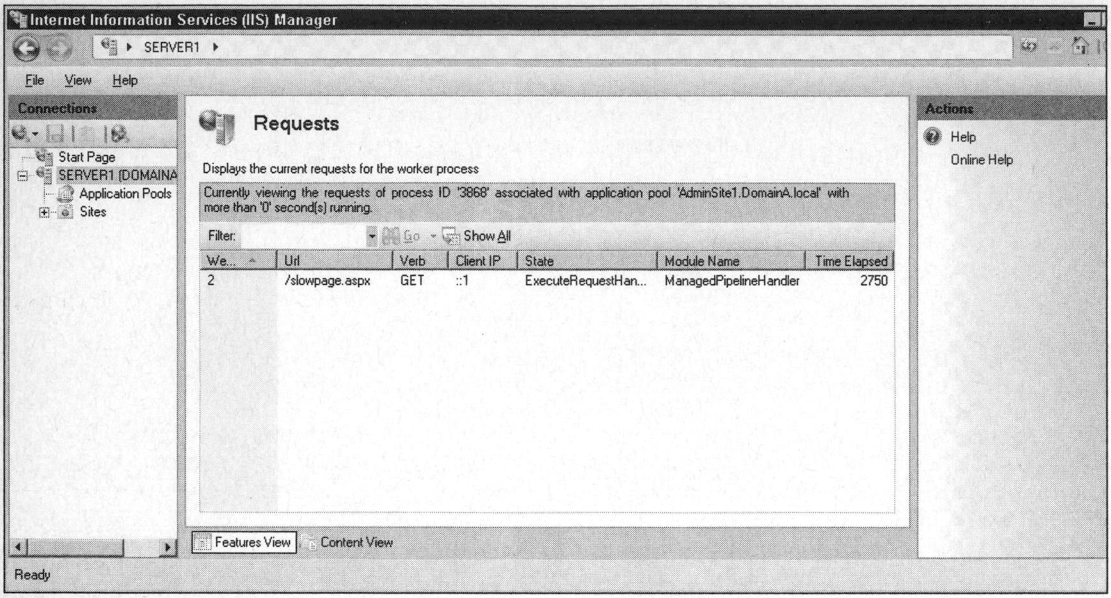

Figure 8-25

Recycling, stopping, or starting an application pool in IIS Manager is a breeze. There are two methods that work equally well. One is to right-click on the application pool and use the dropdown box to take the desired action (see Figure 8-26). The other is to select the application and use the Application Pool Tasks in the Actions pane.

AppCmd.exe is straightforward as well. The AppPool object is used instead of the WP object in this case.

```
appcmd.exe recycle apppool "DefaultAppPool"
appcmd.exe stop apppool "DefaultAppPool"
appcmd.exe start apppool "DefaultAppPool"
```

This can be done from managed code as well, using the Recycle, Start, or Stop method of the ApplicationPools object. The following example shows how to recycle an application pool. Starting or stopping an application pool is just as easy. Simply replace Recycle() with Start() or Stop(), as required.

```
Dim apppool As String = "DefaultAppPool"

Dim sm As ServerManager = New ServerManager
sm.ApplicationPools(apppool).Recycle()
```

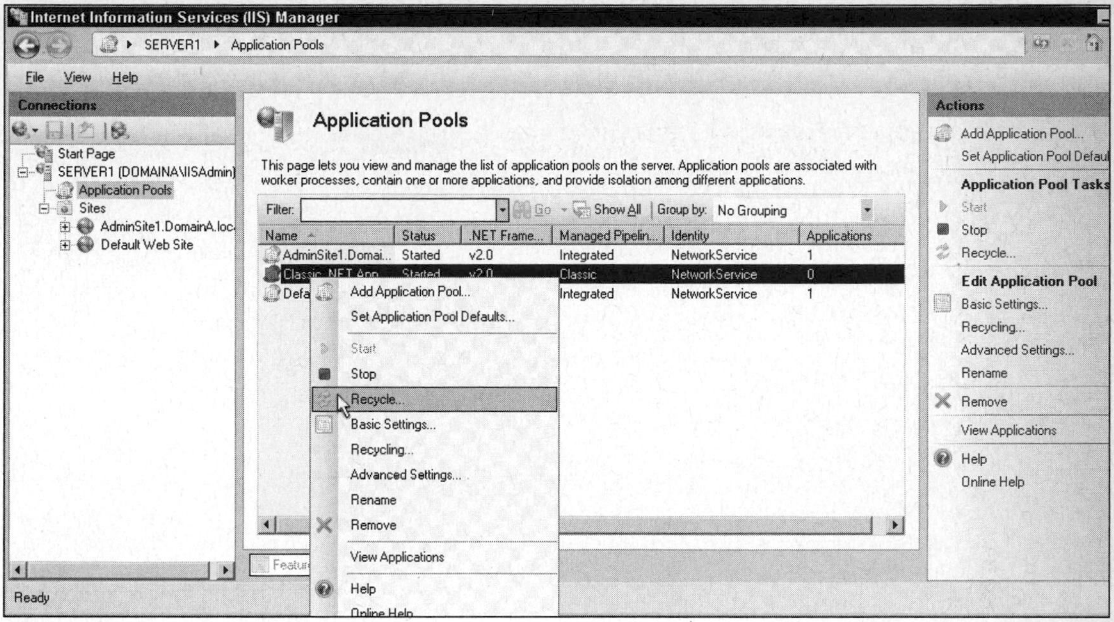

Figure 8-26

Likewise, the `WebAdministration` namespace in WMI allows the same control using the same method names. This example shows how to recycle an application pool. As with the previous example, starting and stopping the application pool is as easy as trading `oAppPool.Recycle` with `oAppPool.Start` or `oAppPool.Stop`, respectively.

```
strAppPool = "DefaultAppPool"

Set oService = GetObject("winmgmts:root\WebAdministration")

'get the app pool instance
Set oAppPool = oService.Get("ApplicationPool.Name='" & strAppPool & "'")

oAppPool.Recycle
```

Application Pool Security

It is essential on a shared server that houses multiple application pools to allow complete isolation between the application pools to ensure that a malicious site cannot harm the other sites, or, if one site is hacked, that the hacker's damage is minimized by ensuring that he or she cannot affect the other sites on the server. There are a few security considerations for managing your application pools.

Application Pool Configuration Isolation

One security consideration with application pools is that the w3wp.exe worker process has to be able to read the IIS configuration data to be able to function properly. It has to know the IIS settings specific to all web sites that it serves. This means that it has to have Read access to the vast majority of applicationHost.config. The issue is that if each application pool can read the entire configuration file, it exposes all the information to all the application pools. Therefore, it is essential that each application pool does not have Read or Write permissions to the entire applicationHost.config file; otherwise, the wrong person could gain access to sensitive information such as site anonymous user passwords or application pool passwords.

To get around this, the IIS development team had to come up with a method to allow the w3wp.exe work process to read all the information pertinent to its needs, without having access to the information for any other application data or sensitive global settings. The result is an impressive method to create complete configuration isolation between application pools.

When an application pool is first started, the *Windows Process Activation Service (WAS)* takes only the information pertinent to the application pool and creates a temporary file in %windir%\inetpub\temp\ appPools\, sets ACLs for just that application pool, and saves the information there. Figure 8-27 shows the folder with the DefaultAppPool.config file.

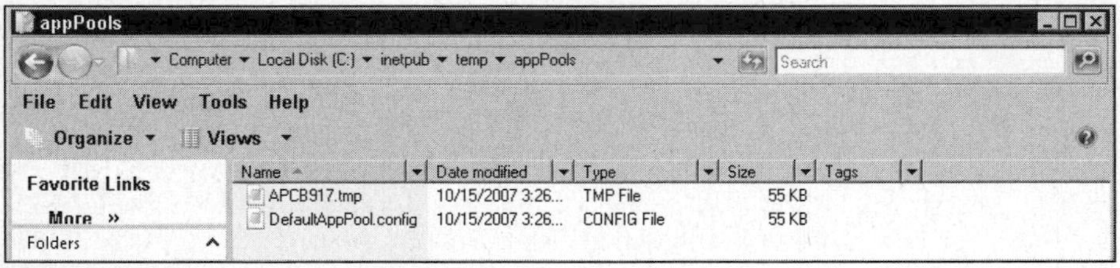

Figure 8-27

The .config file contains most of the same data that applicationHost.config contains, but it does not have any information about the web sites in other application pools and it does not have the application pool settings. It does not need the application pool information, because the w3wp.exe worker process is managed by WAS, and the w3wp.exe worker process does not need information about itself.

This temporary file is updated only when a change is made that pertains to the data in that file; otherwise, it remains in place until IIS is stopped. Deleting this file will cause IIS to fail for that application pool, and it will only be rebuilt when IIS is restarted. Recycling just the application pool will not properly rebuild the file if you delete it, therefore you should not touch these files except under extreme troubleshooting measures and if you understand their purpose and how they function.

This whole process of creating temporary files is new in IIS 7.0 and automatically ensures that no malicious code in one application pool can read sensitive configuration data from other application pools.

Application Pool SID Injection

What happens when all application pools use the Network Service account (which they do by default)? Doesn't this mean that all of the .config files will have ACLs for the Network Service account and will therefore all have access to the other configuration files?

The answer is no! There is a new feature in Windows Server 2008 that allows certain built-in Windows users to have additional unique information injected into the worker process and Windows security token to isolate resources from each other. IIS uses this feature and injects a unique *security identifier (SID)* for each application pool into the header of the w3wp.exe worker process. Each configuration file has the ACLs set to allow access only if both the Network Service account and the application pool SID are a perfect match when reading the configuration file. This ensures that all application pools using the Network Service account are completely isolated from each other automatically.

If you create custom users for your application pool, those custom users will be used to access system resources and the application pool's temporary .config file instead of the Network Service account. Note that if you do create your own application pool identity user, be sure to create a custom user for each application pool, because regular Windows users are unable to use the application pool SID injection. Only the Network Service account has this option. In Chapter 14, "Authentication and Authorization," we discuss this SID injection further. This feature is a part of IIS 7.0 and does not need to be purposefully turned on.

Site Anonymous User

Another security feature that pertains to application pools is also a new feature in IIS 7.0. It is now possible to have a web site's anonymous user identity use the application pool identity instead of the IUSR or custom anonymous user. This means that all code and service calls, local and across the network, will run under the application pool's identity. In IIS 6.0, certain code would run under the anonymous user, and other code would run under the application pool identity. Turning on impersonation would allow you to force most code to use one or the other, but it didn't apply to every situation. Even with impersonation set in ASP.NET, some things would still run under the authenticated user (for example, the site's anonymous user), whereas other things would run under the worker process identity. In addition, CGI applications, static pages, Classic ASP, and ASP.NET all play by different rules and aren't required to run under one user or the other. This new feature in IIS 7.0 allows absolutely everything to run under the application pool identity. If you give each web site its own application pool, it is advisable to enable this so that you don't have to manage both anonymous users and application pool users. Managing one user per application pool/web-site pair makes administration easier.

To enable this, follow these steps:

1. From the site level, double-click the Authentication icon.

2. Click Anonymous Authentication, and then click Edit from the Actions pane.

3. From the Edit Anonymous Authentication Credentials dialog box, select "Application pool identity" (see Figure 8-28).

4. Click OK to save your selection.

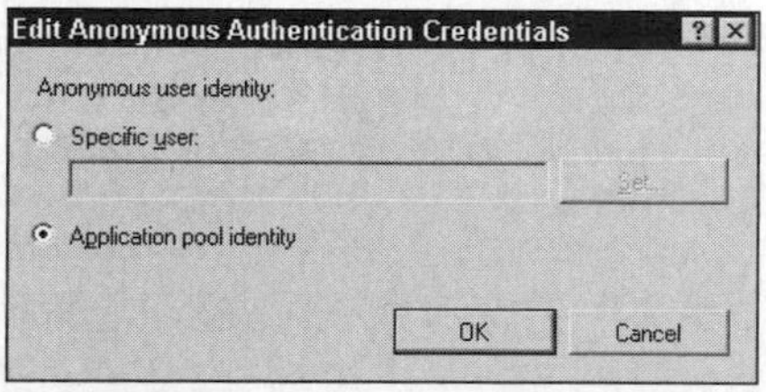

Figure 8-28

To make this the default so that all web sites which don't specifically have this set will use the application pool's identity, you can run the following `AppCmd.exe` command:

```
appcmd.exe set config
-section:system.webServer/security/authentication/anonymousAuthentication
/userName:""
```

Watch word wrapping, as the preceding is a single command. This command sets the `userName` property to nothing, which will cause it to use the application pool identity.

Noteworthy Advanced Settings

It's beyond the scope of this book to detail every available setting because they can be found in the Microsoft Help and in the description section within IIS Manager. But there are some settings that have noteworthy significance.

Bitness

Windows Server 2003, Service Pack 1 offered support in IIS 6.0 to run 32-bit applications on 64-bit Windows. This way you could have 64-bit Windows and set IIS to run in 32-bit mode to run applications that weren't compatible with 64-bit. There was one major limitation with this option in IIS 6.0. You had to make this setting at the global level for all of IIS. You could not have some sites on the same server run 32-bit while others ran 64-bit.

IIS 7.0 supports different bitness settings per application pool. You can set some application pools to run 32-bit and others 64-bit. The operating system must be 64-bit to support both bitness modes, and a 32-bit version of Windows can only support 32-bit application pools. This property does not show up in IIS Manager on a 32-bit version of Windows.

If you are running a 64-bit version of Windows, the Advanced Settings for the application pool has a property called Enable 32-Bit Applications which can be set to true.

You can change this with AppCmd.exe by using the following:

```
appcmd.exe set apppool "AppPool1"
-enable32BitAppOnWin64:true
```

CPU Limits

The CPU limit is one of the easiest settings to misunderstand. At first glance, it would appear that it is possible to set a CPU limit for each application pool so that it is throttled such that it will continue to run without using too much CPU. But that is not what the CPU limit does.

The CPU limit sets the maximum CPU that is allowed in the time frame set by "Limit Interval." If the limit is exceeded, IIS will take the action set in "Limit Action." The "Limit Action" choices are (1) No Action and (2) KillW3wp. "No Action" will write an event to the Event Viewer so that there is a record of the excessive CPU, but no further action is carried out. "KillW3wp" will do just that, kill the application pool worker process that exceeded the CPU limit, to prevent the rest of the server from being affected. A new worker process will immediately start up after the first one is killed. This limit is not a throttle, per se; instead, it is a safety measure to deal with excessive CPU after the fact, but before it goes on too long.

The Limit setting is in 1/1,000-th of a percent of the CPU during the Limit Interval time. To calculate the value, multiply the CPU percentage by 1,000. For example, to have a limit of 60 percent over 5 minutes, set the Limit to 60,000 and the Limit Interval to 5. Setting the Limit to 0 will disable the CPU limit.

Microsoft Windows System Resource Manager (WSRM) can set throttles on CPU and memory usage for each program. This offers a true throttle per worker process and is an alternative to IIS CPU limits if you want more control.

Processor Affinity

IIS supports processor affinity, which means that a worker process can be forced to always run on a particular CPU on a multiprocessor server. Enabling a web garden on multiple processors will distribute the processes across the processors defined in the affinity mask. The following table shows some sample affinity options. The setting in IIS is saved as an unsigned integer (essentially that means that it can only be a positive integer), even though the help mentions that it's a hexadecimal mask. In IIS Manager, in the advanced setting for the application pool, you can enter the value as a hexadecimal number (i.e. 0xF) and it will automatically convert to an integer, or you can enter it directly as an integer.

Be sure to also enable the `Processor Affinity Enabled` property, otherwise the `Processor Affinity Mask` is ignored.

Hex Mask(Binary)	Proc7	Proc6	Proc5	Proc4	Proc3	Proc2	Proc1	Proc0
0x1 (0001)								Yes
0x2 (0010)							Yes	
0x5 (0101)						Yes		Yes
0xF (1111)					Yes	Yes	Yes	Yes
0xF0(11110000)	Yes	Yes	Yes	Yes				
0xFE(11111110)	Yes	Yes	Yes	Yes	Yes	Yes	Yes	
0xFF(11111111)	Yes	Yes	Yes	Yes	Yes	Yes	Yes	Yes

Application Pool Users

Application pools (`w3wp.exe` worker processes) run under the user that you specify, which IIS uses to access various system and network resources. For example, they have access to disk, the ability to perform certain system functions, access to the registry, or access across the network. The default user is the Network Service account, which has limited permissions on the web server and network, but is assigned sufficient permissions to run a standard web site. IIS 7.0 allows you to select from three built-in accounts or to create your own custom user (see Figure 8-29).

The built-in accounts are

- ❑ Network Service
- ❑ Local Service
- ❑ Local System

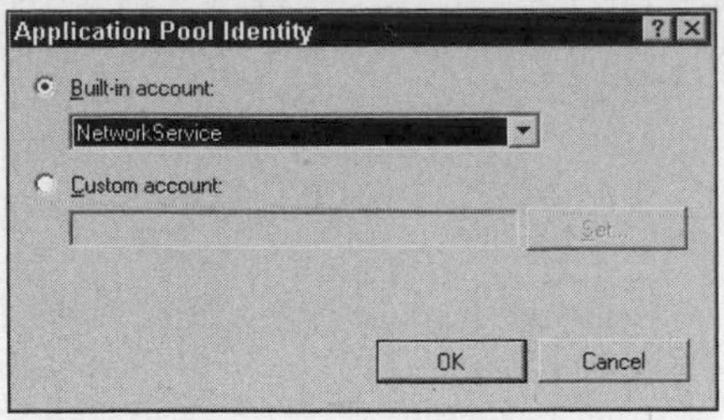

Figure 8-29

The following four sections discuss the three built-in accounts and how to create a custom user account.

Network Service Account

The default application pool user is the built-in *Network Service account*. The Network Service account has minimal permissions on the local computer and network. If you are accessing a resource on another device in the same domain (or in a trusted domain), the Network Service account's network credentials are used to authenticate to the server. This device can be a database, a UNC share, or any other resource that can be accessed across the network. The Network Service account's credentials are in the form of `DomainName\ServerName$`. For example, on the DomainA domain, if a server called WebServer1 was running a site using the Network Service account, and it is doing a database call to SQLServer1, then on SQLServer1, you should grant necessary SQL permissions to the `DomainA\WebServer1$` account.

The following privileges are assigned explicitly to the Network Service account:

❏ Adjust memory quotas for a process.

❏ Bypass traverse checking.

❏ Create global objects.

❏ Generate security audits.

❏ Impersonate a client after authentication.

❏ Replace a process level token.

As a member of the Everyone group, the Network Service account also inherits this privilege:

❏ Access this computer from the network.

Finally, as a member of the IIS_IUSRS group, it inherits this privilege:

❏ Log on as a batch job.

Local Service Account

The *Local Service* built-in user account does not have access to the network like the Network Service account does, but it has similar access to the local system. In Windows Vista and Windows Server 2008, it is given the following additional local privileges that the Network Service account does not have:

❑ Change the system time.

❑ Change the time zone.

You can use the Local Service account if you don't require access to network resources.

Local System Account

The *Local System* built-in user account has full access to the local system. Be sure to use Local System account with caution, and avoid using it permanently if at all possible. Should an unauthorized user exploit a web site on the server or gain the ability to upload his or her own content and if the application pool is running as the Local System, they could do most anything they please on the web server.

> *Although this user poses a potentially large security risk, it has a practical purpose. When troubleshooting an issue on a web site, testing with the application pool identity set as the Local System will confirm whether or not permissions or privileges on the application pool identity are the cause of the issue. Of course, this troubleshooting needs to take into account the possibility of compound issues. Just be sure to set this back to the appropriate user or create a specific user with just the necessary permissions. Also be sure to test this only on a web site for which you know and trust the content and the content developer.*

Custom User Account

Like IIS 6.0, IIS 7.0 allows you to create a custom user. This user can be a local Windows user, or it can be a domain user. Which one you use will depend on your environment and which you prefer for this situation. With a domain user, you can access network resources like UNC shares or a database by giving the application pool identity user access to the network resource. There are a few reasons why you might create a custom user:

❑ **The existing built-in accounts do not adequately meet your needs** — For example, if the Local Service doesn't have enough permission, and the Local System has too much permission, you can create a custom user with the exact permissions needed.

❑ **To separate web sites to protect them from each other** — This is particularly important in a shared environment where one web server hosts multiple sites that do not trust each other. A shared web hosting environment is one prime example. Even within the same organization, web-site isolation is important since, if one web site is compromised, web sites or applications in other application pools will not be affected if configured correctly.

❑ **To access a network resource with the application pool identity** — If you want to access a network resource, you can create a custom domain user and assign it as the application pool identity. Then anything that runs under the application pool identity that requires access to a network resource will use the custom user that you created.

In IIS 7.0, it is easier than ever to create a specific application pool user. In IIS 6.0, you had to remember to add the user to the IIS_WPG group so that it had adequate permissions to the metabase and operating system and for Http.sys to start the application pool. This is handled automatically in IIS 7.0 through a convenient new feature. When IIS starts a worker process, it will automatically add the specific application pool user to the IIS_IUSRS membership at run time. This eliminates the need to manually add the specific user to the IIS_IUSRS group. This process doesn't permanently place the user in the IIS_IUSRS groups, but instead adds it each time for the lifetime of the worker process.

Like so many other features in IIS, this auto-mapping to the IIS_IUSRS group is configurable if you have a reason to disable it. The manualGroupMembership property isn't exposed in IIS Manager, but you can set it through other means, such as through AppCmd.exe, a text editor, or programmatically. To set it using AppCmd.exe, use the following command:

```
appcmd.exe set apppool "DefaultAppPool"
-processModel.manualGroupMembership:true
```

The IIS_IUSRS group is now a built-in group with a unique SID that will always be the same on all Vista and Longhorn servers. In addition, this user and SID will not change when localized to different languages of the operating system. This allows 'xcopy' deployment of web sites if the IIIS_IUSRS group is granted permissions on disk.

Summary

Application pools were one of the most welcome additions in IIS 6.0 and have only gotten better in IIS 7.0. The concepts of application pools remain the same in IIS 7.0, but it is now possible to set the ASP.NET Framework version per application pool, to choose between Integrated mode and Classic mode, and even to set the "bitness" (32-bit or 64-bit) per application pool.

This chapter reviewed key concepts that were introduced in IIS 6.0, including overlapping worker processes during an application pool recycle and web gardens. It covered methods to manage application pools from IIS Manager, AppCmd.exe, WMI, and Microsoft.Web.Administration. It also covered applications and virtual directories and how they can be grouped into application pools or placed into separate application pools for isolation. Additionally, the new Network Service account and application pool SID injection offers complete isolation between application pools, even if they all use the Network Service identity.

Application pools are a foundational part of IIS and require a solid understanding to be able to affectively manage your IIS servers.

The following chapter shows you how to delegate IIS Manager and web.config so that site or application administrators can manage their own part of the server without being given full access to the server.

9

Delegating Remote Administration

Many web environments have a need to separate the roles of the system administrators and the web site development and management teams. Whether there are two people in these roles or hundreds, it is necessary for the server administration team to specify the access level and settings for the developers or deployment teams.

In past versions of IIS, the ability to delegate partial administration of a server, web site, or application was very limited. Unless you developed your own tools, it was not possible to configure partial access to the end developers or administrators.

In the area of delegation, IIS 7.0 breaks revolutionary ground in two areas. First, IIS administrators can specify the access the web site administrators should have and provide the IIS Manager tool for them to manage their settings remotely through a user-friendly interface. Second, this same access in IIS Manager also applies to the `web.config` file. This may seem strange at first because the `web.config` file used to be for ASP.NET, and it wasn't possible to manage IIS from any type of control file. The advantages of managing some IIS features from the web site's `web.config` file are huge, the most prominent benefit being that web site tool vendors and developers can create web sites and then copy them using a simple tool like XCopy or FTP.

Delegation isn't just turning on a switch and allowing developers or web site administrators to start work. It requires a lot of planning and understanding of what can and cannot be delegated. In this chapter, we will explore the various levels of delegation, how to set them, and what to watch for.

Introducing the Main Characters

For the sake of this chapter, it is useful to define two different types of people and their roles. Out in the real world, there are many similar situations. For example, in training, there are teachers and students; in the workplace, there are employers and employees; and at home, there are parents and children. Likewise, in this world of delegation, there are the system administrators, who have full access to the IIS server; and there are the site administrators, who can only do what they have been granted access to by the system administrators. Much to the dismay of the developers and the delight of the system administrators, the parallels here are pretty accurate. It is the job of the system administrator to run a tight ship and only give access where it is absolutely necessary. Henceforth, these two people will be affectionately known as the *system administrator* and the *site administrator*.

> *It is also possible to delegate administration of applications, not just entire web sites; however, it gets a bit wordy to say "site and application administrator" over and over again. Therefore, in this chapter, "site and application" is usually shortened to "site."*

Server Administrator

In the IIS world, the *server administrators* are often those who install the operating system and configure IIS exactly to their liking. They may not be in a management position within the company, but they have full rights to the servers that they manage, and anyone else's access is granted only by their say-so.

This role comes with power, but it also comes with great responsibility. It is absolutely essential in almost any workplace to make sure that no security holes are opened and that every setting, change, and access level is completely accounted for. This is the principle of least privilege. The *principle of least privilege* means that every user or program can access only the information or resources that they need for legitimate purposes, without giving them unnecessary access.

Essentially, this means that each person is given the bare level of access to the system so that they can still get the job done. This often is a tricky balance, where an educated judgment call needs to be made between the level of control someone is given and the security concerns that are introduced with that control.

It is the role of system administrators to ensure that every setting is understood and properly configured to the best setting for their environment. Often their job and their reputation hinge on this being set exactly right.

Site Administrator

The *site administrators*, on the other hand, should not have full access to the server but should only have access to their immediate area of concern. They do not have access to make security settings at the global level or to manage information for any other sites on the server.

Many people can fit in the role of the site administrator. It could be a developer who was given permission to manage his or her own web site; it could be the Quality Assurance (QA) team that needs to test, approve, and sometimes deploy web sites; it could be an individual site owner in a shared hosting environment; or, it could even be the server administrator properly locking down his or her own external access to follow the principle of least privilege.

Regardless of the role, this person is at the mercy of the server administrator and must make do with the permissions granted, or be able to plead his or her case to the server administrator to be granted greater access.

The Two Shall Work as One

Both roles are important in any business situation, but even more important, the two administrators should understand each other. A server administrator who doesn't understand how the site administrator thinks is unable to set up a good environment for him or her, except by sheer luck. Likewise, it's worthwhile for the site administrator to understand as much about the server as possible.

IIS Manager Remote Access

IIS 7.0 offers two methods for allowing site administrators to manage a web site remotely: IIS Manager and the web.config file. In this section, we discuss how to make IIS Manager, with its default settings, available to site administrators. Later, we'll describe using web.config. And, finally, we'll wrap up the chapter by interspersing the two methods.

Installing the IIS 7.0 Management Service

The first thing to do to allow remote access off the server is to turn on the *Management Service feature*. Unless it is installed and enabled, it is not possible to manage IIS 7.0 remotely through IIS Manager. This differs from IIS 6.0, where remote administration through the MMC was installed and enabled by default.

When installed, the Management Service will run as the *Web Management Service (WMSvc)* — a standalone web server and hostable web core (HWC). In case the names seem confusing, *Management Service* is the name that IIS Manager calls the feature, whereas *Web Management Service* (WMSvc) is the name of the Windows service that does the work.

WMSvc listens for the following four types of requests:

- ❑ Login requests to login.axd.
- ❑ Code download requests to download.axd.
- ❑ Management service requests to service.axd.
- ❑ Ping requests to ping.axd.

WMSvc is required to allow remote management of IIS using IIS Manager. To install Management Service, perform the following steps:

1. Click Start, type **Server Manager** in the Search box, and then press Enter. (Note that Windows Vista users should use Programs and Features instead.)
2. Expand Roles in the tree in the left-hand pane.
3. Right-click Web Server (IIS). and select Add Role Services.
4. Select Management Service in the Management Tools section under Role Services (see Figure 9-1).
5. Click Next and Install.

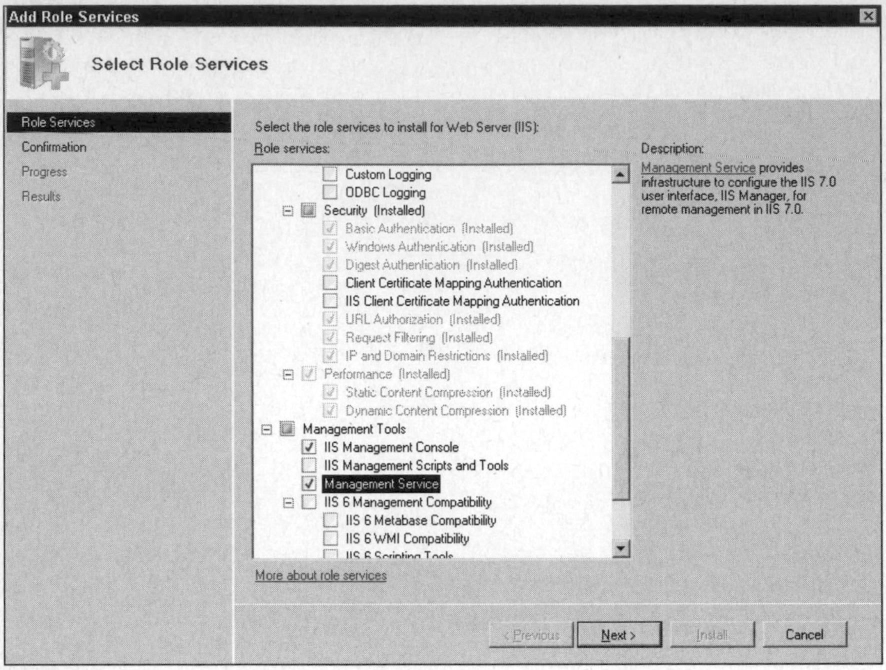

Figure 9-1

Enabling Remote Connections

After installing the management service, you need to enable remote connections, which are disabled by default — obviously the best default setting for the IIS team to make, although it means that no remote access is possible unless you specifically configure it.

When using IIS Manager, only administrators on the local server can manage the Management Service. It is not possible to manage it remotely, even after you have configured the system for remote management.

To enable remote connections:

1. At the server level, double-click Management Service.

2. Check "Enable remote connections" (see Figure 9-2).

3. Optionally, check "Windows credentials or IIS Manager credentials" if you will be using the IIS Manager credentials. This will be covered shortly.

4. The other settings can be left at the default or adjusted, depending on your requirements.

5. Click Apply from the Actions pane.

The Management Service is grayed out when WMSvc is started and cannot be edited until WMSvc is stopped. You can do that from the Actions pane. Obviously, any existing connections will be terminated if you stop the service to make any changes. A warning is presented explaining this, but even the best of administrators can miss the warning and panic when the screen is grayed out.

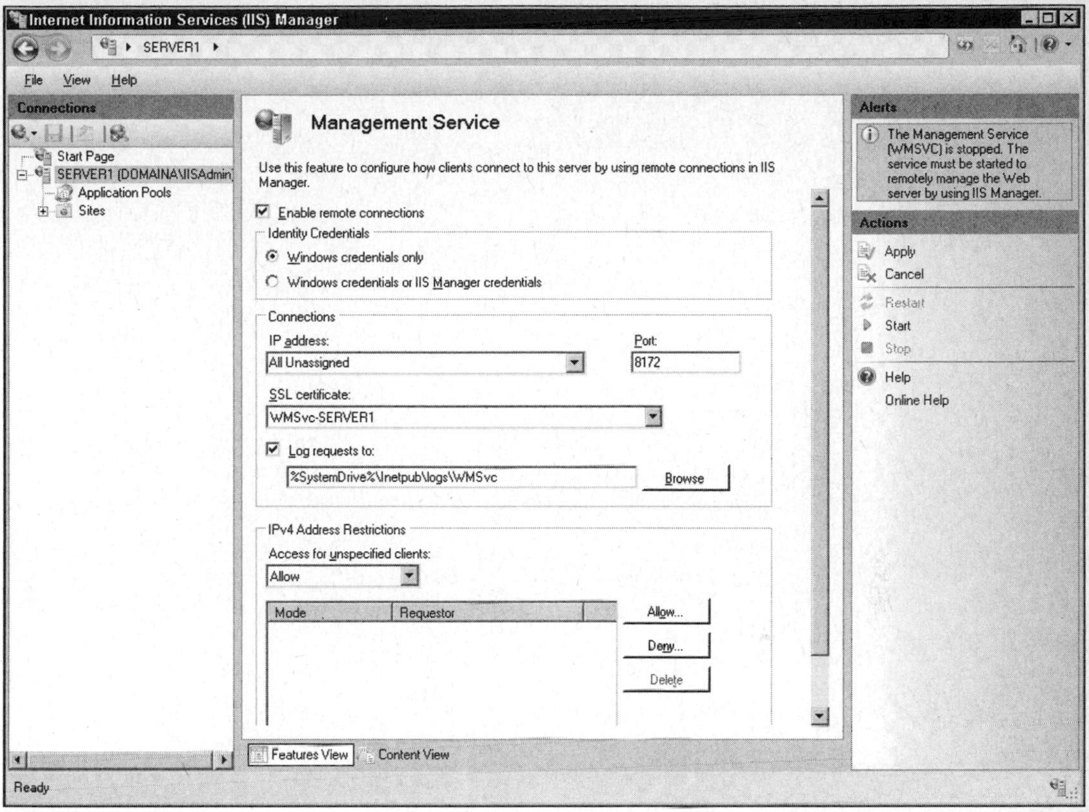

Figure 9-2

After configuring WMSvc, be sure to start it. You can do so from the Actions pane by clicking Start or from the command line by using `net start WMSvc`.

> *By default, WMSvc has a start-up type of Manual. This means that after your first server reboot, WMSvc will not be started as you might expect. (An odd default? Yes!) To set the start-up type to Auto, you can use the Services MMC snap-in from Administrative Tools (or by typing **services.msc** at the command line). Another option is to do it from the command line, as follows (note the spacing):*

```
sc config WMSvc start= auto
```

After starting WMSvc, you can confirm that your server is listening by using `netstat`, as shown in the following example:

```
C:\>netstat -a | findstr 8172
    TCP    0.0.0.0:8172            IIS7:0        LISTENING
    TCP    [::]:8172               IIS7:0        LISTENING
```

The Connections and IP and Domain Restrictions sections enable you to customize how IIS Manager is accessed remotely. The individual settings are as follows:

❑ **Identity Credentials** — This takes a longer description, which will be covered shortly.

❑ **IP Address** — This can be left as All Unassigned or set to a particular IP Address. Multiple bindings are not possible in WMSvc as they are with sites in IIS.

❑ **Port** — This is the TCP port used. Make sure that all firewalls between the client computer and the server allow access to this port. Windows Firewall on the web server will, by default, allow IIS Manager access through port 8172, which is convenient. Yet, if you change the port used, Windows Firewall will not automatically update the port; therefore, make sure to remember to update Windows Firewall whenever you make any port changes to Management Service.

❑ **SSL Certificate** — Windows Server 2008 creates a self-signed certificate when Management Service is installed. This works great as far as encryption is concerned, but it doesn't prove who you are. For that reason, IIS Manager will give a warning if you try to connect using the default certificate. You can change this. The recommended certificate should match the exact URL that you provide to the site administrator. Chapter 15 describes installing certificates in more detail.

❑ **Log requests to** — This is straightforward. By default, logging is enabled and points to `%SystemDrive%\Inetpub\logs\WMSvc`. You can disable logging and/or change the path using this section. Note that this is for traffic coming in, not for errors. Errors with Management Service are logged to Event Viewer, so be sure to also check Event Viewer when troubleshooting configuration errors with Management Service.

❑ **The IP Domain Restrictions** — Lets you allow or disallow access by IP address or range of IP addresses. Without the IP domain restrictions, all that is needed to gain access to the server is the username and password. The IP address, port, site name, and application name come into play too, but they are often easy to guess. With properly configured IP Restrictions, it is much more difficult to gain uninvited access to the server. The settings are fairly easy to understand but are slightly different from IP restrictions in previous versions of IIS.

The "Access for unspecified clients" dropdown list allows you to specify the default permission for anyone not set in this list. When set to Allow, any Allow IP entries will be ignored, and when set to Deny, any Deny IP entries will be ignored. Then why have them? The advantage of this method is that if you have a long list of IPs, you don't lose them if you temporarily switch between Allow and Deny, as you did in prior versions of IIS.

❑ **Restart/Start/Stop** — Be sure to start the service when changes have been completed; otherwise any promises that you made to the site administrators that they can manage their sites will be untrue until you remember to do this.

The settings for Management Service are not set in `applicationHost.config` *like most other settings in IIS. Instead, they are saved in the registry under* `HKEY_LOCAL_MACHINE\SOFTWARE\Microsoft\WebManagement\Server`.

This configuration is stored in the registry and can be manipulated directly in the registry. The following is a sample WSH script that will enable remote management, set remote management to support Windows

and IIS Manager Credentials, set the service mode to start automatically and start the
service (User Access Control (UAC) can interfere with this script since it is making changes to the registry):

```
Const HKLM = &H80000002

strComputer = "."
strService = "WMSvc"

'Connect to the root namespace in WMI
Set objRegistry = GetObject("winmgmts:\\" & strComputer & _
    "\root\default:StdRegProv")

strKeyPath = "Software\Microsoft\WebManagement\Server"

'Turn on Remote Management
strValueName = "EnableRemoteManagement"
strValue = 1
call objRegistry.SetDWORDValue(HKLM, _
    strKeyPath, _
    strValueName, _
    strValue)

'Enable IIS Manager with Windows and IIS Manager Credentials
strValueName = "RequiresWindowsCredentials"
strValue = 0
objRegistry.SetDWORDValue HKLM, _
    strKeyPath, _
    strValueName, _
    strValue

'Connect to the cimv2 namespace in WMI
Set objWMIService = GetObject("winmgmts:" _
    & "{impersonationLevel=impersonate}!\\" & strComputer _
    & "\root\cimv2")

'Get all services called WMSvc (there will only be 1)
Set colServiceList = objWMIService.ExecQuery _
    ("Select * from Win32_Service where Name='" & _
        strService & "'")

For Each objService in colServiceList
    'Change the service account to start automatically
    errChangeMode = objService.Change( , , , , "Automatic")
    'Start the service
    errStartService = objService.StartService()
Next
```

To run this, create a file called *EnableRemoteManagement.vbs*, and put this code into it. You can run it from
the command line by typing cscript EnableRemoteManagement.vbs or by double-clicking on it.

Authentication Types

In past versions of IIS, Windows authentication was the only method of authentication available for IIS related access. This held true in disk-level permissions for the site, application pools, and in IIS FTP. A user needed to be created in Windows Users and Groups before access could be granted to an IIS resource.

With IIS 7.0, there is a new method specific to IIS for remote management. This is *IIS Manager authentication*.

IIS Manager Authentication

The new *IIS Manager authentication* is managed at the server level, and users are assigned authorization at either the site or application level. IIS Manager Users do not require server Client Access Licenses (CALs), and creating an IIS Manager User does not grant any rights to the server except what IIS allows. This makes them ideal for a web host or for a company that needs to manage several users with minimal rights. Within IIS Manager, you can manage the IIS Manager Users at the server level by clicking the server in the left-hand pane and under Management, double-clicking IIS Manager Users, as shown in Figure 9-3.

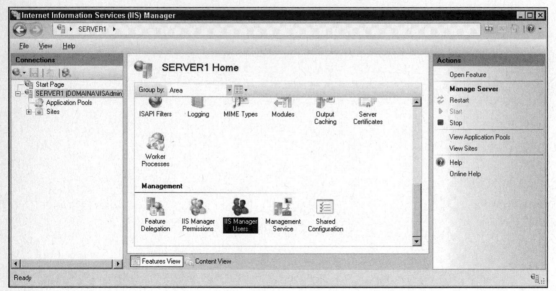

Figure 9-3

From the IIS Manager User dialog box, you can create any number of new users or edit existing users by resetting the password, disabling or deleting them. Setting up authorization for these users comes later and is done from a different area. Figure 9-4 shows the Users tool in IIS Manager.

These users are stored in the `administration.config` file in the `%SystemDrive%\System32\inetsrv\config` folder by default, or they can be saved to a shared configuration location, which is covered in Chapter 16, "Clustering and Load-Balancing Web Farms." The password is never stored anywhere; instead, the SHA256 hash is saved to disk. This enables you to move the hash between servers and ensures that others cannot decrypt and read the password.

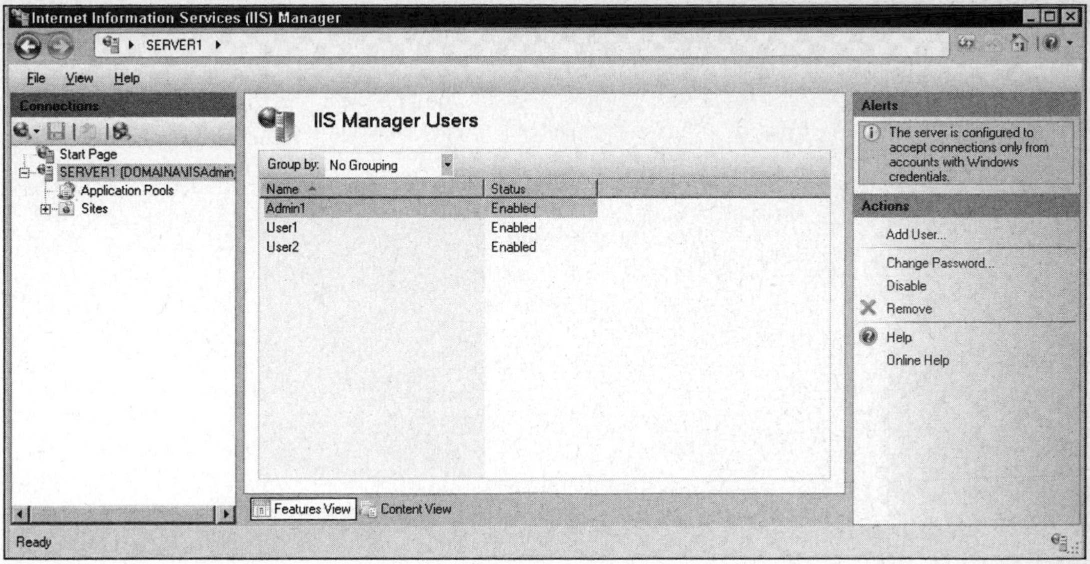

Figure 9-4

When IIS Manager creates users, they are placed in the `system.webServer` section of the `administration.config` file, as shown in the following snippet:

```
<system.webServer>
    <management>
        <authentication defaultProvider="ConfigurationAuthenticationProvider">
            <providers>
                <add name="ConfigurationAuthenticationProvider" type=... />
            </providers>
            <credentials>
                <add name="User1" password="12A303C224C250D07C81691DE6E0FD..." />
                <add name="User2" password="6025D18FE48ABD45168528F18A82E2..." />
                <add name="User3" password="5860FAF02B6BC6222BA5ACA523560F..." />
            </credentials>
        </authentication>
    . . .
    </management>
</system.webServer>
```

Creating IIS Manager Users programmatically is described in Chapter 17, "Programmatic Configuration and Management."

> *Don't forget that the default option for Management Service is "Windows credentials only"; therefore, be sure to select "Windows credentials or IIS Manager credentials" from the Management Service section. Figure 9-4 shows the alert in the top right corner that you will receive if you do not select "Windows credentials or IIS Manager credentials."*

Windows Authentication

Windows Users or Groups is another option for user authentication. Windows authentication can use Local Users and Groups or Active Directory Users and Groups to connect remotely to IIS.

There are many situations in which this is preferred. If you already have a user account for the site or application administrator, you can easily authorize them to manage a site using that user. Additionally, if you plan to give this same user access to other resources or tools, it is worthwhile to use Windows users so that you need only maintain one set of users and passwords. Another key difference between Windows authentication and IIS Manager authentication is how the WMSvc service accesses the configuration files on disk.

When using *Windows authentication*, it is the Windows user token that makes all calls to the configuration files on disk. This means that you must grant the Windows user Write permissions to the configuration files.

When using *IIS Manager authentication*, it is the process identity of the WMSvc NT service that is used to Read and Write to the configuration files. By default, this is *Local Service*. If using shared configuration over a UNC path, make sure to update this service user to one that has access to the configuration files. If you are using *IIS Manager authentication* on a shared server where you need to ensure isolation between sites, be sure to assign a custom Windows user for the WMSvc service to run as, and give that user read/write access to the web.config files for all sites that will be using IIS Manager delegation.

If you want to group users together to give whole groups management access to a site or application, you must use Windows authentication or build your own custom provider because IIS Manager Users does not have a Group feature. With Windows authentication, it is possible to create users, assign them to a Windows group, and give that group permissions to manage a site or application.

Windows users and groups are managed outside of IIS because Windows Users and Groups is a core Windows Server 2008 feature. To add a Windows user:

1. Click Start, type **compmgmt.msc** in the Search box, and then press Enter. Other ways to start Computer Management are to search for Computer Management in the Start menu and click it from the search results, or select it directly from *Administrative Tools*.

2. Expand Local Users and Groups, and create or manage a user or group from there. Figure 9-5 shows the Local Users and Groups tool.

The same concept can be accomplished from Active Directory Users and Computers (ADUC) if you are using Active Directory users instead.

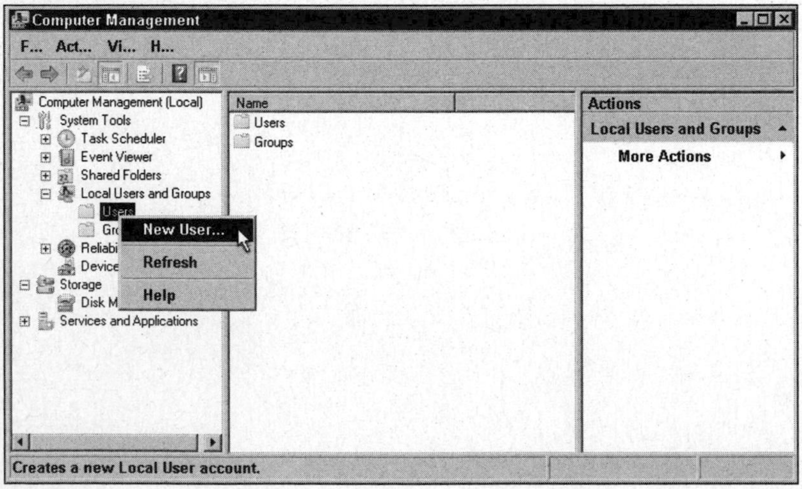

Figure 9-5

Build Your Own

In addition to IIS Manager authentication and Windows authentication, a third option for user authentication in IIS is to build your own. Authentication and authorization are extensible mechanisms implemented on top of a provider model. This means that you can easily (depending on your programming expertise) write your own authentication provider that authenticates against whatever back-end you set.

For example, you can create a SQL back-end so that all your users are maintained in one place, or you can build something on top of the .NET membership provider. This allows you to share the same users with any other tools that you have developed. This is just one example; the sky is the limit as to what you can create.

Authorization at Three Levels

Now that you have created users or groups, it's time to determine the sites or applications to which they have access. Authorization exists at three levels — the server, the site, and the application.

Server Level Authorization

At the server level, users in the Administrators group are automatically given permission to manage the server remotely as long as Management Service is started. IIS 7.0 does not allow you to give an IIS Manager User access to the server level.

Site and Application Level Authorization

You can, however, grant permission to a Windows or IIS Manager User to manage a web site or application. Unlike creating IIS Manager Users, which are managed at the server level, authorization is managed directly within the site or application.

> You can see all permissions for the entire server from the server level. Select the server, and then double-click the IIS Manager Permissions icon. This allows Read Only access to view the site or applications and users that are granted remote management permissions on this server.

To authorize a user in IIS Manager:

1. Navigate to the site or application to which you want to grant management rights.

2. Double-click the IIS Manager Permissions icon (see Figure 9-6).

3. Click Allow User from the Actions pane.

4. Select either Windows or IIS Manager from the radio options. Both options have a Select button to allow you to choose from available users, as shown in Figure 9-7, or you can type in the user directly.

5. When selecting a Windows user, you can select a group instead of a user. It's important to note that the default object type is User, so if you use the Select wizard to assign a group, be sure to click the "Object types" button and check the Groups checkbox, as shown in Figure 9-8.

6. After entering a valid Windows or IIS Manager user or group, click OK.

That user will now have access to the site or application.

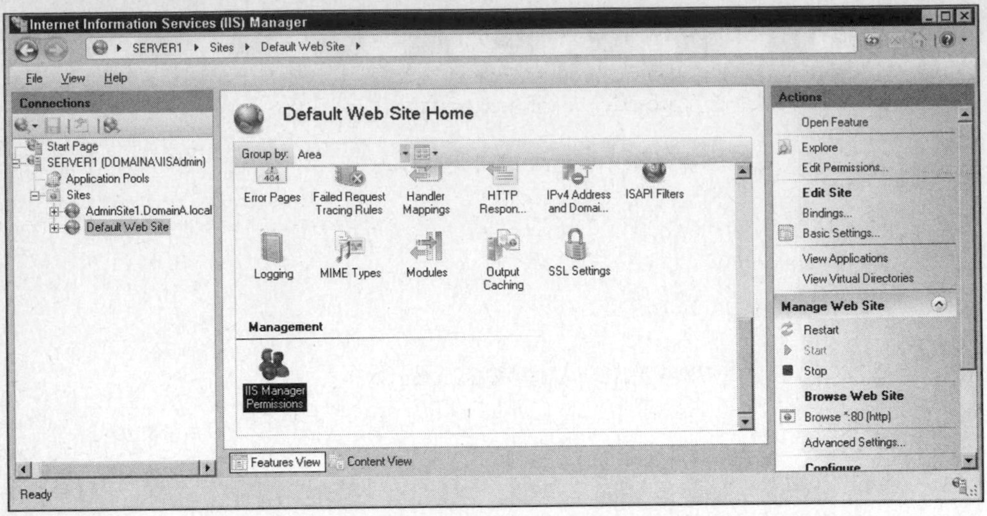

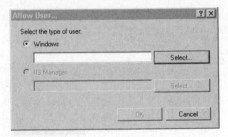

Figure 9-6

Figure 9-7

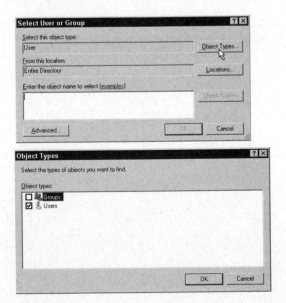

Figure 9-8

Remote Installation and Usage

After configuring the server to allow remote management, the next steps are to make IIS Manager available to the site administrator and to provide the information he or she needs to connect to the IIS 7.0 server.

Both Windows Server 2008 and Windows Vista SP1 ship with the IIS Manager client tool (aka Remote Manager) to connect to an IIS 7.0 web server, although it is not installed by default. The originally released version of Vista does not allow remote management of IIS. It is not available unless you have installed SP1.

IIS Manager 7.0 is compatible and available for Windows XP and Windows Server 2003 through a separate download, available at www.iis.net/go/1524.

Connecting to the Server/Site/Application

After installing IIS Manager, it's time to connect to IIS 7.0 for remote management. The information necessary to connect to the server varies, depending on which level of access you require. Following is a list of the information that you need to provide, or be provided, to connect to IIS 7.0 remotely.

- ❑ Required for all levels of access:
  - ❑ Server name, IP, or domain name
  - ❑ Server Port (if it's different from the default port 8172)
  - ❑ Username (don't forget the server name or Active Directory name if required)
  - ❑ Password
- ❑ Additional information for site or application access:
  - ❑ Web site name (this needs to be spelled exactly right, but it's not case-sensitive). Spaces are allowed because IIS supports spaces in web site names.
  - ❑ Application name

Example Connection Information

It's easy to forget to provide all the necessary information when providing it for your site administrators. The following table is an example of the connection information to provide to the site or application administrator. The port isn't necessary if it is still at the default of 8172; however, if you changed from the default port, then it is required in the server field.

Field	Value
Server	10.0.0.50:8172
Web site	IIS7Site1
Username	IIS7SiteAdmin1
Password	ReallyDifficultPassword
Application	/downloads

Connecting to IIS 7.0 Remotely

There are multiple ways to connect to a server, site, or application via IIS Manager.

❏ From the Start page, click any of the "Connect to a" links — for example, "Connect to a site."

❏ Click the upper-left icon in the Connections pane, and select one of the three choices (see Figure 9-9).

❏ Right-click Start Page, and select one of the three choices.

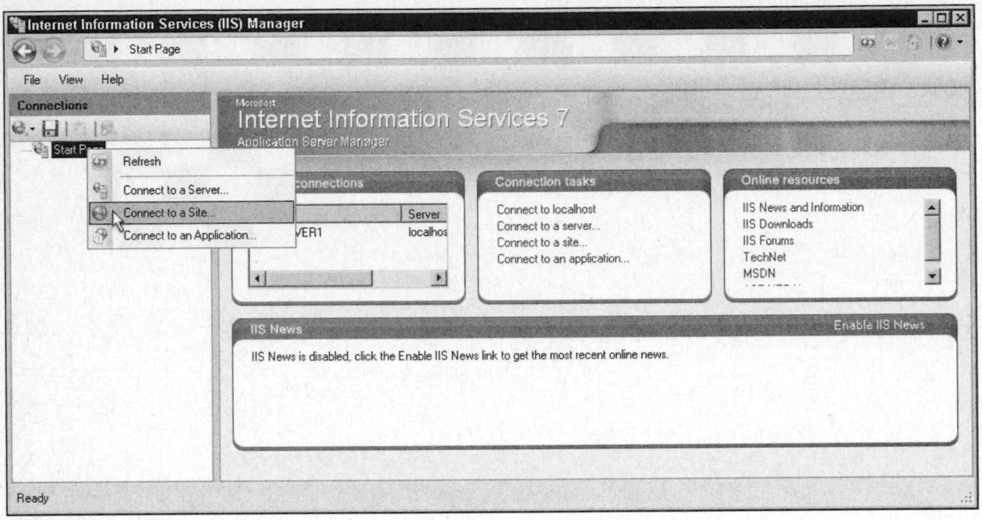

Figure 9-9

Once selected, it's as easy as following the wizard by plugging in the details. The wizard will guide you through the questions and provide some simple examples of the field syntax. You will also be presented with a field asking you for the connection name. This is just a friendly name for your own reference; it doesn't need to correspond with anything on the server.

It is possible to establish a connection to multiple servers, sites, or applications at once and use a single management tool to manage all of them, but you cannot connect remotely to the same site twice from the same server, even if using different methods of authentication. Be sure to save IIS Manager so that your connection is available next time you need to use it to manage a site.

Extending IIS Manager

One of the powerful features of IIS 7.0 is the ability to extend almost every area of the platform. IIS Manager is fully extensible and allows the IIS administrator or developer to extend onto the existing infrastructure. For example, if a new tool or feature is added to IIS, it can be made available remotely through IIS Manager. More impressive yet, all communication is still performed through the same port and then run locally on the web server, ensuring that even complex features do not need additional ports opened on any firewall.

The www.iis.net web site has several custom applications that can extend IIS Manager. They can be accessed remotely just like the native IIS features. Chapter 12, "Core Server Extensibility," takes this further and walks you through extending IIS Manager yourself.

Delegation Settings

So far, we've discussed remote management of IIS 7.0 using IIS Manager. Now it's time to look at the granular control available to you to set access for remote administrators.

IIS 7.0 does not have the ability to control access per user, per site. Each site can be adjusted to your liking, but all users that have permission to manage that site will have the same level of access.

IIS 7.0 enables you to control two types of remote access:

❑ **IIS Manager Features** — No Visibility, Read Only, Read/Write.

❑ **Web.config access** — Read Only, Read/Write.

IIS Manager and web.config remote access can be micromanaged to the finest detail by allowing every setting to be set on a per-site or per-application basis. Management access can be granted for whole sections, elements, collections, attributes, and even individual items within a collection. Additionally, access can be set so that "everything is granted except" or "only grant specific settings." If planned correctly, even the most complex lockdown requirement can be accommodated in IIS 7.0.

It's important to note in this section that only a small part of this managing delegation is available from IIS Manager. Most of the fine-tuning adjustments must be made directly in applicationHost.config *and* administration.config *or with one of the command-line or development methods.*

Delegation of Sections

This can get confusing because IIS Manager has two sides in this discussion. One is for the server administrator using IIS Manager to control access for the site administrator. The other is for the site administrator doing what they have been granted to do.

Moving on from there, we will see what the server administrator is able to set in IIS Manager for the site or application administrator. After looking at what can be achieved in IIS Manager, we will look at the more granular configuration control that can be done directly from the configuration files.

The first thing to do is to open up the Feature Delegation section within IIS Manager, as shown in Figure 9-10, by double-clicking the icon.

The Feature Delegation tool allows you to lock or unlock entire sections. Section examples include Error Handling, Compression, Authentication, and many others. IIS Manager does not allow you to lock or unlock more granular settings like attributes or elements, but they can be done manually, which will be covered below in this chapter. Figure 9-11 shows the Feature Delegation section.

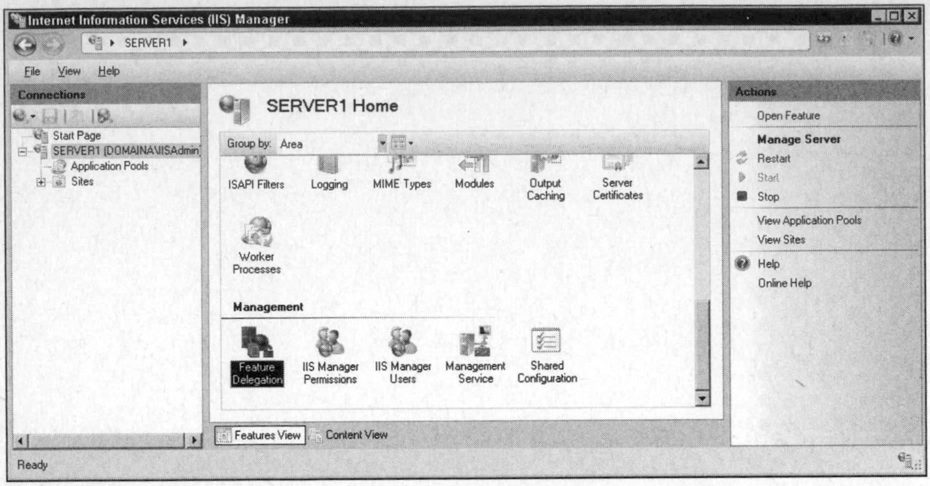

Figure 9-10

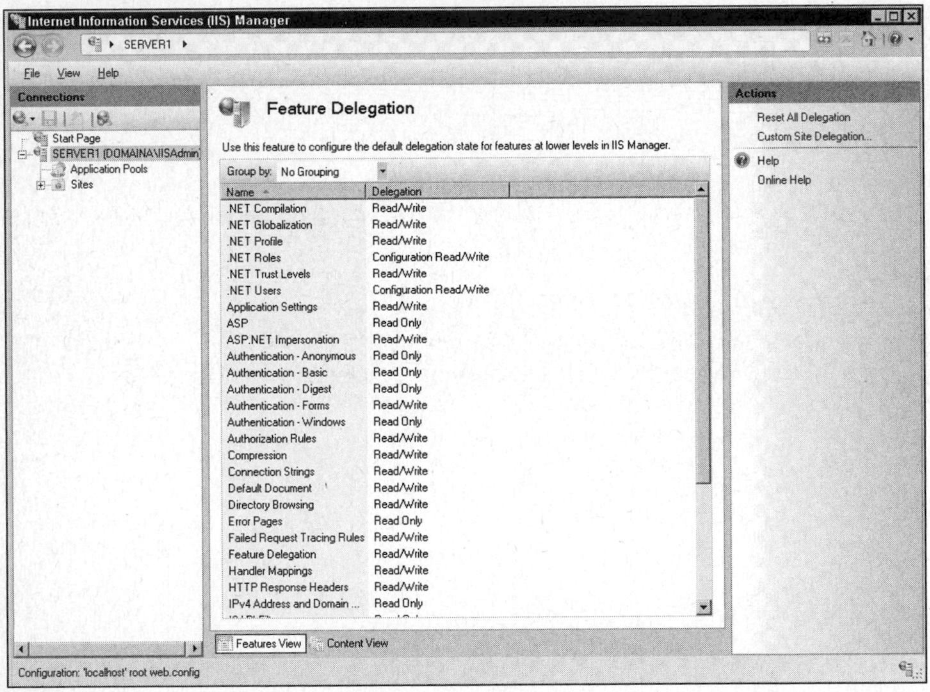

Figure 9-11

Within the Feature Delegation tool, you can change the Delegation setting, depending on the item, to one of the following:

❏ Read/Write

❏ Read Only

❑ Not Delegated

❑ Reset to Inherited

❑ Configuration Read/Write

❑ Configuration Read Only

This can be done by selecting the item in the main window and clicking on the appropriate action in the Action pane, or by right-clicking on the item in the main window and selecting the appropriate action from the dropdown choices.

These three options are covered in more detail later, but to really understand what they are doing, it's important to understand what is happening behind the scenes. The following sections dig in deeper to some of the more subtle settings.

Default Delegation versus Custom Web Site Delegation

The first thing to note is that when you open the Feature Delegation section, you will always start in the Default Delegation mode, labeled "Feature Delegation" at the top. This means that any change you make will apply to all sites (unless the site has its own setting that overrides the default.) To switch to the Custom Web Site Delegation mode, click Custom Web Site Delegation in the Actions pane (see Figure 9-12).

It's easy to get confused here because the differences between the two modes aren't very obvious. Apart from the subtle wording in the Actions pane, the two differences are the title and the existence of the Sites dropdown box only in the Custom Web Site Delegation mode. Figure 9-13 shows the Custom Web Site Delegation mode, whereas Figure 9-12 shows the Default Delegation mode.

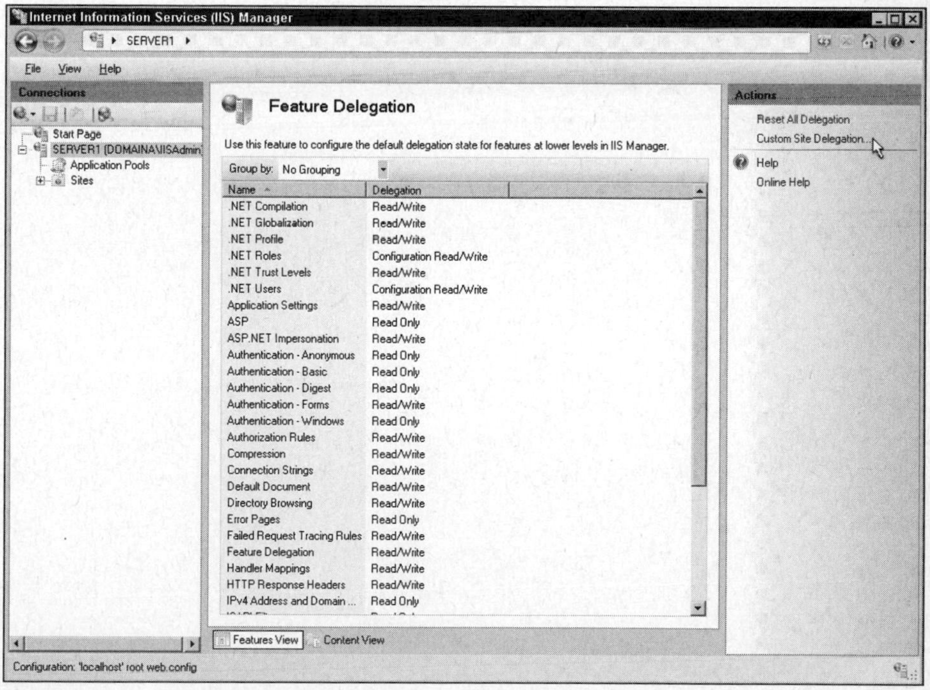

Figure 9-12

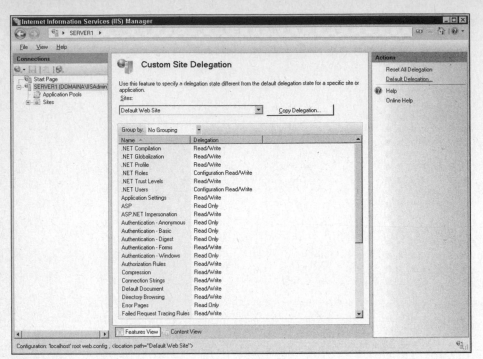

Figure 9-13

It's important to understand these two modes, because changes will be applied differently in each of the modes. In the background, every change is placed in a `<location />` tag in the `applicationHost` `.config` or `administration.config` file, which we cover in the next section (or in `machine.config` or the root `web.config` files for .NET settings). One or more of three location tags may be created, if they aren't already there. One location tag is set with `overrideMode="Allow"`, another with `overrideMode="Deny"`, and sometimes a third with `overrideMode="Inherit"`. When a setting change is made within IIS Manager, that section — for example, `windowsAuthentication` — is placed within one of the location tags.

When you are in Default Delegation mode, all changes are set in a `<location />` tag, where the path is set to `path="."` or `path=""` (both `path=""` and `path="."` function the same), as in the following example. This means that it applies to all sites, unless it is also set at the site or application level.

```
<location path="" overrideMode="Allow">
        <system.webServer>
            <security>
                <authentication>
                    <windowsAuthentication enabled="true">
                        <providers>
                            <add value="Negotiate" />
                            <add value="NTLM" />
                        </providers>
                    </windowsAuthentication>
```

```
                </authentication>
                <ipSecurity allowUnlisted="true" />
            </security>
        </system.webServer>
    </location>
```

In the preceding example, the location path is `" "` with an `overrideMode` of `Allow`, which means that it overrides the default `overrideMode` values. It then specifically grants Read/Write permissions to the `windowsAuthentication` section.

When you are in Custom Web Site Delegation mode, all your changes are placed into `<location />` tags, where the path is set to the web site or application name, as shown in the next example (which is specific for the Default Web Site):

```
<location path="Default Web Site" overrideMode="Deny">
    <system.webServer>
        <security>
            <authentication>
                <windowsAuthentication>
                    <providers />
                </windowsAuthentication>
            </authentication>
        </security>
    </system.webServer>
</location>
```

In this example, the path is `Default Web Site` with an `overrideMode` of `Deny`. This means that Windows authentication cannot be set for the Default Web Site by a site administrator. Because the first location tag allows Windows authentication for all sites, but the second location tag denies it for the Default Web Site, all site administrators except for the Default Web Site administrators can manage Windows authentication. The site administrators for the Default Web Site can view the settings, but they cannot update Windows authentication settings on their site.

In a situation like this, it is always the setting furthest down the configuration hierarchy that takes effect. In this example, the first location section is applied first because it's a generic global section. Then the second location section is applied. This isn't because of the order listed, (although they may be listed in that order) but because the second location is more specific and further down the configuration hierarchy path.

Another thing to notice in the first example above is the `ipSecurity` setting, which the second example does not have. This means that IPSec is allowed for all sites on the server, and because it isn't specifically denied for the Default Web Site, it is allowed there, too.

> *You may be wondering why only a few elements are set in the location tag when there are so many other sections. This is because there are defaults set earlier in the* `applicationHost` *.config file (or* `machine.config` *file for .NET related settings), so if you have not changed a section from the default, it will not show up in the location tag. This is covered in more depth in the next section.*

In IIS Manager, when you switch between the two modes, it does not change any configuration settings in the background. In fact, next time you come back into that section in IIS Manager, it will revert back to the Default Delegation mode. Therefore, don't be afraid to switch between the two modes in IIS Manager and then make adjustments at whatever level you deem necessary.

<section> Settings

At the top of the `applicationHost.config` and `machine.config` files are the `<configSections>` sections. Within them are many `<configGroup>` tags, and under them are `<section>` tags. The `configGroups` are containers that don't do anything except hold `<section>` tags.

The `<section>` tags, on the other hand, define the rules for the section — where they can be configured, what their default `overrideMode` should be, and whether they can be defined in location tags. The following table lists the three properties you can set to control how a section can be managed.

Property	Default	Values	Description
`allowDefinition`	`Everywhere`	`MachineOnly`, `MachineToApplication`, `AppHostOnly`, `Everywhere`	Defines where the section can be set. If not set, or set to `Everywhere`, then this section can be defined in `application Host.config` or any `web. config` file or location tag within the site hierarchy. It can even be set in folders not marked as applications.
			`MachineOnly` applies mainly to .NET and means that this section can only be set in `machine. config`.
			`MachineToApplication` means that this section can be run in `applicationHost.config`, the web site root, or any application folder.
			It cannot, however, run in a regular folder that isn't an application.
			`AppHostOnly` means that it can only run in `application Host.config` and cannot run anywhere under a web site.

Property	Default	Values	Description
overrideModeDefault	Allow	Allow, Deny	This sets the default overrideMode for this section. When set to Allow, changes in location tags or web.config files lower down in the site hierarchy can override the settings higher up. Essentially, it means that the value is Read/Write. Deny means that no sections below this can modify this value. Or, to put it another way, this value is Read Only.
allowLocation	true	true, false	This can be set to false to disallow settings within a location tag. You can still set them in web.config files, but because they cannot be set in location tags, the web.config file needs to reside in the actual folder that you want the setting to apply to.

The combination of these three properties set what is and is not allowed for the section to run at different levels. All three tests need to be passed for a setting to be allowed outside of the main sections of applicationHost
.config, machine.config, or the root web.config files. The default on all three is to allow as much access as possible, but many sections in applicationHost.config have an overrideModeDefault value of Deny.

Although you can change the overrideModeDefault *directly, this may not be the best option. Instead, consider using a* <location> *tag in the bottom area of* applicationHost.config *(or in* machine.config *or the root* web.config *files for .NET settings) with* overrideMode *set to* Allow *or* Deny. *This way, you can leave the IIS defaults untouched while still setting the* overrideMode *at the server, site, or application level.*

The Role of the Configuration Files

The previous section covered changing sections to Read Only or Read/Write permissions. Those changes are applied to the applicationHost.config, machine.config, or root web.config files and apply to both IIS Manager and web.config. The specifics of web.config and IIS Manager will be covered now.

As you are probably well aware by now, IIS 7.0 enables web site developers and administrators to control some IIS settings from the web.config file. Settings such as defaultDocuments no longer require the IIS server administrator or a custom control panel to change them. Consider the following web.config file, which sets defaultDefault to default.aspx. When you or your site administrator places this file in your web site or application root, IIS will pick up the setting and change the default document.

```xml
<?xml version="1.0" encoding="UTF-8"?>
<configuration>
  <system.webServer>
    <defaultDocument>
      <files>
        <clear />
        <add value="default.aspx" />
      </files>
    </defaultDocument>
  </system.webServer>
</configuration>
```

It's important to note that changes by a site administrator through IIS Manager will always be updated in the website web.config file, thus IIS Manager and web.config go hand in hand. IIS Manager is simply a friendly tool to help you do what you could have done in web.config manually.

Changes made by a site administrator in IIS Manager will never be applied to applicationHost .config. (If you happen to have jumped into this section without reading the first couple of pages of this chapter, it's important to note that "site administrator" is referring to someone who is connecting to IIS Manager using specific site or application credentials.) A server administrator, on the other hand, can make changes in IIS Manager that are written to applicationHost.config.

This web.config control allows application developers to create complete web site projects that include everything from the web pages to the IIS configuration, ready for straightforward XCopy deployment. For this to work effectively, it is important that the web site developers and site administrators are not given more permission than they should be trusted with, yet, they need enough access to do their job properly. It is up to the server administrator to implement the necessary settings. Since security best practices are covered in more depth in the security chapters and in other security-specific articles published by Microsoft and other companies, this chapter will not try to make suggestions on which settings you should make in your individual environment, but it will cover how to make the changes that you decide on, and what you should be aware of.

The default configuration allows only a limited amount of control from the site web.config file. The IIS team has tightened it to only the most obviously safe settings. It is up to the server administrator to turn on sections that he or she deems safe. Examples of sections that are allowed changes are:

- ❑ defaultDocument
- ❑ directoryBrowse
- ❑ httpRedirect
- ❑ urlCompression

Some sections that are not allowed by default are:

- ❑ httpCompression
- ❑ windowsAuthentication
- ❑ httpTracing
- ❑ isapiFilters

What happens when a developer uploads a web.config file that violates the rights granted him or her? Since the web site web.config file is not allowed to set windowsAuthentication, as in the following example; when the web site is viewed, a 500.19 error is thrown.

```
<system.webServer>
  <security>
    <authentication>
      <windowsAuthentication enabled="false">
        <providers>
          <remove value="Negotiate" />
          <remove value="NTLM" />
          <add value="NTLM" />
        </providers>
      </windowsAuthentication>
    </authentication>
  </security>
</system.webServer>
```

Fortunately, since the error messages in IIS 7.0 are much more informative than those in the past, it is easy to tell what is wrong. Figure 9-14 shows the error message that is displayed when you view it from the web server (or if you have <httpErrors errorMode="Detailed" /> set in web.config and are viewing it remotely).

Note the Config Error and Config Source sections, which are especially useful, allowing you to tell exactly what is wrong.

It is also worth noting that the windowsAuthentication settings in the site web.config are exactly the same as they are in applicationHost.config. An error will be thrown if there is any attempt to set anything in the windowsAuthentication section, even if the net result doesn't change.

Customizing Application Folders Using Location Tags

You can also configure customized settings for folders set as applications. This is done simply by creating a <location> tag in applicationHost.config with a path attribute pointing to the application. The following example disallows setting the default document within the /app subfolder:

```
<location path="Default Web Site/app" overrideMode="Deny" >
  <system.webServer>
    <defaultDocument enabled="true">
      <files>
        <clear />
        <add value="Default.aspx" />
        <add value="Default.htm" />
        <add value="Default.asp" />
      </files>
    </defaultDocument>
  </system.webServer>
</location>
```

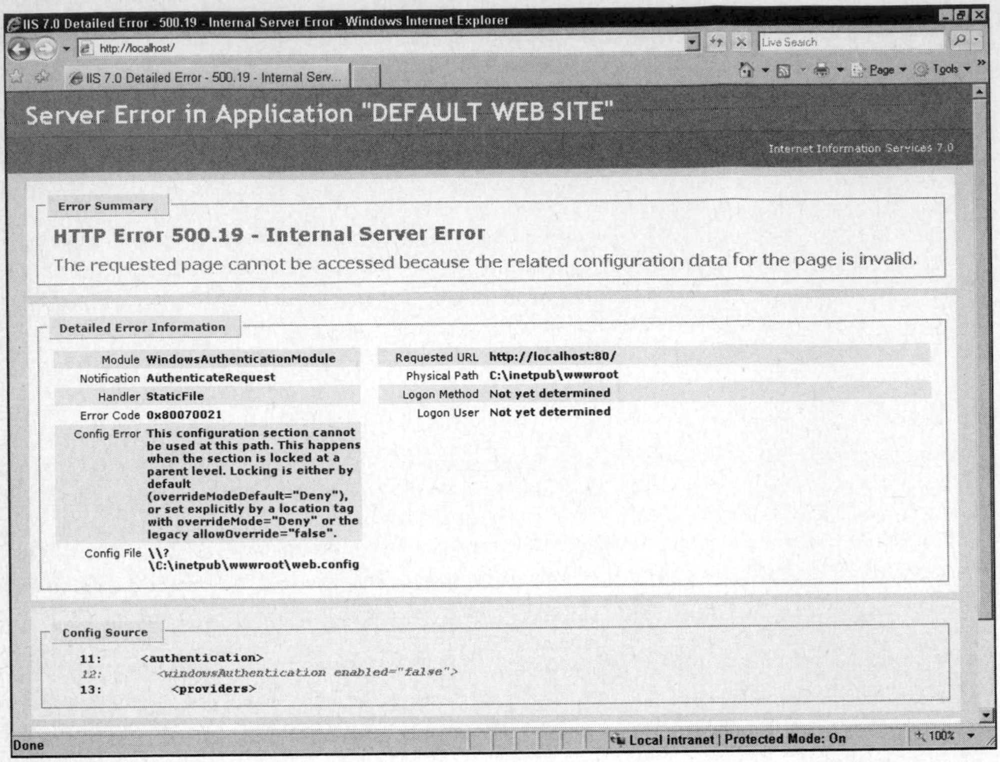

Figure 9-14

If the `web.config` file in the `app` subfolder tries to set the `defaultDocument`, a 500.19 error is thrown because it is explicitly denied the ability to set default documents within the `app` subfolder. If the following `web.config` file in the `app` folder is set, a 500.19 error will be thrown because it violates the policy set in `applicationHost.config`:

```
<system.webServer>
  <defaultDocument>
    <files>
      <clear />
      <add value="default.aspx" />
    </files>
  </defaultDocument>
</system.webServer>
```

The question that arises, then, is how do you set the `defaultDocument` when you don't have permission to set it in the `app` subfolder. The answer? You can still set it in the web site's `web.config` file, assuming that it's not denied access there, too. This is done using the `<location />` tag in the web site's `web.config` file, which is in the root of the site's path, as follows:

```
<location path="app">
  <system.webServer>
    <defaultDocument>
```

```
        <files>
          <clear />
          <add value="default.aspx" />
        </files>
      </defaultDocument>
    </system.webServer>
  </location>
```

Notice that the `location` tag's `path` property is set to `app`, which means that even though it lives in the root of the web site, it sets the default document for the `app` folder. The ability to control different sites and applications from `location` tags is powerful and allows you flexibility to specify IIS settings from locations that make more sense for a server administrator — for example, from `applicationHost.config`, which the server administrator has access to but the site administrator does not.

Where Settings Are Applied

An interesting concept with IIS 7.0's new, delegated configuration structure is that *locking settings define where IIS Manager applies changes*. IIS Manager will always make changes at the lowest level down the path that it is allowed.

If a section is unlocked and you make a change in IIS Manager to an application, IIS Manager will update the `web.config` file located in the application path. If the application does not have permission to make the setting, it will write the setting in a location tag in the site `web.config` file. If the web site is not granted permission to make the setting, then the `applicationHost.config` file is updated instead. Of course, as mentioned above, if a setting needs to be applied to the `applicationHost.config` file, only a server administrator is able to make the change. It is Read Only for all site and application administrators.

IIS Manager does not allow you to specify the location where it applies the change, but it does show you precisely where it makes the setting. This is shown in the status bar at the bottom, as shown in Figures 9-15, 9-16, and 9-17.

> *If you turn off delegation for a particular feature in IIS Manager, it does not automatically move settings around to protect web sites from breaking. It is up to you to go to all web site administrators and make sure that they do not have that setting in their `web.config` files; otherwise, their web sites will fail until they fix it.*

IIS Manager

So far IIS Manager from an administrator's perspective has been covered; now it's time to look at Read Only and Read/Write settings for delegation to site administrators. Let's look at the different IIS Manager delegation options in more depth to see what they really do.

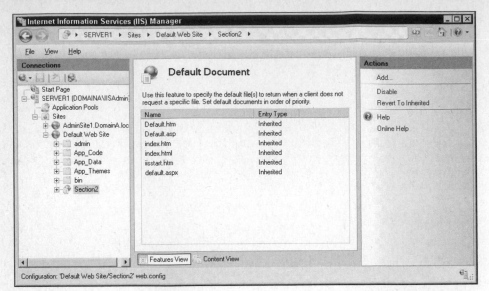

Figure 9-15

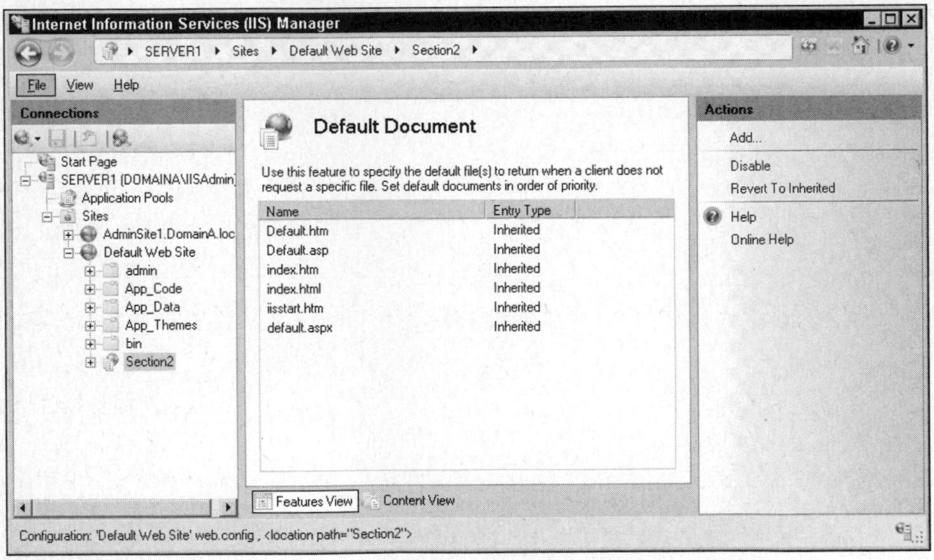

Figure 9-16

Read Only

Read Only access means that for that section, the site administrator cannot make any changes to the web.config file. In IIS Manager the concept is the same. The site administrator can see the settings but is unable to modify them. Figure 9-18 shows the Actions pane for a section that has Read Only permissions.

When the site or application administrator clicks the Edit Feature Setting link, the settings will appear, but they will be grayed out and cannot be changed.

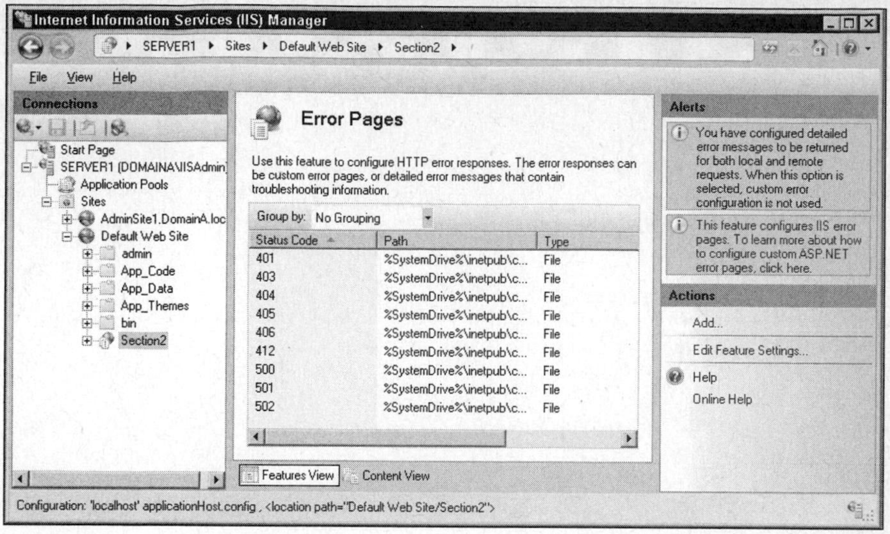

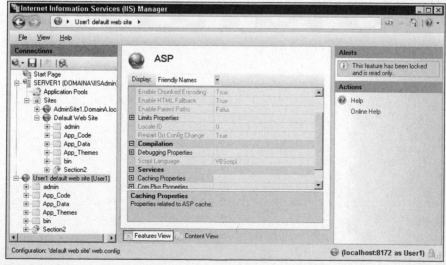

Figure 9-17

Read/Write

With *Read/Write permissions*, a site or application administrator can edit settings in that section, either through `web.config` or from IIS Manager, as covered above in this chapter.

Not Delegated

The *Not Delegated* option is a new one. What if you want to completely hide the icons in IIS Manager so that they don't show at all (for example, if you do not want a site administrator to even see the ISAPI Filters icon)?

Figure 9-18

The `applicationHost.config` file allows you to set `<location />` tags with `overrideMode="Allow"`, `overrideMode="Deny"`, or `overrideMode="Inherit"`. That takes care of Read Only and Read/Write permissions, but it doesn't do anything about the actual icons in IIS Manager.

This is where the `administration.config` file comes into play. The `administration.config` file is specifically for the IIS Manager user interface and various settings that it relies on — for example, management of the IIS Manager Users. In `administration.config`, you can remove modules, which, in turn, hides the icons in IIS Manager. Using this method, you are able to have each site or application show a completely different set of icons/tools.

The following excerpt in `administration.config` can be used to remove the ISAPI Filters icon for just the Default Web Site:

```
<location path="Default Web Site">
  <modules>
    <remove name="IsapiFilters" />
  </modules>
</location>
```

This is specific to just the Default Web Site, and it will remove the IsapiFilters module, which essentially means that the ISAPI Filters icon will not even show up for any site administrator for this web site.

Within the `administration.config` file, concepts for `<clear />`, `<add />`, and `<remove />` apply the same to this as to `applicationHost.config` and even .NET itself. If an object already exists, you must first `<remove />` it or do a `<clear />` to remove all objects in a collection. If you do not do this first, you will run into errors because of duplicate objects.

In Feature Delegation in IIS Manager you can set a section to "Not Delegated" for a particular site or application. When you do this, two changes are made to the configuration files in the background. A `<remove />` tag is added for that section in `administration.config`. Also, in `applicationHost.config`, that section is moved to a `<location />` tag with `overrideMode="Deny"` and the `path` attribute is set to the name of the site or application. This caused it to become Read Only.

If you set a section to "Not Delegated" in Default Delegation mode (for all sites), it will actually remove the tag in `administration.config` rather than using a `<remove />` tag. It will also set it to Read Only in `administration.config`.

To look at it another way, when you select Not Delegated, you are hiding the icon in IIS Manager and you are setting that setting to Read Only for `web.config` administration.

> *By editing the configuration files directly, you can hide the icons but still leave the settings as Read/Write for `web.config` management. Be careful that this doesn't fool you or future administrators into thinking that the section is locked down, just because it doesn't show up in IIS Manager.*

You can switch back to either Read Only or Read/Write, which will add the module back to `administration.config`, and, if you selected Read/Write, it will also update `applicationHost.config` to accommodate your request.

Configuration Read/Write and Read Only

There are two other types of section delegation settings: *Configuration Read/Write* and *Configuration Read Only*. In the future, more sections may exist that use these settings, but for now there are just two of them: .NET Roles and .NET Users. These two sections are specific to ASP.NET users and roles that are stored in a database. Changing them will only affect the configuration settings and not the data itself. The reason they are called *Configuration Read/Write* and *Configuration Read Only* is to serve as a warning to let you know that you aren't locking users out of the data itself, but only the configuration. It's the database part that makes it unique.

The Not Delegated for a .NET User or Role is the same as for any other section. It will hide the icon and set the section to Read Only.

Reset to Inherited

The *Reset to Inherited* option sets the particular section to inherit from its parent. The way it does this differs depending on whether you're in the Default Delegation or the Custom Web Site Delegation mode.

When in Default Delegation mode, if you click *Reset to Inherited* and the section is within a location tag, it will add the tag back to `administration.config` and move the tag back up to the main section in `applicationHost.config` (or the `machine.config` or the root `web.config` files for .NET settings). It will make sure to preserve any of your custom settings. If the section is not within a location tag, meaning that it already has the default setting, it will not change anything.

When in Custom Web Site Delegation mode, it will handle this differently. When you select the *Reset to Inherited* option, it will ensure that the tag is added back to `administration.config` and in `applicationHost.config` it will move the section to a location tag that has `overrideMode` set to Inherit. Even if the section isn't in a location tag already, it will move it down to the Inherit location tag.

Here is what `applicationHost.config` looks like when a section is set to Inherited:

```
<location path="Default Web Site" overrideMode="Inherit">
  <system.webServer>
    <isapiFilters />
  </system.webServer>
</location>
```

The other way to set a section to inherited is to delete it from the location tags using a test editor like Notepad.

Reset All Delegation

The final option in the Actions pane of IIS Manager for delegation is the *Reset All Delegation* link. This also functions differently depending on the situation. Essentially, the rules are the same as for *Reset to Inherited*, covered in the previous section.

If you are in Default Delegation mode and click on *Reset All Delegation*, it will move all sections from location tags and place them back in the main section of `applicationHost.config`, `machine.config`, or the root `web.config`. If there are any specific settings, it will make sure to preserve them for you.

If you are in Custom Web Site Delegation mode, it will copy all of the sections into location tags with `overrideMode="Allow"` or `overrideMode="Deny"`, except that it will leave the `overrideMode="Allow"` untouched. This results in whole new sections being created at the bottom of the configuration files, which you may or may not prefer.

If you would like to ensure that a particular web site always inherits from the master default, you will need to update `applicationHost.config` manually and either delete the location tags if there aren't any specific settings in them or change the `overrideMode` to Inherit.

Copy Delegation

When in Custom Web Site Delegation mode, there is a button called *Copy Delegation*. From here, it is possible to copy the delegation settings from one web site to another.

To do so, select the web site that you want to copy *from* in the dropdown box. Then click the Copy Delegation button. This will open up a dialog box with an option to select any number of the other web sites on the server, as shown in Figure 9-19.

Select the sites that you want to copy *to* and click OK. This will create a duplicate copy of the location tags and section assignments in `applicationHost.config` and `administration.config`. It is also careful to preserve any specific settings on each site.

It's interesting to note, though, that the Copy Delegation tool will create a copy of the entire resultant settings. The following example illustrates this point.

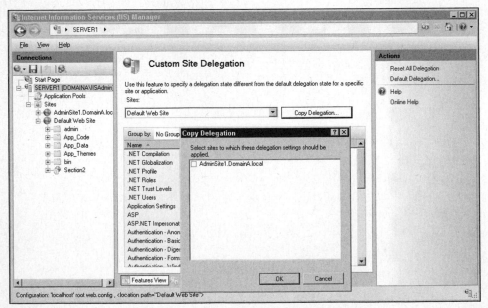

Figure 9-19

Here is a snippet of some example settings in `applicationHost.config` before copying. Notice that `customHeaders` has been set to Read Only for the Default Web Site, and a custom ISAPI filter is configured for WebSite2.

```xml
<location path="Default Web Site" overrideMode="Deny">
    <system.webServer>
        <httpProtocol>
            <customHeaders />
        </httpProtocol>
    </system.webServer>
</location>

<location path="WebSite2" overrideMode="Deny">
    <system.webServer>
        <isapiFilters>
            <filter name="Example" path="c:\windows\system32\file.dll" />
        </isapiFilters>
    </system.webServer>
</location>
```

After copying the delegation from Default Web Site to Site 2, the settings look like this:

```xml
<location path="Default Web Site" overrideMode="Deny">
    <system.webServer>
        <httpProtocol>
            <customHeaders />
        </httpProtocol>
    </system.webServer>
</location>

<location path="WebSite2" overrideMode="Deny">
    <system.webServer>
        <httpErrors />
        <modules />
        <handlers />
        <httpProtocol>
            <customHeaders />
            <redirectHeaders />
        </httpProtocol>
        <isapiFilters>
            <filter name="Example" path="c:\windows\system32\file.dll" />
        </isapiFilters>
        <!---section removed to shorten the example -->
    </system.webServer>
</location>
<location path="WebSite2" overrideMode="Allow">
    <system.webServer>
        <urlCompression />
        <directoryBrowse />
        <security>
            <authorization />
        </security>
        <!--section removed to shorten the example -->
    </system.webServer>
</location>
```

There are three important things to notice here. First, the Copy Delegation tool is careful to preserve the custom ISAPI filter, which we can all be thankful for. Second, the Copy Delegation tool actually fills out the section of the site(s) that it was copied to. Third, the Copy Delegation tool will not copy specific settings to other sites. It will only apply delegation related settings by placing elements in their appropriate location tag. In the example above, the isapiFilter called Example would not be copied to Default Web Site if you used the Copy Delegation tool to copy from Site2 to Default Web Site.

You may or may not prefer how IIS Manager does this. If you do not like how it does the copy, you are free to do it manually in `applicationHost.config` using a text editor like Notepad. There's nothing wrong with this really, except that any changes to the delegation settings further up the hierarchy will not be automatically inherited after a copy is carried out.

AppCmd.exe and Delegation

You can use `AppCmd.exe` to lock and unlock sections and reset them to their inherited settings. It does not handle the advanced attribute, element, and item locking (which are covered in the last few sections), but it does allow most things that IIS Manager supports.

> *The `AppCmd.exe` tool is not set in the server `path` command by default. You might find it beneficial on a new server to type **set path=%path%;%windir%/system32/inetsrv** from the command prompt to add the `inetsrv` folder to the environment path as long as that command prompt window remains open. This way, you don't need to navigate to `%windir%/system32/inetsrv/appcmd.exe` each time you want to run a quick `AppCmd.exe` command.*

To get help for the config management, run the following command:

```
appcmd.exe config /?
```

The `appcmd.exe config` command is used for a lot more than just configuring delegation settings, but the settings that apply to delegation are `lock`, `unlock`, `clear`, and `reset`.

The `lock` and `unlock` commands work the same as in IIS Manager, as covered above. Remember that locking makes a section Read Only, and unlocking makes a section Read/Write.

The syntax to lock a section is straightforward. You can leave out the site or application path so that it applies at the server level, or you can include it to make the section change more specific. Here is an example of how to lock the `directoryBrowse` section at the global level:

```
appcmd.exe lock config -section:directoryBrowse
```

This will place the `directoryBrowse` section in a location tag with `overrideMode` set to `Deny`.

To unlock a section, simply change `lock` to `unlock`. The rest of the syntax is the same. For example, to unlock the `customErrors` section for just the Default Web Site, run the following command:

```
appcmd.exe unlock config "Default Web Site" -section:customErrors
```

This will do exactly what the Read/Write link does in IIS Manager. It will place the `customErrors` section in a location tag with `overrideMode` set to `Allow`.

There is also a clear config and reset config which you can find more details by running `AppCmd.exe clear config /?` or `AppCmd.exe reset config /?`. These are not fully featured, but they do allow the most common changes. For example, `reset config` works only at the global level and does not support resetting inheritance at the site level.

With `AppCmd.exe`, it is possible to lock and unlock sections, reset global level settings, and clear out existing settings to do some housekeeping. In this section, we have looked at section locking and unlocking from IIS Manager, `AppCmd.exe`, and Notepad. Now it's time to look at attribute, element, and item locking.

Delegating the Small Details

So far, we have covered delegation of full sections. But what if you want to lock down more specific elements, collections, attributes, or even individual items? This is possible in IIS 7.0; in fact, the IIS team has you covered. By learning about a half-dozen properties, you can configure customized delegation, not only for sections, but for about anything else you can imagine.

Elements/Collections/Attributes

Before explaining how to lock or unlock elements, collections, and attributes, it's important to understand what they are. An element is a basic building block of XML, comprised of a start tag, the contents, and an end tag. Collections contain multiple elements which can be added or removed individually. An attribute is a parameter used to attach information to the element. The best way to visualize this is to see an example:

```
<anonymousAuthentication enabled="true" userName="IUSR" />
<windowsAuthentication enabled="true">
  <providers>
    </clear>
    <add value="Negotiate" />
    <add value="NTLM" />
  </providers>
</windowsAuthentication>
```

❑ **Element** — In this example, "`anonymousAuthentication`" and "`windowsAuthentication`" are elements. Elements can contain attributes, collections, or other elements within them.

❑ **Collection** — The `providers` collection allows multiple objects to be grouped together. In this case, they are a `<clear>` tag and two `<add>` tags.

❑ **Attribute** — "`enabled`" and "`username`" are attributes. They can only have one value (although the value can be a comma-delimited list of multiple values).

The scheme file `IIS_schema.xml` contains the real definition, where you can specifically see the elements, collections, and attributes. This is shown in the following example:

```
<sectionSchema name="...windowsAuthentication">
  <attribute name="enabled" type="bool" defaultValue="false" />
  <element name="providers">
    <collection addElement="add" clearElement="clear" removeElement="remove">
      <attribute name="value" type="string" isUniqueKey="true" />
    </collection>
  </element>
  <attribute name="authPersistSingleRequest" type="bool" defaultValue="false"
    />
  <attribute name="authPersistNonNTLM" type="bool" defaultValue="false" />
  <attribute name="useKernelMode" type="bool" defaultValue="false" />
</sectionSchema>
```

Now that elements, collections, and attributes have been looked at, it's time to take a look at how to lock or unlock them as needed.

Locking Attributes

The first attribute to look at is `lockAttributes`. This is a comma-delimited list of attributes that you want to lock. When this attribute is set, all child web sites and applications can read the value, but they cannot update it. It can accept an asterisk (*) also, which means that all attributes are locked.

The following example shows how you can use `lockAttributes` to prevent any child sites or applications from changing the `enabled` attribute in `directoryBrowse`.

```
<location path="." overrideMode="Allow">
  <system.webServer>
    <directoryBrowse lockAttributes="enabled" />  </system.webServer>
</location>
```

This allows anything to be changed except for enabling or disabling `directoryBrowse`. As another example, to also lock `showFlags`, you can set `lockAttributes` to `lockAttributes="enabled, showFlags"`.

If an attempt is made to change the `enabled` attribute in a `web.config` file, a 500.19 locking violation error will be thrown when the web site is viewed.

When you attempt to change an attribute in IIS Manager, a warning dialog will pop up, letting you know which line number on which file caused the error (see Figure 9-20).

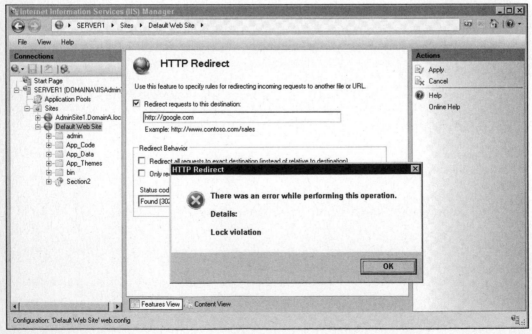

Figure 9-20

Here's an interesting one for you. If the section is set to Read/Write mode, setting changes made in IIS Manager will be applied to the web site or application web.config *file. If the setting that you want to make is not allowed because of the* lockAttribute *setting, you will get the error listed above. However, if the delegation mode is set to Read Only, then IIS Manager will apply the settings to the* applicationHost.config, machine.config, *or root* web.config *files, which aren't blocked by the* lockAttribute *setting. Basically, this means that if a section is set to Read Only, then the* lockAttributes *setting will be ignored by IIS Manager, but for a Read/Write section, the* lockAttributes *will prevent the setting from being changed, even by IIS Manager when running as a server administrator.*

Locking Elements

The next attribute that we'll look at is lockElements. This allows entire elements to be locked. You must place the lockElements attribute in the parent tag, as in the following example:

```
<httpProtocol lockElements="customHeaders">
  <customHeaders>
    <clear />
      <add name="X-Powered-By" value="ASP.NET" />
  </customHeaders>
  <redirectHeaders>
    <clear />
  </redirectHeaders>
</httpProtocol>
```

By setting this in the applicationHost.config file, you can specify that child sites and applications cannot change the customHeaders, but they can still change the redirectHeaders , since you didn't specifically lock it.

Like lockAttributes, the lockElements attribute can use an asterisk (*) to signify all elements, and you can specify multiple elements by separating them with a comma.

Locking Collections

You can also use the lockElements attribute to lock collections. Collections typically have three directives: add, remove, and clear. You can prevent site and application administrators from using any combination of directives. For example, you may want to allow them to add new items to the collection but not to remove or clear out the existing items.

This is done the same way as with locking elements. The following example illustrates this:

```
<requestFiltering>
  <fileExtensions allowUnlisted="true" lockElements="clear,remove">
    <add fileExtension=".asa" allowed="false" />
  </fileExtensions>
</requestFiltering>
```

This will allow elements to be added but not removed. As expected, a 500.19 locking violation will be thrown if an attempt is made to <clear /> or <remove> any items in the collection.

Locking Individual Items

A third attribute that can be used for delegation locking is the `lockItem` attribute. The two values of `lockItem` are `true` and `false`. This allows you to lock a particular item so that it cannot be changed. This is useful in a collection where you require that a particular item always be set. Here is an example of this:

```
<httpProtocol>
  <customHeaders>
    <clear />
    <add name="X-Powered-By" value="ASP.NET" />
    <add name="X-Copywrite" value="Wrox" lockItem="true" />
  </customHeaders>
</httpProtocol>
```

This will allow site or application administrators to change or remove `X-Powered-By` and to add new items, but it will prevent them from changing or removing `X-Copywrite`.

Locking All Attributes and Elements Except Those You Specify

The final two attributes, `lockAllAttributesExcept` and `lockAllElementsExcept`, are counterparts to the attributes just discussed. They enable you to lock all attributes or elements, respectively, except for those you specify. Each attribute takes comma-delimited values, just like their counterparts, but they do not allow the asterisk (*) wildcard because that would be a double negative, which would be confusing and counterproductive. As an example of `lockAllAttributesExcept`, the following line allows the enabling or disabling of the directory browsing but ensures that nothing else can be changed:

```
<directoryBrowse lockAllAttributesExcept="enabled" enabled="false" />
```

The `lockAllElementsExcept` attribute is essentially the same, as shown in the following example:

```
<httpProtocol lockAllElementsExcept="customHeaders">
  <customHeaders>
    <clear />
    <add name="X-Powered-By" value="ASP.NET" />
  </customHeaders>
  <redirectHeaders>
    <clear />
  </redirectHeaders>
</httpProtocol>
```

Notice that the `lockAllElementsExcept` attribute is set with a value of `customHeaders`. This means that if you set a custom header, it will be allowed, but if you try to set the `redirectHeaders`, you would get a 500.19 lock violation error.

The `lock` attributes are useful when you are unsure of what will be added in future versions of IIS or ASP.NET and you want to ensure that no matter what, only the specific attributes or elements that you specify can be changed.

Summary

Delegation of remote access is an important new concept in IIS 7.0, one that takes careful planning. Administrators can manage small subsections of a server, control their own web sites, and update IIS-related settings themselves. This opens up a whole new world of possibility, but also a whole range of potential issues.

Since IIS Manager does not allow remote management by default, this chapter went through the process of setting up a server for remote management, and the information that you must provide for the site or application administrator to connect remotely.

We covered locking or unlocking sections and setting Read Only, Read/Write, or Not Delegated and what happens behind the scenes when these changes are applied. We also looked at inheritance of delegation settings, which is important to understand when managing unique settings per web site.

Finally, `lockAttributes`, `lockElements`, `lockItem`, `lockAllAttributesExcept`, and `lockAllElementsExcept` are new properties that are used to set more granular locking on any object in IIS.

IIS Manager exposes most of the key features of IIS, but there are some advanced settings that cannot be managed directly from IIS Manager. This chapter covered both the settings that can be set in IIS Manager and the ones that need to be manually set outside of IIS Manager.

10

Configuring Other Services

In previous chapters you learned to plan, install, configure, and manage the basic IIS 7.0 web server functions. IIS 7.0 and Windows Server 2008 come with ancillary services that an administrator may want to use, such as an FTP Server and an SMTP Server. There are additional services and third-party tools that may also be helpful to IIS administrators, such as Microsoft's Log Parser and FrontPage Server Extensions. Although the capabilities of Microsoft's additional services might be more limited than those of other commercial products, such as comparing the SMTP Server to Microsoft's Exchange Server, for many functions the included utilities and services provide all the functionality needed and with no additional costs.

Not all IIS servers will benefit from these additional services; thus, an administrator should install only the services required. The security exposure of unneeded services should deter administrators from installing them, but these services can bring additional performance overhead, reducing the performance available for the needed functions of the server. Fortunately, all these services can be installed or uninstalled without affecting the IIS 7.0 functions, either during the IIS installation or at any time after IIS has been installed.

If you are familiar with these services in Windows Server 2003 and IIS 6.0, you should find no significant changes in the versions that ship with Windows Server 2008. The FTP Server that ships with Windows Server 2008 has no changes from the FTP Server in its Windows Server 2003 incarnation, although an upgraded version of the FTP Server can be downloaded from Microsoft's www.iis.net web site. The SMTP service has also seen no change in Windows Server 2008.

There are planning decisions that you need to make before installing and configuring these services, and without the background included in this chapter, the configurations are less than intuitive, especially when configuring FTP. Obviously, each installation environment will dictate how these are configured. For example, intranet use of these services differs from an Internet web hosting service. Plan your installation carefully, and you'll find these services, even with limitations, quite capable and robust. By the end of this chapter, you should be able to

❑   Plan an FTP Server installation, including user isolation and directory structure.

❑   Install and configure the FTP Server, including securing the FTP Server.

❏ Manage your FTP Server both through the GUI interface and programmatically.

❏ Install and configure FrontPage Server Extensions for additional publishing capabilities.

❏ Install and configure an SMTP Server, including securing the SMTP Server.

❏ Manage your SMTP Server both through the GUI interface and programmatically.

❏ Install Microsoft's LogParser tool and perform basic log file analysis.

FTP — Shipping Version

This section describes the version of FTP Server that ships on the installation DVD for Windows Server 2008. This information is for readers who might choose not to install the newer version of FTP Server available as a free download from www.iis.net. In most cases, you will not want to install this version and will instead choose the newer version, covered in a later section of this chapter. You might want to read this section for background, however, even if you intend to install the newer version.

Microsoft's FTP service has been around since the Windows NT days, and the core code has always been a solid implementation of the RFCs describing the FTP service. This has made the FTP service extremely compatible with compliant FTP clients on all platforms. It has also historically caused some limitations in the service, including large file transfers and the lack of secure FTP services that are in high demand today.

Traditionally, Microsoft's FTP service used a single FTP root folder and relied on Windows permissions for securing these folders. This changed somewhat with Windows Server 2003 and the introduction of user isolation in the FTP service in IIS 6.0. User isolation also seems to have caused the most problems for IIS administrators in configuring FTP services.

FTP Basics

At its root, *FTP* is a simple protocol for transferring files between systems. It operates on standard ports — one for control and one for data flow — and the basic functionality has changed little since the early days of networking. The original description for FTP in RFC 114 was written in 1971, and the Internet Engineering Task Force standardized it in RFC 959 in 1985. The PASV command, allowing Passive FTP and also called "Firewall Friendly" FTP, was standardized in 1994.

FTP operates at the application level and uses TCP as the transport protocol. Unlike many common protocols today, FTP uses two ports, one for the data stream and one for control, with TCP ports 20 and 21, respectively, the standard for Active FTP. Passive FTP uses a negotiated port above 1024 for the data, which is initiated by the client and thus normally passes through firewalls with less trouble. By virtue of using a control port and a data port, large transfers can cause problems with FTP when the control port times out with no activity while the data port is transferring the file.

Security has been a concern with FTP since the beginning. By default, logins and passwords are passed in cleartext, allowing network sniffers to retrieve the packets and reveal the logins and passwords. Two separate methods for addressing this issue exist, often referred to as *Secure FTP*. The first, which is true Secure FTP (SFTP), is FTP over SSH, wherein an FTP session is tunneled over an SSH connection. This is a tough act, because FTP uses separate control and data ports, whereas SSH protects a single port.

However, FTP over SSH is available in various products and implementations. The second method, FTP combined with SSL/TLS, is normally referred to as FTPS. The term SFTP, often used to describe either of these methods, actually refers to SSH File Transfer Protocol, which isn't FTP but, rather, a new protocol designed to address FTP deficits. SFTP has not yet been standardized, but SFTP servers and clients exist. The shipped version of FTP does not provide the ability to use SFTP or another Secure FTP method, but FTP 7, available as a free download from www.iis.net, includes FTP with SSL, or FTPS.

FTP on Windows servers can also be a major resource concern. Because each session is persistent in FTP, meaning that it remains open until closed, resources are tied up longer than they would be with an HTTP connection, which is not persistent. The default settings for FTP allow 100,000 connections with a time-out of 120 seconds, and many administrators will extend the time-outs to allow for larger file transfers through firewalls. For that reason, a busy FTP Server should always be a dedicated server and serve no HTTP or other traffic if possible. Installing FTP to allow the upload of content and code to a web site is a common function on web servers, and if this is your purpose, you really want to look at using the FTP 7 download and not the shipped FTP server.

User Isolation

The other major security concern that existed in Microsoft's FTP implementation was the inability to separate users into their own folder structure. While a work-around existed prior to Windows Server 2003 and IIS 6.0, the concept of user isolation introduced in IIS 6.0 eliminated this security concern for administrators. In Windows Server 2003 and Windows Server 2008, FTP users can be "Anonymous or Non-Isolated," "Isolated without Active Directory," or "Isolated with Active Directory." Depending on your specific needs, all three have a place on IIS 7.0 servers, and, in fact, all three can be run on the same server in different sites. When creating a new FTP site, you have three choices for user isolation.

Do Not Isolate Users

Under this setting — "Do Not Isolate Users" — the FTP Server behaves as it did prior to Windows Server 2003 and IIS 6.0. Users may or may not have a home directory under the FTP root, and NTFS permissions determine whether separate users can access each other's files and folders. This setting is primarily used for anonymous access or where multiple users having access to the same files and folders is not an issue.

Isolate Users

The "Isolate Users" setting isolates users, based on their Windows login, into separate home directories. NTFS permissions still affect the users, but they have no direct access to the home directory structure of other users. This setting allows for both local and domain user accounts to be used.

Isolate Users Using Active Directory

The "Isolate Users Using Active Directory" setting authenticates and isolates users through Active Directory and maps their home and root directories based on FTPDir and FTPRoot settings in Active Directory for each user. Naturally, this setting cannot be used outside of an Active Directory domain.

Directory Structure

One of the most confusing and least intuitive settings in configuring a Microsoft FTP site is the directory structure required for each user isolation method. If this directory structure is not used, then user isolation will not function, and clients will receive an error when logging in, indicating that the user's home directory is inaccessible. This is one of those configurations that made sense to a developer somewhere and became a required configuration regardless of usability. It is also one of the distinguishing factors between choosing to use the Microsoft FTP Server and a third-party product.

The directory structure for your FTP site must already exist when you create the site.

Structure if You Do Not Isolate Users

If you choose not to isolate users, the FTP site's root directory becomes the default home directory, unless there is a directory underneath the FTP root that exactly matches the user account login. Whenever there is a matching directory, the user will be dropped into that directory on login, but the only separation between users relies on Windows NTFS permissions on the files and folders.

The directory structure for this setting is the least exclusive of all FTP directory structures. You need an FTP root directory, which is specified in the configuration and can be anything, and that's it. If you want users to be dropped into folders based on their logins, you will also need a subfolder off the FTP root with the exact spelling of the login name. For example, if user John Smith has a login (SAM account name, not UPN) of *user1*, then the folder must be *user1* as well. Figure 10-1 shows examples of FTP folders created for the user account names user1, user2, and user3.

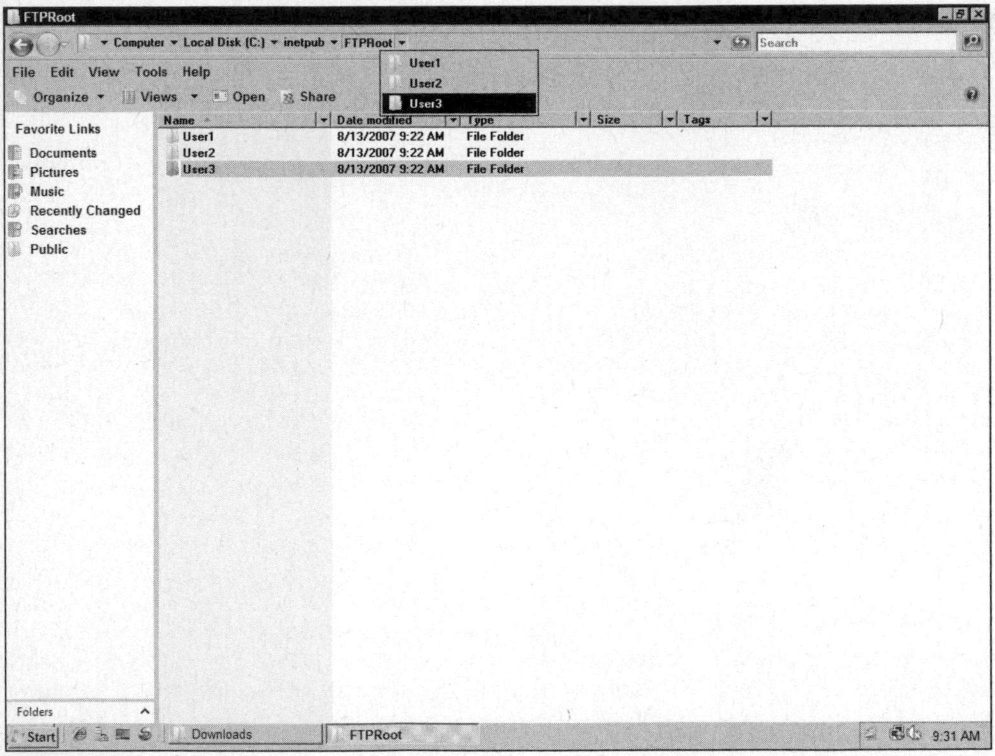

Figure 10-1

One common use of the non-isolated setup is for anonymous user downloads and uploads. When we go through security settings later in the chapter, we'll configure an anonymous upload folder that is invisible and doesn't allow downloads, often called a *blind FTP*. If you will use an anonymous access FTP for uploads or downloads, your best option is to configure a specific site for this and use a specific FTP root that is separate from any other. This setup is most prone to abuse, and instead of isolating the users, you can protect yourself better by isolating the entire site. An even better option is not to allow anonymous access but, rather, use a shared published account — perhaps Upload as a user for anonymous uploads and Download for anonymous downloads. You can then require a login and password and rotate this on a schedule to reduce the opportunity for abuse of the FTP site.

Structure if You Isolate Users without Active Directory

Standard user isolation requires a slightly more specific folder structure. In addition to the FTP root for the site, you need a subfolder off it named *LocalUser* for local accounts and/or the domain name for domain accounts. Off this folder, the subfolders must be named for each user account that will have FTP access. Each user is dropped into their folder on login as their root folder and prevented from navigating up the folder structure to see the other folders. In user isolation, the user's home directory is the root of his or her FTP site.

Figure 10-2 shows examples of FTP folders configured for the local user accounts user1, user2, and user3, as well as for the domain user accounts user4, user5, and user6 in the domain1 domain. There is also a folder named *Public*, which is the home directory for anonymous access when using standard user isolation.

Structure if You Isolate Users Using Active Directory

Active Directory isolation has no required folder structure because the user's home directories map according to entries in their Active Directory accounts. An FTP site using Active Directory isolation for users has no home directory, and only valid Active Directory accounts can access the FTP site.

Installing the FTP Service

Unless you installed FTP as part of the installation of IIS, you will need to install it using Server Manager. Open Server Manager, click Add Role Services, and then choose the entire FTP Publishing Service tree, as shown in Figure 10-3, which includes FTP Server and FTP Management Console. There's no configuration to be done while installing the service; you will set configuration options when you create FTP sites. Because the version of FTP that ships on the Windows Server 2008 DVD was not updated for Windows Server 2008, it is managed through the Internet Information Services (IIS) 6.0 Manager. When you accept the prompt to install required services, the IIS 6.0 Manager will install if it has not been previously installed.

Installing the FTP service creates a directory under \Inetpub on the %SystemDrive% called Ftproot, which is the home directory of the default FTP site. This directory can be changed in the properties of the site, and additional sites on the system will need additional directories created, too. These directories can be on UNC network locations, but valid credentials to the share must be supplied. In other words, if you choose to use a network location and a UNC path, the target server must have that UNC share with proper permissions for the FTP account accessing it. If you choose to do this, the most effective method is with Active Directory accounts and Active Directory isolation.

Creating an FTP Site

The shipped version of FTP Server, along with the SMTP Server, is managed from the "Internet Information Services (IIS) 6.0 Manager" found under Administrative tools, as shown in Figure 10-4. The IIS 7.0 Manager is listed as "Internet Information Services (IIS) Manager," without a version number.

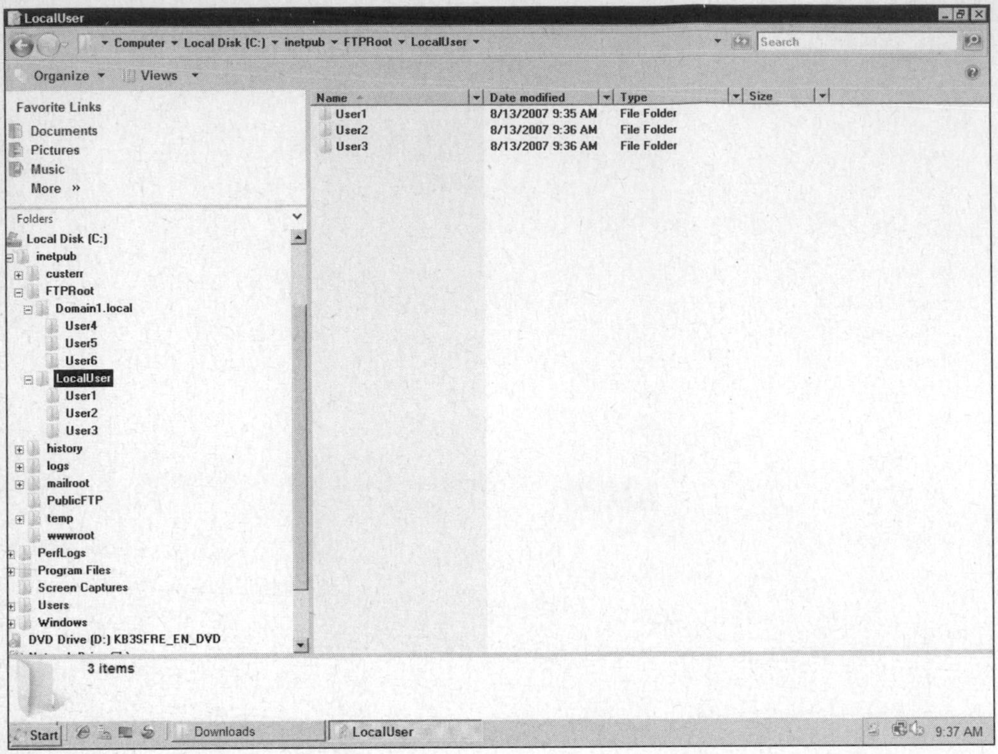

Figure 10-2

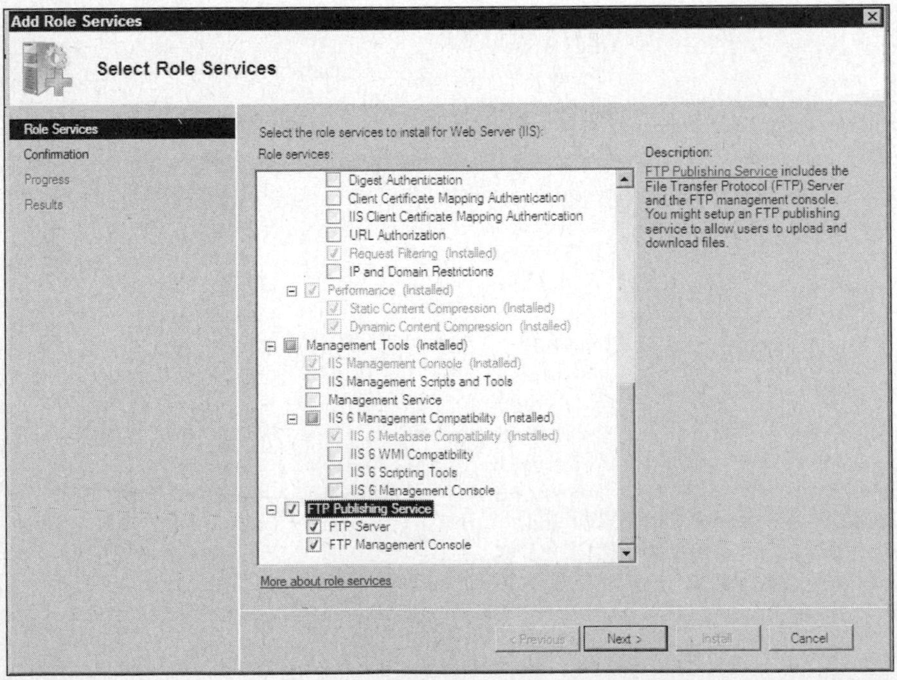

Figure 10-3

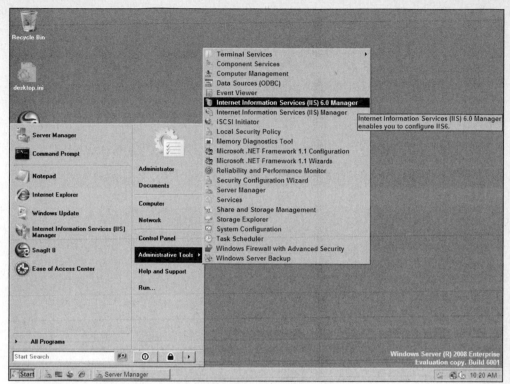

Figure 10-4

To create a new FTP site, expand the local computer in the IIS 6.0 Manager, and expand FTP Sites. On a new installation, you will see the Default FTP Site in a stopped state. You can rename this, or leave the name as is, and configure it, or you can create a new site. Let's walk through creating and configuring a new site. Right-click FTP Sites and choose New, then New FTP Site. This will launch the FTP Site Creation Wizard.

The FTP site description is the title for this site that will appear in the IIS 6.0 Manager under FTP Sites. You should use a name that is descriptive enough to identify the site, such as *Engineering Web Server* or *Public Relations*, so that the site will be easy to find when you have dozens in the list. For our first site, we'll create an anonymous public FTP site for clients to download files using FTP. Therefore, we'll name the site *Anonymous Public Download* so that it is easy to find.

The next wizard step is for IP address and port settings, as shown in Figure 10-5. You'll want to set the FTP site to answer on a specific IP address, even if you only have a single IP address on the system, instead of using (All Unassigned). This helps protect the server from a future IP address being used to provide FTP services and, while this is not a great risk in itself, can help protect the server from unauthorized access. Unless you have a specific need, you should also leave the FTP port at the default of 21. As with web servers, FTP servers answer on a specific IP address and port combination, and the default for the protocol is port 21. If you change this port, the end user must specify the port in the connection, as in `ftp://ftp.domain1.com:2121/` if you set this for port 2121. This is useful for secure FTP sites but can be confusing for end-users, since clients will assume the default FTP port of 21 when a user does not specify one. You must also remember to open the port in your firewall for access.

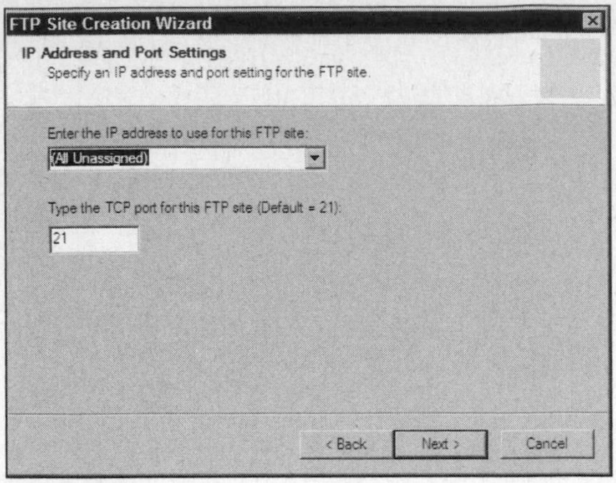

Figure 10-5

The next choice in the wizard is to select the user isolation mode. You need to make a choice, because the isolation method cannot be changed without deleting the site and re-creating it.

❏ **Do Not Isolate Users or Anonymous** — Choosing Do Not Isolate Users creates a single home directory to which all users for this site have access. This is useful for an anonymous access site since the user account doesn't matter. It is also useful for FTP sites that will point to a specific web-site folder structure and be used for uploading content to a web site. In this case, you would want to create a separate FTP site to match each web site and use FTP and NTFS permissions to allow specific user accounts' access. Each user is a local Windows user account.

❏ **Isolated Users** — Choosing to Isolate Users without Using Active Directory is useful to allow individual users to access separate data folders while not having to install an Active Directory structure. Each user is a local Windows user account. Using this mode, you can have a single FTP site with multiple login accounts and still point users to a web-site content folder. You will need to isolate users to provide web-site content access if you use host headers to assign web sites, since host headers share a single IP address, and only a single FTP site can be on a single IP address on the standard FTP port.

❏ **Isolated Users with Active Directory** — Choosing to Isolate Users with Active Directory provides the same benefits as isolating them without Active Directory, with the added benefit of not having a rigid folder structure and needing virtual directories to direct users to specific content folders. The disadvantage is that you will need an Active Directory structure, but, for web farms or other groups of associated web servers, the management tools in Active Directory make this option a worthy choice.

Since we are creating an anonymous public FTP download site, we'll use the Do Not Isolate Users mode. The next step in the wizard is to define a physical folder to hold the FTP site's content. The default is \Inetpub\FTPRoot, but we're going to choose a folder parallel to this, which we have already created, at \Inetpub\PublicFTP. The folder must already exist when you create the site.

The wizard's access permissions step offers two checkboxes: Read access and Write access. This is to the entire site, and site security is checked before the file and folder permissions on the physical files and folders in the site. When site security and NTFS security are combined, the most restrictive permission wins. This is important to remember when you seem to be locked out of a site, or when your FTP site that you thought was secure suddenly becomes a pirated software distribution site. For our site, we're going to grant only Read permission, as this is an anonymous public download and we don't want anyone uploading files to this site. You can change these permissions later in the FTP site configuration.

After completing the wizard, you will have a new site in your FTP sites list. This site will be stopped, but you can start it by right-clicking on it and choosing Start, or you can open the site's properties to continue configuring your new site. In our case, we'll open the properties dialog and adjust the configuration to our need for an anonymous public access site. It is always better to make configuration changes with the site stopped, in case one of your changes opens the site for unrestricted access, but configurations can be done with the site running. To activate most configuration changes, you will need to restart the site.

Setting Site Properties

In the first tab of the FTP Site Properties dialog, you will find the basic settings for the name, IP address, and port number. These can be changed — the IP address dropdown will show the IP addresses available on the server and will require a restart of the site. The second section, FTP Site Connections, allows you to restrict the number of simultaneous connections that the site will accept and the time-out for inactivity on each connection. It is recommended you not set a low number here, the default being 100,000 connections, to prevent a type of denial-of-service attack wherein a connection is made and left open to time out. If you set this to five connections, for example, a malicious script could make five connections to your server, allowing each to time out and restricting the ability of legitimate users to get to the site. A better option is a firewall or intrusion detection system that monitors for these types of attacks and drops them before they reach the server. That way you can limit the number of connections, and thus the amount of resources devoted to the FTP Server, without fear of a denial of service.

Logging

The Logging default is for the W3C extended log file format, and you can choose the location of the log files. Many hosting services will point these logs to a folder accessible through the FTP Server account assigned to the customer with that FTP site. Useful log options include Client IP Address, Method, URI Stem, Bytes Sent, and Bytes Received. This version of FTP has no configuration to restrict the number of bytes transferred or the total drive space, although you can use Windows Server 2008's quotas for limiting the space used by FTP clients.

Security

Use the Security tab to set the anonymous user and to allow anonymous connections. The default setting is to allow anonymous connections. If you don't intend to allow anonymous users into your FTP site, be sure to change this before starting your site. The default anonymous user is the IIS anonymous user account IUSR_{MachineName}, where {MachineName} is the Windows host name of the system. If you intend to have multiple anonymous sites, it is good idea to change this to a known account so that you can track it in security logs.

Messages

The Messages tab enables you to change the default messages returned by the FTP Server. The banner is presented when a connection is made before login is attempted, and the Welcome message is presented after an authenticated login. The Exit message is presented when the server receives the exit command, and the Maximum Connections message is presented when the maximum number of connections has been exceeded.

Home Directory

The Home Directory tab is where you set the physical directory for the FTP content, as well as the permissions to that directory for FTP connections. FTP servers can be pointed to network shares as well as local directories. The key to this is providing access to the share for the authenticated FTP account or using "Connect as" to specify the user account with access to the share. If you use a share, the share permissions also come into play when determining the FTP user account's access to the FTP content.

FTP sites can use virtual directories in the same manner that web sites can. Virtual directories provide two valuable functions for FTP sites: redirection from the forced directory structure of standard isolated user sites, and redirection to common folders for isolated users. You can also use virtual directories to redirect non-isolated sites to alternate drives or folder structures. Virtual directories are below the FTP site home directory, thus you must specify them in the FTP path for access. Many FTP clients allow you to set the default directory on the FTP Server that you will be placed in.

The process for creating a virtual directory in an FTP site is similar to the process for creating a virtual directory in a web site. First, create the physical folder. Then open the IIS 6.0 Manager and browse to the FTP Server where the virtual directory will be. Right-click on the server and choose Bew, then Virtual Directory. The Virtual Directory wizard will open and ask for an alias (the name of the virtual directory). You can then browse to the physical directory, choose it, and assign access permissions for the virtual directory. Virtual directory permissions are in addition to FTP site permissions and NTFS permissions. Remember that all permissions are evaluated, and the most restrictive is used. If you cannot write to an FTP site on a virtual directory, make sure that the account you use has access at all levels.

The directory listing style allows UNIX- or MS-DOS-style directory listings. A UNIX-style format would be similar to

```
drwxrwxrwx   4 FTPUser       0    51200 Sep  10 13:28 FTPRoot
```

with Read, Write, and Execute permissions listed for the owner, group, and public, or world, followed by the links, owner, group, size, date, and time, and finally the name. To Windows users, the more familiar MS-DOS format would look more like this:

```
10/04/2007   11:45 AM     <DIR>              Folder1
10/13/2007   01:38 PM              1,204,415 FTPFileName.doc
```

Whichever style you chose, the FTP client must understand the format. Popular FTP clients will understand either format, and most clients will accept either with no configuration by the user.

Directory Security

The Directory Security tab is inappropriately named in that it doesn't deal with directory security at all. Rather, it determines access based on TCP/IP address restrictions. TCP/IP address restrictions enable you to restrict access to specific IP addresses, or to prevent specific IP addresses from accessing the FTP Server. By default, all IP addresses will be granted access except those listed. This feature is really more useful in restricting FTP access to a single address or range of addresses. For example, suppose that you have a weekly file transfer between systems, using a scripted FTP session. Because you know the address of the other system, denying access to all IP addresses except that one secures the FTP transfer to that single system. This feature is pretty useless at blocking specific addresses or ranges of addresses, especially because the range you'll block is normally far greater than any range you would allow. Since the restrictions apply only to IP addresses and ranges of addresses, not to Internet domains, a domain that spans multiple IP ranges would need all those ranges to be blocked just to block FTP sessions from that domain. All of this is best done in a firewall, although the added restrictions can only increase security in the mentioned server-to-server automated transfer.

Automating FTP Site Creation and Management

For most professional FTP site creation needs beyond creating a single site on a single server, some form of automation will normally be required. Microsoft provides a Visual Basic script as a tool for creating and managing sites through an automated process, IISFtp.vbs. FTP can also be automated using WMI, but that's what IISFtp.vbs does. If you are interested in using WMI directly, from a C# application, for example, look at the source to IISFtp.vbs for details.

IISFtp.vbs

IISFtp.vbs is a command-line script located in the %systemroot%\System32 folder that you can use to create and control FTP sites in IIS. IISFTP.VBS is installed with the IIS 6.0 scripting tools and must be run with elevated Administrator privileges. It should be run using the Run As command from a less privileged account, rather than logging in as the administrator, to maintain Windows Server 2008's security model.

Creating and Managing FTP Sites Using IISFTP.VBS

You can create sites automatically on local and remote systems using IISFTP.VBS. The syntax for the command is as follows:

```
iisftp.vbs /create Path SiteName [/b Port] [/i IPAddress] [/dontstart] [/isolation
{AD|Local} [/ADdomain DomainName /ADadmin [Domain\]User /ADpass Password]]
[/s Computer [/u [Domain\]User /p Password]]
```

The only required argument is /create, with the Path and SiteName to be created. The Path is the path to the FTP directory, and the SiteName is the name the FTP site will be assigned. You must include the path and site name in the order specified to create the site. If the path does not exist, it will be created.

If unspecified by the /b and /i parameters, the FTP site will be assigned to the default port (port 21), and all unassigned IP addresses. The /dontstart parameter leaves the newly created site in a stopped state, which allows further configuration before the site is set online.

The /isolation parameter creates an isolated FTP site, either Active Directory or Local. If AD Isolation is used, the /ADdomain parameter must be used to specify the domain name, and the /ADadmin and /ADpass parameters may be used to specify the administrator account and password. If the /isolation parameter is used, either for AD or Local isolation, the proper directory structure must exist, as mentioned above in this chapter.

The /s parameter allows the script to run against a remote computer. The /u and /p parameters must be used with a username and password that have Administrator permission on the remote system.

Deleting an FTP site is similar, with the following syntax:

```
iisftp.vbs /delete SiteName [/s Computer [/u [Domain\]User /p Password]]
```

As in creating a site, the /s parameter allows the script to run against a remote computer.

Starting, stopping, and pausing FTP sites has a similar syntax, and can also be run against remote computers:

```
iisftp.vbs /start SiteName [/s Computer [/u [Domain\]User /p Password]]
iisftp.vbs /stop SiteName [/s Computer [/u [Domain\]User /p Password]]
iisftp.vbs /pause SiteName [/s Computer [/u [Domain\]User /p Password]]
```

Configuring Active Directory Isolation Using IISFTP.VBS

An Active Directory Isolated site can be created as shown above, but IISFTP.VBS can further configure a user's AD properties related to the site. Remember that the physical directory structure for your user's home directories must exist; setting the property in Active Directory won't create it.

Querying or setting Active Directory properties for users with IISFTP.VBS uses the following syntax:

```
iisftp.vbs /GetADProp UserID [/s Computer [/u [Domain\]User /p Password]]
iisftp.vbs /SetADProp UserID {msIIS-FTPDir|msIIS-FTPRoot} PropertyValue [/s
Computer [/u [Domain\]User/p Password]]
```

Querying the user's FTP properties in Active Directory using the /GetADProp parameter requires only the user's ID. Setting the property with the /SetADProp requires the user ID followed by the property to be set, where msIIS-FTPDir is the user's FTP directory and msIIS-FTPRoot is the FTP root, then the value to set that property to. Again, you can run the script against remote computers.

Examples

To create a non-isolated FTP site named *Download* with a directory of "c:\FTPRoot\Download" using the default port and all unassigned IP addresses, run the following command:

```
iisftp.vbs /create c:\FTPRoot\Download Download
```

To create an AD Isolated FTP site for the domain "domain1" with an Administrator of "JSmth" and a Password of "Passw0rd," and then set the FTP directory for the user "TJones" to "c:\FTPRoot\domain1\TJones\," run the following command:

```
iisftp.vbs /create c:\FTPRoot\domain1 domain1 /isolation AD /ADdomain domain1
/ADadmin domain1\JSmith /ADpass Passw0rd
iisftp.vbs /SetADProp domain1\TJones msIIS-FTPDir c:\FTPRoot\domain1\TJones\
```

Note that the username for any Domain\UserID parameter can also be specified in the UserName@ DomainName format, provided that this has been set as an AD property for the domain and user.

The FTP Command-Line Client

Windows Server 2008, as in previous versions of Windows, includes a command-line FTP client that can be effectively used to diagnose issues with the FTP service. Because the command-line client echoes each command and response, diagnosing the response codes is easier than with other FTP clients, including Internet Explorer, which may not show accurate return codes. Return codes are discussed in the next section.

The default syntax for beginning an FTP session with the command-line client is simply

```
ftp {ServerName}
```

You can designate the server by name or IP address and, if needed for a nonstandard port, append the port address with a colon. The default launching of the FTP client, when followed by a server designation, assumes an open command for that server. If you merely launch the FTP client by typing **ftp [ENTER]**, then you will find yourself at the FTP command prompt without an open connection.

The most commonly used FTP commands are open, close, dir, cd, get, put, and quit. The open and close commands will open or close a connection to the FTP Server specified as a parameter for the command, respectively. The dir command simply displays a directory at the level you are at within the FTP folder hierarchy, and the client also supports the UNIX-style ls command to list directories and files. The cd command enables you to change directories, the same as on the local system at a command prompt. The get and put commands are used to get a file from the FTP Server or put a file on the FTP Server, respectively, essentially downloading or uploading files.

A full FTP session that logs into a site, changes to the upload directory, and uploads the file MyFile.txt, then exits would look something like this (user-typed commands are in bold):

```
c:\>ftp ftp.domain1.com
connected to ftp.domain1.com
220 Microsoft FTP Service
User <ftp.domain1.com:<none>>: jsmith
331 Password required for jsmith
Password: Passw0rd
ftp> cd upload
250 CWD command successful
ftp> put MyFile.txt
220 Port command successful
150 Opening ASCII mode data connection for MyFile.txt
226 Transfer complete
ftp: 10 bytes sent in .01 Seconds 756.00 Kbytes/sec.
ftp> close
221
ftp> quit
c:\>
```

The response codes returned by the server — 220, 331, 250, 150, 226, and 221 — provide a concise path through the transaction. Errors or unexpected response codes are visible in the command-line client so that you can see the exact command that fails along with the response from the server at the point of failure.

For example, if you had entered

```
ftp> cd uplode
```

and the actual physical directory name was spelled correctly, as in our first example, you should have seen a response code of 550, since the directory does not exist. Knowing that the 550 response occurred on that command helps you to diagnose that the directory does not exist or cannot be seen by the client login ID, probably because of permissions.

FTP Logs and Response Codes

The FTP service in Windows Server 2008 follows RFC guides and returns response codes for each command issued to it. Refer to Appendix B for the complete list.

FTP 7

Microsoft customers have switched to third-party FTP Server software over the years because the FTP Server from Microsoft has lacked some technologies that many users need. One of the primary needs was for a secure FTP solution, usually Secure FTP, which was not provided in any Microsoft implementation. For Windows Server 2008, the intention was to ship a new FTP Server that had a secure transfer option as well as several other upgrades or changes. Because of estimated product ship schedules, this new FTP Server was unable to ship on the same installation media as Windows Server 2008. For this reason, the IIS product group decided to provide the new FTP Server, along with many other utilities, on Microsoft's IIS web site at `www.iis.net`.

The new FTP Server, referred to as FTP 7, uses FTP over SSL (FTPS), though not FTP over Secure Shell (SFTP). Although it is not the same as many other FTP servers that use SFTP, FTP over SSL is supported by all the major FTP clients, including the new command-line client that is included in the download. FTP 7 is also integrated with IIS 7.0, including IIS 7.0's extensibility and the use of XML configuration files. FTP 7 does not integrate with IIS 7.0's delegation features, but it does use the IIS 7.0 user interface. FTP 7 also now supports virtual host names, similar to the host headers for web sites. FTP 7 works only on Windows Server 2008; there is no support for Vista or previous versions of Windows Server.

Installing FTP 7

Installation of FTP 7 begins with downloading the installer package from `www.iis.net`. If you already have installed the version of FTP that shipped with Windows Server 2008, you must uninstall it before installing the new version. Be sure to back up any content, as the uninstall will delete the `\Inetpub\ftproot` folder. Removal also requires a system restart. If you are not using the SMTP Server, you can also remove the IIS 6.0 Manager installed with FTP.

Installation of FTP 7 also requires IIS 7.0 to already be installed, and if you intend to manage it using IIS Manager, you must have that installed as well. You must have Administrator privileges to install FTP 7, and if you are installing it on servers in a web farm, you must disable the shared configuration option. You can enable shared configurations again after the FTP 7 Server has been installed. You must also download the appropriate version of the FTP 7 .MSI installer file, x86 for the 32-bit version of Windows Server 2008 or amd64 for the 64-bit version, from the `www.iis.net` Downloads section.

When you run the downloaded .MSI file to install FTP 7, you will be presented with an installation wizard. As you follow through the wizard, you will have a few choices other than whether to install the IIS 7.0 extensibility features, which allow you to use ASP.NET authentication or IIS users in your FTP 7 site. Unless you have a specific reason not to, you should install all features. Installation does not require restarting the server, but it does require a restart of IIS, which it will attempt using the `IISReset` command-line option.

IISReset can be run from a command prompt to stop and restart IIS 7.0. At a command prompt, issue the command:

```
iisreset /noforce ComputerName
```

If you are logged into the server and running the command locally, you can omit the ComputerName parameter. IISReset waits 1 minute for all IIS services to stop before forcing them to stop, potentially losing data. Using the /noforce parameter allows services to stop normally, preserving data, although the reset may take longer.

Creating a New FTP 7 Site

Creating an FTP 7 site in IIS Manager is as easy as creating a new web site. After installing FTP 7, simply browse to the sites tree in the Connection pane, right-click Sites, and choose Add FTP Site. You can also choose Add FTP Site in the Actions pane on the right. This will launch the Add FTP Site wizard.

The first page of the Add FTP Site wizard, as shown in Figure 10-6, will ask for the "site name" and "Physical path." The name is what is displayed in the sites tree in IIS Manager, and the physical path is where this site's content folders will be located. You can use variables in the physical path, such as %SystemDrive%\Inetpub\ftproot\, and when you browse for the physical path, you can create a new folder. The physical path can be on a UNC share as well.

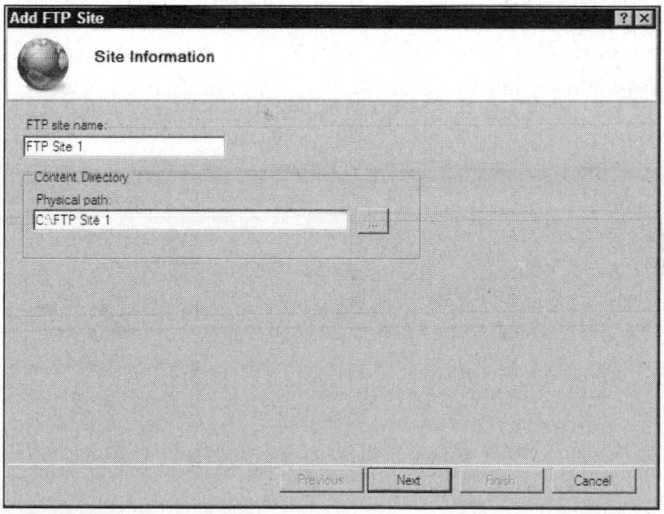

Figure 10-6

The next page of the wizard, as shown in Figure 10-7, allows you to specify an IP Address and Port combination. Unless you have a specific reason not to, you should use the default port of 21. You might change this if you have a scripted FTP transfer that runs automatically, but changing the default port will confuse most users because the port must be specified in the connection unless it is the default of 21. You should not use the default IP address of "All Unassigned," which makes IIS answer on any IP address not assigned to another web site. This can allow unintended connections on other IP addresses, so you should always specify the IP address for the FTP site to respond on. Unlike Microsoft's previous versions of FTP, where the IP address and port combination specified the FTP Server, FTP 7 can use a virtual host setting to allow multiple sites to share the same IP address and port. Virtual hosts are covered in detail later in this chapter, as is configuring SSL settings.

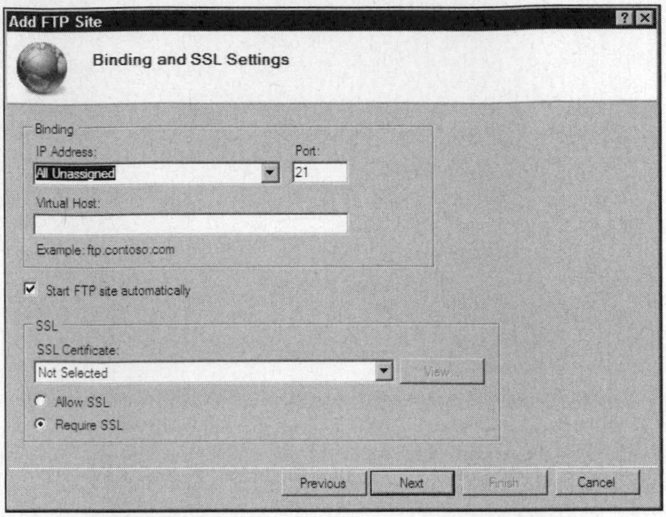

Figure 10-7

The last page of the Add FTP Site wizard, as shown in Figure 10-8, is for Authentication and Authorization. Checkboxes allow Anonymous and/or Basic authentication for the site, and you can choose who to allow access to and what access they receive to the site — Read, Write, or both. Keep in mind that NTFS permissions for the physical files, folders, and any network shares still apply to Windows user accounts, and these permissions combine with the site permissions assigned here. The most restrictive permission wins. As an example, we'll make this an anonymous public FTP site for downloading. Checking the Anonymous authentication box, allowing access to anonymous users, and choosing only Read permission will configure this access. FTP 7 security options are covered later in this chapter.

Adding an FTP 7 Site to an Existing Web Site

One of the most common scenarios for using FTP on an IIS server is to publish content to the web site through FTP. In past versions of the FTP Server, this required using redirection tricks such as a virtual directory with the same name as the user account. FTP 7 does away with all the tricks and redirection by allowing you to bind the FTP site directly to the web site, using the same security accounts for publishing as for administering the web site.

Adding an FTP 7 site to an existing web site is the same process as adding a new FTP 7 site, except that you select the web site in the sites tree of the Connections pane and choose Add FTP Publishing from the Actions pane, as shown in Figure 10-9. The Add FTP Site wizard will walk you through creating the site; as before, only the site will be bound to the specific web site.

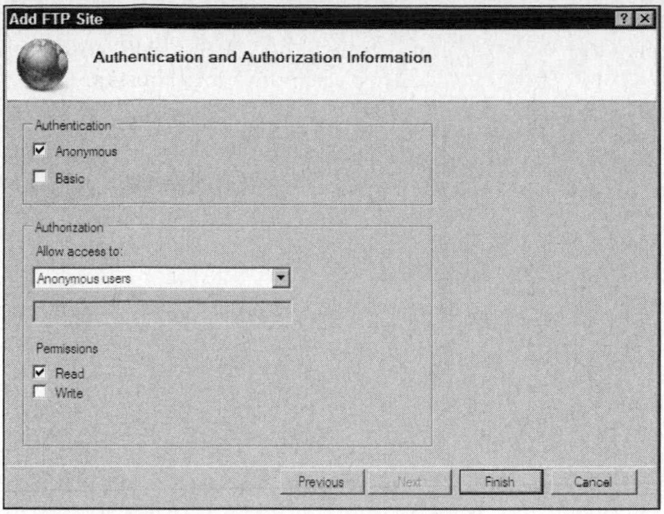

Figure 10-8

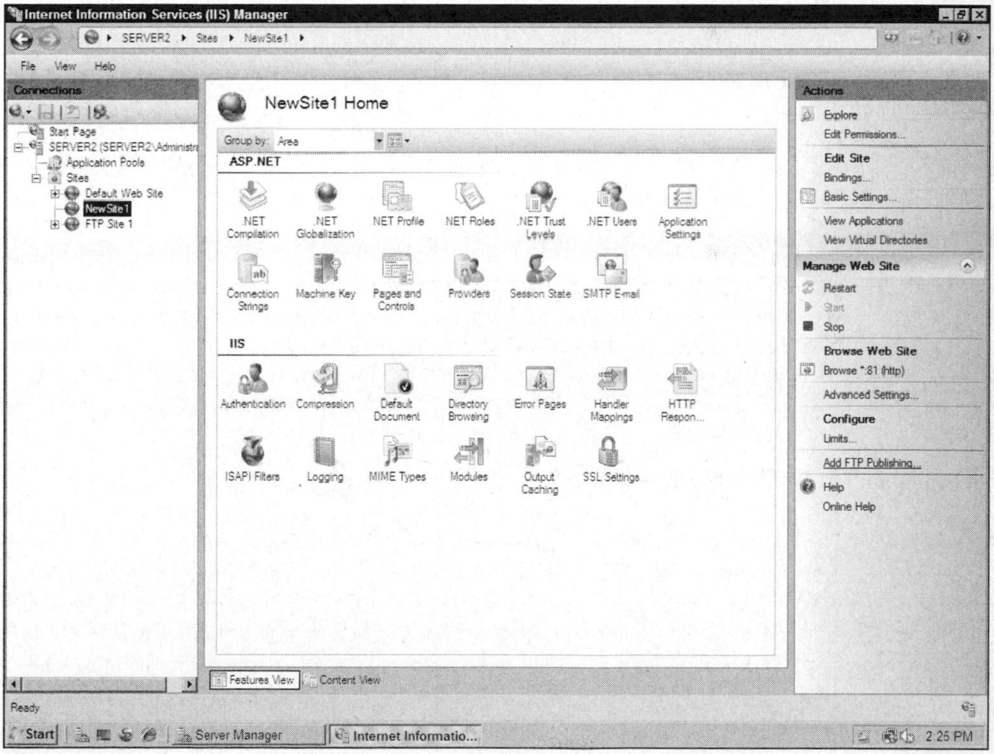

Figure 10-9

Configuring FTP 7 Security

Creating a new site for anonymous access isn't much use for many FTP needs, which require Write access for only specific users. You can configure a range of security options in FTP 7, including authorization and authentication security to provide restricted access for specific users. For example, let's add Read and Write access for the administrator to our FTP site. Start by highlighting the FTP site in the sites tree of the Connections pane, as shown in Figure 10-10, and the FTP features for this site will show in the center pane.

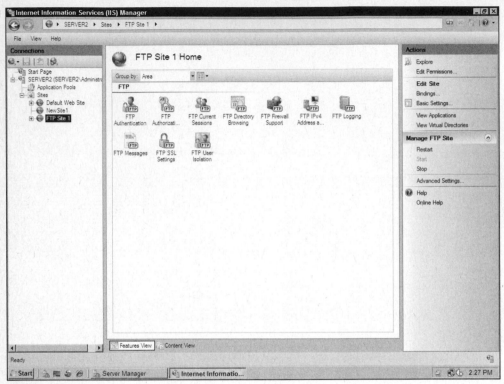

Figure 10-10

Since this site only has Read access for Anonymous, or unauthenticated, users, Authentication and Authorization must be configured for the Administrator account, and it must be granted both Read and Write access. Start by adding Basic authentication in addition to the existing Anonymous authentication so that there is a method for authenticating a user account that logs in. To do this, open the Authentication feature, and you'll see that, while Anonymous authentication was enabled when the site was created, Basic authentication is disabled. Highlight "Basic Authentication," and enable it by choosing Enable in the Actions pane (see Figure 10-11). Now you have a method for authenticating a user account.

After enabling the authentication method, we need to authorize the Administrator account for the FTP site. Opening the Authorization feature, as shown in Figure 10-12, we see that only Anonymous Users are Allowed, and only with the Read Permission. When you click the "Add Allow Rule" action, you will be presented with a dialog to allow specific users or roles access.

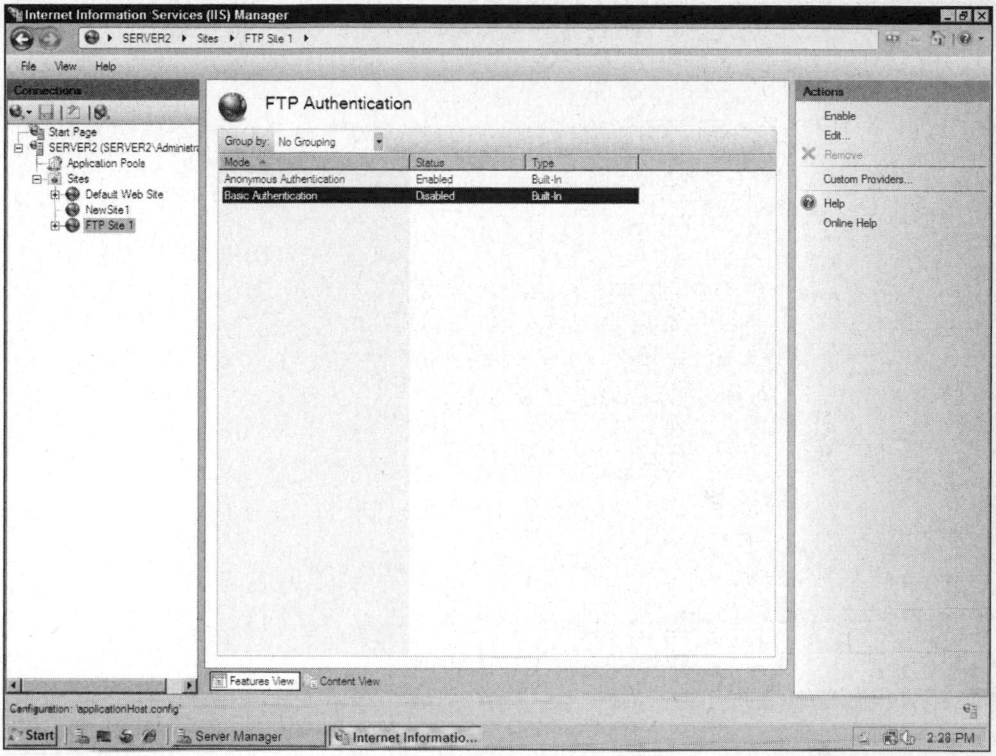

Figure 10-11

As shown in Figure 10-13, you can allow access to all users, all anonymous users, specified roles or user groups, or specified users. The All Users and All Anonymous Users choices are self-explanatory, and naturally should be used carefully because they can allow unintended access to a site. The "Specified roles or user groups" option enables you to assign access to a group, and then user accounts can be allowed or denied access simply by adding or removing them from the group, without ever changing authorization roles for the FTP site. *Roles* are groups of IIS user accounts, whereas *user groups* are standard Windows groups using Windows accounts. Windows accounts will require a client access license, or CAL, and are most useful for intranet situations. IIS users do not require Windows CALs and are useful in hosting situations where accounts only need access to manage IIS or use FTP. For our needs, we are going to add the Administrator account with Read and Write access allowed.

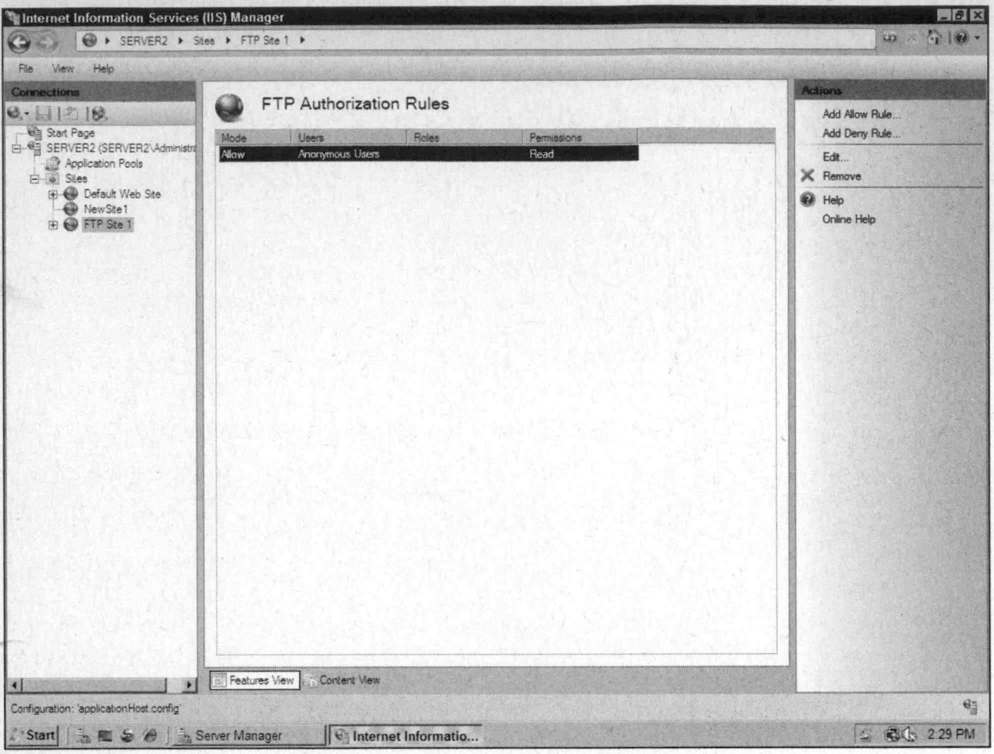

Figure 10-12

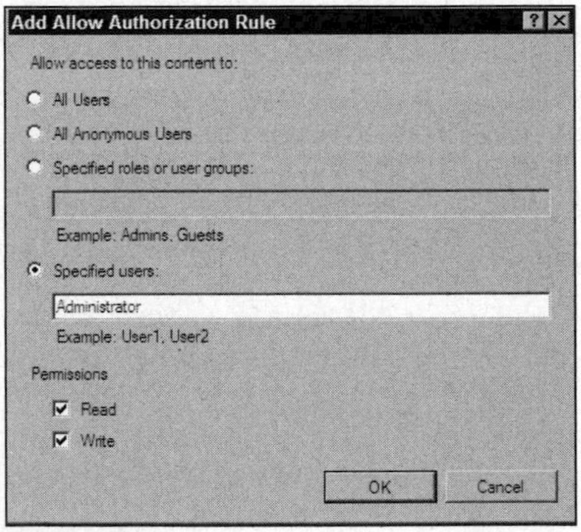

Figure 10-13

Configuring FTP 7 over SSL

One of the most significant changes in IIS 7.0 is the ability to use a secure channel for FTP communications using FTP over SSL (FTPS). Although you still need an SSL certificate to do this, Microsoft has provided simplified self-signed certificates for both IIS and FTP use. Naturally, if you have a certificate from a recognized certificate authority, you can use that, but for simply creating a SSL connection for FTP, a self-signed certificate is both secure and quite usable.

The first step in configuring FTPS is to create the certificate. You can do this in IIS Manager by selecting the server in the Connections pane, and under the Security Category, selecting Server Certificates. When this feature opens, you will see the current certificates or, as shown in Figure 10-14, none. Select "Create Self-Signed Certificate" in the Actions pane to create the certificate for your FTP site.

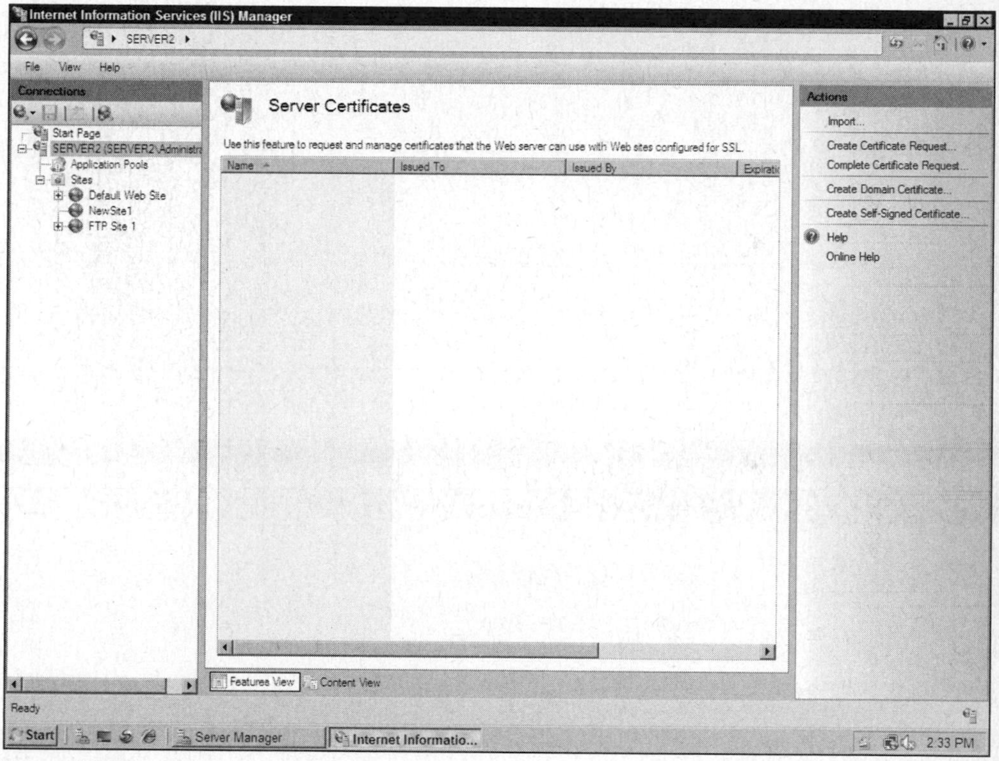

Figure 10-14

You need to enter a Friendly Name for the certificate, as shown in Figure 10-15. Since this is a self-signed certificate, you don't need to send a file to a certificate authority. You simply need to choose OK, and the server will create the certificate for you. See Chapter 15 for more information on using SSL certificates.

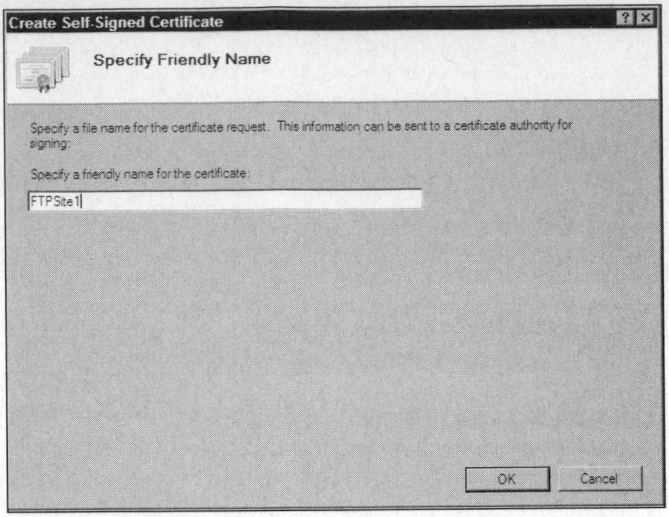

Figure 10-15

The steps to add the SSL certificate to the FTP site are quite simple. Highlight the site in the sites tree of the Connections pane, and choose FTP SSL Settings from the FTP features. In the FTP SSL Settings dialog box, shown in Figure 10-16, select the SSL certificate you just created, and check "Allow SSL connections." This allows the Administrator account to connect with SSL and the anonymous users to connect without using SSL. Connections that don't use SSL could be sniffed on the network for connection credentials, but revealing anonymous credentials is virtually no risk. If you do not allow anonymous users, such as in a web hosting service that uses FTP for clients to upload content to their web sites, then requiring SSL connections will lock down the access to only using SSL. This will protect the connection from network sniffers and from exposing credentials on an unsecured network. You can specify SSL for the credentials only by selecting the Advanced button.

Configuring FTP 7 User Isolation

Although the user isolation introduced in IIS 6.0 is still available in FTP 7, it is less useful because FTP sites can be bound to a specific web site, which was a major reason for user isolation in the past. However, you might still want to isolate users and provide an FTP site for transferring data from client systems. Isolating users in FTP 7 is much easier than in the prior version, and you have options for isolation as well. To isolate users, browse to the FTP site in the sites tree of the Connection pane, and then select the FTP User Isolation feature. The FTP User Isolation configuration, shown in Figure 10-17, offers two basic options — "Do not isolate users" and "Isolate users."

The default option, "FTP root directory," is a new option in FTP 7. All users are started in the same root folder, and NTFS permissions determine what each account can do within that folder structure. The second option, "User name directory," is the same as "Do not isolate users" in IIS 6.0. Users are started in the folder matching their login account name under the root folder, or in the root folder if a folder matching their login does not exist. NTFS permissions are still the only factor determining access differences between users.

Isolating users in FTP 7 restricts users to specific directories, as in IIS 6.0, but there are some additional options. The first option, restricting users to the "user name directory" and disabling "global virtual directories," is new in FTP 7. It behaves like isolating users did in IIS 6.0, with the exception that global virtual directories are also restricted. The second option, enabling global virtual directories, is the same behavior as the FTP Server in IIS 6.0. Isolating users to the home directory in Active Directory is the same as isolating users with Active Directory in IIS 6.0.

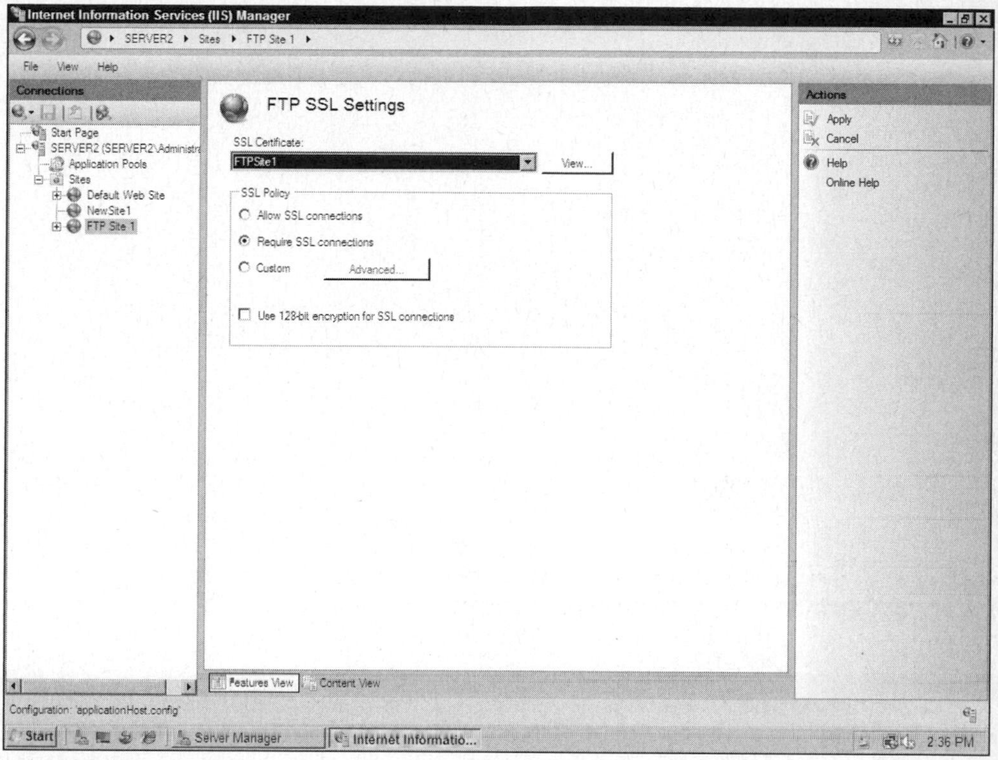

Figure 10-16

As in IIS 6.0, user isolation requires the proper folder structure, and that the folders exist, prior to configuring the web site. Configuration of the IIS 6.0 FTP Server is covered above in this chapter. The following table shows the required directories for each type of access:

User Account Types	Physical Home Directory Syntax
Anonymous users	%FtpRoot%\LocalUser\Public
Local Windows user accounts (requires Basic authentication)	%FtpRoot%\LocalUser\%UserName%
Windows domain accounts (requires Basic authentication)	%FtpRoot%\%UserDomain%\%UserName%
IIS Manager or ASP.NET custom authentication user accounts	%FtpRoot%\LocalUser\%UserName%

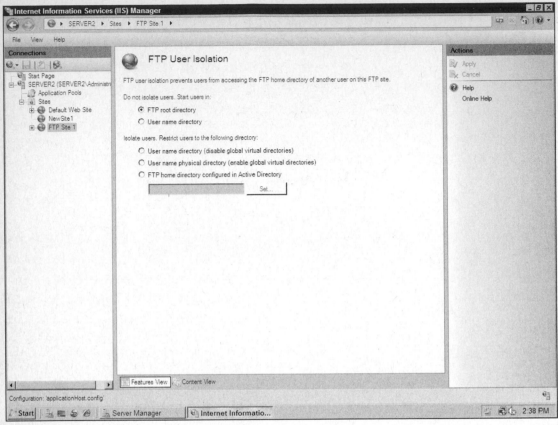

Figure 10-17

Configuring FTP 7 Host Name Support

Host name support for FTP is a second major change in FTP from previous versions. In FTP before version 7, if you wanted a separate FTP site, you had to use a separate IP address and port combination, which in most cases meant a separate IP address, as nonstandard ports can confuse users. Although you could share web sites on a single IP address using host headers, there was nothing similar for FTP.

To add a host name to your FTP site so you can create a separate site on the same IP address and standard port, using a different host name, browse to the FTP site in the sites tree of the Connections pane, and then in the Actions pane, select Bindings. This will show the current bindings for the site, as shown in Figure 10-18. Highlight the FTP binding, and choose Edit to change it.

As shown in Figure 10-19, you have the option to change the FTP bindings, including the host name that this site will answer to. We're going to use ftp.domain1.com as our host name, which means that accessing this site from now on will be done by specifying this host name, not the IP address. In this case, `ftp://ftp.domain1.com/` will open the FTP site, whereas using the IP address or any other host name will not. You must ensure that your DNS has the proper host entry for the FTP host in domain1.com pointing to the IP address this site is configured to answer on.

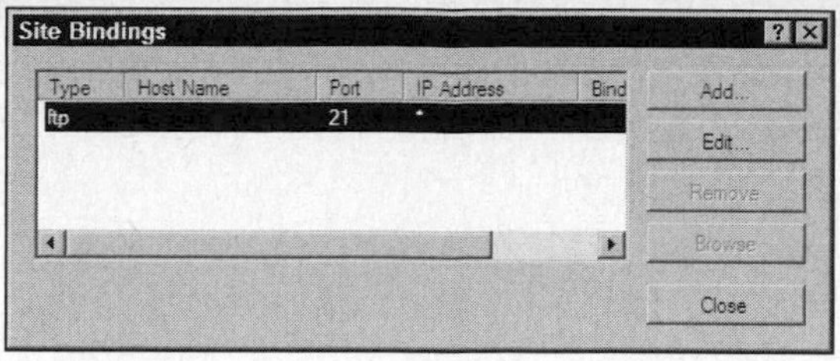

Figure 10-18

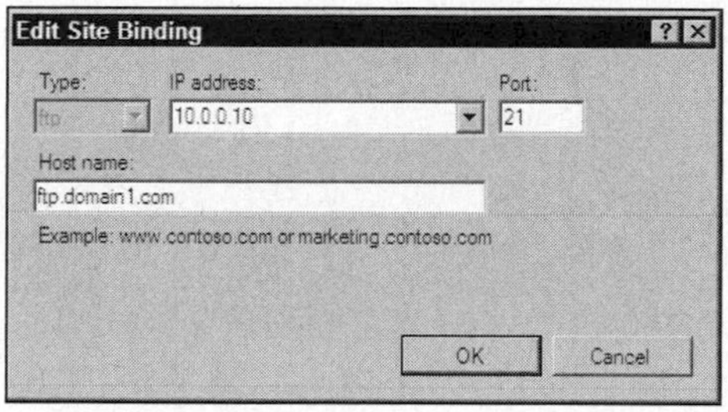

Figure 10-19

When using the virtual host option in FTP, the login process changes for the client. Because the FTP protocol has no concept of a virtual host name, it will not pass the host name to the server as part of the user login. The client must log in using a `{domain}/{username}` syntax, specifying the login domain that the FTP protocol won't pass. There is a proposal for a change to the FTP protocol to allow a HOST feature, which is supported by FTP 7, but FTP clients must support this HOST feature as well.

Administering FTP 7 with Configuration Files

Because FTP 7 uses the same XML-based configuration files as IIS 7.0, you can configure the settings for FTP sites by editing the `applicationHost.config` file, and you can create sites from scratch in the same manner. Although we won't explore every available option, we discuss some of the basic FTP 7 configurations here.

> *Remember that because the configurations are in* `applicationHost.config`, *you can use IIS 7.0's shared configuration option to automatically configure servers across a web farm as soon as the* `applicationHost.config` *file is updated.*

Adding FTP Publishing to a Web Site

Adding FTP publishing to a web site is a simple edit of the `applicationHost.config` file using Visual Studio or any text editor. For example, let's add FTP publishing to Web Site 1 and set it for access by the Administrator account for Read and Write access. In our `applicationHost.config` file, we already have the web-site information, which looks like this:

```
<site name="Web Site 1" id="99">
    <application path="/">
```

```
            <virtualDirectory path="/" physicalPath="%SystemDrive%\inetpub\website1" />
        </application>
        <bindings>
            <binding protocol="http" bindingInformation="*:80:" />
        </bindings>
    </site>
```

Our site name is Web Site 1 with an ID of 99, located in the \inetpub\website1 folder. HTTP is bound to the default port number, 80. First, we add a binding element for FTP on port 21, so that the site information will look like this, with the added line in bold setting the binding:

```
<site name="Web Site 1" id="99">
    <application path="/">
        <virtualDirectory path="/" physicalPath="%SystemDrive%\inetpub\website1" />
    </application>
    <bindings>
        <binding protocol="http" bindingInformation="*:80:" />
        <binding protocol="ftp" bindingInformation="*:21:" />
    </bindings>
</site>
```

We now need to add an FTP Server section to the site with the authentication configured for no anonymous access and Basic authentication for the FTP site. FTP authentication is configured for the site, whereas web-site authentication can be configured for an individual URL. When this section is added, shown in bold in the following code, the site section will be as follows:

```
<site name="Web Site 1" id="99">
    <application path="/">
        <virtualDirectory path="/" physicalPath="%SystemDrive%\inetpub\website1" />
    </application>
    <bindings>
        <binding protocol="http" bindingInformation="*:80:" />
        <binding protocol="ftp" bindingInformation="*:21:" />
    </bindings>
    <ftpServer>
        <security>
            <authentication>
                <anonymousAuthentication enabled="false" />
                <basicAuthentication enabled="true" />
            </authentication>
        </security>
    </ftpServer>
</site>
```

The last thing to do is to add a location section for the web site with the FTP authorization for the Administrator account with Read and Write access to the FTP site. This location section looks like the following:

```
<location path="Web Site 1">
    <system.ftpServer>
        <security>
            <authorization>
```

```
            <add accessType="Allow" users="Administrator" permissions="Read, Write" />
        </authorization>
      </security>
   </system.ftpServer>
 </location>
```

After the `applicationHost.config` is saved, the server will reread it and your site will now have FTP publishing, with Read and Write access for the Administrator account.

Adding FTP over SSL to an Existing Site

To add FTP over SSL to an existing web site, you will need to retrieve the SSL hash to include in the `applicationHost.config` file. This is done by browsing to the web server in the Connections pane, selecting the Server Certificates feature, and then finding the FTP certificate, as shown in Figure 10-20.

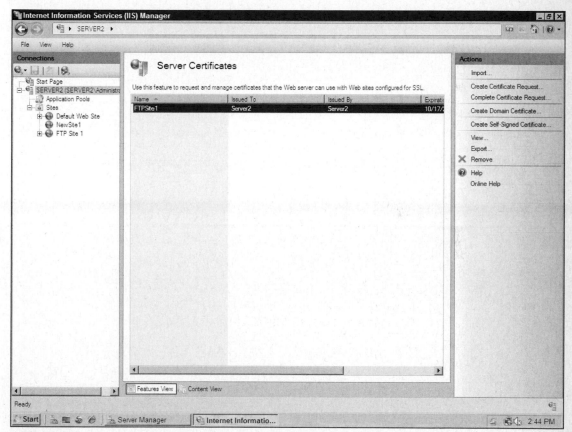

Figure 10-20

Double-click on the certificate, and the properties dialog will open. Choose the Details tab, and scroll until you find Thumbprint, as shown in Figure 10-21. Since this thumbprint is needed in the `applicationHost.config` file, highlight it and copy it to the Windows Clipboard.

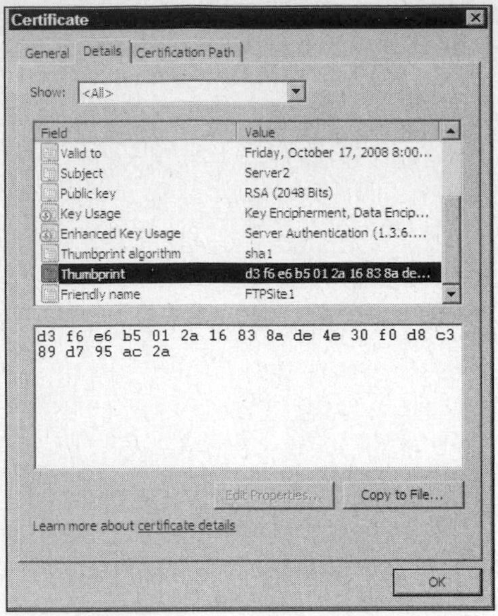

Figure 10-21

Next, open the `applicationHost.config` file in Visual Studio or any text editor, and find the section for your web site with FTP. It should look something like this:

```
<site name="Web Site 1" id="99">
    <application path="/">
        <virtualDirectory path="/" physicalPath="%SystemDrive%\inetpub\website1" />
    </application>
    <bindings>
        <binding protocol="http" bindingInformation="*:80:" />
        <binding protocol="ftp" bindingInformation="*:21:" />
    </bindings>
    <ftpServer>
        <security>
            <authentication>
                <anonymousAuthentication enabled="false" />
                <basicAuthentication enabled="true" />
            </authentication>
        </security>
    </ftpServer>
</site>
```

You need to add the SSL certificate to the site, which is done through an SSL setting below the FTP Server Authentication section. SSL is set for the FTP site level. We are going to require SSL for both the control and data channels of the FTP protocol, so we need to add the following line:

```
<ssl serverCertHash="{Certificate Hash}" controlChannelPolicy="SslRequire"
dataChannelPolicy="SslRequire" />
```

where {Certificate Hash} is the value of the thumbprint without spaces. Ours will look something like this when finished:

```
<site name="Web Site 1" id="99">
    <application path="/">
        <virtualDirectory path="/" physicalPath="%SystemDrive%\inetpub\website1" />
    </application>
    <bindings>
        <binding protocol="http" bindingInformation="*:80:" />
        <binding protocol="ftp" bindingInformation="*:21:" />
    </bindings>
    <ftpServer>
        <security>
            <authentication>
                <anonymousAuthentication enabled="false" />
                <basicAuthentication enabled="true" />
            </authentication>
            <ssl serverCertHash="28d132014f72050177444aa34bba952912f47ff6"
controlChannelPolicy="SslRequire" dataChannelPolicy="SslRequire" />
        </security>
    </ftpServer>
</site>
```

Configuring Host Name Support

Adding host name support to our site can easily be done in the applicationHost.config file as well. Let's start by looking at the FTP site configuration in the applicationHost.config file:

```
<site name="FtpSite1" id="42">
    <application path="/">
      <virtualDirectory path="/"
physicalPath="%SystemDrive%\inetpub\FTPRoot\ftpsite1" />
    </application>
    <bindings>
        <binding protocol="ftp" bindingInformation="192.168.1.10:21:" />
    </bindings>
    <ftpServer>
        <security>
            <authentication>
                <anonymousAuthentication enabled="false" />
                <basicAuthentication enabled="true" />
            </authentication>
        </security>
    </ftpServer>
</site>
```

You just need to add the binding for the host name, thus the edited version will look like this (changes are in bold):

```
<site name="FtpSite1" id="42">
  <application path="/">
    <virtualDirectory path="/"
physicalPath="%SystemDrive%\inetpub\FTPRoot\ftpsite1" />
  </application>
  <bindings>
```

```
        <binding protocol="ftp" bindingInformation="192.168.1.10:21:ftp.domain1.com" />
    </bindings>
    <ftpServer>
      <security>
        <authentication>
          <anonymousAuthentication enabled="false" />
          <basicAuthentication enabled="true" />
        </authentication>
      </security>
    </ftpServer>
</site>
```

Testing FTP with Telnet

One of the easiest tests for determining if the FTP Server is available on port 21 is to try using Telnet to reach the port. From a system outside your network, open a command prompt and type

```
Telnet {ServerName} 21
```

where {ServerName} is the fully qualified domain name or IP address of your FTP Server. You should see a response something like

```
220 Microsoft FTP Service
```

If you see this response, your FTP Server is available and answering connection requests. This means that network connectivity exists between the test system and your FTP Server, including firewalls allowing traffic to pass on port 21.

FrontPage Server Extensions

Whereas FTP is a commonly used protocol for uploading and downloading files, especially in cross-platform situations, FrontPage Server Extensions (FPSE) is an alternate technology that provides file upload and web-site authoring capabilities to end-users. FPSE extends beyond simple uploads, however. Using FPSE, end-users can implement a common look for their web sites (a site theme) or provide various pieces of dynamic content (for example, simple hit counters or the date the file was last modified) without having to write any code. FPSE also provides rudimentary source control features that allow multiple users to work on the same FPSE site. In addition to providing rich authoring functionality, FPSE publishing operates over HTTP (or HTTPS, if secured by SSL/TLS), making it far more "firewall friendly" than FTP.

What Happened to WebDAV?

WebDAV (Web Distributed Authoring and Versioning) was another, alternate, authoring technology that shipped in Windows Server 2003 and IIS 6.0. It is not included on the installation media for Windows Server 2008. Instead, the IIS Product Group has committed to writing a completely new WebDAV server component that fully implements current standards for authoring, and this will be available for download from the www.iis.net web site. Readers are advised to check the www.iis.net web site after the release of Windows Server 2008 to find out more information on the availability of WebDAV for IIS 7.0.

Developed by the Office Product Group, FPSE is a complement for various FPSE clients, such like Microsoft FrontPage, Visual Studio, and Visual InterDev. FPSE ships as part of various Office installations, is included as a separate download from the Microsoft web site, and is included on the installation media for Windows Server 2003.

Because FPSE is included in Office, the IIS Product Group originally had no intention of shipping FPSE with IIS 7.0. Instead, FPSE 2002 was scheduled to be retired as a product. However, the ensuing customer feedback pointed to a continued need for FPSE, and the IIS Product Group has worked with Ready To Run Software to deliver a version of FPSE 2002 that will install and run on IIS 7.0. For readers familiar with FPSE 2002 on Windows Server 2003, there are no significant functionality changes — the product has merely been updated to work with the new IIS 7.0 architecture.

Using the full functionality of FPSE would require a book in itself. In this section, we look at installing FPSE and configuring a web site to support FPSE publishing. We also examine basic user and group configuration to allow secure, authenticated authoring.

Installing FPSE

Prior to installing FPSE, note the following requirements and restrictions. Failure to meet the requirements may result in unexpected behavior or authoring failure:

❑ FPSE must be installed to a NTFS-formatted partition and FPSE-enabled web sites must be stored on NTFS-formatted partitions as well. FAT32 partitions are not supported. Windows Server 2008 ships with the command-line tool `convert.exe`, which you can use to convert an existing FAT or FAT32 partition to NTFS without any destruction of data. Consult the Windows Server 2008 Online Help for more information on using this tool.

❑ FPSE does not support nested published web sites. If you attempt to publish nested web sites, unexpected results may occur. FPSE does support the division of an existing web site into a set of subsites (or *subwebs*).

❑ The following IIS 7.0 components must be installed in order for FPSE to function correctly:

   ❑ **Common HTTP Features** — Static Content and Default Document.

   ❑ **Application Development** — ISAPI Extensions and ISAPI Filters.

   ❑ **Security** — Windows Authentication.

   ❑ **IIS 6.0 Management Capability** — IIS 6.0 Metabase Compatibility.

In addition, the Windows Process Activation Service feature (which is a required feature for installing IIS 7.0) must be installed.

The FPSE set-up process can optionally install the following features to support FPSE functionality beyond authoring support:

❑ **Active Server Pages** — To support the FPSE database component.

❑ **CGI Support** — To support the FPSE hit counters.

❑ **Indexing Service** — To support the FPSE search components.

The FPSE installer will create an Administration web site. This web site can be accessed by using the Microsoft SharePoint Administrator link in the Administrative Tools folder on the server that FPSE is installed on. By default, only users in the local Administrators group are able to load this web site. Additionally, the installer will create an MSSharePointAppPool application pool and place the Administration web site into it.

Adding FPSE to a Web Site

In order for a FPSE client (such as Microsoft FrontPage) to be able to author against a web site, it must be *extended*. This operation is performed on the server using the Microsoft SharePoint Administrator web site. Extended web sites are also known as *virtual servers* in some FrontPage documentation, and you may see the terms used interchangeably.

Before extending a web site, it is worth configuring server-wide defaults. These defaults will affect all web sites extended on the server. To configure these defaults:

1. Open the Microsoft SharePoint Administrator web site using the link in the Administrative Tools folder.

2. Click the Set Installation Defaults link.

3. On the Set Installation Defaults page, as shown in Figure 10-22, you can configure SMTP settings to be used by any web site that needs to send e-mail notifications. You can also configure whether authoring actions are logged (a log file is written to the /_vti_log folder created within each FPSE extended web site), whether SSL/TLS is required for authoring (enabling this requires installing a Server Certificate — see Chapter 14 for more information on configuring SSL/TLS), and whether authors are able to upload .exe files to their web sites.

4. Click the Submit button to commit your changes.

After setting server defaults, individual web sites can now be extended and made available for authoring, as follows:

1. Open the Microsoft SharePoint Administrator web site using the link in the Administrative Tools folder.

2. From the list of available web sites, click the Extend link to enable FPSE authoring. You will need to nominate an account to be the site administrator for that individual web site.

3. Click the Submit button to commit the changes.

Extending a web site can also be automated from a command line by using the owsadm.exe tool, which is located in the %systemdrive%\program files\common files\microsoft shared\web server extensions\50\bin folder.

To extend a specified web site, you must supply the following parameters: the initial user account that should be the Administrator of the site and the IIS 6.0 metabase node name (for example, /LM/W3SVC/1 for the Default Web Site). For example, to extend the second web site created on the machine, use the command:

```
owsadm.exe -o install -u DomainA\Administrator -m /LM/W3SVC/2
```

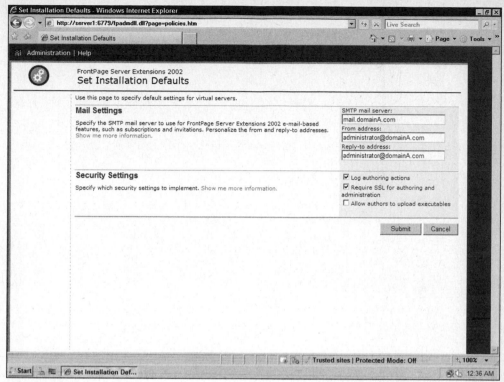

Figure 10-22

After you extend a web site, the following directories are created within the web site's root folder. Some directories have the `hidden` attribute set and thus are not visible in Explorer unless you configure it to show hidden files.

❑ `/fpdb` — Used for holding Microsoft Access database files (.mdb) that may be used by a FrontPage-designed application. Requests for files to the `/fpdb` folder are automatically blocked by the FPSE ISAPI extension. This folder may be created when a user uploads a database-driven project.

❑ `/_private` — Holds private FrontPage files (such as FPSE poll results).

❑ `/_vti_pvt` — Holds FrontPage configuration files.

❑ `/_vti_cbf` — Holds FrontPage metadata about files in the web site (for example, used when versioning is enabled).

❑ `/_vti_scripts` — Holds FrontPage provided scripts (for example, search result generation pages).

❑ `/_vti_txt` — Holds FrontPage catalogs and indices (for FPSE search functionality).

❑ `/_vti_log` — Holds FrontPage authoring log files.

Additionally, in the Microsoft SharePoint Administrator web site, each extended web site now has two links, as shown in Figure 10-23. The Administration link allows you to configure site-wide settings (overriding the defaults supplied earlier), as well as configure a default scripting language or a maximum number of user accounts, or to uninstall FrontPage Server Extensions from the web site.

The web-site name is also a link, which can be accessed by the user account specified as the initial Administrator of that site. This link provides most of the configuration options for FPSE for that web site.

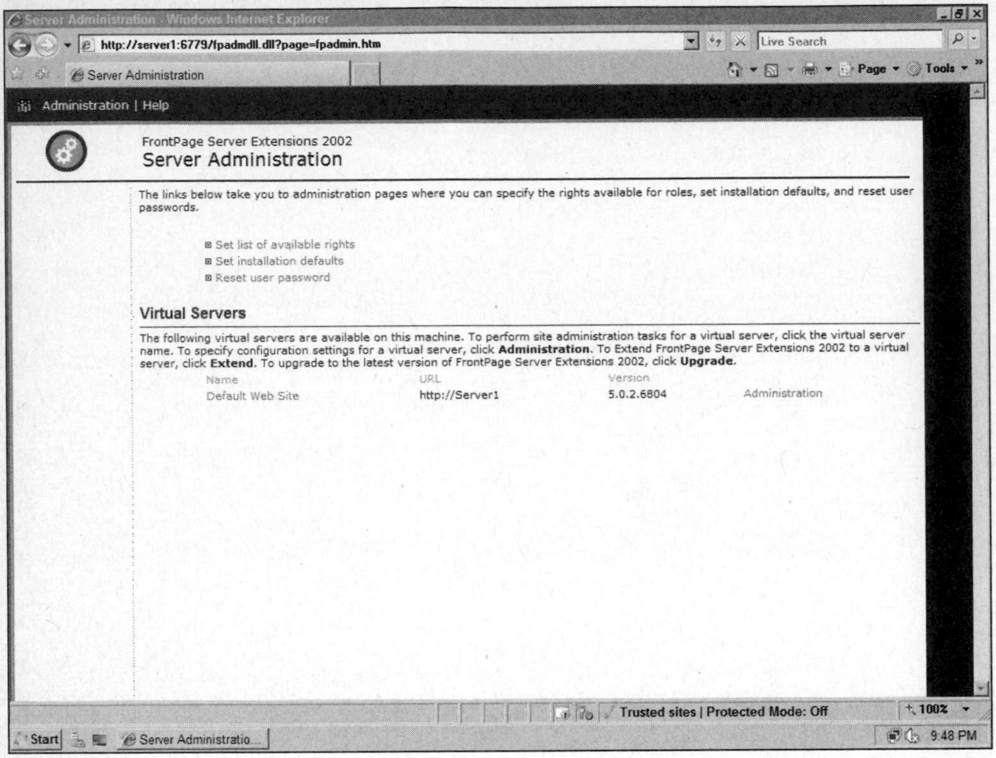

Figure 10-23

Configuring FPSE

After extending an existing web site, click the web site's link in the Microsoft SharePoint Administrator web site to open the individual web site's administration options. If the web site fails to open with an authorization error, ensure that you are attempting to access the site using the account you defined as the initial Administrator of the web site, and also ensure that the /vti_bin virtual directory underneath the web site has an authentication mechanism (Windows authentication, Basic authentication, and so forth) enabled.

The Site Administration page enables you to configure the following options, as shown in Figure 10-24:

❑ **"Change anonymous access settings"** — Allows you to define whether anonymous users are able to access the web site and, if so, which permissions they have. By default, anonymous users are assigned the Browser role, which allows them to view pages only. The configuration can be changed so that anonymous users can author pages, but this is not recommended.

❑ **"Add or delete accounts"** — As FPSE supports both Windows accounts and separate FPSE accounts (that can only be used for FPSE authoring and administration purposes), this section allows the creation and deletion of non-Windows (that is, FPSE only) accounts. To grant access or perform other management tasks with Windows accounts, you should use the next option, as Windows accounts cannot be added or deleted via the FPSE web site.

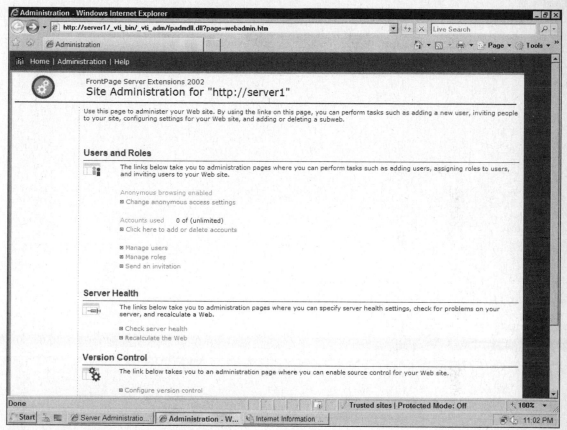

Figure 10-24

❑ **"Manage users"** — This section enables you to add both Windows users and groups, and to create FPSE users. You can assign roles for each user or group that you add. FPSE roles are similar to Windows groups — each role has a set of permissions assigned to it. For example, the Administrator role is permitted to undertake all administrative actions on the FPSE web site, and the initial user account that was specified as the Administrator of the web site was placed into this role. Anonymous users are placed into the Browser role by default, which permits only viewing of pages. Other built-in roles include Author (can upload pages), Advanced Author (can perform advanced authoring actions, such as changing the web-site theme), and Contributor (can contribute to FPSE boards). Additional roles can be defined in the next section.

❑ **"Manage roles"** — This section enables you to add or delete roles, as well as to alter the permissions assigned to each role. FPSE ships with five built-in roles: Administrator, Advanced Author, Author, Contributor, and Browser. There are a total of 12 permissions that can be assigned to roles — the Administrator role has all 12. If the pre-defined roles do not suit the delegation of permissions in your organization, you can create custom roles using this section, and assign an arbitrary set of the 12 permissions. You can then place your users into this custom role.

❑ **"Send an invitation"** — This is a three-step wizard that takes you through the process of adding a new user, assigning his or her permissions, and sending an invitation via e-mail to that user. To use this wizard, the e-mail server settings for the web site must have been configured previously.

❑ **"Check server health"** — This performs a set of automated routines that can verify security, file permissions, and internal settings, and additionally attempt to repair any problems that are discovered. Be aware that having the Tighten Security option repair NTFS permissions can remove any customized NTFS permissions that you have set on your web site, potentially breaking functionality. If you have customized any NTFS permissions, reapply those permissions after running the Tighten Security repair option.

❑ **"Recalculate the Web"** — Use this option if the FPSE-stored metadata no longer match the actual content of your web site. This can occur if non-FPSE-related mechanisms are used to add or remove content from the web site (for example, by using an FTP client, or using Explorer to copy files directly into the web site's folders). This option recalculates the metadata for the web site so that they match the current content.

❑ **"Configure version control"** — Enabling this feature allows users to check out and check in files for editing via a FrontPage-compatible client (for example, Microsoft FrontPage, Visual Studio .NET, and some versions of Office products). Files that have been checked out cannot be edited by other users. Checkout information for files is stored in the /vti_cnf folder. If a file is locked and cannot be checked in, deleting the relevant information in that folder can allow another user to check out the file in question.

❑ **"Create a subweb"** — An existing web site can be broken down into individual subwebs, which incorporate only a specific subsection of the overall web site. These individual subwebs have their own configuration and security settings and can be managed individually. This option can be handy if an organization's web site has discrete sections that need to be managed separately by representatives from each department (for example, for individual departments within the organization).

Securing an FPSE-Extended Web Site

Extending a web site to enable FPSE authoring presents a security risk, as the possibility exists that anyone connected to the Internet who is able to reach the web site may be able to alter content on that web site. Consider the following strategies to help reduce the attack surface of extended web sites:

❑ Do not expose sites intended only for internal use (for example, intranet sites) to the wider Internet. For smaller organizations, a single web server can host both Internet and intranet sites. When extending an intranet site, use IIS 7.0's IP and Domain Restrictions settings to permit access only to internal IP addresses. See Chapter 13 for more information on configuring this setting.

❑ For external facing sites, consider creating two web sites. Internal authors create content on the first web site, and only internal users are permitted access to this web site. A process (either a scheduled batch process or a Windows service) then copies content from the internal site to the externally accessible site. In this way, there is no possibility of malicious external users altering the content of the web site, as FPSE authoring is not enabled on the externally facing site.

If you must enable authoring on an externally facing web site, consider the following action points. First, ensure that anonymous access users do not have authoring permissions. Next, determine which authentication mechanisms you will use for users who should be able to author. IIS 7.0 supports a variety of authentication mechanisms (Basic, ASP.NET Forms-Based Authentication, and so on), but only HTTP-based authentication mechanisms (that is, not ASP.NET Forms-Based Authentication) are supported by FrontPage clients. Chapter 14 covers the advantages and disadvantages of each authentication mechanism. If you choose to use Basic authentication, ensure that you enable SSL/TLS on your web site, and configure a requirement for SSL to be used for authoring actions.

The next step involves evaluating the roles that you need for your web site. In general, the built-in roles are sufficient for most situations, although you might need to define your own custom roles with their own custom permissions. For example, you might need a role that performs account-management tasks for your web site. The duties of this role might be performed by line-of-business managers within your organization. To add a new custom role:

1. Open the Site Administration page.

2. Click the Manage Roles link, and then choose Add a Role.

3. Enter the details of the new role, and select the appropriate permissions for that role (see Figure 10-25).

4. After determining which roles you need, assign users or groups to those roles.

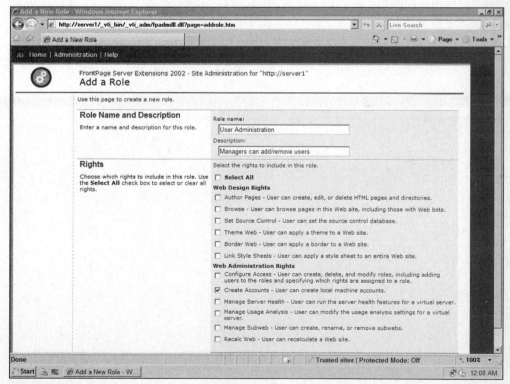

Figure 10-25

For each user (or member of a Windows group) that is assigned permissions on the site, ensure that the account meets an organizationally mandated password requirement (minimum password length, minimum password complexity). Although it is possible to secure FPSE in a way that prevents malicious anonymous attack, anyone who can guess or brute-force the password of a legitimate user will still have access as that user. The use of long or complex passwords mitigates this threat.

You also should run the Tighten Security wizard to ensure that NTFS permissions are configured correctly, which prevents unauthorized users from performing authoring actions. After running the wizard, reapply any custom NTFS permissions that you require for your web site. The wizard also removes IIS 7.0 executable permissions from non-FPSE folders. If you have CGI executables that require Execute permissions, re-enable Execute permissions on folders containing CGI executables. For more information on configuring IIS 7.0 permissions, see Chapter 13.

Finally, determine whether you require logging of authoring actions. The FPSE log records authoring actions by users that are not captured in regular IIS 7.0 log files. To enable authoring logging:

1. Open the Microsoft SharePoint Administrator web site using the link in the Administrative Tools folder.

2. To configure logging for all sites, click the Set Installation Defaults link, and check the Log Authoring Actions checkbox.

3. To configure logging for an individual web site, click the Administration link for that web site, and select Change Configuration Settings. Ensure that the Log Authoring checkbox is ticked.

Connecting Using a Client

After you extend and configure an FPSE web site, users with FrontPage clients will be able to connect and author content.

Additionally, the FPSE ISAPI filter intercepts WebDAV requests from WebDAV clients, which allows WebDAV authoring. A WebDAV client is provided with Windows XP, Windows Server 2003, and Windows Vista. Users can use the Network Locations folder to add an FPSE-enabled web site, as shown in Figure 10-26.

If using Windows Server 2003, the Web Client service must be started. The Windows XP Web Client service does not support authoring of SSL/TLS. Instead, the Internet Explorer 6 or Internet Explorer 7 WebDAV client can be used. To open a site using IE, choose File ⇨ Open, and enter the fully qualified domain name of the FPSE-enabled web site (and ensure that the "Open as Web Folder" checkbox is checked).

Uninstalling FPSE

You can use the Microsoft SharePoint Administrator web site to remove FPSE from an existing extended web site. After opening the web site from the Administrative Tools folder, link the Administration link next to the web site you want to remove FPSE from, and then choose Uninstall FrontPage Server Extensions 2002. The Full Uninstall option will remove FPSE extensibility and all configuration and metadata from your web site.

You can also remove FPSE from an extended web site by using the `owsadm.exe` command-line tool, as follows:

```
owsadm.exe -o fulluninstall -m /LM/W3SVC/1
```

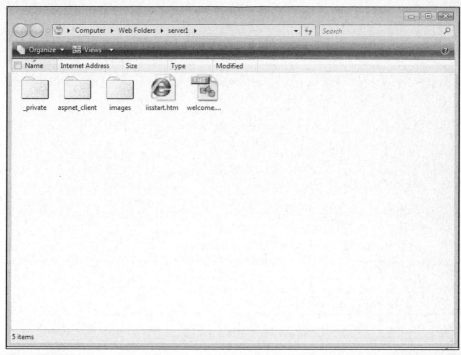

Figure 10-26

If you want to keep the FPSE metadata for the web site, use the `-o uninstall` option rather than the `-o fulluninstall` option. This preserves the various `/vti_` directories within the web site.

To completely uninstall FPSE itself from the web server, use the Programs and Features Control Panel, and choose to uninstall Microsoft FrontPage Server Extensions for Window Server 2008. FPSE cannot be removed using the Windows Server 2008 Server Manager at the time of writing.

SMTP

The SMTP Server in IIS 7.0 provides mail transport functions between servers. It is designed for sending mail from the IIS 7.0 server to another SMTP Server and can act as a relay server as well. Although SMTP does send and receive mail messages, is not designed as a "user" technology to provide a mailbox for messages. That functionality is provided by an e-mail server that implements a mailbox protocol such as POP3 or IMAP.

What Happened to POP3?

In Windows Server 2003, Microsoft included a basic POP3 server that integrated with the SMTP Server (and optionally Active Directory), providing a basic e-mail service. It appears that this solution was never very popular, however, and with the phenomenal growth of third-party e-mail services (including online offerings), Microsoft has decided to discontinue development of a separate POP3 server. This option is no longer available in Windows Server 2008.

How SMTP Works

In Windows Server 2008, SMTP is an in-process service and runs in the `Inetinfo.exe` process. It monitors the SMTP port (25, by default) for incoming messages and the `Pickup` folder for outgoing messages. When a message appears in the `Pickup` folder, SMTP will determine the destination domain from the header. If the domain is local, the message is moved to the `Drop` folder. If not, the destination SMTP Server is determined through a DNS lookup for the mail exchanger, or MX, record for the destination domain. Once the destination SMTP Server is resolved, a connection attempt is made on port 25. If the destination server accepts the connection, the message is transferred to the destination server for delivery to the recipient's mailbox.

If the destination server rejects the message, the SMTP Server will try to deliver a non-delivery report to the original sender. This report will include the original message and the reason that delivery could not be made, such as the destination address not existing. If the message cannot be returned to the original sender, it is moved to the `Badmail` folder.

Installing SMTP

SMTP is not installed by default on Windows Server 2008. It also is not listed as a role service as other IIS 7.0 components are, but, rather, as a server feature. Since SMTP was not updated for Windows Server 2008, it is managed through the Internet Information Services (IIS) 6.0 Manager, as with the shipped version of FTP Server, not the standard IIS manager.

To install the SMTP Server, open Server Manager, choose Features, and run the Add Features Wizard. Select the SMTP Server feature as shown in Figure 10-27, and choose to Add Required Services, which will also install the IIS 6.0 Manager if not already installed. Installing the SMTP Server will configure a default SMTP Server answering on port 25 on all unassigned IP addresses. You will want to configure this server further before you use it.

Installing the SMTP service creates the following on your system. First, a service (Simple Mail Transfer Protocol service) is created. This service runs within the existing `inetinfo.exe` process but can be started and stopped separately from IIS.

Second, an SMTP virtual server is created. This SMTP virtual server is configured to accept mail destined for the fully qualified domain name of the local server, but is not started by default. Additional SMTP virtual servers can be created if desired.

Last, a set of folders is created, by default, within the `%systemdrive%\inetinfo\mailroot` folder, named `badmail`, `drop`, `pickup`, and `queue`. Their purpose is described in detail below in the chapter.

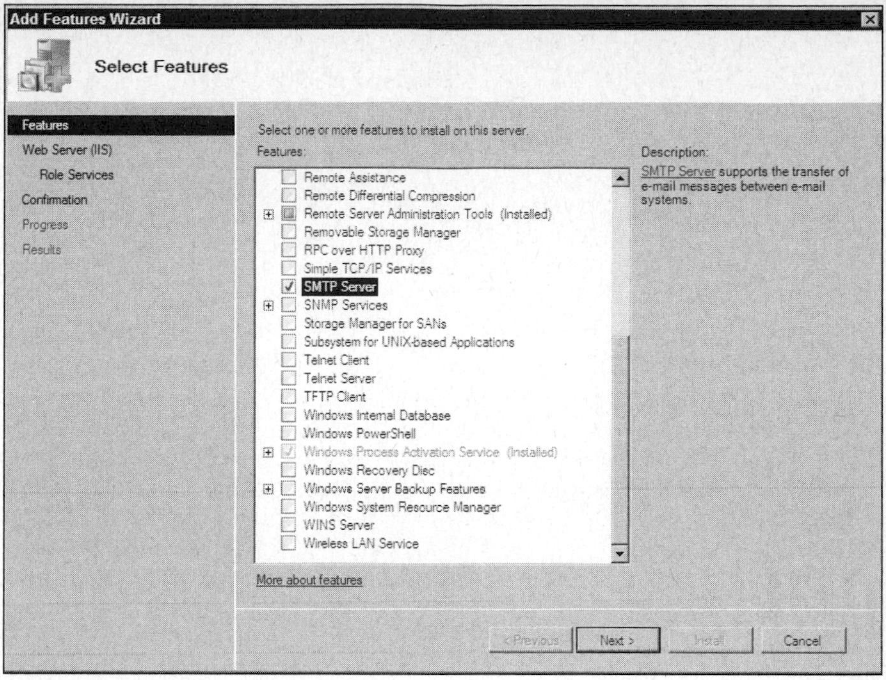

Figure 10-27

The location of these folders can be altered at install time, or moved after installation of SMTP service. If you have already installed SMTP Server and wish to move the folders for the default virtual server to another partition or drive, then the appropriate entries in the IIS 6.0 metabase must be updated. First, use Explorer to create the new folders that you wish SMTP Server to use, and then update the following locations in the metabase:

```
smtpsvc/1/badmaildirectory
smtpsvc/1/dropdirectory
smtpsvc/1/pickupdirectory
smtpsvc/1/queuedirectory
```

If you have created additional SMTP virtual servers on this machine, you will need to change the metabase node (for example, the second virtual server will be located at `smtpsvc/2/`).

You can use a graphical tool such as Metabase Explorer to perform this operation, or you can use the legacy adsutil.vbs tool. For example, to update the `badmail` directory for the default SMTP virtual server, run

```
c:\inetpub\adminscripts\adsutil.vbs set smtpsvc/1/badmaildirectory x:\badmail
```

Configuring the Default SMTP Server

Configuring and administering the SMTP Server is done from the Internet Information Services (IIS) 6.0 Manager on the Administrative Tools menu, a separate menu item from the IIS 7.0 Manager, as shown in Figure 10-28. This is the same management tool used for the shipped version of the FTP Server.

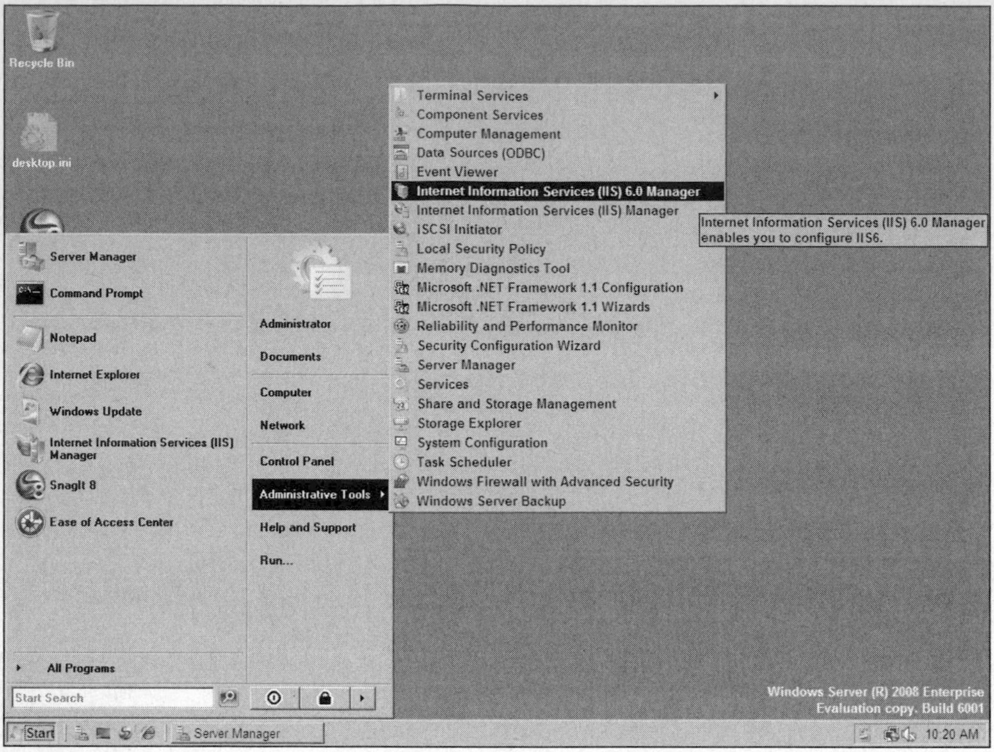

Figure 10-28

Expanding the local computer will show the SMTP servers configured on this physical system. Expanding the SMTP Server will show the SMTP domains and current sessions on that SMTP server. Right-clicking on the server and choosing properties will allow you to configure the server.

General Settings

On the General tab of the SMTP Server Properties dialog, shown in Figure 10-29, there are several important configuration changes that can be made. To begin with, here is where you assign a specific IP address, and the port if you have a reason to change it. You should always assign a specific IP address to your SMTP Server to ensure that you don't accidentally respond to SMTP requests on an unintended address. If you have more than one virtual SMTP Server, you will need to assign separate IP addresses or separate ports, and many programs will assume the default SMTP port of 25. Assigning specific IP addresses to each server addresses this need. You may also wish to assign multiple identities to this server, to provide SMTP services from two separate domains, for example. You can do this through the Advanced button.

You may also restrict the number of connections and set the connection time-out in this dialog. Limiting the number of connections can reduce load on the server, but in most cases it will also cause delays in mail deliveries as connections are unavailable when the mail is sent. Ten minutes is a sufficient time-out for even the slowest mail servers, but you may want to lower this so that dropped connections recycle quicker, especially if you limit the number of connections.

Log files are disabled on the SMTP Server by default, but most administrators will want to enable them. Configuring and interpreting SMTP log files are covered more completely below in this chapter.

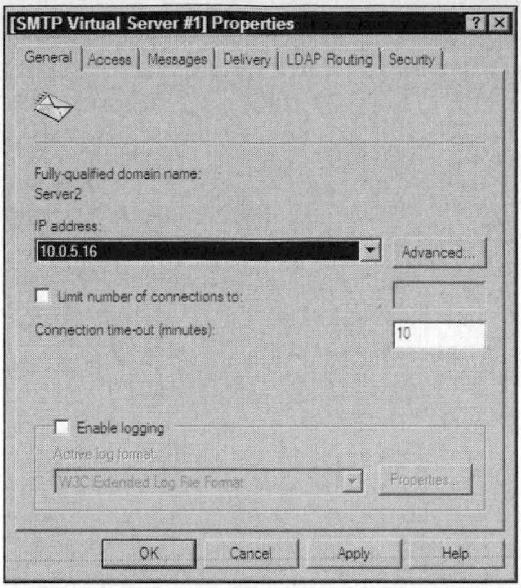

Figure 10-29

Messaging Limit Configurations

The Messages tab of the SMTP Properties dialog, shown in Figure 10-30, allows configuring several message limits to match your needs for this specific SMTP Server. The maximum message size and the maximum session size are both measured in kilobytes (KB). Using these, you can restrict the amount of data that can be sent in a single message or a single session. The defaults are normally adequate for sending messages from ASP.NET applications, but restrict the sending, and receiving, of large files or bulk mail. By increasing the message size limit, you increase the data in a single message, but if you leave the session size limit at the default, you will still throttle performance for sending bulk mail.

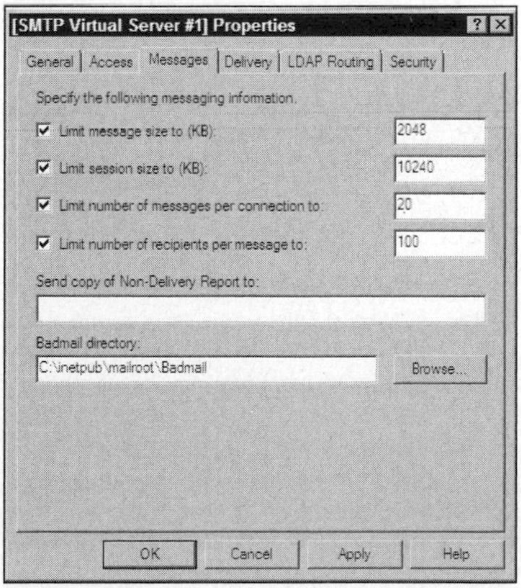

Figure 10-30

Similarly, you can limit the number of messages sent in a single connection, which will force the SMTP Server to renegotiate a new connection after the maximum has been reached. This can increase performance of the server since it will make multiple connections to the destination server, but the destination must also allow multiple connections. You may also limit the number of recipients in a single message. The default is 100, the minimum required by RFC 2821 for an SMTP Server to use this feature.

It is suggested that for most SMTP Server needs, you leave the defaults as is. Increasing the message and session size limits, as well as the number of recipients in a single message, or unchecking the selections so there are no limits, can increase the server's delivery rate for bulk mail, such as found in many newsletter applications or applications that e-mail web-site updates to clients. Increasing these settings and sending one message to many recipients will increase the load on the server and can cause the server to be black-listed by other SMTP Servers as a spam source.

What happens when these limits are exceeded really depends on the remote SMTP Server. For any server supporting EHLO, and most do, the servers will pass their limits to each other for review. This prevents attempts at sending messages outside the limits, and a non-delivery report (NDR) will be generated before a transfer is attempted. If a message exceeding the maximum number of recipients is received by the SMTP Server, it will be split into multiple messages, and no NDR will be generated.

Non-delivery reports are sent to the message sender, but you can have copies sent to another e-mail address as well. This can be useful for notifying an administrator of delivery problems, but in most cases you will only enable this when tracking a problem. There are many legitimate reasons for a NDR to be generated, such as a typo in the recipient's e-mail address, that are not delivery problems that normally need to be addressed by an administrator.

Delivery Configurations

The Delivery tab allows two important configurations to be changed. The first are the retry intervals and options for outgoing messages that cannot be delivered on the first attempt. The defaults, as shown in Figure 10-31, are adequate for almost all situations and should only be adjusted in situations in which network connections might be slow, spotty, or otherwise play havoc with SMTP connectivity. It is important to be aware of the defaults in order to understand SMTP delivery delays. The retry intervals are listed for the first, second, and third attempts at redelivering a message that could not be delivered, and each subsequent delivery attempt. Normally, a server will also send an NDR to the message sender indicating that there was a delivery delay, as defined by the delay notification time. After a default two days of attempts, the server will give up and return the message as undeliverable, with a matching NDR. Consistent SMTP message delivery delays could indicate a problem with connectivity between SMTP servers or a problem with the destination server, such as an overload of messages.

On this same tab, you can set outgoing connection limits as well as the port used, using the "Outbound connections" button. Under the Advanced options, you can specify the use of a smart host for e-mail delivery, relaying through that server to the destination server. The smart host server takes on the responsibility of delivering the message to the destination SMTP Server. You might want to use a smart host outside the firewall to better protect the SMTP Servers inside the firewall from attack. A smart host would also be appropriate where you needed all messages to pass through a central server for archiving and compliance needs, or to add required footer information to all outgoing messages. The smart host entry expects the fully qualified domain name of the smart host SMTP Server, such as smtp.domain1.com. You may also use an IP address by enclosing it in square brackets, as in [192.168.1.10].

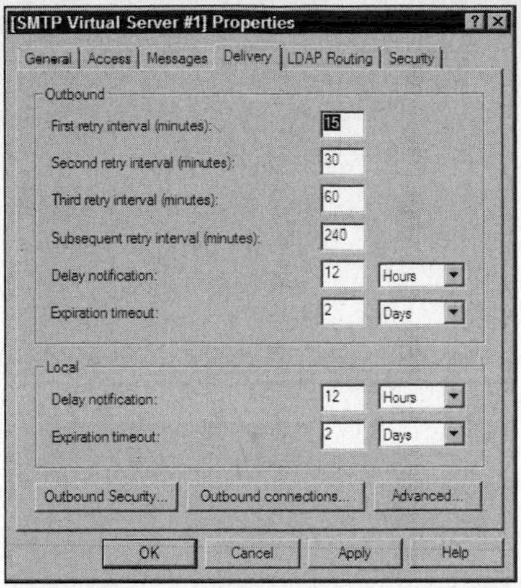

Figure 10-31

The Masquerade Domain and Fully Qualified Domain name configurations may be used to change how the SMTP message is addressed and delivered. The Masquerade Domain will replace the local domain listed in the "Mail From" lines of the SMTP header. Since this can trigger some anti-spam filters, you should test the use of this option carefully. By setting the Fully Qualified Domain name, you override the default domain being used for DNS lookups. This can help speed name resolution by using both the domain's MX record and the host name for resolution.

LDAP Routing

LDAP routing can be used to force the SMTP Server to consult a LDAP server such as an Active Directory server for resolving both senders and recipients. This is really only useful if mail is destined locally within the realm of your LDAP domain, and in almost all cases the use of a mail server such as Microsoft's Exchange Server is a much better option.

SMTP Security and Authentication

SMTP servers provide a risk to organizations for being compromised and used to relay spam and virus attacks. Misconfigured or insecure servers can be used for phishing attacks, denial-of-service attacks, and transportation of pornography and pirated software. All of these mischievous-to-criminal acts are traceable right back to the SMTP Server, putting an organization at risk for lawsuits or criminal charges. In many ways, the worst effect on an organization can be the blacklisting of the SMTP Server, preventing e-mail from being transferred to or from the organization and its clients.

SMTP security is set on the Access tab, as shown in Figure 10-32, not the Security tab as expected from the name. The Security tab is used for determining which users or groups can administer this SMTP virtual server.

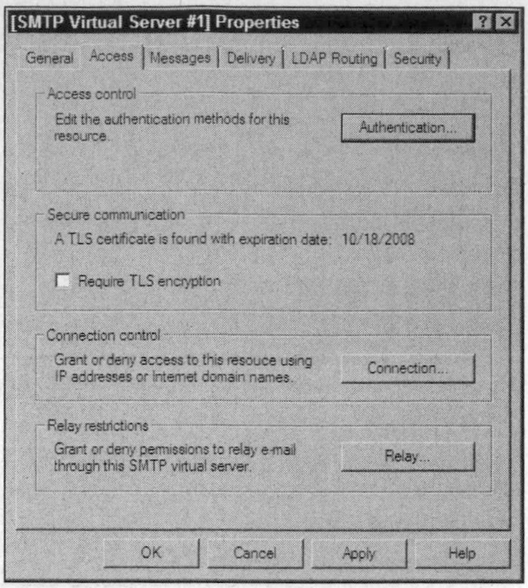

Figure 10-32

Authentication

Clicking the Authentication button on the SMTP Server Properties dialog's Access tab brings up the authentication options, shown in Figure 10-33. You can force incoming connections, whether from an SMTP client such as Windows Mail, another server relaying through this one, or just a message being delivered by a remote server, to authenticate using similar mechanisms to those in IIS 7.0. You can have "Anonymous access," "Basic authentication," or "Integrated Windows Authentication." Each of these behaves as it does in IIS 7.0, with Anonymous Access allowing anyone to connect without providing credentials, and Basic Authentication and Integrated Windows Authentication requiring a valid Windows username and password. The Microsoft SMTP Server does not support ASP.NET authentication or the use of non-Windows user accounts. Basic Authentication has the advantage that most clients support it, and it can be secured using TLS encryption. Integrated Windows Authentication uses NTLM v2 to pass credentials to the SMTP Server, thus enabling this option requires clients that support NTLM v2, such as Microsoft Outlook Express or Windows Mail. In these programs, the use of NTLM is called *Secure Password Authentication*. Enable this option in those clients if you are using IWA on your SMTP Server.

These authentication requirements apply only to inbound SMTP connections. Formatted mail messages dropped directly into the SMTP virtual server's Drop *directory are not affected by these settings. The* Drop *directory is discussed in detail below in this chapter.*

TLS Encryption

TLS encryption is a function of SSL and requires an SSL certificate. You may use the self-signed certificates you can create in IIS Manager, although the SMTP service will only use a single certificate for the server. You must create the certificate or apply for one from a certificate authority and install the certificate before you can use TLS to encrypt transmissions. More information on SSL certificates can be found in Chapter 13.

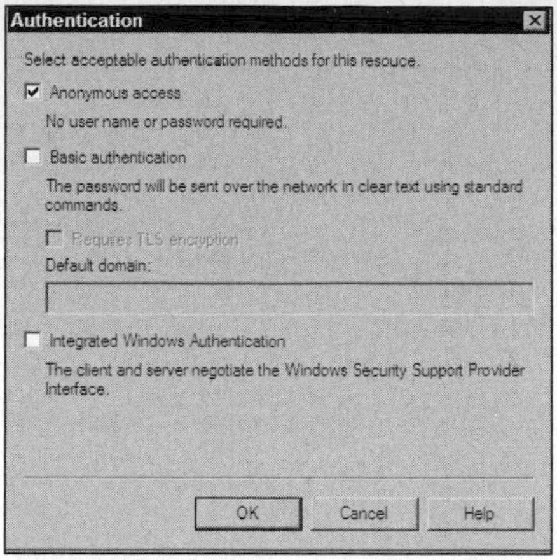

Figure 10-33

Connection Control

The Connection button in the Access tab allows restricting access to the SMTP Server according to the IP address range or domain (see Figure 10-34). You may set the list as systems to exclude from connections ("All except the list below") or as the only systems to include in allowing connections ("Only the list below"). In most cases, you will want to allow all systems to connect so as to be able to accept messages from other networks, but you may want to restrict this if you are only accepting mail from internal clients or if you will be using this server only for outbound messages.

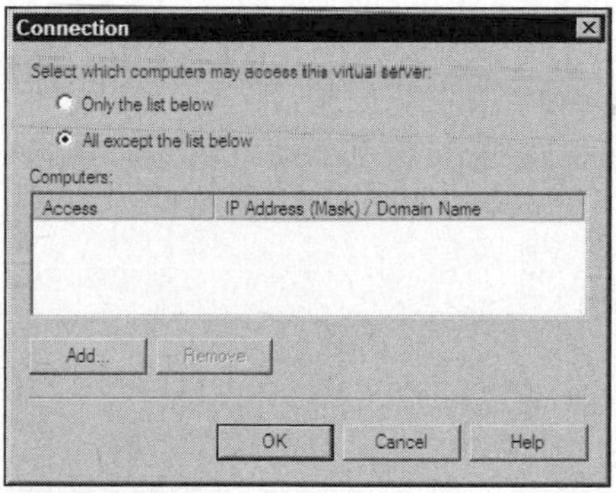

Figure 10-34

Relay Restrictions

More important than connection restrictions are relay restrictions, those systems that are allowed to send mail through this SMTP Server. *Relaying* is the process of sending mail through the SMTP Server that is not destined for final delivery to a remote SMTP Server. Typically, only your legitimate users should be able to relay mail to remote systems. If the system is misconfigured to allow anyone to relay mail, then it is possible for spammers or other malicious users to use your mail server to deliver spam (or worse) to any e-mail address.

337

The default settings, shown in Figure 10-35, allow only those clients that authenticate to your server, by providing a valid username and password, to relay mail through your server. SMTP clients, such as Outlook, as well as an ASP.NET script using `system.net.mail,` *can be configured to provide authentication required by your server. Outside systems will not be able to relay unless they also know the authentication credentials. In more recent times, it has become increasingly common for attackers to attempt to guess passwords for well-known or commonly used user accounts (for example, the built-in Administrator account). If attackers are able to guess a username and corresponding password, they may be able to authenticate to your SMTP Server and relay mail through it. For this reason, unless you have a requirement to allow relay by external roaming users, you should disable the "Allow all computers which successfully authenticate to relay" checkbox.*

If you have systems that will send mail through this server that for some reason cannot authenticate, you can add them into the allowed list. Typically, this would include only the IP addresses of your internal clients. This allows those clients to relay through your SMTP Server, while denying relay privileges to external machines.

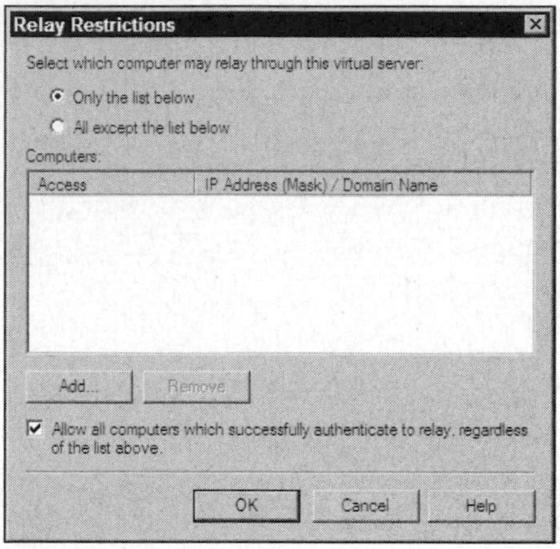

Figure 10-35

Configuring Additional Domains

By default, the SMTP virtual server that is created when you install the SMTP Service accepts mail only for the fully qualified domain name of the local server (that is, mail destined for *@server1.example.com). If you want the SMTP Server to accept mail for your entire organization, or a subdomain of your organization (for example, *@example.com), you will need to configure the SMTP virtual server to accept mail for that domain or subdomain.

To do so, perform the following steps:

1. Open the Internet Information Services (IIS) 6.0 Manager from the Administrative tools folder. Expand the SMTP Virtual Server node that you wish to configure, and locate the Domains node. Right-click and choose New ⇨ Domain.

2. You will be asked to specify whether the new domain you are adding is a local domain or a remote domain. For the SMTP Virtual Server to accept mail for a domain, choose the Alias

domain. Adding a Remote domain allows you to specify how mail should be delivered to that remote domain, overriding the global settings for the virtual server. You may wish to configure a specific Remote domain entry if mail should be delivered to a specific mail server rather than relying on public DNS MX records.

3. Enter the domain name that you wish the SMTP Virtual Server to accept mail from (for example, example.com). Click Finish to close the wizard and commit changes.

SMTP Folders

When SMTP is installed, it will create a folder structure under `%systemdrive%\Inetpub\Mailroot`. This structure becomes the SMTP message store and includes several important folders. Based on where a message file appears in these folders, you can diagnose many mail delivery problems. You can also use these folders to send mail from within your application without using the `system.net.mail` class in ASP.NET 2.0.

Badmail

The `Badmail` folder contains messages that could not be delivered after all delivery attempts have been tried and which cannot be returned to the sender with a non-delivery report. Additionally, all messages from your internal clients that do not have a resolvable From: domain are placed into the `Badmail` directory. Administrators can examine the messages in this folder, as all files can be opened with any text editor, to see why they may not have been deliverable. Undeliverable messages will have a `.bad` extension. The `Badmail` folder can be configured on the Messages tab of the SMTP Server's properties.

Drop

Incoming SMTP messages are placed in the `Drop` folder. Since Windows Server 2008 does not have a POP application that would place messages in individual mailboxes, without an additional application such as Microsoft Exchange Server, users cannot retrieve these messages using POP or IMAP clients like Microsoft Outlook. Since these are text files, they can be read in any text editor, or you could write an ASP.NET application to read these messages. The `Drop` folder for each domain can be configured in the properties for the domain under the SMTP Server in the IIS 6.0 Manager.

Pickup

Outgoing SMTP messages will be placed in the `Pickup` folder. Normally, a message will only stay in this folder long enough for the connection to the destination SMTP Server to be made and the message transferred. If the connection cannot be made for some reason, the SMTP Server will hold the message in the `Queue` folder until the next retry period and attempt delivery again. If the number of retries is exceeded, the message will be moved to `Badmail`, along with an explanation of why the message could not be delivered. Messages destined for the domains served by the local SMTP Server are immediately moved to the `Drop` folder.

The `Pickup` folder can also be used to send mail without using the `system.net.mail` class in ASP.NET 2.0. Because this folder holds text files to be sent by the SMTP Server, any text file with properly formatted headers will be treated as a message and sent. You can create a text file using any text editor, such as Notepad, then save it to this folder, and it will be treated as an SMTP mail message. The format of a SMTP message is governed by RFC 822, which was superseded by RFC 2822.

Queue

Messages that cannot be delivered on the first delivery attempt will be moved to the Queue folder. By default, the server will wait 15 minutes on the first retry, 30 minutes on the second, 60 minutes on the third, and then 240 minutes for each subsequent retry. The default maximum is two days for retrying a connection before moving the message to the Badmail folder. Therefore, if a destination server is down for the weekend, your message may end up in Badmail even if the destination server is eventually available. If you find this is the case, simply rename the file with the .bad extension to have no extension and move it to the Pickup folder. As long as the destination server is now available, the message will be delivered.

Testing and Troubleshooting SMTP

Once SMTP is configured and working, the service itself is pretty bulletproof. SMTP is a simple and time-tested process, and there really aren't many things that can go wrong. When things do go wrong, troubleshooting the problem is usually quite simple with a combination of SMTP logs and non-delivery reports (NDRs) as well as messages left in the \Badmail folder. Many of the problems with SMTP delivery are actually outside the service itself, such as a firewall blocking or network problems between the SMTP Server and the destination.

Testing with Telnet

One of the easiest tests for determining if the SMTP Server is available on port 25 is to try using Telnet to reach the port. From a system outside your network, open a command prompt and type

```
Telnet {ServerName} 25
```

where {ServerName} is the fully qualified domain name or IP address of your SMTP Server. You should see a response something like

```
220 {ServerName} ESMTP Server (Server Type and Version)
```

where the server type and version shown are the same as your SMTP Server. If you see this response, your SMTP Server is available and answering connection requests. This means that network connectivity exists between the test system and your SMTP Server, including firewalls allowing traffic to pass on port 25. To further test the SMTP function, you can follow the process in Microsoft's Knowledge Base article number 323350, at http://support.microsoft.com/kb/323350.

SMTP Log Files

Analyzing log files is an important step to troubleshooting many problems, and SMTP is no exception. By default, the log files for SMTP are not enabled, but any administrator will want log files available for diagnosing problems in connection and delivery of messages. Once the logs are enabled, deciphering the logs can be an adventure in itself. With some simple analysis using nothing more than a text editor, you can diagnose many SMTP connection and delivery problems.

Configuring SMTP Logging

To configure logging of SMTP connections, you need to enable the log files. Log files can be in a text format or logged to an ODBC database. Since ODBC logging will consume resources normally needed for

IIS and SMTP, administrators will want to choose text log files. If the logs need to be maintained in a database for future analysis, then importing the text logs into a database like Microsoft SQL Server is the recommended solution.

In text format, you have a choice of W3C extended log file format, NCSA common log file format, or Microsoft IIS log file format. As with IIS, the most information available will be found in the W3C extended log file format. This format is widely used by many applications, so it can be analyzed using most common third-party analysis tools. The other log file formats mainly exist for backward compatibility reasons. Unless you need to use another format to match an analysis program you already use, the W3C Extended Log file format is recommended.

To configure SMTP logging, you enable logging on the General tab of the SMTP Server Properties and select a log format, as shown in Figure 10-36. The logs are always saved with a filename that includes the date of the log file, but you can specify a directory if you wish. A hosting company, for example, might wish to designate a log directory within the site so that clients can download and process the logs.

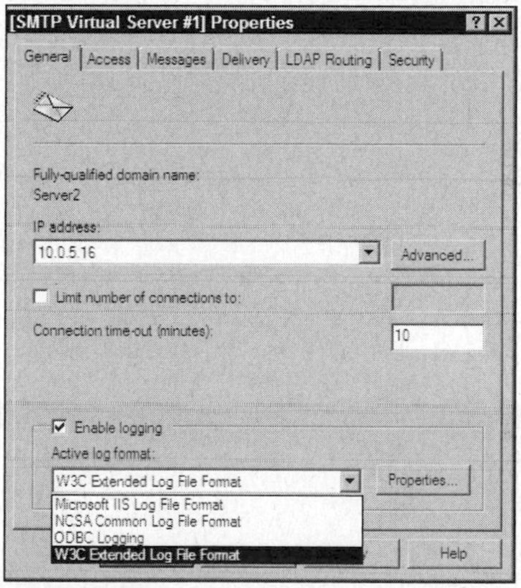

Figure 10-36

You set this directory on the General tab of the Logging Properties dialog (see Figure 10-37). Here you would also set the schedule for starting a new log file, referred to as the *rollover*, as well as whether or not to use the local time for naming and rolling over the file. The W3 Extended specification requires times to be logged in Greenwich Mean Time (GMT). This avoids potential issues arising from changes to local times (for example, when entering or leaving Daylight Savings Time). You will need to use an offset from GMT when you analyze them. Most log analyzer programs allow you to specify an offset when analyzing log files.

The Advanced tab of the Logging Properties dialog allows you to choose the items logged. Most often, you will want to select the Date, Time, Method, Protocol Status, Bytes Sent, and Bytes Received. These are the more useful fields for log analysis in SMTP Server, but you might find that you want to use others as well. The included IIS 7.0 logging utilities do not all work directly with SMTP, but many analysis programs will work fine since the W3C Extended Log file format is a universal standard. You can also use Microsoft's Log Parser utility, described below in this chapter, to analyze these logs.

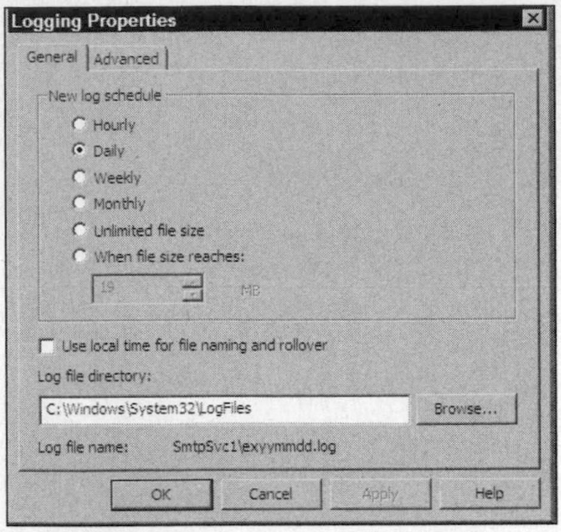

Figure 10-37

Interpreting SMTP Logs

SMTP logs might seem daunting at first, but like IIS logs they are fairly easy to understand once you know what you are looking at. Using the W3C Extended Log file format, you will have a header for each log file with four lines, each preceded by a pound sign. These are, in order, the Software, Version, Date, and Fields. The version is which log file version you chose — 1.0 is the W3C Extended Log file format. The date is year/month/day and hours/minutes/seconds in 24-hour time. Since this time will be Greenwich Mean Time, when you analyze the logs, you will need to use the appropriate offset for your time zone. The configuration for using local time in naming and rollover does not change the GMT setting for the log itself, only for the date used in the file name and the time the log rolls to a new one and archives the old one.

The fields will be those that you chose while configuring the SMTP logs. Although fields like Date and Time have obvious data in them, some of the important fields that are not self-explanatory include

- ❑ **cs-method** — The cs-method is the SMTP command and will be HELO, MAIL, RCPT, DATA, or QUIT. HELO is the initialization of a connection, and QUIT is the termination of the connection. MAIL is the Mail From or reverse path information, and RCPT is the RCPT TO or forward path information for the message — basically, where it's coming from and where it's going to. DATA is the actual data included in the message. Microsoft's SMTP Server supports most EHLO extensions, as well.

- ❑ **sc-status** — The sc-status method is the protocol status, or the codes returned by the SMTP Server. You can use these to determine the connection status and sometimes what caused a connection to drop, such as a time-out being reached.

- ❑ **sc-bytes, cs-bytes** — The sc-bytes and cs-bytes methods are the bytes sent and bytes received, respectively. You can use this to determine the amount of data sent to or received from a particular client or remote SMTP Server. Analyzing this can give you an idea of the total volume of SMTP traffic, and a large jump in traffic may mean your server is being used to send bulk e-mail.

LogParser

LogParser, originally included as an unsupported utility in the IIS 6 Resource Kit, is a simple command-line program that can parse almost any log file and generate output in a wide array of formats. The current version of the resource kit and LogParser can be downloaded from www.iis.net or the downloads section of Microsoft's web site, and support forums for LogParser can be found on the www.iis.net web site.

Installing LogParser

LogParser is probably the easiest add-on to your web server you will ever install. The LogParser download is a Microsoft installation file. Simply double-click the LogParser.msi file and followi the installation prompts to install the entire package. The default installation is to a LogParser folder in \Program Files.

LogParser consists of an executable file and a DLL, and you may want to copy those to a folder in the environment path, such as %WinDir%\System32\. This will allow you to execute LogParser from any folder; otherwise, you will need to specify file paths when using LogParser.

The LogParser installation also includes a compiled HTML help file, LogParser.chm, which includes full instructions and samples for running LogParser. Of particular interest is the reference section of the help file, which includes the query syntax as well as input and output formats.

LogParser Command Line

LogParser is a command line tool, and uses a query language similar to a SQL Server query to parse many types of log files, including IIS, FTP and SMTP logs. The command line for LogParser is simply:

```
LogParser {Command}
```

If the command requires a user-supplied parameter, that parameter follows the command with a colon, as in:

```
LogParser {Command}:{Parameter}
```

If the user-supplied parameter has spaces in it, you need to enclose the parameter in quotes, as in:

```
LogParser {Command}:"{Parameter with spaces}"
```

Log parser has several modes: query mode, conversion mode, defaults override mode and help mode. Help mode is simply prefixing the command with -h, which then displays help on that particular command or command sequence. For example, to get help on using the IISW3C format log file as input, use the LogParser command:

```
LogParser -h -i:IISW3C
```

The defaults override mode allows the LogParser default parameter values of input and output formats, as well as global switches, to be changed by the user. The syntax uses -saveDefaults and -restoreDefaults to save custom parameters or restore the factory default settings.

The conversion mode of LogParser provides for conversion from one format to another, for BIN, IIS and W3C log formats. The mode syntax requires input and output formats, as well as input file and output file information. To convert from IIS to W3C format, the command might look like:

```
LogParser -i:IIS -o:IISW3C iisfile.log w3cfile.log
```

Most useful to IIS administrators is the query mode. Using queries, an administrator can analyze log files for performance issues, error codes or page hits, or just about any other query a user can dream up. LogParser is faster than traditional log analyzers designed to provide site statistics, and can dig deeper into logs based on very specific queries. A simple query to find the top ten requested URI's in a log file would look like:

```
LogParser -i:IISW3C "SELECT TOP 10 cs-uri-stem, COUNT(*) AS Hits FROM ex*.log GROUP
BY cs-uri-stem ORDER BY Hits DESC"
```

This query, entered all as one line, uses the IISW3C format as an input format. The default input format is textline, so the format is specified on the command line. The query selects and counts the cs-uri-stem field entries as hits from the ex*.log files in the folder this command is run in. The ex*.log format will pick up all IIS log files in the folder, which are normally named by the date of the log preceded by "ex" with a LOG file extension. The query groups the output by cs-uri-stem, which is the file and path beginning from the web site's root, and adds the hits for each, displaying the top ten. Reading 200,000 lines of log files and outputting the top ten takes about a half second, far faster than log analyzers designed to provide site statistics.

LogParser queries can be contained in a query file, called on the command line using the file command. For example, the top ten hits query above can be saved as a text file, the SQL extension is a convention used in LogParser query files but any extension can be used. Save the following as Top10Hits.sql:

```
SELECT
TOP 10
cs-uri-stem,
COUNT(*) AS Hits
FROM ex*.log
GROUP BY cs-uri-stem
ORDER BY Hits DESC
```

Run this file with the following command line:

```
LogParser -i:IISW3C file:Top10Hits.sql
```

Saving queries to a file makes repeating the command easier. Note that the input file format is not part of the query and must be entered on the command line.

LogParser Examples

There are any number of queries an IIS administrator might run using LogParser, and there are some examples included with the LogParser installation. More samples can be found in the LogParser forums at www.iis.net. The examples here will be presented in the query file format. You may run them according to the information in the previous section.

Files Not Found

Requests for files that don't exist can indicate a problem with links in the web site. This simple script displays the top ten requested files which generated a 404 response.

```
SELECT
  TOP 10
  Count(*) AS Total,
  cs-uri-stem
FROM ex*.log
WHERE
  (sc-status = 404)
GROUP BY cs-uri-stem
ORDER BY Total DESC
```

This script can be modified for any response code. For example, while 404 errors are files that weren't found, the 404 subcode of 404.3 indicates the request can't be served due to a MIME map policy. Changing the WHERE clause to (sc-status = 404.3) would limit the list to only those requests with faulty MIME maps.

Daily Bandwidth Use

The amount of bandwidth used by a site is a common statistic requested from IIS administrators, and LogParser can provide this quickly and simply. The following script adds the total cs-bytes and sc-bytes, the amount of data coming and going from a web site, then divides those totals by 1,048,567 to change from bytes to megabytes. The results are grouped by day, with the megabytes, both incoming and outgoing, transferred.

```
SELECT
  TO_STRING(TO_TIMESTAMP(date, time), 'MM-dd') AS Day,
        DIV(To_Real(Sum(cs-bytes)), 1048567) As Incoming(Mb),
  DIV(To_Real(Sum(sc-bytes)), 1048567) As Outgoing(Mb)
FROM ex*.log
GROUP BY Day
```

Maximum Time Taken

Requests that take longer to generate a response may indicate a problem with that URI, from a larger than desired file to a problematic script or a poorly formed database query. This script will quickly display the ten URL's with the longest response times. These files may warrant further investigation.

```
SELECT
  TOP 10
  cs-uri-stem,
  MAX(time-taken) AS MaxTime
FROM ex*.log
GROUP BY cs-uri-stem
ORDER BY MaxTime DESC
```

File Leaching

File leaching, the linking to files on your web site from an outside source, is a sore point for many administrators. Especially links to copyrighted material or images, which can pose legal problems as well as representing unauthorized bandwidth use. LogParser can help identify these external systems that link to a web site's resources, through a modification in the top 10 hits query in the previous section. The only change is the addition of a WHERE clause to the query, to limit the results to those from outside referrers. For this example, any file with a JPG or GIF extension will be counted, unless it is requested from the fully qualified domain name of the web site itself. The query changes all file names to lower case so that both "JPG" and "jpg" will be counted, since each will result in serving the same file.

The query also uses the EXTRACT_FILENAME function and the EXTRACT_TOKEN function, to retrieve the filename from the path in cs-uri-stem and to split the cs-referrer string to just the referrer URL. More information on these functions can be found in the LogParser help file. This script will look for referrers who are outside the www.domain1.com domain. Replace that with whatever domain you'll be using.

```
SELECT
  TOP 10
  TO_LOWERCASE (cs-uri-stem) as ImageFile,
  COUNT(*) AS Hits,
  TO_LOWERCASE (EXTRACT_TOKEN(cs(Referer),0,'?')) as OutsideReferer
FROM ex*.log
WHERE
  (EXTRACT_TOKEN(cs(Referer),2,'/') <> 'www.domain1.com')
  AND
  (cs(Referer) IS NOT NULL)
  AND
  EXTRACT_EXTENSION(TO_LOWERCASE(cs-uri-stem)) IN ('gif'; 'jpg')
  AND
  (sc-status IN (200; 304))
GROUP BY ImageFile, OutsideReferer
ORDER BY Hits DESC
```

This script evaluates logged requests that have a status of either 200, which is a successful request, or 304, which indicates that the requested file has not been modified and should be served from the browser's cache. In depth explanations of the query syntax can be found in the LogParser help file.

Additional Examples

The LogParser help file includes examples for most commands, and with a little work they can solve most LogParser query questions. The LogParser forums at www.iis.net are an excellent resource for additional tips and scripts, or for help in adapting a script of your own.

Summary

In this chapter, we covered the installation and configuration of both the shipping version of FTP and the new, downloadable FTP 7. We also covered installing and configuring SMTP, which ships with Windows Server 2008, as well as LogParser and FrontPage Extensions, both of which are available as downloads from www.iis.net. Additional programs useful for running an IIS 7.0 server exist in both the basic server configuration options and as separate downloadable tools. The tools and updates mentioned here are available from Microsoft's IIS site, www.iis.net, in the Downloads section. New tools and utilities are being released all the time, and you should check the web site often for new releases and updates.

Also remember that no book such as this can cover all the optional programs, or any programs released after the publication of the book. The ones we have covered are the more popular and common tools, but you may find a need for others that aren't mentioned. Server administrators are usually quite familiar with finding utilities to meet specific needs — just realize that there are utilities to meet the needs of IIS administration as well. With the extensibility of IIS 7.0, covered in more detail in Chapter 12, "Core Server Extensibility," new modules for IIS 7.0 will be available for many common functions. In Chapter 11, "Core Server," you can find information on changing the core IIS 7.0 configuration by adding or removing modules, creating a custom web server tailored to your needs.

Part III: Advanced Administration

11

Core Server

As you learned in Chapter 2, IIS 7.0 introduces a brand-new architecture to the IIS family. In previous versions, the boundaries between what is part of the web server and what is a plug-in or extension were intuitively apparent. With IIS 7.0 and the new modular structure, the boundaries are less obvious.

In this chapter, we take a closer look at how the underlying IIS web server works, and how it is now possible to define for yourself exactly what functionality is provided by the core server, to maximize performance for your specific applications, and to minimize resource overheads.

Background

In the early days of the Web, a *web server* was nothing more than a single executable. It listened on port 80 for incoming requests, translated the request URI to a local file, and then delivered that file to the client. Figure 11-1 shows this simple web server form.

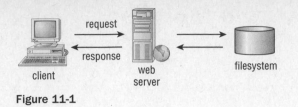

Figure 11-1

The *Common Gateway Interface (CGI)* is an extension of this simple web server form that allows the web server to pass URI parameters (for example, form field data, query strings, and so on) to external programs, and thus deliver dynamic content produced by the external program or script. Figure 11-2 represents how the CGI interfaces between the simple web server and applications running on the web server host.

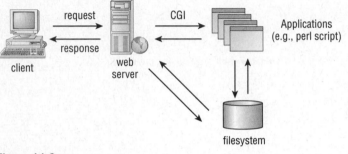

Figure 11-2

Over time, although the web server implementation has become significantly more complex, dealing with performance, scalability, and extensibility factors, the basic functionality remains the same: listener, interpreter, and applications.

Like most other web server platforms, IIS has grown in complexity and sophistication with each major version release. The core server has been enhanced and extended, continually improving the perform- ance characteristics and functionality. Over the years, new IIS releases have boasted new logging options, new authentication capabilities, new methods of caching content, new scripting technologies, and more.

Each version release caused some web server administrators to jump for joy, while leaving others want- ing more.

As more features were added, the system resource overhead grew. For those web applications that do not require or use those advanced features, they become nothing more than a waste of valuable resources and unnecessary or cumbersome overhead.

IIS 7.0 is a major rethink on this direction, putting an end to the wild, resource-hungry web server plat- form, and delivering performance, functionality, and flexibility.

This chapter takes you on a closer inspection tour of IIS 7.0 core server components and highlights why the structure of the new web server can be used to manage that performance and functionality depend- ing on the application requirements.

Core Server and Modules

Unlike previous versions, with core server implementations that were successively larger and more complex, IIS 7.0 provides a sleek core server system cut down to the bare bones of a high-performance and robust processing engine. The basic functionality is broken into three basic components that act as the foundation of arguably the most innovative and flexible web server system ever released:

- ❑ **Http.sys** — The *HTTP Listener* does nothing more than listen on port 80 for inbound web requests and then pass those requests to the IIS 7.0 core.

- ❑ svchost.exe — The *WWW Publishing Service* provides the basic web server functions of identifying the specific web-site destination and managing resources and execution of the relevant worker process(es) used to handle the request.

- ❑ w3wp.exe — One or more *worker processes* that handle all the remaining request processing.

At first glance, the IIS 7.0 core server appears similar to previous versions. IIS 6.0 introduced the concept of *independent worker processes* to isolate independent applications running on the same physical server and thereby prevent a failure in one application from affecting any other. Figure 11-3 depicts the IIS 7.0 structure, highlighting the basic components identified above.

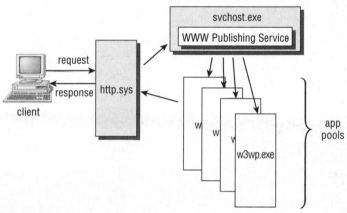

Figure 11-3

If you are familiar with the structure of IIS 6.0, you may recognize the same basic structure of HTTP Listener, WWW Publishing Service, and application pool; but the major difference in IIS 7.0 lies in the implementation of the worker processes. Although IIS 7.0 also executes each request inside independent application pools, the way these processes handle the request is an entirely new approach.

To understand how the new worker process execution in IIS 7.0 is such a major departure from earlier versions, refer to Chapter 2, which introduces the new request-processing pipeline that handles requests in a more linear fashion than previous versions of IIS. Figure 11-4 presents a close-up of the IIS 7.0 application pool processing pipeline.

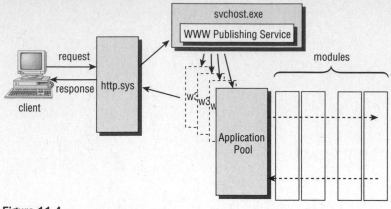

Figure 11-4

Figure 11-4 highlights the modular design of the new application pool structure. Just about every piece of functionality handled by the application pool process in previous IIS versions is now delegated to a module, which can be enabled and/or disabled as required.

The application pool process itself can now be considered as a simple workflow or processing pipeline, as shown in Figure 11-5.

Each stage in the request life cycle is referred to as an *event*, and modules provide the relevant functionality for the event processing. For example, when the worker process reaches the `authenticateRequest` event stage, it will hand off processing to any active module providing that function.

Chapter 12 provides a more detailed treatment of the request-processing pipeline and request events.

HTTP Modules

Out of the box, IIS 7.0 ships with more than 40 individual modules. The default installation activates many of these, which, as you will discover below in this chapter, are not all required. In fact, you can obtain a perfectly functional web server using only a handful of the default modules.

To understand how the core server works, it is useful to take a closer look at each of modules that ship with IIS 7.0. There are two basic categories:

❑ **Native Code Modules** — Generally, a binary .dll file, developed using languages such as VB and C++.

❑ **Managed Code Modules** — Developed using scripted and runtime interpreted languages, including C# and ASP.NET.

The next few pages offer a brief description of the discrete functionality of the modules that ship with IIS 7.0.

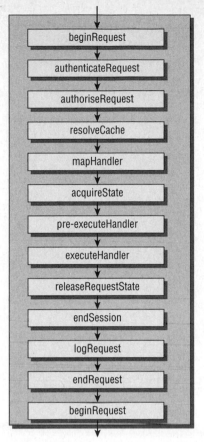

Figure 11-5

Native Modules

The following tables list the native modules that ship with IIS 7.0, grouped into categories by general functionality.

HTTP Modules

The following modules provide HTTP-specific tasks related to client–server interaction.

Module	Description
HttpRedirectionModule	Supports configurable redirection for HTTP requests to a local resource.
ProtocolSupportModule	Performs protocol-related actions (such as setting response headers and redirecting headers), implements the Trace and Options HTTP verbs, and manages keep-alive support via configuration controls.

Security Modules

The following table lists the modules that perform security-related functions. A separate module exists for each authentication mechanism, allowing you to select which authentication mechanisms are supported on your server and to remove those that you don't need.

Note that you must install at least one authentication module. Without at least one authentication module, IIS cannot determine whether the request is authorized to access the relevant system resources. IIS checks for a valid user object after the authentication phase and returns a 401.2 error if it doesn't find one.

Module	Description
AnonymousAuthentication Module	Performs Anonymous authentication when no other authentication method succeeds, or if no other authentication module is present. Typically, this module would be removed for an intranet or secured membership application.
BasicAuthenticationModule	Performs Basic authentication as described in RFC 2617.
DigestAuthentication Module	Performs Digest authentication as described in RFC 2617. The IIS host must be part of an Active Directory domain.
IISCertificateMapping AuthenticationModule	Maps SSL client certificates to a Windows account. SSL must be enabled with the requirement to receive client certificates for this module to work.
CertificateMapping AuthenticationModule	Similar to the previous module, but performs Certificate Mapping authentication using Active Directory. SSL must be configured for this module to work, and the IIS host must be a member of an Active Directory domain. *Caution:* Requests may be allowed if Active Directory Certificate Mapping is configured to protect a directory but the module is removed!
RequestFilteringModule	Performs URLScan tasks such as configuring allowed verbs and file extensions, setting limits, and scanning for bad character sequences. (Refer to Chapter 13 for further details about this feature.) This module is the successor of the ISAPI filter UrlScan.DLL that shipped with IIS 5.0 and 6.0.
UrlAuthorizationModule	Performs URL authorization based on configuration rules.
WindowsAuthentication Module	Performs Windows authentication (NTLM or Kerberos).
IpRestrictionModule	Restricts access to IPv4 clients based on a list of addresses in the IIS configuration. (Refer to Chapter 13 for some further details about this feature.)

Content Modules

The following modules provide functionality related to static web-site content, such as images and plain HTML:

Module	Description
DefaultDocumentModule	Displays a default document from a list of default files in the configuration when no explicit document has been identified in the request. If a matching default document is not found, a 404 result will be returned.
DirectoryListingModule	Lists the contents of a directory if no file is explicitly requested — for example, when the request is something like `http://www.server1.com/path/` or just `http://www.server1.com`. Note that if the DefaultDocumentModule is installed, a default document match will be attempted first. If this module is not installed, and either the default document module is not installed or there is no matching default document found, a 404 (not found) error will result.
ServerSideIncludeModule	Implements server-side includes for those requests ending in .stm, .shtm, or .shtml.
StaticFileModule	Delivers static file content such as plain HTML and images. The list of file extensions supported is determined by the `staticContent/mimeMap` configuration collection. If this module is not present, requests for static content return an HTTP 200 (OK) response, but the entity body (page) will be blank.

Compression Modules

The following two modules perform gzip compression in the request-processing pipeline. Most modern web browsers and search engine indexers support this compression technique.

Module	Description
DynamicCompressionModule	Applies gzip compression to outbound responses produced by applications.
StaticCompressionModule	Performs gzip compression of static content in memory as well as persistent in the file system.

Caching Modules

The following modules manage caching of responses to requests. Note that for user mode caching, the cache resources are defined under the user account mapped to the request, whereas the kernel mode cache is handled by the Http.sys identity.

Module	Description
FileCacheModule	Provides user mode caching for files and handles on files opened by the server engine and modules, reducing file access overheads and improving request delivery times.
HTTPCacheModule	Provides kernel mode and user mode caching in Http.sys and manages the output cache, including cache size and cache profiles as defined via configuration controls.
TokenCacheModule	Caches Windows security tokens for password-based authentication schemes (Anonymous, Basic, IIS client certificate). For example, a password-protected HTML page that references 50 images that are also protected would normally result in 51 logon calls to the local account database, or, even worse, to an off-box domain controller. Using the TokenCacheModule, only one logon event is called and the result is cached, with the remaining reference requests authorized through that cached authentication token.
UriCacheModule	Provides user mode caching of URL information, such as configuration settings. With this module, the server will read configuration data only for the first request for a particular URL, and reuse it on subsequent requests until it changes.

Logging and Diagnostics Modules

The following modules provide support for functions related to web-site and web-application diagnostics and logging. Logging includes ordinary web request logs, as well as application execution logging during run time or failure.

Module	Description
CustomLoggingModule	Provided for legacy support of custom logging modules such as ODBC support. This module also supports the ILogPlugin COM interface, but you should use the new Http Module API for any new development.
FailedRequestsTracing Module	Implements tracing of failed requests, taking definition and rules for failed requests via configuration.
HttpLoggingModule	Implements the standard web-site logging functions by Http.sys.
RequestMonitorModule	Implements the IIS 7.0 Runtime State and Control Interface (RSCA). RSCA allows its consumers to query for runtime information like currently executing request, start/stop state of a web site, or currently executing application domains.

Module	Description
TracingModule	Reports events to Microsoft Event Tracing for Windows (ETW).
CustomErrorModule	Sends rich HTML content to the client on server error, and allows you to customize that default content. Without this module, IIS will send blank pages with minimal information on any server error, including 404.
ConfigurationValidation Module	Validates configuration issues, such as when an application is running in Integrated mode but has handlers or modules declared in the `system.web` section, and displays relevant error information if a problem is detected.

Extensibility Support Modules

The following modules support extending the web server platform to produce dynamic content and special functionality:

Module	Description
IsapiModule	Implements functionality for ISAPI Extensions mapped in the `<handlers>` section (`modules="IsapiModule"`) or called by a specific URL request to the dll.
IsapiFilterModule	Implements ISAPI filter functionality, such as legacy mode ASP.NET or SharePoint.
ManagedEngine	Provides integration of managed code modules in the IIS request-processing pipeline. If this module is not installed, then managed code modules will not work, even if they are installed.
CgiModule	Implements the Common Gateway Interface (CGI) to allow the execution of external programs like Perl, PHP, and console programs to build response output.
FastCgiModule	Supports FastCGI, which provides a high-performance alternative to CGI.

Managed Modules

In addition to native modules, IIS 7.0 ships with several modules developed using managed code. Some of the managed modules, such as UrlAuthorization, have a native module counterpart that provides a native alternative to the managed module. Although modules developed using native code are generally faster and more efficient with memory and other system resources, native code modules can often be a less time-consuming and flexible alternative to develop. Note that managed modules require that the ManagedEngine module be installed.

The following table lists the managed modules that ship with IIS 7.0:

Module	Description
AnonymousIdentification	Manages anonymous identifiers, which are used by features that support anonymous identification such as ASP.NET profile.
DefaultAuthentication	Provides an authentication object to the context when no other authentication method succeeds.
FileAuthorization	Verifies that a user has permission to access the requested file.
FormsAuthentication	Supports authentication by using Forms authentication.
OutputCache	A managed code alternative to the native HttpCacheModule.
Profile	Manages user profiles by using ASP.NET profile, which stores and retrieves user settings in a data source such as a database.
RoleManager	Manages a RolePrincipal instance for the current user.
Session	Supports maintaining the session state, which enables storage of data specific to a single client within an application on the server. Note that without this module, the session state will be unavailable in your applications.
UrlAuthorization	Determines whether the current user is permitted access to the requested URL, based on the user name or the list of roles that a user is a member of.
UrlMappingsModule	Supports configurable mapping of a real URL to a more user-friendly URL (that is, URL Rewrite).
WindowsAuthentication	Sets the identity of the user for an ASP.NET application when Windows authentication is enabled.

Almost all of the feature set of IIS that was implemented as part of the core web server system in previous versions is now delivered as a set of modular plug-in components.

Components can be installed or removed as needed, thus streamlining the server workload and customizing to the specific application. Since this modular structure is based on the worker process object, this customization can be applied to any level, from discrete applications to the global web server environment.

Server Workload Customization

This new modular architecture provides server administrators and developers with the capacity to tune IIS to optimal performance and security by selecting which modules to include and which to "weed out" from the server workload.

For example, if you want to deliver a public web site with only static HTML, including user authentication and CGI handling is not just a waste of system resources, but it may also open your web server to potential threats from attacks against yet-unknown vulnerabilities in those modules.

Many of the examples encountered below assume that several optional components not included in a default IIS installation have been already installed. Please review Chapter 4, "Installing IIS 7," for further information on installing optional IIS components prior to activating those components using the methods demonstrated below.

Eliminating Overheads

Now it is possible to load only those modules required. Try this exercise as a demonstration. Note that you will need administrator privileges.

Performing this exercise on a production system will cause disruption to web-site delivery! You should use a development or test system for this process.

1. On your IIS7 server, open the default IIS home page (`http://localhost`), and then open Task Manager (Start ⇨ Run, enter **taskmgr** in the dialog, and then click OK).

2. Look for the worker process task (`w3wp.exe`) in the processes list, and observe the memory resource usage (around 3 or 4 MB for a default full install). This represents the amount of system memory resource consumed by each worker process task. This may be relatively insignificant for a small web facility, but as the load grows, with potentially hundreds of worker processes, the resource utilization builds and can become quite significant.

Now you will remove *all* modules from the running system.

3. Next, create a backup of the system in case you need to restore it back to the original state, using the AppCmd utility from a command shell:

    ```
    %windir%\system32\inetsrv\appcmd add backup original
    ```

    Now you can restore your configuration to this state at any time by executing the following command:

    ```
    %windir%\system32\inetsrv\appcmd restore backup original
    ```

4. Click Start ⇨ Run, enter **notepad.exe %systemroot%\system32\inetsrv\config\ applicationhost.config** in the dialog, and then press [Enter].

5. Search for the configuration section for HTTP modules `<modules>`.

6. Cut everything between `<modules>` and `</modules>`, and then save the file. (*Note:* Do not close the file just yet so that you can restore with a simple Undo!)

7. Restart the IIS service (Start ⇨ Run ⇨ net stop w3svc ⇨ OK, and then Start ⇨ Run ⇨ net start w3svc ⇨ OK).

8. Refresh the `http://localhost` view.

Like magic, there is nothing but a blank response!

Now take another look at the worker process image in Task Manager. The worker process task now has a significantly smaller memory footprint, thanks to a complete lack of included modules.

Congratulations! You have created arguably the world's fastest and most secure web server! It is fast because it doesn't really *do* anything, and therefore it is secure because it does not expose any system resources.

To restore your IIS install to its former glory, simply Edit ⇨ Undo the changes to the config file and Save. Refresh your browser window, and confirm that the home page is back.

The creation of such a secure and speedy system, of course, is purely academic, but this demonstration provides some indication of the value of fine-tuning the installed modules.

A Basic Real-World Example

For a real-world example of how IIS 7.0 can be tuned to suit a specific purpose, consider a plain old static HTML web site, such as might be made available to schoolchildren to publish their simple web pages. The functionality is essentially the most basic of web server implementations, similar to that pictured in Figure 11-1.

For this application, there is no need for any application processing, no need for individual user authentication or authorization, and no requirement for directory listing or compression. Even logging is effectively optional for this simple application.

For a static HTML web site, only the following modules are required:

❑ **StaticFileModule** — Provides access to the file system.

❑ **AnonymousAuthenticationModule** — Defines the user credentials with which to access the file system.

and optionally,

❑ **DefaultDocumentModule** — Appends a default document (for example, iisstart.htm) to the request URI when a document name is not explicitly requested.

The following exercise demonstrates how to achieve this configuration task.

You will need Administrator privileges to perform the following tasks.

1. Start by creating a backup of the system in case you need to restore it back to the original state, using the AppCmd utility from a command shell:

```
%windir%\system32\inetsrv\appcmd add backup original
```

Now you can restore your configuration to this state at any time by executing the following command:

```
%windir%\system32\inetsrv\appcmd restore backup original
```

2. Click Start ⇨ Run, enter **notepad.exe %systemroot%\system32\inetsrv\config\ applicationhost.config** in the dialog, and then press [Enter].

3. Search for the configuration section for HTTP modules <modules>, and replace the contents with

```
<modules>
    <add name="DefaultDocumentModule" />
    <add name="StaticFileModule" />
    <add name="AnonymousAuthenticationModule" />
</modules>
```

4. Now save the file. (*Note:* Do not close the file just yet so that you can restore with a simple Undo!)

5. Restart the IIS service (Start ⇨ Run ⇨ net stop w3svc ⇨ OK, and then Start ⇨ Run ⇨ net start w3svc ⇨ OK).

This configuration provides just the very bare essential functions to deliver plain, static data from the server file system. With this configuration, you will be able to access the default content by opening a web browser on the server console and browsing to `http://localhost`.

As an exercise, try removing the `DefaultDocumentModule`. Now, when you try `http://localhost`, you will receive a "File Not Found" response. Browse to `http://localhost/iisstart.htm` to view the default page.

For some specific web server applications (for example, an image gallery server), this even tighter configuration might be appropriate.

A More Complex Real-World Example

A more complex example of a real-world web application might take the form of an extranet Perl application using client authentication to the Windows user base.

To support this kind of application, you will want to include the following:

❑ **WindowsAuthenticationModule** — To authenticate the web-site visitor using a Windows-integrated (NTLM) mechanism.

❑ **DefaultDocumentModule** — To display a default document if not provided in the request.

❑ **StaticFileModule** — To display static content, such as images and so forth.

❑ **RequestFilteringModule** — To block suspicious requests. (It is always sensible to block suspicious Web requests, even on a secure, firewalled intranet, and especially when clients are accessing from beyond the secure environment.)

❑ **DynamicCompressionModule** — To reduce bandwidth on the network from ASP pages.

❑ **StaticCompressionModule** — To reduce bandwidth from images and static content.

❑ **FileCacheModule** — To cache file system access.

❑ **TokenCacheModule** — To cache authentication and session tokens.

❑ **UriCacheModule** — To cache URL mapping to local resources.

❑ **HttpLoggingModule** — To log requests in standard file format.

❑ **IsapiFilterModule** — To implement Perl as an ISAPI filter.

The following exercise demonstrates how to use the `applicationHost.config` file to achieve this configuration result.

You will need Administrator privileges to perform the following tasks.

1. Start by creating a backup of the system in case you need to restore it back to the original state, using the AppCmd utility from a command shell:

```
%windir%\system32\inetsrv\appcmd add backup original
```

Now you can restore your configuration to this state at any time by executing the following command:

```
%windir%\system32\inetsrv\appcmd restore backup original
```

2. Click Start ➪ Run, enter **notepad.exe %systemroot%\system32\inetsrv\config\applicationhost.config** in the dialog, and then press [Enter].

3. Search for the configuration section for HTTP modules `<modules>`, and replace the contents with:

```
<modules>
     <add name="UriCacheModule" type="" preCondition="" />
     <add name="FileCacheModule" type="" preCondition="" />
     <add name="TokenCacheModule" type="" preCondition="" />
     <add name="HttpCacheModule" type="" preCondition="" />
     <add name="DynamicCompressionModule" type="" preCondition="" />
     <add name="StaticCompressionModule" type="" preCondition="" />
     <add name="DefaultDocumentModule" type="" preCondition="" />
     <add name="StaticFileModule" type="" preCondition="" />
     <add name="WindowsAuthenticationModule" type="" preCondition="" />
     <add name="DigestAuthenticationModule" type="" preCondition="" />
     <add name="RequestFilteringModule" type="" preCondition="" />
     <add name="CustomErrorModule" type="" preCondition="" />
     <add name="HttpLoggingModule" type="" preCondition="" />
     <add name="IsapiFilterModule" type="" preCondition="" />
</modules>
```

4. Now save the file. (*Note:* Do not close the file just yet so that you can restore with a simple Undo!)

5. Restart the IIS service (Start ➪ Run ➪ **net stop w3svc** ➪ OK, and then Start ➪ Run ➪ **net start w3svc** ➪ OK).

Now all worker processes for all web sites active on your web server will be loaded with the required modules included.

Customizing Individual Web Sites

So far, all the workflow customization demonstrated has been applied to the entire web server, and thus affects all web sites on that system.

It is rare, however, that all web sites on a given server have identical feature and functionality requirements; therefore, you will often want to customize <module> configuration for each web site, rather than (as above) across the entire web server.

The following example assumes that there are two web sites on the server: Site1 and Site2. Site1 delivers a simple web server platform as described in the first example above, "A Basic Real-World Example." Site2 delivers the extranet application described in the second example above, "A More Complex Real-World Example."

It is hardly unlikely that two web sites with such different requirements are running on the same web server. The following process demonstrates how to achieve customization of each.

Refer to Figure 11-4, and notice that the modules are loaded inside the actual worker processes. It is important to understand that in order to customize a specific *web site* different from others on the same server, then that web site must use an independent *application pool*. Fortunately, when using IIS Manager, web sites are created with a unique application pool by default.

The following exercise demonstrates how to first create the two web sites and then customize each application pool, as described above.

> *This exercise assumes a default install with IIS content at* C:\InetPub. *Also, note that you will need Administrator privileges to perform the following tasks.*

1. Open IIS Manager (Start ⇨ Run, enter **inetmgr** in the dialog, and then click OK).

2. Expand the tree to the Web Sites node.

3. Right-click the Web Sites node, choose New Web Site, and then complete the dialog as shown in Figure 11-6. Note how the application pool name changes when you enter the site name.

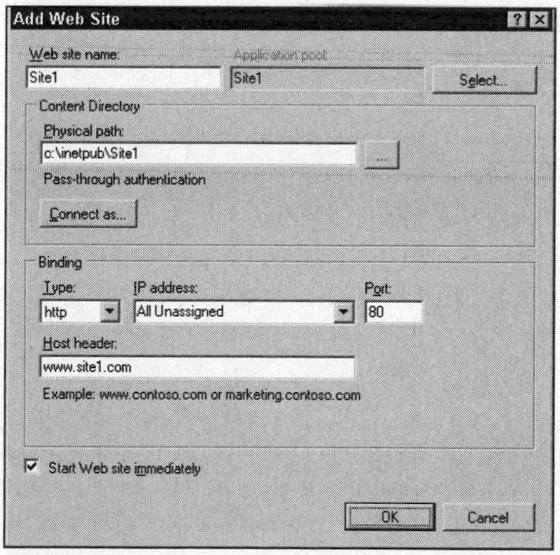

Figure 11-6

4. Repeat Step 3, replacing all occurrences of *Site1* with *Site2*.

Now you need to review the list of modules available on this server, by opening the `applicationHost.config` file and confirming the list of available modules.

5. Click Start ➪ Run, enter **notepad.exe %systemroot%\system32\inetsrv\config\application-host.config** in the dialog, and then press [Enter].

6. Next, make sure that the modules to be enabled for the specific web sites are available to IIS. To make these available to IIS, they must be defined in the `<globalModules>` configuration section of the `applicationHost.config` file.

7. Search for the `<globalModules>` configuration block, and observe the list of available modules. Ensure that all the modules required for the two sample web sites are present in this location:

```
<add name="DefaultDocumentModule" image="%windir%\System32\inetsrv\defdoc.dll" />
<add name="StaticFileModule" image="%windir%\System32\inetsrv\static.dll" />
<add name="AnonymousAuthenticationModule"
   image="%windir%\System32\inetsrv\authanon.dll" />
<add name="UriCacheModule" image="%windir%\System32\inetsrv\cachuri.dll" />
<add name="FileCacheModule" image="%windir%\System32\inetsrv\cachfile.dll" />
<add name="TokenCacheModule" image="%windir%\System32\inetsrv\cachtokn.dll" />
<add name="HttpCacheModule" image="%windir%\System32\inetsrv\cachhttp.dll" />
<add name="DynamicCompressionModule"
   image="%windir%\System32\inetsrv\compdyn.dll" />
<add name="StaticCompressionModule"
   image="%windir%\System32\inetsrv\compstat.dll" />
<add name="WindowsAuthenticationModule"
   image="%windir%\System32\inetsrv\authsspi.dll" />
<add name="DigestAuthenticationModule"
   image="%windir%\System32\inetsrv\authmd5.dll" />
<add name="RequestFilteringModule"
   image="%windir%\System32\inetsrv\modrqflt.dll" />
<add name="IsapiFilterModule" image="%windir%\System32\inetsrv\filter.dll" />
<add name="CustomErrorModule" image="%windir%\System32\inetsrv\custerr.dll" />
<add name="HttpLoggingModule" image="%windir%\System32\inetsrv\loghttp.dll" />
```

You will recognize this list as those modules selected in the two previous examples. It is OK, of course, if there are more than just these modules listed, but any module that is *not* listed under `<globalModules>` will not be available to any web-site application pool to load.

8. Searching for the `<modules>` configuration section, you should confirm that all the available modules are loaded by default:

```
<modules>
    <add name="DefaultDocumentModule" />
    <add name="StaticFileModule" />
    <add name="AnonymousAuthenticationModule" />
    <add name="UriCacheModule" type="" preCondition="" />
    <add name="FileCacheModule" type="" preCondition="" />
    <add name="TokenCacheModule" type="" preCondition="" />
    <add name="HttpCacheModule" type="" preCondition="" />
    <add name="DynamicCompressionModule" type="" preCondition="" />
    <add name="StaticCompressionModule" type="" preCondition="" />
    <add name="WindowsAuthenticationModule" type="" preCondition="" />
    <add name="DigestAuthenticationModule" type="" preCondition="" />
```

```
            <add name="RequestFilteringModule" type="" preCondition="" />
            <add name="CustomErrorModule" type="" preCondition="" />
            <add name="HttpLoggingModule" type="" preCondition="" />
            <add name="IsapiFilterModule" type="" preCondition="" />
        </modules>
```

9. Close the `applicationHost.config` file.

It is important at this stage to clarify the difference between the two configuration sections visited so far:

❑ `<globalModules>` — Determines which modules are available for the application pools to load.

❑ `<modules>` — Determines which modules are actually loaded into the application pools.

Furthermore, the `applicationHost.config` file determined the default configuration for all web sites on that web server. As with the previous examples, at this stage in this exercise, all web sites will load with the same set of modules.

The next step is to define the modules to be loaded for each of the two web sites, beginning with Site1. Because this configuration task is for a specific web site, the local `web.config` file is used.

10. Enter the following configuration elements into a blank text file:

```
<?xml version="1.0" encoding="UTF-8"?>
<configuration>
    <system.webServer>
        <modules>
          <clear/>
          <add name="DefaultDocumentModule" />
          <add name="StaticFileModule" />
          <add name="AnonymousAuthenticationModule" />
        </modules>
    </system.webServer>
</configuration>
```

11. Save this file to the web site root (File ➪ Save As, enter **C:\inetpub\Site1\web,config** for the file name, and then click Save).

Note the use of the `<clear/>` element in this file. By default, the worker processes for this web site will inherit the list of modules from the `<modules>` section of the `applicationHost.con-fig` file. Starting the `<modules>` configuration block with the `<clear/>` element blocks inheritance of the default `<modules>` configuration defined in `applicationHost.config`. After that, it is a simple matter of just adding the modules required in exactly the same format as in the first example above.

12. Next, create the configuration file for Site2. Create a new, blank text file, and enter the following configuration elements:

```
<?xml version="1.0" encoding="UTF-8"?>
<configuration>
    <system.webServer>
        <modules>
            <remove name="AnonymousAuthenticationModule" />
        </modules>
    </system.webServer>
</configuration>
```

13. Save this file to the web site root (File ➪ Save As, enter **C:\inetpub\Site2\web.config** for the file name, and then click Save).

You will notice that this time, instead of using the `<clear/>` tag to remove all inherited modules, one single `<remove name="modulename" />` was used to achieve the same result as `<clear/>` followed by all required module definitions.

After these configuration steps are completed, all worker processes loaded into the Site1 application pool will load up with only those modules required for the simple static web site described in the first example above, yet worker process images loaded into the application pool for Site2 contain all of those additional modules required for the example extranet application.

Using these basic principles of `<globalModules>` configuration sections in `applicationHost.config` and `<modules>` sections of each `web.config` file, you are able to fully customize and fine-tune your application pools independently for each web site on your IIS 7.0 web server.

Customization Using IIS Manager

IIS Manger provides a graphical interface that allows quick and easy results when making ad hoc changes to workflow customization.

The following exercise demonstrates how to add and remove modules that you want to be made available to worker processes, define the default set of modules to be loaded, and customize the server workflow for individual application pools.

You will need Administrator privileges to perform the following tasks.

1. Open IIS Manager (Start ➪ Run, enter **inetmgr** in the dialog, and then click OK).

2. To view and manage the list of modules to be loaded by default into all worker processes across all web sites and applications, in the IIS Administration Tool, click the main Server Node [for example, SERVER1 (SERVER1 \Administrator)], and then double-click the Modules icon in the Features View.

You will see the default set of modules displayed over the Features View pane, similar to that shown in Figure 11-7.

3. To remove a module from the default list, simply right-click on the module to be removed, and choose Remove from the Context menu.

4. To add the module back into the list, click Add Native Module in the Actions pane, select the module to add, and click OK.

Note that removing a module from the list in this way does not remove the availability of that module to application pools, but it does prevent that module from loading *by default* with all applications. If a specific web site or application `web.config` has that module explicitly included using the `<add name="modulename" />` described above, then the module will still be loaded for those worker processes.

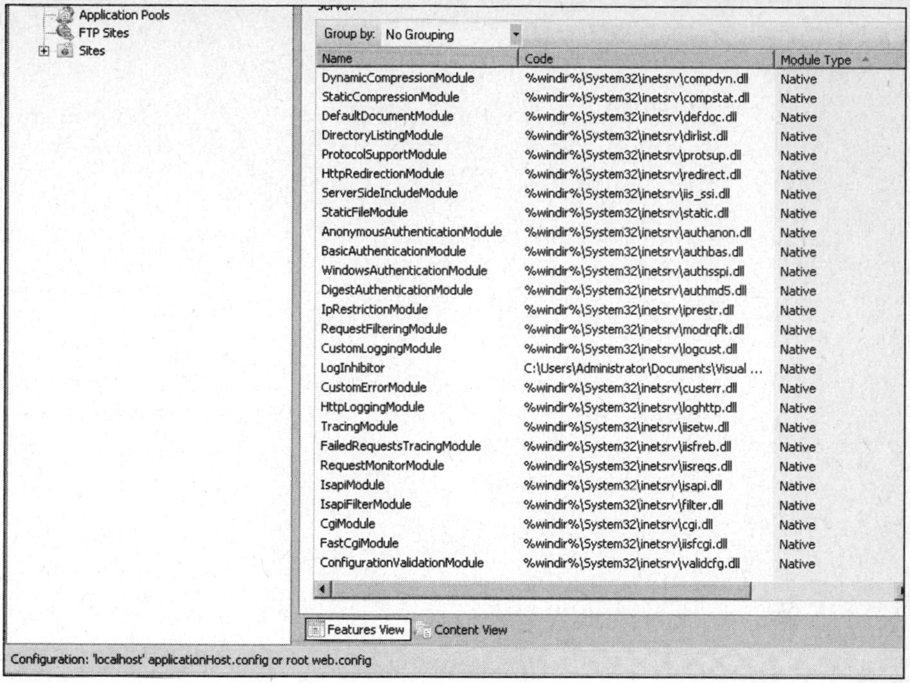

Figure 11-7

Likewise, adding a module to this list does not guarantee that it will be loaded into every worker process for every web site and application root. If the respective web.config file uses the <clear/> directive to remove all inherited module configuration, or if the <modules> configuration section includes a matching <remove name="modulename"/>, then that module will not be loaded in those respective worker process tasks.

5.   To achieve the same outcome as editing the <globalModules> configuration section in applicationHost.config, in the module list described above, first right-click on the selected module, and choose Remove from the Context menu.

6.   Next, click Add Native Module (that's right, *Add* Native Module) in the Actions pane, and again select the module to be removed. Click the Remove button to prevent this module from loading in *any* worker process of any application pool.

Note that if the removed module is explicitly defined in any individual application pool web.config, then IIS will display an error when any visitor attempts to access that web site.

7.   To add a module into the global list, simply click Add Native Module in the Actions pane, and click the Register button. Enter the module details as per the example shown in Figure 11-8, and then click OK.

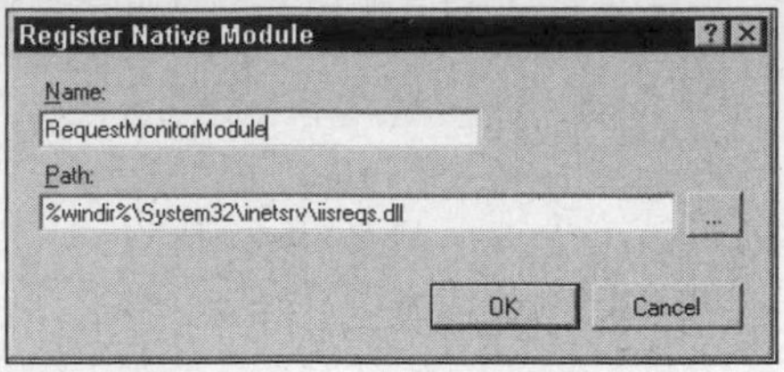

Figure 11-8

8. To customize the modules loaded into a specific web site or application, simply browse to the relevant node in the object tree of IIS Manager, and click on the node to be configured.

9. Double-click on the respective Modules icon to display the module list specific to that application. Any changes to the list of modules under a given web site or application affect only that node and any child node inheriting those settings.

ASP.NET and the IIS Pipeline

Previous versions of IIS provided ASP.NET support as an ISAPI filter. As Figure 11-9 demonstrates, this implementation double-handled many stages of the request processing. Furthermore, some tasks were simply impossible to achieve within the ASP.NET framework. For example, it was not possible to use ASP.NET Forms authentication to manage static content like images without writing complex file-handling routines within the ASP.NET application or mapping images to the ASP.NET ISAPI extension.

Also, basic request processing like mapping the request URL to a local system resource had already been completed before even the ASP.NET framework was loaded, and therefore it was not previously possible to use ASP.NET code to execute tasks like modifying the raw request parameters (for example, rewrite URLs).

With the new request-processing mechanism, however, IIS 7.0 now integrates ASP.NET natively, and thus the ASP.NET framework has become more powerful and pervasive than ever before. Now, with ASP.NET running natively, you can use Forms authentication to secure all content delivered by IIS 7.0, rewrite request URLs before they are mapped to local resources, and do much more that was never before possible using managed code.

Figure 11.10 shows how the new, integrated request-processing pipeline exposes more processing events to the .NET framework than ever before.

Configuring ASP.NET Execution Mode

Although IIS 7.0 provides greater flexibility and tighter integration than previous versions, there may be situations that require you to run an application in the same environment as IIS 6.0. For example, when installing a legacy application under IIS 7.0, you may experience unexpected errors or application misbehavior. A quick solution might be to simply run the application under the old IIS 6.0 execution model. Since the difference between integrated and legacy modes is entirely related to the execution of the worker process tasks, it is not unexpected to find this configuration control under the application pool properties.

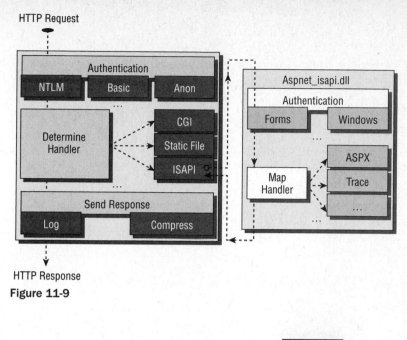

Figure 11-9

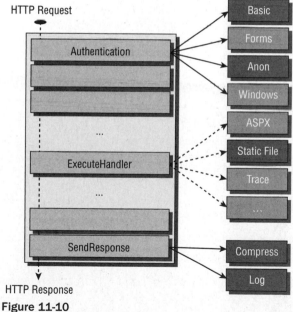

Figure 11-10

Selecting the Execution Mode

When creating your own application pools, you can control the execution mode using the application pool properties configuration:

1. Open IIS 7.0 Manager (Start ⇨ Run, enter **inetmgr** in the dialog, and then press [Enter]).

2. Expand the navigation tree and click the Application Pools node.

3. Double-click on your application pool, and select the required execution state for the Managed Pipeline Mode:

   ❑ **Integrated** — The new IIS 7.0 mode.

   ❑ **Classic** — The IIS 6.0 worker process legacy mode.

Note that those legacy applications written for the IIS 5.0 platform and requiring IIS 5.0 Isolation mode under the IIS 6.0 platform are no longer supported. Those applications must either be recoded or remain deployed to IIS 5.0 and IIS 6.0 platforms.

Setting an Application to Run in Legacy or Integrated Mode

Selecting the required request-processing pipeline mode is as simple as choosing an application pool running in the required mode.

By default, IIS 7.0 installs two application pools:

❑ **DefaultAppPool** — Executes in IIS 7.0 Integrated mode.

❑ **Classic .NET AppPool** — Executes in IIS 6.0 worker process Legacy mode.

If you do not need to create your own application pool, simply choose one of the existing pools:

1. Open IIS Manager (Start ⇨ Run, enter **inetmgr** in the dialog, and then press [Enter]).

2. Expand the navigation tree to your application node under the relevant web site.

3. Right-click on the application node, and choose Manage Application ⇨ Advanced Settings.

4. Click Application Pool, and then click on the ellipsis (...) button to the right of the value field.

5. Select the appropriate application pool from the list provided, and then click OK to all.

If a unique application pool for your application is required or preferred, you can create a new application pool as follows:

1. Open IIS Manager (Start ⇨ Run, enter **inetmgr** in the dialog, and then press [Enter]).

2. Expand the main Server node to expose the Application Pools node.

3. Click the Application Pools node, then click Add Application Pool in the Actions pane.

4. Complete the dialog as shown in Figure 11-11, choosing the required execution mode.

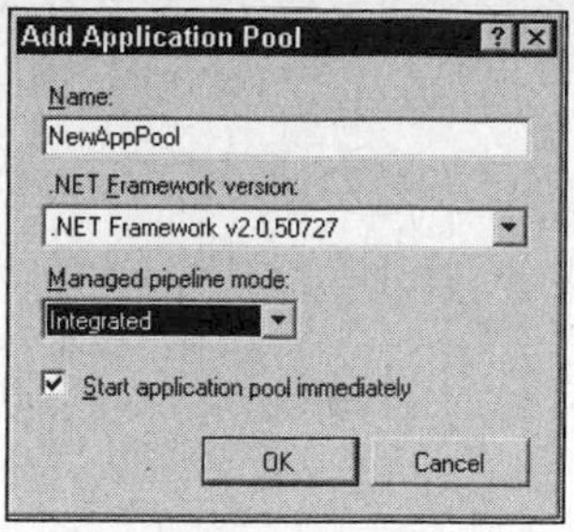

Figure 11-11

After creating the application pool, you can now follow the preceding steps to assign that new application pool to your application.

Migrating Legacy ASP.NET Applications to IIS 7.0

Although the integrated pipeline model of IIS 7.0 is designed to support existing applications seamlessly, there are some configurations that may cause problems under the new framework.

Generally, most scenarios that would cause an application designed to run under IIS 6.0 are related to configuration file layout. IIS 7.0 provides built-in assistance for migrating your application configurations by displaying helpful error text when a Legacy application fails.

You can easily resolve configuration issues by using the AppCmd utility that ships with IIS 7.0. To use the AppCmd utility to check and migrate Legacy .NET applications to take advantage of the new Integrated Mode request-processing pipeline, use the following command syntax:

```
%windir%\system32\inetsrv\appcmd.exe migrate config <Application Path>
```

For example, for an application called *app1* under the IIS *Default Web Site*, you would enter

```
C:\windows\system32\inetsrv\appcmd.exe migrate config Default Web Site/app1
```

It is quite safe to simply install a Legacy application to the IIS platform in exactly the same manner as you have always done with IIS 6.0. If there is any issue with the application configuration, IIS will display an informative error.

Usually, the error message displayed by IIS for a failed application will include the command (similar to the above example) to be executed. Executing the AppCmd instruction will check and correct any configuration issues, and migrate your application to the new platform. Once the migration process is completed, the application will still run properly in Classic Mode.

There may be some cases in which an application will not function correctly in IIS 7.0 Integrated Mode. For example, client impersonation is not available in some early request-processing stages. If your application requires web.config to define <identity impersonate="true" />, which is common with intranet applications, then IIS will generate a warning error message. In most cases, you can simply disable the error as shown below to ignore this error, and your application will run with no adverse repercussions. If, however, problems in application function are experienced or errors are encountered, you will need to configure the application to run using the Classic ASP.NET mode as demonstrated above.

You can disable the configuration migration error messages by adding the following configuration item to the application's `web.config` file:

```
<system.webServer>

    <validation validateIntegratedModeConfiguration="false" />

</system.webServer>
```

Selecting the ASP.NET Version

There may also be conditions that require use of previous ASP.NET framework versions to support some legacy code, sometimes even multiple different versions running side by side on the same server or even under the same web site.

Previously, this flexibility was supported by configuring alternative script maps under the application virtual folder. Because of the limitation that only one ASP.NET version can be loaded into a single worker process, if two applications mapped to different ASP.NET versions were configured to load into the same worker process, only the first application to load would operate under the correct version.

With IIS 7.0, although the same limitation is true, application pool configuration now specifies the ASP.NET version to prevent the common misconfiguration issue from causing difficulty. Therefore, for each application running a different version of the .NET framework, you will also need to create a separate application pool and set the .NET runtime version in the application pool Advanced Properties.

The new request-processing engine of IIS 7.0 provides seamless integration of ASP.NET applications. Although applications designed for previous versions are generally supported, in some cases legacy applications may fail under the new Integrated Mode processing.

It is important to note that the IIS5 Isolation Mode is no longer supported. Legacy applications depending on this mode will no longer run under IIS 7.0 without an appropriate rewrite of the affected code.

Legacy ISAPI Support

When introduced with IIS 4.0, the Internet Server API (ISAPI) opened doors to a whole new world of server programming. ISAPI provided developers with a means to build on the stable and powerful IIS platform to create web applications with virtually limitless functionality.

With IIS 7.0 and the new HttpModule API, ISAPI may well be considered redundant. Although the IIS team has been careful to state that support for ISAPI will not be removed any time soon, there are no strong arguments to compel developers to create new applications using this, now legacy, API.

There are many reasons why the new HttpModule API is superior to ISAPI, including

❑ **New Object-Oriented Design** — The C++ class-based HttpModule API provides a more familiar programming environment with more intuitive objects and structures.

❑ **Improved Resource Management** — New support functions make management of memory and resources more robust and accessible.

❑ **Improved Request State Management** — With ISAPI, passing state information between various event notifications requires construction of custom objects and complex data structures. The CHttpModule class supports global property definitions, offering a more intuitive mechanism.

❑ **Choice of Language** — System-level server programming was previously the exclusive domain of native code developers. Now, with support for managed code HTTP modules, this level of control is open to the widest possible developer audience.

With the vast array of third-party and proprietary components available based on ISAPI, it is safe to expect that ISAPI support will continue to be available for some time. However, developers will most certainly opt for the new HttpModule API from here on. The following chapter takes a detailed look at the new API and how you can take advantage of these new features.

Summary

IIS 7.0 delivers on all of the expectations that might normally be associated with a next-generation release of any server product: improved performance, increased robustness, and greater scalability and flexibility.

All this has been achieved without sacrifice and without major pain to developers and managers of legacy applications. Great care has been taken to maximize support of legacy applications and extensions, and a clear forward direction is defined.

By redesigning the core server platform into just the bare essential functionality and delegating all runtime functions into discrete modules, the IIS 7.0 developers have succeeded in shrinking the resource requirement footprint of the web services engine, resulting in a new generation in web server technology.

In this chapter, you have learned how to take maximum advantage of the fully redesigned request-processing structure, and how to tune the worker processes independently for each specific application on your web server.

In the following chapter, we take an in-depth look at the HttpModule API and some practical demonstrations of how to extend and enhance the IIS 7.0 core server.

12

Core Server Extensibility

You may be getting the idea by now that the new modular structure of IIS 7.0 is probably the most important new feature in the IIS product to date. The previous chapter demonstrated how it is possible to customize the server workload by simply plugging in and unplugging the relevant modules, thereby customizing functionality, reducing resource overheads, and improving performance.

This chapter concentrates on the underlying module system and how independent components can be seamlessly integrated into the core system to enhance or modify the functionality of the basic core system. The following topics are discussed:

❑ An overview of module extensibility.

❑ Basic module concepts.

❑ An example native code module.

❑ An example managed code module.

❑ Event tracing from modules.

❑ IIS configuration extensibility.

❑ Extending the IIS Administration Tool.

Extensibility Overview

The Application Programming Interface provided for developers to extend IIS is quite certainly the most powerful yet delivered by the IIS developer team. This API, in fact, is exactly the same API used by the IIS team itself to create the default modules supplied with IIS out of the box.

This means that the creators and maintainers of IIS are no longer required to wait for a major OS release or service pack, update, or patch to deliver enhanced or new functionality. Cosmetic adjustments, flaws, or security vulnerabilities alike can be addressed by simply replacing the relevant module without affecting the remaining system in general.

As developers, the exciting implication is that we can now not only add our own functionality by creating a custom pluggable module, but we can also completely replace any default module shipped with IIS.

Indeed, if you are so inclined, you could take the basic core server, strip out all default modules, and write your own modules from scratch. (Why anyone would want to do that, though, is questionable!)

Those of you already familiar with the old ISAPI model will find the new API strikingly familiar. The HTTP Module API provides all the notifications available to ISAPI and more, including access to user objects, global notifications such as application startup or shutdown, and change notifications, including changes to configuration and content.

For this reason, although the IIS Developer Team has been careful to state that ISAPI will remain a part of IIS in the future, it is almost certain that developer focus will very quickly move away from ISAPI in favor of the new module API.

To extend core server functionality, two basic module types are available:

❑   **Request Modules** — For extensions that are relevant to request processing (for example, authentication, URL mapping and rewriting, or logging functionality).

❑   **Global Modules** — For extensions that provide additional functionality to the core server that are not necessarily related to request processing (for example, application pool control, configuration, and content change management).

One of the most exciting new features presented by IIS 7.0 is the wide choice of development languages for building server extensions. In previous versions, to extend the core server in ways like new authentication mechanisms, URL rewriting, and so forth, we had little choice other than to use a native development language like C++ or VB. Now, with the new core server, language choices include ASP.NET managed code like C#.

Native code like C++ still provides enhanced control and performance over managed code modules, because of the execution mode, and managed code cannot be used to develop global-level modules, but with support for managed code extensibility, you can create core server extensions with the ease and rapid development cycle attainable from the managed code development environment.

Although there are some important differences between the API for native and managed code, the basic principles are similar, and thus for ease of presentation, this chapter concentrates first on native code and then discusses managed code modules.

IIS Module Concepts

Before you begin developing your own custom IIS modules, it is useful to first review the concepts of events, notifications, priorities, and return codes.

Although the following section describes these concepts in the context of the native code API, it is recommended that those readers more familiar with a managed code development environment continue reading in order to cover some important basic concepts of IIS module design. Once encountering the native code sample, managed code developers may want then to skip to the "Managed Code Modules" section to understand how these concepts relate specifically to a managed code environment.

Events

In earlier chapters, we presented the IIS 7.0 request pipeline and discussed the various stages of request processing. In the context of IIS extensibility, each of these steps can be considered an event.

Pipeline Request-Processing Event	Description
BeginRequest	IIS has received the request and is ready to begin processing.
AuthenticateRequest	IIS is ready to check the supplied credentials.
AuthorizeRequest	The credentials have been checked, and now IIS is ready to determine whether the user is allowed access to the requested resource.
ResolveRequestCache	IIS is ready to check the cache for an existing match to this request.
MapRequestHandler	IIS is ready to determine which handler should be used (static file, ASP, CGI, other) to service the request.
AcquireRequestState	IIS is ready to load state information such as session data and application variables.
PreExecuteRequestHandler	IIS is ready to pass the request to the relevant handler, determined by the MapRequestHandler event.
ExecuteRequestHandler	IIS has executed the request handler, but the handler has not yet commenced processing the request.
ReleaseRequestState	IIS is ready to store and release state information such as session data and application variables.
UpdateRequestCache	IIS is ready to determine whether or not to cache the request.
LogRequest	IIS is ready to pass data to the IIS logging system.
EndRequest	IIS is finished processing the request.

Additionally, the following events are nonsequential and might occur at any place in the pipeline.

Nonsequential Event	Description
AsyncCompletion	An asynchronous processing event has been completed (for example, data written to a response buffer has been sent).
CustomRequestNotification	A custom notification set by a module has been encountered.
MapPath	A URL path has been mapped to a physical path on the system (may occur several times during processing of a single request).
ReadEntity	Data are read from the HTTP request structure.
SendResponse	Data are sent to the HTTP client.

Several global events are also defined that do not necessarily relate to any HTTP request processed within the pipeline.

Global Event	Description
GlobalApplicationResolveModules	When IIS resolves the registered modules.
GlobalApplicationStart	When IIS starts an application.
GlobalApplicationStop	When IIS exits an application.
GlobalCacheCleanup	When IIS clears the cache.
GlobalCacheOperation	When IIS performs a cache-related operation.
GlobalConfigurationChange	When a change is made to a configuration file.
GlobalCustomNotification	When a module raises a user-defined notification.
GlobalFileChange	When a file within a web site is changed.
GlobalHealthCheck	When a health-related operation is executed.
GlobalPreBeginRequest	Before a request enters the integrated request-processing pipeline.
GlobalRSCAQuery	When a Runtime Status and Control query is executed.
GlobalStopListening	When IIS stops accepting new requests.
GlobalThreadCleanup	When IIS returns a thread to the thread pool.
GlobalTraceEvent	When a trace event is raised.

Notifications

When creating your own IIS 7.0 module, you will want to instruct IIS 7.0 to call your own specified code when one or more of the above events are encountered during processing of the request pipeline. Each HTTP module installed into IIS registers to the core server a request for notification of certain events.

For example, suppose you want to create a custom authentication module to check credentials against a local text file or SQL database. For such a module, you would want to register your module to receive notifications of the AuthenticateRequest event.

In the IIS Module code samples provided below in this chapter, you will see how the APIs provide special functions to allow your modules to instruct IIS to pass control to your custom processing upon encountering specified events. IIS will pass control to your module by calling a function provided by your custom module according to the API. For many events, IIS provides two separate notifications: one at the beginning of the event, and one when the event has completed. The functions are implemented in your custom module as methods within your module class.

The following table lists the methods executed at each event notification. Your custom module implementation might register for one or more notifications. For each notification your module registers for, you must implement at least one of the notification methods:

Event Notification	Event Notification Method	Post-Event Notification Method
BeginRequest	OnBeginRequest	OnPostBeginRequest
AuthenticateRequest	OnAuthenticateRequest	OnPostAuthenticateRequest
AuthorizeRequest	OnAuthorizeRequest	OnPostAuthorizeRequest
ResolveRequestCache	OnResolveRequestCache	OnPostResolveRequestCache
MapRequestHandler	OnMapRequestHandler	OnPostMapRequestHandler
AcquireRequestState	OnAcquireRequestState	OnPostAcquireRequestState
PreExecuteRequest-Handler	OnPreExecuteRequest-Handler	OnPostPreExecuteRequest-Handler
ExecuteRequestHandler	OnExecuteRequestHandler	OnPostExecuteRequestHandler
ReleaseRequestState	OnReleaseRequestState	OnPostReleaseRequestState
UpdateRequestCache	OnUpdateRequestCache	OnPostUpdateRequestCache
LogRequest	OnLogRequest	OnPostLogRequest
EndRequest	OnEndRequest	OnPostEndRequest
AsyncCompletion	OnAsyncCompletion	None

Event Notification	Event Notification Method	Post-Event Notification Method
CustomRequest-Notification	OnCustomRequestNotification	None
MapPath	OnMapPath	OnPostMapPath
ReadEntity	OnReadEntity	OnPostReadEntity
SendResponse	OnSendResponse	OnPostSendResponse

Return Codes

After your custom module has completed processing, control will be returned to the IIS pipeline to continue dealing with the request. Depending on the outcome of your custom processing, you may want to allow control to flow back to IIS and other default or custom modules, or to stop processing any further modules for the given event.

This control is achieved by returning one of the following three return codes:

❑ RQ_NOTIFICATION_CONTINUE — Indicates that IIS should continue processing additional request-level notifications.

❑ RQ_NOTIFICATION_PENDING — Indicates that an asynchronous notification is pending (for example, data are added to an output buffer and awaiting delivery to the client) and returns request-level processing to IIS.

❑ RQ_NOTIFICATION_FINISH_REQUEST — Indicates that IIS has finished processing request-level notifications and should not process any additional request-level notifications.

For example, if a custom authentication module determines that the user credentials supplied with the request are invalid, then you will want to instruct IIS to finish the request without any further processing by returning the RQ_NOTIFICATION_FINISH_REQUEST result. If the credentials are considered valid, however, you will want IIS to continue processing the request as usual by returning RQ_NOTIFICATION_CONTINUE.

Notification Priority

It is possible, of course, to install multiple modules that all register for the same event notification. For example, the log inhibitor module described above could be installed together with the default logging module shipped with IIS.

If both modules are installed at the same time and both modules are registered for the LogRequest notifications, then how does IIS determine which one to call first? The answer is priority. The module API provides a `SetPriorityForRequestNotification` function to set the priority of your module to one of the following values:

Priority Value	Description
PRIORITY_ALIAS_FIRST	Indicates that the module should be processed before all other modules.
PRIORITY_ALIAS_HIGH	Indicates that the module should be processed with high priority.
PRIORITY_ALIAS_MEDIUM	Indicates that the module should be processed with medium priority.
PRIORITY_ALIAS_LOW	Indicates that the module should be processed with low priority.
PRIORITY_ALIAS_LAST	Indicates that the module should be processed after all other modules.

Modules that do not call `SetPriorityForRequestNotification` are treated as `PRIORITY_ALIAS_MEDIUM` by default.

Again referring to the example used previously in this chapter, you would probably want to check the IP address of the client before any other request logging actions are taken, and therefore you would set your module priority to `PRIORITY_ALIAS_FIRST`. When more than one module of the same priority value is registered to the same event notification, the module that appears first in the `<globalModules>` configuration section of the `applicationHost.config` file will take precedence. (Refer to Chapter 5 for more details about the contents of the `applicationHost.config` file.)

An alternative method of ordering priority of modules with the same event notification priority is provided in the IIS administration application. Open the IIS manager, and double-click the *modules* icon. In the Actions pane, click View Ordered List. Now the display orders the modules in default priority from first to last. IIS will pass processing control to those modules first by order of priority set using `SetPriorityForRequestNotification`, and *then* in the order shown in this List View, where multiple modules have the same internal priority.

When listing modules in this way, you will also notice that the Actions pane now provides tools to modify the module order with *move up* and *move down* functions.

Following the Native Module Tutorial below, you will see that an individual `SetPriorityFor RequestNotification` call is made for each event registration. Therefore, it is possible to register for different event notifications with differing priorities. For example, you may want to create a module that is first to process `OnAuthentication` events but last to process `OnLog` events.

Figure 12-1 represents how modules interact with the IIS pipeline:

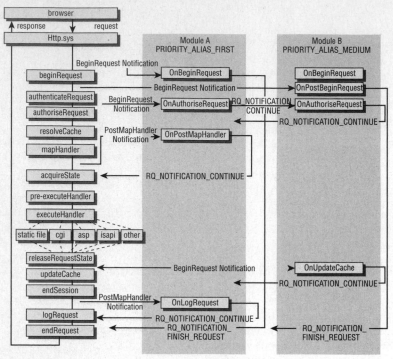

Figure 12-1

Note how Module A returns `RQ_NOTIFICATION_FINISH_REQUEST` after processing `OnBeginRequest` and thus prevents Module B or any other module (even default, out-of-the-box modules) from processing its own implementations. The same is true when Module B returns the `RQ_NOTIFICATION_FINISH_REQUEST` result, bypassing all further modules (except for the `LogRequest` and `EndRequest` notifications).

Now that we've covered the basics, you are ready to proceed to the next section to create custom HTTP modules. The following section explains the steps required to create an HTTP module using C++ native code.

An Example Native Module

For this tutorial, consider a requirement to prevent cross-linking of content on your web site from some other web site. A typical situation in which this might be useful is where your web site contains some graphical content that some other web site includes in its own web pages. Every time someone views the other web page, it causes a hit on your own web server, wasting valuable bandwidth and system resources.

As usual, MSDN is your best friend when it comes to an authoritative and up-to-date reference. For a complete reference to the Native Code Module development API, refer to `http://msdn2.microsoft.com/en-us/library/ms692081.aspx`.

Native Module Design

Note that it is assumed that you are familiar with CGI variables and how to use them to examine certain properties of a web request. In this tutorial, you will use the following CGI variables:

❑ `HTTP_REFERER` — Contains the URI of the web site where the request was initiated. A blank value may indicate that the request was initiated from a bookmark or manual entry, or possibly a search engine robot, and the like. A request that was initiated as a result of following a link on a web page (whether a internal reference such as an image link or actual user click on an href link) will contain the fully qualified URI of the originating web page (if any) — for example, `http://www.iis7.com/path/file.html`.

❑ `SERVER_NAME` — Contains the hostname of the server to which the request is directed — for example, `www.iis7.com`.

Registering a module to receive `OnBeginRequest` notifications will enable you to intercept the request before IIS processes it any further. By examining and comparing the contents of the CGI variables `HTTP_REFERER` and `SERVER_NAME`, it is possible to determine whether the request was initiated from the same web site or from a remote web site. If the value contained in `SERVER_NAME` is found in `HTTP_REFERER`, then it is safe to assume that the request has been initiated from a web page on the local web site. If it is not found, or the `HTTP_REFERER` value is blank, then the request may be treated as if initiated from an external link. If the request is found to be a cross-site link, this module will terminate the request immediately and return a 403 error (http-access-denied) to the client.

The following walkthrough is based on Visual Studio 2008. Although the source code should work under other IDE versions and titles, some of the basic menu and interface options may differ.

Native Module Creation

Before you start, you will need to download and install the Windows Platform SDK for Microsoft Vista, which can be found at `http://www.microsoft.com/downloads/details.aspx?familyid=7614FE22-8A64-4DFB-AA0C-DB53035F40A0&displaylang=en`.

Once you have downloaded and installed the Windows SDK, complete the following steps to create your HTTP module for IIS. The following sections describe these steps in detail.

1. Include SDK files.
2. Create the new project files.
3. Define the `HttpModule` class.
4. Export the `RegisterModule` method.
5. Register the module for event notifications.

6.   Implement the notification method(s).

7.   Set the notification priority (optional).

8.   Build the module.

9.   Install the module.

10.   Test the module.

Including SDK Files

If this is the first time that you have used Visual Studio 2008 with Windows Platform SDK, you will need to make sure that the IDE is aware of the location of the relevant Include files.

1.   Open Visual Studio 2008.

2.   Click Tools ⇨ Options.

3.   Expand the Projects and Solutions node in the tree view, and then click VC++ Directories.

4.   In the Show directories for the dropdown box, select Include files.

5.   Verify that the path where you installed the SDK Include files is listed. If the path is not listed, click the New Line icon, and then add the path where you installed the SDK Include files.

6.   Click OK.

Creating a New Project

The next step creates the new project files. Although you are free to name the project something different from the suggested *BlockCrossLinks*, it is recommended that you follow the sample verbatim at least one time.

1.   Choose File ⇨ New ⇨ Project.

2.   In the Project Types pane, expand the Visual C++ node, and then click Win32.

3.   In the Templates pane, select Win32 Project.

4.   In the Name box, type **BlockCrossLinks**.

5.   In the Location box, type the path for the sample or accept the default, then click OK.

6.   When the Win32 Application Wizard opens, click Application Settings.

7.   Under Application type, click DLL.

8.   Under Additional options, click "Empty project," and then click Finish.

Defining the HttpModule Class

In this step, you will create only the basic source code structure, including only the `HttpModule` class definition as well as construction and export functions.

There are three basic components to the module source code:

❑   The `HttpModule` class — The base class for this module. In this class, you will implement the request notification methods that are called by IIS at the relevant request-processing events.

❑ The HttpModule factory — Manages the creation and removal of the module for each request to be processed.

❑ The RegisterModule function — The exported function to allow IIS to load the module.

Create the basic structure by following these steps:

1. In Solution Explorer, right-click Source Files, point to Add, and then click New Item. The Add New Item dialog box opens.

2. Expand the Visual C++ node in the Categories pane, and then click Code.

3. In the Templates pane, select the C++ File template.

4. In the Name box, type **BlockCrossLinks**, and leave the default path for the file in the Location box.

5. Click Add.

6. Insert the following code:

```
#define _WINSOCKAPI_
#include <windows.h>
#include <sal.h>
#include <httpserv.h>
// Create the module class.
class CBlockCrossLinks : public CHttpModule
{
    //TODO
    // Implement Notification Method/s
};
// Create the module's class factory.
class CBlockCrossLinksFactory : public IHttpModuleFactory
{
public:
    HRESULT
    GetHttpModule(
        OUT CHttpModule ** ppModule,
        IN IModuleAllocator * pAllocator
    )
    {
        UNREFERENCED_PARAMETER( pAllocator );
        // Create a new instance.
        CBlockCrossLinks * pModule = new CBlockCrossLinks;
        // Test for an error.
        if (!pModule)
        {
            // Return an error if the factory cannot create the instance.
            return HRESULT_FROM_WIN32( ERROR_NOT_ENOUGH_MEMORY );
        }
        else
        {
            // Return a pointer to the module.
            *ppModule = pModule;
            pModule = NULL;
            // Return a success status.
```

```
            return S_OK;
        }
    }
    void
    Terminate()
    {
        // Remove the class from memory.
        delete this;
    }
};
// Create the module's exported registration function.
HRESULT
__stdcall
RegisterModule(
    DWORD dwServerVersion,
    IHttpModuleRegistrationInfo * pModuleInfo,
    IHttpServer * pGlobalInfo
)
{
HRESULT hr = S_OK;
UNREFERENCED_PARAMETER( dwServerVersion );
    UNREFERENCED_PARAMETER( pGlobalInfo );
// TODO
// Register for notifications
// Set notification priority
return hr;
}
```

This code lays out the basic framework for the new module. First, the module is defined as an `HttpModule` class with `CBlockCrossLinks : public CHttpModule`. Within this construct, you will implement the runtime functionality, as indicated by the TODO comment placeholder.

Next, the `class CBlockCrossLinksFactory : public IHttpModuleFactory` block defines the factory class called by IIS to construct instances of your module and to later unload them from memory. Any special global initialization can be processed in the `GetHttpModule()` method and then cleaned up in the `Terminate()` method.

Lastly, in this code segment, the `RegisterModule()` function must be provided for use by IIS to obtain runtime information about the module, including which events are required and which functions internal to the module class should be called for each notification. As indicated by the TODO comment placeholders, this is where you will define the notifications and notification priorities for your module.

Exporting the RegisterModule Method

Now that the basic code has been laid out, the following steps are required to export the `RegisterModule` function and thus define the entry point for IIS to access the module:

1. On the Project menu, click BlockCrossLinks Properties.

2. Expand the Configuration Properties node in the tree view, expand the Linker node, and then click Command Line.

3. In the Configuration dropdown box, select All Configurations.

4. In the Additional Options box, type **/EXPORT:RegisterModule**, and then click OK.

At this stage, you can attempt to build the project to confirm correct implementation thus far.

Select Build Solution from the Build menu (or just press F7). You should see the following text in the output window:

```
-Build started: Project: BlockCrossLinks, Configuration: Debug Win32-
Compiling...
BlockCrossLinks.cpp
Linking...
   Creating library C:\Users\Administrator\Documents\Visual Studio
2008\Projects\BlockCrossLinks\Debug\BlockCrossLinks.lib and object
C:\Users\Administrator\Documents\Visual Studio
2008\Projects\BlockCrossLinks\Debug\BlockCrossLinks.exp
Embedding manifest...
Build log was saved at "file://c:\Users\Administrator\Documents\Visual Studio
2008\Projects\BlockCrossLinks\BlockCrossLinks\Debug\BuildLog.htm"
BlockCrossLinks - 0 error(s), 0 warning(s)
========== Build: 1 succeeded, 0 failed, 0 up-to-date, 0 skipped ==========
```

If any errors appear in the output, you will need to resolve those before proceeding.

Registering for Event Notifications

Now it is time to register the module for the required request events. You will recall from the preceding "Native Module Design" section that the BeginRequest notification will be used to deliver the required outcomes.

Notification registration is done in the RegisterModule function by calling SetRequestNotifications. Returning to VS2008, locate the RegisterModule function in your source code file (near the end of the file), and add the following code:

```
HRESULT hr = S_OK;
UNREFERENCED_PARAMETER( dwServerVersion );
UNREFERENCED_PARAMETER( pGlobalInfo );
// TODO
// Register for notifications
// Set notification priority
// Set the request notifications
hr = pModuleInfo->SetRequestNotifications(
        new CBlockCrossLinksFactory,
        RQ_BEGIN_REQUEST, // Register for BeginRequest notifications
        0
);
return hr;
```

This code instructs IIS to call your module whenever a BeginRequest event is encountered. See the table under the "Notifications" section above in this chapter for the full list of notification events available. When this module is installed, whenever a BeginRequest event is encountered, IIS will attempt to call the OnRequestBegin() method of your module class, which must be implemented next.

Implementing the Notification Method(s)

Now that you have registered your module to receive request notifications, IIS will attempt to execute the relevant notification method of your module. Because this module registers for RQ_BEGIN_REQUEST notifications, you must implement one of either OnBeginRequest or OnPostBeginRequest methods.

Refer to the table of available notification events in the "Notifications" section above for a full list of the relevant methods required to register for those notifications.

Again, because this module needs to check the request properties and reject processing depending on the source of the request, the OnBeginRequest method is selected in this case.

Back to VS2008, look for the BlockCrossLinks class implementation, and add the following OnBeginRequest notification:

```
// Create the module class.
class CBlockCrossLinks : public CHttpModule
{
        //TODO
        // Implement Notification Method/s
REQUEST_NOTIFICATION_STATUS
        OnBeginRequest( IN IHttpContext * pHttpContext,
                        IN IHttpEventProvider * pProvider
                      )
        {
            // TODO:
            // Implement Method
        }
};
```

Now it is time to add the code that does the real work! The following code replaces the TODO: Implement Method comment above.

First, assign some buffers and static variables:

```
            // We won't be using this, so confirm that to avoid compiler warnings
            UNREFERENCED_PARAMETER( pProvider );
            // The images folder to be protected
            // Change this value to reflect the images
            // path for your own web site
            PCSTR pszProtectedPath = "/images/";
            // controls whether to permit loading of images from
            // bookmarks or type the url into the browser location
            BOOL permitBookmarks = false;
            // Create an HRESULT to receive return values from methods.
            HRESULT hr;
            // Buffer size for returned variable values.
            DWORD cbValue = 512;
```

Using the AllocateRequestMemory function provided by the API, all memory allocated will be handled by IIS.

```
                  // Allocating buffers for relevant
                  // CGI environment variable values
                  PCSTR pszServerName =
                          (PCSTR) pHttpContext->AllocateRequestMemory( cbValue );
                  PCSTR pszReferer =
                          (PCSTR) pHttpContext->AllocateRequestMemory( cbValue );
                  PCSTR pszPathInfo =
                          (PCSTR) pHttpContext->AllocateRequestMemory( cbValue );
                  if(  pszPathInfo == NULL ||
                       pszServerName == NULL ||
                       pszReferer == NULL
                    )
                  {
                          // looks like a memory allocation problem
                          // bail out and let IIS take care of it.
                          return RQ_NOTIFICATION_CONTINUE;
                  }
```

The `GetResponse` function provides a handle to the HTTP request data. The data structure returned provides access to various request variables, as well the `GetServerVariable()` method used to retrieve CGI variable values. This function is first used to determine whether the request is seeking a file within the protcted path defined at the beginning of this function. If it is not, then the return code `RQ_NOTIFICATION_CONTINUE` is used to send control back to IIS to continue as usual.

It is worth noting at this stage that although this sample tests the PATH_INFO for the existence of the string defined in `pszProtectedPath` above, you could just as easily test the string value for some other property, such as a file extension matching a known image format, such as .jpg, .gif, or .png.

```
                  // Retrieve a pointer to the response.
                  IHttpResponse * pHttpResponse = pHttpContext->GetResponse();
                  // start by inspecting the path
                  hr = pHttpContext->GetServerVariable("PATH_INFO",
                                                      &pszPathInfo,
                                                      &cbValue);
                  if( hr != S_OK )
                  {
                          // Can't determine whether this is an image folder request,
                          // so give it back to IIS to finish it off.
                          return RQ_NOTIFICATION_CONTINUE;
                  }
                  // is it the folder of interest?
                  if( strstr( pszPathInfo, pszProtectedPath ) == NULL )
                  {
                          // not a path of interest - let it go through unchallenged
                          return RQ_NOTIFICATION_CONTINUE;
                  }
```

At this stage, the request is identified as a request for a file within the protected path. The following code retrieves the CGI variables SERVER_NAME and HTTP_REFERER. Note that in the case of any error, control is simply passed back to IIS to continue processing as usual.

```
                  // Look for the "SERVER_NAME" variable.
                  hr = pHttpContext->GetServerVariable("SERVER_NAME",\
```

```
                                              &pszServerName,
                                              &cbValue);
        if( hr != S_OK )
        {
                // No point continuing if we have no SERVER_NAME
                // give it back to IIS to finish it off.
                return RQ_NOTIFICATION_CONTINUE;
        }
        // now retrieve the HTTP_REFERER value
        hr = pHttpContext->GetServerVariable("HTTP_REFERER",&pszReferer,&cbValue);
```

If SERVER_NAME appears within the HTTP_REFERER value, then this request was generated by a link from the same web site. In that case, control is passed back to IIS as before. If not, however, RQ_NOTIFICATION_ FINISH_REQUEST is used to terminate the request immediately — no further notifications for any other modules (including those shipped with IIS) will be processed.

```
        // check for a valid result
        if( hr == S_OK )
        {
                // if the referer is the same web site, then pszServerName
                // will appear in pszReferer
                if( strstr(pszReferer, pszServerName) != 0 )
                {
                        // it is there, so this is a valid link
                        return RQ_NOTIFICATION_CONTINUE;
                }
                else
                {
                        // the referer does not match server_name
                        return RQ_NOTIFICATION_FINISH_REQUEST;
                }
        }
```

If HTTP_REFERER is not found in the list of CGI variables, then the request has not been generated by a web-site link. Possible causes include access from a browser bookmark, directly typing the URI into the browser location, or a request made by a search index robot. The value of the permit_bookmarks variable defined at the beginning of this function determines how to handle this kind of request.

```
        if( hr = ERROR_INVALID_INDEX )
        {
                // the referer value is missing from the header
                if( permitBookmarks )
                        return RQ_NOTIFICATION_CONTINUE;
                else
                        return RQ_NOTIFICATION_FINISH_REQUEST;
        }
        // we only arrive here if there was an error
        // allow IIS to deal with the rest.
        // Return processing to the pipeline.
        return RQ_NOTIFICATION_CONTINUE;
```

You can change the value of the local variable permit_bookmarks to change the default behavior. If you want to allow delivery for requests with missing HTTP_REFERER value, set permitBookmarks = true.

Setting Notification Priority

When several modules (including those shipped with IIS) are loaded, IIS uses a notification priority scheme to determine the order in which to pass request processing. Setting the notification priority for your module is optional. If you do not explicitly set the notification priority here, your module will be treated as the default PRIORITY_ALIAS_MEDIUM priority.

Returning now to the RegisterModule() function, add the following additional code:

```
HRESULT hr = S_OK;
UNREFERENCED_PARAMETER( dwServerVersion );
UNREFERENCED_PARAMETER( pGlobalInfo );
// TODO
// Register for notifications
// Set notification priority
// Set the request notifications
hr = pModuleInfo->SetRequestNotifications(
        new CBlockCrossLinksFactory,
        RQ_BEGIN_REQUEST, // Register for BeginRequest notifications
        0
);
if( hr == S_OK ) // Do this only if there was no error
{
        hr = pModuleInfo->SetPriorityForRequestNotification(
                        RQ_BEGIN_REQUEST,      // which notification
                        PRIORITY_ALIAS_FIRST   // what priority
                        );
}
return hr;
```

Because this module needs to check the request properties and reject processing if the request is determined to be related to a cross-linked request, it makes sense to set the priority to the maximum available so that it will be the first module called by IIS when a request is received.

If, however, you wanted to pre-qualify the request via some other custom module before determining whether to allow or reject a request, then you may want to set a lower priority such as PRIORITY_ALIAS_MEDIUM or PRIORITY_ALIAS_LAST.

Building the Module

Now build the module by choosing Build Module from the Build menu (or simply press F7). Confirm that there are no errors by observing the results displayed in the output window:

```
-Build started: Project: BlockCrossLinks, Configuration: Debug Win32-
Compiling...
BlockCrossLinks.cpp
Linking...
   Creating library C:\Users\Administrator\Documents\Visual Studio
2008\Projects\BlockCrossLinks\Debug\BlockCrossLinks.lib and object
C:\Users\Administrator\Documents\Visual Studio
2008\Projects\BlockCrossLinks\Debug\BlockCrossLinks.exp
Embedding manifest...
```

```
Build log was saved at "file://c:\Users\Administrator\Documents\Visual Studio
2008\Projects\BlockCrossLinks\BlockCrossLinks\Debug\BuildLog.htm"
BlockCrossLinks - 0 error(s), 0 warning(s)
========== Build: 1 succeeded, 0 failed, 0 up-to-date, 0 skipped ==========
```

Installing the Module

Now it is time to install the custom module into IIS. The following steps use IIS Manager for this task. You can also complete this task by editing the applicationHost.config file, as described in Chapter 5.

Note that the following method will install the module to *all* web sites on this server. Refer also to Chapter 11 for more detail on independently managing modules for individual web sites.

1. If IIS 7.0 is running on a different server than your copy of Visual Studio, copy the file BlockCrossLinks.dll generated by the VS2008 build process to some location on the IIS system.

2. To open IIS Manager, click Start ➪ Run, enter **inetmgr** in the dialog, and then press OK.

3. Click the base container (SERVER1/Administrator).

4. Double-click the Modules icon in the Features View.

5. Click Add Native Module in the Actions pane.

6. Click Register.

7. Enter **BlockCrossLinks** as the name, and the full path to the BlockCrossLinks.dll file.

8. Click OK.

9. Confirm that BlockCrossLinks now appears in the list of available modules and that the checkbox is checked.

10. Click OK.

Congratulations! Your first native code HTTP module is installed and ready to test.

Testing the Module

Although there are a variety of ways to test this module, the following process assumes a standard default installation of IIS 7.0. The standard default install will establish the *Default Web Site* referred to in the following demonstration, as well as the default homepage graphic welcome.png. If your own installation is nonstandard, simply modify the following steps accordingly:

1. Open the IIS default web-site root in Windows Explorer by clicking Start ➪ Run, entering **C:\inetpub\wwwroot**, and then clicking OK.

2. Create a new folder called images.

3. Copy (or move) the file welcome.png into the new images folder.

4. Open the iisstart.htm file in a text editor. (Right-click on the file, and choose Open With ➪ Notepad.)

5. Find the text.

```
<img src="welcome.png" alt="IIS7" width="571" height="411" />
```

and replace it with

```
<a href=http://127.0.0.1>
    <img src="http://127.0.0.1/images/welcome.png" />
</a>
```

6. Save the file and exit.

Now open Internet Explorer on the server console (or by a terminal server session), type **http://localhost** in the IE location field (not including the quotes), and hit [Enter].

You will see that the homepage now displays only a broken image icon instead of the IIS Welcome graphic. Now click the broken link icon, and observe the default homepage in all its glory!

Native Module Wrap-Up

When accessing the default homepage that you modified in Steps 4 and 5 above using the URL `http://localhost`, the image link is requested using the IP address (`127.0.0.1`) instead of the hostname (`localhost`). Thus, when the custom module processes the request for the image file, the value of `SERVER_NAME` evaluates to `127.0.0.1`, and the value of `HTTP_REFERER` is `http://localhost/iis-start.htm`.

Since the `SERVER_NAME` value does not exist in the `HTTP_REFERER`, the request is detected as cross-linked and rejected.

When you click on the link to open the homepage now as `http://127.0.0.1`, the value of the `SERVER_NAME` is "127.0.0.1" and the `HTTP_REFERER` is `http://127.0.0.1/iisstart.htm`, and thus the request is allowed to complete.

As a further exercise, you might want to conduct further processing in the `OnBeginRequest` method of your custom module to add further functionality:

❑ Replace the requested image with an alternative image, perhaps containing some copyrighted text alerting the viewers to the fact that the web site they are visiting is (perhaps unintentionally) referring to content delivered to another web site without permission.

❑ Modify the IIS response code to return a more descriptive result, say, 403 (Request Denied), instead of the default 200 (OK).

Managed Code Modules

Although there are several important differences, the Managed Code API shares some basic concepts with the Native Code API, and therefore the earlier section, "IIS Module Concepts" is recommended reading prior to beginning this section. You may also consider reviewing the sections covering the IIS 7.0 pipeline and ASP.NET integrated mode in Chapter 11 prior to proceeding with this section.

For those of you already familiar with `HttpApplication` events in previous versions of ASP.NET, the new IIS 7.0 API will be a familiar and empowering extension.

IIS 7.0 ships with the special ManagedEngine utility module, which acts as a native code module wrapper for managed code modules. Figure 12-2 represents how the ManagedEngine module exposes IIS request-processing pipeline events to the managed code environment.

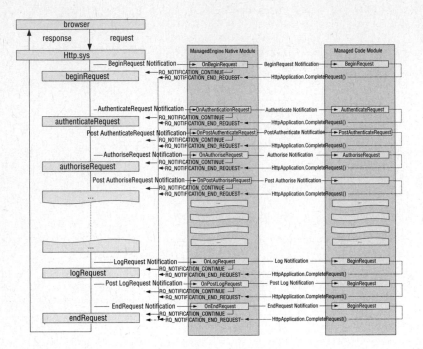

Figure 12-2

Notice that one major difference between the managed and native code functionality is that managed code modules do not set a return code back to IIS; instead, the modules use the `CompleteRequest` method of the `HttpApplication` class to interrupt the request-processing pipeline and go directly to the `EndRequest` event.

Another important difference is that not all the native notification events are available. For example, there is no equivalent of `PostBeginRequest` for managed code modules.

Nonetheless, the ability for managed code to now execute in the same stages as IIS modules makes many tasks previously only accessible to native ISAPI filters and extensions now possible in managed code, using the familiar ASP.NET APIs and full functionality of the .NET platform. For example, it is now possible to use managed code to achieve the following:

❑ Custom authentication modes that replace built-in methods.

❑ Modification of the incoming request contents, such as request headers or rewrite URLs.

❑ Filtering of outgoing responses for all content types, including images and multimedia files.

Managed Event Notifications

The complete pipeline contains the following stages, exposed as `HttpApplication` events in ASP.NET:

Request Event	Description	Post-Event
BeginRequest	The request processing is starting.	<none>
AuthenticateRequest	The request is being authenticated. IIS and ASP.NET authentication modules subscribe to this stage to perform authentication.	PostAuthenticate Request
AuthorizeRequest	The request is being authorized. IIS and ASP.NET authorization modules check whether the authenticated user has access to the resource being requested.	PostAuthorizeRequest
ResolveRequestCache	Cache modules can check whether the response to this request exists in the cache and return it instead of proceeding with the rest of the execution path. Both ASP.NET Output Cache and the new IIS Output Cache features execute here.	PostResolveRequest Cache
MapRequestHandler	This stage is internal in ASP.NET and is used to determine the request handler.	PostMapRequestHandler
AcquireRequestState	The state necessary for the request execution is being fetched. ASP.NET Session State and Profile modules obtain their data here.	PostAcquireRequest State
PreExecuteRequest Handler	Any tasks before the execution of the handler can be performed here.	PostExecuteRequest Handler
ExecuteRequestHandler	The request handler executes here. ASPX pages, ASP pages, CGI programs, and static files are served here.	<none>

Further Reading

Managed module functionality is provided within the `System.Web` namespace. As before, you should allow MSDN to become your best friend when it comes to a concise reference for IIS development. You will find the relevant APIs documented at `http://msdn2.microsoft.com/en-us/library/system.web.aspx`.

This MSDN reference provides details on all the objects and structures available for extending IIS. Probably the best way to learn how to use them is to jump right in and create a sample module.

An Example Managed Module

If you have already completed the previous tutorial in this chapter and completed the development of a custom module using native code, then you will be familiar with the example functionality of the Cross Link Blocker. Otherwise, you should review the information on Module Design above in this chapter.

Managed Module Design

As with the native module design, the `BeginRequest` event will be the notification used to implement this module. Also, the request information used will be the values of the SERVER_NAME and HTTP_REFERER variables provided by the CGI framework.

The example native code module used the `RQ_NOTIFICATION_FINISH_REQUEST` return code to interrupt the request processing when a cross-linked request was discovered. Although this might be a good way to reduce the performance and bandwidth hit that cross-link requests would otherwise create, it does not necessarily provide the most eloquent solution.

The following example delivers an alternative pre-defined image in place of the requested file. The replacement image may be very small, or blank, to minimize bandwidth overheads, or may carry some copyright or "access denied" text. This tutorial demonstrates use of a small text-carrying image, but you can use any file you like — even a nasty surprise for the cross-linker!

Managed Module Creation

Although the IDE used in this sample is Visual Studio 2008, you can use other IDE versions and products. You can even use a plaintext editor like Notepad to complete this sample. Simply replace the IDE steps provided with equivalent steps for your selected IDE.

This example can be completed in five basic steps:

1. Define the `IHttpModule` interface.
2. Register for notifications.
3. Implement the notifications.
4. Install the module.
5. Test the module.

Defining the IHttpModule Interface

The first task is to define the module framework. IHttpModule is a System.Web namespace interface that provides the initialization and disposal methods for IIS modules.

1. Open Visual Studio 2008.

2. Click File ➪ New ➪ File.

3. Select Text File from the General node, and then click Open.

4. Click File ➪ Save TextFile1 As.

5. Use the "File Save As" dialog to browse to the location of your web-site root (for example, C:\inetpub\wwwroot), and create a new folder called *App_Code*.

6. Save the file as BlockLinks.cs.

7. Insert the following code:

```
using System;
using System.Web;
namespace CustomModules
{
    public class BlockLinks : IHttpModule
    {
        public BlockLinks()
        {
            // Class constructor.
        }
        // Classes that inherit IHttpModule
        // must implement the Init and Dispose methods.
        public void Init(HttpApplication app)
        {
            // TODO:
            // Add initialization code
            // Including notifications
        }
        public void Dispose()
        {
            // TODO:
            // Add code to clean up the
            // instance variables of a module.
        }
        // TODO:
        // add event notification methods
    }
}
```

This code simply lays out the basic module framework. All implementations of IHttpModule must provide the basic constructor (public BlockLinks()), initialization (public void Init(HttpApplication app)), and disposal (public void Dispose()) methods.

Next, you will proceed to add the custom functionality of the module.

Registering for Notifications

In this step, you need to determine which event notification will be handled by this module. As outlined in the design discussion, only the `BeginRequest` notification is required for this module.

Find the module's `Init` method, and add the following code:

```
// Classes that inherit IHttpModule
// must implement the Init and Dispose methods.
public void Init(HttpApplication app)
{
    // TODO:
    // Add initialization code
    // Including notifications
    app.BeginRequest += new EventHandler(app_BeginRequest);

}
```

This line registers the module's event handler method `app_BeginRequest` to the IIS request pipeline.

Implementing the Notifications

Now that you have registered the `app_BeginRequest` method, you need to implement it. Add the following code to your class:

```
// TODO:
// add event notification methods
// Define a custom BeginRequest event handler.
public void app_BeginRequest(object o, EventArgs ea)
{
    HttpApplication httpApp = (HttpApplication)o;
    HttpContext ctx = HttpContext.Current;
    NameValueCollection coll;  // to handle the CGI variables
    String ServerName = String.Empty; // variable to store the SERVER_NAME
    String Referer = String.Empty;    // and HTTP_REFERER CGI variables.
```

This code simply sets out a few variables and objects to simplify later manipulation. The `HttpContext` class provides access to the HTTP request details as well as to HTTP response structures if needed.

Notice the use of the `NameValueCollection` class for the `coll` object. This utility class is included to simplify processing of the CGI variables, but you will need to include the namespace in the C# headers to be able to use this:

```
using System;
using System.Web;
using System.Collections.Specialized;
```

Now let's return to the notification method implementation. The next step in this implementation is to inspect the URL requested by the remote client and determine whether it is an image file.

```
String ServerName = String.Empty;
String Referer = String.Empty;
```

```
        // retrieve the URL requested
        String RequestUrl = ctx.Request.RawUrl;
        if (RequestUrl.EndsWith(".jpg", StringComparison.OrdinalIgnoreCase) ||
            RequestUrl.EndsWith(".gif", StringComparison.OrdinalIgnoreCase) ||
            RequestUrl.EndsWith(".png", StringComparison.OrdinalIgnoreCase))
        {
            // Is an image file
        }
    }
```

The next bit of code simply extracts the data of interest from the request structure and then tests whether the request is the result of a link from the local web site:

```
        // Is an image file
        // Load ServerVariable collection into NameValueCollection object.
        coll = ctx.Request.ServerVariables;
        // Get names of all keys into a string array.
        ServerName = coll["SERVER_NAME"];
        Referer   = coll["HTTP_REFERER"];
        if (!Referer.Contains(ServerName))
        {
            // NOT initiated by a link from a local web page!
        }
```

You might already recognize that when `Referer.Contains(ServerName)` is `false` (that is, `!Referer.Contains(ServerName)` is `true`), there are two possible causes:

❑ The `HTTP_REFERER` is a remote web site, for example, the `SERVER_NAME` is *www.mywebsite.com* and the `HTTP_REFERER` is *www.remotewebsite.com/path/page.html*.

❑ The `HTTP_REFERER` is blank. In this case, the request was initiated by a bookmark or direct entry to the browser location, or by a nonbrowser entity (a search engine robot, for example).

If you want to permit access in case of the second cause, you will need to add a further test for a specifically blank string (that is, `Referer == ""`). Otherwise, continue with the following code to deny all requests that are not the result of a local web-page request.

The following code uses the `RewritePath` method of the `HttpContext` class to change the requested file to a different file of your own choosing:

```
        if (!Referer.Contains(ServerName))
        {
            // NOT initiated by a link from a local web page!
            ctx.RewritePath(
                "denied.bmp",   // replacement file
                "/images",      // replacement path
                ""              // replacement query string
                );
        }
```

And that completes the coding for this module.

Installing the Module

Now it is time to install the custom module into IIS. The following steps use IIS Manager for this task. This task can also be completed by editing the `applicationHost.config` file. Refer to Chapter 5 for details of that method.

Note that the following method will install the module to *all* web sites on this server. Refer also to the earlier chapter for more detail on independently managing modules for multiple web sites.

1. To open IIS Manager, click Start ➪ Run, enter **inetmgr**, and then click OK.

2. Expand the node tree, and click on the Web Site container (for example, Default Web Site).

3. Double-click the Modules icon in the Features View.

4. Click on Add Managed Module in the Actions pane.

5. Enter **BlockLinks** in the Name field, and select .CustomModules.CS.BlockLinks from the list.

6. Click OK, and OK again.

7. Click OK.

Congratulations! Your first managed code HTTP Module is installed and ready to test.

Alternative Install

An alternative to installing the managed module as source code in the `App_Code` path under the web-site root is to compile the code as a DLL, copy it to the `bin` folder (for example, `C:\inetpub\wwwroot\bin`) of the web site, and then follow the preceding steps.

Running the module from `App_Code` means that during development, you will be able to make quick modifications to your modules while viewing the results in your web browser, without needing to running the compiler or restarting services. Installing the module as a binary DLL, however, provides some savings on resource overheads, making your modules significantly more efficient when running on production systems, as well as providing some protection of your intellectual property if you are distributing your code on a commercial basis.

Testing the Module

Although there are a variety of ways to test this module, the following process assumes a standard default installation of IIS 7.0. The standard default install will establish the Default Web Site referred to in the following demonstration, as well as the default homepage graphic `welcome.png`. If your own installation is nonstandard, simply modify the following steps accordingly:

1. To open the IIS default web-site root in Windows Explorer, click Start ➪ Run, enter **C:\ inetpub\wwwroot**, and click OK.

2. Create a new folder called `images`.

3. Copy (or move) the file `welcome.png` into the new `images` folder.

4. Open the file `iisstart.htm` in a text editor (right-click on the file, and choose Open With ➪ Notepad).

5. Find the text:

```
<img src="welcome.png" alt="IIS7" width="571" height="411" />
```

and replace it with

```
<a href=http://127.0.0.1>
   <img src="http://127.0.0.1/images/welcome.png" />
</a>
```

6. Save the file, and exit.

7. Right-click inside the `images` folder, choose New ➪ Bitmap Image, and enter the filename **denied.bmp**.

8. Right-click on the new file, and choose Open With ➪ Paint.

9. Use the text tool to add some text (for example, "**Access Denied**"), and save the changes.

Now, open Internet Explorer on the server console (or by a terminal server session), enter **http://localhost** in the location field, then press [Enter].

You will see that the homepage now displays the replacement image instead of the IIS Welcome graphic. Now click on the broken link icon, and observe the default homepage in all its glory!

Managed Module Wrap-Up

When accessing the default home page that you modified in Steps 4 and 5 above using the URL `http://localhost`, the image link is requested using the IP address (`127.0.0.1`) instead of the hostname (`localhost`). Thus, when the custom module processes the request for the image file, the value of SERVER_NAME evaluates to `127.0.0.1`, and the value of HTTP_REFERER is `http://localhost/iisstart.htm`.

Since the SERVER_NAME value does not exist in the HTTP_REFERER, the request is detected as cross-linked and rejected.

When you click the link to open the homepage now as `http://127.0.0.1`, the value of SERVER_NAME is `127.0.0.1`, and the HTTP_REFERER is `http://127.0.0.1/iisstart.htm` — thus, IIS is permitted to deliver the requested image file.

As a further exercise, you might want to further process the custom module to incorporate further functionality, such as adding notification text to the web server log file using the `AppendToLog` method of the `Response` object.

Event Tracing from Modules

Although the sample modules in the preceding examples are relatively simple, they demonstrate how it is now possible to add virtually limitless enhanced functionality to the core web server system as well as web applications.

As you no doubt know, however, the more complex applications become, the more difficult it is to diagnose when something goes wrong. In the past, the diagnosis of misbehaving web applications and extensions was arguably the single-most difficult and time-consuming task in running and managing web applications.

The designers of IIS 7.0 recognized this fact and provided new debugging and diagnostic tools. Chapter 20, "Diagnostics and Troubleshooting," provides an in-depth treatment of the new tracing tools and how to capture and manage tracing information.

For the module programmer, though, the capacity to hook into the built-in tracing subsystem provides some major time-saving capabilities. The advantage of using the tracing system in favor of alternative methods, such as writing debug output to a text file or Event Viewer logging, is that the code has no effect unless a trace listener is attached. Therefore, any diagnostic resource overheads are limited until it is required, and then the diagnostics can be activated by the user when and as required.

Adding Tracing Support to a Managed Code Module

This tutorial expands on the managed code module example, adding some tracing output. You will perform the following steps, as detailed in the following sections:

1. Include a namespace reference.
2. Declare a global `TraceSource` variable.
3. Initialize the `TraceSource` object.
4. Add trace events.
5. Compile and deploy the module.
6. Add a trace listener to IIS.
7. Enable tracing and route trace events to IIS.
8. View the trace results.

> This tutorial requires that the event tracing module is installed and active. For further details on adding and removing optional IIS components, refer to Chapter 4, "Installing IIS 7."

Including a Namespace Reference

The first step to adding event tracing to your IIS module is to include a reference to the relevant namespace. IIS event tracing is supported by `System.Diagnostics`, which you will find fully documented in MSDN at `http://msdn2.microsoft.com/en-us/library/system.diagnostics.aspx`.

In this example, the `TraceSource` class from the `System.Diagnostics` namespace will be used to produce output that can be routed to IIS for display.

To begin, open the C# source created in the previous tutorial (BlockLinks.cs), and include `System.Diagnostics` below the existing `using` declarations:

```
using System;
using System.Web;
```

```
using System.Collections.Specialized;
using System.Diagnostics;
```

Declaring a Global TraceSource Variable

To produce trace output from any location within your module, you need to create a global variable to store the `TraceSource` object.

Add a `Tracesource` object declaration at the beginning of the `Blocklinks` class.

```
public class BlockLinks : IHttpModule
{
    TraceSource ts;
```

Initializing the TraceSource Object

The best place to create the `TraceSource` object is in the `Init()` method of the custom module code. This function is called when the module object is created for each request, and any system resources allocated here will be cleaned up upon request completion.

Initialize the `Tracesource` object with the following code:

```
public void Init(HttpApplication app)
{
    // TODO:
    // Add initialization code
    // Including notifications
    app.BeginRequest += new EventHandler(app_BeginRequest);
    ts = new TraceSource("BlockLinks");
}
```

Note that the text string "BlockLinks" is defined in order to clearly identify output generated by this module.

Adding Trace Events

Now you are free to add trace events at any stage of your module. It is a recommended best practice to always add `Start` and `Stop` events to each of your module notification methods, so that trace output will always confirm module entry to and exit from your custom module.

Precisely where and in how much detail tracing events are added is entirely up to you. For example, the following code includes the recommended `Start` and `Stop` events, plus one `Information` event and one `Warning` event:

Add four trace events with the following additional code:

```
public void app_BeginRequest(object o, EventArgs ea)
{
    ts.TraceEvent(TraceEventType.Start, 0,
            "[BlockLinks] START BeginRequest");
    HttpContext ctx = HttpContext.Current;
    NameValueCollection coll;
```

```
      String ServerName = "";
      String Referer = "";
      int loop1;
      // retrieve the URL requested
      String RequestUrl = ctx.Request.RawUrl;
      if (RequestUrl.EndsWith(".jpg", StringComparison.OrdinalIgnoreCase) ||
          RequestUrl.EndsWith(".gif", StringComparison.OrdinalIgnoreCase) ||
          RequestUrl.EndsWith(".png", StringComparison.OrdinalIgnoreCase))
      {
          // Is an image file
          ts.TraceEvent(TraceEventType.Information, 0,
                  "[BlockLinks] Detected request for image");
          // Load ServerVariable collection into NameValueCollection object.
          coll = ctx.Request.ServerVariables;
          // Get names of all keys into a string array.
          ServerName = coll["SERVER_NAME"];
          Referer   = coll["HTTP_REFERER"];
          if (!Referer.Contains(ServerName))
          {
              // NOT initiated by a link from a local web page!
              ts.TraceEvent(TraceEventType.Warning, 0,
                      "[BlockLinks] Cross-Linked request detected from" + Referer);
              ctx.RewritePath(
                          "denied.bmp",   // replacement file
                          "/images",      // replacement path
                          ""              // replacement query string
                          );
          }
      }
      ts.TraceEvent(TraceEventType.Stop, 0,
              "[BlockLinks] END BeginRequest");
  }
```

Note the use of the `TraceEvent()` method of the `TraceSource` object to generate the trace information. In this sample, the `TraceEvent` method is supplied three arguments:

❑   Trace event type.

❑   A numeric identifier.

❑   A text string message.

The event message is displayed by the connected Event Listener (demonstrated below) and can be any text string. The Identifier is an integer between 0 and 65,535 (inclusive) and used for display purpose only. The Trace Event Type can be one of the following:

Trace Event Type	Description
TraceEventType.Critical	Fatal error or application crash
TraceEventType.Error	Recoverable error
TraceEventType.Information	Informational message

Trace Event Type	Description
TraceEventType.Resume	Resumption of a logical operation
TraceEventType.Start	Starting of a logical operation
TraceEventType.Stop	Stopping of a logical operation
TraceEventType.Suspend	Suspension of a logical operation
TraceEventType.Transfer	Changing of correlation identity
TraceEventType.Verbose	Debugging trace
TraceEventType.Warning	Noncritical problem

Compiling and Deploying the Module

In order to produce tracing events, you must compile the module with the /d:TRACE option. This option is not available in the runtime compiler; thus, you will need to compile and install the module as a binary DLL. One way to achieve this task is to use an Administrator command shell.

An alternative method to build and install your C# code using Visual Studio 2008 is demonstrated below in this chapter with the example in the section, "Extending the IIS Administration Tool."

1. Create a bin directory in the web-site root:

```
C:
cd \inetpub\wwwroot
mkdir bin
cd bin
```

2. Move the source code to the bin folder:

```
move ..\App_Code\BlockLinks.cs
```

3. Compile the module into a binary DLL:

```
%SystemRoot%\Microsoft.NET\Framework\v2.0.50727\csc.exe
    /target:library
    /out:BlockLinks.dll
    /debug
    /d:TRACE
    /R:System.Web.dll
    /R:%windir%\system32\inetsrv\Microsoft.Web.Administration.dll
    BlockLinks.cs
```

4. Click Start ⇨ Run, enter **inetmgr**, and then click OK to open IIS Manager.

5. Expand the node tree, and click on the Web Site container (for example, Default Web Site).

6. Double-click the Modules icon in the Features View.

7. If the BlockLinks module appears in the list, remove it.

8. Click on Add Managed Module in the Actions pane.

9. Enter **BlockLinks** in the Name field, and select .CustomModules.BlockLinks from the list.

10. Click OK to all dialogs.

Adding a Trace Listener to IIS

To make the trace events provided by your module available to IIS, you need to connect an IIS listener to the `TraceSource` that you defined in the module `Init()` method.

Open the `web.config` file in your web-site root (for example, `C:\inetpub\wwwroot\web.config`), and add the following configuration elements:

```
<configuration>
  <system.diagnostics>
    <sharedListeners>
      <add name="IisTraceListener"
          type="System.Web.IisTraceListener, System.Web, Version=2.0.0.0,
              Culture=neutral , PublicKeyToken=b03f5f7f11d50a3a" />
    </sharedListeners>
    <switches>
      <add name="DefaultSwitch" value="All" />
    </switches>
    <sources>
      <source name="BlockLinks" switchName="DefaultSwitch">
        <listeners>
          <add name="IisTraceListener"
              type="System.Web.IisTraceListener,
                  System.Web, Version=2.0.0.0, Culture=neutral,
                  PublicKeyToken=b03f5f7f11d50a3a" />
        </listeners>
      </source>
    </sources>
  </system.diagnostics>
    <system.webServer>
```

Note the use of `name="BlockLinks"`, which corresponds to the use of `ts = new TraceSource` `("BlockLinks")` in the module's `Init()` method.

Enabling Tracing and Routing Trace Events to IIS

Now that your module is ready to produce trace output to any connected listener, you will need to set up IIS 7.0 to capture that information.

Chapter 20 includes some additional detail on administration of IIS using Failed Request Tracing features. The following steps demonstrate one way to achieve this task:

1. Open IIS Manager (Start ➪ Run, enter **inetmgr**, and click OK), and navigate to the web-site node (for example, Default Web Site).

2. Double-click the Failed request Tracing Rules in the Features View.

If the Tracing Rules icon is not displayed, then you will need to install this feature — refer to Chapter 4, "Installing IIS 7," for additional information on installing and managing optional features.

3. Click Add in the Actions pane.

4. Click Next.

5. Enter **100-999** in the Status Codes field to enable tracing for all requests.

6. Select All Sources, and click Finish.

7. Click Edit Site Tracing in the Actions pane, check the box labeled Enable, and then click OK.

Viewing Trace Results

To see the event tracing in action, perform the following steps:

1. Open a web browser on the IIS Server console, and view `http://localhost`.

2. In IIS Manager, click the web-site node, double-click the Failed Request Tracing Rules in the Features View, and then click View Trace Logs in the Actions pane.

3. Open the logs folder to view the list of request trace files. You should see two files for each page request: one for the `iisstart.htm` request and one for the image request.

4. Open the last trace file in the list to see the trace event output.

Extending IIS Configuration

If you have followed through with the examples, you will recall that some of the static variables hard-coded into the module source may vary from application to application.

For example, the native code module example used the variable `pszProtectedPath` to determine which path to protect from cross-link requests. Another web site may store images in a different path, and to use the same module on that other web site, you would need to edit the source code and then recompile a special DLL just for that application.

Obviously, it would be a far better solution to permit configuration of the custom module without requiring access to the source.

The following section demonstrates how you can use IIS 7.0's new extensible configuration to manage and control custom modules, to provide seamless integration of your custom module configuration parameters.

Adding Configuration Support to Custom Modules

This section uses the example managed code module discussed above to demonstrate extending the configuration system.

If you have followed the tutorial above, you will already be familiar with the module design and functionality. You may recall that the BlockLinks module will supply an alternative image if the request for an image file contains a blank `HTTP_REFERER` value. This means that if the request is generated by a non-link source, such as a bookmark or search index robot, the requested image will not be delivered.

It might be useful to allow the Server Administrator to determine whether to allow or deny this type of request, and thus the following walkthrough demonstrates how to extend the IIS configuration to allow the server administrator to control the behavior when a blank `HTTP_REFERER` is encountered, without resorting to changes to the module source code.

This example is accomplished by the following general stages:

1. Extend the configuration schema.
2. Register the configuration extension.
3. Create the configuration entry.
4. Access the configuration information.
5. Include the namespace reference.
6. Define a global configuration variable.
7. Extract the configuration data.
8. Add the processing logic.
9. Install and test the module.

Extending the Schema

First, you need to extend the IIS 7.0 configuration schema. This is achieved by creating a file named CUSTOM_Schema.xml in the IIS configuration schema folder at `%system-root%/system32/inetsrv/config/schema`.

1. Click Start ⇨ Run, enter **notepad.exe %systemroot%\system32\inetsrv\config\schema\CUS-TOM_Schema.xml** in the dialog, and then click OK.

2. Add the following code:

```
<configSchema>
  <sectionSchema name="BlockLinksSection">
    <attribute name="permitBookmarks" type="bool" defaultValue="false" />
  </sectionSchema>
</configSchema>
```

3. Save the file.

Now the IIS configuration schema has been extended to recognize the new item, to expect one attribute named `permitBookmarks`, of Boolean type (`true|false`) and with the default value of `false` if not explicitly set otherwise.

Registering the Extension with IIS Config

Now you need to add this configuration extension into the IIS configuration. This is done using the master configuration file `applicationHost.config` in the configuration path at `%systemroot%/system32/inetsvr/config`.

1. Click Start ➪ Run, enter **notepad.exe %systemroot%\system32\inetsrv\config\ applicationHost.config** in the dialog, and then click OK.

2. Locate the `<configuration>` section.

3. Add the following code:

```
<configSections>
    <section name="BlockLinksSection" />
    <sectionGroup name="system.applicationHost">
```

This step adds the new custom entry to the live IIS configuration. Now you can add configuration information for your module.

Creating the Configuration Entry

Because the custom schema defined above includes a default value (`"false"`) for the `permitBookmarks` configuration attribute, this step is optional if you want to deny requests that have a blank `HTTP_REFERER` value. In this case, however, the attribute will be explicitly set to `"true"`, indicating that requests with blank `HTTP_REFERER` values are permitted access.

Again using `applicationHost.config`, add the following line as the last item before the end of the `<configuration>` section:

```
    <BlockLinksSection permitBookmarks="true" />
</configuration>
```

If you want to deny bookmark links and web robots, of course, you should set the attribute value to `false` or omit this entry to use the default attribute value (also `"false"`).

Accessing Configuration Information

Now it is possible to read the configuration information defined above from inside the sample custom module. This is achieved using the `Microsoft.Web.Administration`, provided by the DLL in the IIS system folder at `%systemroot\system32\inetsvr`.

In the next steps, you will add code to the BlockLinks custom module created earlier in this chapter to access the custom configuration entities created in the previous steps.

Including the Namespace Reference

Open the BlockLinks.cs source code created in the last (Event Tracing) sample, and add the namespace declaration to the top of the file:

```
using System;
using System.Web;
using System.Collections.Specialized;
using System.Diagnostics;
using Microsoft.Web.Administration;
```

Defining a Global Configuration Variable

Next, create a global variable in the module class to store the value of the configuration item.

```
public class BlockLinks : IHttpModule
{
    TraceSource ts;
    String permitBookmarks = "false";
```

Note the default value again set to `"false"`. This default value will be used in case of any problems reading the detail from the configuration system. You can change this default to `"true"` if you prefer, without affecting the basic functionality of this example code.

Extracting the Configuration Attribute

You have a few choices for where to add code to extract the configuration data, but you will want to be careful that the value of the global variable is consistent throughout your module execution. Here, the `Init()` method is used so that the configuration information is retrieved every time the module is initialized as each request is received into the IIS pipeline.

```
public void Init(HttpApplication app)
{
    // TODO:
    // Add initialization code
    // Including notifications
    app.BeginRequest += new EventHandler(app_BeginRequest);

    ts = new TraceSource("BlockLinks");
    // create the server management object
    ServerManager sm = new ServerManager();
    // Open the applicationHost.config data
    Configuration conf = sm.GetApplicationHostConfiguration();
    // Open the configuration section
    ConfigurationSection sect = conf.GetSection("BlockLinksSection");
    // Read the attribute value
    permitBookmarks = sect.GetAttributeValue("permitBookmarks").ToString();
}
```

Here, you will see that the configuration info is retrieved in three steps:

1. Open the IIS configuration using `GetApplicationHostConfiguration()`.

2. Open the custom configuration section with `GetSection("BlockLinksSection")`.

3. Read the attribute value with `GetAttributeValue("permitBookmarks")`.

Adding Processing Logic

Now that the module has initialized with the relevant configuration attribute received into the global variable, all that is required is to add the processing logic.

In the original code sample, if the `HTTP_REFERER` value was blank, the request was treated the same as any cross-linked request. With the new configuration attribute, it is now possible to test for a blank `HTTP_REFERER` and act accordingly.

Therefore, the next step is to modify the original code to include a test for a blank `HTTP_REFERER` and perform the relevant action depending on the value of the `permitBookmarks` attribute global variable.

```
if (!Referer.Contains(ServerName))
{
    // NOT initiated by a link from a local web page!
    if (Referer == "")
    {
        if (permitBookmarks == "false")
        {
            ts.TraceEvent(TraceEventType.Warning, 0,
                    "[BlockLinks] Bookmark request detected");
            ctx.RewritePath(
                            "denied.bmp",  // replacement file
                            "/images",     // replacement path
                            ""             // replacement query string
                            );
        }
    }
    else
    {
        ts.TraceEvent(TraceEventType.Warning, 0,
                "[BlockLinks] Cross-Linked request detected");
        ctx.RewritePath(
                        "denied.bmp",  // replacement file
                        "/images",     // replacement path
                        ""             // replacement query string
                        );
    }
}
```

Installing and Testing the Module

When this new code is compiled in the same way as the previous sample, you will be able to observe the new functionality. Note that if the BlockLinks module is already installed, you may need to first remove the module from the list of installed modules, and then readd as per the method described in the earlier section, "Installing the Module."

Open a fresh web browser (close any open browser windows first) and enter the URL to the IIS 7.0 Welcome image. If you have followed all the previous examples, the URL will be `http://127.0.0.1/images/welcome.png`.

Because this request will carry no `HTTP_REFERER` information, it will be detected as a cross-link.

With the configuration item in `applicationHost.config` set to `true`:

```
<BlockLinksSection permitBookmarks="true" />
```

you will see the image displayed.

Setting the configuration option to `false`:

```
<BlockLinksSection permitBookmarks="false" />
```

will cause the denied image to be displayed instead.

You will recall that a blank HTTP_REFERER variable in a request indicates that the request has been initiated by access to a client bookmark, manual entry to the browser location field, or by a non-browser client such as a search engine or web crawler/robot. To permit delivery of the resource to all these types of requests, set the `permitBookmarks` attribute to `"true"`. To deny all requests of this nature, set the attribute to `"false"`.

As a further exercise, you might like to try extending the IIS configuration to also support configuration of the `pszProtectedPath` global variable via the IIS Configuration System.

Extending the IIS Administration Tool

The ability to extend the IIS configuration to support custom modules provides the IIS developer with a unique capacity to develop custom web service plug-ins with a seamless interface to the core system.

In the previous section, the custom configuration support provided for the sample "BlockLinks" module requires that the end-user edit the IIS configuration files directly in order to control the module behavior.

IIS 7.0 also provides extensibility to the Administration Tool GUI to support simple and intuitive configuration support for your custom modules.

This section provides an example of how to implement GUI control of the `permitBookmarks` configuration item created in the previous section.

Creating an IIS Administration Tool Extension

As above, this walkthrough is based on Microsoft Visual Studio 2008. It is quite possible to use other IDE titles and versions by simply translating the various steps to the equivalent for your selected IDE.

During this example, you will note that the relevant custom GUI component is also called a *module* despite the fact that these objects are very different from the HttpModule encountered in previous sections.

This example is accomplished by the following general stages:

1. Create a new project.
2. Add namespace references.
3. Create a configuration dialog.
4. Add the control to the IIS Administration Tool.
5. Build and install.

Creating a New Project

Start by creating a new project:

1. Click File ➪ New ➪ Project.

2. Under the Visual C# templates, choose the Class Library template, as shown in Figure 12-3.

3. Enter the name **BlockLinksConf** as the project name, and then click OK.

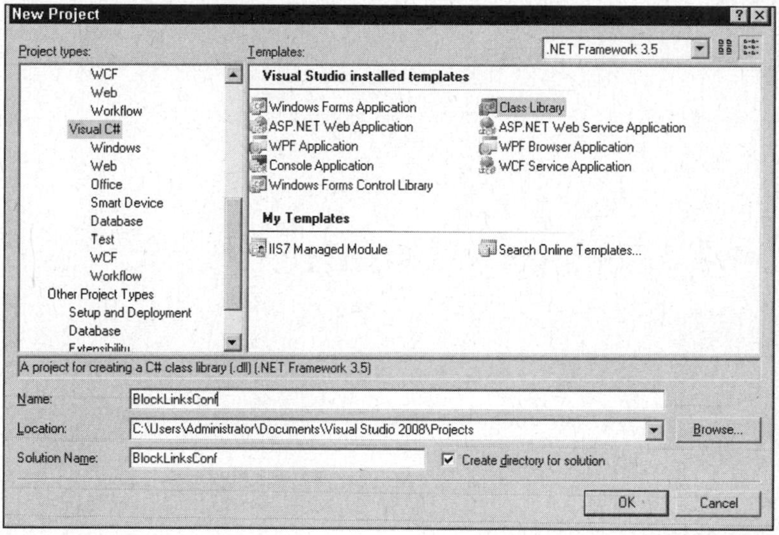

Figure 12-3

Adding Namespace References

Since a couple of namespaces required for this example are not included in the default template, add these as follows:

1. Right-click the References node in the VS2008 project view, and then click Add Reference.

2. Click System.Windows.Forms, and then click OK.

3. Right-click References again, and choose Add Reference.

4. Select the Browse tab, enter **%systemroot%\system32\inetsrv** in the name field, and then press [Enter].

5. While holding down the Ctrl key, click Microsoft.Web.Administration.dll and then on Microsoft.Web.Management.dll, and then click OK.

Creating the Configuration Control

The next step is to create the configuration control that will be used to enter the configuration settings. Because there is only a single attribute used in this example (permitBookmarks value), the control will be very simple, containing just a single checkbox to enable or disable delivery of "bookmark" requests, and a Save button to write the value to the active configuration.

1. In the VS2008 Project View, right-click the BlockLinksConf item, and choose Add ⇨ User Control.

2. Name it BlockLinksConfForm.cs, and click Add.

3. Add two elements to the form: a checkbox with label "permitBookmarks" and a button labeled "save" as shown in Figure 12-4.

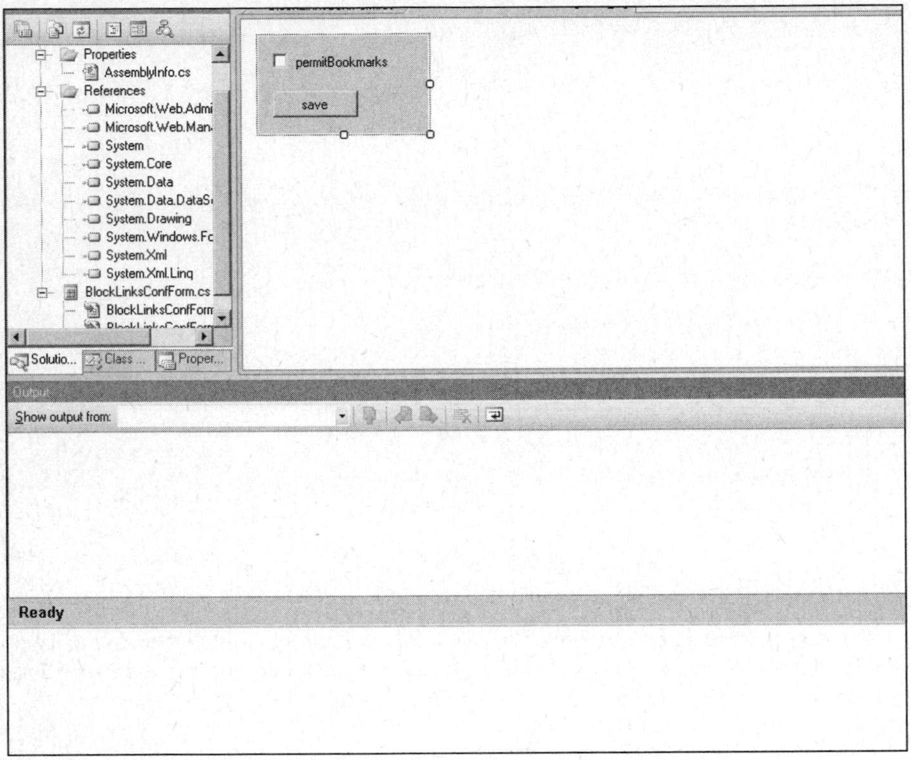

Figure 12-4

4. Open the configuration dialog's code view by right-clicking the BlockCrossLinksConf.cs object and choosing View Code.

5. Add the namespace reference:

```
using System;
using System.Collections.Generic;
using System.ComponentModel;
using System.Drawing;
using System.Data;
using System.Linq;
using System.Text;
using System.Windows.Forms;
using Microsoft.Web.Administration;
```

6. Then declare the following variables:

```
namespace BlockLinksConf
{
    public partial class BlockLinksConfForm : UserControl
    {
        private ServerManager mgr;
        private Boolean permitBookmarks;
```

7. Next, modify the constructor method to take one argument, and set the private member accordingly:

```
        public BlockLinksConfForm(ServerManager mgr)
        {
            this.mgr = mgr;
            InitializeComponent();
        }
```

(*Important:* Note the addition of `ServerManager mgr` in the argument list of the constructor definition.)

8. Next, create a method to read the configuration data:

```
        public BlockLinksConfForm(ServerManager mgr)
        {
            this.mgr = mgr;
            InitializeComponent();
        }
        private void ReadSettings()
        {
            Configuration config = mgr.GetApplicationHostConfiguration();
            ConfigurationSection sect = config.GetSection("BlockLinksSection");
            permitBookmarks = (Boolean) sect.GetAttributeValue("permitBookmarks");
        }
```

You may recognize the functions `GetWebConfiguration()` and `GetSection()`, which are essentially identical to the mechanism used to retrieve configuration item attribute values in the example for the previous section, "Extending IIS Configuration."

9. Create a public initialization function to allow the current value of the permitBookmarks setting to be loaded into the dialog when opened:

```
        public BlockLinksConfForm(ServerManager mgr)
        {
            this.mgr = mgr;
            InitializeComponent();
        }
        private void ReadSettings()
        {
            Configuration config = mgr.GetApplicationHostConfiguration();
            ConfigurationSection sect = config.GetSection("BlockLinksSection");
            permitBookmarks = (Boolean) sect.GetAttributeValue("permitBookmarks");
        }
        public void Initialize()
        {
```

```
            ReadSettings();
            checkBox1.Checked = permitBookmarks;
    }
```

10. Finally, for this stage, implement the action when clicking the "save" button:

```
        private void button1_Click(object sender, EventArgs e)
        {
            ServerManager mgr = new ServerManager();
            Configuration conf = mgr.GetApplicationHostConfiguration();
            ConfigurationSection sect = conf.GetSection("BlockLinksSection");
            sect.SetAttributeValue("permitBookmarks", checkBox1.Checked);
            mgr.CommitChanges();
        }
```

Again, a `ServerManager` object is used to obtain a reference to the `applicationHost.config` configuration entry, but this time `SetAttributeValue()` is used to write the attribute value to active configuration, and then `CommitChanges()` to save those changes.

Creating an IIS Administration Tool Module Container

Now everything is in place to add the control created in the previous steps into the IIS Administration GUI. This is achieved by creating a Module page, which is the middle pane of the IIS Manager console when a module icon is clicked. The Module page is a Windows Forms control onto which the BlockLinksConfForm created above will be added.

The Module page acts as a container (or wrapper) for the custom configuration control.

1. Right-click the BlockLinksConf node in the Visual Studio 2008 project view, and click Add ➪ Class.

2. Name the class BlockLinksConfPage.cs, and then click Add.

3. Add the following namespace reference:

```
using System;
using System.Collections.Generic;
using System.Linq;
using System.Text;
using Microsoft.Web.Management.Client;
using Microsoft.Web.Management.Client.Win32;
using Microsoft.Web.Management.Server;
using Microsoft.Web.Administration;
```

4. Now modify the BlockLinksConfPage class definition as follows, and implement the constructor:

```
class BlockLinksConfPage : ModulePage
{
    private ServerManager mgr;
    private BlockLinksConfForm c;

    public BlockLinksConfPage()
    {
```

```
            mgr = new ServerManager();
            cf = new BlockLinksConfForm(mgr);
            Controls.Add(cf);
        }
    }
```

(Note the addition of ModulePage as the class derived from.)

IIS Manager calls the OnActivated() method of the Modulepage class when opened. You need to override the default OnActivated() method to include a call to the initialization function implemented above. This will make sure that the configuration control dialog will load with the active configration value displayed.

5. Override the default OnActivated() method by adding the following code:

```
public BlockLinksConfPage()
{
    mgr = new ServerManager();
    cf = new BlockLinksConfForm (mgr);
    Controls.Add(cf);
}
protected override void OnActivated(bool initialActivation)
{
    base.OnActivated(initialActivation);
    if (initialActivation) cf.Initialize();
}
}
```

6. Next, add the Module wrapper:

```
class BlockLinksConfModule : Module
{
    protected override void Initialize
            (
            IServiceProvider serviceProvider,
            Microsoft.Web.Management.Server.ModuleInfo moduleInfo
            )
    {
        base.Initialize(serviceProvider, moduleInfo);
        IControlPanel controlPanel =
            (IControlPanel)GetService(typeof(IControlPanel));
        controlPanel.RegisterPage
            (
            new ModulePageInfo
                (
                this,
                typeof(BlockLinksConfPage),
                "BlockLinks",
                "Configuration for the BlockLinks Custom Module."
                )
            );
    }

    protected override bool IsPageEnabled(ModulePageInfo pageInfo)
    {
```

```
            Connection conn = (Connection)GetService(typeof(Connection));
            ConfigurationPathType pt = conn.ConfigurationPath.PathType;
            return pt == ConfigurationPathType.Server;
        }
    }
```

Note that the overridden `IsPageEnabled()` method determines when the configuration control is available. In this case, since the `permitBookmarks` variable is defined globally across all web sites, the `ConfigurationPathType.Server` is defined. Alternative values to make the configuration control available to discrete server items include

❑   `ConfigurationPathType.Site` — Shows the configuration icon on individual web sites.

❑   `ConfigurationPathType.File` — For individual files.

❑   `ConfigurationPathType.Folder` — Physical or virtual paths.

❑   `ConfigurationPathType.Application` — For web application configuration.

7.   Finally, the top level of this hierarchy is the ModuleProvider:

```
class BlockLinksConfModuleProvider: ModuleProvider
{
    public override Type ServiceType
    {
        get { return null; }
    }
    public override bool SupportsScope(ManagementScope scope)
    {
        return true;
    }
    public override ModuleDefinition GetModuleDefinition
            (IManagementContext context)
    {
        return new ModuleDefinition
            (Name, typeof(BlockLinksConfModule).AssemblyQualifiedName);
    }
}
```

Build and Install

The final stage of this example is to build and install the IIS Administration Tool add-in.

Loading the configuration module into the IIS Administration Tool requires strong naming by code signing, thus the first step is to add a signing key to the DLL.

1.   Double-click the Properties node in the VS2008 Project view.

2.   Choose the Signing tab, check the box labeled "Sign the Assembly," and then choose New, as shown in Figure 12-5.

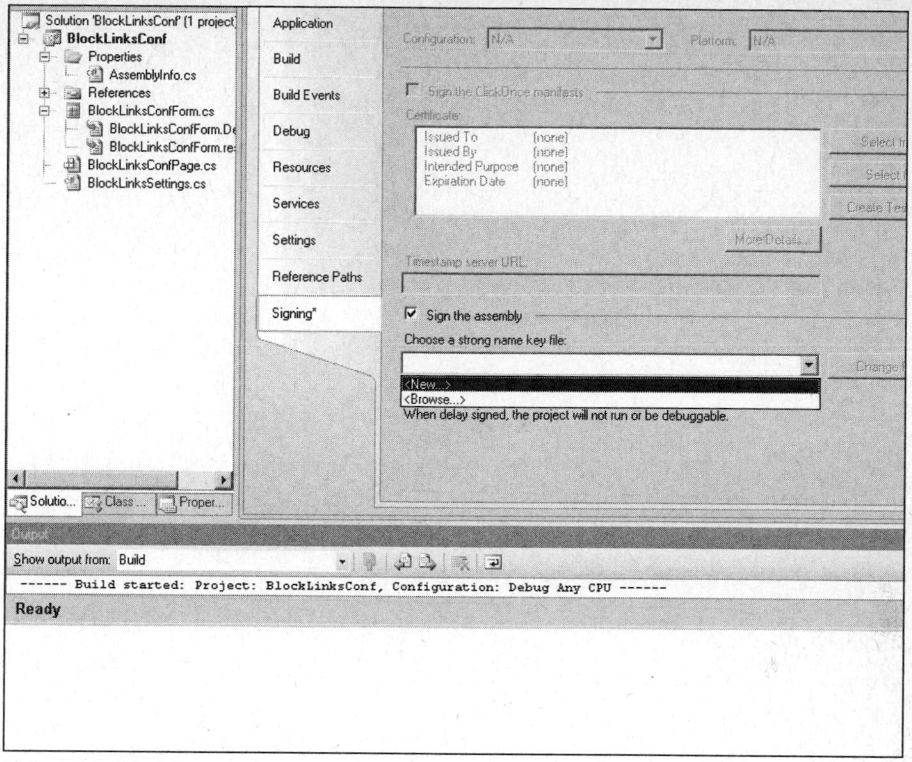

Figure 12-5

3. Enter **BlockLinksConf.key** as the Key File Name, uncheck the password box, and click OK.

4. Now compile the project by right-clicking the BlockLinksConf item in the VS2008 Project view and choosing Build. Unless you have made any changes to the compiler settings, the BlockLinksConf.dll will be saved in the project folder bin/Debug path.

5. Open a command prompt (Tools ⇨ Visual Studio Command Prompt) and change to the dll folder, for example:

```
cd \Users\Administrator
cd Documents\Visual Studio 2008\Projects
cd BlockLinksConf\BlockLinksConf\Bin\Debug
```

6. Install the dll to IIS using the gacutil.exe utility:

```
gacutil -i BlockLinksConf.dll
```

7. Use the gacutil.exe utility again to determine the public key token created by the strong name signing. For example:

```
>gacutil -l BlockLinksConf
Microsoft (R) .NET Global Assembly Cache Utility.  Version 3.5.20706.1
Copyright (c) Microsoft Corporation.  All rights reserved.
The Global Assembly Cache contains the following assemblies:
```

```
BlockLinksConf, Version=1.0.0.0, Culture=neutral,
PublicKeyToken=0a84ead563af042c, processorArchitecture=MSIL
```

The value of the `PublicKeyToken` displayed in this command is needed to install the module to the IIS Administration Tool. Note that this value will be different for every installation!

8. Next open the IIS Administration configuration file. Click Start ⇨ Run, enter **notepad.exe %systemroot%\System32\inetsrv\config\administration.config**, and then click OK.

9. Locate the `<moduleProviders>` configuration section, and add the following, all on one line, directly below the `<moduleProviders>` start tag:

```
<moduleProviders>
    <add name="BlockLinksConf" type="BlockLinksConf.BlockLinksConfModuleProvider,
      BlockLinksConf, Version=1.0.0.0, Culture=neutral,
      PublicKeyToken=0a84ead563af042c" />
```

Note that the `PublicKeyToken` value reflects the value determined from Step 7 above.

10. In the same file, locate the `<location>` section, add the following item, and then save the file and close:

```
<!-- For all Sites -->
<location path=".">
    <modules>
        <add name="BlockLinksConf" />
```

Viewing the Result

Open the IIS Administration tool and click the Server node (for example, SERVER1 SERVER1/Administrator) to display the Features View, and observe the new configuration item displayed, as shown in Figure 12-6.

Click on the BlockLinks config icon to open the configuration dialog, as shown in Figure 12-7. Now you can enable and disable the `permitBookmarks` configuration item created in the previous example ("Extending the IIS Configuration") using this simple and intuitive GUI control.

You can confirm operation of the GUI module by observing the behavior of the web site, as per the "Installing and Testing the Module" section; however, it may be more instructive to observe the effect of modifying the `permitBookmarks` checkbox control on the relevant configuration item in the `applicationHost.config` file.

Checking the custom configuration control checkbox results in `applicationHost.config` to include the following line:

```
<BlockLinksSection permitBookmarks="true" />
```

Clear the checkbox to set

```
<BlockLinksSection permitBookmarks="false" />
```

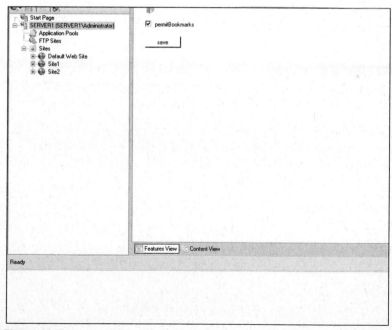

Figure 12-6

Figure 12-7

Summary

In this chapter, you have witnessed the virtually limitless capacity provided by the IIS 7.0 APIs to extend and enhance the core server functionality.

Following the sample tutorials, you will have now created your own starter projects for

- ❏ Native code module.
- ❏ Managed code module.
- ❏ Managed code module with tracing.
- ❏ Managed code module with tracing.
- ❏ IIS Configuration Extension for a Custom Module.
- ❏ IIS Administration Tool Extension for a Custom Module.

Again, MSDN is your best source of a complete reference to the required classes and structures. The tutorials provided in this chapter offer a starting point to begin development of your own custom extensions.

This chapter has demonstrated how IIS 7.0 is certainly the most extensible web server platform ever delivered by Microsoft, providing the developer with a seamless integration opportunity to every area of the core system: functionality, diagnostics, configuration, and management.

The following chapters now move on to IIS security. Read on to learn how to maximize security of IIS 7.0 from unauthorized access and attempts to compromise those security measures. You will also learn about authentication methods and authorization, plus HTTPS and PKI encryption.

13

Securing the Server

"We have just installed Application X onto IIS and would like to know what steps we need to take to make IIS secure." This is one of the most common questions faced in the security arena, and this hasn't changed from when IIS ran on NT to the present day. The question, however, presupposes that there is some set of discrete steps that can be undertaken to secure IIS, and that there is some finite end point that can be described as "secure."

Certainly there are a lot of products and organizations that claim to make your server secure or secure your application or secure your organization. As a security implementer (or even just someone with a dilettante interest), to what extent should you place credence in such claims?

This introductory chapter on security covers the following topics:

❑   The basic principles of network and computer security.

❑   New or improved technologies in Windows Server 2008 that can enhance your overall network security.

❑   Configuring IIS 7.0 to enhance the security of your web server.

❑   Additional items (such as application layer security) that you will need to consider when evaluating overall environmental security.

Beyond this chapter, the next two chapters delve into more specific security areas. Chapter 14 deals with Authentication and Authorization, and Chapter 15 deals with SSL and TLS. These chapters should be read together to get a good understanding of the security technologies and infrastructure that are most important when managing an IIS 7.0 installation.

What Is Security?

Security can be defined as a state of freedom from attack or danger. Current security orthodoxy teaches us that the only totally secure computer is one that is switched off, encased in concrete, and dumped at the bottom of the ocean. And this should tally with any system administrator's experience. There are very few, if any, nontrivial software products that have shipped to date that haven't contained some kind of security vulnerability. Even if the software itself is completely bug-free, it may be compromised because of the way that it interacts with other systems, or because of poor operational practices (for example, the use of easily guessable passwords).

Even the type of totally secure system mentioned above (encased in concrete at the bottom of the ocean) might not be classified as a secure system. A *secure system* will deny access to those who are unauthorized, yet allow access to those who are authorized. In other words, it's usable by those permitted to use it and no one else. The machine at the bottom of the ocean fails this usability test. In fact, this need to distinguish between legitimate users and those who should be denied access is one of the things that makes security difficult. It's easy to write a system that gives access to everyone, or conversely denies access to everyone, but much more difficult to write a system that allows the good guys in but keeps the bad guys out.

What security researchers and books try to focus on is educating readers on security principles and practices that they can apply to their environments that allow them to have "secure enough" computers. This section presents a condensed summary of security principles. With these principles in mind, you can then look over the rest of this chapter, as well as the subsequent two security-related chapters, to determine which policies are best suited to your specific environment.

Managing Risk

When you see a product that claims to be secure or a security guide to secure your system, it's worth asking the following two questions: "secure from whom?" and "secure against what?" Does your new communications system secure you against a casual eavesdropper? A dedicated attacker? Or a national intelligence agency? Is your new application secure against a shoulder surfer (someone who looks over your shoulder to steal a password)? Someone who physically steals your server? Collusion between malicious systems administrators? In some cases, the answer is no — not because the products are necessarily insecure, but because the developers of the product make certain assumptions (conscious or otherwise) about how they would be used. Most server applications assume that the application will be hosted on a machine that is physically secured against attackers. Even well-known security technologies like SSL/TLS assume that the implementer will take the necessary steps to secure the endpoints.

In the computing world, there are almost a limitless number of possible attacks against your systems, ranging from common viruses and worms, through to malicious internal staff. Facing limitless possible attacks without any single way of combating all of them (unless you count the "computer at the bottom of the ocean" idea) requires some kind of framework that security professionals can use to determine whether the security measures being put in place are appropriate for the situation.

To help deal with this challenge, security specialists borrow concepts from risk-management disciplines (among other areas).

The same threat may have differing consequences across differing organizations. For example, a common self-propagating worm may be somewhat more than an annoyance in the average organization if it causes some machines to become unusable; however, it may be fatal in a hospital if it disables a critical machine. Likewise, differing threats can have different consequences within the same organization, and even the same threat can have differing consequences for different parts of the same organization. For example, a compromised public web server at a bank might allow an attacker access to the web application's code, and possibly intercept transactions between the bank and customers — definitely a serious problem, but probably not as serious as if the bank's central customer, accounts, or credit databases were compromised.

To determine which threats to address, at the most rudimentary level, we can look at the concept of risk-weighted costs. We take the expected cost that would result from a threat eventuating and multiply it by the likelihood of that threat eventuating:

(Cost if Risk Eventuates) * (Likelihood of Risk) = Risk Weighted Cost of Compromise

Knowing the risk-weighted cost of compromise helps guide us in prioritizing the threats we face, from the most serious to the trivial. We can then deploy our resources, time, and effort to mitigating the more serious threats.

By no means should you rely on this one simplistic calculation when determining your security design and policies! Especially in more complex environments, you are encouraged to enlist the aid of security and risk specialists in developing and maintaining their security policies.

Security Components

Developing a secure system relies on having, at a minimum, the following components:

❑ **Authentication** — This is the process of remote users identifying themselves and then proving their identity (typically through a shared secret such as a password).

❑ **Authorization** — After a user has been authenticated, the user's requested action is checked against an Access Control List (ACL) maintained on the server to determine if the user is permitted to perform the action.

❑ **Auditing** — The user's actions must be recorded and not be subject to dispute (what is known as "non-repudiation"), so as to definitively determine which users performed which actions.

When determining your security strategy, it is important to verify that your solution encompasses these three components. Although an individual product may perform all three things perfectly, it is important to factor in two other areas where vulnerabilities can creep in — through human error or through one product interacting with another.

Types of Attacks

A complete taxonomy of possible attacks against your IIS server is beyond the scope of this book. Attacks come in all shapes and sizes, and thus it is difficult, if not impossible, to be comprehensive.

Denial-of-Service Attacks

A *denial-of-service (DoS) attack* typically involves an attacker making spurious requests to a server in order to consume resources and deny legitimate users access to the service (hence, "denial of service").

The attack could be as simple as overwhelming the server with a sufficiently large number of requests, or it could involve making requests that consume large amounts of resources (for example, invoking long-running database queries). In the former case, a single attacking machine may not have the necessary CPU or bandwidth to overwhelm a well-provisioned server, thus the attacker may enlist the use of a large number of individual machines to simultaneously attack the server — an attack known as a *distributed denial-of-service (DDoS) attack*.

Privilege Escalation Attacks

A *privilege escalation attack* involves an attacker gaining access to, and performing actions on, resources that they would not otherwise be permitted to. Privilege escalation can involve both gaining additional permissions on a single system (for example, a regular user gaining Administrative privileges) as well as gaining access to other systems in the network that the user wouldn't otherwise have access to at all (for example, getting access to a domain controller or other backend server).

Typically, a privilege escalation attack is merely a precursor to some other form of attack (for example, data theft, data destruction, and so on). By escalating their privileges, attackers are now able to perform a malicious action they wouldn't otherwise have been able to. They may alter files (for example, defacing your web site), they may steal sensitive information, or they may even create additional "backdoor" accounts that can be used to return to the system even after you have closed off the initial attack vector.

There are several ways that a malicious attacker can attempt to gain privileges that they would not otherwise be entitled to. Some of the most common are

❑ **Social Engineering Attacks** — An attacker attempts to convince another user of the system that they should be given access (for example, by pretending to be a Helpdesk technician or by sending an e-mail purporting to be from a legitimate source). The user then provides credentials or otherwise gives the attacker access because they have been fooled into thinking that the attacker is a legitimate user.

❑ **Vulnerability Exploitation** — An attacker exploits a vulnerability in an application or operating system. High-profile worms and viruses that exploited vulnerabilities include Code Red, Nimda, and Blaster.

❑ **Poorly Secured Systems** — Many systems are poorly secured, and this presents an attacker with an easy way in with minimal effort. For example, the use of blank or easily guessable passwords can allow an attacker to gain access without any need to exploit any vulnerabilities or to interact with any legitimate staff. Unfortunately, access gained this way can be very difficult to detect because the attacker (once he or she has access) looks like just a legitimate user.

Preventing, detecting, and combating these types of attacks can be difficult. In an environment that doesn't follow good management practices, it becomes almost impossible to do anything about these attacks. It's not a matter of *if* such an attack will succeed, but *when*.

In this chapter (and the succeeding chapters on security), we will discuss some of the technologies and resources you can use to secure your environment. However, good security relies on good operational procedures:

❑ A **documented baseline** for your environment is necessary. This includes knowing which privileged accounts should exist and what they are for, which services exist on your network, and what they should be doing.

❑   Ensuring that **security patches**, **best practice configuration**, and **appropriate password/access control policies** are in place is a prerequisite for ensuring that the environment can be kept secure.

❑   **Detection tools** (for example, an Intrusion Detection System) and **operations management tools** (such as Microsoft System Center Operations Manager 2007) that enable detection of unusual activity that deviates from your accepted baseline are necessary. This could include detection of services not working, unusual account logons/password guessing, known malicious traffic on the network, and many other symptoms of an attack in progress.

In Chapters 18 and 19, we discuss these concepts in more detail.

Passive Attacks

Passive attacks are much harder to detect than active attacks. Here, attackers are not trying to change anything on your network (although they may have had to perform a previous attack to gain access in the first place). Instead, *passive attackers* are merely observing existing activity. This could be "sniffing" the network for sensitive information or logging keystrokes on a computer to capture usernames and passwords.

Technologies such as SSL/TLS or IPsec can be used to secure traffic in transit and help prevent such passive attacks.

Securing the Server

The remainder of this chapter and the next two chapters focus on technologies, both with Window Server 2008, and IIS 7.0 specifically, that can be used to secure your web servers, your applications, and the data that they use. Specifically, this chapter will outline some technologies in Windows Server 2008 and some basic IIS 7.0 functionality that can be configured to either disable functionality or restrict access, or alternatively may need to be reconfigured from defaults to permit functionality.

In Chapter 14, "Authentication and Authorization," we will look at the various client authentication technologies that IIS 7.0 supports and how these are configured. It will also look at the various user accounts and identities that IIS 7.0 uses for processing requests and how to configure these to support your application.

In Chapter 15, "SSL and TLS," we will look at certificates and PKI management, server authentication, and traffic data encryption for web sites, FTP sites, and SMTP servers.

Securing the Environment

Prior to securing IIS 7.0, it is important that your overall network environment itself is secure. Securing a Windows environment, let alone a heterogeneous environment, is a book (or several) in itself. There are numerous technologies, white papers, best practices, and tools available that will assist in initially configuring the environment, ensuring that the configuration remains and monitoring the environment for any changes.

The TechNet Security portal (www.microsoft.com/technet/security/) is the first stop for administrators seeking guidance on securing a Windows network, including the latest prescriptive advice, security and patch bulletins, analysis tools that can warn of possible misconfiguration, and step-by-step implementation guides.

We have chosen to briefly highlight various technologies that are new or improved in Windows Server 2008 that can be used to secure your network. These are IPsec, Network Access Protection, and Active Directory Federation Services. These technologies are an excellent complement to a hardened IIS 7.0 server and help provide end-to-end security for your web applications.

IPsec (IP Security)

IP Security (IPsec) is an Internet standard that provides multiple protection options for traffic transmitted on IP-based networks, including

- ❏ **Data Encryption** — To prevent passive snooping attacks.

- ❏ **Message Integrity** — To ensure that data have not been modified in transit.

- ❏ **Authentication of Communicating Hosts** — To ensure that a malicious user cannot impersonate a legitimate host.

- ❏ **Replay Protection Mechanisms** — To prevent a malicious user from re-sending previously transmitted information between hosts.

Because IPsec operates at the IP layer (Layer 3 in the OSI model), it is transparent to upper-layer protocols. This reduces the cost of implementation because applications do not need to be remediated in order to take advantage of IPsec. Contrast this to popular Layer 4 technologies (such as SSL/TLS) that require applications to use alternate TCP ports, and incorporate additional security libraries to handle the setup of a secure session.

While IPsec was first introduced in Windows Server 2003 and Windows XP, its configuration was time-consuming, and troubleshooting was difficult. Windows Server 2008 incorporates some additional enhancements to IPsec that make deployment easier for administrators:

- ❏ Incorporation of IPsec configuration into the same administrative MMC as the firewall configuration.

- ❏ Including the IPsec Simple Policy Update that was released for Windows Server 2003 in Windows Server 2008. For more information on the Simple Policy Update and how this simplifies an IPsec deployment, see http://technet.microsoft.com/en-us/library/bb726975.aspx.

- ❏ Support for both IPv4 and IPv6.

Server and Domain Isolation is a Microsoft-approved network security configuration designed to restrict the access of non-legitimate hosts to your network and to sensitive hosts on your network (while also denying access completely to machines that shouldn't be servers, such as client machines). Server and Domain Isolation depends heavily on correctly implementing IPsec. Microsoft has a dedicated web site to assist in implementing Server and Domain Isolation at http://www.microsoft.com/sdisolation.

Network Access Protection

Network Access Protection (NAP) is a new technology in Windows Server 2008 and Windows Vista that provides administrators with the ability to gauge the overall "health" of systems connected to their networks and to isolate those machines that are "unhealthy" until they are brought up to a satisfactory security configuration. Administrators who have used features such as ISA Server 2004's VPN quarantine functionality will be familiar with the concepts, although the technology is completely new. There are plans to ship a Windows XP-compatible client in Service Pack 3.

NAP works by having a client service evaluate various configuration items on the client (for example, firewall configuration, patch level, antivirus configuration) and present this as a *"statement of health" (SOH)* to a *Network Policy Server (NPS)*.

> *NPS is the new name for Microsoft's RADIUS server, formerly known as Internet Authentication Server (IAS).*

The NPS compares the client-supplied SOH with a set of desired configurations determined by the administrator. If the client passes all the tests, it is given access to the network. If the client does not pass all the tests, then it is isolated from the network or given only limited access to a "remediation" network (for example, access to an internal patch server such as Windows Server Update Services or System Center Configuration Manager 2007 to be able to install the latest patches), as shown in Figure 13-1.

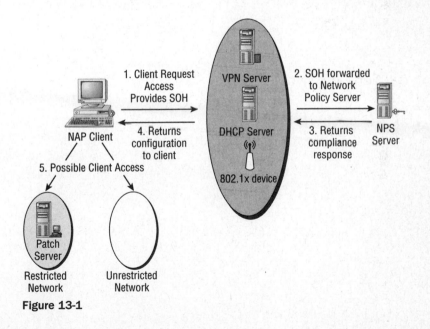

Figure 13-1

The following access technologies are supported with NAP:

❑ **DHCP** — A client requesting a DHCP address that does not meet the defined system policy will be given an IP address on a restricted network with no default gateway and a /32 subnet mask.

Provided that the user is not capable of changing his or her machine's IP address, network access will be limited.

❏ **IPsec** — A client requesting access to the network that does not meet the defined system policy will not be provided with a machine certificate to negotiate IPsec connections with sensitive servers in your environment. Machines that do pass the system policy will be provided with a certificate that is valid for a default of 8 hours.

❏ **802.1x** — In conjunction with compatible 802.1x network infrastructure, the client machine can be placed onto a VLAN that either has full access or access only to a restricted network. Microsoft is working with several hardware vendors to develop compatible network equipment.

❏ **VPN** — Clients connecting to Windows Server 2008 Routing and Remote Access Service (RRAS) or ISA Server 2008 (Codename "Nitrogen") will be provided with network access depending on whether they pass the system policy requirements.

❏ Windows Server 2008 Terminal Services (TS) Gateway — Clients connecting to applications published via a TS Gateway can be subject to Network Access Protection enforcement of minimum requirements. This mechanism does not support allowing clients to access remediation servers though.

In Windows Server 2008, Routing and Remote Access Services (RRAS) can now be found as a role service under the Network Policy and Access Services role in Server Manager.

Active Directory Federation Services

Active Directory Federation Services (ADFS) provides *Single Sign On (SSO)* capabilities for web applications across boundaries that may not support traditional Active Directory trust relationships. This could be between two separate organizations, or perhaps more relevant to IIS administrators, between an internal Active Directory infrastructure and web applications located in the company's DMZ.

ADFS supports two modes of operation to support federation between an internal Active Directory infrastructure and a DMZ-based Active Directory infrastructure. In one situation, a one-way forest trust exists between the two Active Directory forests (Federated Web SSO with Forest Trust), and in the other example, no forest trust exists (Federated Web SSO). The latter mode of operation can also be used for Single Sign On between partner organizations.

Although the Federation Web SSO with Forest Trust mode is the easiest to configure, the alternate mode makes it easier to demonstrate the high-level concepts involved with ADFS. This is shown in Figure 13-2 and described below.

When a client on the internal network wants to access a web application in the DMZ, the following takes place:

1. The client initially contacts the web application. However, because the request does not have an ADFS authentication cookie, the ADFS web agent on the web application redirects the client browser to the external ADFS federation server.

2. The external ADFS federation server does not know who the user is and redirects the client to the internal ADFS federation server to get a token that is acceptable to the external ADFS federation server.

3. The user can authenticate using their Windows credentials to the internal ADFS federation server (which is able to verify those credentials against the internal Active Directory DC). The internal ADFS federation server generates a cookie holding relevant claims information (for example, username) that is acceptable to the external ADFS federation server.

4. The client now makes a new request to the external ADFS federation server, which evaluates the contents of the cookie and determines what username, groups, and other permissions the user has in the external Active Directory forest. It generates a cookie that the client browser can send to the external web application.

5. The client browser makes a second request to the external web application, but this time providing an ADFS-generated cookie that is acceptable to the ADFS web agent, which then permits the user to log on.

Because ADFS works completely over HTTP/HTTPS via the use of cookies included in requests, it provides a securable mechanism for allowing both internal and also roaming external users access to web applications stored hosted in your DMZ while still using their Active Directory credentials.

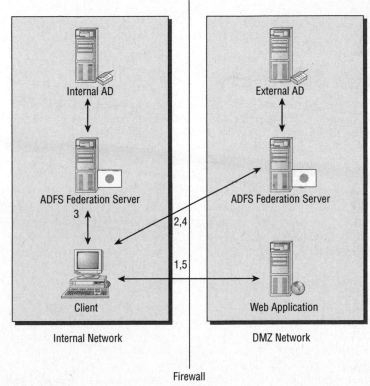

Figure 13-2

Securing IIS 7.0

After securing the environment, you can now look to secure your IIS 7.0 server itself. There are several configuration options in IIS 7.0 that can be used to restrict access or deny certain types of requests without any knowledge of who the end user is. These configuration options are the focus of this security chapter.

Chapter 14, "Authentication and Authorization," examines how to provide protected access to resources based on who the end user is. This covers authentication technologies (such as Basic, Digest, and Kerberos authentication) as well as authorization configuration (how to configure access to resources to permit only certain users access), and also information on the various identities that are used by IIS 7.0 internally to provide access to functionality.

A security best practice is to install only those components that are required for the functionality you need to provide end-users. Beginning with Windows Server 2003, IIS 6.0 has shipped in a locked-down state with only a minimal set of functionalities available in a default configuration. By not installing unnecessary functionality, your server cannot be compromised by possible vulnerabilities in components that you aren't using (or didn't even know were installed). This lock-down mentality should extend to administrator configuration as well. Only install those components that are required to deliver the services end-users need. This reduces the surface area that attackers can attempt to exploit and also reduces the administration overhead of the server by reducing configuration options and reducing the number of patches required to be installed.

IP and Domain Restrictions

Configuring IP address and domain name restrictions allows you to selectively permit or deny access to the web server, web sites, folders, or files. Rules can be configured for remote IP addresses or based on a reverse DNS lookup of the remote IP address. When a remote client that is not permitted access requests a resource, a 403.6 ("Forbidden: IP address of the client has been rejected") or 403.8 ("DNS name of the client is rejected") HTTP status will be logged by IIS.

The IP and Domain Restrictions module (iprestr.dll) is not installed in a default IIS installation. You will need to specifically install this module if you wish to use its functionality. Web-site administrators and web-application administrators can configure IP and Domain Restrictions for web sites and applications that they are permitted to manage, provided that the configuration elements are not locked at a higher level. See Chapter 9, "Delegating Remote Administration," for more information.

Default Policy and Domain Name Restrictions

When configuring IP and domain name restrictions, there is always a default policy. The default policy applies to clients where a specific rule is not defined. It either permits all access except those clients specifically rejected, or rejects all clients except those specifically permitted. When IIS 7.0 is first installed, all clients are permitted unless specifically rejected.

The same dialog that is used to set the default policy is also used to enable or disable the ability to allow or reject clients based on a reverse DNS lookup.

To configure the default rule or to enable a policy based on DNS lookup, perform the following steps:

1. Open the IIS Manager MMC console.

2. At the web server, web site, application, folder, or file node that you wish to configure this setting, select IP and Domain Name Restrictions.

3. Click Edit Feature Settings. The Edit IP and Domain Restrictions Settings dialog box appears, as shown in Figure 13-3.

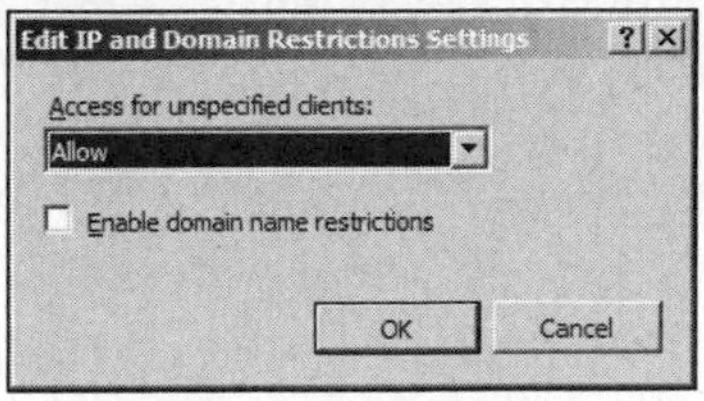

Figure 13-3

4. Select Allow to allow all clients by default, or select Deny to deny all clients by default.

5. Optionally, to configure rules based on the client's DNS name, check the Enable Domain Name Restrictions checkbox. A warning will be presented that performing DNS lookups is a potentially expensive operation. Click Yes to enable DNS lookup restrictions.

6. Click OK to exit the dialog.

Performing reverse DNS lookups is a potentially expensive operation that can severely degrade the performance of your IIS server. DNS lookups may be adversely affected because of slow response times from remote DNS servers or because the remote client does not have an entry in the inAddr.arpa reverse lookup domain. On the other hand, in an intranet scenario where your organization has full control over internal DNS servers and client DNS registration and there are fast links between your IIS servers and internal DNS servers, this can be a useful tool for restricting access to certain client machines within your environment.

You can alter the default rule settings using AppCmd. For example, to change the default settings (that is, disallow all unspecified clients, and also enable Domain Name restrictions), run the following command:

```
appcmd.exe Set config /section:ipSecurity /allowUnlisted:true /enableReverseDns:false
```

This command configures this setting for the entire server. Supplying an optional object parameter permits configuration at an individual web-site or web-application level. For more information on using AppCmd, see Chapter 5, "Administration Tools."

Configuring Rules

You can create rules for specific remote hosts, remote subnets, or remote DNS hosts or domains (if the reverse DNS lookup option is enabled). To create rules that allow or deny access:

1. Open the IIS Manager MMC console.

2. At the web server, web site, application, folder, or file node where you want to configure this setting, select IP and Domain Name Restrictions.

3. Click Create Allow Entry or Create Deny Entry links in the Actions pane. Figure 13-4 shows the interface for creating an Allow Entry.

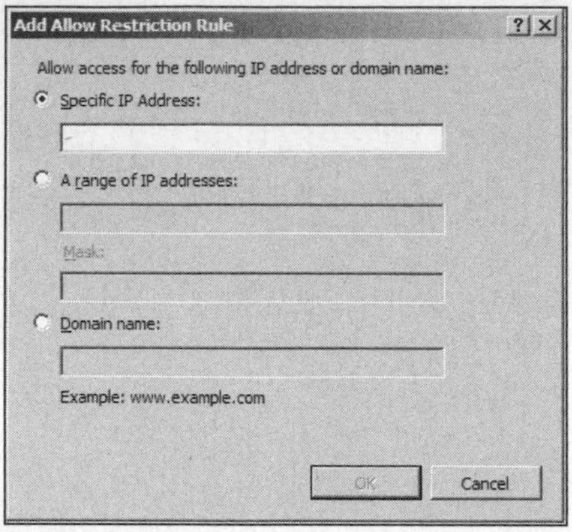

Figure 13-4

To create a rule for a specific remote host, select "Specific IP Address" and enter the remote IP address. This is equivalent to selecting "A range of IP addresses" and entering a specific IP address and a subnet mask of 255.255.255.255.

To create a rule for a remote subnet, select "A range of IP addresses" and enter the subnet and subnet mask. For example, to permit or deny access to all IP addresses in the 127.0.0.0/8 subnet, enter 127.0.0.0 as the subnet and 255.0.0.0 as the subnet mask.

To create a rule for a remote domain name or domain, select "Domain name." Enter the remote reverse DNS name. If you want to permit or deny access to a whole domain, use the * wildcard (for example, ***.example.com** would permit or deny access to all hosts in the example.com domain).

> *When using DNS names, you must use DNS names that have corresponding PTR record in the inAddr.arpa reverse lookup domain. You cannot use any arbitrary DNS name that resolves to the remote IP address. When a client connects to IIS, IIS is only aware of the client's remote IP address. IIS must do a reverse DNS lookup to determine what DNS name the client has. If you wish to determine what reverse DNS name an IP address has, you can use the command* `ping -a xxx.xxx.xxx.xxx` *(where* `xxx.xxx.xxx.xxx` *is the remote IP address). The* `-a` *switch performs a reverse DNS lookup.*

You can also use AppCmd to create Allow and Deny rules. The following code samples explain how to configure global Allow and Deny rules for an individual IP address and for a particular subnet. The first rule permits access from 192.168.0.1, and the second rule denies access to all addresses in the 192.168.2.0/24 subnet.

```
appcmd.exe Set Config /section:ipSecurity /+[ipAddress='192.168.0.1',allowed='true']
```

```
appcmd.exe Set Config /section:ipSecurity
/+[ipAddress='192.168.2.0',subnetMask='255.255.255.0',allowed='false']
```

Rule Priority

A priority system is used to evaluate potentially conflicting rules. Rules are evaluated in order of priority until a rule that matches the remote client is reached. Depending on whether that rule permits or denies access, the resource or an error message is sent back to the client.

It is important to note that Deny rules do not override Permit rules (unlike some systems, such as NTFS Access Control Entries) and that more specific entries do not override more general entries (unlike some systems such as Active Directory subnet definitions). The only consideration is rule ordering. As soon as a rule that matches the remote client's IP (or reverse DNS name if applicable) is reached, that rule is evaluated and no further rule evaluation occurs.

To illustrate this, consider the following scenarios. In each case the remote client is 127.0.0.1.

Rule Priority	Rule	Explanation
1	Allow 127.0.0.0 / 255.0.0.0.	Allow all hosts in the 127.0.0.0 subnet (127.0.0.1 to 127.255.255.254).
2	Deny 127.0.0.1/255.255.255.255.	Deny host 127.0.0.1.

Result: In this scenario, the remote client 127.0.0.1 is allowed access, despite the fact that Rule 2 is more specific. Rule 1 matches the remote client and permits access. No further rule processing is done.

Rule Priority	Rule	Explanation
1	Allow 127.0.0.1/255.255.255.255.	Allow host 127.0.0.1.
2	Deny 127.0.0.0/255.0.0.0.	Deny all hosts in the 127.0.0.0 subnet (127.0.0.1 to 127.255.255.254).

Result: In this scenario, the remote client 127.0.0.1 is permitted access, despite the fact that Rule 2 is an explicit Deny rule. Rule 1 again matches the remote client and permits access. No further rule processing is done.

To view and change rule priority:

1. Open the IIS Manager MMC console.

2. At the web server, web site, application, folder, or file node where you want to configure this setting, select IP and Domain Name Restrictions.

3. Click the View Ordered List option in the Actions pane. The Move Up and Move Down options enable you to reorder the rule priorities. Rules located higher up in the list have higher priority. The Move Up and Move Down options are not visible if no rules are defined that apply to that

server, web site, folder, or file. If rules have been defined at a higher node, the options are available and allow you to override the settings at a lower-level node. To return to the screen that allows you to add and remove rules, click View Unordered List.

Comparing IP and Domain Name Restrictions

While IP and domain name restrictions enable an IIS administrator to determine which remote machines can connect to IIS, other mechanisms that provide the same functionality may be more appropriate, depending on the scenario.

Generally, it is advisable to configure connection restrictions at the lowest level in the ISO OSI model as possible. This prevents a misconfiguration or vulnerability in a lower-level component from allowing an attacker to bypass higher-level restrictions. For example, if a vulnerability in Windows or IIS is discovered, it may be possible for an attacker to compromise the server before any IIS IP and domain name restriction rules are evaluated. To mitigate this scenario, restrictions could be configured on any firewalls in the environment. At the next highest level, routers typically can be configured with routing rules or Access Control Lists (ACLs) that do not permit traffic from hosts. At a host level, IPsec or the Windows Firewall provides a lower level connection control.

IIS IP and domain name restrictions may be more appropriate in the following situations:

❑ As a server, site, or web application administrator, you do not have access to any lower-level options for configuring connection control. For example, you might be hosting your application with a third-party hosting company.

❑ You need to configure differing restrictions for different sites, folders, or files. Most lower-level access restrictions apply filters based on IP address. They are unable to differentiate between different requested URLs all located at the same host. Some firewalls, such as Microsoft's ISA Server 2006, are able to further "application layer" inspection of packets, and are thus aware of HTTP namespaces and able to apply URL-based restrictions.

IIS IP and domain name restrictions are generally more secure than attempting to configure these restrictions within your application. A vulnerability or misconfiguration of ASP or ASP.NET would allow an attacker to potentially bypass any restrictions coded into your application before your code has a chance to run. Prior to IIS 7.0, Administrator Privileges were required on the server to be able to configure IIS IP and domain name restrictions. With IIS 7.0's support for delegated administration, the option now exists for individuals to configure these restrictions within IIS rather than relying on application-level code.

Configuring MIME-Type Extensions

MIME (Multipurpose Internet Mail Extensions)-type restrictions were first introduced in IIS 6.0. These restrictions prevent undefined file types from being served by IIS. This can help protect your server by preventing malicious attackers from downloading sensitive files (such as configuration files, data files, or system binaries).

Although these files would not typically be stored within your web site's root folders, either a system misconfiguration or URL canonicalization vulnerability (for example, that exploited by the NIMDA worm) may allow an attacker to gain access to sensitive files.

When a client attempts to download a file that does not have a defined MIME type, a 404.3 HTTP status is logged in the IIS log files.

> *The MIME Type Extensions security setting only applies to files that are handled by the IIS Static File HTTP handler. If the file extension is handled by a different handler (for example, it is handled by an ISAPI Extension such as ASP or ASP.NET), then a MIME type does not have to be defined. See the section, "Configuring ISAPI Extensions and CGI Restrictions," for more information on HTTP handlers.*

IIS 7.0 ships with approximately 340 defined MIME types that cover files such as text (.txt, .css, .js), HTML (.html, .htm), images (.jpg, .gif, .png), and common audio and video formats. These are enabled if you install the Static File option when installing IIS 7.0.

Adding a New MIME Type

If you have a custom file extension that needs to be downloadable by clients, you will need to add a new MIME type. MIME types can be added at the server, web-site, web-application, or folder level.

To add a new MIME type:

1. Open the IIS Manager MMC Console.
2. At the web server, web site, application, or folder node where you wish to configure this setting, select MIME Types.
3. Click Add to add a new MIME type.
4. Enter the file extension and an appropriate MIME type, as shown in Figure 13-5. MIME types are defined in IETF RFCs 2045, 2046, 2047, 2048, and 2077. Links to these RFCs can be found in Appendix D.
5. Click OK to add the new MIME type and exit the dialog box.

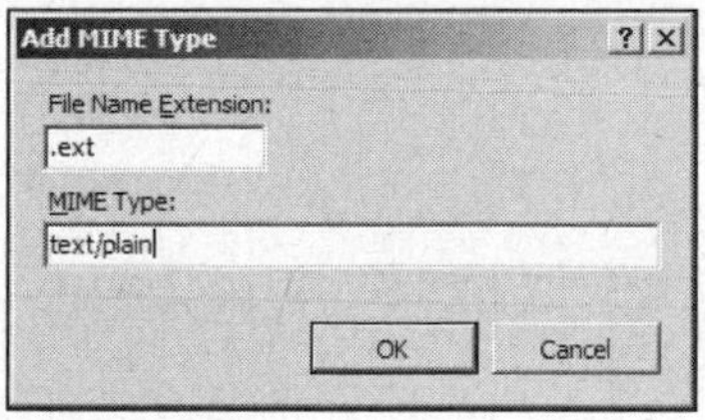

Figure 13-5

Removing an Existing MIME Type

If you are certain that your IIS server should not serve a particular file type, you can remove the associated MIME type to prevent accidental download of that file. To remove a MIME type:

1. Open the IIS Manager MMC Console.
2. At the web server, web site, application, or folder node where you wish to configure this setting, select MIME Types.
3. Select the MIME type you no longer wish to serve, and then click the Remove link from the Actions pane.

Configuring MIME Types using AppCmd

You can configure MIME types programmatically by using AppCmd. To add a new MIME type for a file extension "ext" with a type of "text/plain," run the following code:

```
appcmd.exe SET config /section:staticContent
/+"[fileExtension='ext',mimeType='text/plain']"
```

Configuring ISAPI Extensions and CGI Restrictions

IIS provides a mechanism for extending the functionality of the server via an API known as ISAPI. Developers can write *ISAPI extensions,* which allow for additional functionality when particular types of files are requested. Common ISAPI extensions include ASP.NET and its predecessor ASP (Active Server Pages). A PHP ISAPI extension implementation also exists.

ISAPI extensions work on the basis of file extensions, which can be "mapped" to an ISAPI extension (for example, .aspx files are mapped, by default, to the ASP.NET ISAPI extension). When a file with that extension is requested, processing is handed over to the ISAPI extension, which determines what additional work should be done. In the case of ASP and ASP.NET, these extensions scan the file for custom code that should be run server side.

CGI (Common Gateway Interface) is a platform-independent way of extending web servers. Typically, CGI applications are implemented as .exe files when run on Windows, and read the browser's request from standard input, process the request, and return a valid HTTP response to standard output. CGI is not as popular on IIS as ISAPI extensions because each request spawns a new process and process creation/destruction is relatively expensive in Windows, leading to poor scalability for most CGI applications.

A new CGI implementation (FastCGI) is available as a separate download for IIS 7.0. FastCGI provides the ability to service multiple requests within a single process, either in a single-threaded environment (servicing one request after another) or a multithreaded environment (if the actual CGI executable supports this).

> *For more information about CGI, see Chapter 7.*

IIS 7.0 provides the ability for a server administrator to configure what ISAPI extensions and what CGI applications are permitted to run on the server. This setting can only be configured at a server level by default. For administrators familiar with IIS 6.0, this configuration item corresponds to the Web Service Extensions node in the IIS 6.0 MMC Administrative Tool.

> *The ISAPI and CGI Restrictions option will not appear unless you have installed either the ISAPI extensions or CGI support modules. Neither of these two modules is included in a default installation of IIS 7.0. If you choose to install a built-in ISAPI extension like ASP or ASP.NET, then ISAPI extension support is installed as well.*

To configure ISAPI and CGI restrictions, open IIS Manager and navigate to the server node. If you have previously installed any CGIs or ISAPI extensions, they will be listed, as shown in Figure 13-6.

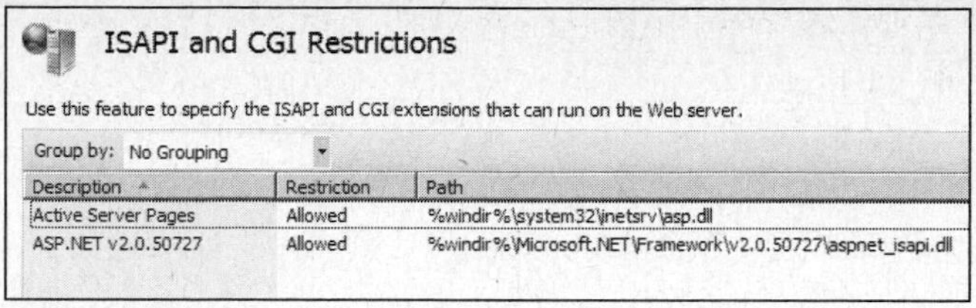

Figure 13-6

IIS 7.0 allows each CGI or ISAPI extension to be set to an Allowed or Disallowed state. For those CGIs or ISAPI extensions that are set to Disallowed, a 404.2 HTTP status will be logged in the IIS log file if a client attempts to request a resource that invokes the ISAPI extension or CGI application.

Adding a New ISAPI Extension or CGI Restriction

To add a new ISAPI extension or CGI restriction:

1. Open IIS Manager and navigate to the server node.

2. Double-click the ISAPI and CGI Restrictions icon to open the feature.

3. Click the Add link in the Actions pane. The Add ISAPI or CGI Restriction dialog box appears, as shown in Figure 13-7.

4. Enter the path to your ISAPI extension (typically, a .dll file) or CGI application (typically, an .exe file). Optionally, add a description.

5. To allow the ISAPI extension or CGI restriction, check the "Allow extension path to execute" checkbox. If this is not selected, the Restriction setting will be set to Not Allowed.

6. Click the OK button to commit your changes.

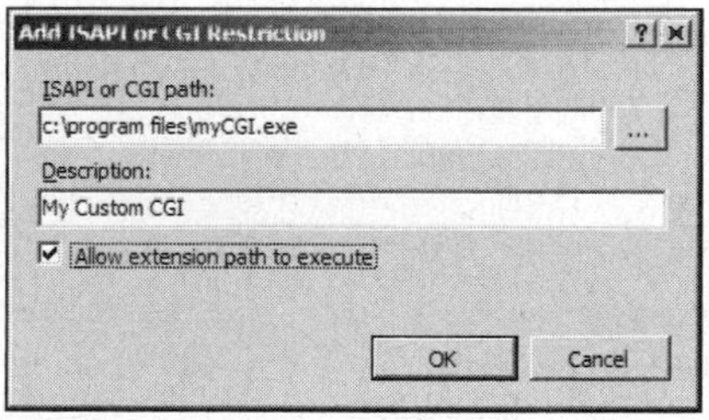

Figure 13-7

Changing Default Settings

By default, only specifically permitted ISAPI extensions and CGI applications are permitted to run; all other ISAPI extensions and CGI applications will be denied. To change these defaults so that all ISAPI extensions or CGI applications are permitted to run except those specifically denied, perform the following steps:

1. Open IIS Manager and navigate to the server node.

2. Double-click the ISAPI and CGI Restrictions icon to open the feature.

3. Click Edit Feature Settings. The Edit ISAPI and CGI Restrictions Settings dialog box appears, as shown in Figure 13-8.

4. Select the "Allow unspecified CGI modules" checkbox to allow all CGI modules except those specifically denied.

5. Select the "Allow unspecified ISAPI extensions" checkbox to allow all ISAPI extensions except those specifically denied.

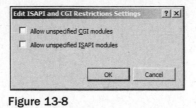

Figure 13-8

Allowing all unspecified CGI applications or ISAPI Extensions is a security risk. If an attacker is able to load a CGI application onto your server (for example, via upload functionality), he will be able to execute it remotely.

Configuring ISAPI and CGI Restrictions with AppCmd

AppCmd can be used to configure the ISAPI and CGI restrictions policy.

❏ To add an additional entry to the ISAPI and CGI restrictions configuration, run the following command:

```
appcmd.exe Set Config -section:isapiCgiRestriction "-+[path='c:\program
files\myCustomCGI.exe',allowed='true',description='My Custom CGI']"
```

❏ To allow unlisted ISAPI extensions, run the following command (be aware that allowing unlisted ISAPI extensions is a security risk):

```
appcmd.exe Set Config /section:isapiCgiRestriction /notListedIsapisAllowed:True
```

❏ To allow unlisted CGI executables, run the following command (be aware that allowing unlisted CGI executables is a security risk):

```
appcmd.exe Set Config /section:isapiCgiRestriction /notListedCGIsAllowed:True
```

❏ To disable unlisted ISAPI extensions or CGI executables, run the listed commands but replace the `True` property with `False`.

Additional Configuration for ISAPI Extensions and CGI Applications

In order for an ISAPI extension or CGI application to process requests, a script mapping must also be configured. This associates files with a certain extension with the ISAPI extension (for example, .asp files with the Active Server Pages ISAPI extension) or CGI application.

If you are familiar with IIS 5.0 or 6.0, this script mapping corresponds with the Mappings tab option in the IIS 6.0 and IIS 5.0 MMC Administrative Tools.

> *If you configure a script map prior to configuring the ISAPI and CGI Restriction Policy setting, IIS Manager will ask you if you want to automatically have an entry placed into the ISAPI and CGI Restriction Policy and have the status set to Allowed. This can save one additional configuration step.*

You can configure script maps at a server, web-site, or web-application level. This allows the flexibility of executing certain ISAPI extensions only within a restricted area. Perform the following steps to configure a script map:

1. Open IIS Manager and navigate to the server, web site, or web application where the script mapping should be added.

2. Select the Handler Mappings option.

3. Select Add a Script Map. The Add Script Map dialog box appears, as shown in Figure 13-9.

4. Enter the path to the ISAPI extension or CGI executable and the file extension or specific file that the ISAPI should handle. To add multiple file extensions, you will need to repeat this process from Step 3 for each additional extension you wish to have processed by the ISAPI extension or CGI application.

5. Optionally, add a name for your ISAPI extension or CGI application.

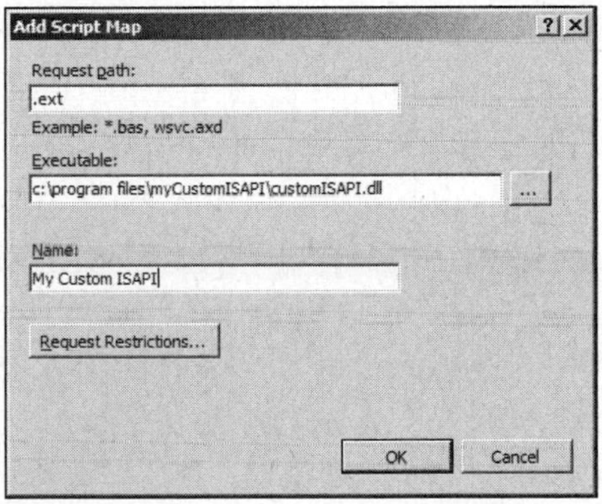

Figure 13-9

6. The Request Restrictions option allows for further restrictions on the operation of the ISAPI Extension. To limit the HTTP verbs (for example, GET, POST, or HEAD) to which the ISAPI extension is permitted to respond, to limit the response to requests for files, or to also allow requests to URLs that have no file (for example, http://servername/folder/), click the Request Restrictions button. Enter the optional restrictions, as shown in Figure 13-10.

7. Click OK to exit the dialogs.

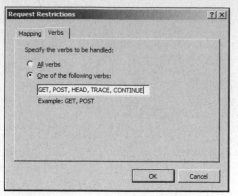

Figure 13-10

IIS automatically configures script mapping to invoke the necessary supporting modules based on the file extension of the executable supplied in Step 4. If the file extension is a DLL, then the ISAPIModule is configured. If the file extension is .exe, then the CGIModule is configured. You can override this by editing the `applicationHost.Config` file.

The following XML configuration snippet shows ISAPIModule (ASP) and CGIModule (PHP) configuration for two popular application programming environments:

```
<handlers accessPolicy="Read, Script">
    <add name="PHP-CGI"
        path="*.php"
        verb="GET,HEAD,POST"
        modules="CgiModule"
        scriptProcessor="c:\setup\php\php-cgi.exe"
        resourceType="File" />
    <add name="ASPClassic"
        path="*.asp"
        verb="GET,HEAD,POST"
        modules="IsapiModule"
        scriptProcessor="%windir%\system32\inetsrv\asp.dll"
        resourceType="File" />
</handlers>
```

For more information on ISAPI extensions and CGI applications, see Chapter 7.

ISAPI extensions and CGI executables provide a powerful way to extend the functionality of IIS 7.0. Out of the box, Windows Server 2008 does not install or enable either ISAPI or CGI support; however, both ASP.NET and ASP are supplied as part of the operating system and can be added from the Server Manager MMC Console.

As with adding any additional functionality to your server, configuring additional ISAPI extensions or CGI executables requires that you take additional steps to ensure the ongoing security of your server. Monitor the vendor's web site for patches that may be released to fix security or configuration vulnerabilities in the product. Additionally, if you install any custom applications (for example, a third-party ASP.NET application), ensure that you monitor that vendor's site to ensure that there are no vulnerabilities in the application itself (see the section, "Application Layer Security," below in this chapter).

Lastly, functionality exists with IIS to allow unlisted ISAPI extensions or CGI executables to be run, effectively disabling the restriction policy. There may be circumstances where this setting may be useful — for example, when developers are uploading new versions of a CGI application that may vary in name. It is a security risk in production environments, as an attacker may be able copy an unauthorized executable or ISAPI extension to your server and then have that run.

Configuring Request Filtering

Request Filtering provides a configurable set of rules that enables you to determine which types of requests should be allowed or rejected for the server, web site, or web application.

Administrators of previous versions of IIS may be familiar with the URLScan tool, which delivers similar functionality. In IIS 7.0, Request Filtering is improved over URLScan for the following reasons:

❑ Request Filtering is implemented as a module rather than an ISAPI filter.

❑ Request Filtering rules can be implemented for specific web sites or web applications, rather than a single set of rules that applies to an entire server.

❑ Request Filtering logging is integrated with IIS logging functionality (rejected requests will be logged to the regular IIS log file), whereas URLScan maintained its own separate log file, making troubleshooting potential issues more time-consuming.

❑ Request Filtering implements functionality that allows for requests for specific namespaces (URLs) to be blocked completely. For example, any request for any file in the special ASP.NET /bin and /app_data folders can be rejected easily. This functionality previously had to be implemented in a separate ISAPI filter (ASPNET_ISAPI).

The Microsoft Technet web site (`www.microsoft.com/technet/security/tools/urlscan.mspx`) provides information on the latest version of URLScan, with more detailed configuration information available in Microsoft KB Article 326444 (`http://support.microsoft.com/?id=326444`). If you are migrating an existing URLScan-protected server to IIS 7.0, these two documents can help with a migration strategy

Request Filtering is implemented in `%systemroot%\system32\intesrv\Modrqflt.dll`.

Request Filtering offers the following options for allowing or denying specific requests. Each type of filter can be applied at the web-server, web-site, or web-application level.

Filtering by File Extension

The `fileExtensions` section allows filtering by file extension. File extensions that are not matched by a specific rule can be set to Allowed or Disallowed (that is, a default rule can be configured). This functionally corresponds to the `[AllowExtensions]` and `[DenyExtensions]` functionality in URLScan.

To configure `fileExtensions` filtering using a configuration file, you can use the following XML tags within a `<system.Web>` section:

```
<security>
        <requestFiltering>
                <fileExtensions allowUnlisted="false" >
```

```
                        <add fileExtension=".asp" allowed="true"/>
                </fileExtensions>
        </requestFiltering>
    </security>
```

The <fileExtensions> parent node enables you to define a default rule. In the preceding example, all file extensions not specifically listed are denied. You can then use the <add>, <remove>, and <clear> tags to manipulate the file extensions that are permitted to be requested. In the preceding example, files with the .asp file extension are permitted to be requested.

If a request is rejected because of a fileExtensions Request Filter, a 404.7 HTTP status is logged in the IIS log file.

The fileExtensions section does provide for an applyToWebDAV attribute to be set. This allows requests that are tagged as WebDAV authoring requests to bypass this filter. To configure this attribute, set

```
<fileExtensions allowUnlisted="false" applyToWebDAV="false">
```

In order for the WebDAV exception to apply, the WebDAV module must be installed. If the WebDAV module detects a WebDAV HTTP request, it sets a server variable. If any applyToWebDAV exceptions have been configured, the RequestFiltering module verifies whether this server variable has been set. If it has, then RequestFiltering rules that have the applyToWebDav attribute set do not apply to the marked requests.

Filtering by HTTP Verb

The verbs section permits or denies requests that use specified HTTP verbs (such as GET and POST). Like fileExtensions above, verbs that are not matched by a specific rule can be set to Allowed or Disallowed. This functionality corresponds to the [allowVerbs] and [denyVerbs] functionality in URLScan.

To configure verbs filtering using a configuration file, you can use the following XML tags within a <system.Web> section:

```
<security>
        <requestFiltering>
                <verbs allowUnlisted="false" >
                        <add verb="GET" allowed="true" />
                        <add verb="POST" allowed="true" />
                </verbs>
        </requestFiltering>
    </security>
```

In this example, all requests that do not use the GET or POST HTTP verbs are denied by IIS. GET and POST requests are permitted.

If a request is rejected because of a Verbs Request filter, a 404.6 HTTP status is logged in the IIS log file.

Similar to the fileExtensions section, the verbs section allows for WebDAV verbs to be exempted from filtering. To configure this attribute, set

```
<verbs allowUnlisted="false" applyToWebDAV="true">
```

Configuring Request Limits

The `requestLimits` option enables you to restrict the size of requests made by clients. This can help prevent malicious requests (for example, requests that send too much data or use too long a URL for your application) from having an adverse impact on your server or application.

There are three specific limits that you can configure:

❑ `maxAllowedContentLength` — This is the maximum size of the HTTP request that can be sent from the client to the server. It is measured in bytes. If a request is rejected because it exceeds a `maxAllowedContentLength` request filter, then a 404.13 HTTP status is logged to the IIS log file.

❑ `maxURL` — This is the maximum size of the URL that can be requested, including the domain name, path, and port, but excluding the query string (the part after a ? in a URL). If a request is rejected because it exceeds a `maxURL` request filter, then a 404.14 HTTP status is logged to the IIS log file.

❑ `maxQueryString` — This is the maximum size of a query string that can be sent by the client to the server. If a request is rejected because it exceeds a `maxQueryString` request filter, then a 404.15 HTTP status is logged to the IIS log file.

```
<security>
    <requestFiltering>
            <requestLimits
                maxAllowedContentLength="1000000"
                maxUrl="260"
                maxQueryString="25" />
    </requestFiltering>
</security>
```

In this example, the maximum allowed content length is 1,000,000 bytes, the maximum URL length is 260 characters, and the maximum query string length is 25 characters.

Filtering by URL Sequence

The `denyURLSequences` section enables you to reject requests that contain certain substrings within the requested URL. A commonly rejected sequence is "..", which may indicate a possible directory traversal attack. In this attack, an attacker attempts to move up or down the directory tree until she can reach a resource she wouldn't otherwise be allowed to reach. The infamous Code Red virus used this technique when attacking vulnerable IIS 5.0 servers.

There is no capability to configure a default rule in this section. You can explicitly configure sequences to be rejected (and all other requests will be accepted). You cannot configure Request Filtering to reject all requests except the specific URLs that you wish to allow.

This functionality corresponds to the `[DenySequences]` functionality in URLScan. When a request is rejected because of a `denySequences` request filter, a 404.5 HTTP status is logged in the IIS log file.

```
<security>
    <requestFiltering>
            <denyUrlSequences>
                    <add sequence=".."/>
```

```
                    </denyUrlSequences>
            </requestFiltering>
    </security>
```

In this example, any request that contains ". ." will be rejected.

Outlook Web Access (OWA) functionality in Microsoft Exchange Server 2000, 2003, and 2007 creates URLs for messages based on the subject line for each e-mail message. If the subject line contains ". .", then the end user will be unable to view the message via OWA if the above example is implemented on an Exchange front-end server (also known as a Client Access Server in Exchange 2007).

Filtering by Segment

The `hiddenSegments` section enables you to reject requests that contain a URL segment. This varies from the previous `denyURLSequences` in that URL segments (for example, folder names) are evaluated rather than raw strings.

Consider the URLs www.example.com/products/water and www.example.com/products/waterbeds. If you want to allow requests to the second URL (waterbeds) but not the first (water), then using `denyURLSequences` would not help, as adding the sequence *water* would result in requests to both folders being denied.

The `hiddenSegments` request filtering section permits us to deny the first URL but allow the second. To configure `hiddenSegments` filtering using a configuration file, the following XML tags may be used within a `<system.Web>` section:

```
<security>
        <requestFiltering>
                <hiddenSegments>
                        <add segment="water" />
                </hiddenSegments>
        </requestFiltering>
</security>
```

Similar to the `fileExtensions` section, the `hiddenSegments` section allows for WebDAV verbs to be exempted from filtering. To configure this attribute, set

```
<hiddenSegments applyToWebDAV="true">
```

When a request is rejected because of a `denySequences` request filter, a 404.8 HTTP status is logged in the IIS log file.

Request Filtering Logging

The new Request Filtering options in IIS 7.0 provide a powerful mechanism for administrators to define known good or known bad requests, and to configure IIS to handle those requests appropriately. Because Request Filtering logging is now integrated with IIS logging, you can use regular log file analysis tools to evaluate the effectiveness of configured Request Filtering policies.

The following table summarizes the HTTP status codes for requests rejected because of a configured Request Filtering policy:

Request Filtering Reason	HTTP Status Code
Request Filtering: URL Sequence denied	404.5
Request Filtering: Verb denied	404.6
Request Filtering: File extension denied	404.7
Request Filtering: Denied by hidden segment	404.8
Request Filtering: Denied because request header is too long	404.10
Request Filtering: Denied because URL doubled escaping	404.11
Request Filtering: Denied because of high bit characters	404.12
Request Filtering: Denied because content length too large	404.13
Request Filtering: Denied because URL too long	404.14
Request Filtering: Denied because query string too long	404.15

Application Layer Security

Even after securing your environment and IIS 7.0 itself, it is important not to neglect application security. Both off-the-shelf (OTS) and custom-developed code may suffer from a range of vulnerabilities. In recent years, more attention has been devoted to breaking applications rather than server software itself because of the larger number of vulnerabilities available. For example, Secunia (an independent vulnerability tracking site) reports just three vulnerabilities in IIS 6.0 in more than four years, and just one in the past year (`http://secunia.com/product/1438/?task=advisories`). On the other hand, SecutyFocus' Bugtraq list announced more than 20 vulnerabilities in various third-party software applications in just a two-week period at the time of writing. (`www.securityfocus.com`).

A wide array of vulnerabilities can affect application layer software. Some of the most common are

❑ **SQL Injection Attacks** — Here, poor input validation allows an attacker to submit carefully crafted input to your application that is then executed inside a database supporting your application. The most trivial would exploit some code such as the following:

```
strSQL = "SELECT * FROM users WHERE username = '" & Request.Form("username") & "'
AND userPassword = '" & Request.Form("Password") & "'"
```

By submitting `';TRUNCATE TABLE Users` as input, the attacker turns the resulting SQL statement into

```
SELECT * FROM Users WHERE Username = '';TRUNCASE TABLE Users — '
```

which would cause the entire Users table to be deleted.

Alternatively, the attacker could enter SQL code that would create a new user (via an INSERT INTO statement) or bypass your authentication mechanism by setting "1=1" as a search criterion.

❏ **Cross-Site Scripting Attacks** — Here, an attacker injects some script into your database, which is then displayed to other users visiting your site. This is a common attack vector against forum/bulletin board software, but could also be used against any software that displays user input to other users (for example, even to administrators). The script runs on the victim's machine and could steal cookies and other data and send them to the attacker.

❏ **Session Replay Attacks** — Here, application software produces predictable session key values, and an attacker is able to easily determine previously good session keys and replay a prior user's session, potentially bypassing the need to authenticate and/or accessing sensitive information that the prior user had access to.

It is important for administrators to subscribe to both vendor update bulletins as well as third-party disclosure forums like Bugtraq (www.securityfocus.com) and Full Disclosure (http://lists.grok. org.uk/mailman/listinfo/full-disclosure).

For custom development, Microsoft publishes both *Writing Secure Code* (www.microsoft.com/ mspress/books/5957.aspx) and *Building Secure ASP.NET Applications* (http://msdn2.microsoft. com/en-us/library/aa302415.aspx), which is also available as a PDF download.

The Open Web Application Security Project (OWASP) produces an excellent, platform-independent guide to application security threats and mitigations. This is available from www.owasp.org/index.php/Category:OWASP_Guide_Project.

Configuring Logging

An effective auditing and logging strategy allows administrators to detect possible malicious activity and possibly prevent compromise. In the event of a successful attack, comprehensive and untainted log files can still help, by identifying the method by which the attacker gained access (and allowing that hole to be closed), and also potentially providing proof of who the attacker was.

IIS 7.0 logging configuration and options are covered in Chapter 6, "Web Site Administration." Windows also provides the Windows Event Logs, where several other important pieces of information are logged (for example, account logon events that might indicate a password guessing attack, or application crash events that might indicate an attempt to exploit an application).

Suffice to say that administrators should consider the following when developing a logging strategy:

❏ Move IIS log files from the Windows system partition (typically, the c: drive). An attack that floods a server with requests could result in the log files growing very large and filling the disk, resulting in a denial of service.

❏ Enable auditing (via the local security policy or domain-based group policy) for account logon events (both successes and failures). A large number of failed logon events can indicate an attempt to brute-force the password for an account. Most operation-monitoring tools (such as Microsoft System Center Operations Manager 2007) can be configured to alert when a certain number of failed logon attempts are detected within a specified period. Successful logons should also be audited, as several failed logons followed by a successful logon may indicate that an attacker has managed to get a password.

❏   In higher security environments, archive your event logs rather than allowing older events to be overwritten as needed. An attacker may generate several spurious events to fill the event log to cover possible incriminating events generated earlier. Windows Server 2008 increases the default log size for the Security and System logs to 20 MB, thus the risk of this happening undetected is lower than previously, but is still a consideration. An automated tool can generate a large number of spurious events in a very short period of time.

Summary

This chapter serves as a primer to security concepts and concerns, introducing some of the more basic configuration steps that administrators can take when enabling or restricting functionality on an IIS 7.0 server. In particular, administrators should be familiar with configuring

❏   IP address and domain name restrictions.

❏   MIME-type extensions.

❏   Request Filtering rules.

❏   ISAPI extension and CGI application restrictions.

❏   Configuring logging for auditing and traffic analysis purposes.

The next two chapters dive deeper into the IIS 7.0 security infrastructure. By the end of Chapter 15, administrators will have a comprehensive understanding of the security-related technologies that concern IIS 7.0 and be able to configure a wide range of security options.

14

Authentication and Authorization

Configuring authentication and authorization for IIS and applications running on top of IIS is one of the more complex IIS security operations. This is in part because of the number of different authentication options available, partly because both the previous version of IIS (6.0) and IIS 7.0 have offered multiple request processing pipelines, and in part because authentication and authorization are often conflated, even though they are distinct concepts.

Authentication is the process of identifying and proving that identity to a remote service (in this case IIS). Typically, a client or user will provide an identifier (for example, a Windows username) and then will be required to prove that identity. Typically, proof of identity takes the form of something you know (a password), something you have (security token), or something you are (some kind of biometric identification). Two-factor or multifactor authentication systems combine these concepts, requiring multiple pieces of authentication information to prove the end-user's identity.

Authorization occurs after authentication, and is the process by which a user requests permission to perform an operation (for example, view a file), and the system verifies that operation against an access control list (ACL) maintained for the file or resource. The ACL consists of a set of access control entries (ACEs) that define which users can or cannot perform certain operations. By "operations," we mean being able to read a file, or modify its contents, or update its properties, or impersonate a user, or perform a backup, or shut down a system, or any other possible thing that can be done. Most operating systems allow the definition of both *Allow* ACEs and *Deny* ACEs, and by default if a user is not explicitly listed on an *Allow* ACE, then he or she is denied access even without a specific *Deny* ACE being present.

The processes of authentication and authorization are often confused because typically they occur at the same time as far as an end-user is concerned. Credentials are supplied, and an immediate answer is provided by the server.

This chapter covers these distinct concepts, enabling you to develop a security strategy for your applications, configure the appropriate settings, and troubleshoot potential issues that arise. In particular, this chapter discusses:

❑ Authentication options available with IIS 7.0.

❑ How to correctly configure permissions on resources to allow permitted users to access resources, while denying unauthorized users.

❑ The built-in Windows accounts that IIS 7.0 uses.

Authentication in IIS 7.0

IIS 7.0 provides six authentication options, plus the ability to configure a fixed user identity for connecting to network resources (making seven in total). These are briefly described below. For each authentication mechanism, more detailed information including configuration options, minimum requirements, and potential weaknesses is described subsequently in the chapter. The following authentication mechanisms are supported by IIS 7.0:

❑ **Anonymous Authentication** — Here the end-user does not supply credentials, effectively making an anonymous request. IIS 7.0 impersonates a fixed user account when attempting to process the request (for example, to read the file off the hard disk). This authentication mechanism would be used for public-facing web sites where visitors are not required to supply credentials.

❑ **Basic Authentication** — The end-user is prompted to supply credentials, which are then transmitted unencrypted across the network. Basic authentication was originally defined in RFC 1945 (the HTTP 1.0 specification) and is thus supported in all current browsers. Links to RFCs can be found in Appendix D.

❑ **Digest Authentication** — The end-user is prompted to supply credentials, but unlike in Basic authentication, the user's password is not passed in cleartext across the network. Digest authentication was originally defined in RFC 2069 and updated in RFC 2619. Digest authentication involves hashing the user's password using MD5. Windows is unable to store MD5 hashes of passwords for local accounts, thus Digest authentication is only available for Active Directory accounts.

❑ **Integrated Windows Authentication** — Technically, this incorporates two separate authentication mechanisms: NTLM v2 (also known as NT Challenge/Response from previous versions of IIS) and Kerberos. Enabling Integrated Windows authentication (IWA) via IIS Manager typically enables support for both of these two mechanisms. Neither mechanism sends the user's password in cleartext across the network. NTLM works in a similar way to Digest authentication (with a hashed version of the user's password). Kerberos relies on shared secrets between the client, Active Directory domain controller, and the IIS server to authenticate the user. Kerberos is only available for Active Directory accounts, whereas NTLM can be used for local accounts as well. IIS 7.0 does not present Kerberos as a discrete authentication option to the client, instead sending a "Negotiate" option, allowing the client to choose Kerberos or NTLM. NTLM can be presented as a discrete authentication option to the client.

❑ **Client Certificate Authentication** — When using Client Certificate authentication, the client presents a certificate to the server. The server is configured to map certificates to one or more Windows user accounts (that is, it is possible to map multiple certificates to a single user account or to map each certificate to an individual user account). IIS logs on the mapped user account. Client Certificate authentication requires that SSL/TLS be enabled for the resource being secured. More information on SSL/TLS, and in particular the handshake that sets up a secured session, can be found in Chapter 15.

❑ **Forms-Based Authentication** — Unlike the previous authentication mechanisms, which rely on the transport of credentials as part of the HTTP headers (technically, client certificate mapping occurs at the TCP level below HTTP), Forms-based authentication (FBA) relies on the user authenticating via an HTML form. In this way, the request for the login form is an anonymous request. After authenticating via the HTML form, an authentication cookie is set by the server. The client must return this cookie with each subsequent request in order for the request to be authenticated. No other HTTP authorization data are carried in the HTTP headers. Although this authentication can be configured in part using IIS Manager, it is effectively ASP.NET's FBA. Forms-Based Authentication can be combined with either ASP.NET's authorization features (available with previous versions of ASP.NET) or IIS 7.0 new inbuilt URL Authorization feature to protect access to resources.

❑ **UNC Authentication** — When IIS 7.0 needs to retrieve files from a remote network resource (for example, a remote file server), a virtual directory in IIS 7.0 can be mapped to a UNC (Universal Naming Convention) path. When configuring this virtual directory, it is possible to specify a fixed user account that will be used to connect to that remote share, regardless of the identity of the end user, or to have the user's credentials passed through to the remote file server for authorization.

What Happened to Passport Authentication?

Microsoft's attempt at a federated identity management system, Hailstorm (and then later known as Microsoft Passport in IIS 6.0, and now known as Microsoft Live ID) has been overtaken by subsequent developments in identity federation technologies. Microsoft now offers Active Directory Federation Services (ADFS) as an identity federation product that is not tied to Microsoft's own identity servers. The relatively low uptake of the Passport service by the wider community has seen Passport authentication removed from IIS 7.0.

These authentication mechanisms (with the exception of UNC authentication, which is per virtual directory that is connected to a remote server) can be configured at a web-site, folder, or individual file level. This provides flexibility in securing a web site. For example, a web site could be largely public, but have a secure section where users are required to authenticate in order to gain access.

How IIS 7.0 Authenticates a Client

Regardless of what authentication mechanism or mechanisms are configured on a resource (web site, folder, or file), the browser begins by making an anonymous request. The exception to this is Client Certificate authentication. This is because Client Certificate authentication occurs during the SSL/TLS handshake, and that handshake occurs before the client browser makes its first HTTP request. Client Certificate authentication is discussed in more detail below in this chapter, and in Chapter 15, we discuss SSL/TLS in detail.

It is possible for users to install third-party utilities that may remember passwords on behalf of the user and automatically submit those to a web site. In that case, the first request may include credentials rather than be an anonymous request.

If Anonymous authentication is configured for the resource being requested, then IIS 7.0 will attempt to log on the configured anonymous user account. If Anonymous authentication is not configured, but one of the other mechanisms is configured, then the server will present a list of available authentication options to the client.

If no authentication mechanism is configured at all for a resource, then IIS 7.0 will respond with a 401.2 ("Unauthorized: Logon failure due to server configuration") HTTP error.

This is done through the use of WWW-Authenticate HTTP headers, one for each possible enabled mechanism. IIS 7.0 will order these from the most preferable to the least preferable (Negotiate, NTLM, Digest, Basic). The client will pick the most preferable authentication mechanism that it supports from the list.

Browsers typically do not support a "fallback" mechanism that allows them to attempt to use a weaker authentication mechanism if using a stronger authentication mechanism fails. Instead, the browser will continue attempting to use the strongest selected authentication mechanism unless or until either the server or browser configuration is changed.

For each subsequent request to the server, the browser will continue sending the same credentials. This means that if the previous request was anonymous, then the next request will also be anonymous. If the previous request involved sending credentials, then the next request will contain the same credentials using the same authentication mechanism. This will continue until either:

❑   The client browser process is terminated. It may not be sufficient to simply close the browser if there are still additional spawned windows that exist in the same Windows process. If using a browser that supports tabbed browsing, closing a tab is generally not sufficient either. When the user next visits the resource, he or she will be prompted to supply credentials again.

❑   The server responds with a 401 Unauthorized HTTP status. This causes the browser to prompt the user to supply alternate credentials.

This has important implications for authentication mechanisms such as Basic authentication that do not encrypt the user's credentials. After accessing a resource that requires Basic authentication, the browser will continue sending credentials for all subsequent requests even if the subsequent file does not require authentication.

There are a few exceptions to this rule. FBA is cookie-based, and as such not reliant on authorization HTTP headers sent from the client. It is possible to create persistent FBA cookies that survive browser restarts, allowing users to authenticate without having to re-enter their credentials. Another exception occurs when using NTLM authentication and a HTTP POST request is made, which is discussed in the NTLM Authentication section.

Now we discuss each authentication mechanism in detail, including a discussion of the way the mechanism works, minimum requirements on the client and server sides, and configuration options for each. The discussion assumes that the default authentication modules supplied with Windows Server 2008 are used, rather than custom authentication modules. For more information on developing custom modules, or replacing supplied modules, see Chapter 12.

Configuring Anonymous Authentication

When *Anonymous access* is permitted, a remote user is not required to supply credentials to access a file. Instead, IIS 7.0 attempts to use a pre-configured account to access the resource (for example, to read a file off the hard disk). If that account has appropriate rights, then the action (typically to read the file) is performed. If the pre-configured account does not have permission to access the resource, but some other authentication mechanism is enabled that both server and client support, then the user has an opportunity to supply credentials that can access the resource. If no alternate authentication mechanism is enabled or there is no alternate authentication mechanism that both client and server support enabled, then a 401.3 ("Unauthorized due to ACL on resource") HTTP status is generated.

By default, the configured anonymous access account is the IUSR account created when IIS 7.0 is installed. This account replaces the IUSR_<machinename> account used in previous versions of IIS.

> *The AnonymousAuthenticationModule (authanon.dll) must be installed and enabled to allow Anonymous authentication. This module is installed by default using an interactive install. Requests for .NET resources (such as ASP.NET ASPX pages or ASMX web services) are not made using the IUSR account. Instead, requests for those resources use the Web Application Pool's identity (by default, NT Authority\Network Service) if ASP.NET impersonation is not enabled. For more information on impersonation, see the Authorization section below in this chapter.*

Anonymous authentication can be configured at a server, web-site, folder (including virtual directories), or file level. You must be an Administrator on the server, or have delegated permissions, to be able to enable Anonymous authentication for the node in question.

To configure Anonymous authentication:

1. Open IIS Manager (Start ⇨ Run, enter **intemgr** in the dialog box, and then press [Enter]).

2. Locate the server, web site, folder, or file that you wish to configure Anonymous authentication for. Select the Authentication Feature option.

3. Select the Anonymous Authentication option, and click Enable in the Actions pane to enable Anonymous authentication. Click Disable in the Actions pane to disable Anonymous authentication (if currently enabled), as shown in Figure 14-1.

4. Click Edit in the Actions pane to edit Anonymous authentication options, as shown in Figure 14-2. By default, the IUSR account is used for anonymously authenticated access for static files and Classic ASP files (ASP.NET file access occurs under the Web Application Pool's identity).

5. Click the Set button to change the Anonymous authentication identity, supplying the username and password to be used. Alternatively, to return the network identity to IUSR, enter IUSR as the username, leaving the password blank. To use any other in-built identity (such as LocalSystem, Local Service, or Network Service), supply the username, leaving the password field blank.

6. To disable the use of a distinct Anonymous user account and rely entirely on the application pool's identity for all requests, select the "Application pool identity" radio option. The implications for disabling a separate Anonymous authentication user account are discussed below in this chapter.

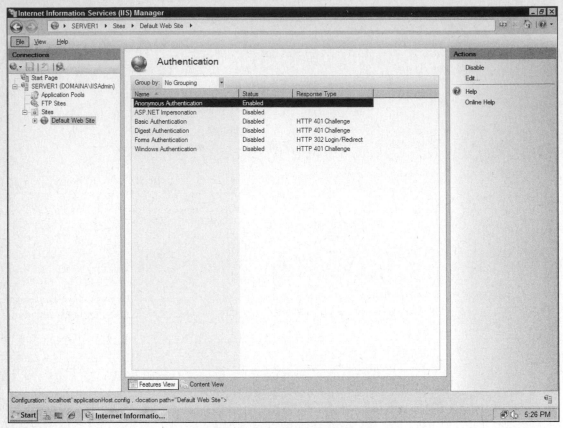

Figure 14-1

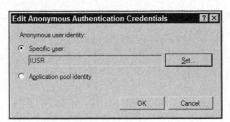

Figure 14-2

7. Click OK to confirm your changes.

Enabling and disabling Anonymous authentication can also be performed programmatically. To enable Anonymous authentication using AppCmd, execute the following line of code:

```
appcmd.exe set config /section:anonymousAuthentication /enabled:true
```

Enabling the use of the application pool identity for requests, rather than relying on a separate Anonymous user identity, can be configured by executing the following AppCmd command:

```
appcmd.exe set config /section:anonymousAuthentication /userName:Username
/password:Password
```

For more information on using AppCmd, see Chapter 5, "Administration Tools."

Configuring Basic Authentication

When *Basic authentication* is enabled, users are prompted to supply a username and password. This password is encoded using Base64 encoding and sent to the server. It is important to note that Base64 encoding is not encryption, and the use of an underlying transport security technology such as SSL/TLS, IPsec, or some VPN technology is recommended to ensure that credentials are not exposed to attackers or devices that are monitoring network traffic.

Basic authentication was introduced as part of the HTTP v1.0 protocol standard, and as such is supported by every major browser. Owing to its simplicity, Basic authentication can safely be used across proxy servers and through firewalls. When using Basic authentication, the server has the user's username and password and can directly access network resources (for example, a remote SQL Server or file server) on behalf of the user.

When accessing a file secured using Basic authentication, the browser will first make an anonymous request. The server will reply with an HTTP 401 (Unauthorized) HTTP status (some HTTP headers are not shown for brevity):

```
HTTP/1.1 401 Unauthorized
WWW-Authenticate: Basic
Server: Microsoft-IIS/7.0
Date: Sat, 08 Sep 2007 07:49:38 GMT
```

The WWW-Authenticate HTTP header indicates that the server supports Basic authentication for clients who want to authenticate.

In the case that multiple authentication mechanisms are supported, multiple WWW-Authenticate headers will be returned; for example:

```
HTTP/1.1 401 Unauthorized
WWW-Authenticate: Negotiate
WWW-Authenticate: Basic
```

To authenticate, the client will take the user's username, append the user's password (separating them with a colon), and Base64-encode the result. For example, for a user User1 and password Password1, the client would append these two, resulting in User1:Password1, which would then be Base64-encoded to give the result: VXNlcjE6RG9tYWluQQ==.

The client then makes a second request, passing these credentials in an Authorization HTTP header. The request would look similar to (again, some HTTP headers are omitted for brevity):

```
GET /default.htm HTTP/1.1
```

```
Host: server1
Authorization: Basic VXNlcjE6RG9tYWluQQ==
```

The server will validate the user's credentials and attempt to access the resource. If the user's credentials are invalid or the user is otherwise unable to access the resource, the server will return another 401 HTTP status response. If the user is able to access the resource and perform the requested action (for example, read the file or write data), the server will return a 200 (OK) HTTP response.

The server will continue to respond to invalid credentials with a 401 HTTP status each time a request is made; however, by default, most browsers will allow a user three incorrect attempts before displaying an Unauthorized message in the browser window. The user would need to make another request for the resource (for example, by refreshing their browser window) in order to attempt to authenticate again.

Basic authentication can be configured at a server, web-site, folder (including virtual directories), or file level. You must be an Administrator on the server or have delegated permissions to be able to enable Basic authentication for the node in question.

The use of Basic authentication requires that Anonymous authentication be disabled. When a browser requests a resource, it does not initially send credentials (the request is anonymous). If Anonymous authentication is also enabled, IIS 7.0 will process the request as is and will not challenge the user for credentials (unless the configured anonymous user does not have access to the resource). To force the user to be prompted, Anonymous authentication should be disabled.

The Basic authentication module (authbas.dll) must be installed and enabled to allow Basic authentication. This module is not installed by default using an interactive install.

To configure Basic authentication:

1. Open IIS Manager (Start ➪ Run, enter **intemgr** in the dialog, and then press [Enter]).

2. Locate the server, web site, folder, or file that you wish to configure Basic authentication for. Select the Authentication Feature option.

3. Select the Basic authentication option, and click Enable in the Actions pane to enable Basic authentication. Click Disable in the Actions pane to disable Basic authentication (if currently enabled).

4. Click Edit in the Actions pane to edit Basic authentication settings (Figure 14-3).

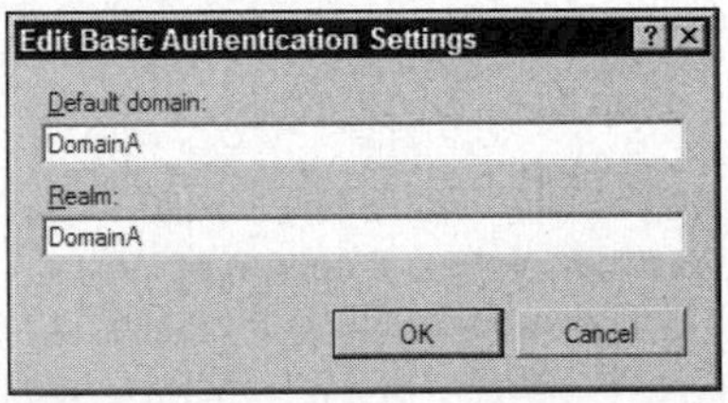

Figure 14-3

5. You may optionally choose to configure a default domain. In the event that a user does not supply a domain (or machine) as part of his or her username, the configured default domain will be inserted by IIS prior to the username. For example, if the user supplies *User1* only as the username and the default domain is configured as *DomainA*, then IIS will attempt to log on the user

as *DomainA\User1*. If no default domain is specified, then the local IIS 7.0 machine's security accounts database (SAM database) will be assumed.

6. You may optionally choose to configure a realm. This information is displayed to the user in the browser's credentials prompt (as shown in Figure 14-4). By making this value the same as the default domain value, users will be aware of which domain IIS 7.0 will be attempting to log on to in the event that a domain is not specified by the user.

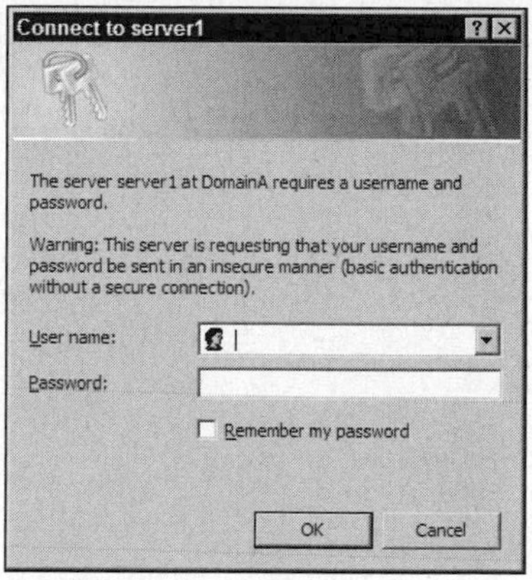

Figure 14-4

7. Click OK to commit changes and exit the dialog box.

Enabling and disabling basic authentication can also be performed programmatically. To enable Basic authentication using AppCmd, execute the following line of code:

```
appcmd.exe set config /section:basicAuthentication /enabled:true
```

To configure the default domain and realm, execute the following command:

```
appcmd.exe set config /section:basicAuthentication /defaultLogonDomain:DomainName
/realm:RealmName
```

Configuring Digest Authentication

When *Digest authentication* is enabled, users are prompted to supply a username and password, similar to Basic authentication. Although the user's username is returned in cleartext to the server, the user's password is not, making Digest authentication significantly more secure than Basic authentication.

Digest authentication was defined in RFC2069 and updated in RFC2619. Digest authentication is supported by all major browsers. Like Basic authentication, Digest authentication works through proxy servers and firewalls and can thus be used in most Internet-facing scenarios.

Digest authentication uses hashing algorithms (MD5 in all the cases seen by the authors) to secure the user's password. A hashing algorithm is a mathematical process that is easy to compute, but given the hash of a value, difficult (or impossible) to determine the original value. For example, when using the mathematical functions Sine and Cosine, a value is easy to compute, but deducing the original value is impossible because, for every given value of $\text{Sin}(x)$, there are an infinite number of starting possible values when attempting to perform the inverse function.

In order to validate the user's identity, the server must also have an MD5 hash of the user's password. The local Security Accounts Manager (SAM) database has no facility for storing the MD5 hash of a user's password, thus Digest authentication cannot be used for local accounts. In a Windows 2000 (or Mixed Mode) domain, passwords must be stored using the "Reversible Encryption" option for the user's Active Directory account. After enabling this option, the user's password must be changed to allow a domain controller to store a copy that can be decrypted. When authenticating a client using Digest authentication, the domain controller can decrypt this copy and perform an MD5 hash on it.

For a Windows Server 2003 (or higher) functional level domain, various hashes of user passwords are calculated automatically when a user's password is set, and stored in the `AltSecID` attribute of the user's account in the directory. For these functional level domains, no additional configuration is required to use Digest authentication.

The previous section looked at Basic authentication, where the server has the user's username and password in cleartext. In that scenario, if IIS 7.0 needs to pass the user's credentials to another back-end server (for example, to a back-end database server like Microsoft SQL Server), it can do so directly. When you use a protocol such as Digest authentication, IIS 7.0 does not have the user's password. In order to access a back-end service using the user's credentials, you need to enable both delegation and protocol transition. These are discussed below in this chapter.

When accessing a file secured using Digest authentication, the browser will first make an anonymous request. The server will reply with an HTTP 401 (Unauthorized) HTTP status (some HTTP headers are not shown for brevity):

```
HTTP/1.1 401 Unauthorized
WWW-Authenticate: Digest
    qop="auth",
    algorithm=MD5sess,
nonce="2fcd0ae920f8c701385153df1e57d19842e5e38c28f173da334776f089bf4e4c1294c328a
    8c4986b",
    charset=utf-8,
    realm="DOMAINA"
Server: Microsoft-IIS/7.0
Date: Sun, 16 Sep 2007 05:17:43 GMT
```

The WWW-Authenticate HTTP header is presented as a single line by the server. Line breaks were added for readability purposes only.

RFC2619 defined two options for the QOP (Quality of Protection) field: *auth* and *auth-int* (authentication with integrity). The second option is not currently supported by IIS 7.0. The algorithm field specifies the hashing algorithm to be used by the client. The Nonce value is randomly determined by the server and is to be used by the client as part of the authentication protocol. The Realm value is also used by the client as part of the authentication process. If the server does not define a Realm value, the value "Digest" is used.

To authenticate, the client performs several operations, resulting in a final authentication code that is returned to the server. (Some HTTP headers are omitted for brevity.) Additionally the Authorization header, when sent from the browser, does not contain line breaks — they have been inserted for readability purposes only.

```
GET / HTTP/1.1
Accept-Encoding: gzip, deflate
Authorization: Digest
    username="User1",
    realm="DOMAINA",
nonce="2fcd0ae920f8c701385153df1e57d19842e5e38c28f173da334776f089bf4e4c1294c328a
    8c4986b",
    uri="/",
    cnonce="eebbf22f9fc23915256ebde6067d0fad",
    nc=00000001,
    algorithm=MD5-sess,
    response="c9891b344053362464d119ca0f40e49a",
    qop="auth",
    charset=utf-8
```

The Response field above contains the authentication information generated by the client. It is calculated as follows:

1. The user's username, realm (in this case, Windows domain), and password are concatenated (each item is separated by a colon) and then hashed to generate a temporary value (Value1).

2. The HTTP method (in this case, GET) and the requested URI (in this case, the root folder /) are concatenated (again separated by a colon) and hashed to generate a second temporary value (Value2).

3. The following items are then concatenated (again with a colon separating each item) and a hash generated: Value1, server-supplied nonce (nonce above), request counter (nc), client nonce (cnonce), quality of protection field (qop), and Value2. This final value is the Response field provided by the client to the server.

As the server has access to the same information (with the exception that a domain controller stores Value1 as a pre-calculated value when the user's account is created in a Windows Server 2003 or higher functional level domain), it is able to perform the same calculations and derive a Response value. If the client-provided Response value matches the one calculated by the server, then the user is deemed authenticated.

Digest authentication protects users and applications against a variety of malicious attacks by incorporating pieces of information about the request as inputs to the hashing algorithm. For example, by incorporating the URI and HTTP method, the response code varies as a user requests different files, preventing an attacker from reusing a captured response code to request other files. Additionally, the client must always supply higher values for the request counter when using the same server nonce (for example, by incrementing the value for each request), resulting in an altered response code, even for subsequent requests for the same file. The server remembers the last received nc (request counter) value for each nonce that it currently has issued, and rejects requests that supply nc values that are the same or lower than the last used value. This prevents replay attacks, where an attacker captures packets on the network and then retransmits them to the server later, effectively impersonating the original user.

Digest authentication can be configured at a server, web-site, folder (including virtual directories), or file level. You must be an Administrator on the server or have delegated permissions to be able to enable Digest authentication for the node in question.

The use of Digest authentication requires that Anonymous authentication be disabled. When a browser requests a resource, it does not initially send credentials (the request is anonymous). If Anonymous authentication is also enabled, IIS 7.0 will process the request as is and will not challenge the user for credentials (unless the configured anonymous user does not have access to the resource). To force the user to be prompted, Anonymous authentication should be disabled.

The Digest authentication module (authmd5.dll) must be installed and enabled to allow Digest authentication. This module is not installed by default using an interactive install.

To configure Digest authentication:

1. Open IIS Manager (Start ➪ Run, enter **intemgr** in the dialog, and then press [Enter]).

2. Locate the server, web site, folder, or file that you want to configure Digest authentication for. Select the Authentication Feature option.

3. Select the Digest Authentication option and click Enable in the Actions pane to enable Digest authentication. Click Disable in the Actions pane to disable Digest authentication (if currently enabled).

4. Click Edit in the Actions pane to edit the Digest authentication settings (Figure 14-5).

   Optionally, you can choose to configure a Realm. This information is displayed to the user in the browser's credentials prompt (as shown in Figure 14-6). Additionally, IIS 7.0 will automatically prefix the configured Realm value to the user's username, obviating the need to supply a domain name.

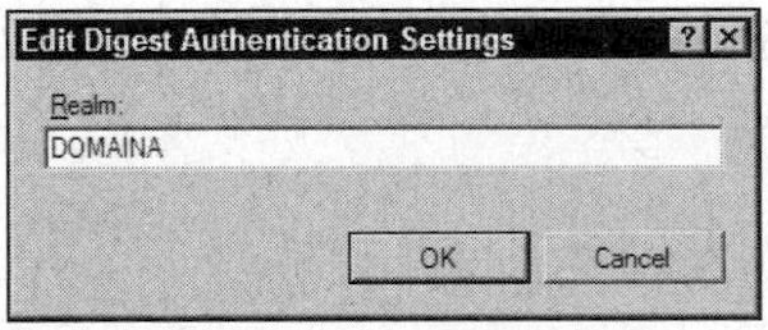

Figure 14-5

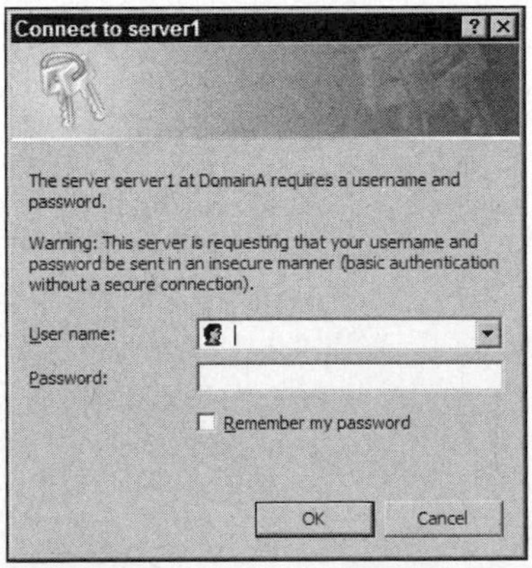

Figure 14-6

5. Click OK to commit changes and exit the dialog.

If a Realm has been configured, users should not supply a Windows domain name as part of the authentication prompt. If users supply their credentials as domain\username and the Realm is then prefixed (forming domain\domain\username), the resulting response value calculated by the server will not match the one supplied by the client.

The MD5 hashing algorithm is case-sensitive. This means that the hash of the value "User1" is different from the hash of the value "USER1" and is different again from the hash of the value "user1." Because a Windows Server 2003 functional level domain does not store passwords using reversible encryption by default, it is not possible for a domain controller to examine the case of the username supplied by the browser and then calculate the appropriate MD5 hash on-the-fly (as the domain controller does not have the password). Therefore, several pre-computed hashes are stored: one hash generated using the exact case of the user's sAMAccountName as well as additional variations (username entirely in lowercase and entirely in uppercase). The user must supply his or her username in one of these cases; otherwise, authentication will fail.

Enabling and disabling digest authentication can also be performed programmatically. To enable digest authentication using AppCmd, execute the following command:

```
appcmd.exe set config /section:digestAuthentication /enabled:true
```

To configure the Realm, execute the following command:

```
appcmd.exe set config /section:digestAuthentication /realm:RealmName
```

Configuring NTLM Authentication

NTLM is one of two authentication mechanisms available when selecting to use Integrated Windows Authentication (IWA) in IIS 7.0 (the other is Kerberos, discussed below). NTLM is a proprietary Microsoft protocol suite that can be used both for HTTP-based authentication and non-HTTP-based authentication. It provides similar capabilities as Digest authentication, but pre-dated the development of Digest authentication. Recognizing the need for a more robust authentication mechanism than Basic authentication, and with the necessary security infrastructure already existing in Windows, Microsoft adapted both Internet Explorer and IIS to support NTLM-based authentication (also known as "NT Challenge/Response Authentication" in IIS 4.0).

Despite being a proprietary Microsoft protocol, most modern browsers in addition to Internet Explorer v3 and higher (such as Mozilla/Firefox and Opera) support NTLM-based authentication. When used to authenticate clients over HTTP, NTLM authentication is a connection-oriented mechanism. This requires that the HTTP connection be maintained through the use of HTTP Keep-Alive functionality. If the server or browser is configured not to use keep-alives, then NTLM authentication will fail. For this reason, it is sometimes said that NTLM authentication does not work through forward proxy servers, because forward proxy servers typically do not permit an end-to-end persistent HTTP connection that can be reused by the end-client for subsequent HTTP requests. In the event that clients are behind a forward proxy server, it must be NTLM-aware in order for NTLM authentication to work.

NTLM authentication can be used for both domain and local accounts, unlike Digest authentication (or Kerberos authentication), which can only be used for domain accounts. This makes NTLM ideal for use in workgroup scenarios or between domains where no trust relationship exists.

Two versions of NTLM exist (v1 and v2). IIS 7.0 only supports NTLM v2; NTLM v1 has been shown to be cryptographically compromised and is not recommended for use. When configuring a Windows computer's local security policy (or configuring its settings via domain-based Group Policy), NTLM v2 support must remain enabled for NTLM authentication over HTTP to work. For brevity, the rest of the chapter will not explicitly mention the NTLM version number — v2 is assumed.

After enabling Integrated Windows Authentication (IWA) in IIS 7.0, two WWW-Authenticate headers are sent to clients by default. The following table outlines under which circumstances NTLM will be used:

Header Sent	Authentication Attempted
WWW-Authenticate: Negotiate	Kerberos, if requirements for it are met; otherwise, NTLM v2. See the "Configuring Kerberos Authentication" section below in this chapter for Kerberos requirements. The Negotiate header uses the Microsoft implementation of SPNEGO and GSSAPI to allow a client to negotiate an acceptable authentication mechanism.
WWW-Authenticate: NTLM	NTLM v2. The NTLM header uses the Microsoft NTLM SSP (Security Support Provider) to authenticate the client using NTLM v2.

Steps to customize which HTTP headers are sent to the client are discussed below in this section.

Internet Explorer, by default, will attempt to automatically log the current user in when a web site is using NTLM or Negotiate security and the web site is in the browser's intranet security zone. This can allow an organization to obviate the need for users to authenticate to their workstations, and then authenticate again to internal web sites, effectively implementing a rudimentary form of Single Sign On (SSO). What Internet Explorer determines to be the intranet security zone automatically is listed in the Microsoft KB article 258063 (`http://support.microsoft.com/?id=258063`).

Internet Explorer's behavior can be altered by editing the settings at Tools ➪ Internet Options ➪ Security ➪ Intranet zone ➪ Custom Level ➪ "Automatic logon only in Intranet zone" (Figure 14-7). This setting can also be set centrally via a Group Policy Object if a large number of machines need to be configured.

> *As NTLM is a proprietary Microsoft protocol, the following discussion of how NTLM authentication works draws heavily on several third-party resources in addition to MSDN documentation. These include Eric Glass's NTLM white paper, the SAMBA project's documentation, and WireShark dissectors. Links to these resources can be found in Appendix D.*

When accessing a file secured using NTLM authentication, the browser will first make an anonymous request. The server will reply with an HTTP 401 (Unauthorized) HTTP status. As NTLM is a three-step challenge/response process, the client needs to send two requests in addition to the initial anonymous request to authenticate successfully. The server's response to the initial anonymous request (some HTTP headers are not shown for brevity) will be:

```
HTTP/1.1 401 Unauthorized
WWW-Authenticate: NTLM
Server: Microsoft-IIS/7.0
Date: Sun, 16 Sep 2007 07:00:44 GMT
```

In this section, IIS 7.0 has been customized to send only the WWW-Authenticate: NTLM header (and omit the WWW-Authenticate: Negotiate header) to ensure that NTLM authentication is used rather than Kerberos. The process for authenticating using NTLM over Negotiate and the data sent between client and server are the same as when using WWW-Authenticate: NTLM.

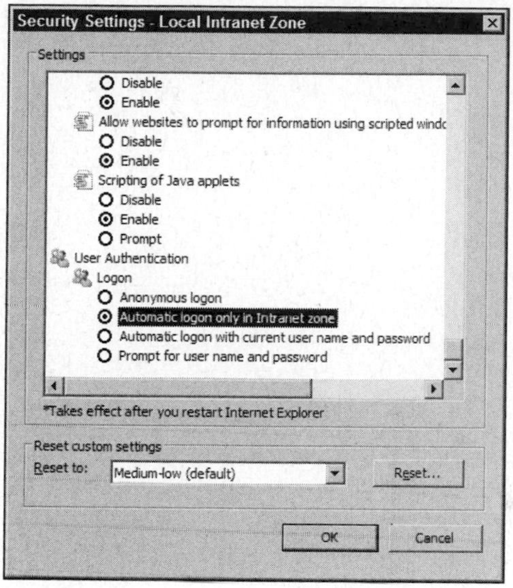

Figure 14-7

The client now replies with an NTLM Type 1 request. This request contains several individual pieces of information:

Bytes	Data	Description
0-7	NTLMSSP <NULL>	Literal text indicating the use of NTLM SSP (Security Support Provider).
8-11	0x01000000	NTLM message type. This is a Type 1 message.
12-15	Varies. Default for Internet Explorer 7.0 is 0xa2088207.	Various flags indicating features that the client supports and that it requires from the server. The default-enabled flags for Internet Explorer 7 are: 56-bit key supported. 128-bit key supported. Negotiate Always Sign (message signed with dummy data). Negotiate NTLM v2 key. Negotiate NTLM key. Request Target (server should identify its authentication realm in its response). Negotiate Unicode (Unicode responses supported in security buffer). Negotiate OEM (OEM strings supported in security buffer).

Bytes	Data	Description
16-23	\<NULL\>	Optional security buffer information indicating the domain that the client is in. This is NULL by default.
24-31	\<NULL\>	Optional security buffer information indicating the workstation name. This is NULL by default.

The data above are Base64-encoded and sent to the server (some HTTP headers are omitted for brevity):

```
GET / HTTP/1.1
Accept: */*
Accept-Encoding: gzip, deflate
Connection: Keep-Alive
Authorization: NTLM TlRMTVNTUAABAAAAB4IIogAAAAAAAAAAAAAAAAAAAAAAGAHEXAAAADw==
```

The server now responds with an HTTP 401 (Unauthorized) HTTP status and a Type 2 NTLM message. The structure of the server's Type 2 message is

Bytes	Data	Description
0-7	NTLMSSP\<NULL\>	Literal text indicating the use of NTLM SSP (Security Support Provider).
8-11	0x02000000	NTLM message type. This is a Type 2 message.
12-29	DomainA	The name of the Realm that the client is authenticating to (could be a domain or server name).
20-23	Varies. Default for IIS 7.0 is 0xA2898205	Various flags indicating features that the client supports and that it requires from the server. The default enabled flags for Internet Explorer 7 are 56-bit key supported. 128-bit key supported. Negotiate Always Sign (message signed with dummy data). Negotiate NTLM v2 key. Negotiate NTLM key. Request Target (server should identify its authentication realm in its response). Negotiate Challenge Initiation. Negotiate Unicode (Unicode responses supported in security buffer).
24-31	Random Data	NTLM challenge. Similar to the Digest authentication server nonce. The client will use this in generating its response.

The data above are Base64-encoded and sent to the client (some HTTP headers are omitted for brevity):

```
HTTP/1.1 401 Unauthorized
WWW-Authenticate: NTLM
TlRMTVNTUAACAAAADgAOADgAAAAFgomiQQLLgzET8xMAAAAAAAAAAJ4AngBGAAAABgBxFwAAAA9EAE8ATQB
```

BAEkATgBBAAIADgBEAE8ATQBBAEkATgBBAAEADgBTAEUAUgBWAEUAUgAxAAQAGgBEAG8AbQBhAGkAbgBBAAC
4AbABvAGMAYQBsAAMAKgBTAGUAcgB2AGUAcgAxAC4ARABvAG0AYQBpAG4AQQAuAGwAbwBjAGEAbAAFABoAR
ABvAG0AYQBpAG4AQQAuAGwAbwBjAGEAbAAHAAgAWrTLUi/4xwEAAAAA
Server: Microsoft-HTTPAPI/2.0
Date: Sun, 16 Sep 2007 07:00:53 GMT

The server HTTP header returns a different value for this particular response. This is due to the new kernel mode authentication functionality in Windows Server 2008. This functionality is described in the next section on Kerberos authentication. If kernel authentication is disabled, the server HTTP header will be Microsoft-IIS/7.0.

In the final part of an NTLM authentication handshake, the client now replies with a Type 3 NTLM message. This contains the client's authentication information derived from the user's password and the challenge sent by the server in the Type 2 message. The following table describes the structure of a Type 3 message:

Bytes	Data	Description
0-15	NTLMSSP<NULL>	Literal text indicating the use of NTLM SSP (Security Support Provider) in Unicode.
16-19	0x03000000	NTLM message type. This is a Type 3 message.
20-43	0x00000000	This is a 24-byte buffer that would store a LANMAN response. As LANMAN responses are not sent as part of NTLM authentication, these bytes are all zero.
44-313	Varies	NTLM v2 response. It comprises the elements in the following rows.
52-59	0x00000000	This buffer stores an optional NTLM session key. This is not used for NTLM HTTP-based authentication.
60-63	Varies. Default for Internet Explorer 7 is 0xa2888205	Various flags indicating features that this request supports. For HTTP-based NTLM authentication, these flags appear to echo the flag set in the Type 2 response but appear to have no discernable effect.
88-101	DomainA	Target realm for authentication. In this case, it is the domain or server that the user is attempting to authenticate to.
102-110	User1	sAMAccountName of the user account attempting to authenticate.
112-117	Workstation1	NetBIOS name of the workstation attempting to authenticate.
142-157	Varies	HMAC-MD5 Value3 (see below).
174-180	Varies	Client nonce (see below).
166-173	Varies	Current time on the client.

The NTLM response data are derived as follows:

1. The MD4 algorithm is applied to the Unicode user password, resulting in Value1.

2. The uppercase username is concatenated with the uppercase target realm (domain or server-name), and the HMAC-MD5 algorithm is applied to this value using Value1 as a key. This results in Value2.

3. A random 8-byte client nonce is created.

4. The server challenge is concatenated with the random client nonce, and the HMAC-MD5 is calculated using Value2 as a key. This results in a 16-byte value (Value3).

The data above are Base64-encoded and sent to the client (some HTTP headers are omitted for brevity):

```
GET / HTTP/1.1
Accept: */*
Connection: Keep-Alive
Authorization: NTLM
TlRMTVNTUAADAAAAGAAYAHYAAAAOAQ4BjgAAAA4ADgBYAAAACgAKAGYAAAAGAAYAcAAAAAAAAACcAQAABYK
IogYAcRcAAAAP3i8A1v3alL72zWiZyER4o0QAbwBtAGEAaQBuAEEAVQBzAGUACgAxAEQAQwAxAAAAAAAAAA
AAAAAAAAAAAAAAAAAAAAAAEKgUqnxPTvsOMEzlfUHyuEBAQAAAAAAFq0y1Iv+McBEs7stuBYC54AAAAAAA
gAOAEQATwBNAEEASQBOAEEAEAAQAOAFMARQBSAFYARQBSADEABAAaAEQAbwBtAGEAaQBuAEEALgBsAG8AYwBh
AGwAAwAqAFMAZQBByAHYAZQBByADEALgBEAG8AbQBhAGkAbgBBAC4AbABvAGMAMAYQBsAAUAGgBEAG8AbQBhAGk
AbgBBAC4AbABvAGMAYQBsAAcACACABatMtSL/jHAQYABAACAAAACAAwADAAAAAAAAAAAAAAAAAwWAAC4D1joWh
dn1+9z+GrU9OYLrAILoE1kzOzUIceswe7n6AAAAAAAAAAAAAAAA==
```

As the server has access to the same information (with the exception that NTLM hashes are stored by default), it is able to perform the same calculations and derive a Response value. If the client-provided Response value matches the one calculated by the server, then the user is deemed authenticated.

Owing to the multistep authentication process, IIS log files will record two 401 HTTP status requests while a client is authenticating, followed by a 200 OK request. This is expected behavior.

NTLM authentication varies from other authentication mechanisms in that the underlying HTTP connection is authenticated. As such, for subsequent requests, no credentials are sent by the client to the server. Instead, the underlying HTTP connection must be keep open via HTTP Keep-Alives functionality (this allows a HTTP connection to be kept open for subsequent HTTP requests). If the connection is closed, the authentication process must begin again.

An exception is when a client needs to send data using the HTTP POST method. Because it is possible that the server may reject the client's credentials (resulting in multiple additional requests, all reposting the same information, consuming bandwidth and delaying the final response), the client does not attempt an authenticated POST request. Instead, it preemptively sends a Type 1 message (but without the POST data). This initiates another NTLM handshake so that the client can verify that the existing credentials are acceptable to the server. Only with the Type 3 message does the client post the form data to the server.

NTLM authentication can be configured at a server, web-site, folder (including virtual directories), or file level. You must be an Administrator on the server or have delegated permissions to be able to enable NTLM authentication for the node in question.

The use of NTLM authentication requires that Anonymous authentication be disabled. When a browser requests a resource, it does not initially send credentials (the request is anonymous). If Anonymous authentication is also enabled, IIS 7.0 will process the request as is and will not challenge the user for credentials (unless the configured anonymous user does not have access to the resource). To force the user to be prompted, Anonymous authentication should be disabled.

The Windows Authentication module (authsspi.dll) must be installed and enabled to allow NTLM authentication. This module is not installed by default using an interactive install.

To configure NTLM authentication:

1. Open IIS Manager (Start ⇨ Run, enter **intemgr** in the dialog, and then press [Enter]).

2. Locate the server, web site, folder, or file that you wish to configure NTLM authentication for. Select the Authentication Feature option.

3. Select the Integrated Windows Authentication option, and click Enable in the Actions pane to enable NTLM authentication. Click Disable in the Actions pane to disable NTLM authentication (if currently enabled).

4. Click OK to commit changes and exit the dialog.

Enabling Integrated Windows Authentication via IIS Manager enables both the WWW-Authenticate: Negotiate HTTP header and the WWW-Authenticate: NTLM header. To force NTLM authentication, remove the WWW-Authenticate: Negotiate header. To do so requires editing the relevant configuration file (`applicationHost.config` or `web.config` if the setting is set at a web-site or application level).

The default configuration (that enables both headers) is

```
<windowsAuthentication enabled="true">
    <providers>
        <add value="Negotiate" />
        <add value="NTLM" />
    </providers>
</windowsAuthentication>
```

You can use the following options to remove the Negotiate header:

❑ Delete the `<add value="Negotiate" />` value if at the `applicationHost.config` root configuration.

❑ Use the `<clear />` option to clear all previously defined providers, and then use the `<add value="NTLM" />` value to readd the NTLM provider if in a delegated configuration file scenario.

❑ Use the `<remove value="Negotiate" />` option to remove the previously defined Negotiate provider if in a delegated configuration file scenario. If the `<add value="NTLM" />` has been defined at a higher level in the configuration hierarchy, then NTLM authentication will be offered to the client.

Configuring Kerberos Authentication

Kerberos v5 authentication is an open, industry-standard, ticket-based authentication method first developed at MIT. It uses a variety of techniques to avoid eavesdropping/passive sniffing attacks and replay attacks. It supports mutual authentication of the client and server to each other.

Kerberos authentication relies on a trusted third party. In a Windows domain, this is a domain controller (DC). For this reason, Kerberos authentication can only be used for Active Directory domain accounts. A client needs to contact a domain controller to obtain the necessary Kerberos tickets. For this reason, Kerberos authentication is commonly said to fail across firewalls. This is not because firewalls cannot pass Kerberos traffic, but because firewalls are typically deployed at the edge of a network (that is, bordering an internal network and the wider Internet), and most firewalls deny traffic from the Internet to internal domain controllers.

Kerberos authentication was first introduced with Windows Server 2000 and can be used for HTTP and non-HTTP authentication. Internet Explorer 5.0 was the first version of IE to support Kerberos authentication. Kerberos authentication can only be used for Active Directory domain accounts and thus is not available in workgroup scenarios or for local accounts. There is currently no way to force Kerberos authentication. Instead, the `WWW-Authenticate: Negotiate` HTTP header allows the browser to negotiate either Kerberos or NTLM authentication. Internet Explorer will attempt Kerberos authentication in the following circumstances:

❑ Enable Integrated Windows Authentication (requires a restart) is enabled under Internet Explorer ➪ Tools ➪ Internet Options ➪ Advanced. This is enabled by default, except under certain circumstances on Windows 2000. For more information, see `http://support.microsoft.com/Default.aspx?id=299838`.

❑ The client operating system must be Windows 2000, Windows XP, Windows Vista, or Windows Server 2003 or 2008. Windows NT and Windows 9x do not support Kerberos authentication by default.

❑ The web site must be in Internet Explorer's Intranet security zone or the Trusted Sites security zone. If the web site is in the Internet security zone, then IE will not attempt Kerberos authentication, as typically the browser cannot contact a domain controller in an Internet scenario. For more information on how IE determines whether a site is in the Intranet zone, see `http://support.microsoft.com/?id=258063`. For the Trusted Sites zone, the web site must be added manually or via Group Policy Object (GPO). To add a site via GPO to the Intranet or Trusted Sites zones, open Group Policy Editor and navigate to Computer/User Configuration ➪ Administrative Templates ➪ Internet Explorer ➪ Internet Explorer Control Panel ➪ Security Page ➪ Site to Zone Assignment (see Figure 14-8).

❑ The client must be able to contact a Kerberos KDC (Key Distribution Center). In an Active Directory domain, this is hosted on domain controllers. The KDC must have a corresponding registered service principal name (SPN) or be able to refer the client to another KDC that does have the SPN registered.

❑ An appropriate SPN must be registered. When installing IIS 7.0, SPNs are automatically registered for `http://servername` and `http://servername.ADDomain` in Active Directory. If you are using a custom name (either NetBIOS or fully qualified domain name) to access the server, you may need to register an appropriate SPN. SPNs are explained in more detail below in this section.

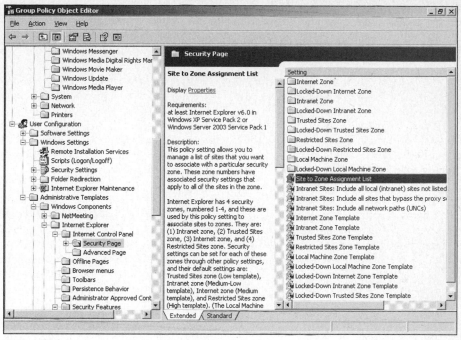

Figure 14-8

How Kerberos Authentication Works

As Kerberos authentication is a far more complex mechanism than previously described protocols, a brief section here will explain the process by which a client authenticates using Kerberos.

Kerberos authentication involves three parties: the client, the remote service that the client wants to access, and a trusted third party. The third party is known as the Kerberos Key Distribution Center (KDC) and is hosted on each domain controller in a Windows Active Directory domain.

To authenticate to the remote service, the client initially contacts the KDC to get a Ticket Granting Ticket (TGT). The TGT enables the client to subsequently contact the KDC for additional authentication tickets. It obviates the need for the client machine to continually ask for the user's password or to cache the user's password in memory. The TGT has a validity of 8 hours by default on a Windows Active Directory domain.

To get a TGT, the client contacts the KDC (specifically, a service called the Authorization Service, or AS), indicating its name. In an Active Directory domain, a process called *pre-authentication* is performed to authenticate the client, but that is beyond the scope of this book. The KDC verifies that the client (user or machine) exists in Active Directory, and if so generates two pieces of information. The first is a session key (Session Key 1) that will be used to secure communications between the KDC and the client. The second is the TGT.

The first piece of information is encrypted using a key derived from the user's password. Since both the KDC and the user know what this is, the user will be able to decrypt the session key. The TGT is encrypted using a secret known only to the KDC. If you have ever wondered what the disabled *krbtgt* user account is for in a Windows Active Directory domain — its password is used to derive the key to encrypt the TGT.

The KDC returns both pieces of information to the client. The client decrypts the session key using its knowledge of the user's password. The client is now able to authenticate to the KDC to obtain service tickets for remote services.

To authenticate to a remote HTTP web site, the client contacts the KDC for a service ticket. As before, the client contacts the TGS. The client supplies its details encrypted with Session Key 1, as well as the previously provided TGT. Since only the client could decrypt the package containing Session Key 1, the KDC knows that the client is legitimate.

The TGS of the KDC now prepares two pieces of information to give back to the client. The first is a new session key (let's call this Session Key 2) that the client will use when talking to the remote HTTP service. These data are encrypted using Session Key 1. The second piece of data contains identifying pieces of information about the client (for example, the username) as well as a second copy of Session Key 2. These data are encrypted using a key derived from data that only the KDC and the HTTP service know (namely, the machine or user account password that the HTTP service is running under). This is known as the "service ticket."

The client receives these two pieces of information. It can only decrypt the first piece, and it extracts the session key that it should use to communicate with the HTTP service.

In the final step of the authentication process, the client now sends two pieces of information to the HTTP service. The first is the service ticket received from the KDC. The second is the current time on the client, and this is encrypted using Session Key 2 (the key used to secure transmission between the client and HTTP service). This is known as the "authenticator."

The HTTP service receives the two pieces of information. It decrypts the first part using its own password. This contains a copy of Session Key 2, as well as the client's identity. The HTTP service uses Session Key 2 to decrypt the authenticator and extract the time stamp. It compares the time to its own current system time. If a significant discrepancy exists (more than 5 minutes, after accounting for time zone differences, in a default Active Directory configuration), then a replay attack is assumed to be occurring. Otherwise, the client is considered authenticated.

Figure 14-9 illustrates the process. The following information is exchanged:

1. Initial client request.
2. Session Key 1 (encrypted with user password) and TGT.
3. Request for service ticket (encrypted with Session Key 1) and TGT.
4. Session Key 2 (encrypted with Session Key 1) and Service Ticket (encrypted with HTTP service's password).
5. Time Stamp/Authenticator (encrypted with Session Key 2) and Service Ticket (encrypted with HTTP service's password).

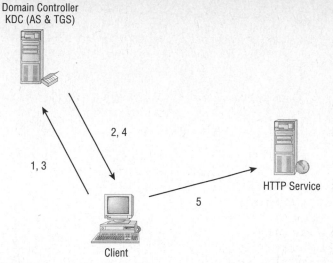

Figure 14-9

Service Principal Names

Kerberos authentication relies on the trusted third party (KDC) to vouch for the authenticity of the client to the server. To do this, the KDC encrypts information about the client using a secret known only to itself and the service.

In order for the KDC to know which secret to use, the client must tell the KDC what service it wishes to access, and the KDC needs some way of determining the appropriate secret for that service. This occurs through the use of Service Principal Names (SPNs).

Service Principal Names (SPNs) are attributes of user or computer objects in Active Directory. When a client wishes to access a particular service, it tells the KDC the SPN of the service it wishes to access, and the KDC searches Active Directory for that SPN. If there is a match, the KDC uses the password of the machine or user that the SPN is registered under as the basis of the secret.

> *For this reason, it is important not to have duplicate SPNs within Active Directory. If an SPN is accidentally registered under two different objects, then the KDC will not know which password should be used to encrypt the service ticket, and Kerberos authentication will fail.*

You can add and remove SPNs by using the SetSPN.exe Resource Kit tool, which you can download from http://www.microsoft.com/downloads/details.aspx?familyid=5fd831fd-ab77-46a3-9cfe-ff01d29e5c46. SetSPN.exe does not need to be run on a domain controller, but rather any domain-joined machine that is Windows 2000 or later.

Registering an SPN requires the following information: a protocol prefix, the machine name (for example, NetBIOS name or fully qualified domain name) used by the client to access the service, an optional port number, and the user or machine account that the SPN should be registered under. For example, to access a web site at www.domainA.local that is running on the machine server1, you would use the following code:

```
setspn.exe -A HTTP/www.domainA.local domainA\server1
```

To remove an existing SPN, use the -D option, as follows:

```
setspn.exe -D HTTP/www.domainA.local
```

To list all SPNs registered under a particular user or computer account, use the -L option:

```
setspn.exe -L domainA\server1
```

When adding a machine to a domain, default SPNs are added for HOST/machinename and HOST/machinename.domainname. This provides Kerberos authentication to web sites accessed using either http://machinename or http://machinename.domainname (HTTPS access also works). If accessing a web site by any other name(s) (for example, a custom FQDN), then an SPN must be registered for that FQDN.

In prior versions of Windows (for example, Windows Server 2003), the SPN was registered under the server's machine account if the web application pool (w3wp.exe process) was running under an inbuilt security principal (LocalSystem, Network Service, or Local Service). If the web application pool was being run under a custom domain user account, then SPN was registered under that domain user account. If the web application pool was being run under a custom local user account, Kerberos authentication could not be used.

Windows Server 2008 offers an option to use *kernel mode security*. In this case, the SPN is registered under the machine account no matter which security principal is used to host the worker process. This simplifies SPN management and also improves performance by moving authentication to kernel mode.

If you elect not to use kernel mode authentication, then the same rules that applied to previous versions of Windows apply. If the web application pool is being hosted under a custom domain account, the SPN must be registered under that user account, rather than the machine account. Additionally, since an SPN is based on a machine name, all web applications hosted at that machine name (for example, www.domainA.local) must run in the same web application pool or separate web application pools running under the same account. That account must be the account that the SPN is registered under.

In a *web farm scenario* (where there are multiple load-balanced web servers, using either Windows Network Load Balancing or an external hardware load balancer), the following rules apply:

❑ The KDC does not know ahead of time which physical machine will receive the request. In order to encrypt the service ticket, it must be encrypted using credentials that can be decrypted on any of the machines in the web farm.

❑ To facilitate this, the web application pools participating in the farm must be run under a custom domain user account, and the SPN for the virtual host name be registered under this domain user account. The KDC can use the password of this account as the basis for encrypting the service ticket.

❑ Kernel mode authentication must be disabled on each web site participating in the web farm. As a result, the custom user account being used as the identity of the web application pool can decrypt the service ticket from the client.

Enabling Kerberos Authentication

You can configure Kerberos authentication at a server, web-site, folder (including virtual directories), or file level. You must be an Administrator on the server or have delegated permissions to be able to enable Kerberos authentication for the node in question.

> *The use of Kerberos authentication requires that Anonymous authentication be disabled. When a browser requests a resource, it does not initially send credentials (the request is anonymous). If Anonymous authentication is also enabled, IIS 7.0 will process the request as is and will not challenge the user for credentials (unless the configured anonymous user does not have access to the resource). To force the user to be prompted, Anonymous authentication should be disabled.*

> *The Windows Authentication module (authsspi.dll) must be installed and enabled to allow Kerberos authentication. This module is not installed by default using an interactive install.*

To configure Kerberos authentication:

1. Open IIS Manager (Start ➪ Run, enter **intemgr** in the dialog, and then press [Enter]).

2. Locate the server, web site, folder, or file that you wish to configure Kerberos authentication for. Select the Authentication Feature option.

3. Select the Integrated Windows Authentication option and click Enable in the Actions pane to enable Kerberos authentication. Click Disable in the Actions pane to disable Kerberos authentication (if currently enabled).

4. Click the Advanced Settings link to enable or disable the use of Kernel-mode authentication (see Figure 14-10).

5. Click OK to commit the changes and exit the dialog.

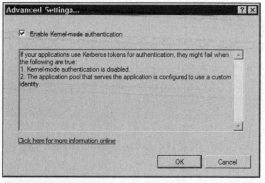

Figure 14-10

Configuring UNC Authentication

UNC authentication allows you to configure IIS to use a specified user account when accessing resources on a remote share. When creating a virtual directory (or web application) that points to a UNC (Universal Naming Convention) share, credentials can be provided for accessing that share. If no credentials are provided, then IIS 7.0 will attempt to use the currently impersonated user. The currently impersonated user may be:

❑ The application pool's user identity (if Anonymous authentication is being permitted). If the application pool's identity is Network Service, then the machine account (machinename$) is used.

❑ The authenticated end-user's account is used, if Basic authentication is used.

❑ The web application pool's user account if Digest or NTLM authentication is used. For these two authentication mechanisms, IIS 7.0 does not have the user's password and therefore is unable to authenticate as the user to the remote resource unless protocol transition is configured and enabled (see the section, "Configuring Protocol Transition," below in this chapter).

❑ The authenticated end-user if Kerberos authentication is used and delegation is configured (see the section, "Configuring Delegation," below in this chapter). Otherwise, if delegation is not configured, or fails, the access will be by the user account hosting the web application pool.

To configure UNC authentication:

1. Open IIS Manager (Start ➪ Run, enter **intemgr** in the dialog, and then press [Enter]).

2. Locate the server, web site, or folder at which you wish to add a new virtual directory or web application. Right-click and choose Add Virtual Directory.

3. Enter the alias that the directory should be accessed under and the UNC path (\\server-name\sharename) to the remote resource. Do not use the drive letters used, as drive-letter mappings are valid for the logged-on user only (see Figure 14-11).

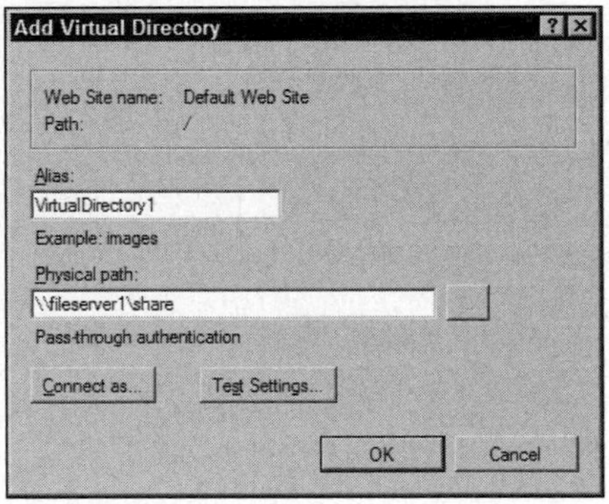

Figure 14-11

4. Click the "Connect as" button to alter the credentials used to connect to the remote share. Choose the Specific User option to set a user account to be used regardless of the end-user. Enter the username and password when prompted. Alternatively, select the Application User ("Pass-through authentication") option if the end-user's credentials (or the web application pool's credentials in the absence of an end-user's credentials) should be used (see Figure 14-12).

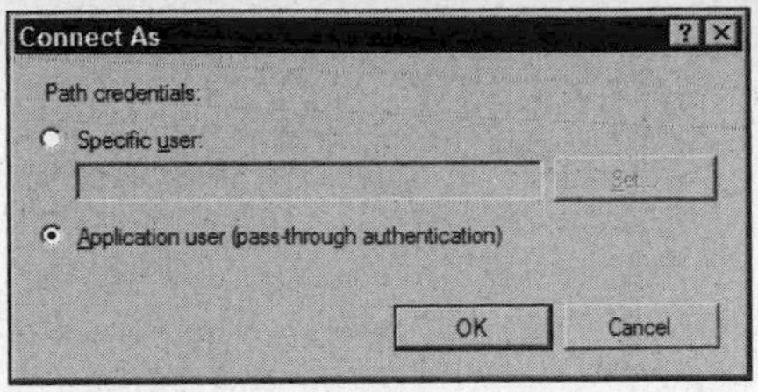

Figure 14-12

5.   Click OK to exit the dialog.

The web application pool's account must also have access to the remote share. This is a new requirement in IIS 7.0 and is a result of that account needing to be able to read any web.config files that may be located on the remote share. In previous versions of IIS, all configuration was stored in the central metabase and therefore no access rights were required for the web application pool identity. If the web application pool identity is Network Service, then granting the machinename$ account access to the remote share is sufficient. This is only possible in an Active Directory domain scenario.

Configuring Client Certificate Authentication

Client Certificate authentication works by having a client present a user authentication certificate issued by a trusted root Certificate Authority, which is then mapped to a Windows security principal (user account).

The Client Certificate is presented by the client to the server as part of an SSL or TLS handshake. As such, use of Client Certificates for authentication requires enabling SSL/TLS on a web site. For more information on SSL/TLS, see Chapter 15.

IIS 7.0 supports three Client Certificate authentication mechanisms:

❑   **One-to-One Client Mapping** — When this is enabled, each individual trusted user certificate is mapped, one by one, to a Windows user account. Some certificates may be mapped to a shared user account, or each certificate may be mapped to an individual user account. When the certificate is presented to IIS 7.0, it logs on the corresponding user.

❑   **Many-to-One Client Mapping** — When this is enabled, multiple trusted user certificates are mapped to a single Windows user account. This is similar to the One-to-One mapping, but doesn't provide the fine-grained options of restricting certain users to certain parts of the web site. Instead, all certificates that are trusted will be permitted the same access. This option provides less flexibility but reduces administration.

❑   **Active Directory Mapping** — When enabled, certificates are passed to Active Directory. If the certificate has been explicitly assigned by a domain Administrator to a user within the directory, then that user is logged on. Alternatively, if the certificate contains a UPN (Universal Principal Name: user@domainA.local) that matches a UPN assigned to a user account in Active Directory, then that user is logged on.

One-to-One and Many-to-One client mappings are most useful when users accessing the site are external to your organization, or your organization does not have an internal PKI (Public Key Infrastructure). In this case, you must manually associate issued certificates with valid Windows users within your internal Active Directory domain or with valid local Windows users on the IIS 7.0 server.

Active Directory mapping is most suitable when your users are internal, and most useful when you have Active Directory Certificate Services (formerly Microsoft Certificate Services) deployed as an Enterprise (AD Integrated) Certificate Authority. Using Group Policy Objects (GPOs), users can automatically be enrolled for certificates, which are then also automatically associated with their Active Directory accounts. These certificates can then be automatically presented to IIS 7.0 and then user-authenticated.

Active Directory mapping cannot be used with either One-to-One or Many-to-One certificate mapping.

> *The Certificate Mapping Authentication module (authcert.dll) must be installed and enabled to use Active Directory certificate mapping authentication. This module is not installed by default using an interactive install. At the time of writing, IIS 7.0 supported enabling Active Directory certificate mapping only at the server level. Configuration at the web-site level should follow the same steps; however, users are advised to consult the released documentation prior to configuring this option.*

1. Open IIS Manager (Start ➪ Run, enter **intemgr** in the dialog, and then press [Enter]).

2. Locate the server or web site that you wish to configure Active Directory Certificate Mapping authentication for. Select the Authentication Feature option.

3. Select the Active Directory Client Certificate Authentication option, and click Enable in the Actions Pane to enable Active Directory Client Certificate authentication. Click Disable in the Actions Pane to disable Active Directory Client Certificate Authentication (if currently enabled).

Like Active Directory Certificate mapping, enabling One-to-One or Many-to-One certificate mapping requires that the web site in question be SSL/TLS-enabled. Steps for requesting and installing a server authentication certificate for SSL/TLS are covered in Chapter 15.

> *At the time of writing, there is no mechanism in IIS Manager to enable or configure One-to-One or Many-to-One certificate mapping. You are advised to consult the released documentation for precise steps on configuring this option. The steps presented below are based on enabling this functionality in IIS 6.0. A programmatic mechanism for enabling this feature is presented subsequently. The IIS Certificate Mapping Authentication module (authmap.dll) must be installed and enabled to use Active Directory certificate mapping authentication. This module is not installed by default using an interactive install.*

1. Open IIS Manager (Start ➪ Run, enter **intemgr** in the dialog, and then press [Enter]).

2. Locate the server or web site that you wish to configure Certificate Mapping authentication for. Select the Authentication Feature option.

3. Select the IIS Client Certificate Authentication option, and click Enable in the Actions pane to enable Client Certificate authentication. Click Disable in the Actions pane to disable Client Certificate authentication (if currently enabled).

4. Click the Configure link to configure mapping between certificates and users. For each user, click the Add button. Browse to the location on the disk where a copy of the user's certificate (.cer file)

is stored and click OK. For the given certificate, enter the Windows username and password that should be logged on when the certificate is presented.

5. Click OK to exit the dialog.

Enabling One-to-One Certificate mapping can be accomplished using the following VBScript code snippet:

```
Set objAdmin = CreateObject("Microsoft.ApplicationHost.WritableAdminManager")
Set objIISCertMap = objAdmin.GetAdminSection( _
"system.webServer/security/authentication/" & _
"iisClientCertificateMappingAuthentication", _
" machine/webroot/apphost/Default Web Site")
objIISCertMap.Properties.Item("enabled").Value = "true"
objIISCertMap.Properties.Item("oneToOneCertificateMappingsEnabled").Value = "true"
```

Adding a Client Certificate to user mapping (with a Base64-encoded .cer file) can be accomplished by the following:

```
' Set variable values here
' Can be supplied via argument scripts, or read from a file
strUser = "DomainA\User1"
strPassword = "Password1"
' Supply contents of Base64 encoded .cer file or read .cer file in using
' the File System Object
strCertificate = "xxxxxxxxxxxxxxx"

Set objAdmin = CreateObject("Microsoft.ApplicationHost.WritableAdminManager")
Set objIISCertMap = objAdmin.GetAdminSection( _
"system.webServer/security/authentication/" & _
"iisClientCertificateMappingAuthentication", _
" machine/webroot/apphost/Default Web Site")
Set obj1t1MappingsElement = objIISCertMap.ChildElements.Item("oneToOneMappings")
Set objMapping = obj1t1MappingsElement.collection.createNewElement()
objMapping.Properties.Item("username").Value = strUser
objMapping.Properties.Item("password").Value = strPassword
objMapping.Properties.Item("certificate").Value = strCertificate
objMapping.Properties.Item("enabled").Value = true
obj1t1MappingsElement.Collection.AddElement(objMapping)
objAdmin.CommitChanges()
```

As no documentation or GUI configuration options exist at the time of writing for configuring this feature, you are advised to consult the Windows Server 2008 documentation released with the product on the exact requirements and steps for enabling and configuring Client Certificate authentication.

Configuring Forms-Based Authentication

Forms-based authentication (FBA) is a non-HTTP-based mechanism for authenticating users. Instead of using HTTP headers, users are redirected to a normal HTML page that contains form elements (such as textboxes) where they can enter credentials. Upon submitting the form, back-end .NET code will process the credentials against a pre-configured user store (for example, Active Directory, an XML file or database). If the user is authenticated, a cookie is set that permits access to further pages.

Although IIS Manager offers an option to configure FBA, this feature is still truly an ASP.NET feature, which has been available with the .NET Framework since v1 was released in 2002. All settings are stored in the `<system.web>` configuration section rather than IIS 7.0's `<system.webServer>` section. Traditionally, ASP.NET's FBA feature has been used in conjunction with ASP.NET's URL authorization feature. This option is still available in IIS 7.0. However, IIS 7.0 now contains a native (non-managed) URL Authorization module as well. The native URL authorization module can be used for requests for all resources (both ASP.NET and other files), whereas the managed .NET URL Authorization module can only be used, by default, when a request is for a .NET resource (similar to how this functionality worked in IIS 5.0 and IIS 6.0)

Although IIS Manager exposes options to configure FBA settings, , if you wish to configure ASP.NET authorization rules, you must still edit ASP.NET configuration files. The following table summaries the main configuration items required to enable FBA:

Configuration Item	Exposed in IIS Manager	Description
Enabling/Disabling FBA	Yes	Enables or disables FBA.
Configuring the Login URL and authentication cookie setting	Yes	The page to which users should be redirected can be configured in IIS Manager, as can various security settings for the authentication cookie.
Users	No	Users must be defined so that access rules (to permit or deny access) can be configured. This must be done manually.
Roles	No	Users can be grouped into roles (similar to groups), and access can be permitted or denied based on role membership. This must be configured manually.
Provider details	No	Configuration information must be provided that tells the FBA module where to look (for example, XML file, SQL database) for user and role information. This must be configured manually.
Access Rules	No	Access rules must be configured that permit or deny access to specified users or roles. This must be configured manually.

FBA is most useful in situations in which a web-site creator does not have the ability to set NTFS permissions or create/delete Windows users accounts, such as in a hosting scenario. FBA provides developers with the ability to configure authentication and authorization rules based simply on ASP.NET configuration files and, optionally, a database to store user and role details.

You are encouraged to examine the IIS 7.0 URL authorization feature as an alternative to ASP.NET's URL Authorization features. The two URL Authorization options are discussed later in this chapter, in the Authorization section.

Forms-Based Authentication

You can configure FBA at a server, web-site, folder (including virtual directories), or file level. You must be an Administrator on the server or have delegated permissions to enable FBA for the node in question.

*The use of FBA requires that Anonymous authentication be enabled. As login credentials need to be entered on an HTML form, forcing HTTP-based authentication will prevent the user from ever being able to load the form unless the user also has a set of Windows credentials. The Forms authentication module (*System.Web.Security.FormsAuthenticationModule*) must be installed and enabled to allow FBA. This module is not installed by default using an interactive install.*

To configure FBA:

1. Open IIS Manager (Start ⇨ Run, enter **intemgr** in the dialog, and then press [Enter]).

2. Locate the server, web site, folder, or file that you wish to configure FBA for. Select the Authentication Feature option.

3. Select the Forms-Based Authentication option, and click Enable in the Actions pane to enable FBA. Click Disable in the Actions pane to disable FBA (if currently enabled).

4. Click the Edit link to edit configuration information for FBA. You can specify the following items in the options dialog box (see Figure 14-13):

    a. **Login URL** — This is the page to which users will be redirected to enter their credentials.

    b. **Cookie Time-out** — After the set period of inactivity (no requests from the browser), the user will need to reauthenticate.

    c. **Cookie Mode** — Allows the Administrator to choose whether to use cookies, store authentication information in the URL, allow .NET to detect whether the device supports cookies via Javascript, or assume cookie support based on the browser's user-agent string (this is the default setting).

    d. **Cookie Name**.

    e. Require SSL for requests.

    f. Whether to use a **sliding cookie renewal** or not. When using sliding renewal, each request resets the cookie time-out setting. If sliding renewal is disabled, the user will have to reauthenticate regardless of whether they are active or inactive when the cookie times out.

5. Click OK to commit changes and exit the dialog.

FBA settings are stored in the ASP.NET configuration section. This can either be the machine-wide root web.config *file or in the* <system.web> *section of a web site's or web application's* web.config *file. FBA settings are not stored in IIS configuration files or sections.*

By default, Forms Based Authentication applies only to requests for files managed by .NET (e.g. ASPX pages), and not to other types of files (e.g. static files). To alter this configuration, so that Forms Based Authentication is used for all file types:

1. Open IIS Manager (Start ⇨ Run, enter **intemgr** in the dialog, and then press [Enter]).

2. Locate the server node, and open the Modules feature.

3. Double click the FormsAuthentication module, and deselect the "Invoke only for requests to ASP.NET applications or managed handlers" option.

4. Click OK to commit your changes, and exit the dialogue boxes.

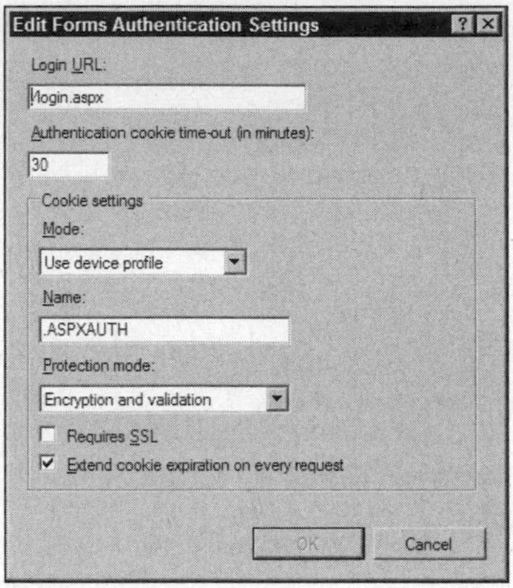

Figure 14-13

This option can be altered in the `applicationHost.config` file by removing the `managedHandler` precondition for the FormsAuthentication module:

```
<add name="FormsAuthentication" type="System.Web.Security.FormsAuthenticationModule"
preCondition="managedHandler" />
```

Configuring Delegation

Delegation is a process by which a server (in this case IIS) can send the user's credentials to another back-end server (for example, to a back-end SQL Server or file server). This may be useful in situations in which the user's credentials should be checked against the access control list (ACL) maintained by the back-end server.

Configuring delegation can be difficult because what's required to be configured depends on what authentication mechanism the client is using. The following table summarizes the major implications:

Authentication Mechanism	User Account Used by IIS	Delegation Configuration
Anonymous	IUSR for non-ASP.NET content. Application pool identity (Network Service) for ASP.NET content	machinename$ account used to access back-end services.

Authentication Mechanism	User Account Used by IIS	Delegation Configuration
Basic	End-user for non-ASP.NET content. Application pool identity (Network Service) for ASP.NET content	IIS has user's username and password in cleartext. Can log on directly as the end-user for remote content. Enable Impersonation for ASP.NET to have .NET access back-end resources as the end-user.
Digest, NTLM	End-user for non-ASP.NET content. Application pool identity (Network Service) for ASP.NET content	IIS does not have user's password. Cannot access back-end resources (except as machinename$) unless protocol transition is configured.
Kerberos	End-user for non-ASP.NET content. Application pool identity (Network Service) for ASP.NET content	Can access back-end content as end-user if Kerberos delegation is configured. Enable Impersonation for ASP.NET to have .NET access back-end resources as end-user.
FBA	IUSR for non-ASP.NET content. Application pool identity (Network Service) for ASP.NET content	In ASP.NET code, impersonate a Windows principal in order to access back-end resources as that user.

This section concentrates on configuring delegation to enable Kerberos-authenticated clients to delegate to back-end services. For NTLM-and Digest-authenticated users, protocol transition enables the IIS server to obtain a Kerberos ticket for a back-end service even though the initial authentication mechanism (from client to IIS) was not Kerberos. The next section focuses on enabling protocol transition.

ASP.NET separates out authentication and impersonation. Although you can configure Windows authentication as an authentication option in ASP.NET, all code still runs as the application pool's identity (Network Service, by default) unless you also enable impersonation. Once you enable impersonation, the end-user's credentials can be delegated to back-end services. For ASP or static files, impersonation occurs automatically.

In a Kerberos delegation scenario, the following takes place (Figure 14-15):

1. The client browser supplies a Kerberos service ticket to the web server. The process that happens in obtaining a service ticket was described above and shown in Figure 14-9.

2. The HTTP service, seeing the need to open a connection to SQL Server using the end-user's credentials, obtains the necessary ticket from the KDC.

3. The KDC returns a ticket if the HTTP service is permitted to delegate.

4. The server opens the connection, sending the ticket obtained from the KDC.

5. The SQL Server permits the connection to be opened or returns an error indicating that the user is not permitted to log in to the SQL Server.

6. The web server returns the web page to the end-user.

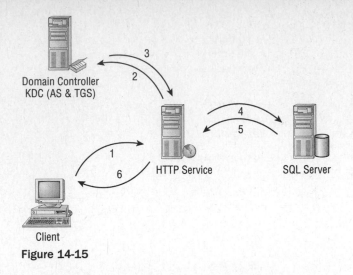

Figure 14-15

To configure delegation requires some configuration within Active Directory. Specifically, the HTTP service must be permitted to delegate, and the end-user's account must not be configured to be non-delegatable.

To configure an IIS server to be permitted to delegate:

1. Open the Active Directory Users and Computers MMC tool.

2. Locate the computer account corresponding to the IIS server (or user account if you are running the worker process hosting the web site under a custom user account).

3. Right-click and choose Properties. Open the Delegation tab (see Figure 14-16).

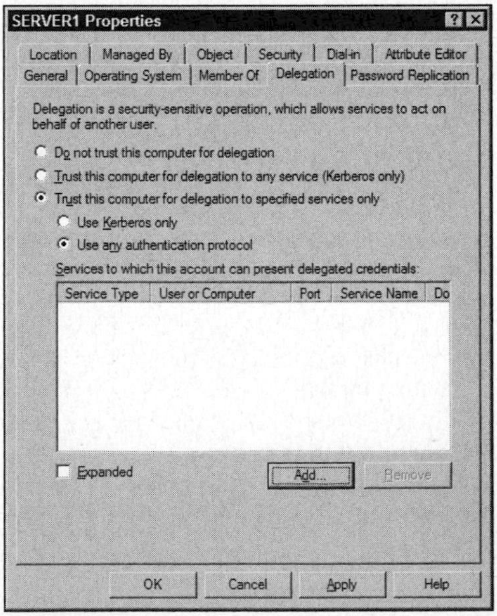

Figure 14-16

4. The "Trust this computer for delegation to any service (Kerberos only)" option corresponds to what was known as *unconstrained delegation*. If the domain functional level is Windows 2000 or Mixed Mode, then this is the only option. The IIS server will be able to delegate to any back-end server; however, protocol transition will not be available. Protocol transition is discussed in the next section.

5. The "Trust this computer for delegation to specified services only" option is a more secure option (because it limits what back-end services this server may attempt to gain access to). The sub-option ("Use any authentication protocol") is what allows protocol transition.

6. Select this option, and click Add to add back-end services that the IIS server should be permitted to delegate to.

7. Enter the machine account name (if the back-end service is running under a built-in principal such as LocalSystem or Network Service) or user account name (if the back-end service is running under a custom account), and click OK to retrieve a list of registered SPNs. For a back-end Microsoft SQL Server, this will be MSSQLSvr. Click OK to add the service (see Figure 14-17).

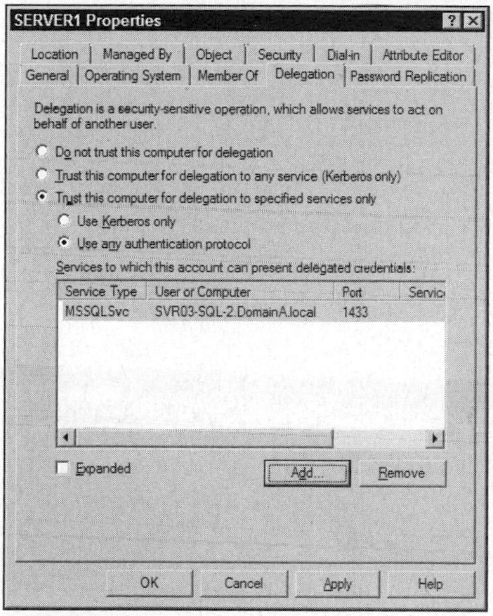

Figure 14-17

8. Lastly, verify that any users that should be able to authenticate are not marked as non-delegatable. To do this, locate the user accounts in Active Directory, right-click and choose Properties. On the Account tab, ensure that the "Account is sensitive and cannot be delegated" option is *not* checked (by default, it is not checked), as shown in Figure 14-18. If this checkbox is checked, delegation for that user account is not possible.

There is an additional configuration step required if:

❑ You are accessing an ASP.NET resource (for example, an .aspx page);

and

❑ The resource is hosting in a web application pool running in Integrated Pipeline mode.

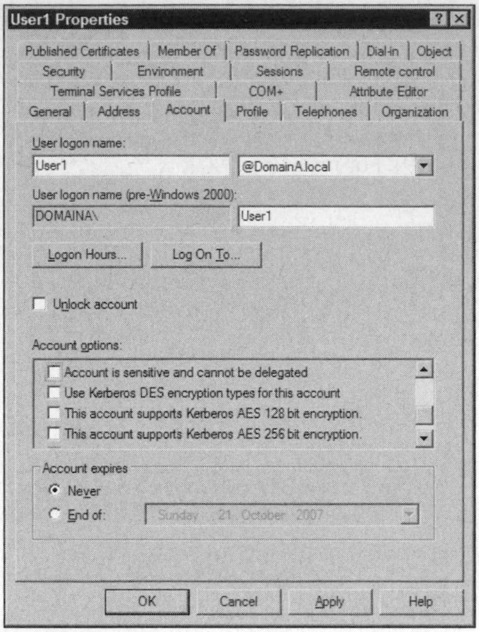

Figure 14-18

In this situation, it is required that you configure <identity impersonation="true" /> for your ASP.NET application. This permits your ASP.NET application to impersonate the end-user and, furthermore, to use those credentials to access the back-end resource.

However, in order for this to work when using the new Integrated Pipeline mode, the validateIntegratedModeConfiguration setting must be disabled. If this setting is enabled, then a 500.24 HTTP status will be sent to the client. This error is thrown because authentication occurs after the BeginRequest and AuthenticateRequest events, and identity impersonation cannot occur during those two events.

You can use AppCmd to disable the validateIntegratedModeConfiguration setting. This setting can be configured for the server, a web site, or an individual web application. For example, to disable this setting for a web application called *Webapp1* located on a web site called *Website1*, run the following command:

```
appcmd.exe config set "Website1/Webapp1" /section:validation
/validateIntegratedModeConfiguration:false
```

As mentioned in the earlier section on configuring Kerberos authentication, service principal names (SPNs) must be correctly registered for the accessed web application. Additionally, when using delegation, correct SPNs must also be registered for the back-end services so that IIS 7.0 can obtain the necessary service tickets. For a product such as Microsoft SQL Server, default SPNs are registered when installing the product. For third-party applications, you might need to register an SPN manually.

Configuring Protocol Transition

First implemented in Windows Server 2003, *protocol transition* is a feature that allows a client to authenticate to IIS 7.0 using a protocol other than Kerberos (for example, NTLM or Digest). By utilizing Services for User to Self (S4U2S) and Services for User to Proxy (S4U2P), IIS 7.0 is able to get a Kerberos ticket to the back-end service (Figure 14-19). For more information on S4U2P and S4U2S, see `http://adopen-static.com/cs/blogs/ken/archive/2007/07/19/8460.aspx`.

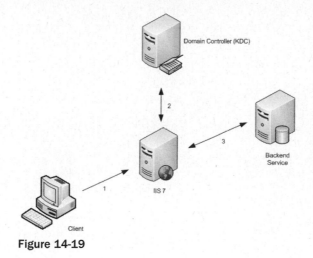

Figure 14-19

In the scenario depicted in Figure 14-19:

1. The client authenticates to IIS 7.0 using an HTTP authentication protocol other than Kerberos (for example, NTLM or Digest authentication).

2. IIS 7.0 obtains a Kerberos ticket on behalf of the user. The process for obtaining Kerberos tickets is discussed above.

3. The IIS 7.0 server authenticates to the back-end server application using Kerberos. The back-end service must support Kerberos authentication.

In a default IIS 7.0 configuration, nothing additional needs to be configured in IIS 7.0 to support protocol transition. The only configuration that is required is on your domain controllers. To support protocol transition, the domain functional level must be Windows Server 2003 or higher. Additionally, protocol transition relies on constrained delegation. This requires that the IIS 7.0 server and back-end server be in the same domain. The client can be in any trusted domain or forest.

To configure Active Directory for protocol transition, ensure that required SPNs are registered, as discussed previously. Then, to configure IIS 7.0 to support protocol transition:

1. Open the Active Directory Users and Computers MMC tool.

2. Locate the computer account corresponding to the IIS server (or user account, if you are running the worker process hosting the web site under a custom user account).

3. Right-click and choose Properties. Open the Delegation tab.

4. Select the "Trust this computer for delegation to specified services only" option, and ensure that the "Use Any Protocol" sub-option is also selected.

5. Click Add to add back-end services that the IIS server should be permitted to delegate to.

6. Enter the machine account name (if the back-end service is running under a built-in principal such as LocalSystem or Network Service) or user account name (if the back-end service is running under a custom account), and click OK to retrieve a list of registered SPNs. For a back-end Microsoft SQL Server, this will be MSSQLSvr. Click OK to add the service (refer to Figure 14-17).

After you have configured these options, users will be able to authenticate to IIS 7.0 using any HTTP authentication protocol, and have IIS 7.0 pass their credentials to the supported back-end services.

Configuring Authorization

As mentioned above, authentication and authorization are discrete steps in determining the final response to be sent to the end-user. The authorization process occurs after the user has been authenticated and involves determining if the user has access to the resource or not. Typically, the resources accessed are files on a hard disk (or possibly a database), and NTFS permissions are used to control access. Once the end-user has been determined, NTFS permissions then determine if the user is able to access the resource in the requested way.

Depending on how the user authenticated, how IIS 7.0 is configured, and what type of resource the user is attempting to access, the actual user account being used is different!

The following table summarizes the common accounts used:

Authentication Mechanism	User Account Being Used by IIS
Anonymous	IUSR for non-ASP.NET content. Application pool identity (Network Service) for ASP.NET content.
HTTP (Basic, Digest, NTLM, Kerberos)	End-user for non-ASP.NET content. Application pool identity (Network Service) for ASP.NET content.
URL authorization	IUSR for non-ASP.NET content. Application pool identity (Network Service) for ASP.NET content.

The IUSR account is used for non-ASP.NET content unless the Application Pool Identity option is configured. See "Configuring Anonymous Authentication" above in this chapter for more information on this setting.

Configuring NTFS permissions to permit (or deny) access can be done using various tools. The Explorer shell provides a useful mechanism for one-off changes. Alternatively, for many changes or on Windows Server 2008 Core edition, you can use the icacls.exe command-line tool.

To be able to load web pages, images, or similar resources, NTFS Read permissions are required. For CGI applications, Execute permissions are required. If your application permits users to upload files (or you are using an authoring technology like WebDAV), then Write permissions are required.

If you are using FBA/ASP.NET URL Authorization or native IIS 7.0 URL authorization, authorization rules are stored in ASP.NET configuration files and IIS configuration files, respectively. For more information on adding, editing, or removing those configuration file entries, see "URL Authorization" later in this chapter.

To alter NTFS permissions using Explorer:

1. Open an Explorer window, navigate to the file or folder that you want to set permissions on, right-click, and choose Properties. Select the Security tab (see Figure 14-20).

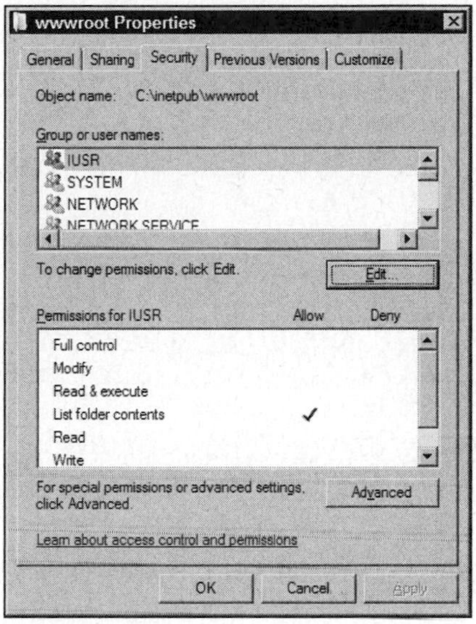

Figure 14-20

2. Click the Edit button to alter permissions. To alter permissions for an existing user or group, select the user or group in the top panel, and check or uncheck permissions checkboxes in the lower panel.

3. To add a new user or group, click the Add button and enter the user or group to add.

4. Click the Advanced button to configure advanced properties, such as propagating changes to all subfolders, enabling auditing, or changing the ownership of the file or folder.

5. Click OK to confirm the changes and exit the dialog.

The `icacls.exe` command-line tool can be used to configure NTFS permissions. It can be used to export permissions for an existing file/folder or configure permissions on an existing file/folder. For example, to grant Read/Execute permissions to User1 to File1.txt, the following command would be used:

```
icacls.exe file1.txt /grant:DomainA\User1:(RX)
```

For more information on using `icacls.exe`, type **icacls.exe /?** at a command prompt.

URL Authorization

URL authorization is a feature in IIS 7.0 that can be used to permit or deny access to resources, by storing access rules in a data store (such as an XML file or database), rather than relying on traditional NTFS permissions.

IIS 7.0 ships with two URL authorization modules. The first is a managed module, which provides the same functionality as ASP.NET has provided when installed with previous versions of IIS, By default, this module is added in applicationHost.Config (in the default <modules> section), and by default, applies only to requests for .NET managed file extensions:

```
<add name="UrlAuthorization" type="System.Web.Security.UrlAuthorizationModule"
preCondition="managedHandler" />
```

IIS 7.0 also ships with a new, native code module, which also implements URL-based authorization. This module is also added in the applicationHost.config file but in the <globalModules> section:

```
<add name="UrlAuthorizationModule" image="%windir%\System32\inetsrv\urlauthz.dll" />
```

The native URL Authorization module applies to all requests, whether they be for .NET managed file or other types of files (e.g. static files or ASP files). Additionally, the IIS Manager MMC console provides a graphical interface for configuring this native URL Authorization module.

> *If you are using the Authorization Manager (AzMan) features in IIS 6.0, URL authorization provides enhanced functionality, over the AzMan implementation in IIS 6.0*

Both URL Authorization mechanisms can be used to secure access to resources through the alteration of configuration stores (e.g. XML files or a database). This makes URL Authorization a viable way of securing access to resources when the site administrator is unable to directly set NTFS permissions (e.g., in a hosting scenario).

Additionally, URL Authorization mechanisms can be used any of the various authentication mechanisms. This means that Forms Based Authentication or some form of HTTP-based authentication, or even Client Certificate Authentication can be combined with a URL Authorization module to permit or deny access to users.

Configuring the Managed (ASP.NET) URL Authorization Module

Configuration of the managed (ASP.NET) URL Authorization module requires editing web.config configuration files – the IIS Manager MMC console does not provide a graphical mechanism for configuring this option. As this functionality is provided by ASP.NET, and hasn't changed with the release of IIS 7.0, you are advised to consult existing ASP.NET v2.0 documentation on how to configure this option. For those new to ASP.NET URL Authorization, a basic overview is provided in the ASP.NET v2.0 QuickStart: http://quickstarts.asp.net/QuickStartv20/aspnet/doc/security/authorization.aspx. More detailed information can be found in the .NET v3.5 SDK: http://msdn2.microsoft.com/en-us/library/wce3kxhd.aspx

> *ASP.NET URL Authorization settings are stored in the ASP.NET configuration section. This can either be the machine-wide root* web.config *file or in the* <system.web> *section of a web site's or web application's* web.config *file. These settings are not stored in IIS configuration files or sections.*

Configuring the Native (IIS 7.0) URL Authorization Module

Fully configuring the native URL Authorization feature is beyond the scope of this book, as URL Authorization can leverage the ASP.NET membership providers to access user and role information in multiple different data stores (e.g. a database, Active Directory, or other authentication store). The steps below involve functionality native to IIS 7.0—rules are stored in IIS 7.0 configuration files. For the more advanced option of using ASP.NET's membership provider model, information on configuring membership providers can be found on the ASP.NET website: http://www.asp.net.

URL Authorization can be configured at a server, web-site, folder (including virtual directories), or file level. You must be an Administrator on the server or have delegated permissions to enable URL authorization for the node in question.

> *The URL Authentication module (urlauthz.dll) must be installed and enabled to allow URL authorization. This module is not installed by default using an interactive install.*

To configure URL authorization:

1. Open IIS Manager (Start ➪ Run, enter **intemgr** in the dialog, and then press [Enter]).

2. Locate the server, web site, folder, or file that you wish to configure URL authorization for. Select the Authorization Rules Feature option.

3. Select the Add Allow Rule from the Actions pane to configure a new permitted access rule. Access can be permitted to any request (including users who have not authenticated), only authenticated users, authenticated users within specific roles, or only specific users (see Figure 14-14).

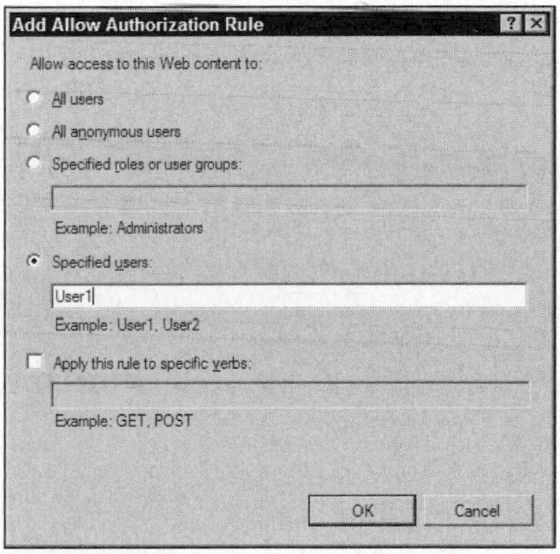

Figure 14-14

4. Optionally, restrict the HTTP verbs that this rule applies to. Click OK to add the rule.

5. To configure a Deny rule, select the Add Deny Rule from the Actions pane.

> *Rules are stored in the IIS configuration file in the order that they were created. Access is either permitted or denied based on the first rule that matches the user's request. It may be necessary to manually reorder rules within the* applicationHost.config *or* web.config *file to gain the desired access rules behavior.*

6. Select the Users or Roles links to configure users or roles. To add a Windows Domain user account, specify Domainname\Username. To specify a local Windows account, use Servername\Username. For other, non Windows accounts, simply use the defined username.

7. Click OK to exit the dialog.

A membership provider must have been configured before users and roles can be managed in an alternative store to IIS 7.0's native configuration files. The default role provider with IIS allows for a connection to a local SQL Server Express database that contains a specially created database suitable for storing users and roles for URL authorization. To create and configure this SQL Server express database, use the `aspnet_regsql.exe` *tool located in the* `%systemdriver%\Microsoft.Net\Framework\ v2.0.50727\` *folder.*

Configuring Application Pool Sandboxing

In previous versions of IIS, it has sometimes been difficult to isolate web application pools from each other. If multiple web application pools are configured to run as the same identity (for example, Network Service), then code running inside one web application pool would be able to use File System objects to access configuration files, web pages, and similar resources belonging to another web application pool. This was because it was impossible to allow one process running as Network Service access to a file, but prevent another process also running as Network Service access to the same file.

In IIS 7.0, it is possible, with some work, to prevent this from occurring. As part of IIS 7.0 built-in functionality, each web application pool has an application pool configuration file generated on-the-fly when that application pool is started. These are stored, by default, in the `%systemdriver\inetpub\temp\appPools` folder. Each web application pool has an additional SID (Security Identifier) generated for it, and this is injected into the relevant `w3wp.exe` process. The application pool's configuration file is ACLed to allow only that SID access. Since each `w3wp.exe` process has its own SID, each application pool's configuration file is ACLed to a different SID. Figure 14-21 illustrates the process.

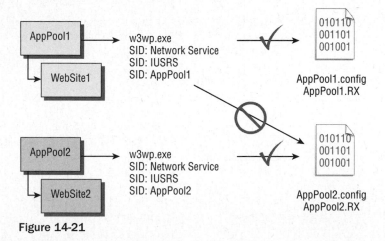

Figure 14-21

You can use the `icacls.exe` tool, as follows, to determine the SID applied to any given application pool's configuration file:

```
icacls.exe %systemdrive%\inetpub\temp\appPools\appPool.config /save output.txt
```

The retrieved SID can now be used to secure web-site content in the same way. To do this:

1. Configure each web site (or web application) to run in its own web application pool.

2. Configure Anonymous authentication to use the application pool identity rather than the IUSR account. See "Configuring Anonymous Authentication" above in this chapter for more information.

3. Remove NTFS permissions for the IUSRS group and the IUSR account from the web site's files and folders.

4. Use the `icacls.exe` tool to permit the retrieved SID Read (and optionally, Execute and Write) access to the web site's files and folders.

After configuring these NTFS permissions, only the SID that has been injected into a particular `w3wp.exe` process will be able to read the contents of the web site in question. All code running in other `w3wp.exe` processes, even though the process identity may also be "Network Service," will be unable to read this particular web site's content.

This technique may be most useful to web hosters or similar administrators that need to accept content from various external or distrusted parties.

Understanding IIS 7.0 User Accounts

User accounts are greatly simplified in IIS 7.0. Because IIS 5.0-style application hosting is no longer supported, previously used accounts such as IWAM_*<machinename>* and `aspnet_wp.exe` no longer exist.

Additionally, the Anonymous User account (previously IUSR_*<machinename>*) is now a well-known security identity called *IUSR*. This means that this account has the same name and the same SID (Security Identifier) on all IIS 7.0 machines.

> *The IUSR_<machinename> account will still be created if you install the legacy FTP Server. It is not created if you install the new FTP 7 server. For more information on FTP, see Chapter 10.*

Lastly, the IIS_WPG group introduced with IIS 6.0 has been replaced with the IIS_IUSRS group. In IIS 6.0, accounts that would be used as web application pool identities needed to be placed into the IIS_WPG group by an administrator. In IIS 7.0, by default, any account configured as a web application pool identity is automatically and dynamically added to the IUSRS group, if required.

> *You can disable this behavior and stop an application identity from being automatically added to the IIS_IUSRS group by editing the configuration for that application pool, as follows:*

```
<applicationPools>
    <add name="DefaultAppPool">
        <processModel manualGroupMembership="true" />
```

```
        </add>
    </applicationPools >
```

This configuration prevents the identity of the DefaultAppPool application pool from automatically being added to the IIS_IUSRS group.

The following table summarizes the user and logon rights granted to the accounts natively used by IIS 7.0. The IUSR account is not specifically listed, as it has no rights specifically assigned to it. Instead, it inherits rights from the default Users group.

The LocalSystem account is used to run IIS 7.0 services, and is also an option for application pool identities. The LocalSystem account has "Act as part of the operating system" privileges (which allows it unfettered access to Windows). It also has many other privileges by default (which are not listed individually below). Suffice to say that a process running as LocalSystem has almost full control over your server. Running application pools as *LocalSystem* is a security risk and needs to be carefully investigated prior to implementation.

Network Service is a low-privilege account and the default web application pool identity. Network Service is able to access network resources using the computer's machine account (machinename$). Local Service is similar to Network Service, but cannot access other resources on the network (except those that permit anonymous access).

	Local System	Network Service	Local Service	IIS_IUSRS
Act as part of the operating system (seTCBPrivilege).	x			
Adjust memory quotas for a process (seIncreaseQuotaPrivilege).		x	x	
Bypass Traverse Checking (seChangeNotifyPrivilege).		x	x	
Change the System Time (seSystemTimePrivilege).			x	
Change the Time Zone (seTimeZonePrivilege).			x	
Create Global Objects (seCreateGlobalPrivilege).		x	x	
Generate Security Audits (seAuditPrivilege).		x	x	
Impersonate a client after authentication (seImpersonatePrivilege).		x	x	x
Log on as a Batch Job.				x
Replace a process-level token (seAssignPrimaryTokenPrivilege).		x	x	

Summary

In this chapter we examined, in detail, the requirements and mechanisms for authenticating end-users. IIS 7.0 has a wealth of options, including traditional HTTP-based authentication (Basic, Digest, NTLM, and Kerberos), Client Certificate authentication, and non-HTTP-based authentication (anonymous and cookie-based techniques such as URL authorization).

Additionally, we looked at techniques that allow you to pass those credentials onto external back-end services via delegation.

After a user is authenticated, authorization is a discrete security step. Configuring authorization is relatively straightforward and typically involves configuring appropriate NTFS permissions. Alternatively, if you are using FBA or URL authorization, rules for permitting or denying access are stored in various configuration files.

By having a solid understanding of authentication and authorization, you are better able to secure your web applications. Security involves ensuring that legitimate users are permitted access, and non-permitted users are denied access. By understanding how to authenticate users and then give them the minimum access needed to perform their work, you ensure that the opportunities to maliciously attack your server are kept to a minimum.

The next chapter covers SSL (Secure Sockets Layer), TLS (Transport Layer Security), and briefly touches upon PKI (Public Key Infrastructure). Although we have covered securing the server and securing access to the server in Chapters 13 and 14, respectively, the next chapter covers securing data in transit between the client and server.

15

SSL and TLS

When looking at a strategy to secure your application server infrastructure, it is important to examine several discrete elements:

❑ Secure the actual server that the application is running on.

❑ Ensure that only permitted users of the application are able to access the allowed functionality (and that all other users, including malicious attackers, are denied access).

❑ Ensure that your users know they are connecting to the correct server, and, if required, secure traffic between the client and server.

In Chapters 13 and 14, we discuss many of the security options available with IIS 7.0. This chapter addresses security between the client and the server. Secure Sockets Layer (SSL) and Transport Layer Security (TLS) are industry standard technologies for authenticating machines (or users) and for encrypting traffic between two devices.

SSL is a technology originally developed by Netscape, with v2.0 being the first publicly available release. TLS is an IETF standard that is the successor to SSL, and the latest draft version is TLS v1.2. Currently, the terms "SSL" and "TLS" are used interchangeably in the popular press when discussing secured HTTP traffic. "TLS" is almost always used when discussing securing other protocols (such as FTP or SMTP).

TLS should be considered whenever there is a need to secure the transmission of data from eavesdropping attacks (including credentials) or to ensure message integrity (that data aren't altered in transit). Additionally, to ensure that the two parties in a conversation (the client and server) are able to trust each other's server (and optionally client), authentication is built into the TLS handshake process.

TLS is a Layer 4 protocol implementation. This typically means that the use of TLS requires the use of an alternate port. For example, when securing HTTP traffic, TLS-secured traffic operates on port 443, rather than port on 80, which is used for unsecured traffic. For internal applications, IPsec should also be considered. As this operates at Layer 3, the security provided by IPsec is transparent to applications, and no modification is required. Instead, routing devices and firewalls need to allow access for additional IP protocols. This is generally not an issue in internal networks.

Securing a Web Site with TLS

TLS uses X.509 certificates and asymmetric (public/private) key cryptography to establish the identity of the server (or client) and to securely encrypt traffic between the client and server. A handshake between the server and client is used to set up a secure session between the two machines. If at any point during the handshake a failure occurs, then either the session is not established or, in the case of recoverable errors, the user is warned of a potential issue and must manually choose to continue with the establishment of the session.

Since Windows Server 2003 SP1, administrators have been able to use kernel-mode SSL, utilizing functionality provided by `ksecdd.sys`*. This significantly cuts processing overhead involved in negotiating an SSL/TLS connection and in maintaining it during the session. When using kernel mode SSL/TLS, the overhead is approximately 10 percent of capacity to service requests. As the SSL/TLS handshake process is far more computationally intensive than the communication afterward, the greater the number of shorter sessions, the greater the impact on a server's performance.*

The SSL/TLS Handshake

The process by which a client and a server establish a secure connection is known as the *SSL/TLS handshake*. The handshake involves the verification of the server's identity (authentication) by the client, as well as a mutual agreement between client and server as to what encryption technologies (ciphers) should be used to secure the connection.

When a user requests a resource using the secured HTTPS URI, and assuming that the server is configured to support SSL/TLS, the client makes the request, indicating the various ciphers that it supports for securing the connection. The server, assuming that it also supports one of the ciphers indicated by the client, returns its certificate as the second step in the handshake.

The client typically performs several checks on this certificate before proceeding. Most browsers will perform all the following checks unless the default configuration is altered by the user. For non-browser clients (for example, automated tools), all, some, or none of these checks may be performed.

❑   The client compares the validity dates embedded in the certificate with the current system time. Each certificate is valid from a starting date to an ending date (typically a period of between 1 and 5 years). If the current client system date and time are outside the certificate's validity period, the user will be presented with a warning.

❑   The client compares the fully qualified domain name (FQDN) of the web site being accessed with the Common Name property of the certificate presented by the server. This helps mitigate DNS poisoning or DNS hijacking attacks, where an attacker may have redirected the DNS entry of a legitimate web site to a server that he or she controls. In such circumstances, the attacker is unlikely to also have a legitimately issued certificate that matches the DNS name.

❑ The client verifies that the certificate has been issued by a trusted certificate authority (CA) and that the certificate has not been tampered with. Each Windows machine stores a list of trusted root and subordinate (or intermediate) CAs. As the certificate presented by the remote server contains the name of the CA that issued the certificate, Windows first verifies that the name of the issuing CA matches one that the machine already trusts. The certificate also contains a verification hash that was generated by the issuing CA and embedded into the certificate. The client can use the public key embedded in the copy of the issuing CA's certificate that is stored on the machine to verify that the details in the certificate have not been altered. Because the hash is created using the issuing CA's signing certificate's private key, which is a secret known only to the CA, it is currently computationally infeasible for someone to create both a fake certificate and matching fake verification code.

Each version of Windows ships with a built-in list of commercial third-party trusted CAs. Deploying Windows Server 2008 Active Directory Certificate Services (formerly known as Windows Certificate Services) in Enterprise mode results in domain-joined clients automatically trusting that CA. Administrators can also manually add trusted CAs (for example, for partner organizations).

To view a list of installed trusted CAs:

1. Click Start ➪ Run, enter **mmc.exe**, and then press [Enter].

2. Choose File ➪ Add/Remove Snapin.

3. Select Certificates and click Add (on Windows Vista), or click Add and then choose Certificates (on Windows XP or Windows Server 2003).

   A prompt will appear offering a selection of the current user's account, a nominated service account, or the machine's account. Each account has its own store of certificates. In a default configuration, the list of trusted root CAs is the same between all options. Select My User Account.

4. Click Finish and OK to exit the Add/Remove Snapin dialog, and then expand the Trusted Root Certification Authorities node to view a list of installed trusted root CAs, as shown in Figure 15-1.

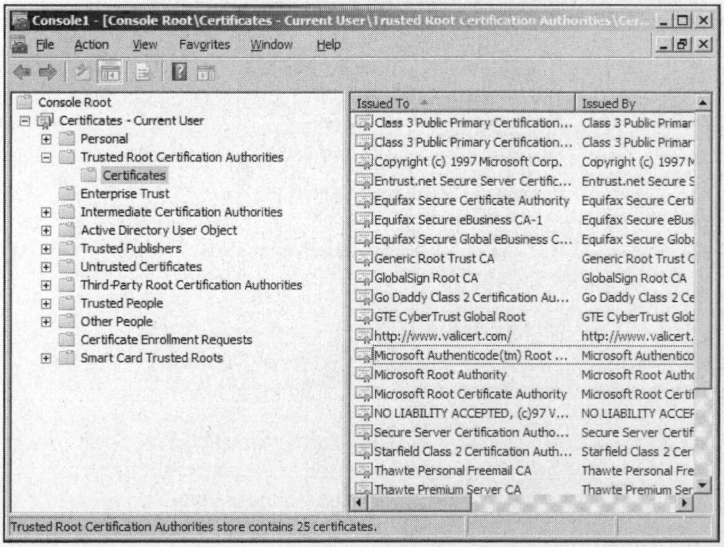

Figure 15-1

Depending on the client operating system, the user may be presented with a variety of error messages if one of these checks fails. Clients such as Windows XP and Windows Server 2003 running the default Internet Explorer 6 browser show the error message shown in Figure 15-2 when connecting to a web site with a nonmatching common name in the certificate.

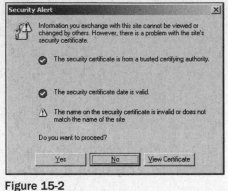

Figure 15-2

Figure 15-3 shows the error message when the certificate is issued by an untrusted CA.

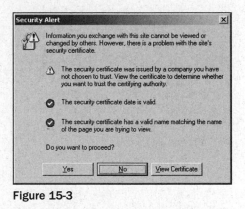

Figure 15-3

For users of Windows Vista or Windows Server 2008 that ship with Internet Explorer 7, the error message is indicated in the first line of gray text, when encountering a web site with a certificate error, as shown in Figure 15-4.

Assuming that the certificate passes the three standard checks, or that the user decides to continue to the site despite the warning, the next steps in the TLS handshake are as follows:

1. The client may optionally contact the CA to determine if the server's certificate has been revoked. A CA can choose to publish a certificate revocation list (CRL), which is used to list certificates that are no longer valid (for example, if they were incorrectly issued in the first place, or a server hosting a certificate has been compromised). Internet Explorer 7 will check published CRLs in a default configuration.

2. If the server's certificate has not been revoked, or the client chooses not to verify the certificate against a published CRL, the client will then generate a random numeric value to be used as the basis for cryptographic work involved in this particular session. Specifically, what is generated depends on the cipher to be used to secure the session.

3. The client extracts the server's public key from the server's certificate and encrypts the generated random numeric value. Because certificates use asymmetric key (private/public key pairs) cryptography, only the server can decrypt this value, using its secret private key.

4. Both the client and the server use the generated random numeric values as a shared secret that is used to derive encryption keys needed for the session (what keys specifically need to be generated depends on the cryptographic ciphers that both client and server support). In general, symmetric keys are generated and used by both client and server. Symmetric keys are used because the overhead incurred when encrypting and decrypting data is far less than when using asymmetric (public/private) key pairs.

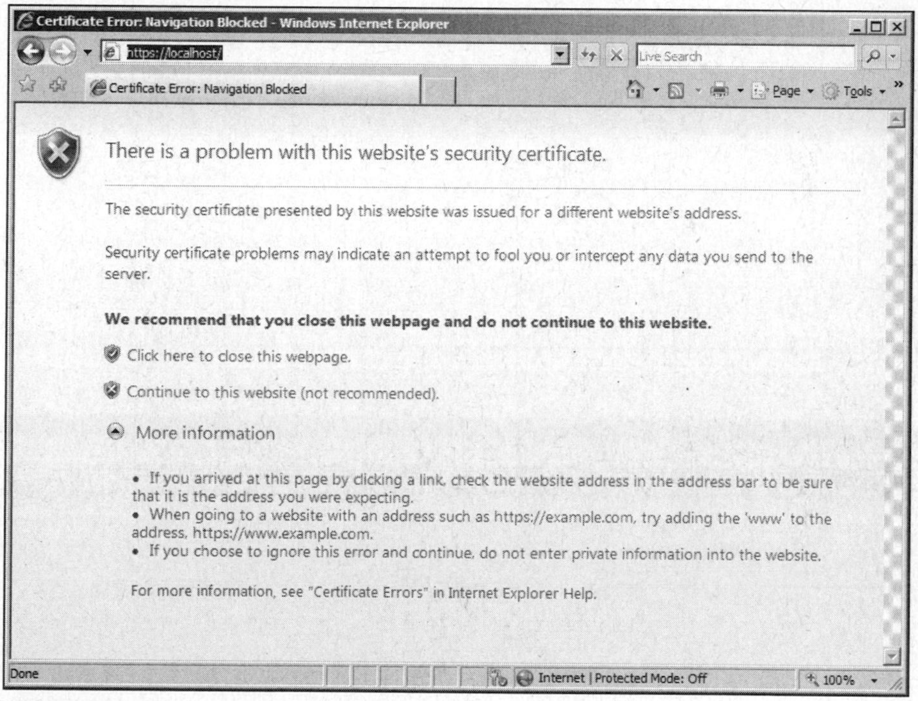

Figure 15-4

Once this exchange has been completed, the SSL/TLS handshake is completed for this session. Information exchange between the client and the server is now encrypted and considered secure against both interception (eavesdropping) and man-in-the-middle attacks.

Generating a Certificate Request

The first step in making content available over HTTPS is to generate a *certificate request*. This request can be submitted to a CA, which will, in turn, generate a certificate that can be installed on the server.

Alternatively, in the absence of a separate CA, a self-signed certificate can be generated. Here the server signs its own certificate; however, such certificates are generally only used for development or testing purposes as no other machines trust the signer of the certificate by default.

IIS Manager provides three options for generating a certificate request:

❑ A certificate request can be generated as a file that is manually submitted to a CA. This method would be used to request a certificate from a third-party CA, or if there is a CA within the organization that is not Active Directory–integrated, or is not otherwise directly contactable by the IIS server.

❑ A certificate request can be generated by IIS 7.0 that is automatically submitted directly to an Active Directory–integrated installation of Active Directory Certificate Services (known as *Microsoft Certificate Services* in Windows Server 2003 and earlier). The Request Domain Certificate option in IIS Manager provides this functionality.

❑ IIS 7.0 can automatically generate a self-signed certificate. Previously, an IIS 6.0 Resource Kit tool (SelfSSL.exe) could be used to create a self-signed certificate. In IIS 7.0, this facility is built into the user interface.

Each of these possible mechanisms for generating a certificate request is discussed in turn below. Full steps for generating a certificate request to send manually to a CA are detailed. For the other, alternate mechanisms for requesting a certificate, only the steps that are different are detailed.

Certificates and certificate requests can only be configured at a server level. Once a certificate has been installed, it can then be configured for use at a web-site level. You must be an Administrator on the IIS server (or delegated permissions to manage the whole IIS server) to be able to generate a certificate request.

To create a certificate request to send to a CA, perform the following steps:

1. Open IIS Manager.

2. At the server-level node, select the Server Certificates option. A list of existing installed server authentication certificates is presented. If the IIS 7.0 Remote Management service is installed, a self-signed certificate issued to WMSvc-<*servername*> will be listed, as this certificate is used to secure connections to the Remote Management service.

3. Select Create Certificate Request to begin the certificate request generation process.

4. Enter the details for the certificate that you want to generate, as shown in Figure 15-5. The Common Name property should be filled in with the server name (either a NetBIOS name or FQDN) that the web site will be answering requests on. If the server's name in the URL being requested by a client does not match the common name in the certificate presented by the server, the client will show an error to the user (refer to Figure 15-4).

   The remaining fields should be filled in according to the legal status of your organization. Depending on the CA you submit this request to and the type of certificate you are requesting, the CA may verify these details before issuing you a certificate.

   Click Next to continue.

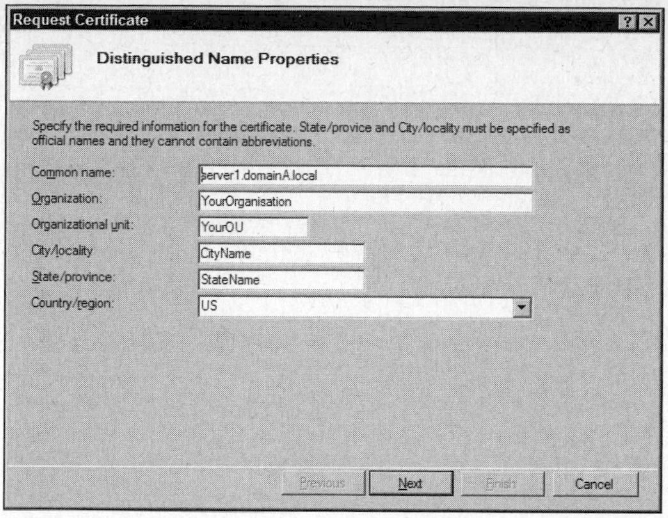

Figure 15-5

5. Select the cryptographic provider and bit length that you want to use for this certificate, as shown in Figure 15-6. RSA is the mostly widely used on the public Internet.

Common current key lengths vary between 1,024 bits and 2,048 bits. As of this writing, RSA key lengths up to approximately 665 bits have been factored and are no longer considered secure. Barring an unexpected breakthrough in mathematics (or computing technology), key lengths greater than 2,048 bits are unlikely to be factored in the foreseeable future. However, selecting a longer key length puts additional load on both the client and server when performing the SSL/TLS handshake. For busy sites, dedicated hardware devices (either add-in cards or separate network devices) to offload the processing of SSL/TLS should be examined.

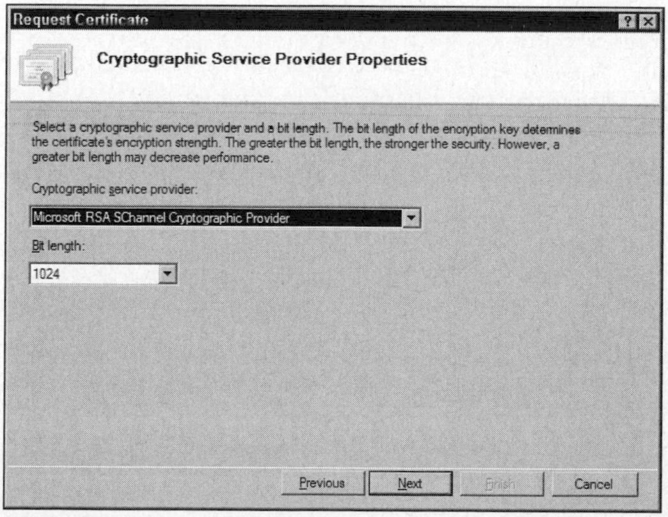

Figure 15-6

6. Choose a filename to save the certificate request to, as shown in Figure 15-7, and click Finish to close the wizard.

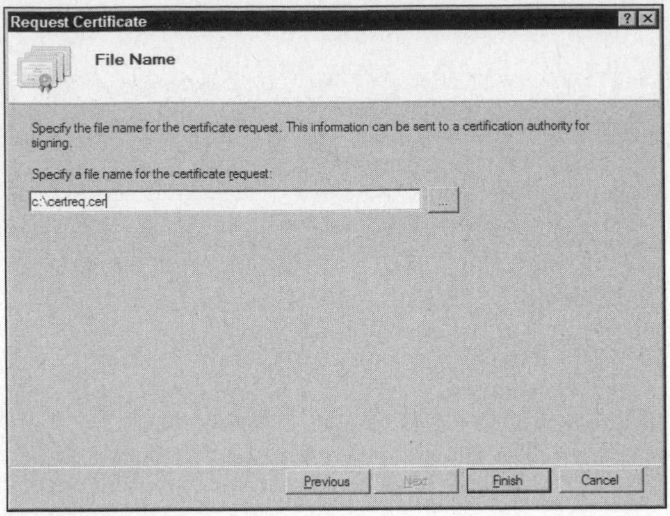

Figure 15-7

At this point, a Certificate Enrollment Request exists in the local machine's certificate store that corresponds with the certificate request file that was just generated. After submitting the certificate request to a CA and receiving your certificate, the new certificate will match the pending Certificate Enrollment Request.

Running the Create Certificate Request wizard again will result in a new certificate request file and a new Certificate Enrollment Request in the certificate store. A certificate resulting from a certificate request file must match a Certificate Enrollment Request in the certificate store for the certificate to be imported. If you delete a pending Certificate Enrollment Request or otherwise overwrite it by rerunning the wizard, then discard the earlier certificate request file and only use the newly created one.

To view the Certificate Enrollment Request:

1. Click Start ⇨ Run, enter **mmc.exe**, and press [Enter].
2. Select File ⇨ Add/Remove Snapin.
3. Select the Certificates snap-in and click Add. Click OK to exit all the dialogs.
4. Expand the Certificate Enrollment Requests node to see all pending requests, as shown in Figure 15-8.

The generated certificate request file is now submitted to a CA, which generates a signed certificate. Most commercial third-party CAs have a range of certificates that vary in price. The higher-assurance certificates (that tend to cost more money) involve additional due diligence by the CA to ensure that the certificate request comes from a legitimate business or individual that is entitled to use the requested certificate common name. In practice, it is debatable whether end-users are sufficiently aware of the different assurance levels offered by various types of certificates. In an attempt to combat this, Microsoft, in conjunction with partners, has launched Extended Validation (EV) certificates. Sites secured using an EV certificate have the URL bar displayed in green, rather than the traditional white. You can find examples and further explanation at www.microsoft.com/windows/products/winfamily/ie/ev/ default.mspx.

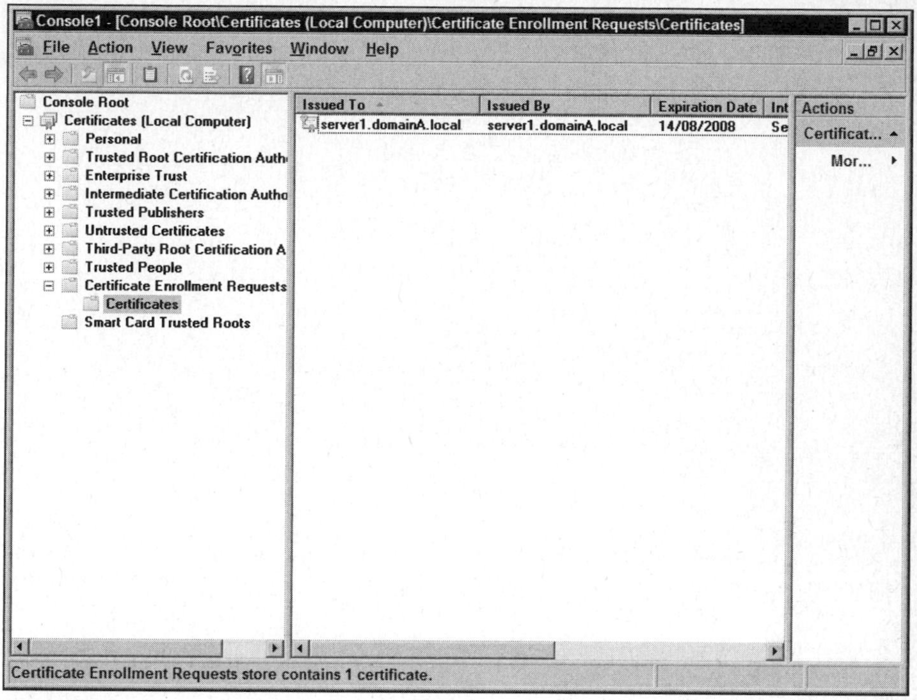

Figure 15-8

A certificate request can also be generated from the command line using the certreq.exe tool. When using the certreq.exe tool to generate a certificate request, the -new option must be specified, and a settings file must be specified that contains information about the request. The full syntax of the command is:

```
certreq.exe [-binary] [-user|machine] policyfile.inf certRequestFileName
```

The policyfile.inf file contains information used to generate the certificate request file. The certRequestFileName is the name of the file that you wish to have certreq.exe save the resulting certificate request as. The optional -binary switch forces certreq.exe to save the resulting certificate request in binary format rather than the Base64-encoded format. The optional -user or -machine determines whether the pending request is stored in the user's certificate store or the machine's certificate store. When creating a request for a server authentication certificate suitable for use with IIS 7.0, the -machine option should be used.

The INF policy file follows standard INF conventions, with section headers delimited by square brackets ([ ]), name value pairs for settings, and comments beginning with the ; character.

The INF for use with `certreq.exe` requires only a single section header:

```
[NewRequest]
```

However, to ensure that the certificate can be used for server authentication, the OID (Object Identifier) for server authentication should be explicitly specified. This is specified in the `[ExtendedUsage]` section.

For name value pairs, only the `subject` value is required — other fields are optional. However, you will most likely want to specify certain fields (for example, key length) to ensure that you are generating a sufficiently secure certificate for the correct purpose. A typical INF would look like this:

```
[NewRequest]
Subject = "cn=server1, o=organization, l=city, s=state, c=country"
KeySpec = 1
KeyLength = 1024
Exportable = true
MachineKeySet = true
PrivateKeyArchive = false
ProviderName = "Microsoft RSA SChannel Cryptographic Provider"
ProviderType = 12
RequestType = PKCS10
KeyUsage = 0xa0

[EnhancedKeyUsageExtension]
; server authentication
OID=1.3.6.1.5.5.7.3.1
```

Running `certreq.exe` using the INF file will result in a PKCS10 certificate request similar to the CER file generated earlier using the wizard in IIS Manager. You can then submit this request file, as detailed in the next section.

Submitting the Certificate Request

The procedure for submitting the generated certificate request and retrieving the resulting certificate varies from CA to CA. For lower-assurance certificates, the contents of the certificate request file are typically sent to the CA, and after some verification of the ownership of the domain, a certificate is generated that can be downloaded and installed into IIS. For higher-assurance certificates, additional physical evidence (such as business-registration papers) may need to be supplied to the CA.

In this chapter, the certificate request will be submitted to a CA running Microsoft Active Directory Certificate Services, which provides an approximation of the process involved.

Certificate requests can be submitted to Active Directory Certificate Services in three main ways:

❑ **By using the Certification Authorities MMC tool** — This MMC console is installed on any server running Active Directory Certificate Services. It can optionally be installed on other Windows Server 2008 machines by using the Server Manager tool.

❑ **By using the optional web interface** — Using the web interface requires that IIS be installed on the same machine running Active Directory Certificate Services. A /certsrv virtual directory is created underneath the Default Web Site to allow users to request and retrieve certificates.

❑ **By using the command-line certreq.exe tool** — Using the command-line certreq.exe tool with the -submit option and specifying your certificate request file, and the name of the CA to submit the request to.

This chapter covers the detailed steps for using the web interface, as this procedure is the most similar to requesting a certificate from a commercial CA.

By default, only users in the Domain Admins and Enterprise Admins security groups are able to issue server authentication certificates. For information on changing this configuration, see the section "Managing a PKI," below in this chapter.

To request a certificate using the optional web interface:

1. Open a browser window and navigate to http://CAServerName/certsrv/, where CAServerName is the name of the server that has Active Directory Certificate Services installed.

2. Click the Request a Certificate link.

3. Click the Submit an Advanced Certificate Request link.

4. Click the Submit a Certificate Request by Using a Base-64-encoded CMC or PKCS #10 File link, as shown in Figure 15-9.

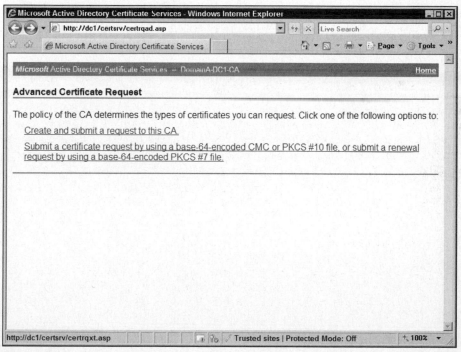

Figure 15-9

5. Using Notepad (or similar text editor), open the certificate request file that was generated previously, and copy the contents of that file into the Base-64-encoded certificate request textbox, including the "-----BEGIN NEW CERTIFICATE REQUEST-----" and "-----END NEW CERTIFICATE REQUEST-----" text.

6. Select Web Server as the certificate template that should be used to generate the new certificate (see Figure 15-10). Click the Submit button to submit the request.

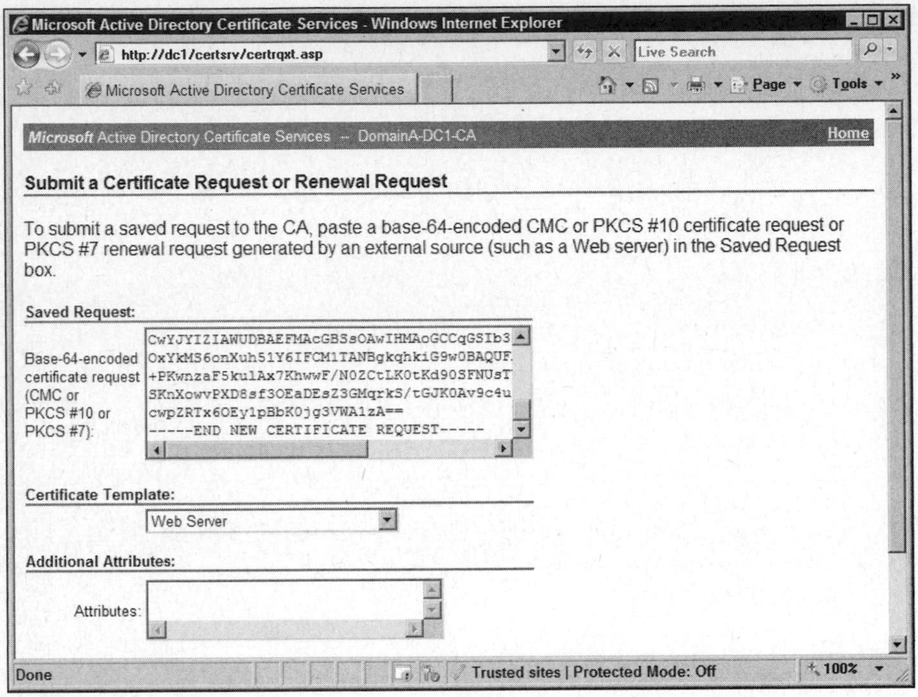

Figure 15-10

Active Directory Certificate Services will process the certificate request and generate a signed certificate that can be downloaded using your browser. Click the DER Encoded link to download the newly issued certificate. The DER Encoded certificate can be imported into IIS 7.0. In some cross-platform situations, it may be necessary to use the Base-64-encoded option instead. Depending on the platform, you may need to decode the Base-64-encoded file prior to importing it. Click the Download Certificate link to download the certificate to the local server.

Importing the Certificate into IIS 7.0

The issued certificate, whether from a commercial CA or from Active Directory Certificate Services, can now be installed on the local machine. This can be done using the Certificate MMC or by using IIS Manager, as follows:

1. Open IIS Manager.

2. At the server-level node, select the Server Certificates option.

3. Select the Complete Certificate Request option.

4. Enter the path to the certificate file that was issued by the CA. Additionally, enter a Friendly Name to describe this certificate. This Friendly Name will be displayed in IIS Manager. The name should help you identify what the certificate is being used for (for example, the name of the web site that will be using the certificate, as shown in Figure 15-11).

5. Click OK to install the certificate.

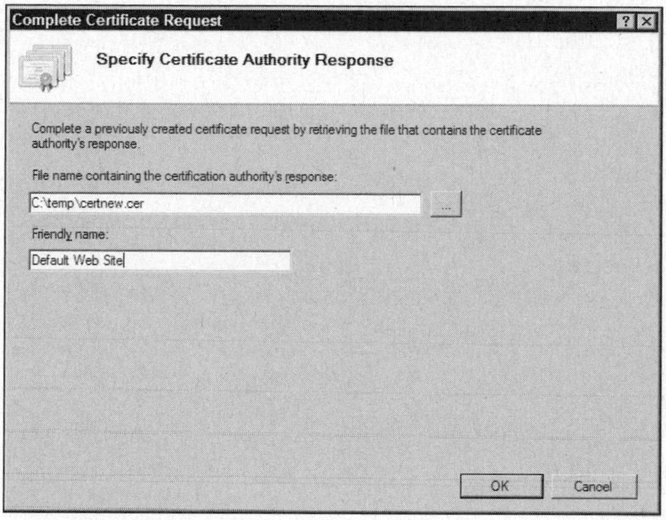

Figure 15-11

Configuring Web-Site Bindings

To use the newly installed certificate, you must update the web-site bindings. This allows a web site to listen on an additional port for SSL/TLS connections — typically, port 443.

Although binding configuration is updated at an individual web-site level, the binding configuration information is stored in the server's `applicationHost.config` *file, not in individual* `web.config` *files under each web site. Allowing individual web-site owners to change the bindings for their web sites is a security risk.*

To update the binding for a web site to allow it to accept SSL/TLS connections, perform the following steps:

1. Open IIS Manager with a user that has permissions to update the `applicationHost.config` file (by default, users in the local Administrators group).

2. Locate the web site to which you want to allow SSL/TLS connections, and click the Bindings link in the Actions pane.

3. Click the Add button to add an additional binding.

4. Set the binding type to https, and, optionally, select the IP address(es) that the web site should listen on for SSL/TLS connections. Alternatively, the "All Unassigned" option can be used to

511

have the web site listen for SSL/TLS connections on any IP address not already assigned to another web site.

5. Select the installed certificate that should be used for this web site, as shown in Figure 15-12.

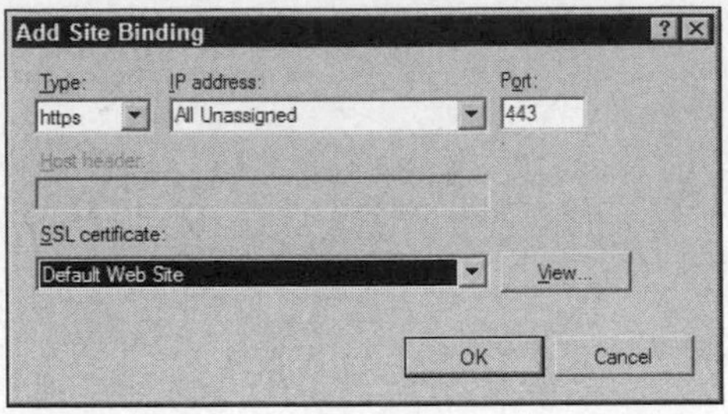

Figure 15-12

6. Click OK twice to exit the dialogs and update the web site's bindings.

You can also update a web site's bindings by using the AppCmd command-line tool. To add an HTTPS binding to an existing site called Site1, run the following command:

```
appcmd.exe set site /site.name:"Site1"
/bindings.[protocol='https',bindinginformation='*:443:']
```

Editing bindings and other web-site configuration details are covered in detail in Chapter 6, "Web-Site Administration."

Generating a Certificate Using Domain Certificate Request

If Active Directory Certificate Services are installed in the organization in Enterprise (Active Directory Integrated) rather than Standalone mode, then the IIS 7.0 Domain Certificate Request feature can be used to automatically submit a certificate request to the CA and have the resulting issued certificate installed on the IIS 7.0 machine.

Because the process uses RPC, this process is not suitable where there are firewalls or similar equipment interposed between the IIS 7.0 server and the ADCS CA. Additionally, by default, only users in the Domain Admins and Enterprise Admins groups have permissions to automatically enroll server authentication certificates. The Domain Certificate Request wizard must be run by a user in a group that has permission to enroll certificates based on the Web Server certificate template.

> *For information on altering the default configuration to allow other users or groups to enroll server authentication certificates, see the section "Managing a PKI," below in this chapter.*

To request and install a certificate using the Domain Certificate Request wizard, perform the following steps:

1. Open IIS Manager. At the server-level node, select the Server Certificates option.
2. Select the Create Domain Certificate option to begin the certificate request generation process.

3. Enter the server's common name and your organization's properties. The information entered here is the same as when creating a certificate request manually (refer to Figure 15-5). Click Next to continue.

4. Enter your CA address, as shown in Figure 15-13. The CA name takes the form of the Common Name entered when installing Active Directory Certificate Services (by default *<domain-name>-<servername>*-CA), followed by the FQDN of the machine that ADCS is running on.

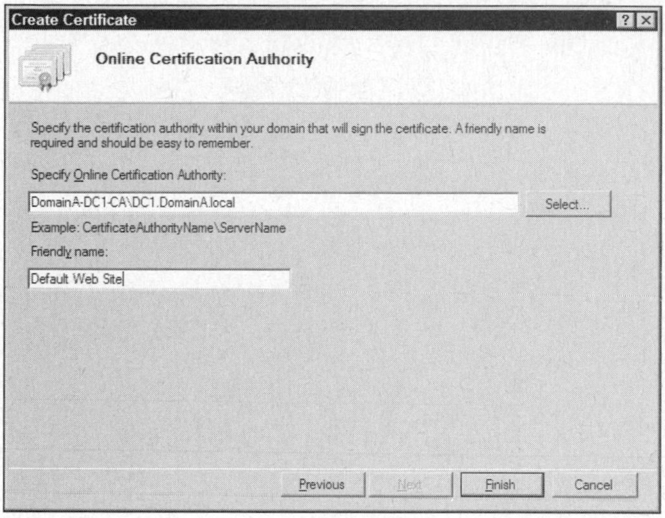

Figure 15-13

5. Enter a Friendly Name to describe this certificate. This Friendly Name will be displayed in IIS Manager. The name should help you identify what the certificate is being used for (for example, the name of the web site that will be using the certificate).

6. Click Finish to complete the wizard and submit the request to the designated CA. The certificate will automatically be issued by the CA and installed into the local machine certificate store on the IIS 7.0 server.

To configure a web site to use this newly issued certificate, follow the steps under "Configuring Web-Site Bindings" above in this chapter.

Generating a Self-Signed Certificate

When a CA is not available, a self-signed certificate may be all that is required. This is particularly true in development environments where a developer may simply wish to test that his application works over SSL/TLS. A self-signed certificate is one where the server signs its own certificate. Because no machine other than the server trusts it as a CA, any remote machine accessing the site will result in a warning being displayed to the user, as shown above in Figure 15-3.

To generate and install a self-signed certificate:

1. Open IIS Manager. At the server-level node, select the Server Certificates option.

513

2. Select the Create Self-Signed Certificate option to begin the certificate request generation process.

3. Enter a Friendly Name for your certificate, as shown in Figure 15-14. This Friendly Name will be displayed in IIS Manager. The name should help you identify what the certificate is being used for (for example, the name of the web site that will be using the certificate).

4. Click OK to generate and install the certificate automatically into the local machine's certificate store. To configure a web site to use this newly issued certificate, follow the steps under "Configuring Web-Site Bindings" above in this chapter.

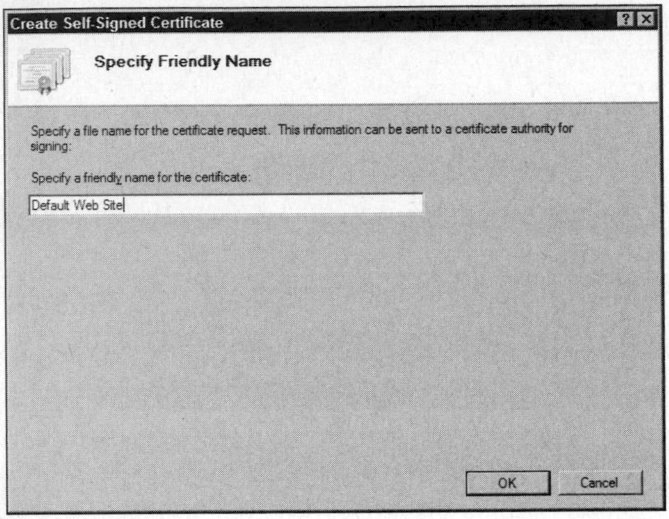

Create Self-Signed Certificate

Specify Friendly Name

Specify a file name for the certificate request. This information can be sent to a certificate authority for signing:

Specify a friendly name for the certificate:

Default Web Site

OK   Cancel

Figure 15-14

Unlike other certificate request mechanisms, there is no need to supply a common name or any organizational details when generating a self-signed certificate. With a self-signed certificate, the common name is automatically set to the FQDN of the local IIS 7.0 server, and the Organizational Unit and Organization details are left blank.

Managing an SSL/TLS-Secured Web Site

After configuring a web site to SSL/TLS connections, additional management or configuration may be required from time to time.

Configuring Additional SSL/TLS Options

An SSL/TLS-secured web site has the following additional configuration options:

❑ **Require an SSL connection** — If this is selected, the web site will no longer listen for HTTP requests, but only access HTTPS-secured requests.

❑ **Require 128 bit key encryption** — Key lengths less than 128 bits are not considered secure, and forcing this option requires the end-client to negotiate a more secure connection. In some countries, U.S. export restrictions prevent technology supporting 128-bit key lengths from being exported from the United States.

❑ **Client Certificates** — The web site can be configured to accept, require, or ignore client certificates. Client certificates can be used in mutual authentication scenarios where the server uses a client certificate to authenticate the end-user. For more information on configuring client certificates, see Chapter 14, "Authentication and Authorization."

To configure any of these additional options:

1. Open IIS Manager and navigate to the web-site node where you wish to configure these settings.

2. Open the SSL Settings feature.

3. Select the options required, and click Apply in the Actions pane to save the changes.

Exporting and Importing Certificates

In certain circumstances, you might need to export an existing certificate (for example, to move it to a new server, or to import into a dedicated hardware device such as an SSL offload device). The following steps can be used to export an existing server authentication certificate and import it into a different IIS 7.0 server.

To export an existing certificate:

1. Click Start ➪ Run, enter **mmc.exe**, and press [Enter].

2. Choose File ➪ Add/Remove Snapin.

3. Select Certificates and click Add. A prompt will appear offering a selection of the current user's account, a nominated service account, or the machine's account. Select Computer Account and click Next. Accept the default Local Computer and click Finish.

4. Expand the Personal node, and then the Certificates node underneath.

5. Select the certificate you want to export from the middle pane, as shown in Figure 15-15.

6. Right-click on the certificate, and choose All Tasks, Export.

7. Click Next on the introductory screen of the wizard. On the second page, choose Yes, export the private key, and click Next.

8. Accept the default Personal Information Exchange PKCS #12 format. If your certificate was issued by a subordinate or intermediate CA and you wish to export the entire certificate chain for import onto the new server, check the "Include all certificates in the certification path." Typically, this is required if you need to install intermediate CA certificates into the local machine store when installing the server authentication certificate. Click Next to continue.

9. Enter a password to secure the private key. You will need this password when importing the certificate on the new device. Click Next to continue.

10. Enter a filename to save the exported certificate as, and then click Next.

11. Review the confirmation screen — click Finish to close the wizard, or click Back if you want to change any of your selections.

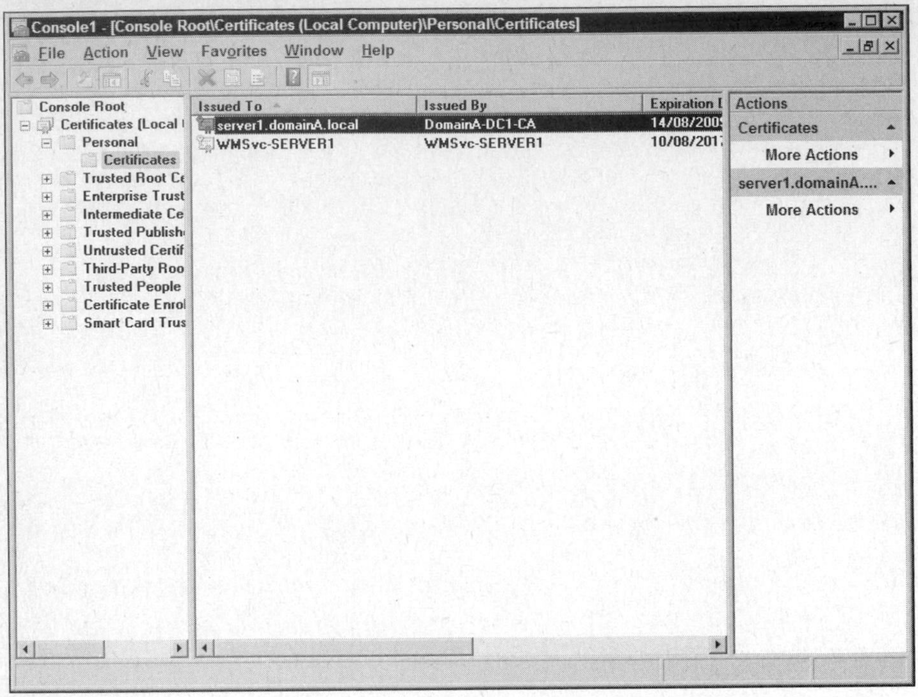

Figure 15-15

To import a certificate on a new IIS 7.0 server, perform the following steps:

1. Open IIS Manager. At the server-level node, select the Server Certificates option.

2. Click the Import link in the Actions pane.

3. Enter the path to the PKCS#12 (.pfx) file that was previously exported, and enter the password to decrypt the private key, as shown in Figure 15-16. If you ever wish to export this certificate in the future, ensure that the "Allow this certificate to be exported" checkbox is checked.

4. Click OK to import the certificate.

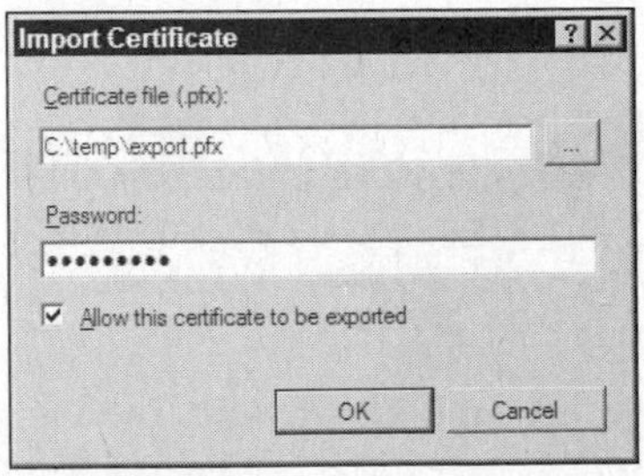

Figure 15-16

The certificate can now be configured for use with a web site. Follow the instructions on configuring web-site binding above in this chapter to configure a web site for SSL/TLS connections.

Configuring SSL and HTTP Host Headers

HTTP Host: headers are a feature of the HTTP v1.1 specification that allows a web server to host multiple web sites on a single IP address and TCP port, while simultaneously allowing HTTP v1.1 clients to specify the web site they wish to connect to. The process requires that the client send a Host: HTTP header as part of the HTTP request specifying a web site it wishes to access, and the web server having a web site configured with a corresponding HTTP Host: header value. For more information on configuring Host: headers for use with web sites, see Chapter 6, "Web-Site Administration."

When using SSL/TLS, the entire HTTP request is encrypted, including the HTTP Host: header. This means that the web server needs some separate mechanism for determining which web site the request should be routed to. Traditionally this has required each SSL/TLS secured web site to be run on a unique combination of IP address and TCP port.

Windows Server 2003 SP1 introduced some limited support for HTTP Host: headers to be used with SSL/TLS secured web sites. The same functionality is present in Windows Server 2008.

To be able to use HTTP Host: headers with SSL/TLS secured web sites, where those web sites run on the same IP address and TCP port, the following conditions must be met:

❑ All hostnames must reside under the same domain name. For example, www1.domain.com and www2.domain.com would be eligible hosts, whereas www1.domain1.com and www2.domain2.com would not.

❑ A wildcard certificate that matches *.domain.com must be installed on the web server. Most major commercial CAs now offer wildcard certificates, although the cost is much higher than for a single hostname certificate. When generating a wildcard certificate request, set the common name to *.yourdomain.com. Alternatively, each specific hostname that your IIS server is responsible for can be listed in the Subject Alternate Name (SAN) field on the certificate.

❑ The same wildcard certificate must be configured for use in the web-site bindings for each web site listening on the common IP address/TCP port combination.

When these three conditions are in place, there is only a single certificate that IIS 7.0 needs to use for all SSL/TLS requests coming in on the specific IP address/TCP port combination. Because the certificate is a wildcard certificate, any hostname in the specified domain will match, ensuring that the end-user does not receive an error. The certificate can be used to decrypt the traffic and extract the HTTP Host: header, and IIS can route the request to the appropriate web site.

Managing a PKI

Implementing and managing a *Public Key Infrastructure (PKI)* is a book in itself; this section merely touches on some considerations. Readers are advised to consider Microsoft TechNet resources or *Microsoft Windows Server 2003 PKI and Certificate Security* (MS Press) for more information on managing a Microsoft PKI.

If you are looking to protect a public-facing web site (for example, an e-commerce site), obtaining a certificate from a major third-party CA is the best route forward. However, if you need to protect internal web sites, then deploying an internal PKI may be more economical, especially if you also need to deploy certificates for other purposes — for example, to permit users to encrypt files via the Encryptable File System (EFS) or to deploy 802.11x network access authentication.

Deploying Microsoft Active Directory Certificate Services in Enterprise Mode (that is, integrated with Active Directory) has several benefits. The CA is automatically added to the trusted root certification authorities store on domain-joined client machines. Additionally, clients can take advantage of auto-enrollment features, to automatically enroll for certificates without intervention by users.

When deploying a PKI, it is essential to know that the CA's certificate is the "key to the kingdom." If an attacker is able to compromise a CA and obtain the CA's certificate, then no certificates issued by that CA can be trusted, nor can the identity of any machine presenting a certificate be guaranteed.

To mitigate this risk, many organizations deploy a two-tier CA infrastructure. A root CA (top-level CA) is initially configured (typically as a standalone CA, not joined to a domain). This CA then signs a certificate for a second CA. This second CA (known as a *subordinate CA*) issues certificates to end-users or computers, and is typically domain-joined (if using Microsoft Active Directory Certificate Services). There may be one, or more, subordinate-issuing CA.

In the event that the subordinate-issuing CA is ever compromised, the subordinate CA's certificate can be revoked by the root CA (thus invalidating any certificates signed by the subordinate CA), and a new certificate issued to the subordinate CA.

To mitigate the risk of compromise of the root CA, the root CA is typically maintained in an offline state (powered off or disconnected from the network). Additionally, tamper-resistant hardware devices (known as hardware security modules, or HSMs) can be used to store the root CA's certificate.

As part of the deployment process, you need to determine your certificate revocation policy. This determines under what circumstances a certificate will be revoked (rendered invalid), and how clients will be advised of that revocation. The first is a decision around what processes to follow within your organization. The second is more a technical consideration. Active Directory Certificate Services can publish certificate revocation lists (CRLs) to various locations (HTTP location, Active Directory, and so forth), and you will need to determine a location that is both highly available and accessible by all clients. Publishing the CRL to Active Directory may be the most useful if all clients are members of your Active Directory domain. However, if you have non-Windows clients, an HTTP location or file share may be more suitable. Windows Server 2008 Active Directory Certificate Services also supports the use of the OCSP (Online Certificate Status Protocol) for responding to client requests on server certificate revocation status.

When issuing certificates from Windows Active Directory Certificate Services (ADCS), each certificate is based on a certificate template. ADCS ships with several built-in templates for common scenarios (for example, server authentication and EFS). If you have Windows Server 2003 Enterprise Edition (or higher), you can edit the supplied certificate templates or create your own. You may need to create additional security templates if you have a need for customized usage, or to facilitate new OIDs (Object Identifiers). For example, if you are deploying Microsoft System Center Operations Manager 2007 and want to use the Gateway Server functionality, you need to create a custom certificate template for that purpose.

Certificate templates also have ACLs that determine who can view the properties for each template and who is permitted to issue certificates based on that template. For web-site server authentication certificates, users in the local Administrators group and the Domain Admins group are able to issue certificates.

Certificate template management can be performed (on your ADCS server) by:

1. Click Start ⇨ Run, enter **mmc.exe**, and then press [Enter].

2. Choose File ⇨ Add/Remove Snapin and select the Certificate Templates snap-in. Click OK to add the snap-in and exit the dialog.

Existing certificate templates are now displayed (see Figure 15-17).

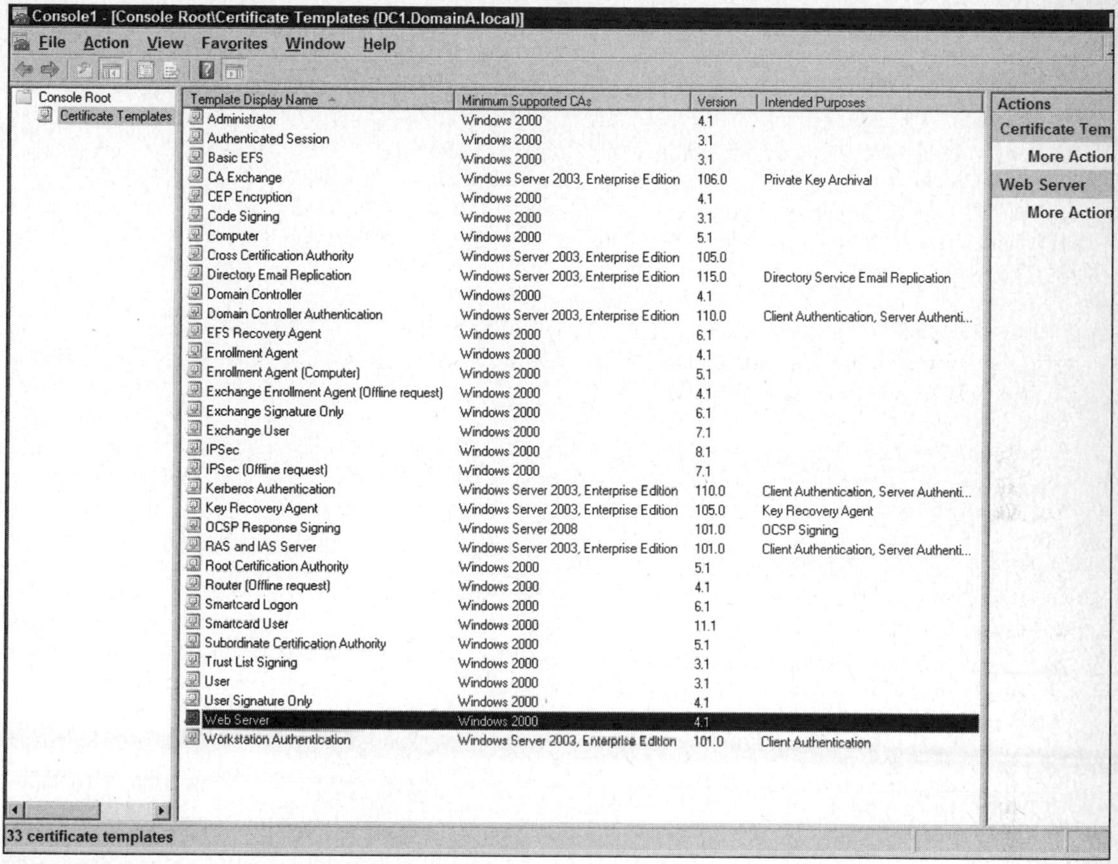

Figure 15-17

3. To duplicate an existing template for editing, right-click an existing template and choose Duplicate Template.

4. To edit an existing template, including issuing permissions, double-click on a template. Enrollment permissions are defined on the Security tab (see Figure 15-18). To permit an additional user or group to issue this particular certificate, add the user or group and grant them the Enroll permission.

Managing a PKI involves good processes. To ensure the ongoing security of your PKI and all the applications that depend on it, it is essential to define clear processes for certificate issuance, new template creation, certificate revocation, CA backup and recovery, and associated tasks. Additionally, a clear delineation of responsibility among IT staff for these tasks is essential. Readers considering deploying their own PKI are encouraged to read the Certificate Services deployment information available on the Microsoft TechNet web site.

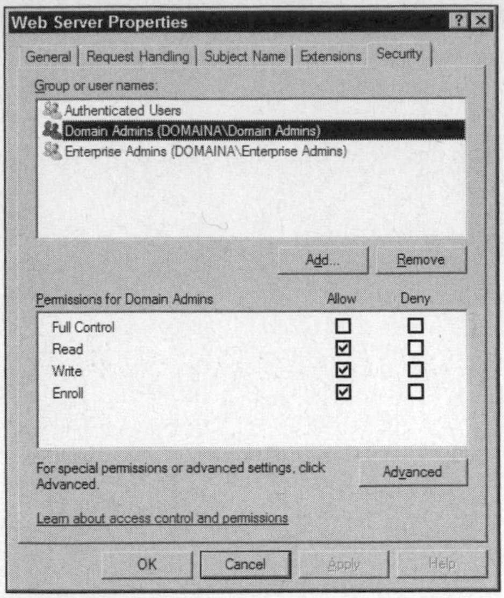

Figure 15-18

Securing an SMTP Virtual Server with TLS

Although SSL and TLS are most popularly used with web sites, the nature of TLS allows it to be used to secure many other protocols as well. The Microsoft SMTP server supplied with Windows Server operating systems has supported TLS for many years now.

TLS can be used to secure both inbound traffic and outbound traffic separately. The encryption offered by TLS can be useful especially if requiring users to authenticate using Basic authentication, since without TLS, the user's credentials would be passed in cleartext across the network or Internet.

Securing connections using TLS requires a suitable server authentication certificate to be installed on the local IIS 7.0 machine. Generating a certificate request suitable for securing an SMTP virtual server is the same as generating a certificate suitable for securing a web site, except that a self-signed certificate should not be used because e-mail clients typically do not have an option to present a prompt to the user about certificates issued by untrusted CAs.

Unlike HTTP/HTTPS, which provides a separate port (port 443) for SSL/TLS secured communications, the Microsoft SMTP Server requires only port 25 to be available. Clients should use the START TLS command to initiate a TLS-secured session over port 25.

After installing a suitable server authentication certificate, you should perform the following steps to secure transmissions:

Managing SMTP virtual servers requires using the IIS 6.0 Manager, rather than the new IIS 7.0 Manager. The IIS 6.0 Manager is installed as a dependency when you install SMTP Server via Server Manager. The IIS 6.0 Manager is located in the Administrative Tools folder beside the IIS 7.0 Manager.

To secure inbound connections:

1. Open IIS Manager (6.0). You must be in the local Administrators group on the machine to be able to use this tool.

2. Locate the SMTP virtual server that is to be secured for inbound connections, right-click and choose Properties.

3. On the Access tab, check the Require TLS Encryption checkbox. The dialog will inform you if a suitable TLS certificate is available for securing inbound connections, as shown in Figure 15-19. Additionally, Event 550 (Source SMTPSvc) will be logged in the Windows Event Log.

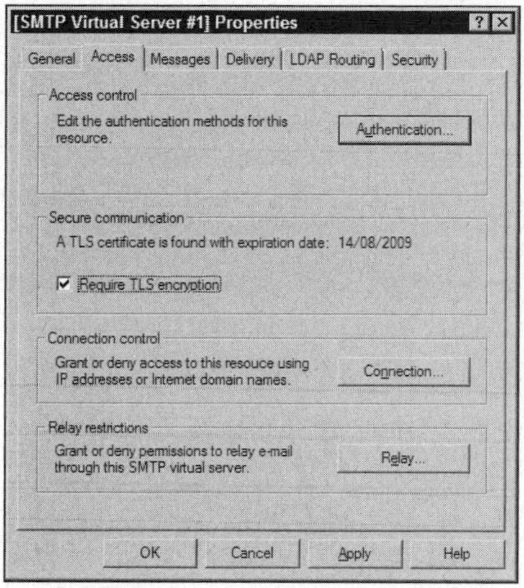

Figure 15-19

To secure outbound connections using TLS, perform the following steps:

1. Open IIS Manager (6.0). You must be in the local Administrators group on the machine to be able to use this tool.

2. Locate the SMTP virtual server that is to be secured for inbound connections, right-click and choose Properties.

3. On the Delivery tab, click the Outbound Security button, and then check the "TLS encryption" checkbox, as shown in Figure 15-20.

4. Unlike the dialog box for securing inbound connections above, no information is presented as to whether there is a suitable certificate available. However, if a suitable certificate can be configured for outbound TLS encryption, Event 2000 will be logged in the Windows System Event Log, as shown in Figure 15-21.

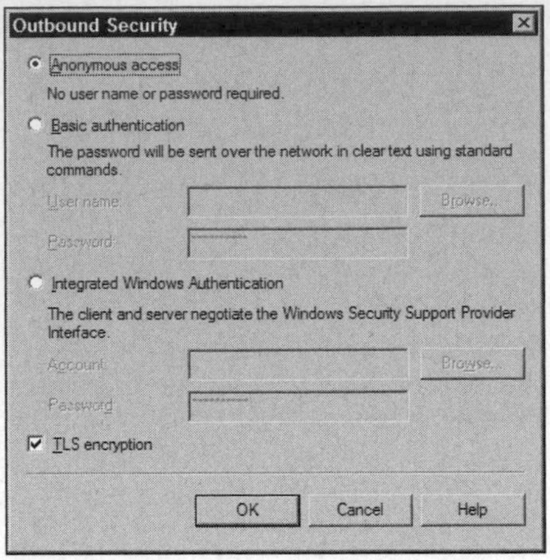

Figure 15-20

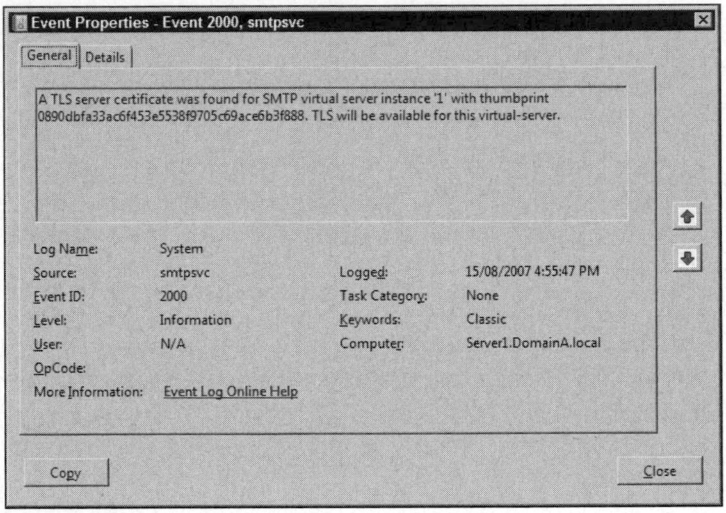

Figure 15-21

Securing an FTP Site with TLS

The Microsoft FTP service supplied with Windows Server 2008 does not support FTPS (FTP over SSL/TLS). However, the separate add-on FTP 7 server from the IIS Product Group does support FTPS. Unfortunately, this new FTP server is a separate add-on component to IIS 7.0 and needs to be downloaded, installed, and configured separately. See Chapter 10 for information on installing and configuring FTP 7.

FTP supports an anonymous access mode, which typically is used for public Read-Only FTP sites. For private sites (Read-Only, or Read/Write–enabled), enabling a password requirement results in the user's username and password being transmitted in cleartext between the FTP client and FTP server. The use of TLS allows the administrator to encrypt the transmission of information between client and server.

The use of TLS to secure transmission of data does incur a processing overhead on both client and server. For a server with many concurrent connections, this can become a significant overhead. To help alleviate this potential problem, FTP 7 supports encrypting the control channel (used for sending commands between client and server), the data channel (used for transferring data), or both channels. Additionally, an option exists to encrypt only the credentials sent across the control channel, and nothing else.

For administrators who want to protect the usernames and passwords of their end-users, the option to encrypt the control channel only will be attractive. Files transferred over the data channel in this scenario will be transferred in cleartext; however, they won't incur any overhead in encryption and decryption.

With FTP 7, it is possible to add an FTP binding to an existing, defined web site. With this option, you can easily enable content to be published to a web site using FTP, and have that secured using TLS. Alternatively, you can explicitly define FTP sites (which need not be related to existing web sites at all) and then configure TLS for those FTP sites.

Securing an FTP site using TLS requires a suitable server authentication certificate to be installed on the local IIS 7.0 machine. The process for generating a certificate request for a certificate is the same for FTP 7 as for web sites discussed above in this chapter. Prior to configuring TLS for an FTP site, follow the steps documented above to request, generate, and install a suitable server authentication certificate.

To configure TLS for an existing FTP site:

1. Open IIS Manager. Because bindings can only be stored in the `applicationHost.config` file, you will need to be in the local Administrators group on the machine, or delegated appropriate permissions.

2. Locate the FTP site you want to configure TLS for, and open the FTP SSL Settings feature.

3. Choose a certificate you want to use to secure connections to this FTP site. Ideally, the Common Name in the certificate should match the NetBIOS name or FQDN that is used to access the FTP site.

4. Choose whether TLS connections are optional for control and data channels or are required for both control and data channels, or click the Advanced button to configure individual settings for both control and data channels, as shown in Figure 15-22.

5. Optionally, choose whether to enforce a minimum 128-bit key length by selecting the "Use 128-bit encryption for SSL connections" checkbox. Key lengths less than 128 bits are no longer considered secure, although in some countries, U.S. export restrictions on cryptography may mean that clients do not support 128-bit SSL keys.

6. Click Apply in the Actions pane to apply the configuration.

FTP 7 supports FTPS (FTP over SSL/TLS). There is a separate protocol SFTP that involves tunneling FTP over SSH (Secure Shell). When evaluating client applications to use with FTP 7, ensure that the clients support FTPS rather than SFTP.

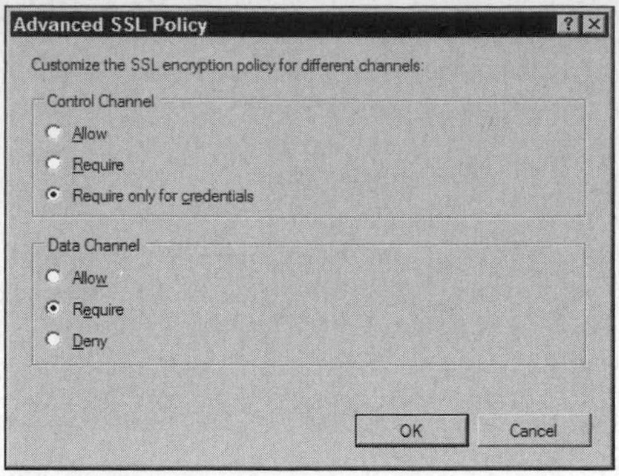

Figure 15-22

To configure a secure FTP binding for an existing web site, perform the following steps:

1. Open IIS Manager. Because bindings can only be stored in the `applicationHost.config` file, you will need to be in the local Administrators group on the machine, or delegated appropriate permissions.

2. Locate the web site you wish to add a secure FTP binding to, and click the Add FTP Publishing link in the Actions pane. The wizard will guide you through the process of adding a new FTP site and configuring TLS.

3. Choose the IP address, TCP port, and virtual hostname that the FTP site should listen on. For more information on configuring FTP 7, see Chapter 10, "Configuring Other Services."

4. Choose the SSL/TLS certificate that should be used for secured connections to this FTP site, and optionally select the Require SSL checkbox to force TLS connections, as shown in Figure 15-23.

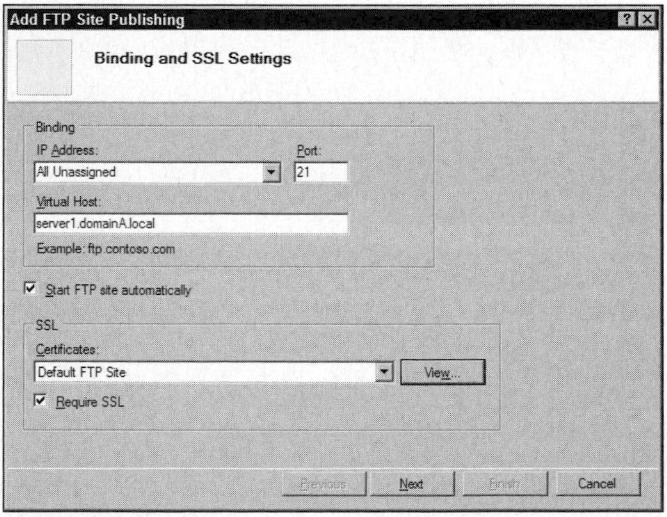

Figure 15-23

5. Click Next to continue, and configure access and authorization restrictions. Click Finish to add the new binding.

6. To configure advanced TLS properties for this secure FTP site, refresh the view in IIS Manager. The FTP SSL Setting feature will now become available, and configuration options described in the previous section can now be configured.

After updating your FTP site's bindings, clients can connect to your TLS secured site by sending an AUTH TLS command when connecting to your FTP site. Detailed information on managing FTP 7 can be found in Chapter 10.

Summary

TLS and SSL are industry-standard technologies for securing communication and authenticating communicating peers. The current version of TLS has withstood the intense scrutiny of researchers, implementers, and attackers and provides a robust, tested mechanism for securing your data between client and server.

In this chapter, we have covered:

❑ The fundamentals of a Public Key Infrastructure and the SSL/TLS handshake process

❑ Requesting and installing a certificate into IIS 7.0

❑ Enabling SSL/TLS for HTTP, SMTP, and FTP communications

By using SSL/TLS, you can secure the transmission of sensitive information between your clients and your IIS 7.0 server against both passive attacks (eavesdropping) and active attacks (data alteration). Although SSL/TLS can secure data in-transit, you still need to ensure endpoint security. Clients need to be free from malware, viruses, and keyloggers, and your IIS 7.0 server needs to be secure. Chapters 13 and 14 cover securing your IIS 7.0 server.

16

Configuring and Load-Balancing Web Farms

At the time of this writing, prior to the final release of IIS 7.0, half of the top ten busiest web sites in the world are running IIS, and within the Fortune 100 sites, more sites are running IIS than any other web platform. This speaks volumes to the scalability and reliability that previous versions of IIS already have in the world of busy web sites.

IIS 7.0 builds on this already solid platform with some welcome additions to web farm support. This chapter covers the new shared configuration infrastructure, which provides centralized IIS configuration files for all servers in a web farm. It also looks at what you need to consider to ensure that there isn't any single point of failure and that your web farm is able to withstand most any type of hardware or software failure, while still maintaining a fully operational web site.

After looking at the new IIS 7.0 features, this chapter will look at content replication, load-balancing options, and several other things to consider to effectively manage a web farm of any size.

IIS 7.0 and Web Farms

IIS 6.0 was capable of scaling out to virtually any number of web servers and had tools like IISCnfg.vbs to keep the IIS metabase in sync between the nodes. With this solid foundation already in place, there are a surprisingly small number of features that IIS 7.0 needs to add.

> IISCnfg.vbs *is no longer available with IIS 7.0 but has been replaced with* AppCmd.exe *and the new shared configuration, which is covered in depth in this chapter.*

Simply put, as a high-level overview, there is one major improvement that IIS 7.0 brings to the table specifically for web farms: *shared configuration*. Shared configuration allows you to store the IIS configuration files in a location of your choosing — either locally or over a UNC path, where multiple IIS servers can point to the same location without any sharing contention. The new configuration mechanism does not hold a lock on the files, so multiple servers can work with the same file simultaneously.

This is powerful when comparing IIS 7.0 to IIS 6.0, which did not have a good solution for easy metabase synchronization. It was possible in IIS 6.0 to keep all nodes in sync, as you can see by the success of the top web sites that rely on IIS, but a lot more work was needed to simplify sharing and/or replication of the configuration files. IIS 7.0 has done exactly that. In fact, when all is said and done, it almost seems too easy! Don't let the simplicity allow you to be underimpressed, though. Behind the scenes, a tremendous amount of work was necessary to make this shared configuration so solid, yet so simple.

Surrounding shared configuration are many other smaller enhancements — for example, the ability to make the configuration file completely machine neutral, new support for system environment variables in the configuration files, and a configuration infrastructure that allows multiple servers to read and write to the same configuration file without any locking or sharing violations.

Shared Configuration

Shared configuration enables you to store IIS configuration files in a location of your choosing: in a local folder or across the network. It also ensures that sensitive information like the IIS user passwords is encrypted.

There is some debate over whether a central configuration location across a UNC path is really the best way to go. The concern is that there are too many variables in play across a network UNC path to cause potential failures. Additionally, a nonredundant UNC path introduces a single point of failure, when a web farm, by nature, usually needs more redundancy, not less. These are valid points because introducing a network path into the mix brings in more potential for a failure. Don't worry, these concerns are addressed throughout the chapter, and good solutions are laid out to work around potential failures.

There happen to be some environments that benefit by pointing to a nonredundant UNC path. A prime candidate is a testing or quality assurance environment where the development and testing servers need to match the production server, but high availability isn't a requirement. While there are some situations like these that will make do to have a nonredundant location, most production environments should have the configuration files in a fully redundant location.

Below in this chapter, this concern is addressed with the discussion about Distributed File System Replication (DSFR) and offline folders, both of which offer excellent methods to plan for potential network and server failures. First, though, the next few sections lay the necessary foundation that applies regardless of whether you use a redundant or nonredundant location for your configuration files. In both situations, you need to understand the shared configuration feature and how to enable it.

Enabling shared configuration is a two-step process:

1. Export the configuration files to the destination location.
2. Set IIS to point to that location.

Note that it is necessary to ensure that the exported configuration does not contain elements that are specific to any of the servers. The items that you need to be aware of are discussed below in this chapter.

Exporting the Configuration Files

IIS Manager allows you to export the configuration files and save them to a location of your choosing. After exporting the files, you can copy them wherever you want, or leave them there. The goal in IIS 7.0 is to make sure that the configuration files are generic text files that can be edited in a simple file editor like Notepad, or copied between locations using simple tools like XCopy. IIS 7.0 has met this goal, making the entire architecture simple and scalable.

When exporting the configuration files, the following three files are saved to the destination that you specify:

❑ `applicationHost.config`

❑ `administration.config`

❑ `configEncKey.key`

From IIS Manager this is done at the server level. Double-click the Shared Configuration icon to open that tool (see Figure 16-1).

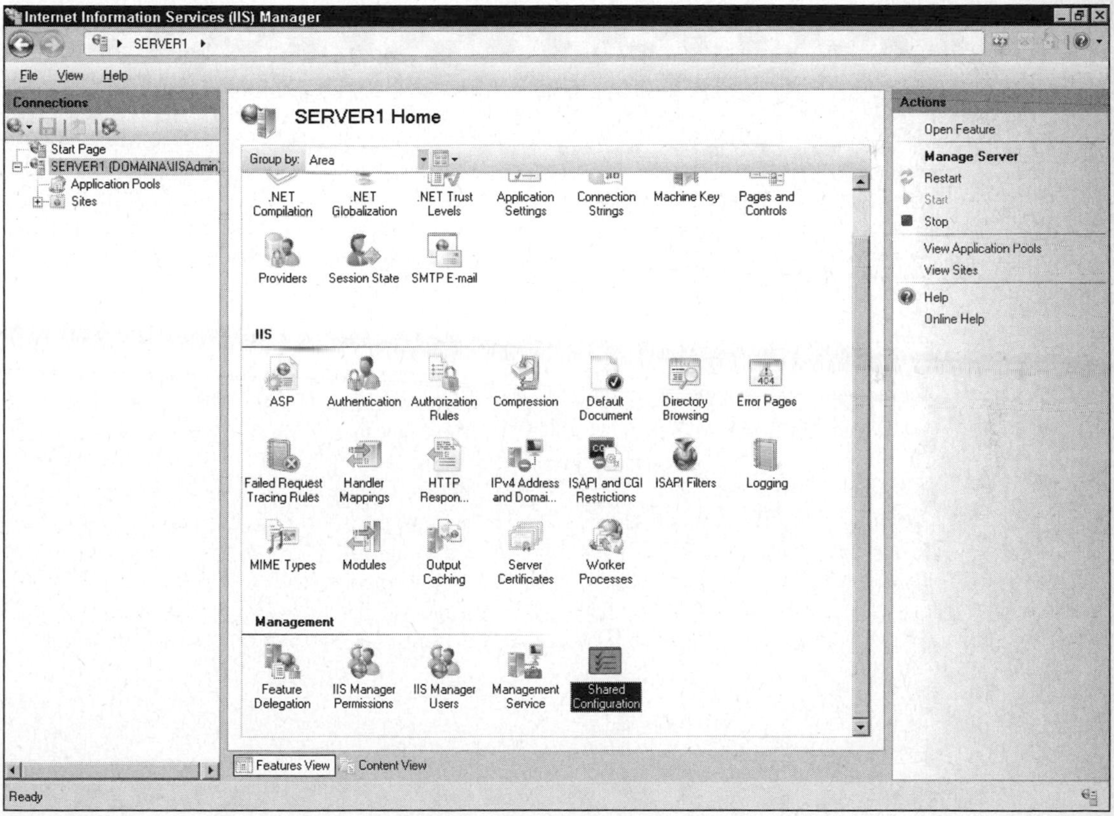

Figure 16-1

The Shared Configuration tool is free from clutter, with the main section used for pointing to the configuration files and the right-hand Actions pane used for exporting the configuration.

529

To export the configuration files, click Export Configuration in the Actions pane. This opens the Export Configuration dialog window, as shown in Figure 16-2.

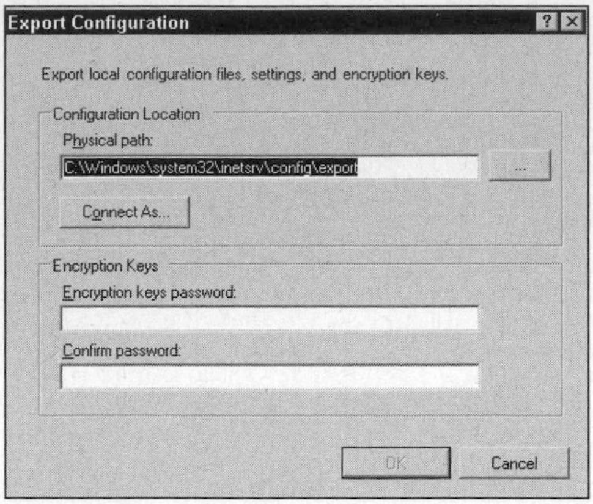

Figure 16-2

The Export Configuration dialog box has three required fields and the optional "Connect As" section.

❑ The "Physical path" can be a local path or a UNC path. The ellipsis (...) opens the "Browse For Folder" dialog box, allowing you to navigate to the folder instead of typing it in. If you want to browse for a box on a UNC path, you can type the first part of the UNC path and click the ellipsis (...) button. This will automatically start you at the path that you entered in the "Physical path" textbox. Obviously, this is only the case if it's a valid path; if you are navigating to a hidden path, the "Browse For Folder" dialog box will not work for you.

❑ The "Connect As" button opens the Set Credentials dialog box. This is an optional setting and often isn't needed. This is only used this once, to connect to the folder and network share that you will export the configuration files to. If you don't set anything in the Set Credentials dialog box, the user that you are currently logged on as will be used instead. You would set credentials here if the user that you are logged into IIS Manager with doesn't have Write permissions to the destination folder or share.

❑ The "Encryption key" is a key that is used to encrypt the `configEncKey.key` file that will be exported through this tool. This will be explained in more depth shortly. The password needs to be a complex password that includes uppercase and lowercase letters, numbers, and symbols, and is at least eight characters. All these requirements need to be met; otherwise, a warning will be displayed, and you will be required to enter a new password. Be sure to remember this password since it is required to configure the other servers in the web farm.

Once you click the OK button, the current configuration is exported to the destination that you specified, whether you are currently using the default configuration or have already set up shared configuration.

It's helpful to understand what the `configEncKey.key` file is. This file contains the RSA keys that will be installed on each of the servers when they are first configured for shared configuration. This ensures that all of the servers in the web farm have the same RSA keys so that they can properly encrypt and decrypt sensitive information like the IIS Manager Users and application pool passwords. Think of it this way — the password entered in the export tool is used to encrypt the `configEncKey.key` file, which, in turn, contains keys that are used to encrypt and decrypt sensitive information in the configuration files.

Completing this dialog box is all that is required for the first step. This exports all of the configuration files that are necessary for this server to share its configuration with other servers. Now the location that you specified is ready to be shared and used by the other servers.

If you will only be using the export tool from IIS Manager, you can tune out for the next few paragraphs until the end of this section. Advanced users who want to export the RSA keys manually rather than using IIS Manager can do so using the `aspnet_regiis.exe` command-line tool. The `<configProtectedData>` section of `applicationHost.config` has three providers, two of which share the same `keyContainerName`. Get the two unique `keyContainerName` values, and then from the command-line in the `\Framework` folder (`%windir%\Microsoft.NET\Framework\<version>\`), enter `aspnet_regiis.exe -px "{keyContainerName}" "{Path and filename}" -pri`.

The `-px` says to export the keys, and the `-pri` says to include the private keys with it. For example, the two commands to export the two keys would be

```
aspnet_regiis.exe -px "iisWasKey" "c:\iisWasKey.xml" -pri
aspnet_regiis.exe -px "iisConfigurationKey" "c:\iisConfigKey.xml" -pri
```

Running this will generate two files in the `c:\` folder. Copy those to the destination server, and run the same two commands again from that server, but this time change the `-px` (for export) with `-pi` (for import) and drop the `-pri`. It should look like this:

```
aspnet_regiis.exe -pi "iisWasKey" "c:\iisWasKey.xml"
aspnet_regiis.exe -pi "iisConfigurationKey" "c:\iisConfKey.xml"
```

*The RSA keys are saved in the All Users Profile in the path `%ALLUSERSPROFILE%\Microsoft\Crypto\RSA\MachineKeys\`. Note that since they are system files, if you want to see them from the command prompt, you must type **dir /as** to show system files.*

After you've completed these steps, the server that you applied this to can work with the same configuration files as the original server.

Relocating the Configuration Files

Now that you have the file exported, you must tell this server and all of the other servers in the web farm where and how to point to those files. Until this point, you are still running off your original configuration files in the `%windir%/System32/inetsrv/config` folder.

Enabling the shared configuration and pointing to the shared configuration files are done from the same shared configuration tool, from the main windowpane. Before walking through this, it's important to understand the two different password prompts.

The first password prompt is the username that is entered into this main window, shown in Figure 16-3. This is the user that is used to authenticate to the shared configuration path during normal operation. Since the Windows Process Activation Service (WAS) Windows service user is Local System by default, it's important to be able to specify a custom user to access network resources. Setting a domain user allows you to access a network share using the permissions that you specify. The domain user must have access to the shared folder; both the windows share and the NTFS permissions. No additional Windows user rights need to be specifically granted to this user besides the share and file access.

Here is an interesting concept. The user entered here in the shared configuration is only used for Read access; by IIS Manager, WAS, and the programming APIs. But, any time that you Write to the configuration files from IIS Manager or the programming APIs, it will not run under this user. Instead, for IIS Manager, it will run under the user that you are authenticated as, or it will run under the WMSvc service account user if you are using delegated administration and IIS Manager Users authentication. When making changes to the configuration using one of the programming APIs, the user account that the code runs under will be used to connect to the shared configuration store for write access. Therefore, it's important that you keep track of the permissions used for Reading from and Writing to the configuration since they can be different users in the shared configuration.

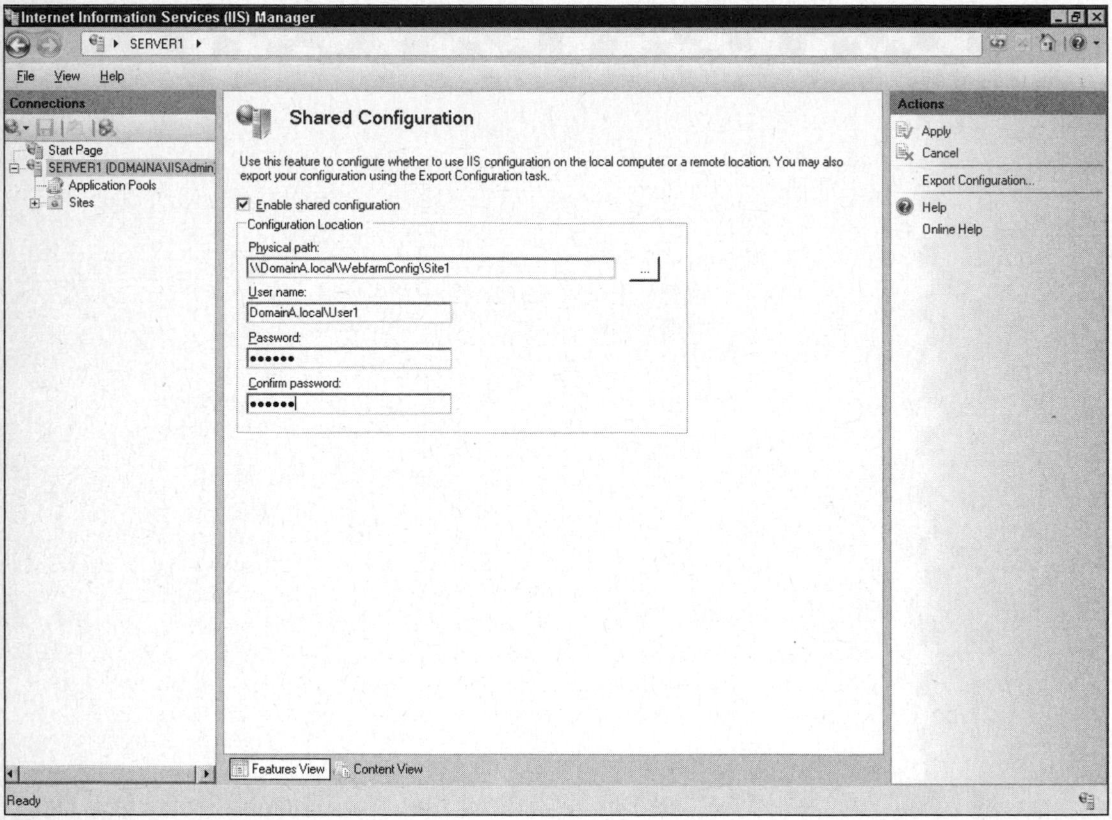

Figure 16-3

After clicking "Apply", a second password prompt will appear, asking you to enter the Encryption Keys Password. This is used to decrypt the `configEncKey.key` file. The password is the same one that you entered in the export configuration tool in the previous section.

To enable shared configuration and have IIS use a different configuration folder, perform the following steps:

1. At the server lever, double-click the Shared Configuration icon to open the Shared Configuration tool.

2. Check the "Enable shared configuration" checkbox.

3. Enter the path in the "Physical path" textbox. This can be a local path or a UNC path. This will often be the same path that was set when using the Export Configuration tool, although it doesn't have to be since you have a lot of flexibility in how you configure this.

4. Enter the username used for authentication to the configuration folder. You can enter the fully qualified domain name (FQDN) or just the name by itself if it's part of the same domain that the server is on — for example, **DomainA.local\User1** or just **User1**.

5. Enter the password and confirmation for the user just entered, and then click Apply.

6. After applying these settings, assuming that you pointed to a valid folder, you will be presented with one of two options.

In most cases, you will be asked to enter another password, as shown in Figure 16-4. This is the Encryption Key password that was entered in the Export Configuration tool. This password is used to decrypt the `configEncKey.key` file, which, in turn, installs the RSA keys on the server. Enter the password that you entered previously and click OK.

Figure 16-4

The other situation is if the physical path points to a folder that has the `.config` files but doesn't have the `configEncKey.key` file. This should only happen if you manually moved files around or tried to point to an existing IIS folder that wasn't properly exported. If this happens, the RSA keys will not be available to decrypt settings like the IIS User's passwords or application pools with custom user identities. Most IIS settings will still work since they aren't decrypted by default, but key passwords cannot be decrypted, which in turn may keep IIS from functioning properly. After clicking Apply in this situation, you will be presented with a warning asking if you want to continue or cancel (see Figure 16-5).

Finally, you will be asked to acknowledge two prompts. The first prompt tells you that the current encryption keys have been backed-up in the current configuration directory on your local computer. The second prompt mentions that both IIS Manager and the Management Service need to be restarted for the change to take effect (see Figure 16-6).

That's it. Well, that's it as long as you followed the instructions to restart IIS Manager and the Management Service. At this point, IIS will be running off the directory that you specified. Repeat this on all servers in the web farm to point multiple servers to this same configuration. After all servers are pointed to the same configuration, any IIS change made to any of the servers will immediately be picked up by all servers.

It's worth noting that the web site and application pool state is per machine and not shared between the servers, even if IIS Shared Configuration is enabled. This means that all the servers can share the same configuration, but if a site or application pool is started, stopped, or recycled, that change isn't made to all of the servers in the web farm.

Additionally, the Runtime Status and Control API (RSCA), which is discussed in Chapter 20, is also per server. Therefore, configuration changes apply to all servers, but site and application pool state is local to the server that you apply it to.

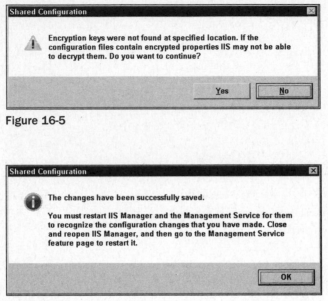

Figure 16-5

Figure 16-6

IIS Manager does two things when enabling shared configuration. First, it imports the RSA keys that were exported through the export configuration tool. Then, it updates a file called `redirection.config` in `%windir%\System32\inetsrv\config`. The `redirection.config` file tells IIS where the rest of the configuration files are and what the user credentials are to connect to them.

Here is an example of the entire `redirection.config` file after enabling shared configuration in IIS Manager:

```
<configuration>

  <configSections>
    <section name="configurationRedirection" />
  </configSections>

  <configProtectedData>
    <providers>
      <add name="IISRsaProvider" type="" description="Uses
        RsaCryptoServiceProvider to encrypt and decrypt"
        keyContainerName="iisConfigurationKey" cspProviderName=""
```

```
            useMachineContainer="true" useOAEP="false" />
       </providers>
    </configProtectedData>

    <configurationRedirection enabled="true"
      path="\\domainA.local\WebfarmConfig\site1"
      userName="domainA.local\User1"
password="[enc:IISRsaProvider:jAAAAAECAAADZgAAAKIUpmPJCNUjMGpYbz0PEdto7bbO5+lYUI5P+
X5YyR5hZogAU82H6LD2qNqWzBWKnb6VFfhHLwkPcFbQh5w43wFFMHkQuosJjFfORJ6US4SKKt3vbSVOyXh1
EqhzaRkc4K0U+aMeY1NjEASwMaBZmDjDyGTjiaFXJi:enc]" />

    </configuration>
```

Notice in the `<configurationRedirection />` section that the path, username, and password are specified. You can manually change this or use IIS Manager to update it.

Now that exporting the configuration and pointing to the new configuration path has been covered, it's time to look at creating machine-neutral configuration files that will work on all servers in the web farm, even with different IP addresses or different paths and settings.

Creating Machine-Neutral Configuration Files

Having a single set of configuration files for multiple servers requires that the configuration files be generic enough to work on all servers, regardless of the unique settings on each server. This takes some forethought and planning. This section explains how to do this and the necessary considerations to accommodate your specific environment.

ACLs

If you are intimately familiar with previous versions of IIS, you know that the metabase has its own set of *Access Control Lists (ACLs)* for each section of the metabase, just as the NTFS file system has ACLs on files and folders. This allowed the administrator to lock down particular settings so that only certain users could read, write, list, or control specified sections.

In concept, this was powerful and allowed a lot of control, but in reality, it was difficult to maintain and to configure properly. For this reason, IIS 7.0 has completely removed ACLs within the configuration and instead depends on ACLs at the file level plus some other configuration improvements.

This was necessary for web farm and shared configuration support. In the past, the ACLs would get in the way when trying to keep multiple servers in sync, and often a tool called `metaacls.vbs` was needed to repair permissions that got out of sync between servers. In IIS 7.0, this is a non-issue, since the configuration file doesn't contain any Windows users or group settings.

No action is required on your part, but it is helpful to be aware of how this has improved over previous versions of IIS.

Environment Variables

System environment variables are an integral part of the Windows operating system and allow unique settings on each server to be defined in a variable that can be called from many different applications. These are commonly used in batch files, .NET applications, Windows programs, and most anywhere else you can imagine.

IIS 7.0 finally supports them as well. New with IIS 7.0, you can set environment variables in the configuration files instead of hard-coding the values. Common system environment variables that you may already be familiar with are `%windir%` and `%SystemDrive%`. In case you aren't already familiar with these two examples, `%windir%` is a system environment variable that points to your Windows directory (which is often `C:\Windows`), and `%SystemDrive%` is usually `C:\`. There are other environment variables, of course, and you can define your own, as discussed below.

By default, `applicationHost.config` already uses several system environment variables. In fact, by default, you won't see c:\ or d:\ hard-coded anywhere in the configuration files. Instead, all paths are relative to the environment variables. For example, the default site's `physicalPath` is set to `%SystemDrive%\inetpub\wwwroot`. Although it's rare to change a system path like the C drive, it's still cleaner to use environment variables every opportunity that you have.

This is especially useful in a web farm environment. Using system environment variables allows you to have unique paths on each server while still sharing the same configuration file. In an ideal situation, all of the servers in a web farm are identical and have the same paths and settings between them. That isn't always possible, though, especially for companies or individuals on a tight budget or who are trying to reuse servers for multiple purposes. It's common enough for web farm environments to have dissimilar settings.

> *IIS 7.0 doesn't support environment variables on all attributes by default — just on the path related attributes like* `physicalPath` *or* `Path`. *This is controlled in the schema files (most likely IIS_schema.xml) by setting the corresponding attribute to* `expanded="true"`. *To find out for sure which attributes support environment variables, open* `%windir%\System32\inetsrv\config\schema\IIS_schema.xml`, *search for* `expanded="true"`, *and take note of the attributes where it's set.*

Because of this support for environment variables, it's a good idea to use environment variables as much as possible for paths. The performance penalty for IIS to get the value of an environment variable is negligible. For example, if you use "d:\websites" as the root folder for your web sites, create an environment variable called `DomainPath` and set it to `d:\websites`. This way, if you ever change the path, or if you build a new machine that doesn't use the same path, you can simply update the server's system environment variable — no other change is required in the configuration files.

If you create your own custom attributes, you can set `expanded="true"` so that you can use environment variables. Here is an example of one line from IIS_schema.xml, where `expanded` is set to `true`.

```
<attribute name="physicalPath" type="string" expanded="true" />
```

To use an environment variable, simply set it surrounded by `%` `%`, as shown in the following example:

```
<site name="Default Web Site" id="1">
  <application path="/">
    <virtualDirectory path="/"
      physicalPath="%SystemDrive%\inetpub\wwwroot" />
  </application>
  <bindings>
    <binding protocol="http" bindingInformation="*:80:" />
  </bindings>
</site>
```

Notice the `SystemDrive` environment variable in `physicalPath` instead of a hard-coded c:\. The complete dynamic path is `%SystemDrive%\inetpub\wwwroot`, which will usually be interpreted by IIS as `c:\inetpub\wwwroot`, depending on what the system environment variable is set to in the system.

This is supported in IIS Manager as well. When entering the path, simply type the environment variable name surrounded by the % %, and it will immediately take effect. Figure 16-7 shows a site's properties with the physical path set to an environment variable.

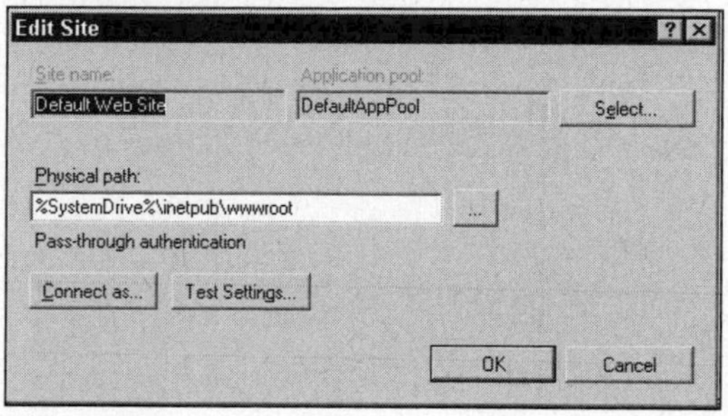

Figure 16-7

To get a list of environment variables on your server, type **Set** from the command line, as shown in Figure 16-8. The `Set` command allows you to set *user* environment variables, but it does not support *system* environment variables. This means that you can use the `Set` command to read the variables but not to write them. To make things a bit trickier, the list shown when typing **Set** is a combination of both system and user environment variables, so be careful to understand the difference. Use `Set` as a quick reference, but to find out for sure which are which, use the Environment Variables interface within Windows to read or set system environment variables.

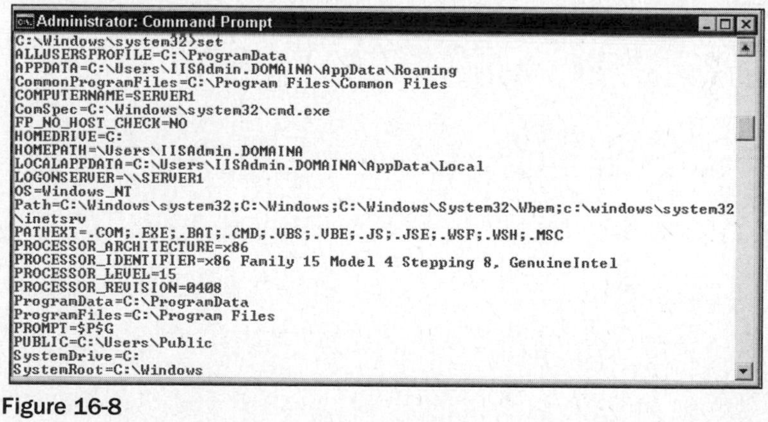

Figure 16-8

The most straightforward way to read or write environment variables is from the Windows environment.

1. Click Start ➪ Search box, enter **System**, and then click System in the list of programs.
2. Click Advanced System Settings in the Tasks pane.

3. In the System Properties dialog box, on the Advanced tab, click Environment Variables. The windows shown in Figure 16-9 will appear.

You can add, remove, or update user or system variables. Only system variables will apply to IIS, since your currently logged-on session will probably not be the one that IIS uses, unless you've purposefully set it up as such.

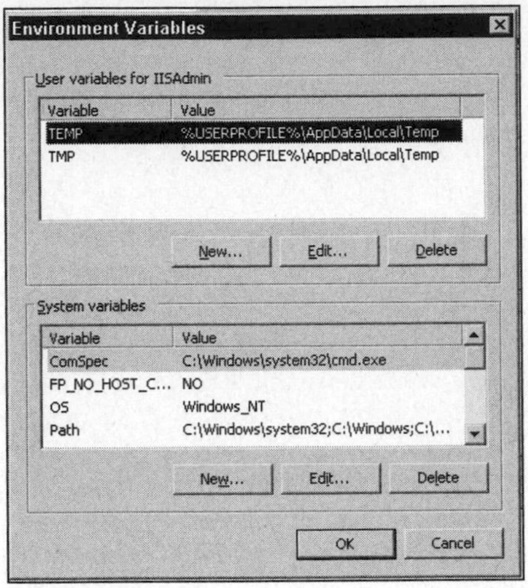

Figure 16-9

Changes to the system environment variables don't take effect immediately. You must restart IIS Manager and the IIS services for IIS to pick up the new environment variable. You can restart IIS by typing IISReset *from the command line.*

Surprisingly, setting system environment variables from the command prompt is not straightforward. As previously mentioned, the Set command will not allow you to set system-level environment variables, only user-level variables. One method to set system-level variables is to add to the Registry directly from the command prompt by creating a file called *SetEnvironmentVariable.vbs*, placing the following code into it, and saving it:

```
Const HKLM = &H80000002

strComputer = "."
Set objRegistry = GetObject("winmgmts:\\" & strComputer & _
    "\root\default:StdRegProv")

strKeyPath = "System\CurrentControlSet\Control\Session Manager\Environment"
strValueName = WScript.Arguments.Item(0)
strValue = WScript.Arguments.Item(1)

objRegistry.SetStringValue HKLM, strKeyPath, strValueName, strValue
```

Note that this code is a bare-bones example without any error checking. Feel free to enhance it.

This uses WMI to set or update the registry. `WScript.Arguments.Item()` gets a value that is passed as a parameter from the command line or batch file. `Item(0)` is the first value, and `Item(1)` is the second. The final line sets the string.

To add a system environment variable with this script, from the command prompt folder where this exists, type `SetEnvironmentVariable "DomainPath" "D:\websites"`. Be sure to start the command prompt as administrator so that User Access Control (UAC) doesn't prevent this from working properly.

Just like when using the Windows interface, this change does not take effect until you restart IIS and IIS Manager.

In your quest to neutralize the configuration files, environment variables play a large role because of their ability to have unique settings per server while still having a single shared configuration.

Handling IP Addresses

A common question with web farm configuration is how to handle the different IP addresses across a web farm. Your web farm load-balancing method (covered in the "Load Balancing" section below in this chapter) may require a unique IP address per server, but even if you can use the same IP for all sites, you will probably want to have a method of testing each server directly so that if there are intermittent issues, you can tell which server is to blame. The way to accomplish this is to have a unique binding per server for each site, which is described below in this section. The trick with shared configuration is to be able to have unique bindings on each server but still share the same configuration.

It's surprisingly easy to manage this as long as you understand a simple principle: *Invalid site bindings are ignored; they will not throw an error*.

Even IP addresses that don't exist on the server will be ignored. When using IIS Manager and setting up a new site binding, you will be offered a dropdown list of all of the IP addresses on the server. Don't let this fool you. That is a handy method of quickly selecting a valid IP that is already on the server, but you can type in another IP address free-form instead of using the options in the dropdown box.

This means that the unique site bindings on each server can be added to all servers and will be ignored on the servers that they don't apply to. With this in mind, to properly manage a web farm of servers using shared configuration with different site bindings on each server, simply add all the bindings at once. A more detailed example is covered below.

Furthermore, the ability to add all site bindings to all servers offers another benefit. Using this principle, it's possible to set up a handy set of testing URLs using host headers. This is particularly useful if you support multiple web sites on the same web farm.

To illustrate both of these points at once, consider a web farm of three servers and two web sites (see Figure 16-10) and five IP addresses available. One IP address is assigned to each server, and for each site, one is assigned as the virtual IP address. The server names and IP addresses are Server1/10.0.0.10, Server2/10.0.0.11, and Server3/10.0.0.12. The virtual IP addresses are Site1/10.0.0.20 and Site2/10.0.0.21. The web sites are called Site1 and Site2.

The first step is to set up a DNS wildcard so that {everything}.Server1.DomainA.com points to 10.0.0.10. Do the same with Server2 and Server3 for 10.0.0.11 and 10.0.0.12. Once this wildcard configuration is set up, no DNS changes are necessary in the future if additional web sites are added to the web farm.

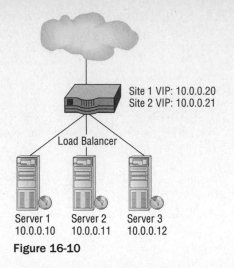

Figure 16-10

Once the DNS step is completed, the next step is to add the site bindings to IIS. Since this web farm is using shared configuration, any of the servers can be used to add the site bindings. Entering the IP address is optional since the host header is unique enough to apply only to the one web site. The four site bindings on Site1 will be

IP Address	Port	Hostname
10.0.0.20	80	{blank}
All Unassigned	80	Site1.Server1.DomainA.com
All Unassigned	80	Site1.Server2.DomainA.com
All Unassigned	80	Site1.Server3.DomainA.com

Next, the three site bindings on Site2 will be

IP Address	Port	Hostname
10.0.0.21	80	{blank}
All Unassigned	80	Site2.Server1.DomainA.com
All Unassigned	80	Site2.Server2.DomainA.com
All Unassigned	80	Site2.Server3.DomainA.com

This will result in DNS pointing the domain name to the correct server, and then IIS will know which site to serve up based on the binding. Essentially, each server will have all of these bindings, and the appropriate server will know what to do when it receives a page request.

Figure 16-11 shows the site bindings on Site1.

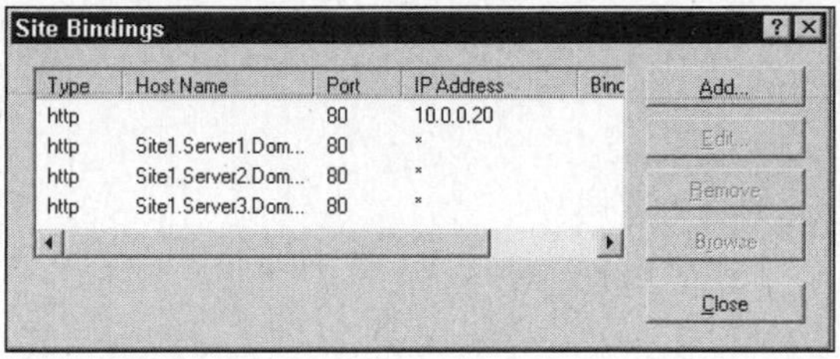

Figure 16-11

The same principle applies not only to host headers but also to IP addresses. Not all load-balancing solutions share the same virtual IP address, so it's often necessary to apply the same concept with different IP addresses per server.

Now that you know that unused site bindings are ignored, you can set up almost any environment to have neutral configuration files so that all servers can share the same set of configuration files.

Diversified web.config files

With the diversified `web.config` file structure in IIS 7.0, it's possible to use the `web.config` files to separate unique settings from each server in the web farm so that each server can have a unique configuration specific to its differences.

With the ability to pull settings out of `applicationHost.config` and set them in the web-site `web.config` file instead, it is possible to have different `web.config` files for each server on the web farm. See Chapter 9, "Delegating Remote Administration," for more information on applying settings in the `web.config` file instead of `applicationHost.config`.

Since most web farms will have shared or replicated content, it's not common to have a unique `web.config` file per server. This makes diversified `web.config` files a non-solution in many web farms, but it's good to be aware of the options.

configSource

The new `configSource` attribute is mentioned here more to say that it's a non-option than to say that it's an option. But since at first it appears that it may be a good solution, it's worth mentioning.

The `configSource` attribute can be applied to configuration sections or individual items of the `web.config` file to pull sections out of the `web.config` file and store them in their own configuration files. This is particularly useful if you want to protect certain sections from being overwritten or if you want to set NTFS ACLs on sections so that only certain people can manage them.

The following example shows how to create a separate configuration file for the defaultDocument section of a site.

Create or update your web site's `web.config` file so that it looks like the following:

```
<?xml version="1.0" encoding="UTF-8"?>
<configuration>
    <system.webServer>
        <defaultDocument configSource="defaultDoc.config">
        </defaultDocument>
    </system.webServer>
</configuration>
```

Next, create a new document called `defaultDoc.config` and place the following in it:

```
<defaultDocument>
    <files>
        <clear />
        <add value="default.aspx" />
    </files>
</defaultDocument>
```

Notice that this allows the `<defaultDocument>` section to be placed in its own file rather than being managed from the `web.config` file.

The list of default documents will now be controlled from `defaultDoc.config` instead of `web.config`. Unfortunately, in the original release of IIS 7.0, IIS Manager will not update a `configSource` file properly. In this example, when you update the list of default documents in IIS Manager, they will be deleted from `defaultDoc.config` and will be saved in `web.config` instead. Therefore, if you do use `configSource`, be sure that you don't use IIS Manager to update any of the settings that are saved in their own configuration files.

The biggest issue on a web farm is that `configSource` is not supported within `applicationHost.config` because of the relative paths that the new application pool isolation introduced. Without this being supported at the `applicationHost.config` level, it's not a common solution for web farms.

Additionally, `configSource` will only work with *relative* paths; therefore, even in the `web.config` files, it's not possible to point to an *absolute* physical path on the server.

Be aware of this, though; in case you do have a unique requirement, you can use this as part of your solution. Also, watch for future versions of IIS to improve and build on the `configSource` attribute.

childSource

The `childSource` attribute, on the other hand, does have some potential for a web farm. It only works for the `<site>` section in `applicationHost.config`, but that just may be the section that you want to save out to a different file. The concept is the same as the `configSource` attribute mentioned in the above section.

The `childSource` attribute's path is relative to the temporary application pool's folder (`%systemdrive%\inetpub\temp\apppools`), so it's best to use an absolute path. That's probably better, however, because it means that you can point to a configuration file on your local server, which achieves the purpose of having unique site settings on each server while still sharing the same general configuration files.

The `childSource` attribute differs from `configSource` in that it doesn't manage any of the attributes for the parent. It only manages the child elements. Here is what `applicationHost.config` should look like:

```
<site name="Site1" id="1" childSource="c:\SiteConfig\site1.config" >
</site>
```

Notice the absolute path to the file on disk, and notice that the name and ID are still set in `applicationHost.config`. The `site1.config` file looks like this:

```
<site>
  <application path="/">
    <virtualDirectory path="/" physicalPath="%SystemDrive%\inetpub\wwwroot" />
  </application>
  <bindings>
    <binding protocol="http" bindingInformation="*:80:" />
  </bindings>
</site>
```

Notice that the `<site>` element is completely empty in `site1.config`. That is a requirement of the `childSource` because the attributes are defined in `applicationHost.config`. Changes you make to this file will be immediately picked up by IIS Manager, but they will not be picked up by Windows Process Activation Service (WAS) until IIS is restarted or `applicationHost.config` is "touched" in some way. The best way to deal with this if you are making changes to the child config file directly is to add an irrelevant space to `applicationHost.config` to cause the change to take effect. When making changes from IIS Manager, they take effect immediately. Interestingly enough, unlike configSource, IIS Manager fully supports updating a section that uses childSource.

So far, this chapter has covered the shared configuration mechanism introduced in IIS 7.0 and how to make the configuration files machine-neutral so that they will work successfully on all servers of the web farm.

Additionally, the bulk of the IIS features for web farms have been covered. Everything else in IIS will work on single servers and on web farms without any specific consideration. Keep reading, though, because there are some specific considerations to keep in mind, and there will be some discussion about content replication and protecting the IIS configuration files from any network hiccup.

It's time to switch gears and move away from IIS specific settings and take a look at content replication, which can be applied to various aspects of the web farm to keep the servers in sync. The rest of this chapter is mostly non-IIS-specific and covers the tools necessary to build and maintain a web farm environment.

Content Configuration

Before diving into the technologies that support a web farm, it's important to understand some high-level concepts for configuring the content for a web farm, and to know which method you will use.

There are essentially three web farm file content configurations:

❑ Local content.

❑ Shared network content.

❑ Shared SAN content.

The solution that you choose will often be based on the project requirements, budget, your previous experience, and/or available hardware. Each has its own set of advantages and disadvantages.

Local Content

Figure 16-12 shows a web farm configuration using *local content*. Each of the web servers keeps the content locally, and therefore it's up to the System Administrator to set up either an automatic method of replication or a way to push content to all nodes after it has gone through the quality assurance team and is ready for deployment. In the case of code from the web site writing to disk, it's important that the content is immediately replicated to the other servers so that they remain in sync.

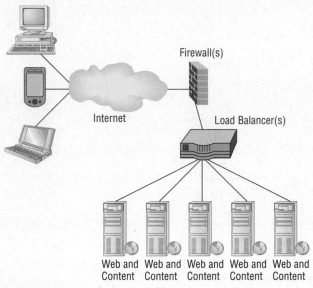

Figure 16-12

There are several advantages and disadvantages of a web farm file content configuration using local content. Some advantages are:

❑ There is complete isolation between servers. If something goes wrong, usually only one of the servers is affected, and if the load balancer properly takes it out of rotation, end-users won't be affected.

❑ It has the ability to distribute load evenly. Each server handles its own load, removing disk I/O pressure from a central location.

❑ Because there are fewer moving parts, local content is straightforward to configure.

❑ It can be less expensive since another content server isn't required.

❑ Testing and troubleshooting can sometimes be easier because taking a server out of the web farm allows modifying the content without affecting any of the other servers.

This method has some disadvantages:

❑ A solution for replication between servers is required. The more servers there are the more complex this can become.

❑ If the web site writes to disk (for example, with a wiki), the other servers won't have that content available until the replication software copies it to the other servers. Depending on the replication solution and/or file locking, this may take a while.

❑ There are more copies of the data, which costs more if the web site content is very large; that is, for a very large web site (in terms of disk space usage), there will be as many copies of the data as there are servers (plus backups).

The advantages and disadvantages need to be considered within your particular environment to see if this is best for you. Many high-traffic web sites on the Internet today use local content.

Shared Network Content

Shared network content utilizes a central location to manage the content, often using a Network Attached Storage (NAS) server, and all the web servers point to that location. Often they are mirrored to another server with some method of failover, but the web servers primarily point to a single location.

In contrast to local content, Figure 16-13 shows shared content using a NAS device. All the servers on the web farm point to the network storage over a UNC path. This is fully supported in IIS 7.0 (as it was in previous versions). Network shares are easy to configure on Windows or non-Windows servers, so using a network device for sharing content is easy to do for most any size web farm.

Shared network content has its own set of advantages and disadvantages. The advantages of a single shared network content storage location are:

❑ Anything written to disk is immediately available on all of the servers. In addition to web-site content, FTP and other means of transferring the web-site data only need to write to the one place for it to become immediately available to all of the web servers.

❑ Adding the content on additional servers is as easy as pointing to a UNC path.

❑ Only a few copies of the web site need to be kept. For web sites that use a large amount of space, this can be beneficial. The hard drives on the web servers need to contain only the operating system; it's up to the content servers to maintain all the content. For a large web farm, this may mean two copies of the data (plus backups) instead of having copies for each of the web servers.

The disadvantages of this method are:

❑ There becomes a single point of failure. This can be minimized with a good solution like DFS, which is discussed below.

❑ More pressure is placed on the content location. As the site gets busier, if it overtaxes the content server, it's often difficult to scale out quickly to address the load. Disk I/O can become a bottleneck quite easily.

❑ Network bandwidth can become a concern on a busy web farm because in addition to the bandwidth generated from the web-site visitors (common to all methods), there is additional traffic, between the web servers and the shared network devices, that can be quite substantial.

❑   Cost can be a consideration since a set of content servers is required.

❑   The network device must support Server Message Block (SMB) File Change Notifications, which are not supported by all operating systems. Most Windows versions from Windows 2000 Server and on support at least SMB v1. Windows Server 2008 has enhanced support with SMB v2 and should be considered for the network server, if possible.

❑   There are more moving parts. For example, ASP.NET requires some CAS settings to work over a UNC path. (This is covered close to the end of this chapter.) There are also more share and NTFS permissions to maintain.

❑   The new feature that injects the application pool SID into the NETWORK SERVICE token does not work across the network, so you should use custom application pool identity users instead.

❑   There can be potential locking issues because multiple servers use the same files. Be sure that your web site considers this.

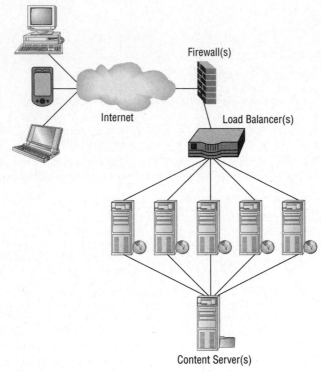

Figure 16-13

Don't let the list of disadvantages scare you. There are many environments where shared content over a network share is the best solution. Weigh the pros and cons of each method to decide which is best for you.

There is an important set of settings that need to be made if you have multiple web sites on your server using different UNC paths and you are using the 32-bit version of Windows Server 2008. You will quickly run out of work contexts and start to receive intermittent failures on your web sites. This was a problem with previous versions of Windows and is still a problem with Windows Server 2008. The Knowledge

Base article at `http://support.microsoft.com/default.aspx?scid=kb;en-us;Q221790` explains this in depth. Note that although the KB article is for previous versions of Windows, it still applies to Windows Server 2008.

To apply the fix, follow these steps:

1. Create a file on the desktop (or anywhere you prefer) of your web servers called *Client.reg*, and add the following to it:

```
Windows Registry Editor Version 5.00

HKEY_LOCAL_MACHINE\SYSTEM\CurrentControlSet\Services\lanmanworkstation\parameters]
"MaxCmds"=dword:00000800
```

2. Double-click the file and acknowledge the prompts. A reboot is required for this to take effect.

You also need to make changes on your NAS server if it is a Windows server. Repeat the preceding steps on that server, but instead use the following registry entries. Name this file *Server.reg*.

```
Windows Registry Editor Version 5.00

[HKEY_LOCAL_MACHINE\SYSTEM\CurrentControlSet\Services\lanmanserver\parameters]
"MaxMpxCT"=dword:00000800
"MaxWorkItems"=dword:00002000
```

Once these have been applied and you have rebooted your servers, you should not run out of work contexts needed to maintain connections to multiple UNC paths. The KB article explains in more depth which performance information you should watch to ensure that you don't use up your non-paged memory; however, in most situations, this is a safe change that is required for the successful operation of your web farm.

Shared SAN Content

The third method of managing the content of a web site on a web farm is using a *Storage Area Network (SAN)* device. A SAN is often a highly redundant, high-performing network device devoted solely to disk storage (refer to Figure 16-13 again, which also applies to a SAN).

SANs are typically used for high-end storage. They offer benefits by having the ability to house a large number of hard drives, thus creating more hard drive spindles working at the same time, which, in turn, offers much better disk I/O. They often offer additional benefits like the ability to carve out new drives on the fly and increase the size of existing partitions, powerful snapshot features, replication across a wide-area network, extensive redundancy, error handling, and much more. Each vendor offers its own set of advantages.

A SAN allows each server on the web farm to see the content as if it were a local drive. For example, the SAN can be configured to add an F: drive on each server. As far as each server is concerned, that content is local. Yet, while it appears to be local to the server, all of the servers are using the same content at the same time.

> *Not all SAN environments will allow multiple servers to access the content simultaneously. Be sure to confirm with your SAN vendor to ensure that it will allow multiple servers to use the SAN at the same time. Alternately, if your SAN supports it, you can consider using a UNC path as covered in the last section. This will allow you to take advantage of the highly scalable and redundant features of a SAN, while accessing it simultaneously from multiple web servers.*

There are a few methods of connecting the servers to the SAN. The most common method in the past has been *Fiber Channel SCSI*. Fiber Channel has dedicated hardware and cabling but is quite pricey. At the time of this writing, Fiber Channel is still the most common method of connecting SANs to servers.

The second most common method of SAN connectivity is *iSCSI*. iSCSI uses the SCSI protocol over TCP/IP networks. This is advantageous because most networks depend on TCP/IP and have existing infrastructures already in place. Using iSCSI, existing networks, which so many network administrators are already familiar with, can be utilized. iSCSI is quickly gaining momentum and will probably overtake Fiber Channel within a short time. Early versions of iSCSI weren't as efficient as Fiber Channel SCSI because they required extra processing overhead, but that has changed with iSCSI controllers and the option of specialized network adapters that handle that overhead without robbing any CPU from the server itself.

SANs share many of the advantages and disadvantages of local content and network storages. The advantages that SANs offer above local content and network storage are:

❑   Usually much higher-end content solution with a high level of redundancy and flexibility to scale up and out.

❑   Easier to manage and adjust for growth using the built-in tools and features.

There are a few disadvantages, of course:

❑   **Up-front cost** — Some will argue that a SAN is less expensive in the long run, but a small web farm may never get to that point. While prices on SANs have been dropping considerably, the up-front costs for a good SAN solution have caused SANs to generally be available only in larger enterprises.

❑   **Initial implementation overhead** — Researching, training-for, and implementing a SAN can be a daunting task. If it's the first in the company, it's not an easy decision or process. Once implemented, it has many advantages that usually outweigh the initial time investment.

A good SAN solution can be costly up-front, but it has many advantages. Yet even if you have a bottomless bank account, it's not always the best solution; so careful consideration should be given in determining which of the methods works best in your environment.

Content Replication

A key part of virtually any web farm is keeping the various nodes of the web farm in sync. This applies to each of the three types of web farm configurations described above.

There are various components that make up a web farm's web site. They include, but aren't limited to, the IIS configuration, content, session state, database, components in the Global Assembly Cache (GAC), and COM+ components. Often it is necessary to automatically keep this content in sync between the server nodes.

Various tools and programs exist to support this. Microsoft provides a few options, and there are many third-party vendors that have created extensive applications to take care of content replication. This section covers three of Microsoft's solutions and briefly discusses additional tools.

The two most obvious aspects of a web farm that would use replication are web-site content and IIS Shared Configuration files. Both are stored at the disk level, so a disk replication tool is necessary to keep them in sync.

You might be asking why replication is necessary when the IIS configuration can point to a UNC share. Without redundancy of the configuration files, the web farm hinges on a single point of failure, and therefore the content store needs to have a good replication and failover solution. This is covered in depth during this section.

Distributed File System

With the introduction of Windows Server 2003 R2, Microsoft released an impressive set of updates to *Distributed File System (DFS)*. There are some improvements in Windows Server 2008, particularly the support for greater than 5,000 folders, which was a limitation in prior versions, but, for the most part, the features introduced in Windows Server 2003 R2 are the same as in Windows Server 2008.

DFS is made up of DFS Namespaces (DFSN) and DFS Replication (DFSR). The two work together, using the same management interface, and as a whole are parts of the DFS family. Together they offer a powerful solution for high availability and redundancy.

If one entire server fails, the other will immediately take over without any configuration changes required on your part. DFS Namespaces uses Active Directory (itself a fully redundant system if configured as such) and provide a fully redundant UNC path. This UNC path can be used from IIS, or elsewhere, and will continue to work even if the primary content server fails. It's worth noting that DFS also supports stand-alone DFS roots, which can also be used in a web farm, but they do not use Active Directory, and they do not offer the redundant DFS Namespaces described here.

It is also possible to use the two independent of each other. For example, it's possible, and fairly common, to just use DFSR without using DFS Namespaces. It is also possible, although less common, to use DFS Namespaces without DFSR. Examples of the former will be covered shortly.

Figure 16-14 shows an image of the DFS Management tool that is configured with a pair of replicated folder targets. The UNC path \\DomainA.local\WebfarmConfig\Site1 is a redundant path that can handle a failure on either server with almost instant failover capability.

DFS is part of Windows Server 2008 and doesn't require a separate download. To install, go to Server Manager, add a new role, and select File Services as the Role, and then the wizard will lead you through the rest. Much more can be said about DFS than is covered in this chapter — be sure to research it well and test it well before depending on it in a web farm environment — but this information and the next few sections will get you pointed in the right direction.

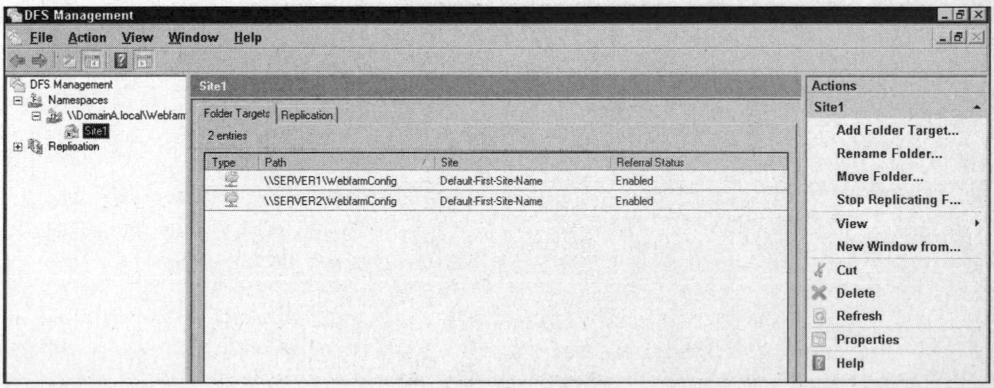

Figure 16-14

DFS Replication

DFSR offers the ability to replicate data over either a LAN or a WAN with support for remote differential compression (RDC), a client-server protocol to efficiently replicate data over a limited-bandwidth connection by detecting insertions, removals, and rearrangements in files to only replicate changes when the files are updated.

This makes DFSR extremely efficient over long distances, or on a local network. Once set up, DFSR "just works." Little maintenance is required after it is properly configured. There are a few options for handling the replication method. You can have two-way replication or use a full mesh, or you can use a combination of these to create your own style of replication between all of the servers. DFSR offers a lot of flexibility for almost any environment.

Changes made to one server are immediately replicated to the other servers as long as there aren't any locks on the file. DFSR supports file creation, renames, deletions, or changes to the file itself.

DFSR isn't for every situation, however. You should not use it if you have multiple servers writing to the data at the same time, or if there are often locks on the file. Microsoft Exchange and SQL Server will not work with DFSR for that reason. Web applications tend to be prime candidates for DFSR, and the new IIS 7.0 shared configuration is another technology that works well on DFSR; it is discussed in more depth below.

DFS Namespaces

DFS Namespaces offer failover support for when a server becomes unavailable by immediately switching over to use the next server in the priority order. There are two modes for DFS Namespaces. The more robust is using domain-based namespaces, and the second is stand-alone namespaces.

Domain-based namespaces benefit from the redundancy of Active Directory and store the namespace information both in Active Directory and in a memory cache on each of the namespace servers. If configured currently, there is redundancy in Active Directory, multiple namespace servers, and multiple target folders, thus allowing redundancy at every part of the system.

Priorities can be placed on each folder so that a particular folder is always used first, as long as it's available. Additionally, DFS Namespaces can be configured so that the highest-priority server becomes the primary server again when it has recovered.

DFS Namespaces enable you to point to a UNC path (for example, `\\DomainA.local\WebfarmConfig\Site1`), which will always be available, even if any single server on the network fails.

DFSR and the IIS Configuration Files

DFSR is an excellent solution for the new IIS Shared Configuration. It can be used in one of two ways.

❑ Use DFS Namespaces and DFSR together to provide a single UNC path that all servers point to. This path is fully redundant and can handle a failure on any server on the network (or more if configured for additional redundancy) and still provide uninterrupted service.

❑ Use DFSR, but don't use DFS Namespaces. DFS must be installed on each web server and will keep the configuration files in sync locally on each server. Set the IIS Shared Configuration to point to a physical path on each server instead of using a UNC path.

Both options are fully acceptable, and really there aren't too many advantages or disadvantages for each one. The one that you choose is more a matter of preference.

The first option depends on the stability of the network since IIS will be continually reading the configuration across the network. It's convenient in that there is a central place that all new servers can be pointed to, and it doesn't require DFS to be installed on all of the web servers.

The second option is potentially more stable because a network failure won't affect the IIS configuration, as long as general Internet traffic can still get through. If there is a network failure, the configuration may get out of sync until the network connection is available again, but IIS will continue to run normally since the configuration is local on the same server.

When using the second method, it is advisable to pick one server that you consider the configuration master server, and you should only make changes from that server. This ensures that changes aren't made to two servers at the same time when they are disconnected from each other, causing conflicts that DFS may not be able to resolve.

In either situation, be sure to use the IIS Export Configuration tool in IIS Manager to ensure that the encryption keys are exported and will work on all of the servers. The first part of this chapter covered that in depth.

Whichever option you choose, be sure to test it well before releasing into production so that you are well aware of how it will respond in every situation.

DFSR and Content Replication

Keeping the web content (files, folders, images, etc) in sync between nodes is also key to any web farm environment. DFS can be used for any of the three web farm configurations. Just like in the previous section on the IIS configuration files, it can be used for replication between servers without using DFS Namespaces, or it can be used to mirror a server to provide redundancy in case of a failure.

If used for replication of local content, DFS needs to be installed on all of the web servers. Once configured, a new server can be added to the mix at any time. Just be extra careful when adding a new server that you don't make it the master server by mistake, causing it to replicate a blank or invalid folder, which, in turn, will blow away all of the files on the rest of the web farm. It's important to test this in advance to be sure you can join this correctly to the domain 100 percent of the time.

Robocopy

Another tool that Microsoft has had for many years is *Robocopy (Robust File Copy for Windows)*, which is available by default in Windows Server 2008. *Robocopy* is a command-line tool that will replicate content between servers, either one-way or two-way. It is not nearly as robust as DFS, but it's been around for years and has proven itself worthwhile.

Unlike DFSN, Robocopy doesn't offer a method to redirect to the backup server if the primary server fails. Where it really shines is in easy-to-configure replication between folders. It can be set up in a batch file, scheduled using Windows Task Scheduler, and left alone. No installation is needed on the servers, and it will work with previous versions of Windows.

There are dozens of command parameters and ways to use Robocopy, including the ability to: copy or move folders; choose how many subfolders to traverse; copy NTFS permissions; add or remove file attributes; determine which files, folders, or types to include or exclude; and much more. It is very powerful and flexible, but it has its limitations, as well.

One of the shortcomings of Robocopy is that it runs when you tell it to run, often from Windows Task Scheduler if you configure it as such. Therefore, it does not have a file handle on the files to know when they are created, updated, or deleted. This means that if a file is created on a server but that file is not on the other server, it does not know if it was just created on Server1 or just deleted on Server2. This means that two-way mirroring is not completely trustworthy. One way to handle this is to consider one of the servers as the primary and the other as just a copy of the primary server. You can create a true copy with the /PURGE or /MIR (mirror) properties. With these properties set, Robocopy will delete files on the destination server if they are not on the source server. In the event that you need to failover to the secondary server, you should immediately disable /PURGE or /MIR so that new files that are created are not deleted again on Robocopy's next run. Another way to deal with this is to not use /PURGE or /MIR so that new files on either server will not be deleted by mistake. This will result in a need to do housekeeping over time because deleted files will not truly be deleted unless you delete them from both servers.

Here is an example of a batch file that does two-way replication between two servers. Create a file called *robocopyexample.bat*, and add the following to it:

```
robocopy.exe "D:\Domains" "\\10.0.0.10\domains$" /LOG+:"D:\Robocopylogs\Example
Logs To.txt" /E /W:10 /R:3 /SEC /XO

robocopy.exe "\\10.0.0.10\domains$" "D:\Domains" /LOG+:"D:\Robocopylogs\Example
Logs From.txt" /E /W:10 /R:3 /SEC /XO
```

Be careful on the word wrapping; there should be just two lines in your batch file. This is just a small sample of the commands possible. The usage is ROBOCOPY source destination [file [file]...] [options].

If you have spaces in your path, make sure to surround the path in quotes, as shown in this example. The /LOG+:{path} logs the operation to the path that you specify, and the + says to append instead of overwrite. The /E property says to copy all subfolders even if they are empty. The /W:10 says to wait 10 seconds between retries (the default is 30 seconds), and the /R:3 says to retry three times before giving up (the default is 1 million). The /SEC copies all of the NTFS security settings. Make sure that both systems are using NTFS as the file system. Finally, the /XO says to exclude files with older time stamps, which will result in the files with the newest time stamp taking precedence. Notice that there are two commands, one for each direction.

To see a complete list of commands, run Robocopy.exe /??? from the command line. With other tools like DFS, Robocopy has less of a place in a web farm than it did in times past, but there are times when Robocopy might be the tool for you, whether because of corporate policy, the inability to install DFS on your production content servers, or whatever other factors drive your decision.

You can also use Robocopy for the IIS Shared Configuration. You can have configuration files that are pushed to all other servers on the web farm using Robocopy. Whatever the use, it's important to be aware of Robocopy and what it can bring to the table.

Offline Folders

Another option for the IIS Shared Configuration is to use offline folders instead of calling the UNC path directly. This will allow the configuration files to always be available, even if there is a problem with the network. During a network failure, or a failure with the remote server, it will use the cached version until the network connection is restored. Windows takes care of this seamlessly once it is properly set up. It's recommended to do this if you are accessing a UNC path for the IIS Shared Configuration.

To set up an offline folder for the IIS Shared Configuration, there are a few steps to configure the first time. Offline folders aren't enabled by default, so the first step is to enable and reboot. Here are the steps necessary for offline folders:

1. Click Start ➪ Search box, enter **control.exe cscui.dll** in the dialog, and then press [Enter], or double-click on Offline Files in the Control Panel. Note that after using this for the first time, Windows Search will allow you to go to the Start ➪ Search box and type **Offline Files** and **Enter**, but you may not find it available the first time you use Windows Search to open the Offline Files tool.

2. If Offline Files haven't been enabled on this server yet, click Enable Offline Files. Since a reboot is necessary before offline files are active, perform a reboot before the next step.

3. After the reboot, from Windows Explorer open the UNC path to the IIS configuration files.

4. Right-click in an empty place in the main window and choose Properties.

5. Check the "Always available offline" checkbox, as shown in Figure 16-15.

6. Click OK.

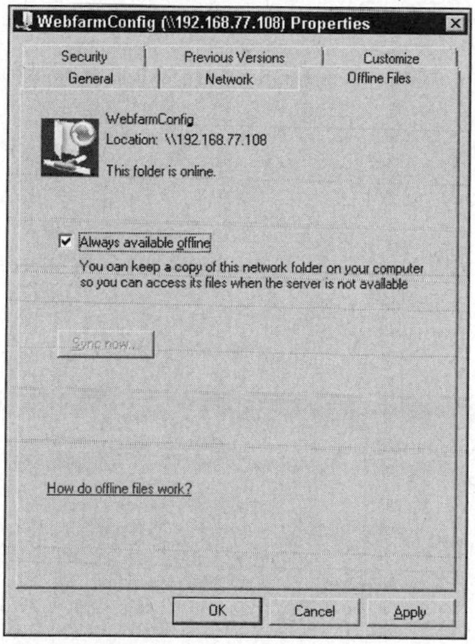

Figure 16-15

Configuring and using offline folders will protect the configuration files against any network hiccup and ensure that IIS can read or write to the configuration even when disconnected from the main UNC share.

Offline folders can be used along with DFS Namespaces and Replication to give even greater resiliency to network blips. A general principle worth considering for the IIS Shared Configuration is: if you are pointing to a UNC share, enable offline files for that folder.

Keep in mind that if you are in Offline mode for any period of time that neither you nor anyone else that manages IIS makes configuration changes to this server and another server while offline. Otherwise only one set of changes will take effect, while the other will be overwritten. If you specify one of the web servers as the primary configuration server, it will help avoid this issue and ensure that all servers have the same configuration at all times.

Additional Tools

The three tools mentioned so far for redundancy and failover are by no means the only options available. There are many mature third-party solutions on the market that will help with not only the file-level content, but also many other aspects of deploying your applications from your testing environment to your production environment. If these solutions mentioned so far don't meet your needs, with a bit of research, you can find many other good options available to you.

Additionally, Microsoft had a product called Application Center 2000. This was a powerful solution for deployment, monitoring, and management of web farms. For example, App Center will completely manage COM+ replication, removing the burden from the web-site administrator to ensure that all servers are in sync. That is just one example of what App Center offers that the solutions mentioned above lack.

As of July 2006, it can no longer be purchased, although Microsoft has extended support for existing App Center 2000 customers until 2011. Unfortunately, there is no direct replacement for App Center 2000. Instead, several products replace most of the functionality, but other features do not yet have a replacement. Microsoft is working on enhancing their toolset so that eventually everything that App Center 2000 offered will be available through other products.

The product family that partially replaces App Center 2000 is called *System Center*. It includes System Center Operations Manager (formerly known as "Microsoft Operations Manager"), System Center Configuration Manager (formerly known as "Microsoft System Management Server"), and four other products.

If you are looking for additional tools, take a look at Systems Center and keep an eye on this product family over the next few years as it will continue to evolve to help with web farm management.

Microsoft Web Deployment Tool

At the time of publication, Microsoft has just released the first technical preview for the Microsoft Web Deployment tool (the name may change before it's released). This is the long rumored tool used for deployment and migration of IIS sites, content and dependencies, and that will eventually replace Application Center 2000.

This tool is very versatile and has many uses that pertain to your IIS 7.0 administration. It will migrate IIS 6.0 sites to IIS 7.0, IIS 6.0 sites to another IIS 6.0 server, and IIS 7.0 sites to another IIS 7.0 server. You can migrate single sites or the entire server. In addition to migration and syncing of IIS settings, it can copy web content, registry settings, COM+ components, GAC component, SSL certificates and even specific metabase or configuration sections between servers.

In fact, by the time this book is released, some of the sections later in this chapter will be handled better by Microsoft Web Deployment than the currently available tools mentioned below.

The Microsoft Web Deployment tool is a command line tool which can work in Offline or Remote mode.

In Remote mode, one of the servers is set up as the server and listens for incoming requests (by default over port 80), while the other functions as the client, so that you can do a migration or sync between the servers in one step.

In Offline mode, no installation is necessary and you can export to a saved path, manually copy to the other server, and import on the other end. These options grant a lot of power and flexibility.

In the future, possibly by the time that you read this, there will be full support using PowerShell and .NET programming APIs.

The tool's blog homepage is `blogs.iis.net/msdeploy/`.

Complete Redundancy

A web farm is only as strong as its weakest link. If any part of the architecture fails that is not prepared to handle a failure, the entire architecture fails. It almost seems too obvious to say, but there are many web farms that have redundancy built into part of the system but not the entire system. A fully resilient web farm needs to be planned all of the way through.

Each item has a different failure rate and also a different cost to make it fully redundant, therefore the cost/risk decision needs to be determined by you and the decision-makers around you. You may find that it's worth the risk to leave some parts without redundancy, or you may have double or triple contingencies at each part of the process.

Here are some things to consider if you haven't already. Do you have redundancy or failover options at network feeds from upstream providers, power, all network equipment, firewalls, domain controllers, DNS servers, web servers, content servers, database servers, session state, documentation, and processes or staffing?

You may have a requirement for geographical redundancy so that if an entire city were to be taken out by a natural (or unnatural) disaster, your web sites would remain online. This is fully doable, but make sure to size the geographically redundant location to be able to handle the entire peak load. Often this means a complete copy of your primary location with equipment that sits idle, waiting for the once-in-a-lifetime failure to occur.

The point in all of this is to make sure to sit back, put your feet up, and think through every part of your architecture. Simply having a web farm with multiple web servers doesn't make a fail-proof system. Your network team, firewall team, web team, database team, Active Directory team, and your management team need to have a well-thought-through plan for each and every type of situation. The old saying to plan for the worst and pray for the best is very true here. Don't be caught with unexpected downtime because one part of the system failed that you didn't have a contingency plan for.

One more thing: test, test, test! Make sure to schedule regular testing windows where you can "pull the plug" (virtually or literally) on different devices in your web farm and watch it continue to hum away just as if nothing happened.

Load Balancing

Where would a web farm be without some type of method to load balance the web servers? It wouldn't be a web farm actually. This section discusses, at a high level, various load-balancing options.

Although redundancy and load balancing have been used somewhat interchangeably so far in this chapter, the two really aren't the same. *Redundancy* talks about duplication or having a complete copy of equipment, while *load balancing* can have the exact number of servers necessary to handle the load, or only have a small number of extra servers.

For high availability, a web farm must have at least $N+1$ servers in the web farm, where N is the number of servers to handle the peak traffic. For example, if five servers are required to handle peak load, a web farm with six servers is said to have $N+1$ servers. For additional redundancy, even more servers can be added.

Web farms are often set up in a load-balanced configuration, where all servers are actively set up to handle the load. If one of the servers fails, the rest of the servers pick up the slack. This is called *load balancing*.

There are many different ways to set up load balancing for a web farm. The next few sections discuss a few different options, ranging from Microsoft's Network Local Balancer (NLB) to third-party hardware load balancing.

Network Load Balancer (NLB)

Network Load Balancer (NLB) is Microsoft's solution to load balancing. Actually, it's one of three solutions for Windows Clustering solutions, but it's the one used for stateless applications like web servers.

It is a robust, yet easy to configure, solution to enable a farm of servers to function together to handle a single (or multiple) web site(s). New servers can be added without taking the site down for maintenance, and problem servers can be replaced "on the fly."

NLB uses its own algorithm to balance the load across all of the servers. Incoming traffic is routed to all of the servers, but only one of them will actually handle the traffic while the others ignore the traffic. Therefore, it doesn't have any load-balancing device in front of the web servers. All of the servers work together as peers, together for a shared cause.

NLB's main strengths are that it is easy to configure and set up, it's free since it is included in the OS, and it has enough features to handle many common web farm environments. It lacks some of the powerful features that the third-party hardware vendors have, but for straightforward web farms, it does an impressive job.

A limit of 32 servers can be included in each NLB cluster, but see the next section on DNS load balancing for a way to handle more than 32 servers by using NLB and round-robin DNS load balancing together. To install NLB, perform the following steps:

1. Click Start ⇨ Search box, enter **Server Manager** in the dialog, and then press [Enter]. (Note: In Windows Vista, use Programs and Features instead.)

2. Right-click Features in the tree in the left-hand pane and click **Add Features**.

3. Check Network Load Balancing, as shown in Figure 16-16.

4. Click Next and then Install.

After installing NLB, you can access it from Start ⇨ Administrative Tools ⇨ Network Load Balancing Manager. It can be managed locally or remotely. In fact, generally one server is a good place to manage the entire NLB cluster.

It's outside the scope of this book to explain how to fully configure NLB, and covering just a small bit is enough to make someone dangerous. But as long as you understand that this is a high-level overview, a simple NLB configuration walkthrough will be beneficial.

To create a NLB cluster using the default settings, perform the following steps:

1. Click Start ⇨ Administrative Tools, and then click Network Load Balancing Manager.

2. Click Cluster and New, as shown in Figure 16-17.

3. Enter the hostname (IP, DNS, or NetBIOS name) of the first server in the cluster, as shown in Figure 16-18.

4. Select the network adapter that you will use as the cluster interface from the choices at the bottom, and then click Next.

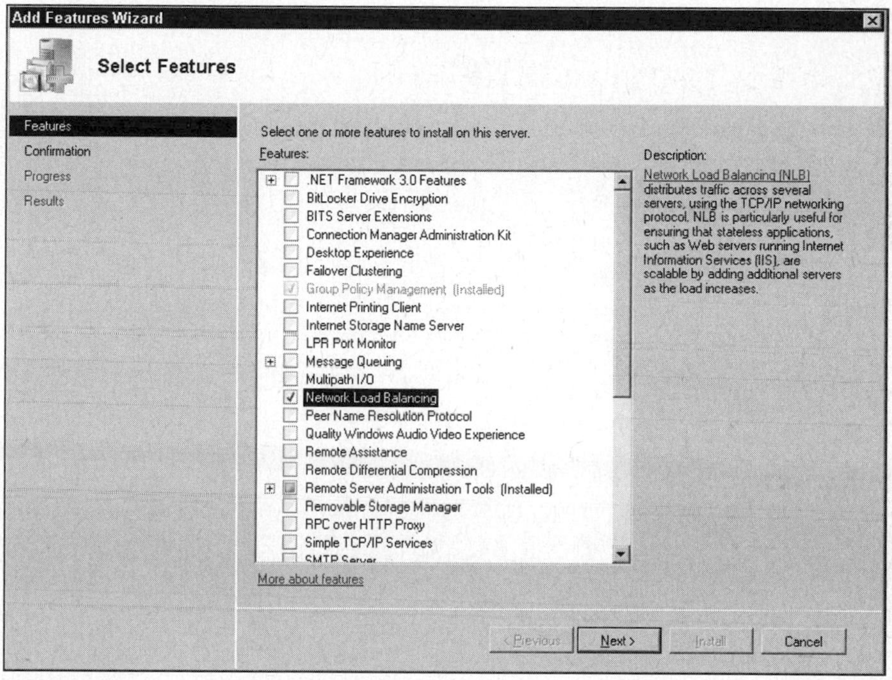

Figure 16-16

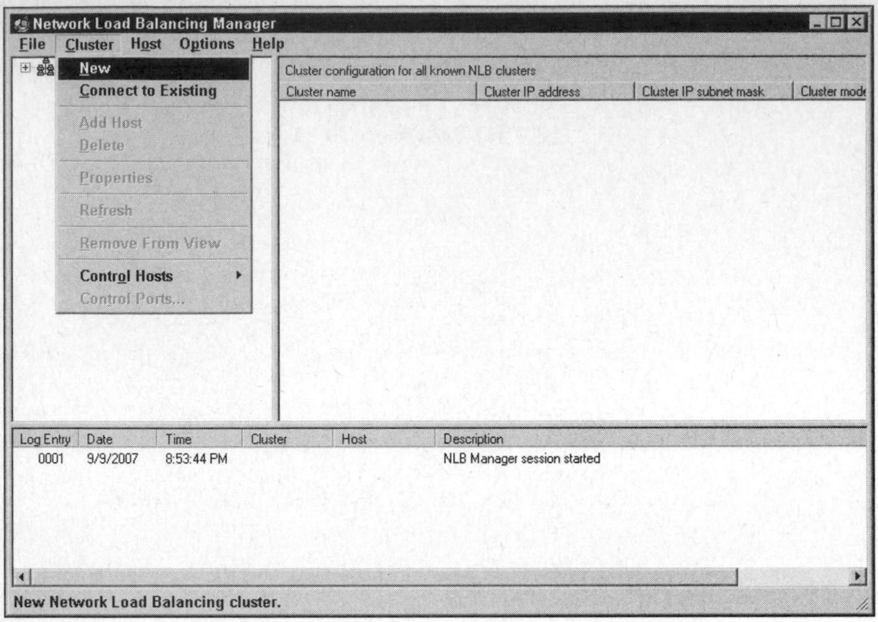

Figure 16-17

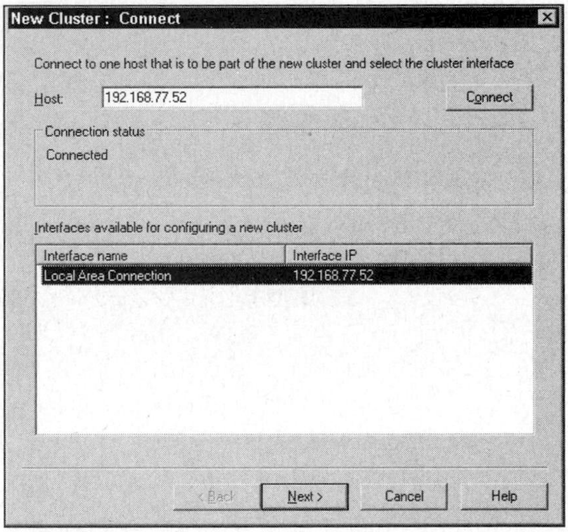

Figure 16-18

5. In the "New Cluster : Host Parameters" dialog box, you can select the priority. Even though the servers generally function as peers to each other, they need to be assigned a unique host identifier, which also serves as the priority. Normally, the default here is good (see Figure 16-19).

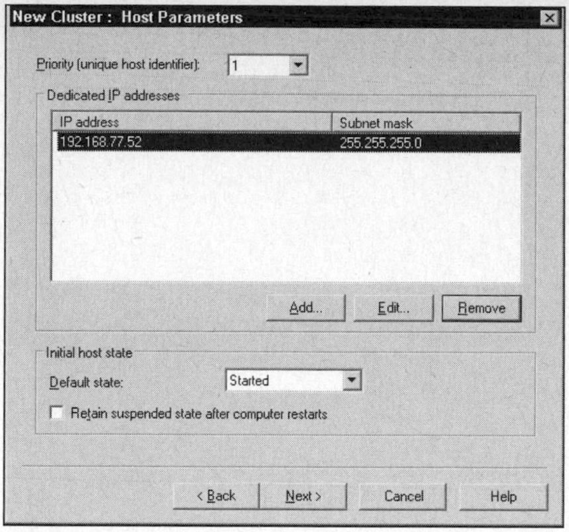

Figure 16-19

The Dedicated IP address is the IP address for that particular server. You will enter the Cluster IP address on the following screen. Ensure that the IP address and subnet are correct.

You can change the default state or leave it as Started.

6. Click Next. Enter a cluster IP address in the "New Cluster : Cluster IP Addresses" dialog box, as shown in Figure 16-20. This is the virtual IP address that is shared by all servers in the cluster. It is also used for the cluster heartbeat.

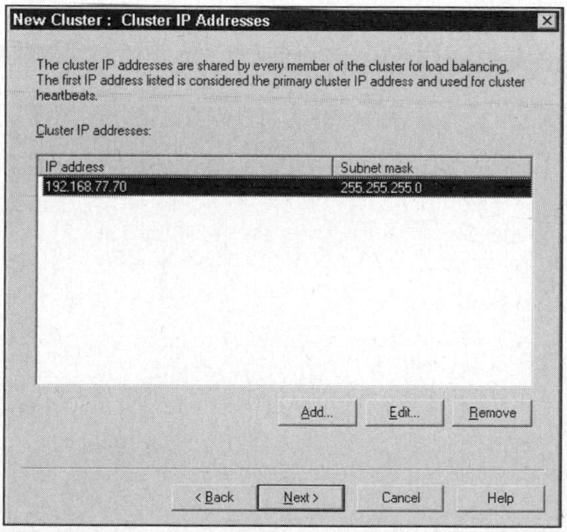

Figure 16-20

7. Click Next. In the "New Cluster : Cluster Parameters" dialog box, in the "Cluster IP configuration" section, ensure that the settings are correct. The "Full Internet name" should be the domain name that points to the cluster IP address specified in that section (see Figure 16-21).

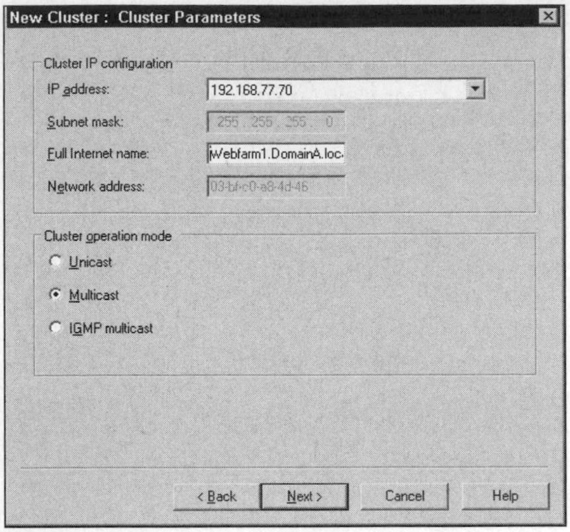

Figure 16-21

Now you are presented with one of the more difficult questions in this wizard. The "Cluster operation mode" has three choices: "Unicast," "Multicast," and "IGMP multicast." If your network supports it, usually "Multicast" or "IGMP multicast" is the best solution. NLB does its magic by messing with the MAC address of the network adapters on the servers. Unicast and Multicast work differently at both the switch layer and the network adapter on the server. The biggest issue with Unicast mode is that it will not allow the same network adapter that is used for the cluster IP address to also be used to manage the server using the server's original IP address. Essentially, that means that the NLB virtual IP will take over the network adapter and render the other IP address useless. Therefore, unless you're guaranteed to never want to manage a cluster node directly (highly unlikely), you must configure a second network adapter on the server to be used for directly managing the server. Multicast doesn't have this limitation and is preferred unless your network doesn't support it (most networks support multicast). This is the one time in the wizard where it's usually best to break away from the NLB default, as long as your network supports it.

8. Click Next. The "New Cluster : Port Rules" dialog box is where most of the rules are configured. If you click Next too quickly, you will accept the defaults and miss a lot of the customization that NLB offers.

9. Instead, click Edit on the default port rule. You can limit the rule to a particular "Cluster IP address," "Port range," and protocol, as shown in Figure 16-22.

You can change the filtering mode to "Multiple host," "Single host," or "Disable this port range". If you select "Multiple host," you have three suboptions for the level of affinity. Or, to put it another way, you can choose if you want users to come back to the same server on their repeat visits and whether "users" means everyone with the same IP address or everyone in the same network (class C), or if you don't want any affinity at all. The default of "Single" (host) means that the same IP address comes back to the same server on each subsequent visit. The default is often good. After your first server is added, the Port Rules section will also have an option for the load weight. With this you can give some servers a higher weight (and thus more traffic) than the others.

10.   Click OK and then Finish to complete the wizard.

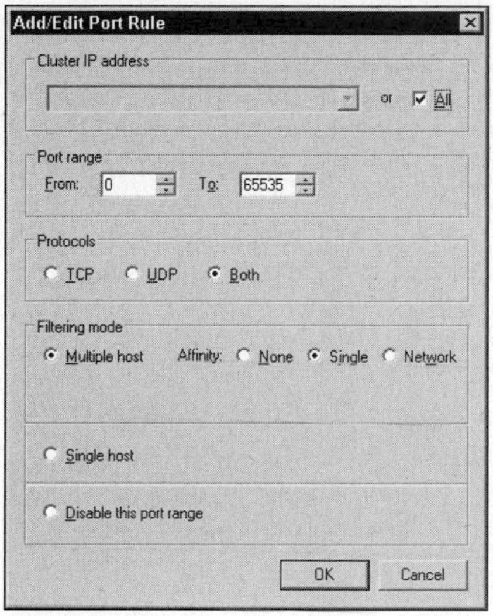

Figure 16-22

Since the preceding steps set up only one of the cluster servers, you must add additional servers to NLB now.

To add additional servers to the cluster, either with a new configuration or a currently active web farm cluster, select the cluster node and click Cluster ⇨ Add Host, and complete the wizard using the same principles as for the original setup. Repeat for each of the servers that you want added to the cluster.

That gives a high-level overview of how to configure NLB. It is straightforward to set up a web farm using the native technologies included in the operating system. This is just the start, however. Using this same tool, you can control the existing cluster servers by starting them, by stopping them doing a drain-stop (basically a graceful stop), or by temporarily suspending them.

NLB in Windows Server 2008 has some enhancements over previous versions, including

- ❏   Support for IPv6.
- ❏   Support for NDIS 6.0. The NBL driver for NDIS has been completely rewritten to offer enhanced driver performance and scalability and a simplified NDIS driver mode.
- ❏   Multiple dedicated IP addresses per node are now supported.
- ❏   Enhanced functionality with ISA Server — Multiple improvements have been made with the ISA integration ranging from supporting multiple dedicated IP addresses per node to ISA providing NLB with SYN and time starvation notifications.
- ❏   The `MicrosoftNLB` namespace and `MicrosoftNLB_NodeSetting` class have support for IPv6.

❏ In addition, NLB in Windows Server 2008 provides increased performance, enhanced interoperability, better security, support for new industry standards, and more flexibility for application deployment and consolidation.

Server failures are handled with ease and grace on an NLB cluster. There is a heartbeat pulse between the servers, and when one fails, the others will immediately take over. Because the HTTP and HTTPS protocols are so forgiving, when there is a failure, the application (usually a web browser) will retry for a period of time before giving up. Since NLB recovers from a failure much more quickly than the standard timeout in most browsers, the end-user just sees a bit of a delay while waiting for the page to load. This essentially means that there will be zero downtime when a server fails.

There are other types of failures that aren't as graceful, though. If there is an ASP.NET or IIS failure, NLB will not be aware of it, and it will continue to handle traffic on that server. The only way around this is to develop your own testing and, through code, disable a server if it fails any of the tests that you specify. System Center Operations Manager 2007 and ISA server can be used together with NLB to enhance its intelligence and functionality.

There isn't anything in NLB that specifically works with IIS. The two products are completely independent of each other. That said, they also complement each other nicely.

Overall, NLB offers a good solution that anyone can set up as long as they have at least two web servers. NLB scales well and is worth considering as your load-balancing method if you are planning for a new web farm or reevaluating your current solution.

Round-Robin DNS Load Balancing

Another method for load balancing is called *round-robin DNS load balancing* (also known as a "poor man's load balancer"). To be true, it's not really load balancing because it doesn't "balance" based on the load of the server. Instead, it sends each new request to the next server in the list regardless of the state of the server. In fact, it will continue to send traffic to servers even if they are partially or fully unavailable.

Additionally, it's not possible to have any type of stickiness when using DNS load balancing because DNS doesn't have any intelligence for maintaining information about the traffic.

So, when is DNS load balancing worth considering? For a small web farm in a Windows environment, DNS load balancing is rarely worth considering. With NLB and third-party solution, DNS load balancing doesn't bring much to the table.

Where it is worth considering is if you scale larger than a single NLB (or third-party) cluster can handle. If you outgrow NLB in terms of scalability, you can consider having multiple NLB clusters and use DNS load balancing to balance the clusters. DNS should have a Host (A) record for each cluster's virtual IP, and it will send the traffic evenly to each cluster.

When configuring DNS load balancing, make sure that the time to live (TTL) is set low so that new requests continue to distribute around the servers or clusters, and so that if you make a change, it will take effect as soon as possible.

DNS load balancing isn't the most common method, but it does have its place, especially if you need to create multiple clusters.

Third-Party Load Balancing

Third-party companies have created very powerful and robust solutions for load balancing. Some of these will offer more features than you can dream of, or at least more than NLB and DNS load balancing offer. Generally, the high-traffic web sites on the Internet today tend to use third-party load-balancing devices because of their flexibility to work with even the most complex and high-trafficked environment.

In contrast to NLB, which doesn't have a device out front, most third-party hardware devices sit in front of the web farm with dedicated hardware and will take the incoming requests and forward them on to the server that they feel is ready for that particular request.

These can work with ISO Layers 2 to 7, both for monitoring and for distribution of traffic. Layer 4 switches will balance by IP and port, whereas Layer 7 switches will read inside of the network packets and distribute to the appropriate server. Layer 7 checking can distribute traffic by host header, cookies, text in the URL, SSL session ID, text in the page, or even the protocol.

Layer 2 to 4 load balancing is relatively easy to do, and most reputable vendors can handle it with ease. Higher-end load balancers allow inspection at Layer 7 (the Application layer). They dig into the packets and distribute the load based on information at that level. Because of the greater demands on the load balancer for Layer 7 load balancing, there is a drastic difference between vendors, separating the low-end vendors from the high-end vendors.

In addition to Layer 7 load balancing, many Layer 4 switches will do health checking at the Layer 7 level. They can check the status of a page to watch for a status of 200, for example, to ensure that the page is functioning properly. Or, they can dig further and check for particular words or patterns of characters on a page. If it fails any of its tests, then it will take a server out of rotation and only send traffic to the fully functioning web servers.

Other features that some third-party solutions offer are global load balancing across geographical boundaries, SSL offloading, scripting and APIs, compression, caching, and powerful performance acceleration. Be sure to be aware of each of these when deciding on the solution so that you don't get a load balancer that can't handle your current and future requirements.

Some other considerations when deciding on the best solution include scalability (can it handle your peak load both now and in the future?), features (can it handle all your requirements?), API and programming support, reputation, staff expertise (is someone on your staff already familiar with a particular brand and model?), the vendor's reputation for support, brand name (yes, sometimes the brand is used in the decision-making), and price.

Another thing to consider when choosing your load balancer is the session affinity and balancing distribution. Will the load balancer send equal amounts of traffic to each server, or will it distribute it by some other method? Or, will it ensure that subsequent page requests go back to the same server? Different vendors call them by different terms, but some common affinity options include:

- ❑ **Round-Robin** — Each request is assigned to the next server in the list in a round-robin fashion.
- ❑ **Weight-Based** — Each server is given a weight so requests are assigned to the servers in proportion to their weight.
- ❑ **Random** — Each request is randomly assigned to a server.
- ❑ **Sticky Sessions (Affinity)** — The load balancer keeps track of the sessions and ensures that return visits within the time-out period always return to the same server.

❏ **Response Time** — The load balancer regularly queries the server and keeps track of the server that responds the fastest. It sends new requests to the server with the fastest response time.

You can use a combination of these options, plus others.

Weakhost Required for the Loopback Adapter

If your load-balancing configuration uses the Microsoft Loopback Adapter, a change with Windows Server 2008 default settings keeps it from working as it used to. By default, `stronghost` is enabled, which prevents cross-interface forwarding. This means that a request coming in through a network adapter cannot be handled by the loopback adapter since it's a different network adapter from the one that the original traffic came in on. To switch from `stronghost` to `weakhost`, run the following from the command line:

```
netsh int ipv4 set int "Local Area Connection"
weakhostreceive=enabled weakhostsend=enabled
```

Be sure to change the name of the network adapter from *Local Area Connection* to the name of your network adapter that receives the Internet traffic for that web site.

Choosing a hardware load balancer is a big decision with lots of options to choose from, but with careful planning and research, you should be able to find the product that will fit your environment well.

Other Considerations

Just setting up load balancing and IIS Shared Configuration isn't all that is required to effectively configure and manage a web farm. The following few sections discuss other applicable technologies and how to configure them for your web farm.

Replication

Not everything will copy between servers as easily as the IIS Shared Configuration files or the web content. This section touches on a few things to keep in mind that DFS, Robocopy, and offline folders don't address.

SSL Certificates

Secure Socket Layer (SSL) certificates need to be installed on all servers. While it's not overly complex, there are a couple of rules of thumb to be aware of.

First, as long as the same certificate is installed on each server, then the shared IIS configuration will correctly use the right certificate, regardless of the server. As long as you ensure that this is true, you should be set, but there are some common misunderstandings about SSL certifications that are addressed here.

After you create a *Certificate Signing Request (CSR)* and send it to a CA, the certificate that the CA generates will work only on the server where the CSR was generated. You cannot apply the certificate from the vendor on any of the servers on the web farm except for the one that generated the CSR.

The solution is to go through the entire SSL issuing process on one of the servers on the web farm. After you have successfully installed the certificate on the one server, you can export it and use it all you want on the other servers. In other words, the CSR can be used only on one server, but an exported certificate can be used on multiple servers. Be sure to guard the certificate carefully and password-protect it so that no one else is able to gain access to it.

> *See Chapter 15, "SSL and TLS," for detailed instructions on creating and working with certificates.*

Be sure that you don't install a new unique certificate for each server on the web farm since the certificates will not work correctly with the IIS Shared Configuration. The only way for SSL certificates to work with the IIS Shared Configuration is to create the certificate on one server and then export that to all of the other servers.

> *While copying the certificate to different servers is technically possible, be sure to check the service agreement with your certificate authority to ensure that you aren't breaking any of their requirements by doing so. If they do require that you order a certificate for each web farm server, be sure to arrange with them a way to pay for their licensing, but still only use one actual certificate.*

Registry Settings

Windows *registry settings* may need to be updated for one reason or another. Obviously, registry settings aren't replicated between servers by default. This is probably a good thing because it gives a chance to pull back the changes if something goes wrong with the first server updated. However, this also means that changes need to be applied to all servers somehow.

Registry keys generally aren't changed very often, so even a manual system can be acceptable, but here are some things to keep in mind that may be beneficial to you in your environment.

It is possible to export a part of the registry to a text file and import just that particular key, or set of keys. This is easy to do and can be pushed out using a tool like System Center Configuration Manager (formerly "Microsoft System Management Server").

To export a single key from within the Registry Editor, right-click on the key and click Export. Then specify the path and filename and click Save.

This will save a file with a .reg extension to the place that you specified. You can edit this file using Notepad and scale it down to only include the specific registry information that you want applied to the other servers. To push that setting to all users, you can use System Center Configuration Manager or WMI. Or, if you don't have too many servers and you want the plain and simple method, you can copy this to a network share, log into each of the servers on the network, and double click on the .reg file. After having you accept a confirmation, it will add the registry information to the Registry.

GAC

Files installed in the .NET *Global Assembly Cache (GAC)* also need to be kept in sync between the nodes of the web farm.

This can be done manually from the Fusion Cache Viewer by navigating to `%windir%\Assembly\` or by using `gacutil.exe` (which is available after installing Visual Studio or one of the Visual Studio Express editions).

Often an assembly is part of a larger install, therefore be sure to understand the full installation process so that you can either install it manually on all nodes or run the vendor's (or your development team's) installer.

> *One word of warning: When viewing the GAC through the `%windir%\assembly` folder, you will see a unique interface that masks the disk-level folder structure. This is called the Fusion Cache Viewer. Interestingly enough, when viewing this over a UNC path, for example, `\\machinename\windows\assembly\`, it will show you the local GAC and not the remote one. Be careful that this doesn't cause you to update the wrong GAC. You should either log on locally to each server that you're managing the GAC for, or on the server that you're working from, disable the Fusion Cache Viewer by creating a DWORD under HKLM\Software\Microsoft\Fusion\ called `DisableCacheViewer` with a value of 1.*

Installing IIS Features and Third-Party Tools

Installing additional IIS features and third-party IIS-related applications can potentially make registry key changes, install components locally, and make changes to the IIS configuration files. This adds complexity to a web farm environment using the shared configuration, because whatever is set on one server needs to be set on all of the others, and if they are set out of order, errors can occur.

For example, consider a case in which an install is done on the first server in a web farm where the installer places files in the GAC, makes a registry change, and then updates the configuration files. Because the configuration files are shared by all servers in the web farm, this will result in only one server having the necessary GAC components and registry changes, while all other servers use the updated configuration. This can cause serious problems until the installer is run on the other servers. To make matters worse, when you attempt the install on the other servers, it may check the IIS configuration files first, determine that it is already installed, and not complete the install. Yet another potential issue is that it may complete the install but add redundant entries to the configuration file, causing new errors.

A final potential concern with using third-party installers is that not all installers are intelligent enough to reference the `redirection.config` file to find out the actual location of the shared configuration files. They may cut corners and update `%windir%\system32\inetsrv\applicationHost.config` directly. This will mean that although it might appear that the installer has completed the install, nothing takes effect.

There are a few ways to address these install issues. One is to work with the vendor and get a manual install. With that manual install, you can create a script that can be applied to all of the servers. If the vendor doesn't have a manual install, you may need to dig into the application or the vendor's documentation to find out what the installer does. Then you can script your own manual way to push the installs out across the web farm.

The obvious other solution is to use the installer on all of the web farm servers. Be careful with something like this because you're at the mercy of the application vendor. You're particularly vulnerable running the installation as an administrator because the installation program can do pretty much anything the vendor dreams up, malicious or otherwise. A lot can go wrong, and you're putting your trust in someone outside of your control. It is generally good practice to get a manual install for each third-party package to ensure that you are in control of everything added to the server.

If you must use an installer Server Manager to install IIS features from Server Manager, here is a suggested method that will address all the issues mentioned above:

1. The first step is to notify all other administrators that you have moved this web farm to a lockdown state and that they must not make any changes to IIS until you have finished. If they do make changes while you have only partially completed the install, the configuration can be out of sync, and their changes will be lost.

2. Take one of the servers out of the web farm so that it is not handling new traffic. Wait until all current page requests have finished and the load balancer is not sending any further traffic to that server.

3. Turn off shared configuration. This is done in reverse to how it was described in the "Shared Configuration" section at the beginning of this chapter. From the server level, double-click the Shared Configuration icon. Uncheck the Enable Shared Configuration checkbox and click Apply. You will be prompted with two choices (plus Cancel), as shown in Figure 16-23. You are asked if you want to import the current shared configuration into your local server or if you want to use the old one that is already on your local server. Unless you have some reason to use the old configuration from before you enabled shared configuration, you should click Yes. The shared configuration files will be copied to your `%windir%\system32\inetsrv\config` folder. This means that your server will function with the same settings as it did while using shared configuration even though it is reading them from the local configuration. As long as no one makes any changes to the configuration on any of the servers, it is OK if the servers are reading from local configuration files for this period of time.

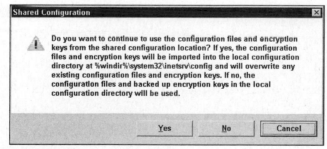

Figure 16-23

4. Now it is time to run the installer or add the IIS feature. This will install everything locally and update the local configuration files without touching the other servers in the web farm.

5. At this point, you can go down multiple paths, depending on the size of your web farm and how many servers need to be active to handle your traffic during this maintenance window. You can leave the server using local configuration files but allow it to handle traffic, or you can set this server to use the shared configuration again. If you set it to use the shared configuration, make sure *not* to export the configuration. This will mean that this server is prepared to use the new features but will not use them until all other servers in the web farm have completed and the shared configuration file is updated.

6. Repeat this process for all servers in the web farm. Since only you know your web farm well enough to plan the specifics, you can do half of your servers while transferring your load over to the other half, or you can take them out and replace them one by one, or you can point your traffic to a "Down for maintenance" web site during this maintenance. Whichever method you decide, make sure to plan it well so that you don't cause failures during the install.

7. When you have completed the install on all servers in the web farm, you can take one of the servers that is not using the shared configuration yet and export the configuration to the shared configuration location. This will cause the changes to the configuration files to be made live, and all servers on the web farm will start using the new feature, assuming that shared configuration is enabled on all of them.

8. After finishing the previous steps, you can complete your final cleanup. Bring all servers back into the web farm, notify all other administrators that the maintenance is complete, and complete any documentation and post-project housekeeping.

As with everything else, be sure to thoroughly test the whole process in a staging environment first before installing it in production. Don't allow a lack of processes or planning to be the weak link in your web farm environment.

COM+

With the advent of .NET and managed code, *COM+* is quickly fading from existence, but there are still some legacy applications and code around that require COM+ support, or, if you have developers who are set in their COM+ ways, it's possible that new development may still use COM+.

There are a few ways to keep the COM+ catalog and files in sync between servers.

On a smaller web farm, you can manually register the rare COM+ component that needs to be registered or updated. This is done using whichever steps you currently use for individual servers.

Microsoft provides the `comrepl.exe` tool, located in `%windir%\System32\com`, to help keep the COM+ catalog completely in sync between servers without needing to register the components on all servers manually. It will also copy files between the servers, although it doesn't give you flexibility to set the path for the components on disk; instead, it will handle this automatically as seen in the example below. Running it is as simple as navigating to that path and entering the following:

```
comrepl.exe <source server> <list of servers separated by spaces>
```

The two optional parameters are potentially helpful. The `/n` parameter disables any confirmation prompts. Ensure that you use this in any batch files, but be careful because the prompts are there for a reason. The `/v` parameter gives verbose log information in the command line rather than forcing you to dig it out of the log file.

Here is an example that will copy the COM+ catalog and files without any confirmation prompts:

```
%windir%\system32\Com\comrepl.exe localhost 10.0.0.10 /n
```

The following is an example of using `comrepl.exe` from the command line with the `/v` parameter:

```
C:\WINDOWS\system32\Com>comrepl localhost 10.0.0.10 /v
```

```
WARNING: The entire catalog on 10.0.0.10 will be
replaced with the catalog from localhost
Replication is an irreversable action.

Please enter YES (upper case) to continue:YES

Replication started - logging to C:\Program Files\ComPlus
Applications\Replication\comrepl.log
COM REPLICATION LOG  - [DATE:10,13,2007 TIME: 03:54 pm]

STATUS [localhost]: Preparing to replicate from source computer.
STATUS [localhost]: Exporting application 'ASPEasyPDF' to 'C:\Program Files\ComPlus
Applications\Replication\ReplicaSource\Def\{41E90F3E-56C1-4633-81C3-6E8BAC8BDD70}\{
E6223F6B-A7B3-4386-9EEE-E71B5D3C15F6}\comrepl.msi'
STATUS [10.0.0.10]: Preparing to replicate to target computer.
STATUS [10.0.0.10]: Copying all exported application files from the source computer
to 'C:\Program Files\ComPlus Applications\Replication\ReplicaNew' on the target.
STATUS [10.0.0.10]: Removing old replica files in 'C:\Program
Files\ComPlusApplications\Replication\ReplicaOld'.
STATUS [10.0.0.10]: Renaming 'C:\Program Files\ComPlus
Applications\Replication\ReplicaCurrent' to '\ReplicaOld'.
STATUS [10.0.0.10]: Renaming 'C:\Program Files\ComPlus
Applications\Replication\ReplicaNew' to '\ReplicaCurrent'.
STATUS [10.0.0.10]: Installing application from 'C:\Program Files\ComPlus
Applications\Replication\ReplicaCurrent\Def\{41E90F3E-56C1-4633-81C3-6E8BAC8BDD70}\
{E6223F6B-A7B3-4386-9EEE-E71B5D3C15F6}\comrepl.msi'.
STATUS [10.0.0.10]: Setting identity for app 'ASPEasyPDF'.
STATUS [10.0.0.10] : Replicating Partition Users.
STATUS [10.0.0.10]: Removing the computer list.
STATUS [10.0.0.10]: Copying computer list from 'localhost'.
STATUS [10.0.0.10]: Copying local computer properties from 'localhost'.
Replication succeeded.
```

This example shows all the steps that comrepl.exe takes to copy over the components, user permissions, and catalog. This should be run only on systems that are configured virtually the same, as the change is made to all COM+ packages and does not allow you to pick and choose.

To create an automated solution, create a batch file to do this for you. You can then run it manually after each install on the primary or staging machine, or schedule it to run at regular intervals. Be careful, however, as this will copy the entire catalog over to the target servers.

.NET Configuration Files and machineKey

The .NET and ASP.NET configuration files live in the .NET framework config folder. Be sure that all changes made to these files are applied on all other servers. Also, don't forget that there are configuration files for each version of the framework. If you will support multiple versions of the framework, be sure that all configuration files for all versions of the framework are applied to all servers.

Another important configuration item is the .NET machineKey. For all of the servers to work together as one, ASP.NET requires that the machineKey be the same on all servers. This ensures that if something like "viewstate" is encoded on one server and the user's second page request is handled by a different server, the different server is able to successfully decode "viewstate." The same applies to everything else that depends on the machineKey.

The `machineKey` tag has two keys:

❑ `validationKey` — Used to validate encrypted data like "viewstate" to ensure that it hasn't been tampered with.

❑ `decryptionKey` — Used to encrypt and decrypt forms authentication data and viewstate data when validation is set to TripleDES.

The default setting for each key is `AutoGenerate, IsolateApps`. `AutoGenerate` is as it sounds; it means that a key will be automatically generated rather than you specifying one. In a web farm, you don't want this because you want each server to have the same keys. `IsolateApps` generates a unique encrypted key for each application by using the application's ID. `IsolateApps` is OK in a web farm.

To configure this using the IIS Manager GUI, perform the following steps:

1. At the server, web-site, or application level, double-click the Machine Key icon.

2. Uncheck the two checkboxes for "Automatically generate at runtime," as shown in Figure 16-24.

3. Click Generate Keys from the Actions pane.

4. The "Generate a unique key for each application" box is optional. The default is often good unless you have a site that needs to use Forms authentication across application boundaries.

5. Click Apply.

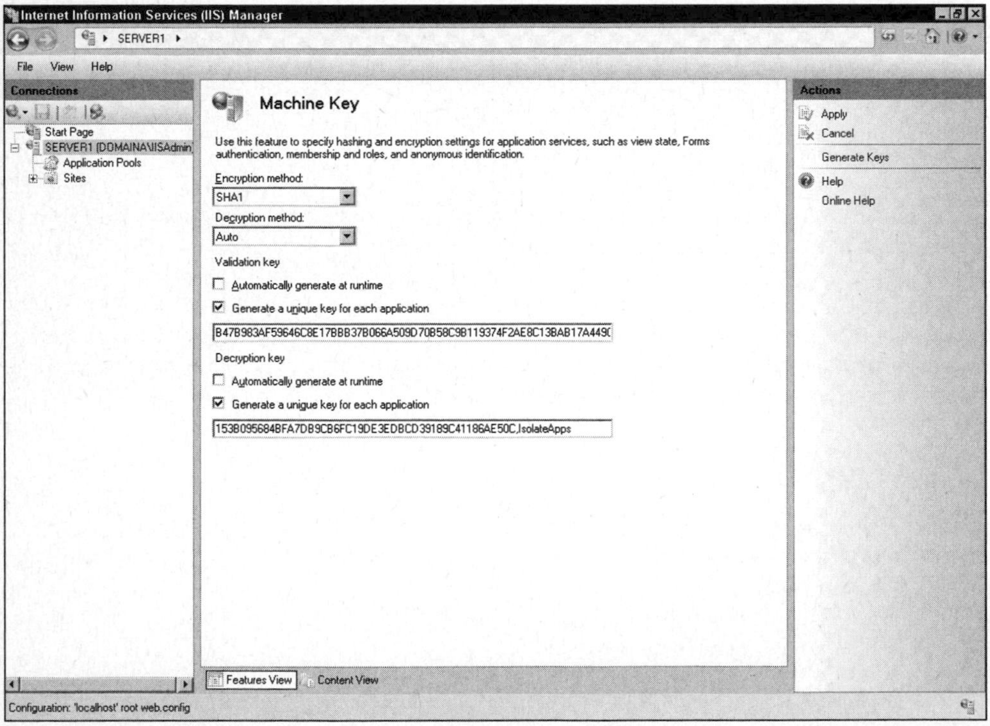

Figure 16-24

This will apply the change to a `web.config` file at the server, site, or application level. Any time `web.config` is touched, all sites and applications affected by that file will have their AppDomains reset. In other words, don't do this during the day unless you're aware of the brief AppDomain recycle (InProc session state will be lost) and slow first load.

Session State

Many web sites require a way to maintain state between pages so that variables, like user settings, can be passed around the web site throughout a person's visit. A common situation that often uses session variables is a shopping cart that needs to know the user and what they have added to their cart. Session variables are common, and the web sites that you support may have a requirement for session state.

Session variables are maintained by the web server, and a small cookie is saved to the client. This way when a new page request is made, the cookie will let the server know who this is, and the server will retrieve the session information from wherever it stores it.

The issue on a web farm is that if one page request is handled by one web server but the next page request is handled by another web server, the two web servers each need to have that same data available.

There are three solutions for this:

❑ Have your load balancer implement sticky sessions so that the same user gets the same server each time. This way the session information can be stored locally on each server and is only lost if a server fails. It only affects the users on that server when it does fail. This may be required for Classic ASP, which doesn't have any built-in session state solution that works with a web farm.

❑ Don't support session state. This isn't necessarily feasible, but technically it's a solution. In fact, many web-site developers do decide to build their web sites without a dependency on session state because of the web farm requirements.

❑ The third option is to ensure that your session state provider saves the session state off the server, or that it replicates the session data so that each server has all of the data. It's this third option for ASP.NET that will be discussed more now.

Since the most commonly used development platform on IIS web servers is ASP.NET and since it is Microsoft's solution for dynamic data-driven web sites, it will get preference in this discussion. Many other development platforms or languages support a session state solution for web farms; thus, be sure to check with their documentation for the best solution.

ASP.NET has five options for session state:

❑ InProc
❑ StateServer
❑ SQLServer
❑ Custom
❑ Off

InProc

InProc saves the state In-Process, in the `w3wp.exe` worker process. This means that the data is stored on each server and is not available on the other servers. It also means that an application pool recycle will cause the session state to be lost. While it's the fastest solution (not counting Off), it won't work on a web farm unless sticky sessions are applied. If sticky sessions are applied and you are not using a web garden, then InProc is a workable solution.

> *See Chapter 8, "Web Application Pool Administration," for more information on web gardens, which can be confusing because they differ from web farms.*

You can change the session state from IIS Manager, from code, or from editing the config files directly. To edit it in IIS Manager at the server, site, or application level, double-click the Session State icon to open the Session State tool. Figure 16-25 shows the Session State tool with the default setting of InProc.

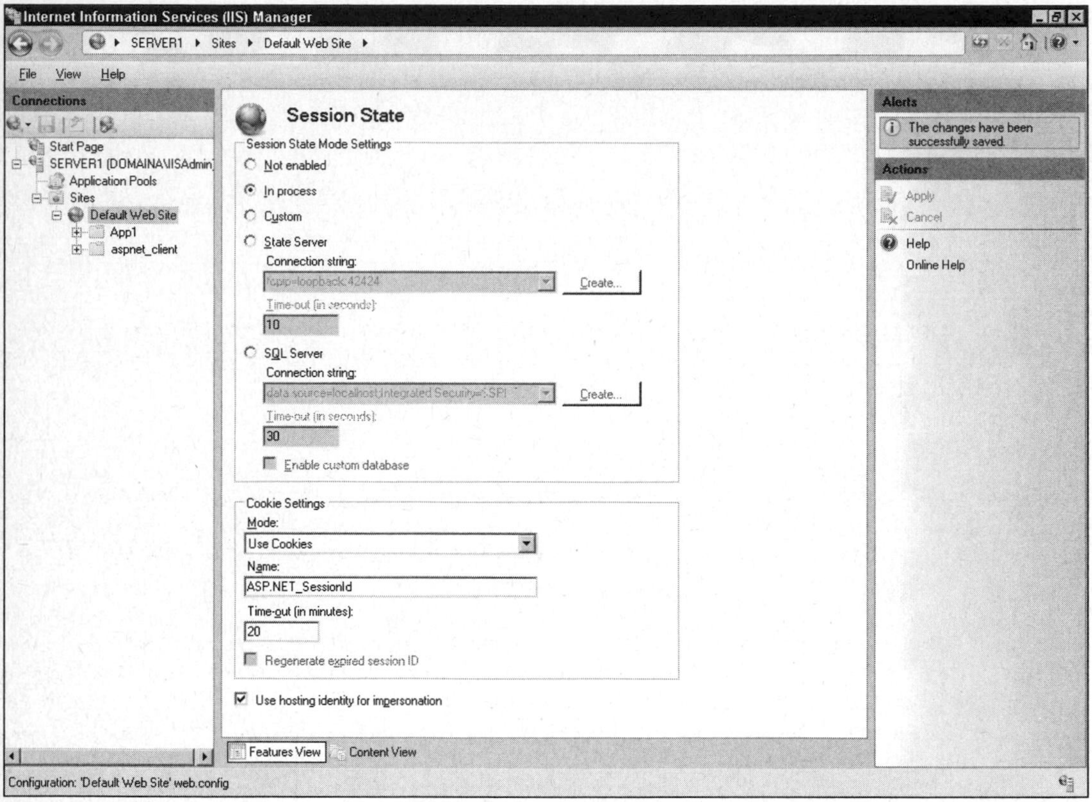

Figure 16-25

To set the session state to InProc from your `web.config` or other config file, add a `sessionState` tag to the `<system.web>` section of your configuration file, as follows:

```
<configuration>
    <system.web>
        <sessionState mode="InProc" />
```

```
    </system.web>
  </configuration>
```

StateServer

StateServer is another solution provided by Microsoft, but it doesn't have any failover option. When ASP.NET is installed on a server, there is a service called *ASP.NET State Service* that is installed in Windows Services. This is disabled by default but can be easily enabled. Be sure to set the start-up mode to Automatic so that it starts after every reboot.

By default, the ASP.NET SessionState can't be accessed remotely. To enable it to run remotely, set HKEY_LOCAL_MACHINE\SYSTEM\CurrentControlSet\Services\aspnet_state\Parameters\ AllowRemoteConnection to 1 in the Registry.

To enable StateServer from IIS Manager, follow the steps described in the "InProc" section above, but select StateServer instead. If you prefer to change this from a text editor, the setting will look like the following:

```
    <sessionState mode="StateServer" />
```

If you are not using the default state server on the local server, you can set the parameters to what you need, as seen here:

```
    <sessionState mode="StateServer" stateConnectionString="tcpip=10.0.0.10:42424" />
```

This configuration tag must be in the `<system.web>` section of your configuration file.

While StateServer is easy to configure and can manage session state in a web farm because all servers can share it, it doesn't have any sort of redundancy. You should use it only if you can accept that risk and have a way to switch to another state server if the first one fails.

SQLServer

The third solution provided by Microsoft is *SQLServer session state*. If you have a SQLServer cluster in place, this is a good solution. SQLServer session state has the most performance overhead of any of the built-in options, but the added redundancy is often worth the performance penalty. Be sure to test in your environment to ensure that it performs and scales well.

To use SQLServer session state, you must prepare your database to have the SQL Server state schema. This can be done from `aspnet_regsql.exe`, which is in the `framework` folder. This can only be done from the command prompt. The `aspnet_regsql.exe` GUI (opened by double-clicking the icon from Windows Explorer) is for other database features of ASP.NET and is not for SQLServer session state.

You can run `aspnet_regsql.exe` by using Windows credentials (the credentials that your command prompt is running as) or by using SQL authentication with a username and password that you provide. A third option is to generate a SQL script file, which you can run manually on the server.

Unfortunately, you cannot run this with just dbo permissions on the database because `aspnet_regsql.` *exe uses msdb system stored procedures and makes changes to the msdb database. None of the SQL Server roles are sufficient except for sysadmin. People have successfully used the* `-sqlexportonly` *parameter of* `aspnet_regsql.exe` *to generate the SQL script file and manually modified it to work in an environment where the database user only had dbo permissions. It requires several changes and is not supported by*

Microsoft. A detailed walkthrough of this hack is outside the scope of this book except to say that it is possible should you have that requirement.

In addition to the authentication options for `aspnet_regsql.exe`, there is another decision that needs to be made. This decision is for the `-sstype` parameter, which is the SQLServer session type. The three options are `t` (temporary), `p` (persistent), and `c` (custom). The difference between them is where the database is stored. Both `t` and `p` create a database called *ASPState*. This means that you cannot have two SQLServer session state instances on the same server because the database name is not unique. The `t` option saves the session state data in the *tempdb* database and does not persist the data through a reset. The session state data is lost if SQL Server is restarted.

Several stored procedures are created in the ASPState database. The `p` option causes both the session state data and the stored procedures to be saved in the ASPState database and allows the session data to be persisted even if SQL Server is restarted.

The third option, `c` (custom), enables you to specify the database name that is used for both storing the session data and for the stored procedures. This allows multiple instances of SQLServer session state management to use the same SQL server.

It's worth seeing a few common examples.

Run the following in the `framework` folder (`%windir%\Microsoft.NET\Framework\<version>\`) from the command line. You can run it from any server with the .NET framework installed; it does not need to be run from the SQL Server. Be sure that port 1433 is opened on the firewall.

```
aspnet_regsql.exe -ssadd -sstype c -S sql.domainA.local -d SQLState -U User1 -P
Pa$$word1
```

The `-ssadd` parameter says to add SQLServer session state (note: the `-ssremove` parameter is the opposite and will remove it again). The `-sstype c` parameter is the option that was just described to specify the type. You specify the server with the `-S sql.domainA.local` option. The `-d` is for the database, `-U` for the user, and `-P` for the password. Note that the parameters are case-sensitive, so be sure to match the case correctly.

The following example does the same, except that the `-E` causes it to use Windows authentication instead of SQL authentication:

```
aspnet_regsql.exe -ssadd -sstype c -S sql.domainA.local -d SQLState -E
```

The following example is the same as the previous example, except that that the `sstype` is `p`, which means that it will create a database called *ASPState* instead of one that you specify. Notice that the `-d` parameter is not used in this case.

```
aspnet_regsql.exe -ssadd -sstype p -S sql.domainA.local -E
```

Once the database has been prepared, you must change your configuration file to point to SQLServer session state management. You can do this as described in the "InProc" section from IIS Manager or by editing the configuration file directly.

When using IIS Manager, you must select SQL Server and set a valid connection string. The Create button will open a dialog box that will help you create the connection string.

The config file section should look like this:

```
<sessionState mode="SQLServer" sqlConnectionString="Server=sql.domainA.
local;Database=sqlstate;User ID=User1;Password=Pa$$word1" />
```

Once this has been completed, your web site will be using SQLServer session state management, and if SQL Server is properly configured in a cluster, it will provide a fully redundant session state solution for your web farm.

Note that as with most command-line tools, `aspnet_regsql.exe` allows you to view the detailed help with `aspnet_regsql.exe /?`.

Custom

ASP.NET supports implementing your own session state provider, so if you want to implement something other than Microsoft's solution, you can do so. As with the others, once you've developed it and installed it on the server, either your site `web.config` or root `web.config` file can be updated to point to your custom provider.

Off

Session state can be turned off completely, and this is worth doing if you don't use session state since there is a slight performance penalty to using session state, even if you don't use it. To turn it off, follow the instructions in the "InProc" section above, except turn it Off instead of setting it to In Process. IIS Manager calls this *Not enabled*. In your config file, it should look like this:

```
<configuration>
   <system.web>
      <sessionState mode="Off" />
   </system.web>
</configuration>
```

Third-Party Session State

ScaleOut Software (`www.scaleoutsoftware.com`) and Alachisoft (`www.alachisoft.com`) are two reputable third-party vendors who have developed session state solutions for web farms. Their products are built for highly available, highly scalable web farms and either maintain session data in-process and replicate all changes immediately, or store the session data out-of-process through a custom worker process that resides on each server.

Security

By default, the IIS application pools run as the Network Service user. This means that if you are accessing remote content over a UNC path, the computer machine account must have permission to access the remote resource.

It may not be desirable to use Network Service as the application pool identity, however, because if you give access to the machine account, everything on that server now has access to it. It's an all-or-nothing permission setting. While it may be acceptable in some situations, it's more advisable to create a custom user for each application pool and assign that user to the remote resources instead.

Using Active Directory accounts makes this easier to manage because you only need to maintain the passwords in Active Directory and IIS. If you create a new server to add to the web farm, you can point to the same IIS Shared Configuration, and it will work immediately.

Using local users and groups is also acceptable; it just means that the same username and password need to be assigned to each server. As long as the password is the same, it will use pass-through authentication, which allows the different servers to function together even though they don't share a central username/password configuration store.

CAS

There is one final consideration when planning or growing a web farm that utilizes ASP.NET and uses UNC paths — ensuring that the code does only what has been approved. ASP.NET implements *Code Access Security (CAS)* to ensure that web-site content resides on the local server or an approved UNC path. You must be sure to tell ASP.NET that the UNC path that you are using is approved; otherwise, it will fail.

The `CasPol.exe` tool adds the UNC path to CAS's approved list. It is located in the .NET `Framework` folder (`%windir%\Microsoft.NET\Framework\<version>\`). To approve a UNC path, run the following command:

```
CasPol.exe -m -ag 1 -url "file://\\{NAS1.DomainA.local}\*" FullTrust -exclusive on
```

Running this will modify the `security.config` file in the framework's `config` folder. If `security.config` does not already exist, it will create the file. Once run, your web site will allow a UNC path to the web-site content. The URL that you entered into the command is approved. In the example above, this is the `\\NAS1.DomainA.local\` path.

You can view the parameters for `CasPol.exe` by typing `CasPol.exe /?`, but it's worth briefly touching on them now. The `-m` parameter says to apply this to the machine level instead of the user, enterprise, or custom level. The `-ag 1` parameter means that it should add to group 1 (meaning that it applies to all code). To see a list of possible groups, type `CasPol.exe -listdescription`. The `-url` parameter and the URL itself are obvious. That is the URL that is to be granted CAS rights. The `-exclusive on` sets an Attributes property in `security.config` to Exclusive, which narrows the focus to the permissions associated with the code group. The `FullTrust` says that you fully trust all code from this location. If you use CAS in partial trust, you can consider using `Everywhere` instead of `FullTrust`, which means that it trusts this location but doesn't skip the CAS code validation.

Once this has been run, the following will be added to the `security.config` file:

```
<CodeGroup class="UnionCodeGroup"
version="1"
PermissionSetName="Internet"
Attributes="Exclusive">
<IMembershipCondition class="UrlMembershipCondition"
version="1"
Url="file://\\NAS1.DomainA.local\*"/>
</CodeGroup>
```

There are a few things to watch for:

❑ Replace {NAS1.DomainA.local} (including the curly brackets) with your server name. You don't need the whole path; that's what * is for. You just need to enter the UNC path to the server.

❑ Enter the command exactly as written. If you put a domain name here but an IP address in the IIS path, it won't work.

❑ Run the command for all versions of the framework that you support.

❑ Run the command for all servers that you trust and that will be used by this server. If you have backup or alternate servers, be sure to add them as well.

❑ Don't run the command twice, or ASP.NET will fail because of a duplicate entry. CasPol.exe isn't smart enough to check if you already made that entry. The command will update a file called security.config in the config subfolder off the framework folder.

To get detailed help from the command prompt, within the framework folder type CasPol.exe /?.

Summary

IIS is a powerful web-hosting platform, able to grow with you. Whether you are scaling to two servers so that you have a failover option during a failure or scaling to dozens of servers because of your site's success, you will need to take measures to ensure that the IIS configuration, content, and all other aspects of your site are in sync.

The new IIS Shared Configuration, along with some work on your part to neutralize your configuration files, is a powerful yet easy-to-configure solution for keeping your web server IIS settings in sync. IIS Shared Configuration allows you to export the configuration, including RSA keys, so that it can be used from all other servers on the web farm.

Distributed File System (DFS) is a robust solution for keeping the data on your web farm in sync, whether you're just using the replication feature and using local content on each web server, or are using DFS Namespaces to have a fully redundant UNC path that all servers point to. DFS can be used for content replication and for replication of the IIS configuration files.

Once the servers are set to work well together, there needs to be a way to balance the load across all servers and to be able to respond accordingly when there is a failure. Microsoft's Network Load Balancer (NLB) is available with the operating system without any extra download, and it works well with many environments. Or, if you have need of something more robust, there are many third-party solutions that offer many more powerful features.

All in all, IIS is a powerful platform to host your demanding web site needs.

17

Programmatic Configuration and Management

No previous version of IIS has offered nearly the same level of management and programmatic configuration as IIS 7.0. The latest release of IIS has taken large steps in the area of management and laid a foundation for extensive customization.

The configuration infrastructure is leaps and bounds above IIS 6.0, with the ability to extend the schema, thereby allowing all the programming methods to immediately use the custom extensions. The schema is no longer hard-coded into IIS; instead, it's fully extensible.

Additionally, with the move away from the metabase and toward the XML configuration structure, mimicking the ASP.NET structure, IIS 7.0 fully supports many of the configuration methods familiar to .NET developers.

If you have invested into custom programs in previous versions of IIS, you will be happy to know that the IIS development team has taken great care to ensure that IIS 7.0 is backward-compatible with existing scripts, allowing you to continue to use your existing code.

This chapter is broken into two main sections: direct configuration and programmatic configuration. *Direct configuration* refers to understanding the configuration model and many of the underlying principles that can be managed using a simple text editor. After a detailed explanation of the configuration model, we discuss *programmatic configuration* and methods such as the new managed AHAdmin that lies at the programming API core, the new .NET-managed code wrapper, and IIS 7.0 Windows Management Instrumentation (WMI). Additionally, ABO, IIS 6.0 WMI, ADSI, and legacy code support are covered.

We also discuss the configuration file hierarchy, `location` tags, and how to reference configuration files or `location` tags specifically. Some areas of IIS tend to mask this complexity, but there are times when it's important to modify a particular `location` tag within a particular configuration file. This chapter covers how this is done from a manual configuration perspective and how to do this programmatically.

The goal of this chapter isn't to give multitudes of code examples, but rather to give you the tools that you need to understand the configuration files and the programmatic APIs so that you can do far more than what is shown in the examples here.

Direct Configuration

IIS can be managed in many different ways. You are probably very familiar with using IIS Manager to configure and administer IIS, and you may have edited the metabase directly or developed some applications that manage IIS. With so many new features in IIS 7.0, it's well worth your time to understand the entire configuration structure and many of the features that are available so that you can tackle even the most complex situation with relative ease.

IIS 7.0 has taken great strides to ensure that the entire schema can be extended and configured and that all programming APIs have full access to the extended configuration.

This section lays a foundation that is necessary for both the administrator and the IIS programmer to be able to understand the configuration files, why they are configured as they are, the benefits that they have over previous versions, and how to manage them well.

Configuration File Hierarchy

With the new Integrated Pipeline, ASP.NET isn't a second-class citizen anymore. This means that ASP.NET plays a much larger role than at any time in the past. It also means that IIS and ASP.NET need to work together in a cohesive way.

The decision that led up to the new IIS configuration structure could be considered a battle of configuration dominance between IIS and ASP.NET. The IIS development team had to decide which configuration structure should become the new standard. In this case, it was ASP.NET. The configuration structure that has been ASP.NET's since day one is the one that IIS has now moved toward. The old metabase is done away with, and a new XML-based method has taken over.

This is a welcome change for those who are familiar with ASP.NET because there is little relearning necessary. The schema structure and rules that have guided ASP.NET now guide IIS too, and by the time the configuration files have been read and a web site is displayed, the two are merged into one joint system. This means that the `web.config` files of the web sites and applications control both ASP.NET and IIS configuration.

There are three root configuration files and some other administration files that live at the global level. The hierarchy of configuration files contains the following:

File	Path	Description
machine.config	%windir%\Microsoft.NET\ Framework\<version>\config\	Contains most of the .NET Framework sections and settings. This isn't new to IIS 7.0, but shows how IIS and the .NET Framework now function as one.
web.config (root)	%windir%\Microsoft.NET\ Framework\<version>\config\	Contains more of the ASP.NET-specific sections and settings. Like machine.config, this is not new to IIS 7.0.
applicationHost.config	%windir%\System32\inetsrv\ config (by default)	Contains the IIS global web server, configuration sections, and site settings using location tags. Unlike machine.config and web.config, this is brand-new.
administration.config	%windir%\System32\inetsrv\ config (by default)	Contains the configuration for IIS Manager and the IIS Manager users.
redirection.config	%windir%\System32\inetsrv\ config	This is used for shared configuration, which allows applicationHost.config and administration.config to be relocated.
web.config (site)	Web-site root path	Contains ASP.NET or IIS settings for the site. Or if a location tag is used, it can manage the setting for subfolders or files. This file is not new to IIS 7.0, but it now supports IIS 7.0 settings, which is a new concept.
web.config (application)	Web-site application path	The same as the site web.config file, except that it can be specific to an individual application.
Web.config (folder)	Web-site folder path	Although it's not commonly placed in a regular folder, some sections in web.config can run at the folder level.

Figure 17-1 shows how IIS and .NET work together and the order in which they are loaded. The .NET framework configuration files are processed parallel to the IIS configuration files. After all global configuration files are loaded, the site's `web.config` file is processed.

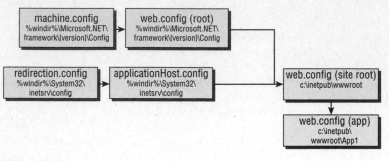

Figure 17-1

Order of Operation

As the configuration files are loaded, it's possible to have the same setting exist in multiple places at the same time. For example, you can set directory browsing settings in `applicationHost.config`, in site `web.config` files, and in location sections within those files. When settings exist in more than one place at a time, it's the last one loaded that actually takes effect.

Additionally, there are location sections within each configuration file that can also exist. Location sections are processed with the file that they live in, but after any generic section within that file.

Consider the following example:

applicationHost.config

```
<system.webServer>
   ...
   <directoryBrowse enabled="false" />
   ...
</system.webServer>
```

applicationHost.config location tag

```
<location path="Default Web Site">
   <system.webServer>
      <directoryBrowse enabled="true" />
   </system.webServer>
</location>
```

site web.config

```
<system.webServer>
   <directoryBrowse enabled="false" />
</system.webServer>
```

In this example, the `directoryBrowse` element will first be processed by the general section of `applicationHost.config`, causing the value to be set to `"false"`. Then the `location` tag (still in `applicationHost.config`) will be processed, causing the value to become `"true"`. Finally, the site's `web.config` will be processed, setting the actual value back to `"false"`. The final result of `directoryBrowse` will be `"false"`.

This is not unlike Active Directory or NTFS permissions. The settings closest to the final object are the ones that are applied last, and ultimately win the fight.

To look at it another way, the more generic default settings are applied at the global level, whereas the specific settings are applied at the site level. The site owner knows best what the site needs, but the server administrator knows best what the server defaults should be.

> *Even though the site administrator makes the decision on settings the server administrator needs to be able to deny the ability to override certain settings. This is covered below in the section on locking.*

Collection Items

The earlier directoryBrowsing example is a simple "attribute." That is an easy example because an attribute can be set in multiple configuration locations at once without any conflict. Although an attribute is as simple as it gets, collection items are a different matter. You cannot add the same collection item multiple times without throwing an error.

A *collection item* is part of a group of items that can be added, removed, or cleared. For example, the `defaultDocument` element contains a `files` section, which often contains multiple collection items, as illustrated by this example:

```
<defaultDocument enabled="true">
   <files>
      <add value="default.aspx" />
      <add value="default.htm" />
      <add value="default.asp" />
      <add value="index.htm" />
      <add value="index.html" />
   </files>
</defaultDocument>
```

In this example, the `<add />` element adds to the collection, resulting in five default documents specified by this configuration section.

The issue arises when the same items are added again, either right there in the same tag or in another configuration file or location section down the structure hierarchy.

> *Some common collections are* `modules`, `handlers`, `defaultDocuments`, `httpErrors`, `customHeaders`, `filesExtensions`, *and* `windowsAuthentication` *providers.*

The solution is easy enough, but you must understand it to master the IIS and ASP.NET configuration model. If a collection item already exists and you want to replace it with your own item, you must first "remove" the individual item or "clear" the set of items and add back what you want.

This is best understood with an example. Consider setting a customHeader. By default, there is already one with a name of X-Powered-By and a value of ASP.NET set in applicationHost.config. If you want to change the value of X-Powered-By in your web site's web.config file and add a second collection item called X-Managed-By, you might erroneously try the following:

```
<httpProtocol>
    <customHeaders>
        <add name="X-Powered-By" value="ASP.NET v3.5" />
        <add name="X-Managed-By" value="The Best Admin" />
    </customHeaders>
</httpProtocol>
```

Because the X-Powered-By collection item already exists, you would run into the error seen in Figure 17-2.

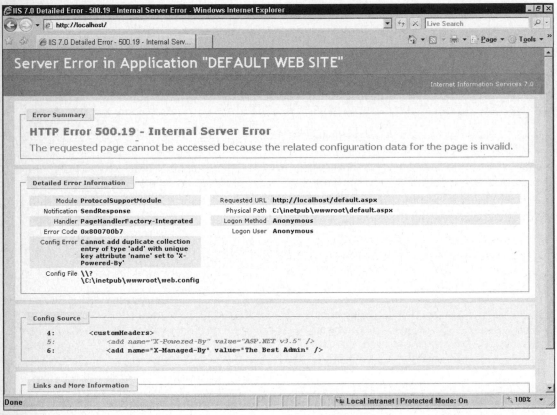

Figure 17-2

To configure your web.config file properly, you would need to *remove* the X-Powered-By collection item first or *clear* the whole section and add back what you need. Both of the following examples are valid:

Valid Option 1

```
<httpProtocol>
   <customHeaders>
      <remove name="X-Powered-By" />
      <add name="X-Powered-By" value="ASP.NET v3.5" />
      <add name="X-Managed-By" value="The Best Admin" />
   </customHeaders>
</httpProtocol>
```

Valid Option 2

```
<httpProtocol>
   <customHeaders>
      <clear />
      <add name="X-Powered-By" value="ASP.NET v3.5" />
      <add name="X-Managed-By" value="The Best Admin" />
   </customHeaders>
</httpProtocol>
```

In the first example above, you may have noticed in the Remove tag that the *value* property isn't set like it is in the Add tags. This is because the value is not required to specify an item uniquely and to remove it from the collection. In fact, an error will be thrown if you have the value in the Remove tag. Only enough information to identity the item uniquely is necessary.

In these examples, when IIS processes all the configuration files, it will first add the X-Powered-By collection item at the global level when applicationHost.config is processed. Then, in the first example, it will remove the item again, causing it to not exist anymore. Then it will add it back and also add X-Managed-By. In the second example, when web.config is processed, it will clear *all* of the previous collection items (in this case there is only one) and then will add both items in the example. In neither situation is there a time when a duplicate entry exists.

> It is possible to have duplicate collection items with the same key if it is specifically allowed in the schema. This is possible when a collection element has the allowDuplicates attribute set to "true". This doesn't occur often, and applicationHost.config doesn't have any duplicate collection items allowed. The ASP.NET 2.0 configuration files allow three.

There is one more thing worth noting about collection items. There are three commands that can be applied to a collection item. They can be added, removed, or cleared, although IIS doesn't always call them *add*, *remove*, and *clear*. In fact, the schema file allows those command names to be changed, as shown in the following excerpt from IIS_schema.xml:

```
<sectionSchema name="system.webServer/httpErrors">
   ...
   <collection addElement="error" clearElement="clear" removeElement="remove">
   ...
</collection>
```

The httpErrors section uses *error* for the Add command instead of *add*. As you can see from that excerpt, it's possible to create a custom command name for Clear and Remove too, although it's never changed by default in any of the configuration files.

Section Structure

The IIS and .NET configuration files are made up of section groups, sections, elements, attributes, and collections. It's helpful to understand the structure of each of the global configuration files, both for IIS and .NET. The following subsections describe the core configuration files.

applicationHost.config

At the core of IIS is the `applicationHost.config` configuration file, which contains settings that pertain to the activation service like application pools, sites, logging settings, listeners, and the like. By default, it is located in `%windir%\System32\inetsrv\config`, but it can be redirected to a different location, as explained in Chapter 16, "Configuring and Load-Balancing Web Farms." Figure 17-3 shows the structure of `applicationHost.config`.

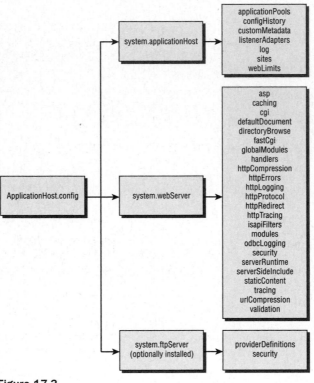

Figure 17-3

administration.config

The `administration.config` file is for the IIS Manager user interface (UI) and settings that pertain to that, such as the IIS Manager users. Like `applicationHost.config`, this file is located in `%windir%\System32\inetsrv\config` but can be redirected to a local or network folder. Figure 17-4 shows the configuration structure for `administration.config`.

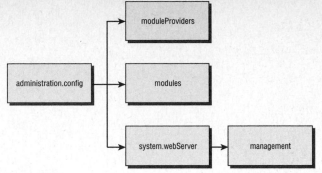

Figure 17-4

redirection.config

The `redirection.config` file is used to configure the location where `applicationHost.config` and `administration.config` are located to allow the shared configuration mechanism to function. Located in the `%windir%\System32\inetsrv\config` folder, `redirection.config`'s structure is very simple because of its narrow focus, as shown in Figure 17-5.

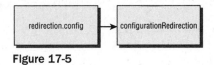

Figure 17-5

machine.config

The `machine.config` file is specific to .NET and isn't new to IIS 7.0, but because of the tight integration between .NET and IIS, it is a key player in IIS 7.0 now. It is located in the `%windir%\Microsoft.NET\Framework\<version>\config\` folder and contains most of the .NET framework sections and settings. Since this file exists for each version of the framework, there is often more than one on each server.

web.config (Root)

The root `web.config` file is similar to `machine.config` except that it has ASP.NET-related sections and settings. It is also located at `%windir%\Microsoft.NET\Framework\<version>\config\`. Like `machine.config`, there will be one root `web.config` file for each version of the framework.

location Tag

An essential part of configuring ASP.NET, and now IIS, is the `location` tag. This has been covered already in previous chapters, but it's worth covering again now because of its central role in the IIS configuration.

Within any of the configuration files, the settings within the top-level `<configuration>` tag are applied to the directory that the configuration file resides in, and all the child paths beneath it. In the case of global configuration files, the settings in the `applicationHost.config` and the other root configuration files are the default settings for all sites.

The `location` tag enables you to specify unique settings to specific child paths without needing a `web.config` file to actually exist at that level. This is done by setting the `path` property to the site, application, folder, or file that you want to configure, as seen in the following `applicationHost.config` section example:

```
<location path="Default Web Site">
   <system.webServer>
      <defaultDocument enabled="true">
         <files>
            <clear />
            <add value="default.aspx" />
         </files>
      </defaultDocument>
   </system.webServer>
</location>
```

The `path` in this example is set to Default Web Site, which means that everything in that tag will be applied to the site located at `c:\inetpub\wwwroot`, even though the configuration is set in `%windir%\System32\inetsrv\config`.

When set in the global configuration files, the `path` property must start with a reference to the site and then optionally include the path to folders or files under the site. If the `.config` file is for a site instead of being a global configuration file, it cannot include the web-site name but instead it must start with a relative path under the `web.config` file. Absolute paths are not supported; everything must be relative to the `.config` file where the `location` tag exists.

The following table explains the possible values for the path attribute:

Value	Global Configuration Example	Site or Application Example	Description
`"."` (or `""`)	path="."	path="."	The current level. In the global configuration files, this refers to the defaults. In a site or application's `web.config` file, this refers to the location where the `web.config` file resides. Since this is the default value, leaving the `path` attribute off will do the same.
`"sitename"`	path="Default Web Site"	N/A	The *sitename* specifies a site and is valid from any of the global configuration files. You cannot set the path to a sitename from a site's `web.config` file.
`"application"`	path="Site1/App1"	path="App1"	At the site or application level, the application name must be a relative path.

Value	Global Configuration Example	Site or Application Example	Description
"vdir"	path="Site1/ Vdir1"	path="Vdir1"	At the global level, the sitename must be included, but at the site level, the sitename cannot be included.
"physicaldir"	path="Site1/ PhysicalDir1"	path="Physical Dir1"	A simple folder doesn't need to be an application or vdir to have IIS or ASP.NET settings applied, but understand that most settings are locked so that they cannot be set outside of an application root.
"file.ext"	path="Site1/ default.aspx"	path="login. aspx"	Files can also be configured. In fact, using a location tag is the only way to configure settings for a file.

Multiple location tags can exist in the same configuration file, and it's even possible to have multiple location tags with the same path as long as they don't reference the same sections, or if they have a different overrideMode as described in Chapter 9, "Delegating Remote Administration."

The order in which the location tags are listed isn't important to the configuration system, but you may want to consider keeping it organized for your own sake.

You cannot nest a location tag in the top-level sections or under other location tags. When creating a location tag, the entire path to the section must be included. For example, if you want to set the default document for Site1 in the applicationHost.config file, you would create a location tag that looks like this:

```
<location path="Default Web Site">
    <system.webServer>
        <security>
            <authentication>
                <basicAuthentication enabled="true" />
            </authentication>
        </security>
    </system.webServer>
</location>
```

Notice that even the <system.webServer></system.webServer> must be included within the location tag.

You can use the location tag for various reasons:

❑ To control the settings for a site or application that is different from where the configuration file is located.

❑ To centralize all settings into a single file for neater housekeeping.

❑ To apply settings to a file (instead of a folder).

❑ To lock certain sections, as will be explained shortly.

❑ To disable inheritance, as will also be explained shortly.

❑ To apply default settings in the global configuration files while still leaving the default installation settings untouched.

Inheritance

By default, all settings that are applied at any level will *inherit* down to all child sites, applications, folders, and files, wherever the setting is relevant. What's interesting when working with ASP.NET applications is that the application folders and files do not inherit across application boundaries. This means that files in \bin and \app_code and other system folders will only be processed within the bounds of that application.

This can cause some issues when there are references in web.config that are inherited by its child applications, but when the files and classes that are referenced don't exist at that level. Consider a situation in which a module exists in the root of the site in \bin and is referenced in web.config in the <module> section, but a subfolder called App1 is marked as an application. The reference in web.config to the module would still be there in the App1 application because of the web.config inheritance, but the module binary itself wouldn't be loaded as long as it only exists in the root \bin folder. This would cause an error in the App1 application, preventing anything from working.

To look at it another way, consider the following:

❑ \web.config — Contains a reference to a HTTP module

❑ \bin\module.dll — The module itself

❑ \App1\ — Marked as an application

In the App1 application, the web.config settings will still be the same as in the root application, since the web.config files inherit across application boundaries. But the \bin\module.dll will not be loaded in the \App1\ application because ASP.NET files and folders do not inherit across application boundaries. Because the web.config reference is looking for the classes within the module.dll file but cannot find it, an error will be thrown.

There are a few ways to work around this (purposely) inconsistent inheritance where web.config is inherited, but not the other ASP.NET system files and folders:

❑ Under the App1 folder, place a copy of the \bin folder and other necessary system folders. This will keep ASP.NET happy even if it doesn't use the module. Of course, make sure to understand your application to know if the module would be helpful or if it would hurt having it load in the App1 folder.

❑ "Remove" the module as described in the "Collection Items" section above. As of ASP.NET v2.0, if you remove a module, it will not load the module at any time. Note that prior to v2.0, this didn't work because the module would be loaded into memory when the site's web.config file was processed before the application's `web.config` file had a chance to remove it. Either `<remove />` or `<clear />` will work, but when using `<clear />` be sure to add back any modules that you need for the site to operate properly.

❑ ASP.NET v2.0 introduced a new attribute called `inheritInChildApplications`. This is extremely useful in these situations where you don't want something to inherit to the child applications. It will be explained further now.

The `inheritInChildApplications` attribute allows you to wrap a section within a `location` tag, mark it so that it doesn't inherit, and then put in whatever settings you want to only live at that level. The path attribute can be "." or something more specific, whatever your needs are. Consider the following example from the `web.config` file in the root of the site:

```
<location path="" inheritInChildApplications="false">
  <system.webServer>
    <modules>
      <add name="CustomModule" type="…"
        preCondition="managedHandler" />
    </modules>
  </system.webServer>
</location>
```

This will only be applied to the root of the web site and not to any child applications because of the `inheritInChildApplications` setting.

One caveat is that a section cannot be in two places at once. This means that you cannot have the top-level section contain some modules and a `location` tag with `inheritInChildApplications="false"` contain the rest of the modules. It's all or nothing for each unique section within the path.

Locking

Often the server administrator has full access to the server, while the site owners need to be isolated to their own area and are given only as much access as they need to manage their sites properly. One of the main ways to ensure that this happens is through section, attribute, and element *locking*. This is explained in depth in Chapter 9, "Delegating Remote Administration" but will be briefly reviewed here.

Using the `location` tag, you can set configuration items so that they cannot be overwritten. The attribute name that controls this is `overrideMode`. The three options for `overrideMode` are *Allow*, *Deny*, and *Inherit*. The following example shows how to set the windowsAuthentication section so that it cannot be overwritten further down the path hierarchy:

```
<location path="Default Web Site" overrideMode="Deny">
    <system.webServer>
        <security>
            <authentication>
                <windowsAuthentication>
                    <providers />
                </windowsAuthentication>
            </authentication>
        </security>
    </system.webServer>
</location>
```

Usually this is set in the global configuration files so that web-site and application operators cannot change those settings. Many sections are locked down by default but can be changed to lock or unlock sections of the configuration files.

childConfig/sourceConfig

The configuration system can be further configured by using the `childConfig` and `sourceConfig` attributes to break out parts of the configuration into other `config` files. There are several reasons why you may do this.

❑ **Security** — Sections of the configuration can be delegated to different administrators and have NTFS ACLs applied so that only the necessary users or roles have access to make changes.

❑ **Manageability** — Separating the configuration into sections can allow different people to manage different parts of the configuration without stepping on each other's toes.

❑ **Section Isolation** — Breaking the configuration into parts can protect parts of the configuration from being overwritten when unrelated changes are uploaded to the server. This is especially useful for the `web.config` files in a web site because it is common to use FTP or some other remote deployment method to upload an old copy to the `web.config` file. This upload can potentially overwrite changes that were made through IIS Manager on the server.

Updating the `childConfig` *or* `sourceConfig` *files will not cause an AppDomain recycle like changing the other* `.config` *files will. This means that the changes will not take effect until the next time the configuration files are reloaded, or until you purposefully "touch" the main configuration files. To touch a configuration file, add a space to an insignificant place and save the file. This will cause an AppDomain recycle, causing the configuration change to take effect.*

By default, the three main global configuration files (`applicationHost.config`, `machine.config`, and root `web.config`) don't utilize either `childConfig` or `sourceConfig`. It's important to note that `sourceConfig` doesn't work in `applicationHost.config` and `childConfig` doesn't support the section's attribute values.

Both `configSource` and `childSource` are described further in Chapter 16, "Configuring and Load-Balancing Web Farms."

Configuration Path

Understanding the configuration paths in IIS 7.0 is important, both from tools like `AppCmd.exe` and for programming with the programming APIs. The configuration paths have changed considerably from IIS 6.0 to IIS 7.0.

In IIS 6.0 and prior versions, the configuration path was in the form of LM/W3SVC/1/ROOT, where 1 is the site ID. Since there was just the one metabase file for the entire configuration, there wasn't a need to reference the configuration file from any tool or programming API.

In IIS 7.0, with ASP.NET working as such an integral part, there are multiple configuration files. Plus, it is possible to have settings at multiple levels, so it's necessary to have a method to specify where a particular setting should be applied. This is done by offering a method to target specific locations of a given setting.

In the new system, the configuration path has the following syntax:

```
MACHINE/WEBROOT/APPHOST/{Sitename}/{Vdir or App}
```

MACHINE corresponds to machine.config, WEBROOT to the root web.config file, and APPHOST to applicationHost.config, and when referencing the site, the MACHINE/WEBROOT/APPHOST is optional. What is interesting about this configuration path structure is that it never references a setting directly. It only references the configuration file and location tag. This is different from IIS 6.0, which often required the whole path direct to the property — for example, LM/W3SVC/1/ROOT/ServerComment. The IIS 7.0 configuration settings are set as a separate step.

You can use just part of the path to access specific configuration files. For example, machine.config's path is simply MACHINE. Additionally, the redirection.config file's path is MACHINE/REDIRECTION.

A good way to illustrate how this works is by using AppCmd.exe, which makes use of the configuration path. The directory browsing setting makes for a good example because by default it is allowed to be set in the site's web.config. This means that changing the setting in IIS Manager will result in the site's web.config file being changed rather than setting it in a location tag in applicationHost.config. This may not be your preference, so using the configuration path, you can have the setting apply to a location tag within applicationHost.config instead. This can be done with the following command:

```
AppCmd.exe Set Config "Default Web Site/" /section:directoryBrowse /enabled:true
/COMMIT:MACHINE/WEBROOT/APPHOST
```

Notice the /COMMIT property, which allows you to force AppCmd.exe to apply the setting to the place of your choosing. This is optional and often isn't needed, but in this situation it is used to ensure that the setting is applied directly to applicationHost.config instead of the site's web.config file. For additional information about AppCmd.exe, see Chapter 5, "Administration Tools."

Understanding this configuration hierarchy is important when using AppCmd.exe and for programming, which is covered below in this chapter.

Schema Extensibility

In versions past, there wasn't a consistent schema or configuration structure to the metabase. Much of this was hard-coded into IIS and wasn't available to be modified or extended. There was an MBSchema.xml file, which enforced some data integrity, but there was room for improvement. IIS 7.0 builds substantially on this and has a schema folder that includes schema files for IIS and the .NET Framework. These can be extended by Microsoft, third-party companies, or by you directly.

The four core schema files are:

❑ IIS_schema.xml — This covers the Windows Process Activation Service (WAS) and settings for the IIS web server.

❑ FX_schema.xml — This covers the .NET framework configuration sections.

❑ `ASPNET_schema.xml` — This covers the ASP.NET settings.

❑ `rscaext.xml` — This is the schema for the Runtime Status and Control API (RSCA) extension configuration. This works along with `IIS_Schema.xml` but adds the runtime state schema.

It is strongly recommended that you don't change any of the native schema files. Instead, you should use your own schema file to extend it. This ensures that you don't make any changes that will keep IIS from starting and also ensures that hot fixes and upgrades will not override the changes that you make.

These schema files, along with the configuration sections in the config files, define rules and guidelines that IIS and .NET must abide by. What makes this even more powerful is that it can easily be extended to include anything that you need, such as web-site contact names or phone numbers.

In addition to the built-in schema and the extensible schema, there are dynamic properties that allow properties and their values to be generated dynamically, as needed. Together this makes a powerful, extensible infrastructure. Although there is no high-level programmatic method to get and set schema files except using traditional XML APIs, it is easy to do this from a text editor and easy to deploy by using XCopy and other common tools.

The best way to understand this is to see it in action. Suppose you want to add owner information to the web site so that your custom tools can tell who the owner is and have information about them. In this example, it's desirable to add an element section called *OwnerInfo*. This section will include two attributes: name and e-mail, both of type string. Finally, it will have a role attribute of type enum that has three possible options: Admin, Tech, and Billing.

To extend the schema, you can place a file with any name into the schema folder as long as it has an extension of .xml. To create this and write code to update the site with the new owner information, follow these steps:

1. Create an empty text file in the schema folder (`%windir%\System32\inetsrv\config\schema`) called **OwnerInfo.xml**. You can do this from the command prompt or from Windows Explorer.

2. Add the following text to the file:

```xml
<configSchema>
  <sectionSchema name="system.applicationHost/sites">
    <collection addElement="site">
     <element name="OwnerInfo" >
        <attribute name="name" type="string"/>
        <attribute name="email" type="string"/>
        <attribute name="role" type="string">
           <enum name="Admin" value="0" />
           <enum name="Tech" value="1" />
           <enum name="Billing" value="3" />
        </attribute>
     </element>
    </collection>
  </sectionSchema>
</configSchema>
```

Your schema has been extended and is ready to use. This will extend onto the existing `system.applicationHost/sites` schema. A good way to find out the correct syntax is to use the `rscaext.xml` file as an example. It already extends onto many existing sections and has examples for the sectionSchema, collections, elements, attributes, and enums.

> *Here's a side tip for you. If you ever have a hard time getting IIS to start after you make a bad change, and doing an iisreset doesn't show you the real error, there is hope. The best way to find out what is wrong with a schema file or any of the configuration files is to use IIS Manager. Even if IIS can't be started, IIS Manager will continue to work, and if there are any errors, it will do a good job of telling you what is wrong.*

This schema addition will add to the existing `Site` collection and create a new element called **OwnerInfo** with the three attributes.

> *When you save the file in the schema folder, it will be immediately noticed by IIS. No reset of IIS is necessary. Be careful because an error here could cause IIS to fail, so, at the risk of stating the obvious, be sure to test this extensively in a testing environment before releasing it to production.*

Because the `sites` section is already in `applicationHost.config`, no changes need to be made there at this time. The next example in this section covers how to add a new section that doesn't already exist in any of the configuration files.

The next step is to create a tool to Write the owner information to the site. You can use any of the programming methods described below in this chapter or edit the configuration file directly from a text editor. The following example will work with the managed code API, which is described below in this chapter. If IIS programming is new to you, you should jump to the programming section of this chapter and come back to this later. Also, as covered in more depth later in the chapter, be sure to reference `Microsoft.Web.Administration.dll` from `%windir%\System32\inetsrv` and import the `Microsoft.Web.Administration` namespace. Using whichever programming tool you choose, add the following code:

```
Dim SM As New ServerManager
Dim config As Configuration = SM.GetApplicationHostConfiguration
Dim section As ConfigurationSection = _
    config.GetSection("system.applicationHost/sites")

Dim mySite As Site = SM.Sites("Default Web Site")

Dim ownerInfo As ConfigurationElement = mySite.GetChildElement("OwnerInfo")

ownerInfo.GetAttribute("name").Value = "Abraham Lincoln"
ownerInfo.GetAttribute("email").Value = "16@whitehouse.gov"
ownerInfo.GetAttribute("role").Value = "Admin"

SM.CommitChanges()
```

Finally, run your program. That's all there is to it. You will notice in the `Microsoft.Web.Administration` section that the code to manage your custom schema is exactly the same as the code used to manage built-in IIS settings.

You can see the new settings by opening `applicationHost.config` and looking in the sites section. It should look something like this:

```
<site name="Default Web Site" id="1">
  <application path="/">
    <virtualDirectory path="/" physicalPath="%SystemDrive%\inetpub\wwwroot" />
  </application>
  <bindings>
  <binding protocol="http" bindingInformation="*:80:" />
  </bindings>
  <OwnerInfo name="Abraham Lincoln" email="16@whitehouse.gov" role="Admin" />
</site>
```

Notice the `OwnerInfo` element with the values filled in. This is amazingly easy and powerful!

The previous example showed how to extend onto the existing sites section in `applicationHost.config`. The next example will show you how to create a *new* section. First, add a file into the schema folder called *MyCustomSection.xml* and add the following to it:

```
<configSchema>
  <sectionSchema name="myCustomSection">
    <attribute name="name" type="string" />
    <attribute name="Length" type="int" defaultValue="100" />
    <attribute name="IsActive" type="bool" defaultValue="true" />
    <attribute name="Color" type="enum" defaultValue="Red" >
        <enum name="Red" value="0" />
        <enum name="Yellow" value="1" />
        <enum name="Green" value="3" />
        <enum name="Blue" value="4" />
    </attribute>
  </sectionSchema>
</configSchema>
```

Since this is a new section, you must also add it to the `configSections` section of the configuration file. This example will add this to `administration.config` to show that it's not just `applicationHost.config` that can be extended. Since this is a main section, it must be placed directly under `<configSections>`, as follows:

```
<configuration>
    <configSections>
        <section name="myCustomSection" />
        <section name="moduleProviders" ... />
    ...
    </configSections>
    ...
</configuration>
```

The code to work with your new custom section is essentially the same as before. Here is a code sample to set these four attributes:

```
Dim SM As New ServerManager
Dim config As Configuration = SM.GetAdministrationConfiguration
```

```
Dim section As ConfigurationSection = _
config.GetSection("myCustomSection")

section.GetAttribute("name").Value = "TheName"
section.GetAttribute("Length").Value = 200
section.GetAttribute("IsActive").Value = True
section.GetAttribute("Color").Value = "Blue"

SM.CommitChanges()
```

After running this, it will add a new section to the configuration file:

```
<myCustomSection name="TheName" Length="200" IsActive="true" Color="Blue" />
```

It is possible to create a strongly typed class that will provide IntelliSense support for your custom schema. To do so, you would create a class that corresponds to the custom schema that you just created. Then use one of the GetSection overrides that allow you to set the System.Type of the section. This will provide full IntelliSense support as if you were using Microsoft's managed code APIs directly.

As you can see, the schema is a foundational part of IIS, is used for many of the tools and programming within IIS, and can be extended to fit your needs. The sky is the limit on what you can do with IIS to make it more customized for your environment.

This completes the direct configuration section, which covered many of the key concepts of the configuration files. Now it's time to move on to *programmatic configuration*, where you will learn the various programming API choices, which you would want to use, and how you would do so.

Programmatic Configuration

When dealing with a small number of web servers and infrequent changes, IIS Manager and manual methods of administrating IIS work well, but it doesn't take long to outgrow this manual administration and look for a better way to manage the server.

Programmatic configuration is nothing new in IIS, but it's been greatly improved while keeping full support for legacy code. There is no need to throw out your old code, yet you can use the latest and greatest methods of programming to manage your IIS servers from now on.

Virtually everything that can be done through IIS Manager and through editing the configuration files directly can be done programmatically. You can program to automate monotonous tasks like the creation of new sites, managing many servers at once, or to develop tools so that non-administrators can make changes — for example, to shut down a site because of non-payment. Whatever the reason, pretty much anything that you dream up can be built.

Since there are code samples scattered throughout the book, this section focuses more on the key concepts so that, coupled with the code snipped throughout the book, you will have the tools necessary to program whatever you need. It's hard to cover everything that you need for programming without writing at least a full book, but the key foundational concepts for various programming methods are covered.

You as the reader of this book may be a seasoned developer who just needs reference material, or you may be a programmer who needs to know how to program against IIS 7.0, or you may be a system administrator who has never programmed before but who is looking to create some tools to simplify your work.

The next few pages are targeted at the person who is not yet a programmer but would like to know how to take advantage of many of the coding examples that have been scattered throughout the book. You will be taken on a walkthrough to create a tool that will use a web page to create an application pool and web site. This will be done using free tools that you can easily download online.

For the more seasoned programmer, stick around, because there is a lot to cover that will benefit you too, but feel free to skim parts that you already know well.

My First IIS 7.0 Programming Walkthrough

This walkthrough will take you on a brief journey to get your feet wet in the world of IIS administration programming. It is by no means a detailed walkthrough — full books have been written for that — but it will lay a foundation on which you can build.

System Requirements

This walkthrough uses only three tools: Visual Web Developer 2008, IIS 7.0, and any commonly used web browser. Additionally, it is much easier to develop when the development machine has IIS installed, rather than doing development remotely. The assumption is that you are doing your development on a Vista SP1 or Windows Server 2008 server that has IIS installed. It is possible to set up remote debugging, but explaining how to do so is outside of the scope of this book.

> *The full Visual Studio 2008 is even better than Visual Web Developer because of the extra tools and features that it comes with. This walkthrough uses features that both products have, so you can use whichever one you have access to. Since the steps are pretty much the same, you should have no problem using either tool and still following this walkthrough. Visual Studio 2005 and Visual Web Developer 2005 are also acceptable for this development and work great. The tools have changed somewhat but are close enough that you should be able to follow along with ease. For this walkthrough, Visual Web Developer is used.*

To obtain Visual Web Developer, a good place to start is www.asp.net or with a Google search. Searching for Visual Web Developer 2008 should get you a good download page within the top few links. Be sure that you're downloading it directly from www.asp.net or www.microsoft.com and not some third-party download.

Installing Visual Web Developer is straightforward. SQL Server Express is not required for this walkthrough, so selecting that during the Visual Web Developer installation is optional and up to you.

Getting Started with Visual Web Developer

Before starting Visual Web Developer, you need to decide on the disk location where you will develop the web site. Visual Web Developer has its own web engine, called ASP.NET Development Server (aka Cassini), so IIS does not need to be used for development. However, once you have it developed, you will probably want to run it under IIS on either the same server or a different server.

Be sure to prepare a folder that makes the most sense for both development and operational use. This demo uses `C:\inetpub\WebSite1`.

> *When running Cassini, your currently logged-in user will need access to disk and to make changes to IIS. With User Access Control (UAC) in Windows Server 2008 and Vista, you may run into an issue where you need to elevate to Administrator rights, even if you are logged in as a user who is an administrator. To get around this, there are three potential solutions:*

1. One is to make sure that the folder where your web site exists has specific permissions for your currently logged-in user. Just having the Administrators group will not be enough. This is usually the preferred method since it doesn't require bypassing UAC.

2. Right-click the Visual Web Developer icon before you start it and click "Run as administrator." This will ensure that everything within Visual Web Developer, including Cassini, will run as the Administrator.

3. In theory, you could disable UAC so that it doesn't get in the way, but that's not the recommended workaround.

After Visual Web Developer or Visual Studio is installed, fire it up. It's time to begin:

1. Click File ➪ New Web Site.

2. Ensure that ASP.NET Web Site is selected.

3. Ensure that File System is selected in the Location dropdown box.

4. In the Location textbox, enter **C:\inetpub\WebSite1**.

5. You can develop in Visual Basic or C#. Both will accomplish the same — it's just a matter of syntax. This walkthrough is in Visual Basic. Ensure that Visual Basic is selected. Figure 17-6 shows this dialog box completed.

6. Click OK.

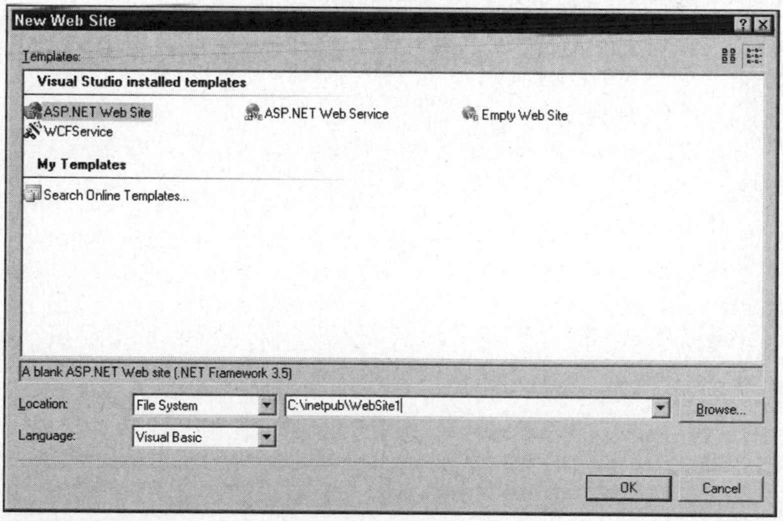

Figure 17-6

This will create a new web site with a couple of default documents. Default.aspx and Default.aspx.vb are the starting files in the new web-site template. For simplicity in the walk-through, they will be used instead of creating new files. Note: Default.aspx.vb may be collapsed under Default.aspx. If it is, click the plus (+) beside Default.aspx to expand it. App_Data will not be used, so you can ignore or delete that folder.

7. `Microsoft.Web.Administration.dll` needs to be added as a reference to the project. To add the reference, click Web Site from the top menu and then Add Reference.

8. Go to the Browse tab and navigate to `%windir%\System32\inetsrv` (`%windir%` is usually `C:\Windows`).

9. Select `Microsoft.Web.Administration.dll` and click OK, as shown in Figure 17-7. To save time navigating through the folders and files, you can directly type **%windir%\System32\ inetsrv\Microsoft.Web.Administration.dll**.

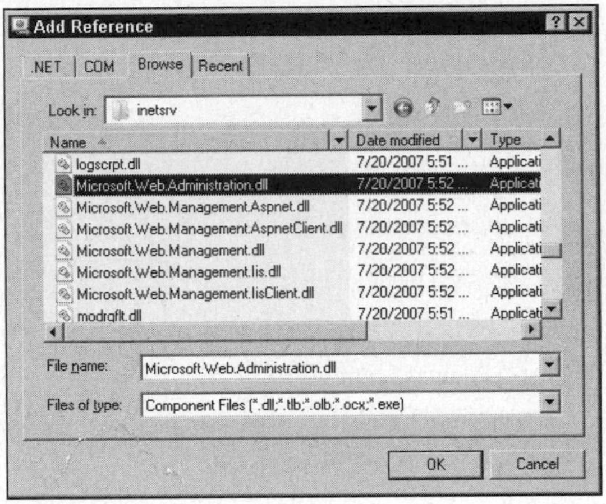

Figure 17-7

Designing the Web Form

Now that Visual Web Developer is started and the reference to `Microsoft.Web.Administration.dll` is in place, it's time to design the web form that takes the information about the web site.

1. Open Default.aspx from Solution Explorer on the right. If Solution Explorer is not shown, you can open it from the top menu by clicking View ➪ Solution Explorer.

2. Click the Design tab at the bottom of the main window. This will switch to Design View, which is a graphical representation of the web page.

3. Right-click in a fresh place on the design surface and click Properties. This will place you in the Properties menu, which is usually on the right side.

4. Change the Title property to **Create Web Site**.

5. On the design surface, type **Create Web Site** inside the `div` tag (the dotted square box), and press [Enter] twice.

6. From the toolbox on the left, drag a Label control to the empty space below the words you just typed (still inside the `div` tag). If the toolbox isn't displayed, you can show it by clicking View from the top menu and clicking Toolbox.

7. Position your cursor after the Label and press [Enter] twice.

8. Next, create a table to make the page look better. To create the table, from the top menu click Table ➪ Insert Table.

9. In the dialog box that appears, enter **6** for the rows and **2** for the columns as shown in Figure 17-8. The defaults are good unless you feel the urge to clean it up further.

10. Click OK to accept the settings.

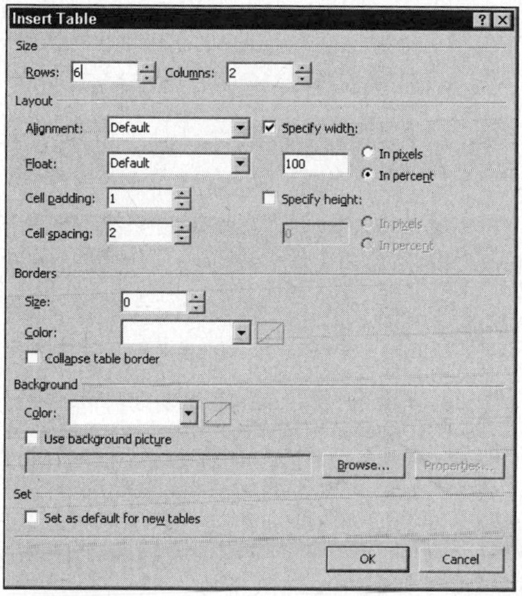

Figure 17-8

11. In the top five left-hand column cells, enter the following text: **Site Name**, **Site IP**, **Site Port**, **Site Host Header**, and **Site Path**, respectively.

12. Drag a TextBox control from the toolbox to each of the top five right-hand column cells.

13. Drag a Button control from the toolbox to the bottom left-hand column cell.

14. Now it's time to name the controls properly. Right-click on the Label control and select Properties.

15. In the Properties windows delete everything in the Text property.

16. Still in the Properties window, change the ID to StatusLabel.

17. The third change to make to the Label is to enter **Red** for the ForeColor property.

18. Each of the TextBoxes needs to be renamed. Just as you changed the ID property for the Label, do the same for the TextBoxes. They should be named **NameTextBox**, **IPTextBox**, **PortTextBox**,

HostHeaderTextbox, and **PathTextBox**. Be certain to name these exactly right, as they need to match the code later in this walkthrough.

19. Edit the properties for the Site Port TextBox, and set the Text value to **80**. This is the standard default port for HTTP.

20. Change the Button Text property to Create Site, and the Button ID to CreateSiteButton.

21. On the right-hand side of the TextBox beside Site IP, type **Leave blank for (all unassigned)**.

22. On the right-hand side of the TextBox beside Site Host Header, type **Leave blank for all host headers**.

23. Feel free to adjust the column widths to improve the aesthetics.

24. This completes the design area of the web page. Finally, double-click the Create Site button to be positioned in the code section of Default.asp.vb, and prepare to write some code.

Writing the Code

Now that the web page UI has been completed, it's time to write some code. This is surprisingly easy with Visual Web Developer and the IntelliSense, which will auto-complete the namespaces, classes, and objects for you.

Copy and paste the following code into the code window, or type it manually so that you get a chance to understand it better. A further explanation is coming shortly. Note that there is already some code in the code window. That should all be replaced with this:

```
Imports Microsoft.Web.Administration

Partial Class _Default
  Inherits System.Web.UI.Page

  Protected Sub CreateSiteButton_Click(ByVal sender As Object, _
                                       ByVal e As System.EventArgs) _
                                       Handles CreateSiteButton.Click
    'Declare and instigate ServerManager
    Dim SM As New ServerManager
    Dim bindingInfo As String
    Dim mySite As Site

    'Create the bindingInfo variable which will be in the
    'form for "IP:Port:HostHeader".  Example ":80:" is
    'everything on port 80.
    bindingInfo = IPTextBox.Text & ":" & _
      PortTextBox.Text & ":" & _
      HostHeaderTextBox.Text

    'Create an App Pool for this site
    SM.ApplicationPools.Add(NameTextBox.Text)

    'Create the Site
    mySite = SM.Sites.Add(NameTextBox.Text, _
             "HTTP", _
             bindingInfo, _
             PathTextBox.Text)
```

```
        'Add site to app pool.  Application(0) is the first and only
        'application in the site so far.
        mySite.Applications(0).ApplicationPoolName _
            = NameTextBox.Text

        'Changes will not take effect until CommitChanges is called.
        SM.CommitChanges()

        StatusLabel.Text = "Website " & NameTextBox.Text & " was created."

    End Sub
End Class
```

It's worth stopping here for a minute to explain the code.

The `Imports` command at the top will import the `Microsoft.Web.Administration` namespace, so you don't need to type it each time you need to reference any of its classes. For example, notice the line that says `Dim SM As New ServerManager`. You could instead enter `Dim SM As New Microsoft.Web.Administration.ServerManager`, which is the full name of the class. Since it can be pretty monotonous to type `Microsoft.Web.Administration` every time, especially if it's used more than once, importing the namespace is a good practice.

The `Protected Sub CreateSiteButton_Click` is an Event subroutine that is called when the Create Site button is clicked. This will not run when the page is first loaded. It will only run when someone specifically clicks on the Create Site button.

Next, three variables are declared: the `ServerManager` object, which is the main entry point for managing the server, the `bindingInfo` string variable, and the `mySite` site variable.

Next the `bindingInfo` variable is populated in the format that IIS needs. The format is `IP:Port:Host Header`. For example, to create a site binding for IP address 10.0.0.10 on port 80 and using a host header of `Site1.DomainA.local`, the site binding would be `10.0.0.10:80:Site1.DomainA.local`. The IP and host header are optional, but the port is required; therefore, `":80:"` is also valid.

The add method only allows you to set one binding. If you need to add multiple bindings, you must add them after the site has been created. This simple example supports only a single host header and binding when initially creating the web site.

Be sure to add `SM.CommitChanges()` as it is the method required to actually apply the changes to the server.

Finally, the StatusLabel is updated with a message to state that the web site was created.

Running the Create Web Site Web Site

No, that title isn't a typo. Now that you've created a web site that creates an IIS site, it's time to try it out. To run this using the ASP.NET Development Server (aka Cassini) that is part of Visual Web Developer:

1.   Choose Debug ⇨ Start Without Debugging. Alternately, you can start with debugging if you want, and then acknowledge the prompt asking you if you want to enable debugging in `web.config`.

This will start the ASP.NET Developer Server and start your web browser running your new application.

2. Enter in the values that you want for your new web site. Note that this example doesn't do any error checking, so be sure to enter only valid values. The site name can contain spaces, but most other special characters are not supported. The site IP should be an IP address on the web server. Leaving it blank is supported. The default port of 80 is often good, but feel free to change that. The site host header can be set or left blank, which essentially gives a wildcard host header. Finally, the site path needs to be a valid path on disk to your web site, for example, `c:\inetpub\Site2`. Figure 17-9 shows a picture of what your Create Web Site web site should look like with some possible values filled in.

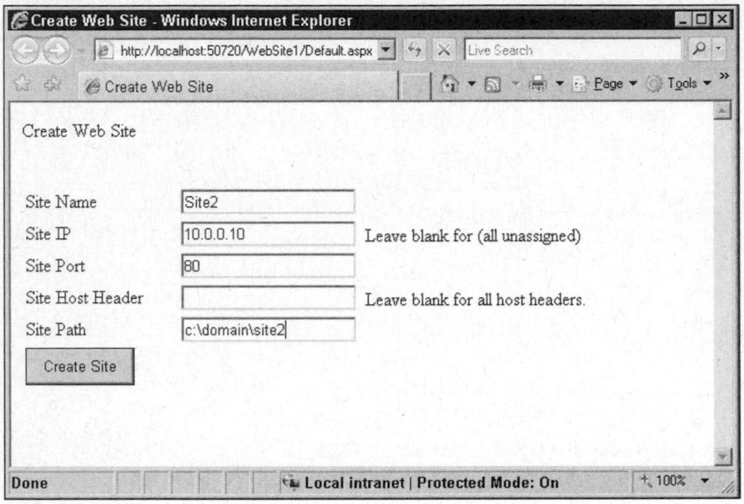

Figure 17-9

3. Once everything is filled in, click on the Create Site button, and the site will be created in IIS!

This is a bare-bones example showing the essentials to installing Visual Web Developer and creating a simple web site that will create a site in IIS. To keep the code example clean and easy to understand, this does not include error checking, and it does not attempt to use all programming best practices. Use this as a stepping-stone to get you started in IIS 7.0 administrative programming.

That's it! That was easy, wasn't it? Whether you're a seasoned programmer or this is your first program, I'm sure you can see the powerful simplicity that is available at your fingertips. Now, use this along with the other references in this chapter to start dreaming up and developing your own tools to help yourself and those around you be even better IIS administrators.

Microsoft.Web.Administration (MWA)

New to IIS 7.0 is the `Microsoft.Web.Administration` API, which offers a strongly typed set of .NET classes for IIS administrative programming. It is a wrapper over the Application Host Administration API (AHAdmin) native code interface library, which is discussed in its own section below. These sets of classes make programmatic management of IIS extremely easy. With tools like Visual Studio or Visual Web Developer, it's easy to create anything from a few simple scripts to a full-blown corporate program to manage IIS. Since the classes are strongly typed, IntelliSense and design-time error checking make programming so much easier than in past versions.

The walkthrough above in this chapter used `Microsoft.Web.Administration` and will most likely be the preferred programmatic method for .NET developers. Unless you have a specific need for using any of the other APIs or WMI, `Microsoft.Web.Administration` is well worth considering as your primary programming method.

This API needs to be referenced in your project or `web.config` file. It's located at `%windir%\System32\inetsrv\ Microsoft.Web.Administration.dll`, so be sure to add this after you first create a project.

It's important to understand the class structure in this namespace. There are a set of predefined classes that make management of the most common IIS objects straightforward, but you also have the ability to change individual elements and attributes directly. Additionally, from code, you can specify the configuration file and the `location` tag that you want to manage.

The root level class is `ServerManager`, which is the foundation for the other classes (see Figure 17-10).

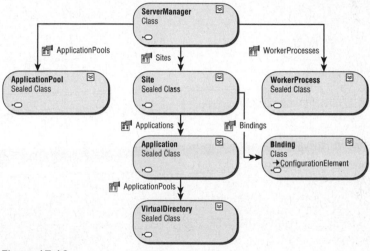

Figure 17-10

The class structure is easy to visualize. Picture five main objects: `Site`, `Application`, `VirtualDirectory`, `ApplicationPool`, and `WorkerProcess`. There are also some matching classes which enable you to set the default settings for these objects.

An `Application` belongs to a `Site`, and a `VirtualDirectory` belongs to an `Application`. None of these objects lives on its own; they must be part of their parent.

The `WorkerProcess` class allows you to view real-time configuration data about the server! You can gain access into the currently running worker processes and even the running requests.

Additionally, the `ServerManager` class has a set of methods to manage the configuration files directly. Don't worry if you aren't a seasoned programmer and this seems overwhelming. At first you may imagine a complex XML-based configuration method, but it's really quite simple. If you are a seasoned developer, you'll be equally impressed with the power that you have.

The next three sections cover programming the configuration setting, dynamic runtime data and how to directly edit attributes and elements.

Configuration Classes

The core *configuration classes* include `ApplicationPool`, `Site`, `Application`, and `VirtualDirectory`, and a matching set of classes to set the default values for each object. Creating these various objects in IIS couldn't be easier.

The following example shows how to create a site in IIS. (Don't forget to import the `Microsoft.Web.Administration` namespace, as `ServerManager` is really `Microsoft.Web.Administration.ServerManager`.)

```
Dim SM As New ServerManager
SM.Sites.Add("Site1", "http", ":80:", "c:\websites\Site1")
SM.CommitChanges()
```

This creates an instance of the `ServerManager` class and uses the `Sites` collection's `Add` method to create the "Site1" site.

To create an application pool, use the following:

```
Dim SM As New ServerManager
SM.ApplicationPools.Add("Site1AppPool")
SM.CommitChanges()
```

Once created, you can change various settings — for example, to set the application pool's framework version back to version 1.1, you could add the following code. Note that SM is not defined again because this is meant to be a continuation of the previous code example.

```
Dim apppool As ApplicationPool
apppool = SM.ApplicationPools("Site1AppPool")
apppool.ManagedRuntimeVersion = "v1.1"
SM.CommitChanges()
```

Another way to accomplish the previous two code examples would be to set the new application pool as a variable of type `ApplicationPool`. This will give you a handle to the application pool so that you can immediately make changes to it.

```
Dim SM As New ServerManager
Dim apppool As ApplicationPool

apppool = SM.ApplicationPools.Add("Site2AppPool")
apppool.ManagedRuntimeVersion = "v1.1"
SM.CommitChanges()
```

To create a new application, (not an application pool) all that is needed is:

```
Dim SM As New ServerManager
Dim site As Site

site = SM.Sites("Site1")
site.Applications.Add("/app1", "C:\websites\Site1\App1")

SM.CommitChanges()
```

As you can see, development with the `Microsoft.Web.Administration` managed code API is straightforward. This is just the beginning of what you can do. Using this as a springboard, the sky is the limit on the possibilities available.

Dynamic Runtime Classes

In addition to the classes that configure sites and application pools (static data), you can start and stop sites, recycle application pools, and even see the currently running worker processes, application domains, and page requests.

Here's an example of how to view all of the running processes on the server. Remember that this data is dynamic and changes based on what is running at any given time. Applications that exist in IIS don't always have a worker process running at all times.

```
Dim SM As New ServerManager

For Each wp As WorkerProcess In SM.WorkerProcesses
  Console.Writeline(wp.AppPoolName & " " & wp.ProcessId)
Next
```

In this example, the method used for writing the information to the screen is `Console.Writeline`, which makes sense for a console application. If you are developing this for the web, you can write the information to a Label control, or the quick and easy way if it's for testing is to use `Response.Write` instead of `Console.Writeline`.

> User Access Control (UAC) can fight with you here. If you don't get any results, be sure to elevate your permissions to an Administrator so that UAC doesn't prevent you from gaining access to the process information.

The following code shows all running page requests. Notice `GetRequests(0)`. The 0 is the time that the page has been running in milliseconds. Setting it to 0 means that it will get all page requests, but you can set it to a higher number, for example, 10000 for 10 seconds, to see all pages that have been running for longer than that period of time.

```
Dim SM As New ServerManager

'loop through each running worker process
For Each wp As WorkerProcess In SM.WorkerProcesses
   Console.Writeline("App Pool Name: " & wp.AppPoolName")
   Console.Writeline("Worker Process PID: " & wp.ProcessId")

   'loop through each running page request
```

```
        For Each request As Request In wp.GetRequests(0)
            Console.Writeline("   Request:" & request.Url")
        Next
    Next
```

Additionally, you can start and stop sites and start, stop, and recycle application pools. To recycle the application pool called AppPool1, you can do the following:

```
    Dim SM As New ServerManager
    SM.ApplicationPools("Site1").Recycle()
```

You get the point. It doesn't take much to figure out each of these from scratch, plus there are code examples scattered throughout this book.

Accessing a Remote Server

Connecting to a remote IIS server is as simple as calling `ServerManager.OpenRemote`. The following example shows how to define a variable of type `ServerManager` and connect to a remote host:

```
    Dim SM As ServerManager = ServerManager.OpenRemote("10.0.0.10")
```

In the previous code examples in this chapter, you will notice that SM is defined as: `Dim SM As New ServerManager`. Just replace that line with the line in this code example, and you will be able to connect to a remote server instead of the local IIS server. You can use an IP address, hostname, or domain name for `OpenRemote`'s `serverName`. This is a good place to add a `Try...Catch` block to handle any failures connecting to the remote server.

Direct Attribute and Element Editing

In addition to the classes for the most common configuration objects, you can view, create, update, or delete any attribute or element within the configuration files using the base class `ServerManager`. You can edit any of the IIS configuration files, which include `applicationHost.config`, `administration.config`, `redirection.config`, and all site and application configuration files.

To do so, as you are used to by now, you must declare and instigate a variable of type `ServerManager`, as follows:

```
    Dim SM As New ServerManager
```

Then you have a few choices for the various configuration files:

- ❑ `ServerManager.GetApplicationHostConfiguration`
- ❑ `ServerManager.GetAdministrationConfiguration`
- ❑ `ServerManager.GetRedirectionConfiguration`
- ❑ `ServerManager.GetWebConfiguration`

The `GetWebConfiguration` method enables you to specify a specific site's configuration file. The other three don't take any parameters and point directly to the corresponding configuration file that is obvious from the method name.

To get the `applicationHost.config` file, for example, you would do something like this:

```
Dim config As Configuration = SM.GetApplicationHostConfiguration
```

To get a specific site's `web.config` file, you would use this:

```
Dim config As Configuration = SM.GetWebConfiguration("Site1")
```

And to get an application's `web.config` file, you would use this:

```
Dim config As Configuration = SM.GetWebConfiguration("Site1", "/App1")
```

Now that you've created the configuration object for the configuration file that you want, it's time to call the section. Picking a particular `location` tag is covered in the next section. For now, only the default section will be covered. Using the section structure covered above in this chapter, you can pick the section that you want to change. For example, to pick the `defaultDocument` section from the `system.webServer` section group, you would do the following:

```
Dim section As ConfigurationSection = _
          config.GetSection("system.webServer/defaultDocument")
```

As you can probably tell already, the `system.webServer` in this code example corresponds to the `<system.webServer>` section group in the configuration file. The `defaultDocument` corresponds to the `<defaultDocument>` section.

Once you have chosen the group, then it's time to pull out an attribute or element. The following example pulls this all together into a complete example and reads the enabled attribute value from Site1's `web.config` file.

```
Dim SM As New ServerManager
Dim config As Configuration = SM.GetWebConfiguration("Site1")
Dim section As ConfigurationSection = _
    config.GetSection("system.webServer/defaultDocument")

Dim enabled As ConfigurationAttribute = section.Attributes("enabled")

Console.Writeline(enabled.Value)
```

You can also read, update, and delete elements and collections. The following example gets the default documents for a site:

```
Dim SM As New ServerManager
Dim config As Configuration = SM.GetWebConfiguration("Site1")
Dim section As ConfigurationSection = _
    config.GetSection("system.webServer/defaultDocument")

Dim filescollection As ConfigurationElementCollection

filescollection = section.GetCollection("files")

For Each item As ConfigurationElement In filescollection
    Console.Writeline(item.Attributes("value").Value")
Next
```

Don't forget to change `Console.Writeline` to `Response.Write` if you are creating a web page instead of a console application. Notice the `filescollection` variable, which gets all of the collection elements. Then the `For Each` loop writes out the value (name) of each of the default documents.

Dealing with location Tags

Many times you will need to make a change to a specific `location` tag instead of the default section. This is fully supported and fairly straightforward once you know how to do it.

The thing to keep in mind is that it's when you choose the section in the configuration file that you also choose the location. In the previous code example, it's the line that starts with `Dim Section` that can be tweaked to specify the `location` tag. The `GetSection` method has an override to allow you to specify the `locationPath`. The `locationPath` is in the form of *Site1* or *Site1/App1*.

To set the `defaultDocument`-enabled attribute to `false` in the `location` tag for "Site1" in `applicationHost.config`, you can use the following example (notice that this example is also managing a remote server at IP address 10.0.0.10):

```
Dim SM As ServerManager = ServerManager.OpenRemote("10.0.0.10")
Dim config As Configuration = SM.GetApplicationHostConfiguration
Dim section As ConfigurationSection = _
    config.GetSection("system.webServer/defaultDocument", "Site1")
```

Notice that the `GetSection` method has the site name as the second parameter. For the `GetSection` method, the following:

```
GetSection("system.webServer/defaultDocument")
```

is identical to

```
GetSection("system.webServer/defaultDocument", "")
```

A question comes to mind. What happens if there are multiple `location` tags for the same path, but with different `overrideMode` values? Suppose, for example, that you have the following three sections in `applicationHost.config`:

General Section

```
<system.webServer>
    . . . {various sections} . . .
</system.webServer>
```

Locking location Tag

```
<location path="" allowOverride="false">
    <system.webServer>
        . . . {various sections} . . .
    </system.webServer>
</location>
```

Allowing location Tag

```
<location path="" allowOverride="true">
    <system.webServer>
        . . . {various sections} . . .
    </system.webServer>
</location>
```

That's a trick question actually. Configuration elements can only appear once per unique path, so it's not possible to have a section in all three locations at the same time. When updating a section, you only need to specify the configuration file and the site or application. If you do need to indicate a specific location tag with a specific overrideMode setting, you can do that by using the overrideMode property of ConfigurationSection, as follows:

```
...
Dim section As ConfigurationSection = _
    config.GetSection("system.webServer/defaultDocument", "Site1")

section.OverrideMode = OverrideMode.Deny

...
```

As you can see, you have granular control over the location tag paths and even the overrideMode specific tags within any of the configuration files.

Microsoft.Web.Administration offers a powerful programming solution for IIS 7.0 administration. The IIS team has done a tremendous job of making it very powerful and flexible, yet easy to work with.

Microsoft.Web.Management (MWM)

The second managed code API that IIS offers is Microsoft.Web.Management. This provides the framework to create user interface (UI) features in IIS Manager and create and manage IIS Users and permissions. Since many of the built-in features and icons in IIS Manager use this same namespace in the background, you can use it to create features that look and feel identical to the built-in IIS features.

There is both a server side and a client side to this API, including rich features for lists, properties, grids, group panels, and wizards, and access into the action and other panes within IIS Manager. IIS User management allows you to create users, update users and passwords, and assign either IIS Manager users or Windows users to sites and applications for remote delegation.

You must reference %windir%\System32\inetsrv\Microsoft.Web.Management.dll within your project or web.config file to use Microsoft.Web.Management. There are four subnamespaces within the Microsoft.Web.Management namespace: Client, Features, Host, and Server.

Extensive development in Microsoft.Web.Management is not covered here, but one example will be provided. This example creates an IIS Manager user and grants it permissions to a specific Site1. Additionally, a Windows user will also be granted permissions to the same site.

First, be sure to import Microsoft.Web.Management.Server, which is the namespace for ManagementAuthentication and ManagementAuthorization, as follows:

```
Imports Microsoft.Web.Management.Server
```

The code to create the IIS Manager user and grant the two users to the site is straightforward:

```
Dim user As ManagementUserInfo
'create IIS Manager user
user = ManagementAuthentication.CreateUser("IISUser1", "password")

'grant the freshly created user permissions to the site
ManagementAuthorization.Grant(user.Name, "Site1", False)

'additionally, grant the Windows user permission to the site
ManagementAuthorization.Grant("DomainA.local/User2", "Site1", False)
```

In Chapter 12, "Core Server Extensibility," we discuss this further and give a walkthrough using `Microsoft.Web.Management` to extend IIS Manager.

ABO, ADSI, and Legacy API Support

Anyone who has existing scripts for their IIS 6.0 (or older) web servers will be pleased to know that IIS 7.0 maintains support for existing APIs. Even though the IIS 7.0 underlying structure is substantially different, the IIS team has created an emulation layer that maps Admin Base Objects (ABO) (aka IMSAdminBase) and code calls to the new configuration system using a new component called *ABOMapper*. This means that your existing code can function as it always did without needing to rewrite your code before migrating to IIS 7.0.

The ABOMapper works as an intermediary layer between legacy code and the new IIS configuration system. It does this by taking and interpreting all the code, discovering the differences between the old and the new and making the appropriate Read or Write operations directly against the configuration files. It does not work against the in-memory configuration like it did in previous versions.

Active Directory Service Interface (ADSI) and IIS 6.0 WMI depend on ABO and are fully supported in IIS 7.0. The whole set of ABO APIs and dependency APIs are included in this discussion. This applies to the .NET `System.DirectoryServices` namespace, too, which works on top of ADSI.

> *IIS 6.0 WMI support and IIS 7.0 WMI support are two different things. Make sure to take note of which version of WMI is being referred to whenever "WMI" is mentioned. There is legacy support for existing WMI code, which is called IIS 6 WMI. The new syntax for the IIS 7.0 API is much improved, as described further in the next section.*

To be able to support ABO, the metabase compatibility components need to be installed, as they are not installed by default. This is done in the Add Role Services section of Server Manager. The three relevant options are:

❑ IIS 6.0 Metabase Compatibility

❑ IIS 6.0 WMI Compatibility

❑ IIS 6.0 Scripting Tools

The IIS 6.0 Metabase Compatibility option is a requirement for the other two, and IIS 6.0 WMI Compatibility is a requirement for IIS 6.0 Scripting Tools.

There are some things to keep in mind with the IIS 6.0 scripting options. They do not support the new features of IIS 7.0, only features that already existed in IIS 6.0. This also means that the new distributed configuration is not supported. You cannot specify which `location` tag or which configuration file is being used. You must leave that decision to the ABOMapper. Additionally, the ServerComment field in IIS 6.0 wasn't a required field, and it wasn't required to be unique, but the site name is a required field in IIS 7.0; therefore, the ABOMapper takes care of that new requirement by adding numbers to the name to ensure uniqueness. This means that the site name will end up different from what was entered in the script. Also, calls that ABO makes to back up, restore, import, and export will be ignored since the new configure files work much differently in IIS 7.0. For these reasons, it's advisable to migrate to the new API options when possible.

Some features — namely, the FTP version that is shipped with the product, NNTP, and SMTP — will still use the regular call to `metabase.xml`. Everything else will go through the ABOMapper.

When developing or troubleshooting using any of the IIS 6.0 scripting APIs, the error logs will not be recorded to the Event Log. Instead, they will be saved to `%windir%\System32\Abomapper.log`, so be sure to watch that log file for any clues to issues that you may run into.

IIS 7.0 WMI Provider

Windows Management Instrumentation (WMI) is used for managing various aspects of the Windows operating system. You were able to manage IIS with WMI in previous versions of IIS, and support is still maintained for existing IIS 6.0 scripts, as seen in the last section.

IIS 7.0 introduces some nice improvements in the syntax for the WMI provider, ensuring a greater consistency across the whole provider and making scripting with WMI easier and more powerful. There are now two blends of WMI to be aware of. One is the IIS 7.0 WMI provider, and the other is the IIS 6.0 WMI provider. The IIS 6.0 WMI API is maintained for backward compatibility, but it has its limitations and shouldn't be used for new development unless you have a compelling reason to do so. The previous section discussed this in more depth. IIS 7.0 WMI is the new WMI provider, and through the rest of this chapter, any time that *WMI* is mentioned without specifying the version, it will always refer to the IIS 7.0 WMI provider.

One of the most common uses for WMI is within Windows Scripting Host (WSH), which gives you the ability to create a script that can be run right from the computer, almost like an executable program except that you can edit it directly from Notepad.

Probably the best tool for WMI development is CIM Studio, which is a Microsoft tool and a free download. CIM Studio enables you to fully navigate the classes, properties, methods, and associators of any of the WMI namespaces so that you can know what is available for you to use from code. CIM Studio also gives you the ability to see active instances of real data and to write your own WQL commands directly. *WQL (WMI Query Language)* is named after and follows similar syntax to SQL (Structured Query Language used in databases). The "Select * from {something}" syntax that you may already be familiar with can be used within WMI.

Throughout the next couple of sections, you will be given an introduction to CIM Studio and will learn how to create some simple WSH scripts that you can run yourself.

First, make sure that you have the required components installed to support WMI. They are installed from Server Manager by Adding a Role. The IIS7 WMI provider feature is under Management Tools ⇨ IIS Management Scripts and Tools.

Once you have that installed, you are ready to start creating your own WMI scripts. The next section introduces you to CIM Studio so that you can learn how to find the classes, properties, and methods yourself; the following section will give a walkthrough of how to create an application pool and a site and then add the site to the application pool.

CIM Studio

CIM Studio is part of the WMI Administrative Tools kit. You can download it from www.microsoft. com/downloads/details.aspx?FamilyID=6430f853-1120-48db-8cc5-f2abdc3ed314&display lang=en. It is a 4.7 MB download and takes up only about 14 MB of space, so it's a quick program to download and install.

CIM Studio runs as a web page on your local computer using your web browser. You must be running as an Administrator, which User Access Control (UAC) doesn't do by default, even if your user is in the Administrators group. Therefore, be sure to follow this next step correctly.

Start a command prompt window with elevated permissions, start CIM Studio, and then connect to the WebAdministration namespace. Here is how to do so:

1. Click Start, and type **cmd** in the search box.

2. Right-click cmd.exe, which should appear at the top of the search choices.

3. Click "Run as administrator."

4. From the command prompt window, type **"%ProgramFiles%\wmi tools\studio.htm"** (including quotes).

5. If you are using Internet Explorer as your default browser, you will need to acknowledge the warning at the top of the browser's main window to allow the Active X control to run.

6. In the "Connect to namespace" window that opens by default, enter **root\WebAdministration**.

7. Click OK, and then click OK again on the WMI CIM Studio Login prompt. You may need to press the spacebar once during this process to activate the Active X control.

Figure 17-11 shows CIM Studio at this point.

At first there may seem to be an overwhelming number of objects in the left-hand pane and a confusing right-hand pane. Don't worry — you will get used to this quickly.

On the left you'll see various classes that make up the WebAdministration namespace. The first place to look is under Object ⇨ Configured Object. This contains the Application, Site, and Virtual Directory objects. If you click the Site class, it will show the list of properties in the right-hand side. The properties are a mixture of inherited properties and properties specific to the Site class. The properties that you see here — for example, Bindings, Id, and name — are available from code, making WMI Studio a powerful tool to serve as a reference guide for your programming.

The Methods tab shows all the methods that you can execute for that particular class. For the Site class, there are methods like Create, Start, and Stop.

CIM Studio also allows you to run WQL queries directly. This is done through the second icon from the right that looks like a database with a magnifying glass. After clicking this, you will be presented with a

Query window, which you can use to save and/or execute queries. For example, type **select * from site** and click the Execute button. That may be too generic, so try something like **select name, id from site**. WQL has the basic select syntax of SQL. Figure 17-12 shows the Query window with a SELECT statement and with the instances behind the Query window showing the results.

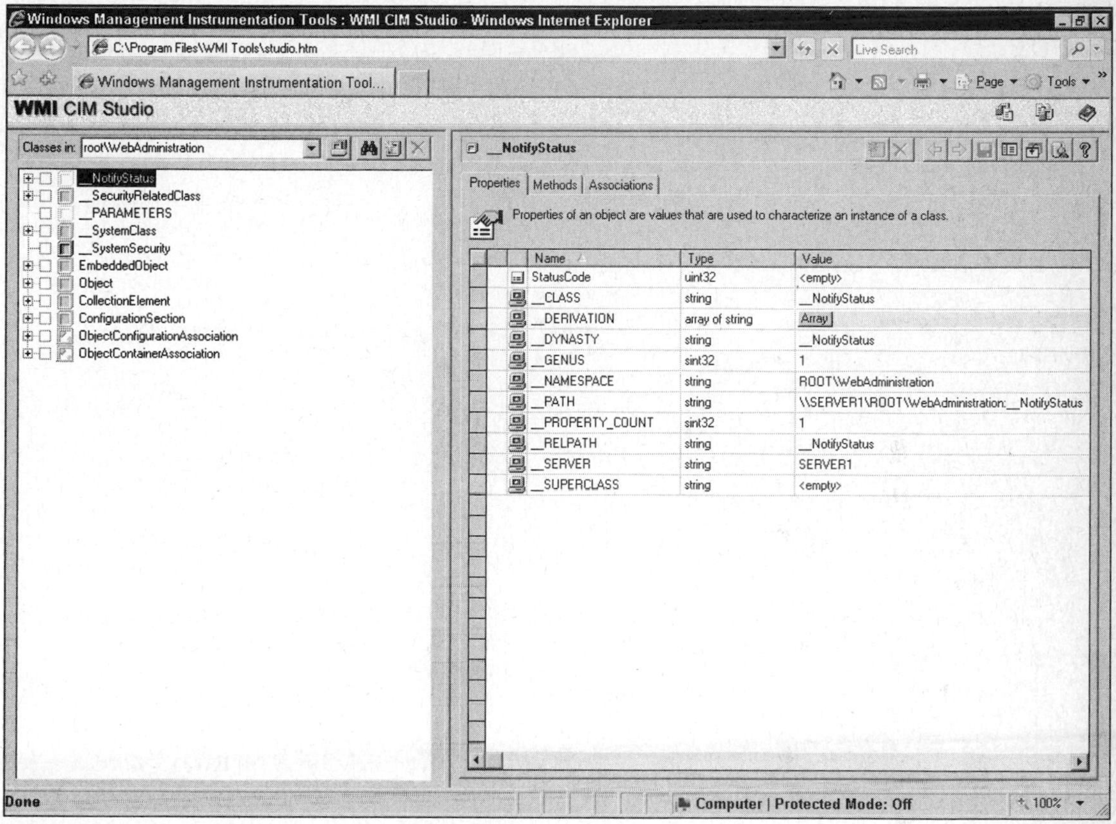

Figure 17-11

The other valuable part of CIM Studio is seeing actual instance data. This is similar to the WQL query shown previously except that the data is available with a click of the mouse. The icon is the fourth from the right that looks like a lopsided book. After clicking the Instances button, you will be shown all the available instances for the object you are in. For example, in the case of the Site class, you will be shown all the actual site instances directly from IIS 7.0.

As you can see, CIM Studio is a tool that allows you to see the properties, methods, and associations for a WMI class, but it also allows you to run WQL queries and get the live instance data directly. This proves to be a valuable tool for programming because you can reference CIM Studio to get properties and methods that are necessary to write your scripts.

WMI Walkthrough

Now that you have seen CIM studio, it's time to write a WMI example script to create an application pool and a web site and add the web site to the application pool.

WMI can be used in many different ways, but a common programming method is to use WSH, which is what will be used in this example.

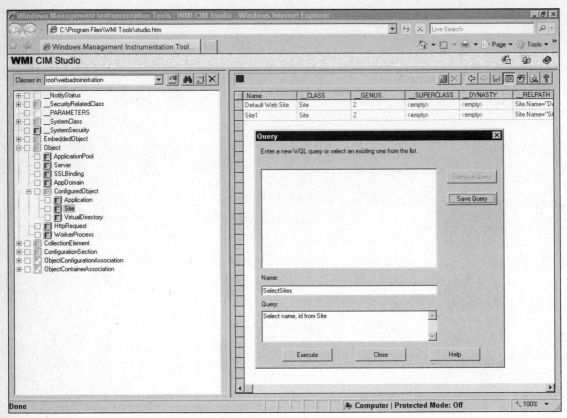

Figure 17-12

To start, open Notepad or your favorite text editor. Enter the following code sections, in order.

```
Option Explicit

Dim oIIS, oBinding, oApp
Dim siteName, physicalPath, bindings
siteName = "Site1"
physicalPath = "c:\inetpub\wwwroot"
bindings = ":80:Site1.DomainA.local"
```

First, `Option Explicit` is set, ensuring that all variables are declared. If they aren't, an error is thrown early. This is generally a good practice and makes it easier to catch typos early.

Once the variables are defined, they are populated with the desired values.

```
' Set oIIS to the WebAdministration class
Set oIIS = GetObject("winmgmts:root\WebAdministration")
```

The `oIIS` object is set to the `WebAdministration` class. This will be used many times throughout this script.

```
' Create application pool
oIIS.Get("ApplicationPool").Create(siteName)
```

To create the application pool, that is all there is to it! Running the script will be covered shortly. Remember that you can find out the method names and parameters from CIM Studio. Now it's on to creating the site bindings.

```
'Create the binding for the site
Set oBinding = oIIS.Get("BindingElement").SpawnInstance_
oBinding.BindingInformation = bindings
oBinding.Protocol = "http"
```

The bindings are set in the `BindingElement` class to be used shortly in the next step. Notice the variable called `bindings`, which was set at the beginning of the script.

```
' Create the site
oIIS.Get("Site").Create siteName, array(oBinding), physicalPath
```

Creating the site is also easy. The `Create` method takes the site name, the `BindingElement` object as an array, and the physical path.

```
' Get the application that was created
Set oApp = oIIS.Get("Application.SiteName='" & siteName & "',Path='/'")

' Assign the new app pool to the application
oApp.ApplicationPool = siteName

' Commit the changes
oApp.Put_
```

To add the new site to the application pool, you must first get the application of the site that was created., then update the application's application pool. To ensure that the change is applied, you must run `oApp.Put_`, which commits the changes.

```
' Write out a message
WScript.Echo "Site " & siteName & " has been created."
```

Finally, it's helpful to output something so that you have feedback on the status of the script.

This code example doesn't have any error handling so that it is a concise example, but if you try to create this and the application pool or site already exists, it will fail. To properly create this for a production environment, it's wise to check first if the application pool and site already exist and handle any other errors that may occur.

Now, take all the preceding code and piece it together into the text document. Then save the text document to your computer with an extension of .vbs.

WSH runs in two modes, either WScript or CScript. If it is set to run in WScript on your computer, then everything will run the same, but the final message saying that the site has been created will display in a Windows message box. If there are any error messages, a Windows message box will be used for them also. If you are using CScript and you ran the program by double-clicking on it, then you will probably see the message flash on the screen briefly and then disappear. That is because it displays it in a command prompt instead of a pop-up window. Essentially, the differences between CScript and WScript are just in the output method. CScript is command-line-based, while WScript is more Windows-based. The actual code execution is the same.

To control which script host you are using, you can either change the default or you can start the script from the command prompt using the script host that you choose. In this example, start by opening the command prompt. If you forget the syntax, you can always get it by typing **cscript /?**. To change the default script host:

❑ For Cscript, type **cscript //H:CScript**.

❑ For Wscript, type **cscript //H:WScript**.

The way to run it without permanently changing the default script host is to start it from the command prompt and prefix the filename with the script host that you want it to run under. For example:

❑ cscript CreateSite.vbs

❑ wscript CreateSite.vbs

Although WScript can be more friendly in some ways because of the Windows message boxes, be careful about running a script that outputs a lot of information in individual pieces, for example, if you are testing something within a while loop and doing a wscript.echo often. If you aren't careful, you'll need to click the OK button a lot of times. If you use cscript, it will output the data in the command prompt without waiting for you to acknowledge anything. That makes CScript better when you have a lot to output.

This has given a brief overview of how to create a script using WSH and some differences between WScript and Cscript and how to use each script host.

Connecting to a remote server is also fully supported in WMI. For the line in the preceding code sample that has set oIIS = GetObject("winmgmts:root\WebAdministration"), you can use the following instead, and replace the serverName with your server name or IP:

```
set oIIS = GetObject("winmgmts://ServerName/root/WebAdministration")
```

Much more could be said about WMI programming, but this is enough to get your feet wet and give you the tools that you need to start creating scripts in your enterprise to manage IIS 7.0.

AHAdmin

The *Application Host Administration API (AHAdmin)* interface is the new foundational native code COM-friendly interface, which you can use directly from native code applications and module development, or indirectly using the IIS 7.0 WMI provider or the managed code wrappers. AHAdmin replaces the role of ABO, although ABO is still supported, as discussed above.

AHAdmin is straightforward to develop with and builds on the configuration path and `location` tag principles already discussed in this chapter. With it you can target a specific `location` tag and use the distributed configuration system introduced in IIS 7.0.

When developing using AHAdmin, you start by getting an instance of `IAppHostAdminManager` for Read-Only access to the config. To have Read/Write access, you use `IappHostWritableAdminManager`, which derives from `IAppHostAdminManager` but has additional methods: `CommitChange` to commit the changes to disk and `CommitPath` to specify where the configuration settings are written.

For example, in VbScript in WSH, you can write the following:

```
Set ahRead = CreateObject("Microsoft.ApplicationHost.AdminManager")
Set ahWrite = _
    CreateObject("Microsoft.ApplicationHost.WritableAdminManager")
```

The `ahRead` object can read the configuration, whereas the `ahWrite` object can read and write to the configuration.

Here's an example of how to disable the anonymous user using AHAdmin from a WSH file using VbScript. Create a file called `DisableAnonymousAuth.vbs` and save the following to it.

```
configFile = "MACHINE/WEBROOT/APPHOST/"
siteName = "Default Web Site"
configPath = configFile & siteName
configSectionName = _
    "system.webServer/security/authentication/anonymousAuthentication"

'create the ahManager object
Set ahManager = CreateObject("Microsoft.ApplicationHost.WritableAdminManager")

'get the anonymous authentication section
set anonymousAuth = _
    ahManager.GetAdminSection(configSectionName, configPath)

'set the enabled attribute to false
anonymousAuth.Properties.Item("enabled").Value = False

'commit the changes
ahManager.CommitChanges()
```

Notice that you can specify the configuration file and `location` tag that the configuration is written to. See the Configuration Path section above in this chapter for more discussion on setting that. See the WMI Walkthrough section in this chapter to get an overview of writing and running WSH scripts.

The AHAdmin `WritableAdminManager` object is created, and the enabled property is set. Finally, the changes are committed.

WSH can also use Jscript instead of VbScript simply by naming the file with a .js extension instead of a .vbs extension and, of course, using Jscript for your development instead of VbScript. Following is an example of how to enable shared configuration and set the path, username, and password. Save the file with the filename `SetSharedConfiguration.js`.

```
try{

var configPath = "c:\\SharedConfig";
var username = "User1";
var password = "User1";

var config =
WScript.CreateObject(
    "Microsoft.ApplicationHost.WritableAdminManager" );

config.CommitPath = "MACHINE/REDIRECTION";

var section = config.GetAdminSection(
    "configurationRedirection",
    config.CommitPath);

section.Properties.Item( "enabled" ).Value = true;
section.Properties.Item( "path" ).Value = configPath;
section.Properties.Item( "userName" ).Value = username;
section.Properties.Item( "password" ).Value = password;

//comment the changes
config.CommitChanges();
}
//catch and output any error
catch(e)
{
WScript.Echo(e.number);
WScript.Echo(e.description);
}
```

This example uses `MACHINE/REDIRECTION` for the commit path, which means that the changes are made to the `%windir%\System32\inetsrv\config\redirection.config` file.

IIS Manager, IIS 7.0 WMI, `Microsoft.Web.Administration`, and `Microsoft.Web.Management` use AHAdmin under the covers, so as you can guess, AHAdmin can do almost anything you dream up and is recommended by Microsoft for native code applications and module development. If you aren't using .NET and the managed code APIs, or WMI, then AHAdmin is the API that you should consider for your development needs.

Summary

IIS 7.0 builds on an extremely configurable and customizable architecture and one that can be distributed across UNC shares and across many web sites. Unlike IIS 6.0, which had the entire configuration in a single file, IIS 7.0 distributes the configuration to where it makes the most sense. This offers a tremendous amount of control, delegation of administration, and flexibility.

From a configuration perspective, this chapter covered the IIS configuration files, `location` tags, sections, locking, extending the schema, the configuration paths, and more. Understanding these allows you to better manage your IIS environment and also prepares you for programming against IIS.

From the programming perspective, AHAdmin has become the new underlying API for development. If you are writing core modules, then you can program using AHAdmin directly. Or, if you are using IIS 7.0 WMI, it utilizes AHadmin behind the scenes. The new managed code wrappers (`Microsoft.Web.Administration` and `Microsoft.Web.Management`) use AHAdmin, as well. While there are new and much-improved methods of programming in IIS 7.0, there is still full support for the old methods of programming using ABO, IIS 6.0 WMI, and ADSI.

This chapter discussed backward compatibility for existing scripts, but probably more importantly, it covered how to program with the new programming APIs. There was a full walkthrough on developing with Visual Web Developer, using the new managed code API targeted to a non-programmer who wants to get started in IIS administration development. IIS 7.0 WMI using the `WebAdministration` class and AHAdmin development was also covered with some code samples provided. Additionally, CIM Studio, which is a powerful tool to aid in WMI development, was covered.

Through the understanding of the IIS configuration structure and the programming APIs available to you, it is possible for you to manage and extend your IIS server in ways that far surpass what you were able to do in previous versions of IIS.

Part IV: Managing and Operating IIS 7.0

18

IIS and Operations Management

After a web site has been built and deployed into a production environment, what then? How do you ensure uptime for your web application in an environment that is subject to ongoing changes, is exposed to the hailstorm of the Internet, or is subject to more traffic than any other server? How do you keep an IIS 7.0 server operational? The answers to these questions have many forms. After deploying a web server, in some ways, the work has just begun.

Maintaining a web site involves a range of knowledge, skills, and abilities. There are a few different approaches to managing the operations of IIS servers, and all of them have some merit. You will, undoubtedly, want control and predictability from your site on an ongoing basis. Most technicians involved in managing operations will value a constant flow of information and metrics.

In this chapter, we introduce some important topics related to managing production IIS servers. To keep your servers up and the hosted applications functioning properly, you need a way to organize your team differently from when the application was under development. You need a system and organization suited to respond to the daily troubles that plague today's web server, and to be proactive about ensuring the viability of your investment in the hosted application. We review some of the best sources for putting together a world-class structure for ensuring uptime. We begin by looking more at organizational processes, and then return to a more technical focus later in the chapter. Toward the end of the chapter, we cover the mechanics of two important operation tasks: approving hotfixes and conducting backups.

Management Approaches and Principles

The requirements for a professional web site will always imply some level of predictable uptime and minimum performance goals. No one would expect a web site to respond inconsistently or sporadically every day. Of course, the margin of error, or window of acceptable downtime, will vary greatly depending on the nature of the web site and the role it plays in fulfilling the mission of a business. A professional web site is a business tool, whether it's used occasionally for simple text updates or used extensively by customers to conduct eCommerce transactions.

In many cases, a particular web site is just one site among many, and is hosted on a server that depends on a network infrastructure with ties — complex and often fragile — to other systems in your organization. The point here is that not only may a web site break on its own, but also it can be hosted in the middle of a network that can be susceptible to any number of failings. In this kind of environment, ensuring uptime and performance is a matter of operational management.

Managing operations for IIS applications and servers is about meeting the expectations for the web site every day. Control, predictability, and information flow are all key elements of web server operations management. If you have web servers in operation, yet lack operational systems, where can you turn to get started?

Two excellent sources of some great tools for bringing operational systems to bear are the widely recognized authorities on technical management: the IT Infrastructure Library (ITIL) and the closely related Microsoft Operations Framework (MOF).

ITIL Standards

Within the last 20 years, technical managers have consolidated their thinking, to varying degrees, into a body of management practices. The *IT Infrastructure Library*, or ITIL (www.itil.org.uk/), has become a leading authority for technical management practices. Based in the United Kingdom and deployed across the globe, the ITIL offers a body of knowledge, training practicum, and certification that is known as the standard for technical management assets and templates.

Chartered in the 1980s under the British government, and originally written as 31 volumes, the foundation publications were retitled in the 1990s to be seen as guidance and not as a formal method, and since then ITIL adoption has gained world-wide momentum. This wider adoption and awareness have led to a number of other standards, including ISO/IEC 20000, which is now the conceptual framework within which the latest version of ITIL operates.

ITIL v3 became available in May 2007. The new version recasts the ITIL assets against the modern business and technical landscape and organizes the body of knowledge into five core texts, including:

❑ Service Strategy

❑ Service Design

❑ Service Transition

❑ Service Operation

❑ Continual Service Improvement

With v3, ITIL extends its relevance to cover the technical priorities of modern business, including technical service management. Part of the framework is the all-important toolkit. The ITIL Toolkit is a collection of resources brought together to accompany the principles of ITIL and help you accomplish them in your daily operations. The materials included in the toolkit are intended to assist in both understanding and implementation and are therefore targeted at both existing ITIL users and beginners alike. The toolkit includes:

❑ A detailed guide to ITIL and service management.

❑ The ITIL Factsheets — 12 two-page documents, serving as a concise summary of each of the ITIL disciplines.

❑ A management presentation for ITIL (which doubles as a proposal for service management).

❑ A service management audit/review questionnaire and report in Microsoft Excel workbook form.

❑ Materials to assist in the reporting of the above results (for example, templates).

When developing applications on the IIS 7.0 platform, ITIL can bring you two levels of benefits. First, you can take the ITIL templates and use them to identify the common requirements, risks, and techniques used across the globe for building, deploying and maintaining web applications. The templates are comprehensive aides to planning. Second, you can base your designs and directions on the strategic guidance found in the ITIL white papers, ensuring that your application plans are based on proven principles.

ITIL is a terrific source for many things, but it's not the only recognized source for guidance. Other widely used frameworks include the Information Services Procurement Library (ISPL), the Application Services Library (ASL), the Dynamic Systems Development Method (DSDM), the Capability Maturity Model (CMM/CMMI), the Control Objectives for Information and related Technology (COBIT), the Project Management Institute's Project Management Body of Knowledge (PMBOK), and the Microsoft Operations Framework (MOF). MOF is a Microsoft-centric superset of ITIL, and it makes perfect sense to use MOF when talking about managing IIS operations.

MOF: Microsoft's ITIL Superset

Before we apply the MOF processes to a couple of sample IIS operations, let's take a moment to properly introduce it. *Microsoft Operations Framework (MOF)* is a set of publications providing both descriptive and prescriptive guidance on IT service management. It's an actionable version of ITIL for Microsoft servers. Where ITIL is a consortium of expertise, MOF is limited to Microsoft's perspective on managing IT using Microsoft's software. This limited focus is also the benefit of MOF, since the framework has the benefit of Microsoft's insider knowledge of their own products. You can get everything you need from MOF by visiting www.microsoft.com/technet/solutionaccelerators/cits/mo/mof/default.mspx.

Microsoft published the first elements of MOF in 2000 to help their customers achieve reliability, availability, and manageability for mission-critical systems that operate on the Microsoft platform. MOF is definitely one of the best sources for guidance covering operational systems for IIS servers. Built from the precursor standards found in the ITIL, MOF provides in-depth technical guidance covering the spectrum of technology. MOF addresses the people, process, and technology issues that define today's complex and heterogeneous environments.

MOF includes operational knowledge captured in white papers and guidance presented through three formats: Service Improvement Programs (SIPs), Service Management Functions (SMFs), and Solution Accelerators (SAs). All these components are centralized into these foundation elements of MOF:

❑ MOF Team Model for Operations

❑ MOF Process Model for Operations

❑   MOF Risk Management Discipline for Operations

❑   MOF Service Management Functions

❑   MOF Operations Management Reviews

The MOF Process Model provides the description of processes that operations teams perform in order to manage and maintain IT services. It is organized around four quadrants and 20 Service Management Functions.

The MOF Team Model simplifies the view of team roles and helps management focus on organizing people effectively. It supports the Process Model by providing guidelines for organizing people into operational teams, or *role clusters*, and describes the key activities within each role cluster. The MOF Risk Model helps organizations manage risk while running their businesses. It is composed of a set of guiding principles and a risk management process.

There is another organizational layer to MOF. To show the stages of applying MOF, Microsoft uses a circle divided into four quadrants. Figure 18-1 shows the four quadrants and their relationships.

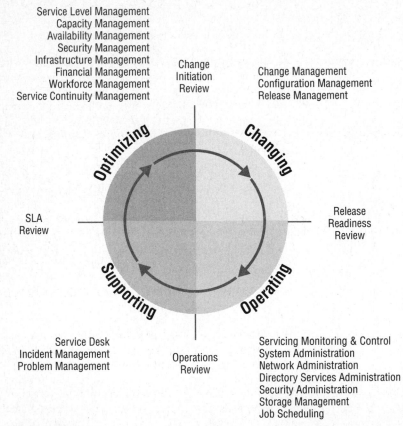

Figure 18-1

❑ **Optimizing Quadrant** — The optimization practices found in MOF guide teams toward more effective service-level management, capacity planning, and other longer-range planning efforts. Practices outlined in the associated MOF Change Initiation Review help teams put recommendations into action.

❑ **Changing Quadrant** — MOF guides you through initiation, analysis, planning, and deployment stages to ensure that change creates the desired effect without undesired consequences.

❑ **Supporting Quadrant** — The MOF Supporting Quadrant describes the processes and practices required to fully support the efficient usage of an IT infrastructure. Team roles defined in this quadrant focus on solving end-user issues and resolving broader IT problems.

❑ **Operating Quadrant** — Improvements in operations processes have the intended consequence of reducing costs while enabling agility. The demands for availability and security mean that operations have to be focused and effective. Regular operations reviews promote continuous improvement in operations processes.

The following table outlines the different *Service Management Functions (SMFs)* and their goals:

MOF Function	Benefit to IIS Operations
Availability Management	Maximizes uptime of IIS servers.
Capacity Management	Ensures responsiveness by matching IIS server resources to visitor demand levels.
Change Management	Controls the impact of maintenance and improvement activities.
Configuration Management	Governs the settings that determine the security and performance of your IIS servers.
Directory Services Administration	Offers guidance on deploying and managing AD in the enterprise, which is often a dependency service for IIS systems.
Financial Management	Covers budgeting, cost accounting, cost recovery, cost allocations, charge-back models, and revenue accounting. The key aspects of financial management that ITIL and MOF address are its linkage to other service management functions.
Incident Management	Detects incidents and then targets the correct support resources to resolve the incidents.
Infrastructure Engineering	Develops and uses consistent standards and policies for infrastructure. Helps to ensure that releases are compatible with the existing infrastructure systems.
Job Scheduling	Ensures the efficient processing of data at a pre-determined time and in a prescribed sequence to maximize the use of system resources and minimize the impact to online users.

MOF Function	Benefit to IIS Operations
Network Administration	Defines procedures to operate network services on which IIS servers depend — including DHCP, WINS, and DNS — on a day-to-day basis. It also covers maintaining the hardware layer on which the services reside.
Problem Management	Identifies and resolves the root causes of any significant or recurring incidents to keep IIS servers more stable.
Release Management	Provides the processes and controls that ensure that all changes made to IIS systems are deployed successfully into the production environment in the least disruptive manner.
Security Administration	Provides processes for maintaining a safe computing environment. The six basic requirements, or tenets, that ensure confidentiality, integrity, and availability are: **Identification** — Describes how users identify themselves to the system. **Authentication** — Describes how users prove to the system that they are who they claim to be. **Authorization** — Ensures that the appropriate privileges are granted to users so that they can perform certain functions on the system. **Confidentiality** — Ensures that only authorized people can see data stored on the network. **Integrity** — Ensures that data are not garbled, lost, or changed when traveling across the network. **Nonrepudiation** — Provides proof of data transmission or receipt.
Security Management	Builds processes used for web security planning and management in an organization. The overall objective of the SMF is to describe "what" to do rather than "how" to do it.
Service Continuity Management	Ensures constant availability of web services at all times. This availability is won through resilient IIS and dependent systems, and recovery options for your IIS servers.
Service Desk	Provides an organized and coordinated front line to technical support staff members who are working independently in various geographical locations. Stitching this capability together right means quick answers, straightforward resolutions, and accurate results.
Service Level Management	Increases service continuity by adding formal processes. The six major processes of Service Level Management are setup activities, service catalog, service level agreements, service level monitoring, service level reporting, and service level agreement review.
Service Monitoring and Control	Provides for real-time observation and alerting of health conditions and, where appropriate, automatically correcting any exceptions.

MOF Function	Benefit to IIS Operations
Storage Management	Leverages the optimum storage array to support the performance needs of IIS, and manages the life of information over its life cycle of relevance.
System Administration	Provides day-to-day administrative services for the computing environment. This entails managing network accounts (users, groups, distribution lists, and so on) and network resources (servers, printers, storage devices, and so on).
Workforce Management	Attends to all areas of management by partitioning work among appropriately skilled personnel.

MOF service functions have detailed documents that offer rich process definitions, templates, and other collateral that can flesh out how you shape your IIS operations. Visiting www.microsoft.com and searching for MOF content will help you find everything you need to get your IIS operations into a predictable, efficient program. If you are interested in a more thorough and expert inculcation, there are several professional training options made available through Microsoft and a network of training partners. Use your favorite search engine to search for "MOF training."

Making use of the SMFs is definitely a terrific start to defining your IIS operations program. If any program is made of people, process, and technology, then the MOG library, found at the Microsoft web site, will satisfy the process leg of the triangle. The remaining legs are addressed by the MOF Solution Accelerators and the MOF Team Model.

The Solution Accelerators are available on Microsoft's TechNet web site (www.microsoft.com/technet) and provide concentrated advice and tools on specific solutions, such as AD and IIS. At the time of this writing, Microsoft has yet to provide IIS 7.0 specific guidance via solution accelerators; you can check for the latest advice using the full catalog of the accelerators at www.microsoft.com/technet/solutionaccelerators/listings/product.mspx. Note that you can reuse plenty of the guidance written for IIS 6.0 for your IIS 7.0 operations. Many processes will work regardless of the IIS platform on which you operate.

The MOF Team Model is about defining roles and responsibilities, to ensure coverage across the breadth of projects and tasks that you need to manage for smooth operations. We cover the MOF Team Model in more detail in the "Role-Based Administration" section below. Figure 18-2 presents the relationship of the MOF assets.

Now that we have given you a general introduction to MOF, here are some more specific ways you can leverage it for IIS operations.

Applying MOF to IIS Operations Management

The following sections describe just a few ways in which you can use the MOF library to structure your operations to meet your requirements for uptime and performance (for example, SLA obligations). The two sections we picked are especially relevant to IIS. We first cover role-based administration to show how operations teams can be layered to provide full coverage of your IIS operations challenges. Afterward, we cover change management to illustrate how operations teams can reduce the risks of downtime when deploying changes to their web servers.

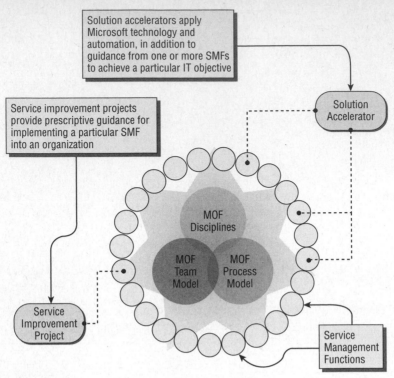

Figure 18-2

Role-Based Administration

IIS operations usually involve a team-based approach. Many players can be involved in managing web applications, including developers, system engineers, service desk personnel, and managers of all types. To keep your environment secure and performing well, each person involved in the operations program should only have the rights and privileges necessary to do the job at hand. The widely accepted network administration concept of *Least-Privilege User Account (LUA)* provides a great justification for limiting access, both from a security point of view as well as managing your SLA responsibilities. The following table describes the roles that your web application team might consider for managing the operations of all their web servers. The roles listed map to the "role clusters" from the MOF Team Model, which is described in the "MOF Executive Overview" document found at www.microsoft.com/technet/ solutionaccelerators/cits/mo/mof/mofeo.mspx.

MOF Role Cluster	Role Name	Role Responsibilities
Operations	IIS Admin	Routine maintenance, audit, lockdown, enable extensions, and aid in the deployment of new Web applications as per the organization's policies. Ensure that the web server is maintained in a state so that it can satisfy all SLA requirements. Participate in monitoring and audit processes.

MOF Role Cluster	Role Name	Role Responsibilities
Security	IIS Security Admin	Implement Active Directory policies. Lead security audit. Ensure IIS security by implementing best practices.
Operations	IIS Application Admin	Administer applications and web sites (does not have rights to all IIS, only to particular web sites). Configure resources for web sites. Participate in monitoring and audit processes and take care of all security concerns raised by the application.
Infrastructure	IIS Deployment Admin	Deploy the web servers. Ensure that service packs and patches are current and that configuration settings conform with organization rules. Ensure that the web servers have antivirus protection.
Support	IIS Incident Admin	Implement incident response for incidents. Provide web server incident management policy. Isolate and resolve problems and issues from incidents and propagate requests for changes. Interface with partners if there are issues regarding hardware or technology they have provided and maintain a support loop with them.

Additional roles can be added to support application-specific needs, such as publishing files or making changes to the config files. IIS 7.0 makes it easy to delegate tasks to application owners and infrastructure engineers alike. Application roles usually require fewer privileges and should not interfere with any of the organization roles. They also need to be restricted to the application or applications in scope for the personnel and have boundaries to block access to areas outside their charge. For this purpose, IIS 7.0 provides highly granular access to resources through adaptation of Group Policy Objects (GPO), inheritance of permissions on folders, and integration with the Windows Server security mechanisms. Delegating rights for the IIS server, web sites, and application pools is covered in detail in Chapter 9, "Delegating Remote Administration."

One context in which roles are important is when a change to an IIS platform has to be deployed. Some changes, such as new versions of IIS applications, can present high levels of risk for downtime should the change have unknown and undesired consequences upon deployment. The next SMF we look at is Change Management.

Change Management

Like many of the SMFs, huge tomes have been written on the subject of *change management* — both by Microsoft and by other venerable institutions. If you don't have a mature change management process, then you should develop a system to support both your web-site development processes and the ongoing operations that keep your production site going. If you have a change management process already and it hasn't been crafted specifically for web solutions, review it for appropriateness for web-site applications and servers.

A good change management system provides a disciplined process for introducing changes into the web-server environment and maintains minimal disruption to ongoing operations when the change is introduced. Keeping your servers up while they undergo software or hardware upgrades, for example, can best be done when you have a realistic plan. To achieve this goal, a change management process includes the following objectives:

❑ Formalize the process of initiating change through the submission of a *request for change (RFC)* and a *change approval board (CAB)*.

❑ Assign a priority and a category to the change, and appraise urgency and impact on tertiary services, the infrastructure, and end-users.

❑ Plan the deployment of the change. Be careful to include "go no-go" checkpoints where the change deployment progress can be verified or delayed depending on the new levels of risk that you may uncover as the change plan matures.

❑ Work with the Release Management SMF, which manages the release and deployment of changes into the production environment. For more information about the Release Management SMF, see www.microsoft.com/technet/solutionaccelerators/cits/mo/smf/default.mspx.

❑ Conduct a post-implementation review of whether the change has achieved the goals that were established for it and determine whether to keep the change or roll it back.

The MOF Change Management SMF extends these objectives into specific tasks, and it's worthwhile to view those and incorporate the relevant tasks into your IIS operations program. An important principle of how the SMF sets up and relates change managements tasks is that you don't take anything for granted. Be sure you have all the relevant people reviewing the change and the deployment plan, and be sure everyone involved understands and agrees on what to expect after the change is implemented.

To that end, the following table lays out how you may wish to involve team members in change management decisions. The first column calls out the different teams that can be involved in IIS operations as defined by the MOF Team Model. The remaining columns indicate whether the team should be involved based on the severity (that is, scope, risk, impact) of the change.

MOF Role Cluster	Change Type	Change Type	Change Type	Change Type
	Minor Change	Standard Change	Significant and Major Change	Emergency Change
Infrastructure	Not involved	Preauthorized	CAB member	CAB member
Operations	Not involved	Preauthorized	CAB member	CAB member
Partner	Not involved	Preauthorized	CAB member	CAB member
Release	Authorizer	Authorizer	CAB member	CAB member
Security	Not involved	Preauthorized	CAB member	CAB member
Support	Not involved	Preauthorized	CAB member	CAB member
Service	Not involved	Preauthorized	CAB member	CAB member

To make both the Team Model and Change Management SMFs more palpable, let's go through two examples of how these important MOF principles can help you manage your IIS operations. First, we will look at how to scope, plan, and manage an emergency change. Then we will look at a typical change management task: applying server hotfixes.

MOF Example: Change Management for Emergency Updates

Emergency updates to an IIS environment are those that need to be applied to restore performance or to avoid an imminent loss of performance. This is the kind of change that usually accompanies pressure to skip the normal considerations you would take before introducing change. The process outlined in the example below, taken from the MOF Change Management SMF, will help you deploy changes to an IIS environment without losing confidence in your results.

For this example, let's assume you have received alerts from your IIS server base that indicate an unexpected spike in CPU and I/O utilization. Let's assume that an application team has recently deployed a web site onto the same shared IIS 7.0 server cluster from which you have received the alerts. Furthermore, let's assume that the cluster includes three web servers in a load-balanced configuration. The cluster provides key services for financial and marketing personnel who report to executives in your company and are dissatisfied with the responsiveness. Upon approaching the application team who recently added the web site, you have been informed that they have a fix they would like to apply immediately. You communicate to the application team that this fix must first be applied through your group's change management process, which is based on MOF and is illustrated in Figure 18-3.

The first thing to talk about is the *change manager (CM)*. The CM, as we may think of the role, is the pivot point for the entire process. The CM pushes and redistributes all communications between the CAB members and stakeholders and ensures that the CAB establishes a plan and governs execution of the change deployment according to the terms set by the CAB. The CM is usually a technical manager but can be a project manager or a team leader from either the infrastructure or application group who is familiar with the entire environment. The CM is involved with the change from start (request) to finish (debrief), and although the CM is not responsible for the decisions made by the CAB, the CM is responsible for the time it takes for the CAB to act and progress.

Taking our example, the upcoming sections describe the following steps for progressing through the deployment of your application fix:

1. Appoint CAB members.
2. Notify CAB members.
3. CAB members review the request for change.
4. CAB members vote on the RFC.

Appoint CAB Members

The CAB includes several standing members, including subject matter experts from your systems engineering team, the application group that manages web sites on your servers, security representatives, networking specialists, and hardware representatives. Depending on the nature of the emergency, you can add or remove members from this core list. For our change, we will want the following team members represented in our CAB:

❑ Network administrator responsible for the IIS cluster

❏ Networking engineer or architect who is responsible for the IIS cluster

❏ Application engineers from all teams that host applications on the applicable cluster

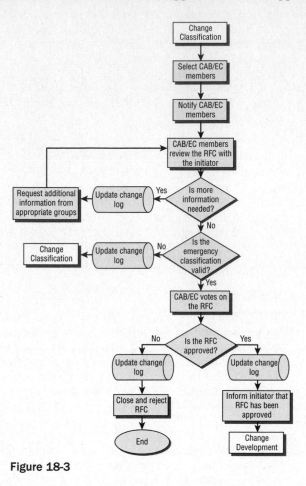

Figure 18-3

We will exclude the security and hardware representatives. The more people who are asked to join an emergency CAB meeting, the more difficult it becomes to schedule a meeting that all members can attend, especially when given short notice and if such a meeting is not part of the normal working day. Extra members of the CAB should be invited to join only if absolutely necessary. An example of when you would extend the circle of the CAB to include others would be when a change affects areas that lie outside the knowledge and authority of the standing members. The change initiator for a particular change request is an exception. This person needs to be a member of the CAB to provide quick answers to their questions. Ideally, the standing members alone should possess sufficient knowledge and authority to make a decision.

The CAB has a short time frame in which to meet and act. An emergency change can be requested at any time, for any number of business and technical circumstances, and because the emergency change must be deployed quickly, the CAB must be large enough to have enough authority to act without impediment, and be small enough to decide how to act very quickly. Since voting requires a quorum (when adhering strictly to MOF), the standing members or appointed deputies of the CAB must always be able to attend the meetings for emergency changes given short notice. This demand for instant availability can be ensured by using second and third parties who can back up the primary when he or she is not available. Depending on the nature of an emergency change, the CAB members may be called into duty anytime, at any time of day or night — either in person, over the phone, or by using other technology solutions.

For an emergency change, the recommended voting is that the change requires unanimous approval. Given this recommendation, this is another good reason to keep the CAB members to a minimum.

Notify CAB Members

The CM is responsible for contacting each CAB member personally to inform him or her of the emergency change request, and arrange for when it will be reviewed, and what form the meeting will take. The CM has to be aggressive about communicating and organizing. Normal communications methods may not be sufficient to get the CAB aligned in the time frame necessary for an emergency change. If e-mail meeting requests are used, invitees should be given a short time period to acknowledge the meeting to the CM; otherwise, more direct methods of contacting CAB members must be used.

In all cases, the CM would contact enough of the members from the standing CAB membership roster to cover the required teams.

CAB Members Review the Request for Change

In our example, an initial review meeting has to happen within 4 hours to ensure that follow-up tasks can be accomplished following the initial meeting. In the initial review of the RFC, the CAB applies the same common-sense approach and criteria used for all changes. A key difference between the emergency change and most other changes is that the testing effort will not be as exhaustive, if it is done at all. The risk assessment, as factored by the likelihood and impact estimates, may be more important for an emergency change because the risks are typically higher given the available — or unavailable — room for testing.

Having all the right resources at the review will facilitate the decision-making process. The presence of the change initiator at the review allows questions about the change and its impact to be put directly to the initiator and to be answered quickly. There may be a need to collect additional information and re-present the RFC to the CAB before a decision can be made. In this case, the RFC is placed in a pending state until the CAB can reconvene, likely within a very short time (an hour, for example).

The outcome of the initial review can range from canceling the change to accepting the change as a fast-track candidate. The CAB may decide that the change is not an emergency change and should be handled by the normal change process. In this case, the CM reclassifies the change and updates the change log with the reason for reclassification. If the change initiator wants the RFC to be considered again as an emergency change, this person must provide additional supporting evidence to justify the need and resubmit the RFC to the CM. The CM can then bring the RFC, containing the new information, back to the CAB.

The decisions and actions of the CAB for an emergency change happen as quickly as possible. In our example, the CAB meets at the behest of the CM who received your change request, which you initiated based on the alerts you received concerning the resource constraints. The change request that the CAB has been called to review includes your personal testimony about the resource metrics (alerts) and complaints proffered by the finance and marketing departments. In addition, you include log files that describe the activities of the web services since the application team applied their web site to the cluster, which show that the services used by the financial and marketing personnel are interrupted whenever the new application that shares the IIS server is in use. The final data point that the CAB considers as part of the request for change is the change description. In our case, your change request is to roll back the new application off the server cluster until it can be system-tested in a lab environment and proven compatible with the services used by the finance and marketing teams.

Along with the recommended change, you include both a risk assessment and a risk mitigation plan. The risk assessment includes the likelihood and impact of several undesired outcomes that are unlikely but possible. In our case, you would indicate that rolling back an application can cause damage to other systems if too many files or configurations are removed, or other elements of the application are removed on which the remaining applications rely. Your mitigation plan includes running RegMon and FileMon on a lab server during a test install of the problem application to identify the relevant files and registry keys. You also will back up the server and ensure that you can completely restore it should you need to roll back the change.

You will want to present your recommendation and supporting points in an organized brief. The following is a sample form that you can use to present your case:

REQUEST FOR CHANGE SUMMARY				
Division		Date		
Current State				
Desired State				
Change Recommendation				
Type	Priority	Services Affected	Impact	
Risks		Likelihood x Impact (1–5)	Mitigation	
			1. 2.	
			1. 2.	
Change Owner:		Technical Lead:		
Project Manager:		Business Liaison:		

Some of the fields in this template are more intuitive than others, and one cannot overlook the need for training across your entire team on this and other aspects of your change processes. Here are some descriptions of the fields that you would use in this form.

- ❏ **Division** — Include the business or technical division name where the change will take effect.

- ❏ **Current State** — A short narrative that describes the deficiency in the affected system that needs to be changed.

- ❏ **Desired State** — A short narrative that characterizes the intended functionality.

- ❏ **Change Recommendation** — The steps needed to change from the current state to the desired state.

- ❏ **Type** — The MOF change types include:

  - ❏ **Major** — A change where the impact on the group could be massive — for example, a department- or corporate-wide change, or a network-wide or service-wide change.

  - ❏ **Significant** — A change where the effect is widespread, but not massive — for example, a change affecting a group within a department or a specific group of CIs.

  - ❏ **Minor** — A change affecting small numbers of individuals or CIs — for example, a change to a printer used by a department consisting of just a few members.

  - ❏ **Standard** — A change that has been performed before and is part of the operational practice of the business — for example, an update to a user profile.

As with the change priority, the change category will also vary with the makeup of the business. A change affecting a particular department may be deemed significant in some organizations but may only be considered a standard category in another organization in which that department is regarded as less critical to the business.

A set of standard changes and standard procedures for implementing them is normally predefined by the CAB. This set of standard changes can be automatically approved without needing to be voted on by the CAB or the CM, thereby taking a shorter route through the change approval process.

- ❏ **Priority** — The suggested priorities include:

  - ❏ **Emergency** — A change that, if not implemented immediately, will leave the organization open to huge risk — for example, applying a security patch.

  - ❏ **High** — A change that is important for the organization and must be implemented soon — for example, an upgrade in response to new government legislation.

  - ❏ **Medium** — A change that should be implemented to gain functional benefits from the upgrade — for example, adding a customer feedback service.

  - ❏ **Low** — A change that is not pressing but would be advantageous — for example, a "nice to have" addition to a user profile.

These definitions will mean different things to different organizations. Depending on organizational size, structure, and the underlying SLAs between IT and the business it serves, organizations might need to modify their own priority definitions. There is also the matter of perception and political influence. It's a well-known practice to escalate changes that come from certain managers for reasons other than business optimization.

It is important to note, however, that an emergency priority change differs from the other change priorities in that it takes a different path through the review process in order to implement the change as quickly as possible. This priority is reserved for only those changes that, if not implemented quickly, might seriously affect service levels or result in a large cost to the business.

❑ **Services Affected** — Outline the technical systems or services that will or may be affected. Be sure to include all the services that depend on the servers you plan to change, not just the services that are tied directly to the server. By identifying tertiary services, you empower the CAB to fully evaluate the scope and therefore the impact and risk of the change.

❑ **Impact** — Share the goal of the change and how the business services will be positively or negatively affected.

❑ **Risks** — Think through the unintended consequences that may occur as a result of the intended change. List the possible outcomes that would affect the uptime and performance of the target server and of the systems that depend on it.

❑ **Likelihood x Impact** — These are numerical values that can be multiplied to provide a weighted measure of severity.

The *likelihood* is a measure of the probability of the risk turning into an issue. A rating of 1 represents the lowest probability, whereas a rating of 5 represents the highest level of certainty.

The *impact* is a measure of the risk's scope, or breadth and depth of effect. Again, a rating of 1 is the low end, which means you can tolerate this risk if it materializes. A rating of 5 would indicate that the end-users of the system would not tolerate the risk if it happened.

Note that if a risk has a high likelihood of occurring but has a low impact — an undesired but negligible consequence — then the value for this field is $5 \times 1 = 5$. In another case, if a risk has a moderate likelihood but a fairly problematic consequence if it does happen, then you could expect a value approximating a $3 \times 4 = 12$. The point here is that just because a risk is likely to occur doesn't necessarily mean that you need to expend resources to mitigate the risk, if the impact is low.

❑ **Mitigation** — These are the steps you will take to either reduce the likelihood of the risk actually coming to pass, or steps you will take to lessen the impact in the case where the risk materializes.

❑ **Change Owner** — This is the person who is accountable to the rest of the organization for the success of the change. This person will usually be the direct supervisor of the Technical Lead identified below.

❑ **Project Manager** — The Project Manager (PM) is the person responsible for managing scope, staffing, and communication for the team that is planning and deploying the change.

❑ **Technical Lead** — Having responsibility for the technical design, deployment, and transfer to operations, the Technical Lead is the person responsible for the quality of the technical solution.

❑ **Business Liaison** — This person or persons represents the class of end-users who will be most affected by the change. The Liaison ensures that their constituents are informed about the change deployment and represented in the change planning process. Liaisons can tell you what the work schedules are, what the workers' priorities are, and many more details about the constraints you'll have to work around to keep from interrupting operations during the deployment of the change.

Now look at the following form, which is filled out for our particular situation in the running example of processing an emergency change. The form shows how you might present your argument in a formal request to the CAB for an emergency update.

REQUEST FOR CHANGE SUMMARY				
Division	eComm	Date	Aug 19, 2007	
Current State				
IIS 7.0 Server Cluster X is intermittently unresponsive. The downtime is linked to resources required by a recently installed application.				
Desired State				
IIS 7.0 Server Cluster X must comply with the SLA expectations for the finance and marketing systems.				
Change Recommendation				
Restore the IIS Server Cluster X to the pre-application state, where resources were sufficient to accommodate the financial and marketing systems.				
Type	Priority	Services Affected		Impact
Emergency	High	IIS 7 Server Cluster X: +Finance App XYZ +Marketing App XYZ +New App XYZ		Restore SLA compliance w/ finance + mkt systems. Tmp end service for the problem application and launch compatibility testing project.
Risks		Likelihood x Impact (1–5)		Mitigation
Finance + mkt systems will be disabled during roll back of the new application.		2 x 5 = 10		1. Validate new app footprint using RegMon and FileMon. 2. Back up server for possible restore.
Removing the new application does not resolve the issue.		1 x 5 = 5		1. Plan to restore the server to a point prior to the detection of the service failure. 2. Activate application engineers standby for possible triage duty.
Change Owner:	Ken Schaefer, x3845	Technical Lead:		Dennis Glendenning, x3123
Project Manager:	Ken Schaefer, x3845	Business Liaison:		Mike Everest, x4572

Note that this form can provide only an overview or summary; it's a good way to get the CAB review started and to keep it structured. It is not all that you would want to present, or have ready to present. Be sure to include supplemental evidence including log files, best practice articles, and testimony from business leaders in the form of e-mails or your own personal notes. These supplemental data will round out your argument and provide substance to position against the inevitable questioning that a good CAB review will provoke.

CAB Members Vote on the RFC

Once the CAB members agree that all the necessary information has been collected and reviewed, a vote on whether to continue fast-tracking the change can take place. For an emergency change to be approved, a unanimous vote should be required. In this case, a majority is not sufficient, considering the risks involved in making an emergency change.

When a change is approved, it moves on to the change deployment stage, which follows an expedited path to implement the change as soon as possible. Whichever decision is made, the change initiator and all other interested parties are informed of the decision, and the change log is updated.

For our example, the CAB approves your change request to roll back the problem application, provided you follow through with your risk mitigation plan. Upon this decision, the CM communicates the decision throughout the organization and documents the disposition (for or against) of the CAB pertaining to the emergency change request.

In following this MOF Change Management SMF, your team has accomplished the following:

❑　Involved leaders with sufficient authority to approve change

❑　Included subject matter experts with sufficient knowledge to evaluate the change request

❑　Consulted with the stakeholders (i.e. the application teams)

❑　Communicated the final disposition to all team members and end-users

The above example illustrates how emergency changes to an IIS application can be enacted with predictable results. By enabling a team of informed representatives to communicate and to track progress, the MOF Change Management SMF reduces the risk of a problem with deployment affecting uptime.

MOF Example: Change Management for Applying Hotfixes

Applying hotfixes to IIS servers is considered by many as the single most important security task involved in maintaining a web server. As the type of server with the most exposure to external attacks in many organizations, and the kind of server that often handles more network traffic, IIS servers require every possible defense.

Although the task of installing a hotfix is usually simple, the effect of not applying the hotfix can be disastrous. The possible impact aside, installing a hotfix is a minor change. In an overwhelming majority of cases, applying a hotfix to a server poses only a minimal risk to the server.

Any minor change to a server, by definition, has both low impact and low risk. A change of this nature differs from a standard change in that the change may not have been performed before and therefore has to be approved. What actually constitutes a minor change depends on the criteria set by your organization. Because the impact and risk of a minor change are low, as is the need for deployment resources to implement the change, a minor change does not normally need to go before the CAB for review. Instead, the area leader or CM has the authority to approve or reject the change.

Figure 18-4 shows the process that the CM uses to authorize minor changes.

Comparing the process for approving and deploying a minor change to that for an emergency change, you can see that there are less steps and less concern and that the process for a minor change is more streamlined. The complexity and scale of the change approval process should reflect both the complexity and scale of the change under review. Although there is a definite need for some process regardless of the scope of change, the simple change does not justify the effort required of most other types of changes.

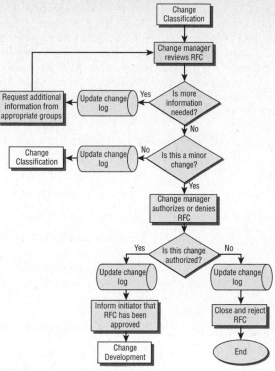

Figure 18-4

The priorities of the change review board remain the same, however, when considering major or minor changes. The board must, in both cases, be concerned that the change has been correctly classified, that the unintended outcomes have been identified and mitigated, and that — above all else — communication and organizational processes will be enacted correctly.

Operational Tasks

The first half of this chapter covered the management approaches you can use to build an operations program that yields a higher rate of success in meeting the uptime and performance demands of your web site. In the remaining sections of this chapter, we cover some specific tasks to which every IIS administrator must attend: backing up and restoring web servers.

Backup and Restore Program

One operation that stands at the top of priorities for any administrator of any server is ensuring an adequate back-up/restore program. Should an administrator fail in this task, the server and the applications that it hosts are in serious jeopardy of failing miserably should anything unfavorable occur to the server. Although IIS 7.0 is the most secure and stable web platform that Microsoft has released to date, IIS servers are more susceptible than any other infrastructure server to attack or failure, given their position in the perimeter network and their high traffic profiles. In this light, maintaining operational fallbacks (backup) and defense (antivirus) are relatively inexpensive insurance policies against the likely faults to which any IIS server is susceptible.

In this section, we outline a disaster recovery program sufficient for enterprise-class SLAs. The program we present below is just a sample, though, and you should take this as a starting point only. Our discussion includes a stepwise review of some basic back-up tasks, and an approach to backups as an operational program with checks and balances.

Backup Scope

When designing a backup/restore program, the first element to consider in your design is what exactly needs to be backed up. The answer, in general terms, comes in two parts:

1. First, back up all data and configurations that are important to the mission of the server.

2. Second, back up everything that would restore more efficiently from back-up media than from the original installation media.

Your two top priorities for selecting back-up points are then *coverage* and *convenience*. Those are the general terms. More specifically, when backing up an IIS server, you need to consider these main categories of data:

❑ **Web-Site Data** — Files that contain code and configurations necessary to present the user with interfaces, manage data, and apply the computational logic of the hosted application. Examples include HTML, ASP.NET, and .DLL files.

❑ **Transaction Data** — Data collected in the course of using the web site, such as logs, session data, user credentials, product data, and sales records. Transactional data can be stored on the local server in the form of log files, on a dedicated session state server, or on a special database server (for example, Microsoft SQL, Sybase ASE 15, Oracle 10g).

❑ **IIS 7.0 Configurations** — Settings that customize the service for the hosted applications, including settings that define the web-site object, application pool, and core IIS service. Example configurations include authentication schemes, file directories, and modular switches that are found in the .config files. These files are introduced in Chapter 1 and reviewed in detail in Chapter 5.

❑ **OS and Dependent Services** — Any configurations and supporting files that help provide the working engines for your hosted applications. Examples include resource kit tools, monitoring agents, and local/group policies.

Be sure that you review all of the above categories and include the appropriate files in your back-up set. Use the list above as a basic checklist to reduce the chances that you will leave anything out that is mission-critical to your IIS server.

Back-up Methods and Media

Now that you have an introduction to what data to back up, the next item to consider is the back-up method and media. The following list covers the main options for back-up media in a business setting.

❑ **No Backup** — In rare cases, all files come straight from installation media and you have only to reinstall from a CD-ROM disk. An example of this scenario is an e-mail relay server that uses a simple SMTP and IIS service and is not mission-critical. It's hard to beat the convenience of reinstalling from CD-ROM, but be sure you have an infallible system for storing and retrieving your CD-ROM media.

❑ **Tape or Cartridge** — Tape drives have been staples for backing servers for IT administrators for decades. Tape media have the benefits of providing high storage capacities and the portability of moving backups off site. Tapes come in a range of technologies and are affordable enough to allow you to leverage a library of tapes to accommodate normal, differential, and incremental backups.

❑ **Local Disk** — Backing up data on a separate disk is affordable and fast. Restoring data from a separate disk is as easy as it gets. Adding a secondary hard disk drive is easy for most administrators and offers a low-maintenance solution.

❑ **External Disk Array** (for example, Storage Area Network, or SAN) — An array of disks is more expensive than using local storage but comes with the added benefits of better management options and a much higher fault tolerance. Most disk arrays can withstand one or more drive failures while maintaining operations. Robust and highly engineered arrays, such as SANs or Network Attached Storage (NAS), provide the most scalable and tolerant solutions.

❑ **Array of Servers** — This option includes posting data to two separate servers that are clustered together to appear as the same server. Use the integrated Microsoft Clustering Service to evoke Network Load Balancing (NLB) for IIS servers, or a dedicated clustering appliance such as those offered by Cisco, F5, and Citrix. Using more than one server to provide a service can also increase performance.

The following table compares the back-up media options that are presented above:

Option	Pros	Cons	Speed	Cost
No backup	Economical, convenient	Risk of lost installation media; applicable in rare cases	Restores can be very slow, depending on the installation times and complexity	None
Tape	High-capacity media; removable for off-site storage	Drives can be expensive and are slow; media fail periodically without notice	1–10 MBps (megabytes per second)	$0.25–$0.50 per gigabyte
Local Disk	Fast; highest capacity for unattended, automated backup	Not portable, server remains as a single point of failure	100–320 MBps	$1 per gigabyte
External disk array	Fast; highest capacity for workgroup back-up program; fault-tolerant	Fitting disks for fault tolerance (RAID 1, 5, or 10) can be expensive	100–320 MBps	$4–$10 per gigabyte
Server array	Highest level of fault tolerance; smallest response time for restorations	Expensive; highest maintenance and operations burden	Ethernet 100 MBps to Gigabit Ethernet 1,000 MBps	Varies

Approaches

Your approach to backups has to reflect the expectations that your end-users have for restoration times. For example, if you have an agreement with a customer or another workgroup in your company that specifies your availability and performance boundaries, such as a Service Level Agreement (SLA), that promises 99.999% uptime, then you can afford no more than 5 minutes per year of downtime.

Your back-up and restoration program needs to be part of an overall program for high availability. If your end-users accept up to 4 hours or more of downtime a few times a year, then your back-up approach can be very different from the one where you have to guarantee 99.999% uptime. Both scenarios are covered below. To round out the scenarios, let's start with the situation where there are few or no expectations.

Low Service Expectations

When your server can be down for extended periods of time, the hardware used is typically not redundant and may not have fault tolerance. Often, the IIS platform with low service expectations is a single server with one or more hard disk drives. For this scenario, backups should be thorough although your users can tolerate a flexible window for restoring the service. The following table shows the backup priorities for IIS systems with low service expectations.

Scope	Priority	Period	Method/Media
Web-site data	High	Monthly–yearly	Tape or install files
Transaction data	Low	Never	None
IIS 7.0 configurations	Low	Never	None (checklist)
OS and dependent services	Low	Never	None (checklist)

When you have plenty of time to restore a server, you can simply rebuild it from scratch using the Windows media, a checklist, and any back-up media that have the web-site content.

Moderate Expectations

If your end-users need your faulty IIS server back within a fixed window of time, then you should focus on being able to recover the web-site data and IIS service configurations quickly. The following table shows the backup priorities for IIS systems with moderate service expectations.

Scope	Priority	Rate	Method/Media
Web-site data	High	Daily–hourly	Tape–disk
Transaction date	High	Daily–hourly	Tape–disk
IIS 7.0 configuration	Moderate	Monthly	Tape
OS and dependent services	Moderate	Monthly–yearly	Image

When you have a fixed amount of time to restore a server, you can rebuild the server from scratch or from an image file that you create using Symantec Ghost, Microsoft Automated Deployment Services (ADS), or another similar imaging technology.

High Availability

For the IIS servers that are critical to business continuity, those that must continue to provide service regardless of whatever technical difficulties may arise, a back-up program may focus less on recovering from a hardware fault and more on maintaining history. The following table shows the backup priorities for IIS systems with high service expectations.

Scope	Priority	Rate	Method/Media
Web-site data	High	Hourly–constant (Mirror)	Tape–array of servers
Transaction data	High	Hourly–constant (Mirror)	Tape–array of servers
IIS service configuration	High	Never	None
OS and dependent services	High	Never	None

Conducting Backups

Having covered the scope and media options, the next area to cover is the specifics of conducting a backup of your IIS server, and how to restore data from backups. For IIS operations, you can pick from many excellent options for back-up software. Windows Server 2008 is new as of this writing, and there are few back-up solutions that are compatible. However, the leading providers will undoubtedly keep pace and release compatible solutions. Some of the best options you can consider are in the following table:

Vendor	Software	Web Site
Symantec	Backup Exec	www.symantec.com
CA	ARCServe	www.ca.com
EMC	Retrospect, HomeBase, Networker, AlphaStor, Backup Advisor	www.emc.com
IBM	Tivoli Storage Manager	www.ibm.com
WysDM	WysDM for Backups	www.wysdm.com
Bocada	Bocada Enterprise (consolidator)	www.bocada.com

Continued

Vendor	Software	Web Site
Aptare	StorageConsole	www.aptare.com
CommVault	Galaxy Backup & Recovery	www.commvault.com
Hewlett-Packard	OpenView Storage Data Protector	www.hp.com/storage

For the purposes of this chapter, we follow up with Microsoft's Windows Server Backup. Microsoft's embedded backup tools come in three forms:

❑ **Windows Server Backup** — Volume backup and restore center (http://technet2. microsoft.com/windowsserver2008/en/library/00162c92-a834-43f9-9e8a-71aeb25fa4ad1033.mspx).

❑ **Wbadmin.exe** — Command-line backup and restore management tool; replaces ntbackup.exe (http://technet2.microsoft.com/windowsserver2008/en/library/4b0b3f32-d21f-4861-84bb-b2eadbf1e7b81033.mspx).

❑ **Recovery Disks** — As in past releases, a system disk for recovering the operating system of a failed server.

These tools replace ntbackup.exe in the Windows platform and are the Windows Server complement to Windows Vista's Backup and Recovery Center. Administrators that are experienced with Ntbackup will note that the feature set for Windows Server 2008 backup tools is a small subset of what used to be available. However, having integrated VSS and leveraging the new Task Scheduler will make this version of the integrated backup tool far more reliable. To install Windows Server Backup and the command-line support tool:

1. Click Start and mouse over the Administrative Tools link.

2. Click Server Manager to launch the Windows Server Manager.

3. On the left pane of the Server Manager, click Features.

4. In the top-right pane, click Add Features to activate the wizard.

5. In the Add Features wizard, which may pop up depending on your configuration, click Add Required Features and then click Next.

6. In the Select Features pane, shown in Figure 18-5, open the Windows Server Backup Features node and select the desired options. (Note that Windows PowerShell is required for the command-line tools.)

7. On the Confirm Installation Selections page, review the choices you made and choose Install.

8. After the features are installed, click Start again and mouse over the Administrative Tools to access the Windows Server Backup option.

9. Launch the Backup Schedule wizard by clicking on the Backup Schedule in the right Actions pane of the Windows Server Backup Manager. This is illustrated in Figure 18-6.

10. Using the wizard, you have the option to select from among the volumes you have loaded on the local computer (unless you have connected to a remote computer).

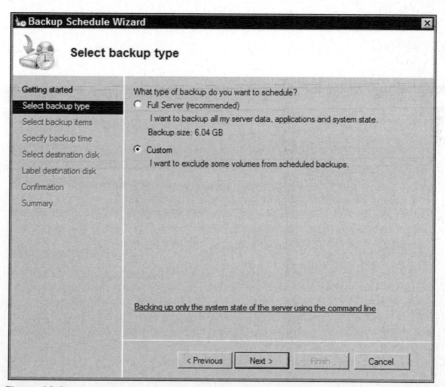

Figure 18-5

Figure 18-6

Note that Windows Server Backup is based on the Volume Shadow Copy Server (VSS). Using VSS, it will take snapshots of an entire volume and allow you to restore either the entire volume or individual files. For more details on how to leverage the Windows Server Backup tool, see Microsoft's Step by Step Guide by following the link at `http://technet2.microsoft.com/windowsserver2008/en/library/00162c92-a834-43f9-9e8a-71aeb25fa4ad1033.mspx`.

Alternatively, you can use the command-line tool to set up and manage your back-up and restore tasks. To use the command-line WBadmin tool, click the Start button and in the search field type **cmd** and hit [Return]; in the new command shell, type **WBadmin /?** and hit [Return]. This is illustrated in Figure 18-7.

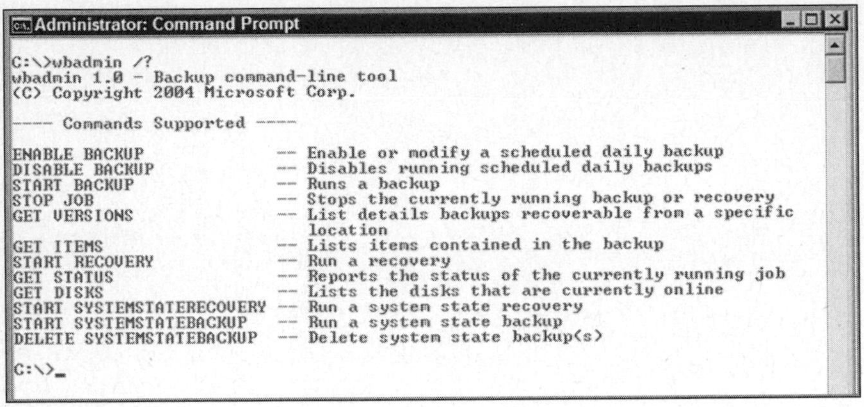

Figure 18-7

Unlike the Windows Server Backup tool, you can use the `wbadmin` command-line tool to back up and restore the system state, which contains many of the IIS configuration settings. To make a backup of the system state, create a .CMD file with the following command:

```
Wbadmin start SystemStateBackup -backupTarget:[volume name]
```

Summary

Chapter 17 covered an extensive set of options that can be used to manage IIS servers. This chapter helps you develop a sense of when and why to use those techniques. Having covered the technical basics of installing and deploying an IIS 7.0 web server in the preceding chapters, we changed emphasis briefly in this chapter to explore the organizational approaches to ensuring that your servers maintain their performance objectives over time.

The lessons of this chapter are focused on maintaining an IIS server through the longer stabilization and production stages of the IIS-service life cycle by keeping your team organized with standards, guides, and process from the ITIL and MOF programs. Use these world-class references as guides when building organization and process for managing operations, including the important topics of scope, quality, and the communications required to maintain a web server infrastructure.

Adding to that, we choose two core operational tasks to cover in some detail, including the MOF approval process for applying hotfixes and the important task of conducting backups. Keeping a backup and restore program current is critical to most IIS implementations, and in this chapter we covered the main kinds of data you would want to back up and the common media options in use today, and included some of the common software options used by today's enterprise organizations to ensure timely and thorough backups.

In the next chapter, we cover another important operational area: concepts and techniques you can use to monitor and tune your servers.

19

Monitoring and Performance Tuning

After covering operations processes in the previous chapter, it's time to talk about the technical changes that you can make to improve performance and ensure the uptime of your web site. In this chapter, you will learn how to track the status of the IIS services and how to make performance improvements to your web server.

The value to your business of monitoring computer systems is widely accepted by professional organizations. To this end, monitoring tools automate the capture and reporting of performance data. Using a monitoring tool installed on your web server, you can track the history and status of the applications and web-site engines and track the state of operating system services, including IIS. Simply put, *monitoring* is about collecting data, and *optimizing* is about using that data to build the best configuration.

Administrators are often unable to act on the data they collect. With *performance data*, you can establish patterns that will define peak periods of activity, audit capacity, build detailed upgrade plans, and learn how all the parts of your system interact. The adjustments you make to your web site and servers to improve performance are the subject of the later sections of this chapter. The goal of this chapter is to help you tune your system in the process of maximizing performance across the entire system.

Monitoring Web Sites

When you install IIS 7.0, you get a service with default settings designed for reliability, security, and performance. IIS 7.0 also employs several features that allow IIS to "self-heal" and perform well in different environments. At the same time, every web server is different, and you need to measure and track performance over time to ensure that your server is delivering as promised. To help you with your task, the following major performance and optimization areas are discussed in this chapter:

- ❑ `Http.sys` (Kernel mode request processing).
- ❑ Memory usage.
- ❑ Processor utilization.
- ❑ Disk I/O.
- ❑ Network bandwidth.
- ❑ Bandwidth throttling.
- ❑ Web connections.
- ❑ HTTP compression.
- ❑ Site configuration.

We dig deeper into each of these areas and provide everything you will need to know to get started on a comprehensive monitoring program. Before going into the details of what aspects to monitor though, it makes sense to first talk about *how* you monitor an IIS server. After all, the tools you use will dictate the options you have for monitoring. The following section covers the native tools that you can use on a Windows Server 2008 computer.

How to Monitor IIS 7.0

For complex web applications that span two or more servers, with business demands for consistent performance, you can invest in a commercial monitoring solution. The leading options offer a great menu of features, including customizable reports covering both platform and Web services data, alerting and auto-correction scripts, and other management functions — all of which will provide you with a consolidated, comprehensive toolset for monitoring your application. Some of the main points to consider in selecting a monitoring solution include

- ❑ **Business Value of the Application** — Critical to casual, you should align your investment with the relative importance of your web site.
- ❑ **The Sophistication of Your Application** — Match it to the feature set of the monitoring solution.
- ❑ **Monitoring** — Can have an impact on performance.
- ❑ **Consolidation of Logs** — Is of great benefit when tracking performance of distributed application.
- ❑ **Granular Metrics** — Are of use only if your tuning options are equally granular. Collecting data that you cannot act on is a waste of resources.

Some of the major providers for computing-system monitoring are named in the following table. Each application offers terrific options for monitoring web applications of all types. Many include a per-server fee, an investment that will return dividends many times over if your application has scale. The list is not meant to be comprehensive, but it should get you started with a list of best-of-class options.

Software	Vendor	Description
i³ for Web Applications	Symantec	i³ correlates activity across web servers, application servers, and databases to identify performance problems in a distributed system. Accommodates data from web clients, web servers, Microsoft .NET, or Java EE platforms.
System Center Operations Manager 2007	Microsoft	Operations Manager is an extensible monitoring and alerting platform by Microsoft for the Windows server environment. Includes rich instrumentation for nearly all Microsoft servers and services, written by the Microsoft product teams, including Active Directory, DNS, and IIS. The instrumentation for IIS, embedded in what is called a "management pack", includes detailed models that cover both the system design and health aspects of an IIS application. Microsoft's health models are based on the Systems Definition Model (SDM) that enables Operations Manger to analyze the performance, availability, configuration and security of IIS applications. Accommodates many leading hardware vendors' instrumentation including HP, IBM, Dell, Cisco, Nortel, EMC, and many others.
Mercury SiteScope	Hewlett-Packard Development Company	SiteScope is a popular monitoring and alerting solution and is based on an agentless architecture. Monitors more than 65 different targets for critical health and performance characteristics such as utilization, response time, usage, and resource availability. Sets thresholds to receive proactive alerts before end-users experience problems. Specialized solution for web-site monitoring and management, including unique features such as URL content monitoring, URL sequence monitoring, and link checks.
Mercury SiteSeer	Hewlett-Packard Development Company	SiteSeer monitors system availability from outside the firewall, polling as often as every five minutes from outside the network. Monitors URLs from multiple endpoints to detect ISP performance issues.
Performance Manager for Internet Servers *and* PATROL	BMC Software	Performance Manager monitors and manages web servers using either centralized aggregation or stand-alone agents. Facilitates root-cause analysis to pinpoint server problems using automated log parsing. Simulates activity to help validate the content delivery of dynamic web pages.

Continued

Software	Vendor	Description
Tivoli Monitoring for Web Infrastructure *and* Tivoli Monitoring Express	IBM	Tivoli is another popular solution that equips you with the resources for identifying issues and alerting appropriate personnel. Includes automated problem correction using a bank of IBM's best practices.
WebTrends Analytics	WebTrends, Inc.	WebTrends Analytics measures and tests the online experience, capturing metrics from both the visitor's point of view and the system metrics. Does more with session context, providing details surrounding the source and nature of web sessions. Ties analysis into other reporting and business solutions via industry-standard open-access technologies.

The options listed in the table above are all terrific, proven solutions for distributed eCommerce applications and can make all the difference between success and failure when keeping such a complex system running uninterrupted. Again, the list isn't meant to be comprehensive but an illustration of what is available today.

If your application is smaller in scope or its importance to your business doesn't justify further investment, there are reliable options within the Windows platform. Windows Server 2008 offers a rich set of native performance tools. Even if you install a commercial-grade solution, you will find that you need to use one of the native tools to supplement your real-time data needs.

Software	Description
Task Manager	Provides real-time data on locally running processes and services, and metrics on CPU and memory.
New command-line tools	Windows Server 2008 includes a few new command-line tools that can expose targeted performance data in a pinch.
Reliability and Performance Monitor	The center for all performance monitoring functions in both Windows Vista and Windows Server 2008.

Having reviewed a few commercial options, it's time to focus on the many native tools that accompany Windows Server 2008. Some are included in legacy operating systems, whereas some of them are new to the Windows Server 2008 platform. We start off with the venerable Task Manager, which has been updated for the new operating system.

Task Manager

Task Manager, shown in Figure 19-1, holds a wealth of information. You can get real-time data on resources and processes, as well as information covering logged-on users and applications. Some of the uses of Task Manager include

- ❑ **Performance Monitoring** — View real-time performance of key server components, including processor, memory, network throughput, hard disk drive I/O, and more.

- ❑ **Performance Tuning** — Associate processes with processors using the Processor Affinity option for running processes. Also terminate any process that may be causing problems for server performance.

- ❑ **Managing Services** — View and change the running state of services, and associate services with processes.

- ❑ **Managing Processes** — View details on the running processes, including the resources allocated, descriptions, and associated files.

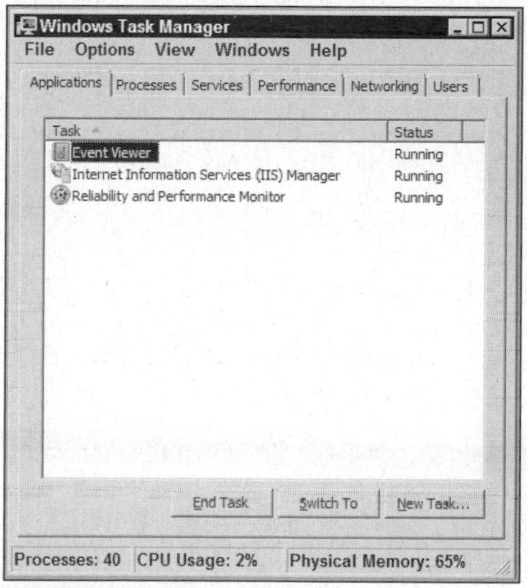

Figure 19-1

You can open Task Manager in one of two ways:

- ❑ **Using the Mouse** — Right-click on the taskbar and from the Context menu, click Task Manager.

- ❑ **Using the Keyboard** — Press *Ctrl+Alt+Delete*, and then click Task Manager from the options on the system screen. Or, simply press *Ctrl+Shift+Esc*.

Managing Services from Task Manager

The *Services tab* is a new addition to Task Manager for Windows Server 2008. You can use the Services tab to start and stop services and to view several important aspects of the services, both running and available, on your computer. You can see the processor ID (PID), description, status, and group associated with each service (see Figure 19-2). You can also use this pane as a shortcut to the Services MMC console using the Services button at the bottom of the window.

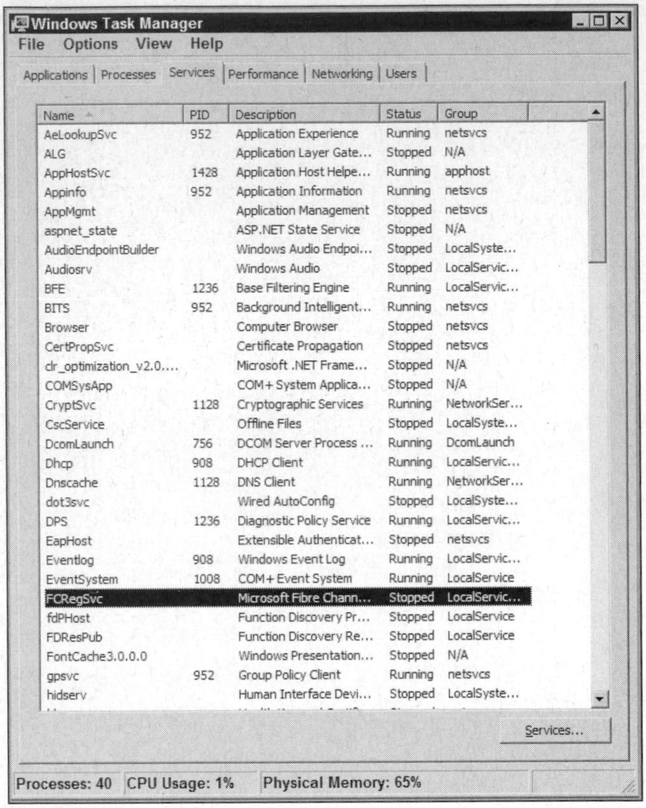

Figure 19-2

To start or stop a service, right-click on its name on the Services tab, and then click either Start Service or Stop Service. Using the Services tab, you can map a running service to its process identifier (PID), which is useful in running scripts to automate the management of services.

You can also map services to running processes. When you right-click on one of the services, you'll find two options: one to stop the service and another called Go To Process. Click Go To Process, and the Processes tab is opened with the particular process highlighted that is associated with the service. Most service-related processes run under an account other than your own and therefore aren't available when you attempt to use the Go To Process option. To view these processes, use the "Show processes from all users" option on the Processes tab in Task Manager before clicking Go To Process.

Managing Performance from Task Manager

The *Performance tab* provides real-time performance data in graph and table formats. CPU and RAM usage is monitored in an easy-to-view graph that depicts details on other CPU and RAM metrics. This tab also is used as a shortcut to the Resource Monitor MMC console by clicking the Resource Monitor button, as shown in Figure 19-3.

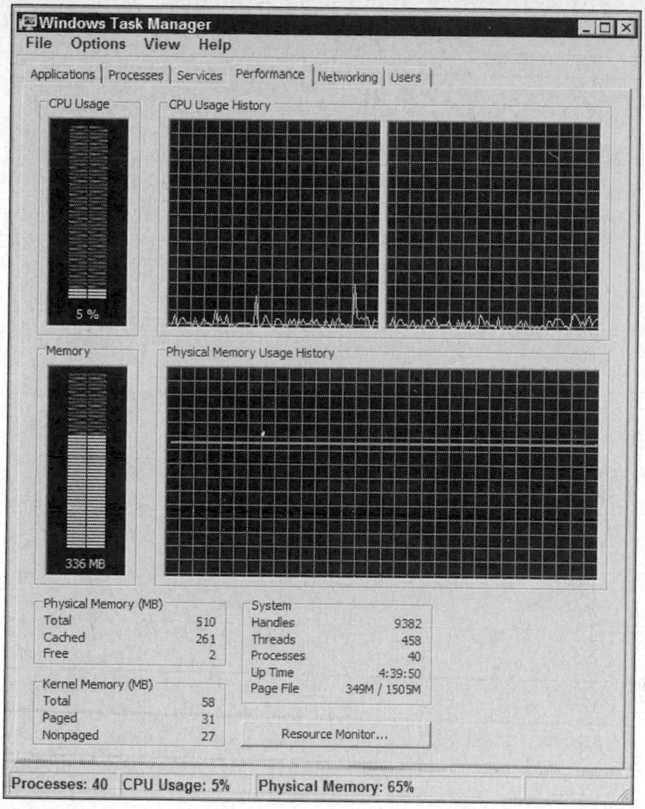

Figure 19-3

New Command-Line Tools

There's more to Windows functionality than what you can point to and click on. Often, it's easier — and more powerful — to run a command directly from the command line. Windows Server 2008 includes several new command-line tools that include new features. Some of these tools, which were previously available from operating system resource-kit downloads, are now integrated with Windows Server 2008. The following table describes some of the new commands:

Tool	Description
clip	Redirects the output of command-line tools to the Windows clipboard.
cmdkey	Creates, displays, and deletes stored usernames and passwords.
dispdiag	Displays diagnostics.
quser	Displays information about users logged on to the system.
rpcping	Pings a server using the Remote Procedure Call (RPC) protocol

Continued

Tool	Description
Timeout	Accepts a time-out parameter to wait for the specified time period or until any key is pressed.
TraceRpt	Parses event logs, such as those produced by Performance Monitor, and helps format and convert data.
Waitfor	Sends or waits for a signal on a system.
Whoami	Returns username and group information along with the respective security identifiers (SID), privileges, and logon identifier (logon ID) for the current user (access token) on the local system.
WinRM	The Windows Remote Management tool, a firewall-friendly WMI helper, reads and writes configuration data on a remote Vista or Windows Server 2008 computer using the new Windows Management Service over port 80.
WinRS	The Windows Remote Shell tool, a firewall-friendly management tool, enables you to launch processes and execute commands on a remote Vista or Windows Server 2008 computer using WinRM over port 80

Reliability and Performance Monitor

In Windows Server 2008, the hotspot for performance tasks is the *Reliability and Performance Monitor*, a collection of tools available from the Control Panel.

Reliability and Performance Monitor identifies how programs affect computer performance. You can look at real-time data through the graphic interface of Performance Monitor or analyze performance over time using log data. Like System Monitor in Windows Server 2003, Reliability and Performance Monitor uses performance counters, event trace data, and system configuration information.

You can launch the toolset in one of the following three ways:

❑ Choose Start ➪ Run, type **Perfmon.exe**, and then press [Enter].

❑ Right-click the Computer link in the Start menu, and choose Manage to open Computer Management console. Click the Reliability and Performance node.

❑ Click the Control Panel link in the Start menu, double-click the Administrative Tools link, and then double-click Reliability and Performance Monitor.

Figure 19-4 shows the main console of the Reliability and Performance Monitor.

The Performance Log Users group is a built-in group in Windows Server 2008 that enables users who are not local Administrators to perform many of the functions related to performance monitoring and logging. In order for members of the Performance Log Users group to initiate data logging or modify Data Collector Sets, the group must first be assigned the user right to log on as a batch job. To assign this user right, use the Local Security Policy MMC snap-in.

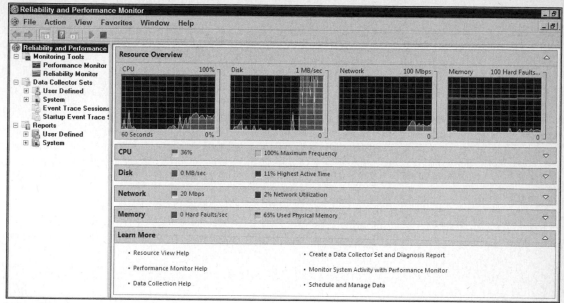

Figure 19-4

Membership in the local Administrators group, or equivalent, is the minimum required to complete this procedure.

To assign the "Log on as a batch job" user right to the Performance Log Users group, follow these steps:

1. Click the Start button ➪ Run, enter **secpol.msc**, and then press [Enter]. The Local Security Policy snap-in will open in Microsoft Management Console.

2. In the navigation pane, expand Local Policies and click User Rights Assignment.

3. In the console pane, right-click "Log on as a batch job," and click Properties.

4. In the Properties page, click "Add User or Group."

5. In the Select Users or Groups dialog box, click Object Types. Select Groups in the Object Types dialog box and click OK.

6. Type **Performance Log Users** in the "Select Users or Groups" dialog box, and then click OK.

7. In the Properties page, click OK.

Performance Monitor

Performance Monitor enables you to view performance data, both in real time and from historical data stored in log files. You can render the data in graphs, histograms, or tabular reports. Performance Monitor for Windows Server 2008, although similar to the version found in previous operating systems, is hosted in the new version 3 of the Microsoft Management Console (see Figure 19-5).

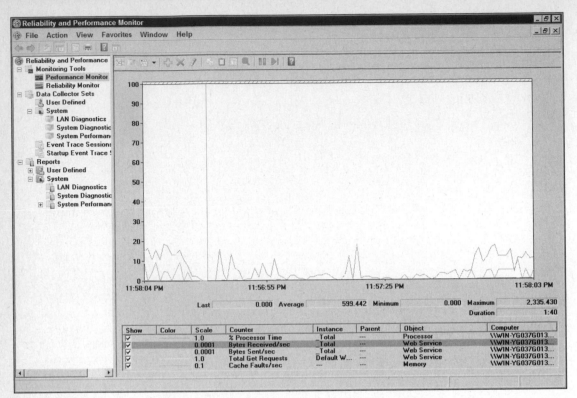

Figure 19-5

Access Performance Monitor by following these steps:

1. Choose Start ➪ Run, enter **Perfmon.exe**, and then press [Enter] to open the Performance and Reliability console.

2. To connect to a remote computer, right-click the Performance and Reliability node and select "Connect to another computer."

3. Click on the Performance Monitor node under the Monitoring Tools node.

To configure Performance Monitor, add counters by clicking the green plus sign (+) on the top menu bar and using the Add Counters screen to select performance objects and counters to monitor. Be sure to check the box next to "Show description" to view a description of the counters as you browse through them (see Figure 19-6).

The following table describes how to perform common tasks in the Add Counters dialog box.

Task	Procedure
Choose the source computer for counters.	Select a computer from the dropdown list, or click Browse to find other computers. You can add counters from the local computer or another computer on network to which you have access.

Task	Procedure
Display a description of the selected counter group.	Select "Show description" in the lower left corner of the page. The description will update as you select other groups.
Add a group of counters.	Highlight the group name and click Add.
Add individual counters.	Expand the group by clicking the down arrow, highlight the counter, and click Add.
Search for instances of a counter.	Highlight the counter group or expand the group and highlight the counter you want to add, type the process name in the dropdown below the "Instances of selected object" box, and click Search. The process name that you type will be available in the dropdown list to repeat the search with other counters. If no results are returned and you want to clear your search, you must highlight another group. If there are not multiple instances of a counter group or counter, the Search function will not be available.
Add only certain instances of a counter.	Highlight a counter group or counter in the list, select the process you want from the list that appears in the "Instances of selected object" box, and click Add. Multiple processes can create the same counter, but choosing an instance will collect only those counters produced by the selected process.

Once you have added counters to the Performance Monitor display, you can adjust the view from the tool menu bar to help identify information that you are looking for.

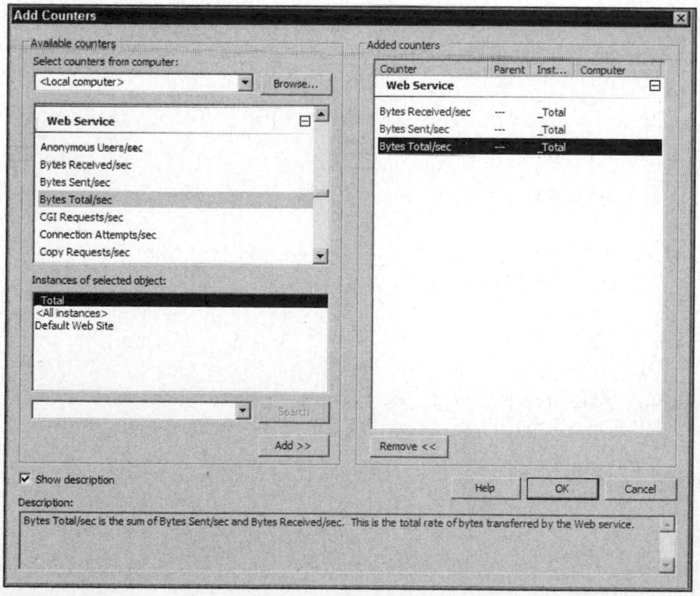

Figure 19-6

Reliability Monitor

Reliability Monitor provides an overview of system stability and shows event details of activities that have an impact on system reliability. You are presented with a Stability Index, which is calculated over the lifetime of the system based on daily measures that are displayed in a graph on the main pane. The *index* is an integer that ranges between 1 and 10, where 10 means that the system is most stable. The *daily index* is a weighted measure derived from the number of specified failures seen over a rolling historical period.

Access Reliability Monitor by following these steps:

1. Click the Start button and in the Start Search field, type **Perfmon.exe**, and then press [Enter] to open the Performance and Reliability console.

2. To connect to a remote computer, right-click the Performance and Reliability node, and select "Connect to another computer."

3. Click the Reliability Monitor node under the Monitoring Tools node.

Another main area of the Reliability Monitor console is the System Reliability Report. Reliability events in the System Stability Report describe the specific failures that have been logged, as shown in Figure 19-7.

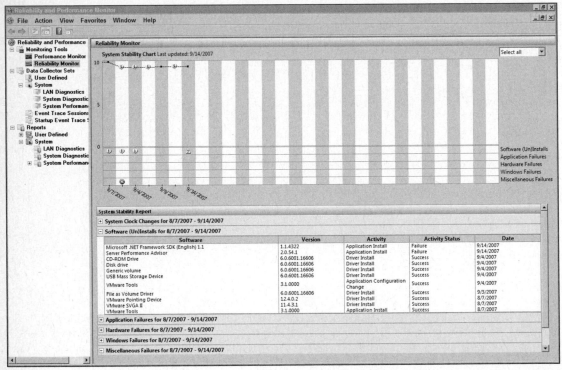

Figure 19-7

The top portion of Reliability Monitor is a chart that plots the system uptime and performance over time. Stop events that halt either the server or one of its services are mapped out so that you can quickly identify failures within the displayed time frame. You can adjust the focus of the chart from All Data to a particular day. Unfortunately, you cannot choose a date range. Under the chart are the detailed data that the chart represents. The data are partitioned into the following main categories:

❑ **System Clock Changes for [date range]** — Displays changes to the system time. These data are displayed only if you have picked a day on which to report that includes a change to the system clock.

❑ **Software (Un)Installs for [date range]** — Displays software installations and removals, including operating-system components, Windows updates, drivers, and applications.

❑ **Application Failures for [date range]** — Displays application failures, including the termination of a non-responding application or an application that has stopped working.

❑ **Hardware Failures for [date range]** — Displays disk and memory failures.

❑ **Windows Failures for [date range]** — Displays boot and operating system failures.

❑ **Miscellaneous Failures for [date range]** — Displays failures that impact stability and do not fall under previous categories, including unexpected operating-system shutdowns.

Each of the preceding categories, when expanded, shows the detailed records of events that caused trouble for the server. In Windows Server 2008, you can roll the counters and trace data and configuration into a Data Collector Set, which is covered in the section below.

Data Collector Sets

With Windows Server 2008's Reliability and Performance Monitor comes a new configuration concept known as *Data Collector Sets*. A *Data Collector Set* organizes multiple data collection points into a single component that you can use to review or log performance. A Data Collector Set can be created and recorded, grouped with other sets, incorporated into logs, viewed in Performance Monitor, configured to generate alerts, and used by non-Microsoft applications.

There are three ways to create a Data Collector Set:

❑ **From Performance Monitor** — Create a Data Collector Set using the counters loaded in Performance Monitor by right-clicking anywhere in the Performance Monitor display pane, pointing to New, and then clicking Data Collector Set to launch the wizard. More details on how to do this follow below.

❑ **From a Template** — This is the simplest way to create a new Data Collector Set. There are several templates from which to choose. Templates are XML files and can be exported and imported. To build a collector set from a template, open Reliability and Performance Monitor, locate the "Data Collector Set" node in the navigation pane, and double-click it to expand it. Right-click the "User Defined" node and choose New, then "Data Collector Set" to start the wizard. After providing a name for your new Data Collector Set, choose "Create From A Template," click Next, and then complete the wizard.

❑ **Manually** — Open Reliability and Performance Monitor and double-click the Data Collector Sets node to expand it. Then right-click the "User Defined node" and point to New and click Data Collector Set to start the wizard. After providing a name for your new Data Collector Set, choose Create Manually, click Next, and then complete the wizard.

You can obtain system diagnostics and generate a report detailing the status of local hardware resources, system response times, and processes on the local system, along with system information and configuration data. This report includes suggestions for ways to maximize performance and streamline system operation.

You must be a member of the local Administrators Group to run the default Data Collector Set.

Here are the missing details on how to create a Data Collector Set from within Performance Monitor. Before you begin, though, add some counters to collect data against. Begin with the display of counters in Performance Monitor. If you are unsure about adding additional counters, see the "What to Monitor" section below for advice on which counters to use.

1. Right-click anywhere in the Performance Monitor display pane, point to New, and click Data Collector Set. The Create New Data Collector Set wizard starts. The Data Collector Set created will contain all of the data collectors selected in the current Performance Monitor view.

2. Type a name for your Data Collector Set and click Next.

3. The Root Directory setting will contain data collected by the Data Collector Set. Change this setting if you want to store your Data Collector Set data in a different location from the default. Browse to and select the directory, or type the directory name.

If you enter the directory name manually, you must not enter a backslash at the end of the directory name.

4. Click Next to define a user account for the Data Collector Set to run as, or click Finish to save the current settings and exit.

5. After clicking Next, you can later update the Data Collector Set to run as a specific user. Click the Change button to enter the user name and password for a different user from the default listed.

If you are a member of the Performance Log Users group, you can configure Data Collector Sets that you create to run under your own credentials.

6. Click Finish to complete the wizard and to return to Windows Reliability and Performance Monitor.

To view the properties of the Data Collector Set or to make additional changes, select Open Properties for this Data Collector Set. You can get more information about the properties of Data Collector Sets by clicking the Help button in the Properties page.

❑ To save and start the Data Collector Set immediately (and begin saving data to the location specified in Step 4), click "Start this data collector set now."

❑ To save the Data Collector Set without starting collection, click Save and close.

Reports

Reliability and Performance Monitor includes two default system reports for assessing system health and diagnosing system-performance issues. It also includes a third report for network issues. The three default reports correlate to the default collector sets and are described below:

❑ **LAN Diagnostics** — Details on the status of network components, connections, and activity.

❑ **System Diagnostics** — Details on the status of hardware drivers, system services, security systems, and disk drives.

❑ **System Performance** — Detailed metrics covering the resource utilization of hardware devices, and the impact of running applications.

In the scenario we use below to show you how to collect data and view reports, you will collect data to view the System Diagnostics Report.

Keep in mind the prerequisites for viewing a report. To view system reports, ensure that you meet the following requirements:

❑ You are logged on as a member of the local Administrators group, or you have started Windows Reliability and Performance Monitor with elevated privileges.

❑ Windows Reliability and Performance Monitor is running.

The System Diagnostics Report uses the Windows Kernel Trace provider, which can only be accessed by members of the local Administrators group.

After launching Reliability and Performance Monitor and ensuring that you have data to report by enabling the Data Collector Set, perform the following steps to view a diagnosis report:

1. In the navigation tree, expand Data Collector Sets and then expand System.

2. Right-click System Diagnostics and click Start. Data collection will begin.

3. In the navigation tree, expand Reports, expand System, expand System Diagnostics, and click the current date.

4. When data collection and report generation are complete, the System Diagnostics Report will appear in the console pane (see Figure 19-8).

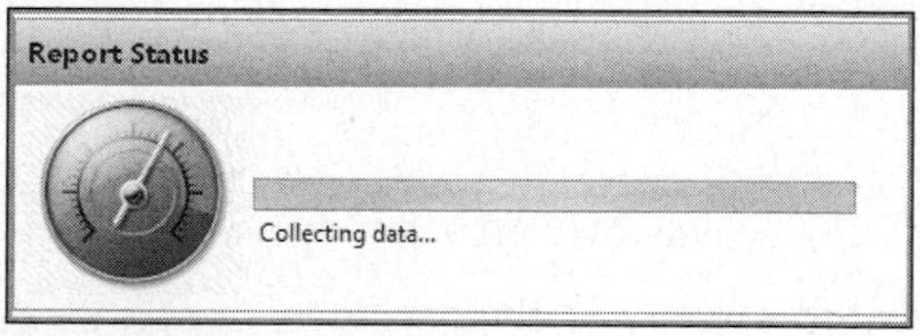

Figure 19-8

Using the reports, you can get to the full details of how your web server and web application are performing over time. Figure 19-9 shows an example report.

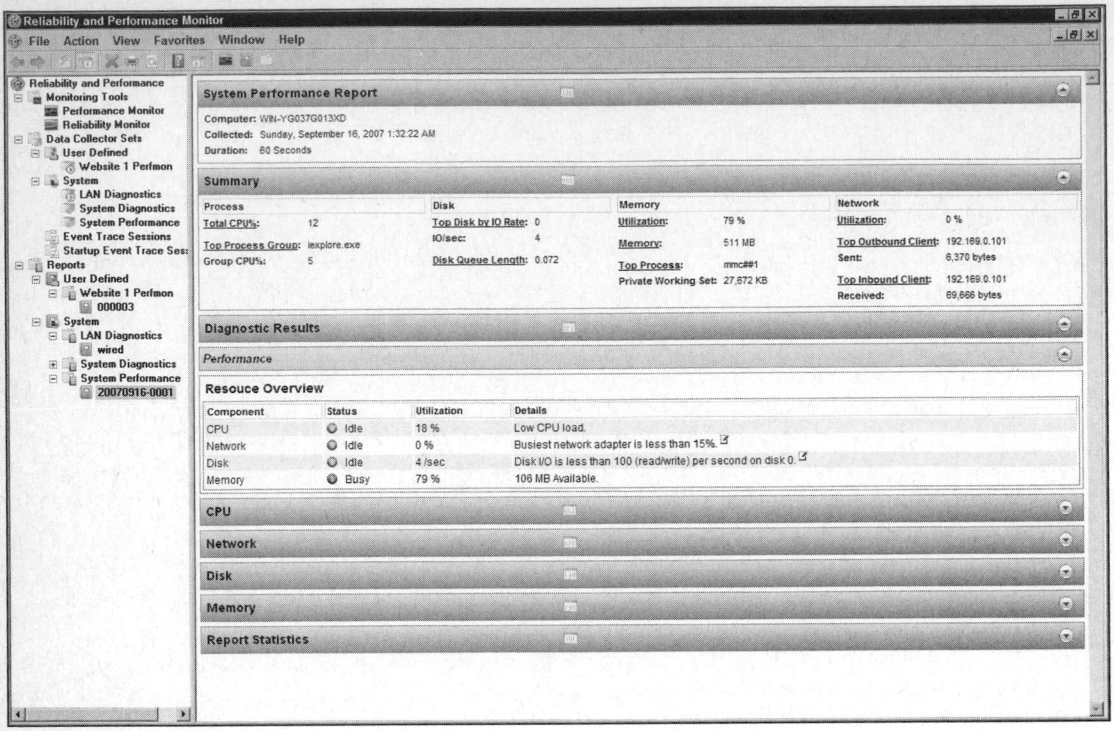

Figure 19-9

Each report presents data in categories and subcategories. Here are a few tips on navigating through a Reliability and Performance Monitor report:

- ❑ Use the blue arrow icons on the right side of a category bar to expand and collapse the category.

- ❑ Use the data icons on the center of a category to pull up a summary menu of all the data points in the report and navigate using the quick links therein.

- ❑ Toggle between Report view and Performance Monitor view by clicking on the desired icon on the top menu bar. Click the black icon with the red line to view the data in graph form. Click the green icon with the white box to see the data in report form (see Figure 19-10).

Figure 19-10

Note an important caveat about logging: using Performance Monitor on the local server will add to the load that the server must handle. Usually, you can assume that logging increases most of the captured data by 5 percent, but that can vary greatly, and the best thing you can do to ensure that your perform- ance data are accurate is to monitor from another server. Open Performance and Reliability Monitor on a

Windows Server 2008 server that does not host your web application and point the monitoring counters toward the remote web-host server. The data you collect, then, will not be tainted by the demands of the monitoring and logging process. Creating and viewing reports on collected data can also spike the demand for resources on a server, thus doing that on a server other than those that are hosting your web application will further protect your web server's resource load.

What to Monitor

When picking objects and counters to monitor, you will find that you have tens of objects and hundreds of counters from which to choose. Picking counters that have meaning to you can be a daunting task. The following sections are based on Microsoft's best practices and will help you pick meaningful counters that will become the basis for useful reports on your system.

We cover the main components of the server as well as the core services that make an IIS server tick. In each case, we offer a description of the counters that you will find in both Windows Server 2003 and Windows Server 2008. As we mentioned in the Monitoring sections above, these counters are performance objects that are written into the operating system by Microsoft and enable you capture the metrics over time.

Memory Usage

Memory can be a source of performance degradation. Memory issues should be reviewed prior to investigating other web server components (for example, processor utilization). The following table provides an overview of the counters that can be tracked to find memory, caching, and virtual memory (paging) bottlenecks.

Area	Counters	Description
Physical and virtual memory usage	Memory\Available Kbytes Memory\Committed Bytes	Memory\Available Kbytes is the amount of physical memory available to processes running on the server. Memory\Committed Bytes is the amount of committed virtual memory. If the server has little available memory, you may need to add memory to the system. In general, you want the available memory to be no less than 5 percent of the total physical memory on the server. Generally, the committed bytes value should be no more than 75 percent of the total physical memory. Capture data during peak periods.
Memory caching	Memory\Cache Bytes Internet Information Services Global\Current File Cache Memory Usage Internet Information Services Global\File Cache Hits %	Memory\Cache Bytes represents the total size of the file system cache. Internet Information Services Global\Current File Cache Memory Usage represents the current memory used by the IIS file cache. Internet Information Services Global\File Cache Hits % represents the ratio of cache hits to total cache requests and reflects how well the settings for the IIS file cache are working. A site with mostly static files should have a very high cache hit percentage (70%–85%).

Area	Counters	Description
Memory page faults	Memory\Page Faults/sec Memory\Pages Input/sec Memory\Page Reads/sec	A "page fault" occurs when a process requests a page in memory and the system cannot find it at the requested location. If the requested page is elsewhere in memory, the fault is called a *soft page fault*. If the requested page must be retrieved from disk, the fault is called a *hard page fault*. Most processors can handle large numbers of soft faults. Hard faults, however, can cause significant delays. Page Faults/sec is the overall rate at which the processor handles all types of page faults. Pages Input/sec is the total number of pages read from disk to resolve hard page faults. Page Reads/sec is the total disk reads needed to resolve hard page faults. Pages Input/sec will be greater than or equal to Page Reads/sec and can give you a good idea of your hard page fault rate. If there are a high number of hard page faults, you might need to increase the amount of memory or reduce the cache size on the server. Memory used by IIS can be controlled by the `MaxCachedFile Size` registry settings. The default value for `MaxCachedFileSize` is 256 KB.

Processor Utilization

Before you review processor utilization, first ensure that any memory issues have been resolved. Processor utilization on an IIS server is a factor of processing HTTP requests, code execution, and I/O writes. Note that each processor installed in a server will have its own counter objects. The following table lists the most valuable counters to include in your data set:

Area	Counters	Description
Thread queuing	System\Processor Queue Length	System\Processor Queue Length displays the number of threads waiting to be executed. These threads are queued in an area shared by all processors on the system. If this counter has a sustained value of 10 or more threads, you'll need to upgrade or add processors.
CPU usage	Processor\% Processor Time	Processor\% Processor Time displays the percentage of time the selected CPU is executing a non-idle thread. Track this counter separately for each processor instance. If the values are high (greater than 75%) while the network interface and disk I/O throughput rates remain low, you'll need to upgrade or add processors.

Area	Counters	Description
ASP performance	Active Server Pages\Request Wait Time Active Server Pages\Requests Queued Active Server Pages\ Requests Rejected Active Server Pages\Requests/sec	These counters indicate the relative performance of IIS when working with ASP. Active Server Pages\Request Wait Time is the number of milliseconds that the most recent request was waiting in the queue. Active Server Pages\Requests Queued is the number of requests waiting to be processed. Active Server Pages\Requests Rejected is the total number of requests not executed because there weren't resources to process them. Active Server Pages\Requests/sec is the number of requests executed per second. Optimally, queues will be empty, and if requests are queuing, then the wait time should be very low. You also don't want to see requests rejected because resources aren't available.

Disk I/O

Disk throughput is not a common cause of performance degradation because of the high performance of today's storage systems. If a server has heavy disk read and write duties, the server's overall performance can be degraded first by memory constraints, since memory reads and writes are much faster than disk I/O. To reduce the disk I/O, manage the server's memory to ensure that the page.sys file is used only when necessary. The following table includes the counters you should monitor to measure disk I/O performance:

Area	Counters	Description
Overall drive performance	PhysicalDisk\% Disk Time	PhysicalDisk\% Disk Time is the percentage of elapsed time that the selected disk drive was busy servicing Read or Write requests. If the % Disk Time value is high and the processor and network connection remain nominal, the system's hard disk drives may be contributing to performance degradation. For example, if the system's processor utilization was at or below 50 percent, network utilization was at 20 percent and % Disk Time was at 90 percent, this would indicate a problem.
Disk I/O	PhysicalDisk\Disk Writes/sec PhysicalDisk\Disk Reads/sec PhysicalDisk\Avg. Disk Write Queue Length PhysicalDisk\Avg. Disk Read Queue Length Physical Disk\Current Disk Queue Length	PhysicalDisk\Disk Writes/sec and PhysicalDisk\Disk Reads/sec are the number of Writes and Reads per second and measure disk I/O activity. PhysicalDisk\Avg. Disk Write Queue Length and PhysicalDisk\Avg. Disk Read Queue Length — In combination, these counters tell you how many Write or Read requests are waiting to be processed. In general, you want there to be very few waiting requests. Keep in mind that the request delays are proportional to the length of the queues minus the number of drives in a redundant array of independent disks (RAID). In most cases, the average disk-queue lengths should be less than 4.

Network Bandwidth

To determine the throughput and current activity on a Web server's NIC, monitor the performance counters in the following table:

Area	Counters	Description
Network traffic	Network Interface\Bytes Total/sec	Network Interface\Bytes Total/sec is the rate at which bytes are sent and received over each network adapter, including framing characters. If the total bytes-per-second value is more than 50 percent of the total bandwidth under a typical load, you might have problems under peak times.

Web Service Counters

The following counters describe the main ways in which a web site posts activity. From these counters, you can get a great sense of the demands your web-site visitors are placing on your web-site components, and the utilization of your web-site service. The following table lists the most valuable counters to include in your data set:

Area	Setting	Description
Web service demand	Web Service\Current Connections Web Service\Connection Attempts/sec	Web Service\Current Connections is the current number of connections established with the Web service. Web Service\Connection Attempts/sec is the rate, in seconds, at which connections to the WWW service have been attempted since the service started.
Web service utilization	Web Service\Bytes Total/sec Web Service\Total Method Requests/sec	Web Service\Bytes Total/sec is the total rate at which bytes are transferred by the Web service. Web Service\Total Method Requests/sec is the rate at which all HTTP requests are made.
Web service utilization	Web Service\ISAPI Extension Requests/sec Web Service\CGI Requests/sec	Web Service\ISAPI Extension Requests/sec is the rate at which ISAPI extension requests are received by the web service. Web Service\CGI Requests/sec is the rate at which CGI requests are received by the web service. If these values decrease because of increasing loads, you might need to redesign the applications.

Area	Setting	Description
Web service utilization	Web Service\Get Requests/sec Web Service\Post Requests/sec	Web Service\Get Requests/sec is the rate at which HTTP requests using the GET method are made. GET requests are the most common HTTP request. Web Service\Post Requests/sec is the rate at which HTTP requests using the POST method are made. POST requests are generally used for forms and are sent to ISAPIs (including ASP) or CGIs. GET requests make up almost all other requests from browsers and include requests for static files, ASPs and other ISAPIs, and CGI requests.
Web server storage capacity	Web Service Cache\File Cache Hits %	Web Service Cache\File Cache Hits % is the total number of successful lookups in the user-mode file cache (since service startup). If the cache is performing its function well, this counter will be high for static content. This value might be low if the counter known as the "Kernel URI Cache Hits % Age" is high.
Web server processor capacity	Web Service Cache\Kernel:URI Cache Flushes Web Service Cache\Kernel:URI Cache Misses Web Service Cache\Kernel:URI Cache Hits %	Web Service Cache\Kernel:URI Cache Flushes should be as low as possible, relative to the number of requests. Note that his number increases every time a file is flushed from the Http.sys response cache, which means that the content has not been accessed in the past two to four minutes. The only way to decrease this number is to flush the cache less often, although frequent flushing can cause Http.sys to use more memory for content that is not being accessed. Web Service Cache\Kernel:URI Cache Misses is the total number of unsuccessful lookups in the kernel URI cache (since service startup). The lower misses the better. (Each request for dynamic content increases the value of the counter by one.) Web Service Cache\Kernel:URI Cache Hits % is the ratio of kernel URI cache hits to total cache requests (since service startup). The higher the ratio the better — up to 100. (This counter applies to static unauthenticated content and dynamic content that is marked as cacheable.)

ASP.NET Counters

You can audit your capacity, stability, and throughput metrics for your ASP.NET code using the counters in the following table:

Area	Setting	Description
ASP.NET stability	ASP.NET Apps vX\Errors Total ASP.NET vX\Application Restarts ASP.NET vX\Worker Process Restarts	ASP.NET Apps vX\Errors Total, where X is the .NET version number, is the total number of errors that have occurred in ASP.NET applications. ASP.NET vX\Application Restarts is the number of times the application has been restarted during the web server's lifetime. ASP.NET vX\Worker Process Restarts is the number of times a worker process has restarted on the machine.
ASP.NET throughput	ASP.NET Apps vX\Requests/Sec ASP.NET vX\Requests Queued	ASP.NET Apps vX\Requests/Sec, where X is the .NET version number, is the number of requests executed per second for ASP.NET applications. ASP.NET vX\Requests Queued is the number of ASP.NET requests waiting to be processed.
ASP.NET capacity	ASP.NET vX\Requests Rejected ASP.NET vX\Worker Process Running	ASP.NET vX\Requests Rejected, where X is the .NET version number, is the total number of requests that were not executed because of insufficient server resources. This counter represents the number of requests that return a 503 HTTP status code. ASP.NET vX\Worker Process Running is the number of worker processes running on the machine.

Centralized Binary Logging

When an IIS server hosts many web sites, the process of creating hundreds or thousands of formatted log files can consume valuable CPU and memory resources from the server. When using a production web server as your basis for monitoring and logging, you can actually create performance and scalability problems.

Centralized binary logging is an option that minimizes the amount of system resources that is used for logging. With this format, IIS creates one log file for all sites on the web server. Every site writes request hit information as unformatted binary data. The binary output file, which is a far more efficient file system than other logging formats, takes up to 50 percent less space than an ANSI text file.

Centralized binary logging is a server property, not a site property. When you enable centralized binary logging, you cannot record data from individual web sites in a different format. The centralized binary logging log file has an Internet binary log (.ibl) file name extension.

To enable centralized binary logging, perform the following steps:

1. Open IIS Manager.

2. Click the Web server node in the Connections pane.

3. In the center pane, locate the Logging icon within the IIS section and double-click on it.

4. In the Log File pane, select Binary, as shown in Figure 19-11.

5. Make any other changes as necessary, including the log path and name and rollover details.

6. As you click away from the Logging settings, IIS Manager will ask you if you want to save your settings. Click Yes.

7. Restart the World Wide Web Publishing service (WWW service) so that the change can take effect. In a command console:

   a. Type **net stop W3SVC** and hit [Enter].

   b. Type **net start W3SVC** and hit [Enter].

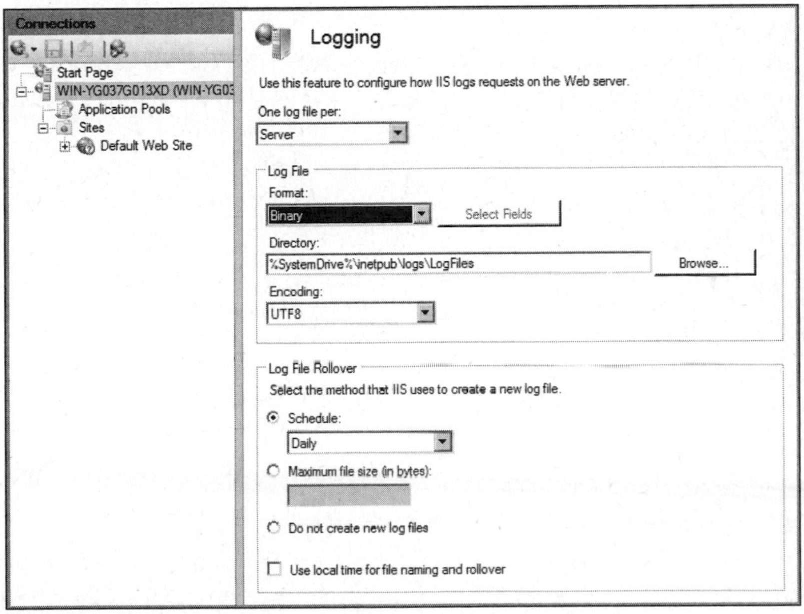

Figure 19-11

The log file is created in the W3SVC folder, which by default is located at systemroot\System32\ LogFiles\.

When you are ready to extract data from a raw log file, you can do one of the following:

❑ Create a custom application (for example, VB, VB.NET) that locates and extracts the data that you want from the raw file and converts the data into formatted text. You can view header file and log file format descriptions in the IIS 7.0 SDK.

❑ Use the Log Parser tool to extract data from the raw file. The Log Parser tool and its accompanying user documentation are included in the IIS 6.0 Resource Kit tools or as a separate download from www.microsoft.com/downloads.

Centralized binary logging records the following information, which is similar, but not identical, to the W3C Extended log file format:

- ❑ Date.
- ❑ Time.
- ❑ Client IP address.
- ❑ User name.
- ❑ Site ID.
- ❑ Server name.
- ❑ Server IP address.
- ❑ Server port.
- ❑ Method.
- ❑ URI stem.
- ❑ URI query.
- ❑ Protocol status.
- ❑ Windows status.
- ❑ Bytes sent.
- ❑ Bytes received.
- ❑ Time taken.
- ❑ Protocol version.
- ❑ Protocol substatus.

Note that the following fields are reported in W3C Extended log files, but they are not recorded in centralized binary logging log files:

- ❑ **Host** — The host header.
- ❑ **User Agent** — The browser type of the client; this string is too large to be practical for the binary format.
- ❑ **Cookie** — The content of the cookie that was sent.
- ❑ **Referrer** — The site that the user last visited.

At this point in the chapter, we change topics from *collecting* data to *using* data. Using the data collected from your monitoring solution, you can make incremental changes to your web-site configuration, hardware platform, or operating-system services with confidence that your changes will actually amount to improved performance.

Performance Tuning

The mandates for tuning web sites range from emergency fixes to creating more headroom for growth in an existing environment. One of the most compelling reasons for tuning performance is that your visitor base goes up, but your budget for hardware does not. By fine-tuning your application, you can get more life from your existing platform as demands go up.

Ideally, you would conduct your first round of *performance tuning* before the web site is released into production. That way, you can be sure that when your application goes into production, it will perform well, and you will know what that application's limitations will be before they are reached. In any event, the main configuration points that you can consider when making incremental changes are listed first in brief below, then in detail in the sections that follow. For each category of configuration change, we included a few examples of what can be done for illustration purposes. It's not a comprehensive list, but it should give you a good idea of what to consider.

Tuning your web server and site involves these areas:

❑ **Network Components** — Increase or stabilize bandwidth and packet processing; add fault tolerance using NIC teaming and clustered routers, using the Windows Server 2008 network processing offloading feature; add Wide-area Data Services (WDS) layer 4-7 compression (for example, as from Riverbed Technologies).

❑ **Storage** — Expand storage capacity and I/O speeds, and deploy fault tolerance.

❑ **Processor** — Change the processor type or add processors to the server.

❑ **Memory** — Change the memory type or add memory to the server.

❑ **Operating System** — Stop unnecessary services from using resources, and adjust settings to prioritize IIS traffic processing.

❑ **Load Balancing** — Add system capacity and fault tolerance by pairing servers and clustering servers to handle extra demands.

❑ **Application Partitions** — Add system capacity by partitioning your web application into tiers and hosting those tiers on separate, dedicated servers.

❑ **IIS and Web Site** — Configure IIS and your web sites to maximize performance and stability.

In the next sections, we cover the details of the areas introduced above, starting with some of the more important operating-system configurations, and will later go into detail on how to tune IIS and web sites.

Operating System Optimizations

We mention just a couple of areas related to optimizing the operating system here, but you should give thought to how you can do more. Pick up a book on Windows Server 2008 or do an online search. You can uncover an entire universe of settings that are beyond the scope of this book. The areas of the operation-system configurations that are covered include the operating-system architecture, service hardening, data throughput, application performance, TCP stack tuning options, and storage settings.

For higher demands, consider using the 64-bit version of Windows Server 2008. The 64-bit systems offer direct access to more virtual and physical memory than 32-bit systems and process more data per clock cycle, enabling more scalable, higher-performing solutions. Regardless of the architecture you use, keep the operating system up-to-date with hotfixes and service packs that affect stability and performance.

Disable Unnecessary Services

Because Windows Server 2008 has a modular architecture, there should not be many services running that are not necessary. You may have installed modules that you don't need, though, and by removing those modules, you make more resources available to IIS and to your web sites. Use the Services console (click the Start button, type **services.msc** into the Start Search box, and then hit [Enter]) to disable any unnecessary services by right-clicking on the service and updating the Startup Type to "Manual" or "Disabled." The following table lists the services that you normally will not need on an IIS server:

Service Name	Description
Application Experience	Processes application-compatibility cache requests for applications as they are launched.
Base Filtering Engine	The Base Filtering Engine (BFE) is a service that manages firewall and IPsec policies and implements user-mode filtering. Stopping or disabling the BFE service will significantly reduce the security of the system. It will also result in unpredictable behavior in IPsec management and firewall applications.
Desktop Window Manager Session Manager	This provides part of the new Windows themes and reverts back to basic styles when running applications that are not compatible with Vista Aero. If you decide to disable this service, you might check into also disabling the Themes Service to make the desktop look more like classic Windows 2000.
Distributed Link Tracking Client	Maintains links between NTFS files within a computer or across computers in a network.
IKE and AuthIP IPsec Keying Modules	The IKEEXT service hosts the Internet Key Exchange (IKE) and Authenticated Internet Protocol (AuthIP) keying modules. These keying modules are used for authentication and key exchange in IPsec. Stopping or disabling the IKEEXT service will disable IKE and AuthIP key exchange with peer computers. IPsec is typically configured to use IKE or AuthIP; therefore, stopping or disabling the IKEEXT service might result in an IPsec failure and might compromise the security of the system. It is strongly recommended that you have the IKEEXT service running.
IP Helper	Provides automatic IPv6 connectivity over an IPv4 network. If this service is stopped, the machine will only have IPv6 connectivity if it is connected to a native IPv6 network.
IPsec Policy Agent	IPsec supports network-level peer authentication, data origin authentication, data integrity, data confidentiality (encryption), and replay protection. This service enforces IPsec policies created through the IP Security Policies snap-in or the command-line tool `netsh ipsec`. If you stop this service, you may experience network connectivity issues if your policy requires that connections use IPsec. Also, remote management of Windows Firewall is not available when this service is stopped.

Service Name	Description
Net.Pipe Listener Adapter	Receives activation requests over the `net.pipe` protocol and passes them to the Windows Process Activation Service.
Net.Tcp Listener Adapter	Receives activation requests over the `net.tcp` protocol and passes them to the Windows Process Activation Service.
Network List Service	Identifies the networks to which the computer has connected, collects and stores properties for these networks, and notifies applications when these properties change. Note that the SL UI Notification Service depends on the Network List Service and may be required for activating your operating system.
Print Spooler	Loads files to memory for later printing. Most IIS servers do not have printer access, thus you can effectively disable this service.
Remote Registry	Enables remote users to modify registry settings on this computer. If this service is stopped, the Registry can be modified only by users on this computer. If this service is disabled, any services that explicitly depend on it will fail to start.
Secondary Logon	Enables starting processes under alternate credentials. If this service is stopped, this type of logon access will be unavailable. If this service is disabled, any services that explicitly depend on it will fail to start. Usually, Administrators that log on to IIS servers have the necessary rights required to administer the server and do not require the Run As service.
Windows Error Reporting Service	Allows errors to be reported when programs stop working or responding and allows existing solutions to be delivered. Also allows logs to be generated for diagnostic and repair services. If this service is stopped, error reporting might not work correctly, and results of diagnostic services and repairs might not be displayed.
Windows Firewall	Windows Firewall helps protect your computer by preventing unauthorized users from gaining access to your computer through the Internet or a network. Most organizations have a perimeter network firewall. Including a host-based firewall can provide defense in depth, but if you are not following such a strategy, turn off this service.

Disable the preceding services only after giving careful thought to whether the web server requires them.

Application Performance

The configuration options on the *Application Performance* area of the System Properties console (sysdm.cpl) determine the responsiveness of foreground and background applications. To adjust the configuration options for application performance, follow these steps:

1. Click the Start button, type **Sysdm.cpl** into the Start Search box, and hit [Enter].

2. In the System Properties dialog box of the Control Panel, select the Advanced tab, and then click Settings in the Performance section.

3. On the Visual Effects tab, you can select "Adjust for best performance." This will reduce the load on the system when displaying windows and menus.

4. On the Advanced tab, ensure that Background Services is selected. This setting is used since the IIS processes runs as a background service. By default, Background Services is selected.

5. Also on the Advanced tab, click the Change button in the Virtual Memory section, and configure the paging file according to the following principles:

   ❑ Ideally, place the paging file on a different disk or disk array than the one that holds the system and/or boot partitions. You should use the RAID-0 (Stripe Set) array to store the paging file.

   ❑ Avoid placing a paging file on a fault-tolerant drive, such as a RAID-1 or a RAID-5 volume. Paging files do not need fault tolerance, and some fault-tolerant systems suffer from slow data writes because they write data to multiple locations.

   ❑ Do not place multiple paging files on different partitions on the same physical disk drive.

   ❑ Set the initial paging file size to be at least 1.5 times larger than the amount of physical RAM.

   ❑ Set the maximum paging file size to be equal to the initial size, which stops the paging file from changing sizes and fragmenting the hard disk drive.

TCP Stack Tuning Options

Microsoft has improved the network stack considerably in Windows Server 2008. Network performance is more stable and flexible, and faster. Here is an abridged list of benefits over previous operating systems:

❑ Automated TCP/IP performance tuning, using improved algorithms to accurately assess the best way to communicate with networks.

❑ An ability to offload TCP/IP processing away from the CPU onto a compatible NIC adapter, saving CPU cycles for other services.

❑ Receive-side scaling (RSS) allows faster network performance by spreading the packet reception processing load across multiple processors.

❑ Dual layer implementations of IPv4 and IPv6 network stacks.

In addition to the improvements in the network stack, you can configure settings to fine-tune the server. You should thoroughly test any and all changes you make to the Registry, and rarely will you want to introduce such a change into a production environment without first proving the value (and stability) of the change in a controlled lab environment.

The following table shows some of the ways you can optimize the TCP network services stack for your IIS server:

Registry Value	Description

`TCPWindowSize`	The maximum data (in bytes) in a TCP transmission burst; the range is from 1 to 65,535 bytes using the following registry value:
	`HKEY_LOCAL_MACHINE\System\CurrentControlSet\Services\Tcpip\`
	`Parameters\TcpWindowSize`
	
	The default values for common interfaces are
	Gigabit (1,000 Mbps) — 65,535
	Ethernet (100 Mbps) — 16,384
	Others — 8,192
	
	This value should be set to
	`End-to-end network bandwidth (bytes/s) x Bandwidth-Delay`
	`product (the round-trip delay in seconds)`

`Tcp1323Opts`
(Window Scaling)
	To raise the TCP window size past 65K using the TCPWindowSize value in the row above, set the following registry value to equal 1:
	`HKEY_LOCAL_MACHINE\System\CurrentControlSet\Services\Tcpip\`
	`Parameters\Tcp1323Opts`
	
	Without this registry value, the TCPWindowSize value is capped at 65,535 bytes.

`MaxHashTableSize`	The TCP hash table tracks open TCP connection states. Set during installation, the default size is figured by multiplying the number of processors times 128.
	`HKEY_LOCAL_MACHINE\System\CurrentControlSet\Services\Tcpip\`
	`Parameters\MaxHashTableSize`
	
	The maximum is 0x10000 or 65,536 bytes for this Registry value. For high-performance servers, use the maximum value regardless of the number of processors.

`MaxUserPort`	Windows makes 5,000 port connections available for each IP address. Your site may require more concurrent port connections and can raise the below Registry value up to 65,534.
	`HKEY_LOCAL_MACHINE\System\CurrentControlSet\Services\Tcpip\`
	`Parameters\MaxUserPort`

Storage Tuning Options

Optimizing disk reading and writing can make a huge difference in the performance of your server. Start with the right hardware and choose the best backplane solution that you can afford. Today's options include the high-speed technologies Serial Advanced Technology Attachment (SATA) with 1.5–3 Gbits/second throughput and Small Computer System Interface (SCSI) with 1.6–2.5 Gbit/seconds throughput.

Make use of performance and tolerance options such as RAID 1, 1+0, or 5, to provide the best hardware level platform. In the operating system itself, you have several options for tuning disk I/O. The options are listed in the following table:

Registry Value	Description
CountOperations	Enable or disable process and system counters that measure disk and network I/O. Turn off these counters on systems when these counters are redundant, which they often are when I/O rates are analyzed at the physical, logical, network interface, IP and TCP levels. To turn off the process and system I/O counters, create a Registry value and set the value to 0 (REG_DWORD) in the following registry value: `HKEY_LOCAL_MACHINE\System\CurrentControlSet\Session Manager\I/O System\CountOperations` Note that this setting does not affect the physical and logical disk counters, network interface, IP and TCP counters. A reboot is required for this setting to take effect.
DontVerifyRandom Drivers	Stop storage drivers from auditing storage configuration randomly by setting the below registry value to equal 1 (REG_DWORD): `HKEY_LOCAL_MACHINE\System\CurrentControlSet\Session Manager\Memory Management\DontVerifyRandomDrivers`
NumberOfRequests	Control the I/O requests for a specific network adaptor by setting the NumberOfRequests value. Disk array performance improves when setting the below Registry value to a number ranging from 16 to 255. `HKEY_LOCAL_MACHINE\System\CurrentControlSet\Services\ MINIPORT_ADAPTER\Parameters\DeviceN\NumberOfRequests` Replace `MINIPORT_ADAPTER` with the adapter name.

IIS Service Optimizations

Having optimized the other aspects of the operating system, the next area to think about before we cover web-site configuration is the IIS 7.0 service. As you read through these options, keep in mind that most of the tuning options covered here are set at the *server* level and will apply uniformly to all the web sites hosted on the server. If your web server hosts more than one site, be careful to consider the requirements for all the sites on the server before making any changes to the IIS service.

Http.sys

Http.sys, the front end of IIS, is defined in Chapter 2, "IIS 7.0 Architecture." Because of the separation of the HTTP protocol stack in *kernel mode* from the worker processes in *user mode*, Http.sys uses its own error-logging scheme that is controlled by the Kernel mode conventions. Examples of events that use Kernel mode error logging are

❑ Connection time-outs.

❏ Worker process in user mode unexpectedly terminates or closes its application pool; outstanding requests are logged.

❏ When IIS does not immediately destroy connections that the client terminates before a response for the last request on these connections is complete ("Zombie sessions").

The Kernel mode request processing handled by the Http.sys stack has a separate log file than those files that log web-site activity. The default location for the Http.sys error log is

```
%SystemRoot%\System32\LogFiles\HTTPERR
```

To change the configuration of Http.sys error logging, you have to edit the Registry. Http.sys reads the configuration only once during startup. The Http.sys error-logging configuration is global and will affect all Web traffic.

Three parameters control Http.sys error logging. They are located under the following Registry Key:

```
HKEY_LOCAL_MACHINE\System\CurrentControlSet\Services\HTTP\Parameters
```

The three registry values that can be set are described in the following table:

Registry Value	Description
EnableError Logging	The default value is True. It is not recommended that you change this value.
ErrorLogFile TruncateSize	The default value is 1 * 1,024 * 1,024 bytes. The value cannot be smaller than this, and it must be specified in bytes. By increasing this number, you minimize the processor and disk I/O overhead used in cutting over to new log files as they reach the truncate size.
ErrorLoggingDir	The default value is \systemroot\System32\LogFiles. When specified, this value must be a fully qualified directory string, but you can use \system root. For example: C:\LogFiles is the same as \systemroot\LogFiles. Change the location of this file to a dedicated disk that holds log files only, to maximize disk I/O performance by aggregating sequential disk operations onto a single disk spindle.

In addition to the logging optimizations listed above, you can make adjustments to other values within the HTTP\Parameters key to further tune how the Http.sys service receives and responds to raw requests. To optimize the Http.sys I/O processing, review the options in the following table:

Registry Value	Description
UriEnableCache	This Registry value enables the Kernel mode response and fragment cache. For most workloads, the cache should remain enabled. Consider disabling the cache if you expect very low response and fragment cache utilization. To disable the fragment cache, change the data for this value to 0.

Continued

Registry Value	Description
UriMaxCache MegabyteCount	Specifies the maximum memory available to the Kernel cache. When set to 0, the operating system adjusts the amount of memory available to the cache. Note that specifying the size only sets the maximum, and the system may not allow the cache to grow to the specified size.
UriMaxUriBytes	This is the maximum size of an entry in the Kernel cache, which offers a faster response to requests by keeping them in memory and off the hard drives. Responses or fragments larger than the data set in this registry value will not be cached. The default value is 262,144 bytes (256 KB). You should increase this limit to take advantage of installed memory greater than 2 GB. If memory is limited, and large entries are crowding out smaller ones, it may help to lower this limit.
UriScavenger Period	The Http.sys cache is flushed by a scavenging process, which fires according to the time period set in this Registry value. Setting the scavenger period to a high value reduces the number of scavenger scans. However, the cache memory usage may grow as older, less frequently accessed entries are allowed to stay in the cache. Setting this period to too low a value causes more frequent scavenger scans and may result in excessive flushes and cache churn. The default value is 120 seconds. Consider increasing that amount by as much as 100 percent if your data are static.

This last set of Http.sys registry values is centered on connection options. You can tune the connection parameters to make the most of the installed resources on the local server. The Registry-based tuning options for connections are listed in the following table:

Registry Value	Description
IdleConnectionsHighMark IdleConnectionsLowMark IdleListTrimmerPeriod	Manage the structures that handle Http.sys connections, ensuring a minimum and maximum capacity as well as the polling period where capacity is audited.
MaxConnections	Number of concurrent connections that the Http.sys will allow. Each connection uses non-paged-pool memory. On a dedicated web server, the value can be set higher than the default, which is set conservatively, to enable the server to handle more simultaneous requests.

Application Pool Optimizations

IIS 7.0 builds on the options first introduced in IIS 6.0 for optimizing application pool and worker process performance. Chapter 8, "Web Application Pool Administration," explains how pooling applications into a common worker process benefits web sites, and how to manage the pooling feature using code, configuration files, and IIS Manager.

You can tune application pools using the same tools, including WMI scripting, `web.config` files, `appcmd.exe`, and IIS Manager.

To view the options for setting application pool settings using AppCmd, type the following line into a command window (replace `DefaultAppPool` with the name of any application pool on your server):

```
appcmd.exe set AppPool "DefaultAppPool" /?
```

To use IIS Manager, perform the following steps to access the tuning window:

1. Open IIS Manager.
2. In the Connections pane, double-click on the server that you want to manage.
3. Click the Application Pools node under the target server.
4. In the center pane, right-click on the application pool that you want to tune, and select Advanced Settings to view the tuning options (see Figure 19-12).

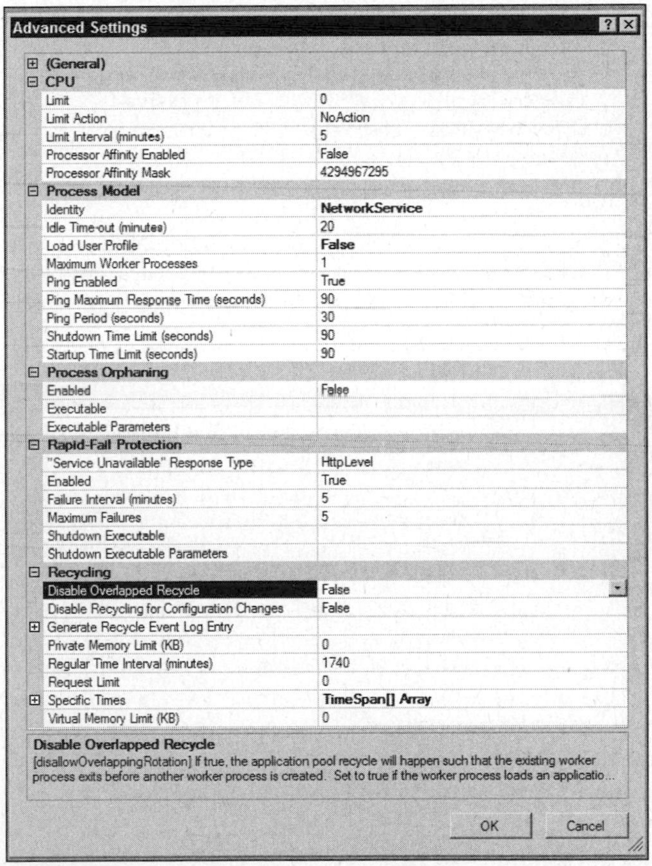

Figure 19-12

The following three tables list some of the key settings to consider when tuning IIS application pools. Use the values suggested in the following tables as a baseline, and further fine-tune these settings based on the performance data collected.

This first table covers application pool CPU tuning options:

Parameter	Description
Limit	Maximum percent of CPU time (in 1/1000-ths of a %) that the worker processes in an application pool are allowed to use within the interval specified below. 0 disables this limit and is the default setting. Use this setting if code in the web site is unstable and consumes CPU resources over time.
Limit Interval (minutes)	Interval for monitoring the limit of CPU time that the application pool is allowed to use, as specified above. At the end of this interval, the counter is reset. 0 disables CPU monitoring, and 5 minutes is the default setting.
Processor Affinity Enabled	Force the worker processes for this application pool to spawn as a thread on a particular processor. Use this setting on multiprocessor systems that host web sites that are not written using .NET managed code (which is multi-threading aware).
Processor Affinity Mask	Hexadecimal value, or CPU ID, that represents the target CPU to which the application pool will assign new worker processes

The next table includes options for application pool process model tuning. These settings affect the worker process behavior and can have a big impact on the user's experience.

Parameter	Description
Idle Time-out (minutes)	Shut down a worker process after being idle for more than a specified amount of time. This can save some resources on limited-memory systems, but it is not recommended in situations that will require frequent spawning of new worker processes under heavy CPU load, because of the overhead associated with process creation.
Load User Profile	When True, IIS will load the user profile of the account specified in the Identity field. This is new to IIS 7.0 and allows you to further configure security and logging based on the application pool identity account profile.

Parameter	Description
Maximum Worker Processes	You can control the total number of worker processes in a Web Garden mode of operation. In Web Garden mode, several worker processes handle the request load under a single application pool. There is no pre-assignment of worker processes to web sites via different app-pools. In some cases, one worker process is not enough to handle the load (indicated by poor CPU usage and long response times), and increasing the number of worker processes may improve throughput and CPU usage. One case in which the Web Garden mode may be considered is with hosting multiple sites. Multiple worker processes can also offer more reliability in case of an incidental crash of one of them, with little chance of total service disruption. Web Garden mode is easier to set up and control than multiple pre-assigned application pools. The default is one worker process to handle all requests.
Ping Enabled	Enables health monitoring of the application pool using a periodic request for acknowledgement that is sent to the pool (according to the two settings below). If the pool is unresponsive, it is recycled. True by default, this is an excellent option for most pools.
Ping Maximum Response Time (seconds)	Maximum time that a worker process is given to respond to a health-monitoring ping. The process is terminated by IIS if it does not respond. This is set to 90 seconds by default.
Ping Period (seconds)	Interval between health-monitoring pings.
Shutdown Time Limit (seconds)	Period of time a worker process is given to finish processing requests and shut down. If the process exceeds the limit, it will be forced to terminate by IIS. Set to 90 seconds by default.
Startup Time Limit (seconds)	Period of time a worker process is given to start. If the process exceeds the limit before it becomes responsive, it will be restarted by IIS. Set to 90 seconds by default.

The final table in this section covers the application pool recycling tuning options. Like the settings in the preceding table, the options in the table below can affect the user's experience significantly and deserve careful consideration.

Parameter	Description
Disable Overlapped Recycle	When True, the existing worker process will be shut down first before another is started. Use this setting when your application does not support multiple instances.
Disable Recycling for Configuration Changes	Stops the recycling act that would accompany a configuration change to the application pool.
Private Memory Limit (KB, kilobytes)	Maximum amount of private memory a worker process can consume before causing the application pool to recycle. A value of 0 means that there is no limit.

Continued

Parameter	Description
Regular Time Interval (minutes)	Periodic recycling based on time. The default value is 1,740. Use this value if your application is unstable and becomes inoperable over time. Otherwise, set this to 0 to stop the application pool from automatically recycling based on this time interval.
Request Limit	Periodic recycling based on the (cumulative) number of requests. 0 means that there is no limit. Use this value to cap the number of requests as a means to reset your application pool in the case that the server ceases to be responsive.
Specific Times	Recycling at given time settings. You can provide several times during the day, or one entry. Use to recycle the application pool during a maintenance window.
Virtual Memory Limit (KB, kilobytes)	Memory-based recycling (disabled by default) allows recycling of a worker process if it has reached the limit defined here. 0 indicates no recycling based on virtual memory usage.

Web-Site Optimizations

Having covered the tuning options for the operating systems and for the IIS service, it's now time to work directly with the web-site configurations. Tuning a web site is not as complex as writing optimized web-site code, but it's every bit as important. Each of the tuning options covered below will apply to the web site where you make the change; other web sites that you may host on the server will not be affected.

HTTP Page Headers

Every web page that IIS sends includes *HTTP page headers*, extra data that are prefixed to the page stream before it is sent. The extra data in the page headers tell the visitor's browser how to handle the web page. There are two types of HTTP page headers that you can use to help optimize your web-site performance: Content Expiration and HTTP keep-alives.

HTTP Keep-Alives

A browser typically makes multiple requests in order to download an entire web page. To enhance server performance, most web browsers request that the server keep the connection open across these multiple requests, which is a feature known as *HTTP keep-alives*.

Without HTTP keep-alives, a browser that makes numerous requests for a page containing multiple elements, such as graphics, might require a separate connection for each element. The additional connections also make a browser much slower and less responsive, especially across a slow connection.

HTTP keep-alives are required for integrated security or connection-based authentication services, such as Integrated Windows Authentication (IWA). If you disable HTTP keep-alives for web sites that use Integrated Windows authentication, requests to the web site fail.

Content Expiration

Consider setting file expiration dates where possible. *Content expiration* is how IIS determines whether or not to return a new version of the requested web page if the request is made after the web-page content has expired. IIS will mark each web page before it's sent using the settings you provide for content expiration. The end-user's browser will translate the expiration mark. The options for expiring content are

❑ **Immediately** — Expires content immediately after it is delivered.

❑ **After** — Sets the number of days after which the content will expire.

❑ **On** — Sets an exact date when the content will expire.

By setting content expiration other than immediately, you can reduce second-access load times by 50 to 70 percent. This setting will not affect dynamically generated content.

Enabling HTTP Header Tuning

To enable Content Expiration or HTML Keep-Alives, follow these steps:

1. Open IIS Manager.

2. Double-click on the target server that you want to administer. To set the options to apply to all servers, continue to Step 3. To apply these settings to a single web site, double-click the Sites node under the target server, and then select the web site you want to administer.

3. Ensure that your center panel shows the Features View tab (located at the bottom left of the center pane).

4. In the HTTP Response Headers pane, right-click on an empty space, and select the Set Common HTTP Response Headers option from the context menu.

Figure 19-13 shows the "Enable HTTP keep-alive" and "Expire Web content" options.

5. Select the configuration options most suitable for the web site and click OK.

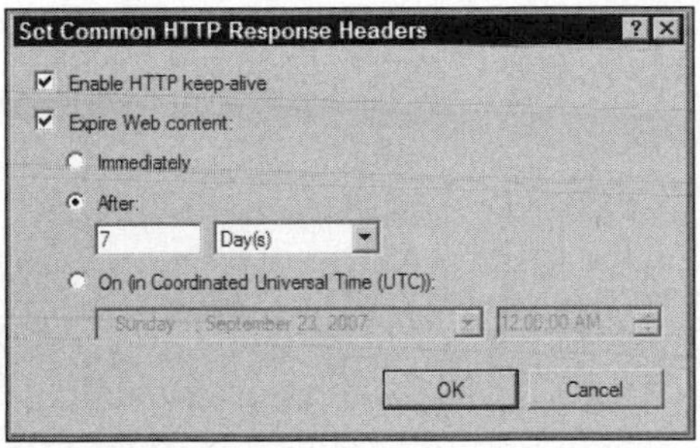

Figure 19-13

Bandwidth Throttling

Bandwidth throttling can be set at the global web-sites node and at each individual web site. At the global web-sites level, you can limit the total network bandwidth available for all web sites on the server. Bandwidth throttling can also be set at the web-site level, allowing you to limit the amount of bandwidth consumed by each site. The default for bandwidth throttling at any level is disabled and is the recommended setting.

If a minimum amount of bandwidth for a particular site is required, or a site uses too much bandwidth that affects other sites, then bandwidth throttling is an optional solution. Also, adding server NICs or offloading the web site/application to another server would alleviate bandwidth bottlenecks.

1. Open IIS Manager.

2. Double-click on the target server that you want to administer.

3. Double-click on the Sites node under the target server.

4. Select the web site you want to administer.

5. Ensure that your center panel shows the Features View tab (located at the bottom left of the center pane).

6. In the Actions pane, in the Manage Web Site\Configure group, click the Limits link. The following options are available for controlling bandwidth usage for the site:

- ❑ **Limit bandwidth usage (in bytes)** — Select to limit the amount of traffic allowed to a web site based on bandwidth usage. In the corresponding box, enter a value, in bytes, at which you want to limit the web-site traffic. The value must be an integer between 1,024 and 2,147,483,647.

- ❑ **Connection timeout (in seconds)** — Type a number in the box to set the length of time, in seconds, before the web server disconnects an inactive user. This setting guarantees that all connections are closed if the HTTP protocol cannot close a connection.

- ❑ **Limit number of connections** — Select to limit the number of connections allowed to a web site. In the corresponding box, enter the number of connections to which you want to limit the web site. The value must be an integer between 0 and 4,294,967,295 (unlimited). Setting the number to be unlimited circumvents constant administration if your connections tend to fluctuate. However, system performance can be affected if the number of connections exceeds your system resources. Restricting a web site to a specified number of connections can keep performance stable.

Output Caching

New to IIS 7.0, you can configure output caching to improve performance. As you know, when a user requests a web page, IIS processes the request and returns a page to the client browser. With output caching enabled, a copy of that processed web page is stored in memory on the web server and returned to client browsers in subsequent requests for that same resource, eliminating the need to reprocess the page each time it is requested. This is helpful when your content relies on an external program for processing, such as with a Common Gateway Interface (CGI) program, or when the site includes data from an external source, such as from a remote share or a database.

With the new output caching management in IIS 7.0, cached items are retained in memory, but they are dumped if resources run low on the server. The page will then be re-cached the next time a user requests that resource if the server determines that the page is sufficiently popular to be cached.

To access the tuning options for output caching, follow these steps:

1. Open IIS Manager.

2. Double-click on the target server that you want to administer.

3. Double-click the Sites node under the target server.

4. Select the web site you want to administer.

5. Ensure that your center panel shows the Features View tab (located at the bottom left of the center pane).

6. In the center pane, double-click the Output Caching Rules icon in the IIS grouping.

7. In the Actions pane, click the Edit Feature Settings link. Figure 19-14 shows the resulting Edit Output Cache Settings dialog box.

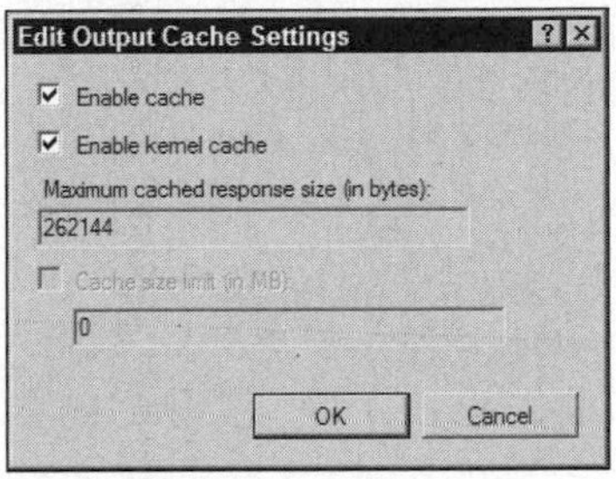

Figure 19-14

The options for caching are as follows:

❑ **Enable cache** — Enables the IIS output cache, which stores cached responses in user mode. The IIS output cache is similar to the ASP.NET output cache. However, the IIS output cache is a native output cache that offers increased performance over the managed output cache in ASP.NET.

❑ **Enable kernel cache** — Enables the kernel cache, which stores cached responses in Kernel mode. Performance is improved when responses are returned from the kernel cache without transitioning to user mode.

❑ **Maximum cached response size (in bytes)** — Specifies the maximum size of a cached response for both the user-mode and Kernel-mode caches. The default value is 262,144 bytes.

❑ **Cache size limit (in MB)** — Configures the size limit of both the user-mode and Kernel-mode caches.

8. Make any changes and click OK.

After establishing the feature settings, you can add caching rules. To create a new caching rule, click Add in the Actions pane and complete the configuration window. The options are listed and explained in the following table:

Element Name	Description
Extension	Displays the filename extension for which the caching rule applies.

Continued

Element Name	Description
User-Mode Behavior	Displays the user-mode caching behavior for the rule: **Cache until change** — Content is cached until IIS receives a file change notification. **Cache for time period** — Content is cached for a specific duration. **Prevent all caching** — User-mode caching has been disabled. **Do not cache** — User-mode caching has not been configured.
Kernel-Mode Behavior	Displays the Kernel-mode caching behavior for the rule: **Cache until change** — Content is cached until IIS receives a file change notification. **Cache for time period** — Content is cached for a specific duration. **Prevent all caching** — User-mode caching has been disabled. **Do not cache** — User-mode caching has not been configured.
Entry Type	Shows the scope of the output caching rule. The value is either Local or Inherited.

HTTP Compression

If network bandwidth is a concern, consider using the IIS compression service. *HTTP compression* will shrink data before the IIS server sends it; the client's browser decompresses the data before rendering them for the web-site visitor. Using HTTP compression gives you these benefits:

❑   Reduces the amount of data sent (improves bandwidth utilization).

❑   Increases the page display speed (increases transfer times).

❑   Allows for consolidation of web applications into a smaller web farm (reduces server sprawl).

HTTP compression requires support of HTTP 1.1 by the client's browser. Most current browsers support HTTP 1.1 and have the feature enabled by default; older browsers may not support HTTP 1.1. *Older browsers will still be able to retrieve files from your site; they will not take advantage of HTTP compression.* Before enabling HTTP compression on production servers, it is imperative that all the applications on the web server are tested fully.

Using IIS Manager, you can apply compression settings at the global web-site level. IIS Manager allows you to configure global compression for

❑   Static files only.

❑   Dynamic application responses only.

Here are the steps to install the IIS compression services, which are required if the server will use HTTP compression:

1.   Open the Windows Server Manager wizard (appwiz.cpl) using the Windows Start menu.

2.   Double-click the Roles node in the Connections pane.

3.   Locate and open the Web Services (IIS) grouping in the center pane.

4.   In the Role Services subgroup of the Web Services (IIS) group, click Add Role Services.

5. From the available services, check the box next to these modules:

❏ Web Server\Performance\Static Content Compression.

❏ Web Server\Performance\Dynamic Content Compression.

6. Click Next, and then Install. Click Close after the role services are installed.

Now that the services are installed, you can configure compression for a web site. Here are the steps for enabling HTTP compression in IIS:

1. Open IIS Manager.

2. Double-click on the target server that you want to administer. If you want to set the options to apply to all servers, continue to Step 3. To apply these settings to a single web site, double-click the Sites node under the target server, and then select the web site you want to administer.

3. Ensure that your center panel shows the Features View tab (located at the bottom left of the center pane).

4. In the center pane, double-click the Compression icon in the IIS grouping.

5. In the center pane, click the checkboxes of the kind of compression you want to employ.

When setting compression settings at the server level, you have more options to consider. Figure 19-15 shows the options for server-level compression settings.

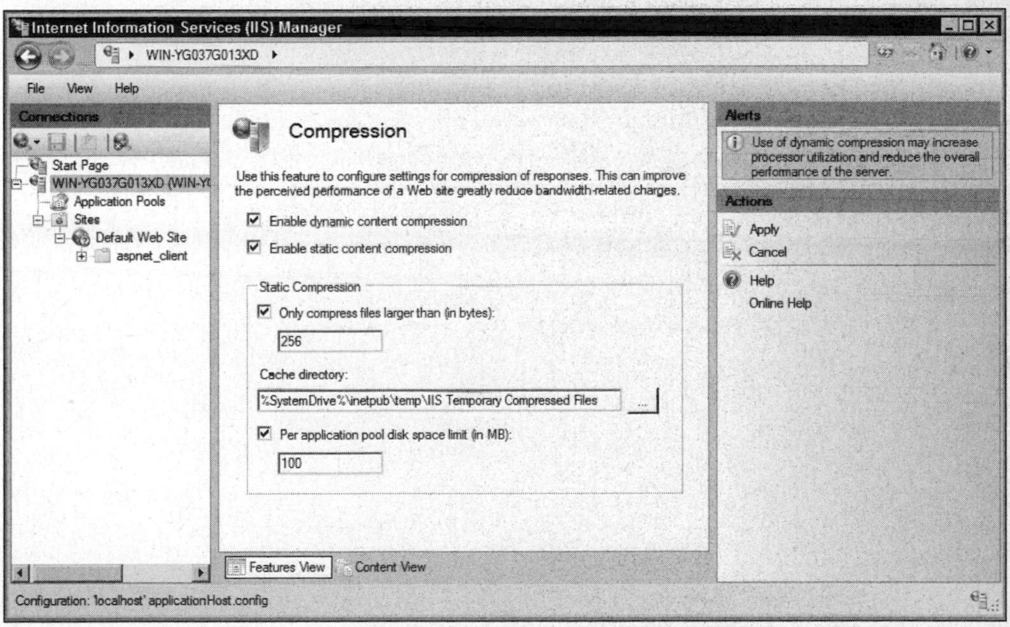

Figure 19-15

You can set the following compression settings at the server level:

❑ **Enable static content compression** — Configures IIS to compress static content. Unlike dynamic responses, compressed static responses can be cached on disk across multiple requests without degrading CPU resources. On the next request, a compressed file can be retrieved from disk, which improves performance because the CPU does not have to compress the file again.

❑ **Enable dynamic content compression** — Configures IIS to compress dynamic content. Compression of dynamic application responses can affect CPU resources because IIS does not cache compressed versions of dynamic output. If compression is enabled for dynamic responses and IIS receives a request for a resource that contains dynamic content, the response that IIS sends is newly compressed every time it is requested. Because dynamic compression consumes significant CPU time and memory resources, use it only on servers that have clients with slow network connections but that have CPU time to spare.

❑ **Only compress files larger than (in bytes)** — Defines the minimum file size that you want IIS to compress. The default size is 256 bytes.

❑ **Cache Directory** — Defines the path of a local directory where a static file is cached after it is compressed, either until it expires or until the content changes. For security reasons, this temporary directory must be on a local drive on an NTFS-formatted partition. The directory cannot be compressed and should not be shared.

❑ **Per application pool disk space limit (in MB)** — Sets the maximum amount of space, in megabytes, you want IIS to use when compressing static content. When the "Limit disk space usage" setting is defined, IIS automatically cleans up the temporary directory when the set limit is reached. The default limit is 100 MB per application pool.

When tuning at the web-site level, you only have the option to turn compression on or off by selecting the checkbox next to either "Enable dynamic content compression" or "Enable static content compression."

6. In the Actions pane, click Apply.

Note that dynamic content cannot be compressed and then later cached. An important caveat about compressing dynamic content is that it must be generated and compressed on every hit to the web page. When hosting dynamic content, you should evaluate the cost/benefit ratio of compressing dynamic content. You benefit from better bandwidth management, but it comes at the cost of CPU processing. If your site uses dynamic content extensively and processor utilization (% Processor Time) is already high, you may have to first upgrade the server's processors before enabling HTTP compression.

Web-Site Connections

Using the web-site Performance tab, IIS provides a means for an unlimited number of concurrent connections and an option to limit the number of connections at both the *web server* (global) level and for a particular *web site*. For internal IIS servers, setting the value to an unlimited number avoids additional benchmarking and administration if your connection loads burst beyond anticipated levels. For internal IIS servers, this setting should remain set to unlimited by default, unless the application is mission-critical and high demand.

For externally facing sites, IIS performance will plummet if the number of connections exceeds your system resources — affecting all sessions. All IIS systems have a performance ceiling. For Internet-facing servers, provide a maximum connection figure to protect against denial-of-service scenarios. To arrive at a realistic figure, establish a benchmark for concurrent connections during peak performance, and then add 10%–20% as a margin of error.

To access the web-site tuning options, follow these steps:

1. Open IIS Manager.

2. Double-click on the target server that you want to administer.

3. Double-click the Sites node under the target server.

4. Select the web site you want to administer.

5. In the Actions pane, under the Manage Web Site group, click Advance Settings. The Advanced Settings window is shown in Figure 19-16.

6. In the Behavior group, make any necessary adjustments to the Connection Limits field as appropriate to the nature of your web site.

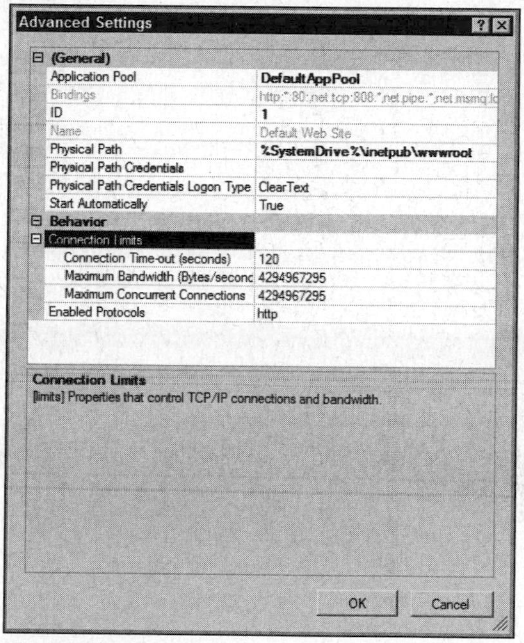

Figure 19-16

Ideally, your web application(s) and server(s) will be tested to identify performance expectations at given connection/activity levels. For example, if an Internet-facing application realizes 200 concurrent connections and performance indicators point to 100% utilization of the server farm, then capping the connection rate to 95% — or 190 concurrent connections — will ensure that servers will remain responsive during a burst in requests.

Summary

Today's technology teams are under constant pressure to do more with less. Getting the most out of your web server is one way to give your company a leg up competitively, and a good way to free your team from having to add and manage expensive capacity. The way to maximize the benefits of any web application is through a good monitoring program and intelligent performance tuning.

This chapter covered some of the monitoring solutions available today, and then covered Microsoft's native tools in some detail. Remember, even if you have a commercial tool, you will still need to open Reliability and Performance Monitor from time to time.

Of course, the purpose of monitoring an IIS server is to collect and present performance data. The main uses for performance data are capacity planning, diagnostics, and performance tuning. To get the data, you can use one of the commercial packages that are available, such as Symantec's i^3 or HP Mercury's SiteScope, along with some terrific tools integrated in Windows Server 2008. Some of those tools that you should become familiar with include Task Manager for quick access to live data on services and applications, and the new Reliability and Performance Monitoring console for rich reports on event traces.

After collecting and reviewing your performance data, you have to put that knowledge to work for you by tuning your platform. You can make major adjustments that may have a drastic impact on capacity and performance. Be sure to consider the range of options, including those settings found under the following sections in this chapter:

❑   Operating system optimizations.

❑   IIS Service optimizations.

❑   Web-site optimizations.

While working our way through the configuration options in this chapter, we offered guidance on how to set them based on the demands of the server, and we provided some specific settings. The advice is offered based on years of experience and Microsoft's best practices, but should be tested and validated in your company before you put your improved configurations into production. After reading this chapter, you are ready to get started with the process of transforming your default web servers into optimized investments.

20

Diagnostics and Troubleshooting

At first glance, "Diagnostics and Troubleshooting" might not strike you as a very interesting chapter. Let's put you at ease from the beginning. Whether you are a casual IIS administrator or an IIS professional, you have probably run into many situations in which you wanted to find out why a page was taking a long time to load, why it hung, why it was consuming so much CPU, or why it failed. In this chapter, we will explore together many of the new and existing features and tools that will help you better manage your web platform.

IIS 7.0 brings with it a wealth of new troubleshooting features which greatly enhance this latest version of Microsoft's web platform. It is easy to get excited about the ability that IIS now gives us to get behind the scenes and gain access to a wealth of information.

This chapter will start off with many new features that IIS 7.0 offers and then will branch off into various other tools built into the operating system and some additional tools that can be downloaded, to make your troubleshooting skills the envy of your fellow administrators.

Types of Issues

It is important to gain an understanding of the type of failures that can be encountered on your web server. IIS 7.0 has built-in support for the following types of errors:

- ❑ Specific errors
- ❑ Hang/time-out issues
- ❑ Resource-intensive issues

Specific Errors

The first type of error is a *specific error*. These are the errors that usually fail quickly and will show an HTTP Error page corresponding to the error (see Figure 20-1). Some errors (for example, those with a 500 HTTP status code) will have customized error pages with extensive information used for troubleshooting and debugging. Specific errors are often the easiest to troubleshoot, as the error message will immediately narrow down the issue, and usually they are easy to reproduce and will fail the same way every time.

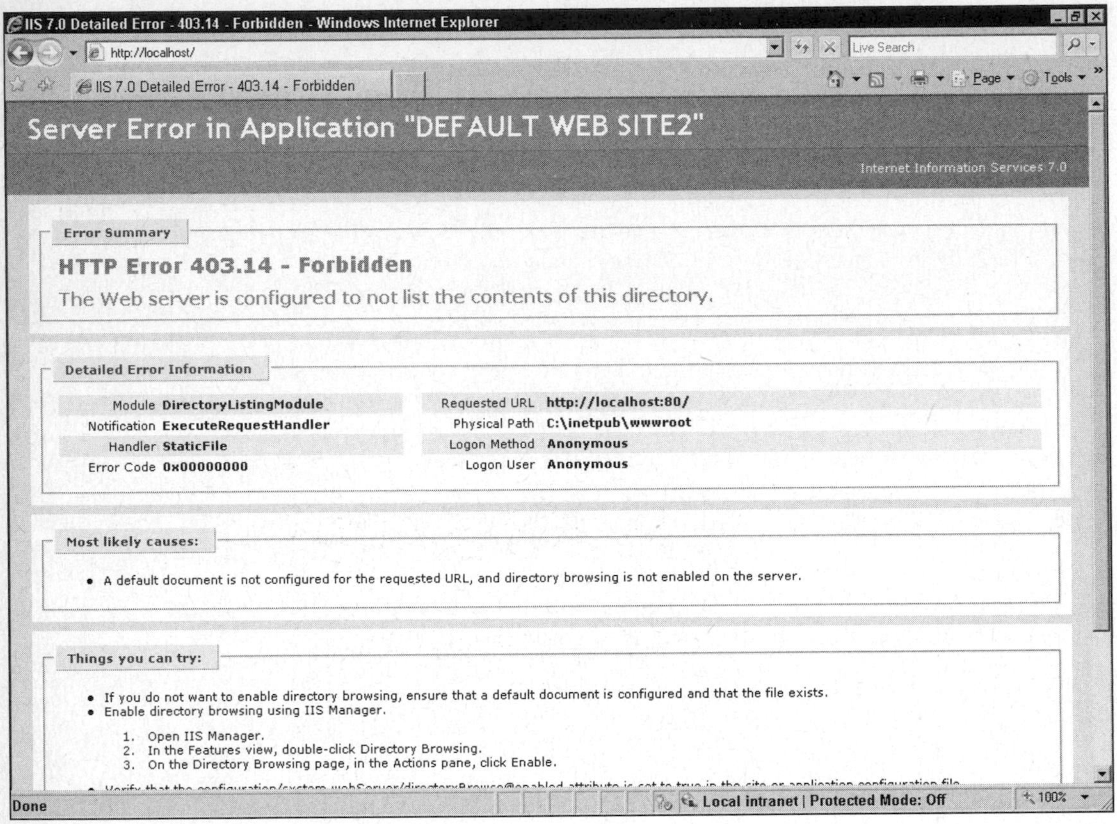

Figure 20-1

IIS 7.0 goes out of the way to give better information than ever before. Take, for instance, a case in which you forget to put in a default document. The error page that IIS 7.0 serves up will tell you exactly what is happening, providing detailed error information, most likely causes, suggestions on what you can try, and links to further information.

Hang/Time-out Issues

The second type of error is a *hang* or *time-out error*. In past versions of IIS, these were often very difficult to troubleshoot. The error would often simply say that there was a time-out, without giving any clues as to the cause. What makes these even more difficult to troubleshoot is that they can be hard to reproduce, and these type of errors will often take a long time before failing (90 seconds is a common time-out value used by IIS and various web browsers); thus, each time you want to test or see the error again, you may need to wait a long time.

With IIS 7.0, troubleshooting hang and time-out issues gets much easier with Failed Request Tracing and RSCA, which are covered in-depth later in the chapter.

Resource-Intensive and Slowness Issues

The final category of errors is *resource-intensive* and *slowness issues*. They can cause the server's CPU to spike, cause excessive disk usage, high memory usage, or overutilize almost any resource. These are generally the most difficult issues to resolve. The negative effects of this issue are often not noticed immediately, and sometimes are not even caught during pre-production load testing if the issue occurs in a situation in which the testing team did not think to test. Instead, after heavy load on the server or under certain unique circumstances, the site can start to bog down. When you start to troubleshoot the error, the only clue that you might have is that the site is running slower than normal. Now it is your responsibility to find out what is causing the slowness. It could be the server, the network, the database server, a third-party component — it could be nearly anything. Figure 20-2 shows Windows Task Manager during an issue of intermittent but heavy CPU usage.

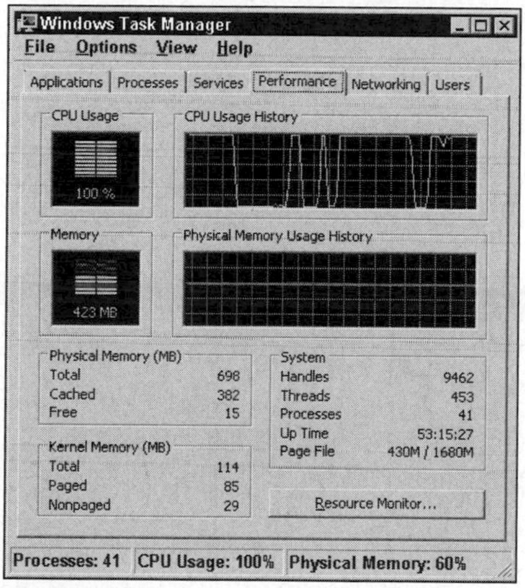

Figure 20-2

As with hang and time-out issues, Failed Request Tracing is at your service. IIS 7.0 enables you to determine which pages are taking a long time to run and what part of the page is currently being processed, usually leading to the cause of the issue.

It is also possible to have a combination of issues, either one error causing another error, or multiple independent issues that need to be solved at the same time. The rest of this chapter covers tools and troubleshooting steps to solve all three of these types of issues.

Runtime Status and Control API (RSCA)

IIS 7.0 allows you to look into the real-time state of the server, including all running page requests, application domains, and active sites. This is a major leap forward from IIS 6.0 and makes troubleshooting long-lasting page requests much easier. This is done through the Runtime Status and Control API (RSCA). Don't let the term "API" (application programming interface) in the name scare you. RSCA is used many different ways, including with IIS Manager and AppCmd.exe.

IIS Manager is one of the most straightforward means of viewing the RSCA data. Although the location in IIS Manager for RSCA makes sense when you think about it, it's not easy to find the first time. The next section shows how RSCA is used to view running worker processes.

Viewing Worker Processes

You can view the running requests at the server level in IIS Manager by double-clicking on the Worker Processes icon (see Figure 20-3).

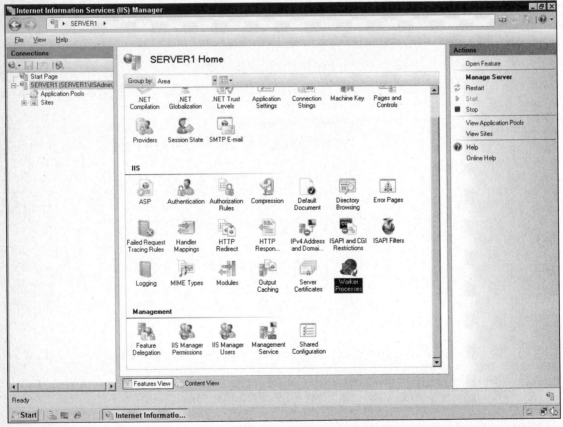

Figure 20-3

Double-click the Worker Processes icon at the server level to bring up a view of all running worker processes. Figure 20-4 shows the Worker Processes screen with one worker process running. Obviously, this can have many more than one worker process. There can be dozens or even hundreds of running worker processes, depending on how many sites and application pools you have on your server.

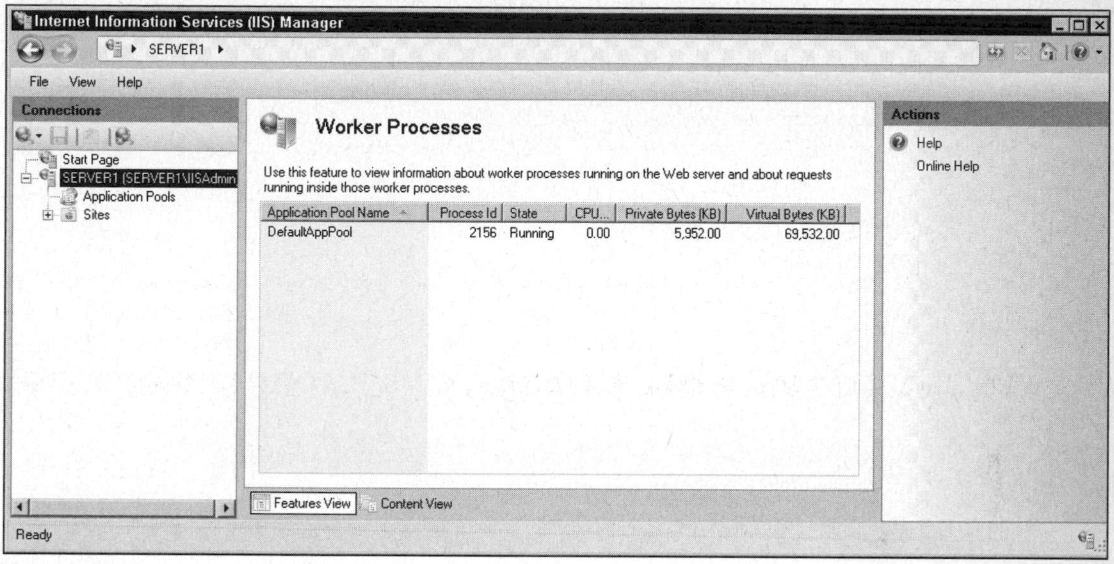

Figure 20-4

Because this is active data, only current worker processes will be shown here. This may change often. In Chapter 8, we discuss application pools in depth, but as a general rule, if web gardens are not enabled, there should be one worker process for each application pool, and often not all applications pools will have a running worker process. Application pools will not start until the first time they are used, and if the idle-time-out value is reached because a site has not been visited in a while, an application pool will shut down. In these cases, there will not be a worker process for that application pool.

In addition, since this is real-time data, if an application pool is recycled or killed, the process ID will change, and the worker process that you are watching may seem to disappear. This is the nature of real-time process information.

The Worker Processes view will show the Application Pool Name, Process ID, current State, CPU, Private Bytes, and Virtual Bytes.

Virtual bytes and private bytes are interesting counters to understand. Virtual bytes refers to the size in bytes of the virtual address space that the process is using. This doesn't necessarily correspond to physical memory or disk usage. Private bytes refers to the size in bytes of memory that the process has allocated. This space cannot be shared by other processes. Since different tools in Windows Server 2008 display them differently, it is helpful to know the Private bytes and Virtual bytes values and what they correspond to within the different tools.

❑   **Task Manager** — In Task Manager, the Commit Size column corresponds to the Private Bytes value in RSCA. The Commit Size column is not shown by default, however. To display it, go to View ➪ Select Columns, and add it. There is no matching column in Task Manager for Virtual Bytes.

❑ **Performance Monitor** — In Performance Monitor, both names match the RSCA names. The only difference between the two tools is that RSCA reports the value in kilobytes, whereas Performance Monitor reports it in bytes. To have the value match exactly, divide the Performance Monitor value by 1024.

In Performance Monitor, you can view the memory usage for each worker process by selecting the Process counter and the w3wp Instance. On a busy server, there may be multiple w3wp processes, which can make this more difficult. You will need to view the Process ID (PID) value to confirm which worker process it really is.

To see a list of all running worker processes using `AppCmd.exe`, run the following (see Figure 20-5):

```
appcmd.exe list wp
```

AppCmd.exe is in %windir%\system32\inetsrv, which isn't in the system path; thus you must either add it to the system path, navigate to %windir%\system32\inetsrv, or enter the full page like so: %windir%\system32\inetsrv\appcmd.exe list wp. To add the inetsrv folder to the system path for the duration of the life of that command prompt session, you can run the following command: path=%path%;%windir%\system32\inetsrv.

Figure 20-5

This will do the equivalent of what IISApp.vbs did in IIS 6.0. If you were not familiar with IISApp.vbs, it was new to IIS 6.0 and had a single purpose, which was to list or recycle running worker processes on the server.

It is possible to filter based on the application pool name or worker process ID. For example, `appcmd.exe list wp /apppool.name:DefaultAppPool` or `appcmd.exe list wp /wp.name:2668` (`appcmd.exe list wp 2668` is a shorthand way to do the same), respectively.

Here is a simple VBScript example using WMI that will create output similar to `appcmd list wp`:

```
Set oService = GetObject("winmgmts:root\WebAdministration")

Set oWorkerProcesses = oService.InstancesOf("WorkerProcess")

For Each WP In oWorkerProcesses
   strPID = "WP """ & WP.ProcessId & """"
   strAppPool = "(applicationPool:" _
      & WP. AppPoolName & ")"
   WScript.echo(strPID & " " & strAppPool)
Next
```

This will make a call to the `WebAdministration` namespace, get a list of all worker processes, and then loop through each worker process and output its Process ID and application pool name.

Viewing Page Requests

Now it's time to enter a hidden world that goes even deeper. At first glance, it's easy to miss that you can drill into the worker processes to see all running page requests. Double-click on the worker process that you want to drill into to see all the page requests for that worker process (see Figure 20-6).

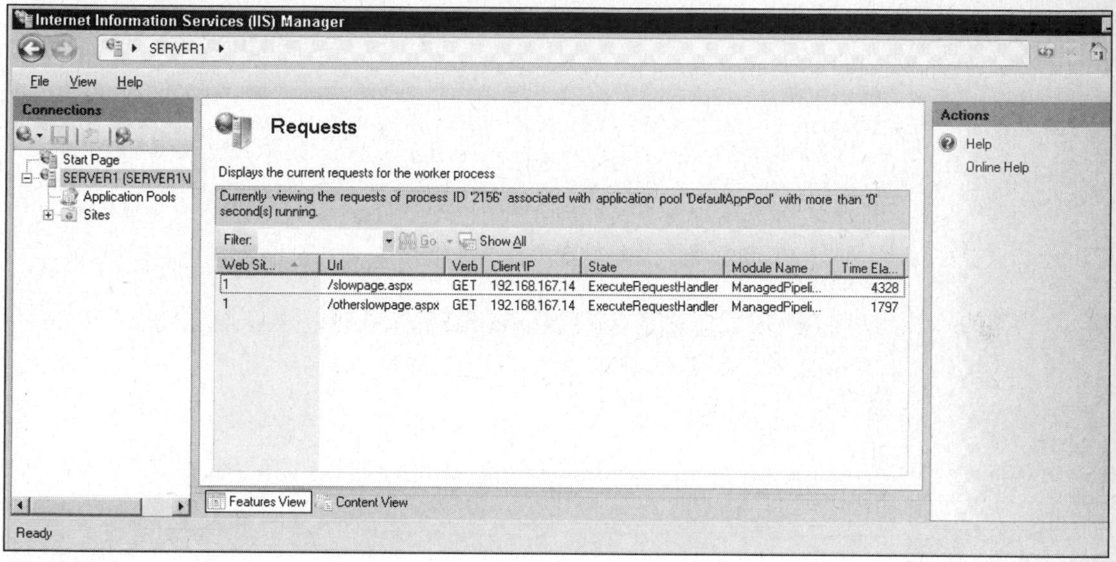

Figure 20-6

Here you can find a list of all running page requests. These are active pages, so it will be difficult to catch any page that lives for less than a second. For testing, you can write a simple page that calls a Sleep command. Create a file, call it sleep.aspx and place the following in it::

```
<% System.Threading.Thread.Sleep(10000) %>
Done
```

Since the time is in milliseconds, a value of `10000` will cause the page to sleep for 10 seconds.

After double-clicking on the worker process in the Worker Processes section, you will be taken to the Requests section, which shows the Web Site ID, Url, Verb, Client IP Address, State, Module Name, and Time Elapsed for each running page request. It is also interesting to note that if you hit a default page without putting the full path (for example, `http://localhost/`), it will show two requests: one for the default and one for the specific page.

Requests can be filtered based on the time that they take to run; known as the Time Elapsed. Although it is not obvious, the Filter field in the Requests section is for the Time Elapsed. Enter a number of seconds between 0 and 2,147,482 into the Filter field and press Go. This will show all page requests that have been running for as long as or longer than the time you entered in the filter. To clear the filter, click the Show All button.

You can also use `AppCmd.exe` to obtain the same information. You can pass additional parameters to filter for the request ID, site name, worker process ID, application pool name, and time elapsed. To view all running requests on the server, run the following:

```
appcmd.exe list request
```

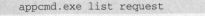

```
Administrator: Command Prompt                                    _ □ ×

C:\Windows\System32\inetsrv>appcmd list request

C:\Windows\System32\inetsrv>appcmd list request
REQUEST "f700000080000016" <url:GET /otherslowpage.aspx, time:4296 msec, client:
192.168.167.14, stage:ExecuteRequestHandler, module:ManagedPipelineHandler>
REQUEST "f600000080000004" <url:GET /slowpage.aspx, time:2984 msec, client:192.1
68.167.14, stage:ExecuteRequestHandler, module:ManagedPipelineHandler>

C:\Windows\System32\inetsrv>_
```

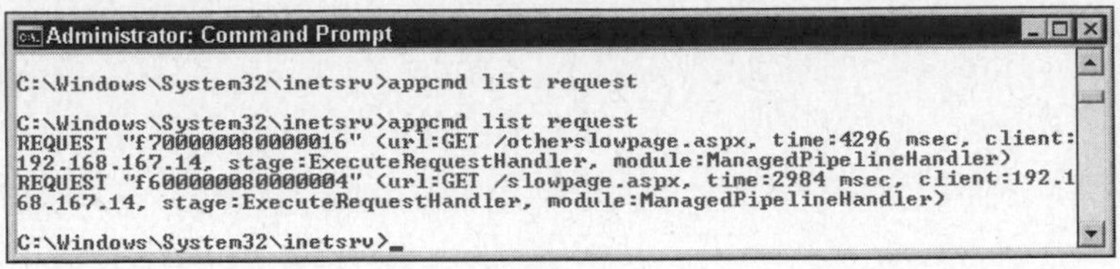

Figure 20-7

Figure 20-7 shows `AppCmd.exe` run from the command line with two long running requests. There can be many more than two running requests on a server at any given time, so it is often useful to narrow it down further. The length of time that the pages have been running is a useful filter. You can also filter based on the identifier, worker process PID, application pool name, and web-site name. To get the syntax and examples for each, type `AppCmd.exe list request /?` from the `%windir%\system32\inetsrv` folder. To see page requests that have been running for more than 5 seconds (5,000 milliseconds), run the following command (see Figure 20-8):

```
appcmd.exe list request /elapsed:5000
```

```
Administrator: Command Prompt                                    _ □ ×

C:\Windows\System32\inetsrv>appcmd list request /elapsed:5000
REQUEST "f600000080000009" <url:GET /slowpage.aspx, time:8531 msec, client:192.1
68.167.14, stage:ExecuteRequestHandler, module:ManagedPipelineHandler>

C:\Windows\System32\inetsrv>_
```

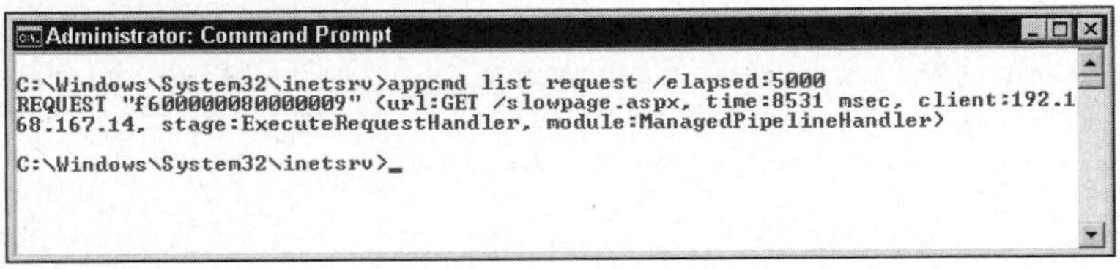

Figure 20-8

The same information can be retrieved using WMI or `Microsoft.Web.Administration`, and is explained in more depth in Chapter 17, "Programmatic Configuration and Management."

Viewing Application Domains

Application domains (aka "AppDomains") are a key part of ASP.NET, but they have been mostly hidden in the past. An *application domain* is an isolated environment where applications exist. IIS creates separate AppDomains for each folder that is set as an application. Additionally, from code, developers can set their own AppDomains for code isolation.

The `WebAdministration` WMI namespace, and `Microsoft.Web.Administration` each expose application domains and give the ability to unload them.

Here is a simple VBScript example using WMI that will allow you to view all the running application domains:

```
Set oService = GetObject("winmgmts:root\WebAdministration")

Set oAppDomains = oService.InstancesOf("AppDomain")

For Each AppDomain In oAppDomains
  WScript.echo("ID: " & AppDomain.Id)
  WScript.echo("  ApplicationPath: " & AppDomain.ApplicationPath)
  WScript.echo("  PhysicalPath:    " & AppDomain.PhysicalPath)
  WScript.echo("  Process Id:      " & AppDomain.ProcessId)
  WScript.echo("  SiteName:        " & AppDomain.SiteName)
  WScript.echo("  IsIdle:          " & AppDomain.IsIdle)
  WScript.echo("")
Next
```

This example uses the WebAdministration namespace, gets all AppDomains on the server, loops through them, and outputs key information on the AppDomain.

As you can see, RSCA offers a lot of information through a variety of methods. Using RSCA, the system administrator can view running processes, page requests, application domains, and much more. This can all be accessed in real time without installing a third-party product and without a system restart to install it.

IIS 7.0 Error Pages

Like previous versions of IIS, IIS 7.0 can point to customized error pages. These can be created uniquely for your environment to allow you to customize what the end-users see when they encounter an error — to hide the error details and display a friendly page that looks like the rest of the site. You can also create it to send detailed information to you when there is a failure. Custom error pages can be set for each HTTP status code and optionally sub-status codes (status codes are covered in a later section).

There are two types of errors that IIS 7.0 can return:

❑   **Custom Errors** — Custom Errors are errors that regular end-users of the web site will see. They contain a brief description of the error, but should not contain any sensitive information that you do not want an end-user to see. You can customize this, so you can put as little or as much on this page as you want. Generally, though, it should hide the real error and display a friendly page to the end-user.

❑   **Detailed Errors** — Detailed Errors contain a wealth of information meant for local administrators and developers. Because it can contain sensitive information about the error, it should not be shown to end-users. The Detailed Errors are meant to provide valuable information to the administrators and developers to help troubleshoot failures and errors on the server.

IIS 7.0 has a convenient method of displaying a different error to end-users than to administrators and developers. This method was modeled by ASP.NET, so if you know ASP.NET, you will already be familiar with this concept. By default, IIS 7.0 will display a Detailed Error when the page request comes from the local server, and display a Custom Error when the page request comes from anything but the local server. This allows the local administrator or developer to view the page while on the local server and receive a helpful and detailed error message, while the end-users will receive a different error message that doesn't expose the sensitive information about the error.

Internet Explorer's default setting is to show a friendly error message. Microsoft implemented this feature because many web servers would return a plain HTTP status code and a one- or two-word description (such as "Internal Error"), which many novice users would struggle to understand. Internet Explorer shows the error message returned by the server if it exceeds a certain size (indicating that the server is returning a descriptive error message). The sizes can be found in Microsoft KB218155 (`http://support.microsoft.com/?id=218155`*). To disable this feature, select Tools ⇨ Internet Options ⇨ Advanced and uncheck the checkbox titled "Show friendly HTTP error messages."*

The default behavior can be changed so that, rather than different error pages depending on where the page request originated from, you can have all requests be Detailed Errors or all requests be Custom Errors. This will be explained shortly.

While IIS 7.0 has greatly improved the error page handling, it hasn't taken over the error handling for ASP.NET pages by default. All pages that are handled by ASP.NET will still use the ASP.NET error handler and will still receive the Custom and Detailed Error pages that ASP.NET provides. This can be confusing, since some pages have the new IIS 7.0 Custom Error pages while others have the ASP.NET error pages. This is by design, but it can be changed. The `existingResponse` attribute on the `httpErrors` element can be set to the following:

❏ **Auto** — This will allow the application (in this case ASP.NET) to determine whether it should use its own error pages or allow IIS to use its error pages. This is the default, which means that ASP.NET pages will use the ASP.NET error pages while most non-ASP.NET pages will use the IIS 7.0 Custom Error pages.

❏ **Replace** — This forces IIS to always use the IIS 7.0 Error Pages. The benefit is that the error pages will be consistent and will always be controlled in the same manner, but IIS 7.0 doesn't provide the same detailed information on ASP.NET requests as ASP.NET does.

❏ **PassThrough** — This will allow the error pages of the application to pass through without IIS 7.0 intercepting them and displaying its own error pages. With this setting selected, not even static and other generic pages will display the IIS 7.0 Custom Error pages.

You can change between modes by using `AppCmd.exe`. Here is how you can set the mode to `Replace`:

```
appcmd.exe set config /section:httpErrors /existingResponse:Replace
```

To change back to `Auto`, or to change to `PassThrough`, just run the same command but change the `Replace` with `Auto` or `PassThrough`.

Customizing Custom Error Pages

IIS 7.0 Error Pages can be changed in IIS Manager at the server, site or application level. The interface is essentially the same. Figure 20-9 shows the Error Pages icon at the site level.

To manage Error Pages in IIS Manager, double-click the Error Pages icon. This will bring you to a list of status codes and their settings (see Figure 20-10). From here you can change any of the existing error pages, or add new error pages. It's important to note that this allows you to change the Custom Error pages only, and not the Detailed Error pages.

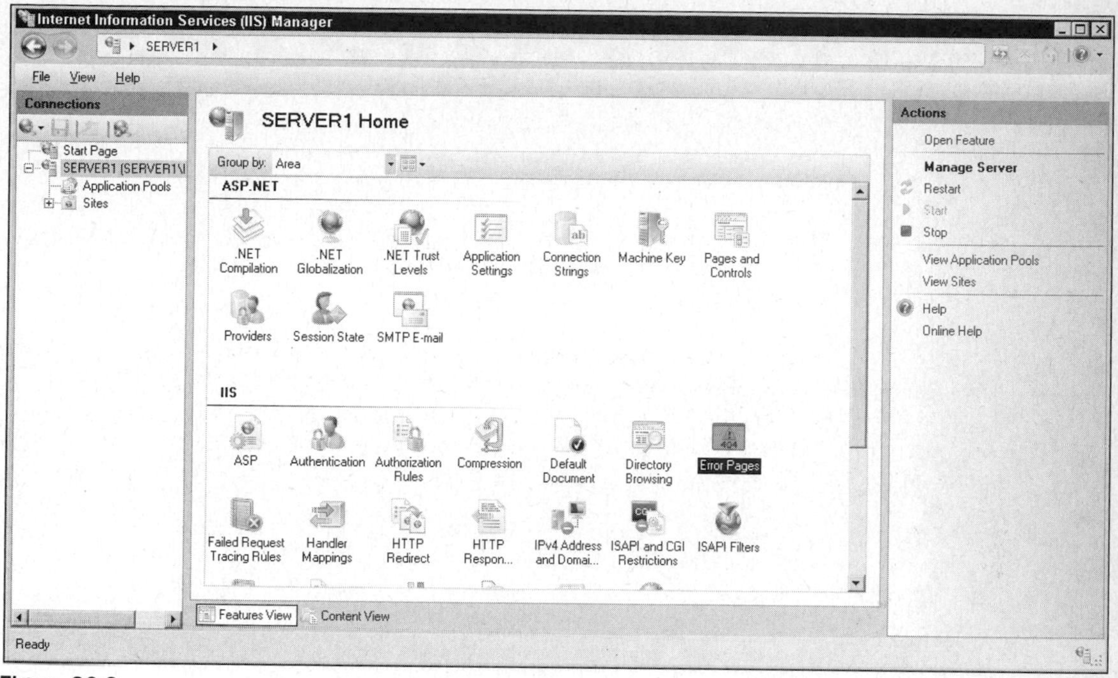

Figure 20-9

The Detailed Error pages cannot be changed unless you replace the CustomErrorModule (custerr.dll) Module in IIS 7.0, but you generally won't need to change the Detailed Error pages since they are meant to be seen by the system administrator or developer only, and don't need to be customized to look like the rest of the site.

From the IIS Manager Error Pages tool, you can edit the existing error pages or add a new error page. When adding new error pages, you can set the major status code, and have the option to set the sub-status code as well. This means, for example, that a 403.1 and 403.3 error page will return the same error page. Appendix B shows a detailed list of status codes and a description of what they mean.

When creating or editing an error page, you can choose from one of three ways that IIS will display an error page. They are:

❑ **Insert content from static file into the error response** — Displays a simple static page. This is the default, and it is fast because it is not preprocessed by the ASP.NET engine. You can select a file anywhere on the system. You can also serve up a different page for different languages, which will be covered in the next section.

❑ **Execute a URL on this site** — Displays the page that you specify, but it will process it with the ASP.NET engine to allow you to have dynamic content. It's important to note that this page must be a relative URL, and it must be in the same application pool as the page that caused the error.

Part 4: Maintaining and Operating IIS 7.0

❑ **Respond with a 302 redirect** — Redirects the page request to a new page, which can be on the same server or on a different server, so there is no requirement to be in the same application pool.

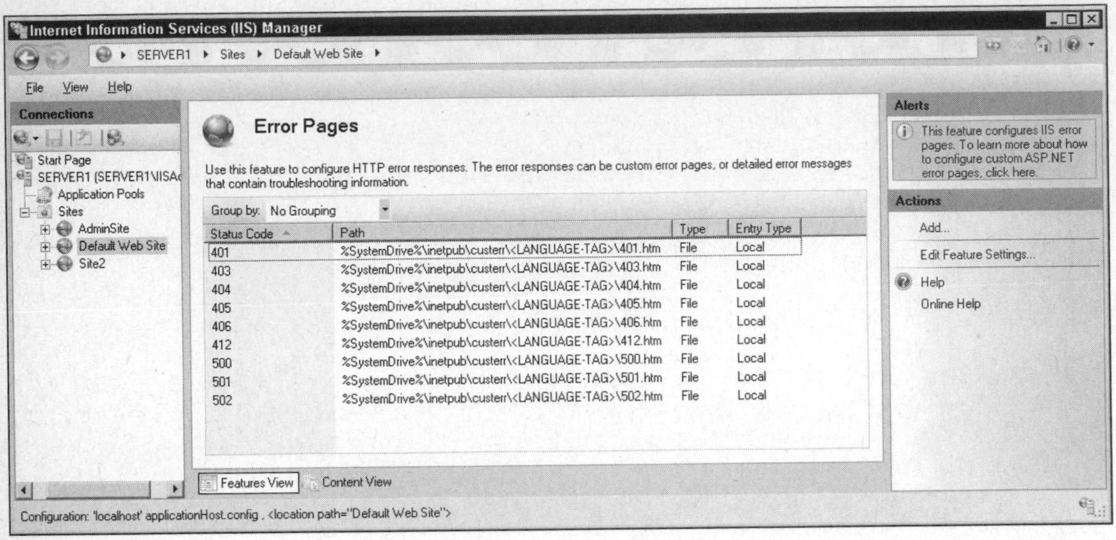

Figure 20-10

Within this same tool in IIS Manager, you can change between the three error response types: *Custom error pages, Detailed errors,* and *Detailed errors for local requests and custom error pages for remote requests.* You can get to this setting window by clicking on "Edit Feature Settings" from the right-hand Actions pane. Figure 20-11 shows the Edit Error Pages Settings window.

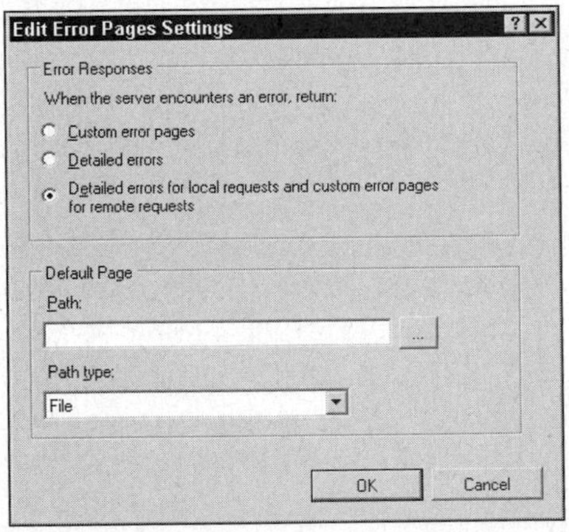

Figure 20-11

Multiple Language Support

IIS 7.0 supports multiple languages so that different error pages can be displayed for different browsers. Modern browsers send an HTTP header with the web request that specifies the language of the client. For example, a browser with a client language of English will send the following HTTP header: `Accept-Language: en-us.`

When setting Custom Error pages in IIS as described in the last section, if you select "Insert content from static file into the error response" for the Custom Error type, there is a checkbox that says "Try to return the error in the client language." If you check that, click on the "Set" button for a new dialog box which allows you to set the *Root directory path* and *Relative file path*. With this setting, when an error occurs, IIS will piece together the root directory + language + relative file path. The default Custom Error folder on an English version of Windows Server 2008 is `%SystemDrive%\inetpub\custerr\en-US\.`

Additional Language Packs can be obtained from `www.microsoft.com/downloads`.

The way that IIS handles sub-status codes is by first checking if there is a specific error page set for the sub-status code, and if there is not one set, it will check if there is a specific error page for the major status code. If there is no custom error page set for the major status code, it will check to see if a default error page has been set and use it.

HTTP Status Codes

When users try to access content on a server that is running IIS through HTTP or File Transfer Protocol (FTP), IIS returns a numeric code that indicates the status of the request. This status code is recorded in the IIS log, and it may also be displayed in the Web browser or FTP client. The status code can indicate whether a particular request is successful or unsuccessful and can also reveal the exact reason that a request is unsuccessful.

Appendix B shows all the status and sub-status codes in more detail. Here is a list of the major status code categories:

- ❑ **1xx — Informational** — These status codes indicate a provisional response. The client should be prepared to receive one or more 1xx responses before receiving a regular response.

- ❑ **2xx — Success** — This class of status codes indicates that the server successfully accepted the client request.

- ❑ **3xx — Redirection** — The client browser must take more action to fulfill the request. For example, the browser may have to request a different page on the server or repeat the request by using a proxy server.

- ❑ **4xx — Client Error** — An error occurs, and the client appears to be at fault. For example, the client may request a page that does not exist, or the client may not provide valid authentication information.

- ❑ **5xx — Server Error** — The server cannot complete the request because it encounters an error.

FTP Status Codes

In addition to the HTTP status codes, there are several FTP status codes that can be used for troubleshooting FTP-related issues:

- ❏ **1xx — Positive Preliminary Reply** — These status codes indicate that an action has started successfully, but the client expects another reply before it continues with a new command.

- ❏ **2xx — Positive Completion Reply** — An action has successfully completed. The client can execute a new command.

- ❏ **3xx — Positive Intermediate Reply** — The command was successful, but the server requires additional information from the client to complete processing the request.

- ❏ **4xx — Transient Negative Completion Reply** — The command was not successful, but the error is temporary. If the client retries the command, it may succeed.

- ❏ **5xx — Permanent Negative Completion Reply** — The command was not successful, and the error is permanent. If the client retries the command, it receives the same error.

Failed Request Tracing

Failed Request Tracing is one of the most welcome features in IIS 7.0. It enables you to gain detailed information about any page request and to be able to capture data based on the criteria that you define. This is not simply a tool for your development computer; this is a full-fledged, production-ready method of troubleshooting failures.

But what is even better is that as complex as it sounds, it really is not difficult at all. In the past, an IIS administrator would be required to rely on third-party tools to get inside the ASP.NET events to gain real-time insight into potential issues. These tools are usually expensive, have a steep learning curve, and often require a reset of IIS during installation. Tracing in Windows Server 2003 SP1 brought the ability to see detailed debugging information free of charge and without installation downtime on the server, but the steps required to figure it out would scare the casual user.

With Failed Request Tracing in IIS 7.0, however, troubleshooting can be done at any time without downtime, with intangible performance overhead on the server, and with such ease of use that anyone can figure it out in a few minutes.

Failed Request Tracing was formally nicknamed *FREB*, or *Failed Request Event Buffering*, by the IIS development team. It is used to watch for all incoming requests that meet certain criteria and will save detailed information about the entire page request to disk in an easy-to-read XML format.

Three steps are required to start FREB logging to disk:

1. Ensure that Tracing is installed on the server. You can do this by going to Start Í Search box, typing **Server Manager**, and pressing Enter. Expand the Roles section in the left-hand section, right-click on Web Server (IIS) and click Add Role Service. Check Tracing in the Health and Diagnostics section. Click Next and then Install to complete the install.

2. Create a new tracing rule, as detailed in the following "Failed Request Tracing Rules Setup" section.

3. It is easy to miss the second step, which is to actually *turn it on*. Creating a rule does not automatically enable it, as you might assume. To enable FREB, go to the site level and double-click the Failed Request Tracing Rules icon. Then, in the Actions pane, click Edit Site Tracing. There is a checkbox labeled Enable that is off by default. Enable that and select OK.

Failed Request Tracing Rules Setup

It would not be practical to have all requests saved to disk, especially on a busy production server. You will want to narrow it down to capture the exact problem page. FREB provides filter options to narrow it down quite significantly. There are three steps to the wizard in IIS Manager:

- ❏ Specify Content to Trace.
- ❏ Define Trace Conditions.
- ❏ Select Trace Providers.

To begin creating a FREB rule from the server, site, or subfolder level, double-click the Failed Request Tracing Rules icon. This will open the Failed Request Tracing Rules tool as shown in Figure 20-12.

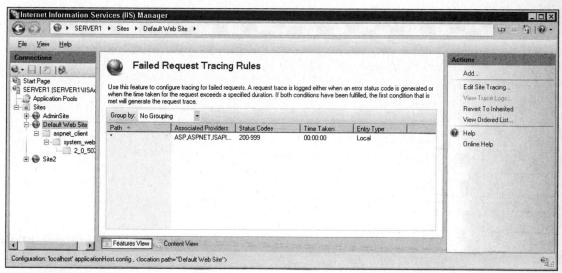

Figure 20-12

To create a new Failed Request Tracing Rule, click on the Add link in the Actions pane. The following three subsections will take you through the three pages of the wizard and cover the various options available to you.

Specify Content to Trace

The first step of the wizard gives you the ability to choose all content, or a specific type of content. You can choose All content, ASP.NET, Classic ASP, or Custom (see Figure 20-13).

This step is pretty straightforward. If you would like to narrow down to a single failed page, select Custom and enter the page name. For multiple pages, you must set up a new rule for each page. The Custom field does not allow you to enter multiple content types, although an asterisk (*) is allowed for wildcard characters. For example, staff*.aspx will catch staff.aspx, staff_edit.aspx and any other pages that start with staff and have an extension of aspx.

Click Next to go to the next step.

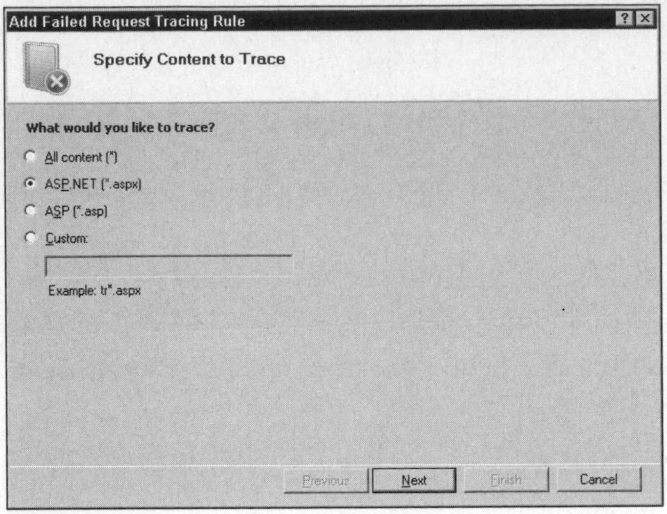

Figure 20-13

Define Trace Conditions

The second filter step sets the *status code*, time taken and event severity. The status code field allows selecting multiple status code types, separated by a comma. For example, if you want to select all 500 errors, simply enter **500**. If you want to narrow down to 500 and 401.5 errors (Authorization failed by ISAPI/CGI application), then you can enter **401.5,500** in the "Status code" box (see Figure 20-14).

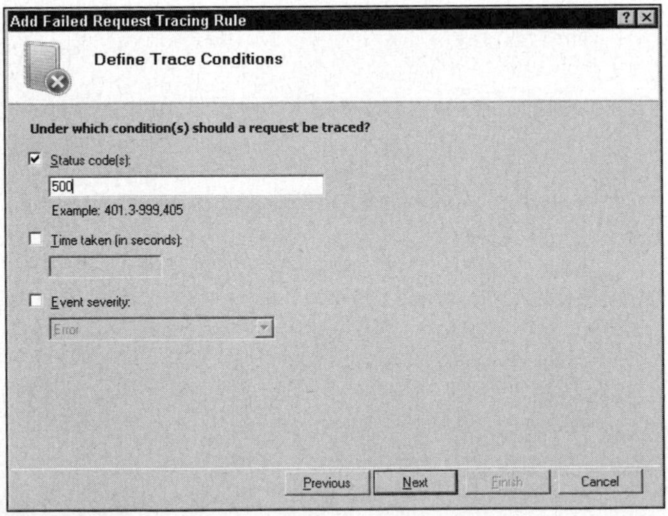

Figure 20-14

HTTP 200 status codes are also allowed. Even though the name of the tool is "Failed" Request Tracing, it will allow successful pages to be saved as well. This is a great way to find out how fast your code is running and which part of your code is taking the longest to process.

The Time taken field allows you to set the minimum time (in seconds) that the page must take to complete before it is reported on. This is as easy as it seems. Since it is optional, if desired, check the checkbox to enable it, and enter the number of seconds that it should take before a request page trace is saved. Set it to whatever you feel is low enough to catch the issue, but high enough to capture the least amount of non-relevant pages as possible.

Click Next to go to the next step.

Select Trace Providers

The final step of the wizard is to select the trace providers and the verbosity (see Figure 20-15). There are four providers by default — ASP, ASP.NET, ISAPI, and WWW Server — but, like virtually everything else in IIS, these can be extended or added to. Some providers overlap each other, and some are mutually exclusive. For example, the WWW Server provider gains information about every page request, whereas the ASP and ASP.NET providers will not both capture information for the same request.

The default configuration has all providers selected with a Verbosity setting of "Verbose." This will capture everything possible, but you can turn off anything that you do not require so that you can minimize the information that is captured.

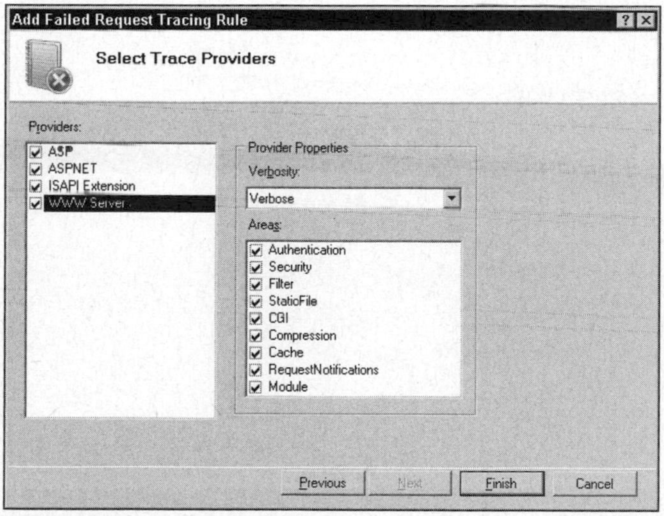

Figure 20-15

After making your choices, select Finish. If tracing has not been enabled yet, finishing the wizard will not enable it for you. From the Failed Request Tracing Rules screen, click Edit Site Tracing. The resulting screen allows you to enable tracing for that site. You can also set the path and maximum number of trace files to store. Tracing is disabled by default. This is so that if you set certain tracing rules at the global level, tracing will not start writing to disk for all web sites unless you purposefully turn them on.

Make sure to take note of the path where the trace files are placed. By default they are in `%SystemDrive%\inetpub\logs\FailedReqLogFiles\{subfolder}\`. When tracing writes to disk, it will place the trace files in a subfolder for that web site (for example, W3SVC1).

Reading the XML Trace Logs

Once you have set up the files and captured some data, you can view the XML trace file by navigating to the logging folder. The files are numbered in successive order, with the file date stamp giving out the precise time that it was captured. Open the XML file that you want using your favorite XML viewer (for example, Internet Explorer). The trace files include a wealth of information about the page request, ranging from the time that it takes to the failures that occur in each event. The `freb.xsl` file that comes with Windows Server 2008 has a number of tabs including the Performance View tab that shows details about each event of the page lifecycle, sorted by the duration of time spent in each event (see Figure 20-16).

The first time that you attempt to view one of the FREB trace files in Internet Explorer, you may receive a warning that content is being blocked for "about:internet." Be sure to add "about:internet" to either the Local intranet or Trusted sites zone. If you don't, you will receive an error that says "Security settings do not allow the execution of script code within this stylesheet." You will get this message because the freb.xsl file has scripts in it which Internet Explorer will not run without specific authorization.

If you have User Account Control (UAC) enabled, you may not see the "Add" button in the warning dialogue box, so you will need to manually go to Tools ➪ Internet Options ➪ Security to add it.

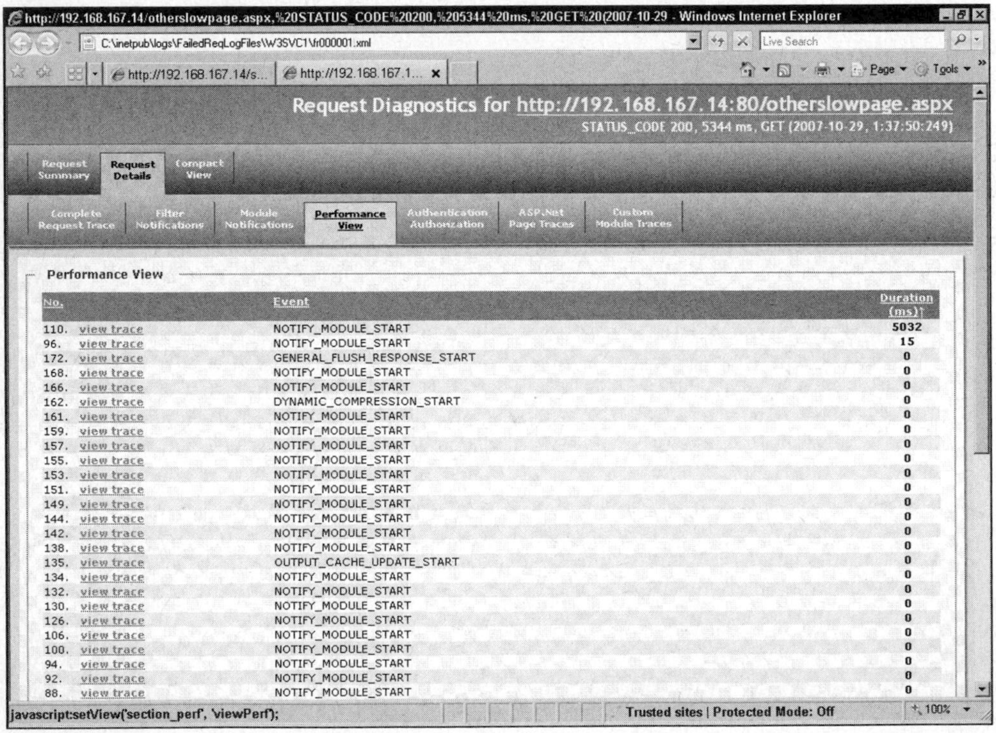

Figure 20-16

With this information in hand, you can tell which page caused the issue, if you didn't know that already, how long it took to run, and which event in the page lifecycle took the most time.

> *The top line in the XML output file (see Figure 20-16) shows the URL that was used to make the request. It will not automatically include the default document name if the original request didn't include it. Therefore,* `http://yoursite.com/` *is the request for whatever your default document is, which is commonly default.aspx.*

The other sections of the XML file contain valuable information about that particular page request. Failed Tracing, which is new in IIS 7.0, may turn out to be a favorite for many system administrators trying to solve hang/time-out and resource-intensive and slowness issues.

Logging

No web server would be complete without detailed logging of every hit to the server. This includes not just page requests but images, files, HEAD requests, and virtually every request made to the web server. IIS has always had logging, and IIS 7.0 is no exception.

The default location for the log files has changed from previous versions. It is now `%SystemDrive%\inetpub\logs\LogFiles`. By default, each web site has its own set of logs, but this can be changed so that logging is per server.

> *The per-site logs are placed in their own folder, which is named by the site ID. Therefore, by default, a site with a site ID of 10 would have its log files saved to* `%SystemDrive%\inetpub\logs\LogFiles\w3svc10\`.

The log settings can be changed in IIS Manager at the server, site, application or file level. However, not all settings are applicable at all levels. For example, the server level is the only place where you can set the encoding type and whether logging is per site or per server.

To change the log settings, double-click the Logging icon in IIS Manager. Most settings are set in the main Logging pane, but enabling and disabling logging is set in the Actions pane on the right.

> *Beside the Format drop-down list is a Select Fields button. This allows you to specify which fields are logged to disk. Three fields that aren't enabled by default that we recommend enabling are Bytes Sent, Bytes Received, and Referrer (Time Taken was another good setting to add in IIS 6.0 but is now a default in IIS 7.0). These fields will be read by most statistics programs and provide valuable information that is worth recording. It is worth adding these fields with every new server build.*

Log files can be read in various ways and provide valuable information for troubleshooting. Logs can also be used by the web site design team and marketing team, to know how many people have visited the site, where they spent time, how they got there, and what browser or tool they used to view the web site.

The following are some common means of reading the log files:

❑ Using third-party programs such as Google Analytics, SmarterTools SmarterStats, WebTrends Analytics, or any of the multitude of choices out there.

❑ Viewing the files in their raw format using tools such as Notepad, WordPad, or UltraEdit.

❑ Using a log reader tool like Log Parser. (Log Parser is explained in more detail below in this chapter.)

Log data files can be used for marketing and to know how visitors are using the site, but they can also be used to track hacking attempts, find out which pages are viewed when server resources spike, or to gather other valuable information.

ASP.NET Tracing

ASP.NET tracing is a powerful tool to gain valuable information when troubleshooting dynamic code. While there isn't anything new to IIS 7.0 in this tracing section, it is a key tool to understand.

ASP.NET Tracing provides detailed information about each page that is run. Unlike Failed Request Tracing, which records the information to an XML format saved to disk, page-level tracing can be displayed within the page itself, by using the ASP.NET trace viewer, or through code. This enables the developer or system administrator to easily view detailed information about the entire page request, including the precise time-stamps of all of the page events, cookie and session state information, request and response and header information, and plenty of other information.

Figure 20-17 shows a small portion of a page-level trace. This trace is added to the bottom of the existing page, below your normal content. This is ideal during development, but obviously not meant for pro-duction because of the detailed information that is embedded into the page for everyone to see. Notice the custom trace information and the timestamps, which are approximately 1000 milliseconds apart from each other. The following code was added to the page in Figure 20-17:

```
' Trace.Write information before the pause.
Trace.Write("Custom", "We are Sleeping for 1000 milliseconds")

' Pause/Sleep for 1 second.
System.Threading.Thread.Sleep(1000)

' Trace.Write to show when the pause has completed.
Trace.Write("Custom", "Done sleeping, time to wake up.")
```

As you can see, the custom information from the page is displayed in the trace report, including the time before and after the 1-second sleep. Notice that the "From First(s)" column increased by 1 second, which is what we instructed the page to do. As you can see, tracing allows you to troubleshoot the length of time that various parts of the page take to run, potentially uncovering performance issues on the web sites that you troubleshoot. With ASP.NET tracing, it makes it easier to tell if a slow loading page is caused by a web service call, a database call, the time to render a custom image, or something else within the code.

Enabling ASP.NET Tracing

Neither page-level nor application-level tracing is enabled by default, so it must be enabled for you to use it. ASP.NET tracing can be enabled in several ways. The most straightforward is to enable it at the page level by adding the following directive to the top of the ASP.NET page code:

```
<%@ Page Trace="true" %>
```

This will enable it at the page level and will append the trace input to the bottom of the page. The page directive can also have the `traceMode` property set, which can set to either SortByCategory or SortByTime. The default is SortByTime.

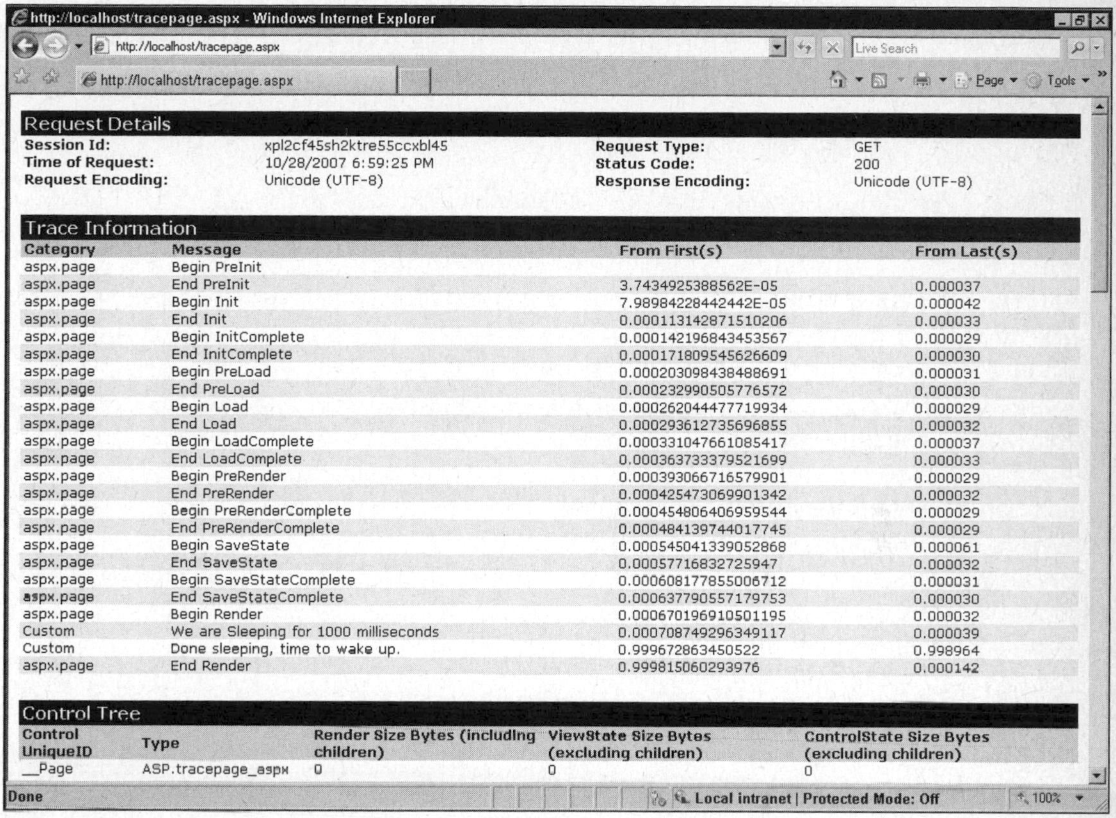

Request Details

Session Id:	xpl2cf45sh2ktre55ccxbl45	**Request Type:**	GET
Time of Request:	10/28/2007 6:59:25 PM	**Status Code:**	200
Request Encoding:	Unicode (UTF-8)	**Response Encoding:**	Unicode (UTF-8)

Trace Information

Category	Message	From First(s)	From Last(s)
aspx.page	Begin PreInit		
aspx.page	End PreInit	3.7434925388562E-05	0.000037
aspx.page	Begin Init	7.98984228442442E-05	0.000042
aspx.page	End Init	0.000113142871510206	0.000033
aspx.page	Begin InitComplete	0.000142196843453567	0.000029
aspx.page	End InitComplete	0.000171809545626609	0.000030
aspx.page	Begin PreLoad	0.000203098438488691	0.000031
aspx.page	End PreLoad	0.000232990505776572	0.000030
aspx.page	Begin Load	0.000262044477719934	0.000029
aspx.page	End Load	0.000293612735696855	0.000032
aspx.page	Begin LoadComplete	0.000331047661085417	0.000037
aspx.page	End LoadComplete	0.000363733379521699	0.000033
aspx.page	Begin PreRender	0.000393066716579901	0.000029
aspx.page	End PreRender	0.000425473069901342	0.000032
aspx.page	Begin PreRenderComplete	0.000454806406959544	0.000029
aspx.page	End PreRenderComplete	0.000484139744017745	0.000029
aspx.page	Begin SaveState	0.000545041339052868	0.000061
aspx.page	End SaveState	0.00057716832725947	0.000032
aspx.page	Begin SaveStateComplete	0.000608177855006712	0.000031
aspx.page	End SaveStateComplete	0.000637790557179753	0.000030
aspx.page	Begin Render	0.000670196910501195	0.000032
Custom	We are Sleeping for 1000 milliseconds	0.000708749296349117	0.000039
Custom	Done sleeping, time to wake up.	0.999672863450522	0.998964
aspx.page	End Render	0.999815060293976	0.000142

Control Tree

Control UniqueID	Type	Render Size Bytes (including children)	ViewState Size Bytes (excluding children)	ControlState Size Bytes (excluding children)
__Page	ASP.tracepage_aspx	0	0	0

Figure 20-17

Alternately, you can enable ASP.NET tracing at the application level within your `web.config` file. Within the `<system.web>` section, add the `<trace />` attribute as seen in the following example:

```
<system.web>
  <trace enabled="true" pageOutput="true" localOnly="true" />
  . . . .
</system.web>
```

In this example, tracing is enabled with the `enabled` attribute. The `pageOutput` then sets the trace data to be appended to the bottom of each page, which is useful during development or non-production troubleshooting. The `localOnly` attribute instructs the ASP.NET trace viewer to be available only on the local server, and not for anyone trying to view it from another computer.

The following table shows the possible ASP.NET tracing attributes and their values. These attributes can be set in your `web.config` file, from code, within your global.asax page or from an HTTP module.

Property	Description
Enabled	Optional Boolean attribute. Read/Write value that specifies whether tracing is enabled for an application or a page. The default is `false`.
localOnly	Optional Boolean attribute. Specifies whether the ASP.NET trace viewer is available only on the host web server. If `false`, the ASP.NET trace viewer is available from any computer. The default is `true`.
mostRecent	Optional Boolean attribute. When `true`, the most recent page requests are displayed, while the oldest are rolled off the bottom end. When `false`, only the number of requests set in `requestLimit` are saved. New requests will be discarded if the `requestLimit` has been reached. The default is `false`.
pageOutput	Optional Boolean attribute. When `true`, the trace output is rendered at the end of each page. When `false`, it is only available from the ASP.NET trace viewer, and the page output is not affected. The default is `false`.
requestLimit	Optional Int32 attribute. Specifies the number of trace requests to store on the server. See the `mostRecent` attribute description to see how to change the behavior when the `requestLimit` value is reached. The maximum value is 10,000. The default is 10.
traceMode	Optional TraceDisplayMode attribute. This attribute sets the "Sort by" value, to be used by the ASP.NET trace viewer. There are two possible values: SortByCategory and SortByTime. The default is SortByTime.
writeToDiagnosticsTrace	Optional Boolean attribute. This new .NET v2.0 attribute can be set to `true` to forward trace messages to the `System.Diagnostics` tracing infrastructure for further tracing abilities.

The ASP.NET Trace Viewer

When application-level ASP.NET tracing is enabled, the ASP.NET trace viewer is available. Accessing the ASP.NET trace viewer is straightforward. By default, you can only view the ASP.NET trace viewer on the local host server, but using the attributes discussed in the previous section, you can override the default setting.

Accessing the ASP.NET Trace Viewer

Navigate to the application root, and append `trace.axd` to the end of the URL. Example: `http://www.sitename.com/trace.axd`.

If you are unsure of your application root, use this simple method to find out what the path to the ASP.NET trace viewer would be.

Add the following to your web-site:

```
<%= "Trace Viewer Path: " & Request("SERVER_NAME") _
    & ":" & Request("SERVER_PORT") _
    & Request.ApplicationPath _
    & "/trace.axd" %>
```

The `trace.axd` file is a virtual file that is handled by an HTTP handler set in the root `web.config` file in the framework config folder. It is handled by the ASP.NET engine as if it were a real file, even though it does not physically exist.

The ASP.NET trace viewer provides the same information as the `pageOutput` tracing information, but it is not as intrusive since it is available from a separate tool and doesn't show in the webpage itself (see Figure 20-18). From the List page in the ASP.NET trace viewer, click the page to view its trace report. The trace report provides the same information as the `pageOutput` tracing information, but the advantage is that it does not affect the look of the pages. Instead, it saves it to a report to be viewed by the system administrator.

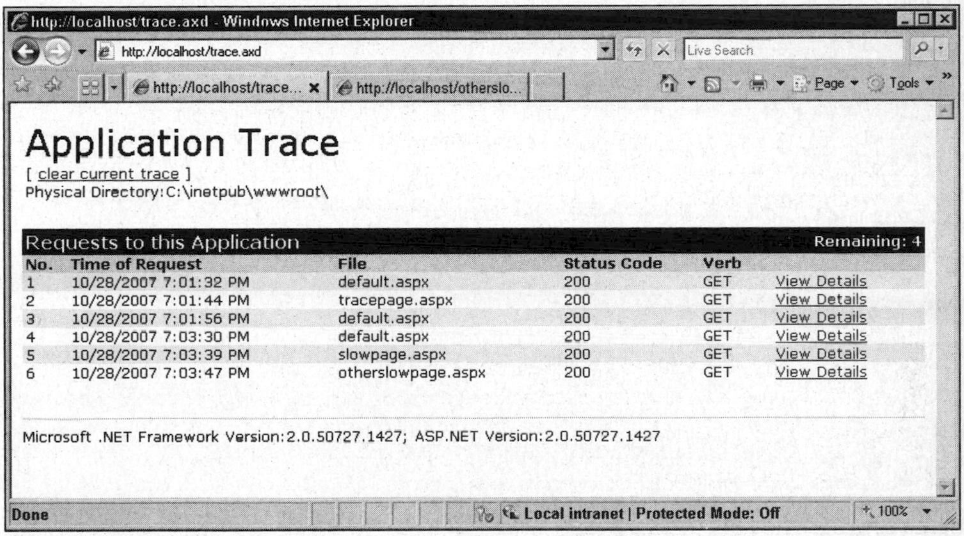

Figure 20-18

Password Protecting the ASP.NET Trace Viewer

If you set the `localOnly` attribute to false, allowing the ASP.NET trace viewer to be viewed from any computer, it is important to secure the ASP.NET trace viewer so that unauthorized people cannot gain access to privileged information. This can be done from `web.config` in the application root. Use the `<location>` element, which allows you to password-protect a specific file or folder.

```
<location path="trace.axd">
  <system.web>
    <authorization>
      <allow users="BillGates" />
      <deny users="*" />
    </authorization>
  </system.web>
</location>
```

You can add as many `<allow>` lines as you want. Attributes for `<allow>` are users and roles. For example, you can set `<allow roles="admin" />` to allow everyone in the admin role to have access to trace.axd. Be sure to place this outside of the current `<system.web>` section, under the main `<configuration>` section.

When you are using Windows authentication in `web.config`, the user and password will be a Windows or Active Directory user. When using Forms authentication, you must use ASP.NET usernames and passwords.

With your password-protected ASP.NET trace viewer, you are now able to view full trace information for pages that your viewers view without them being able to view this sensitive information.

The ASP.NET trace viewer information is stored in the IIS worker process so that when the application pool is recycled or an application domain is restarted, the information will be lost. This also means that any change to `web.config` will cause previous ASP.NET trace viewer data to be lost.

Extending Output Data

The ASP.NET trace viewer or the page-level pageOutput attribute can be extended to include information that you provide. This is similar to what developers often use with `Response.Write`, except that it has several advantages.

When debugging information is outputted to a trace report, it can be quickly and easily turned off or hidden from the casual user but still be available in the trace report. This allows you to leave your tracing output in place, even when your web site is in production, without a performance penalty. When insight into your application is required, you can turn on the ASP.NET trace viewer and see the outputted information.

There are two methods for outputting the trace information — `Trace.Write` and `Trace.Warn`. The only difference is that `Trace.Write` is outputted with black text, and `Trace.Warn` is outputted in red.

```
' Write key information to the trace output
Trace.Write("The querystring information is: " _
   & Request.Querystring)

If Request.Querystring = "" Then
   Trace.Warn("No valid querystring is set.")
End If
```

This will show in the trace report when it is run.

You are able to programmatically determine if tracing has been enabled by checking the `Tracecontext.Enabled` or `Context.Trace.IsEnabled` property. This will allow you to output non-trace information conditionally. For example, if you want to display a table only if tracing is enabled, you could do something like this:

```
If Tracecontext.Enabled = True Then
  DataTable.Visible = True
Else
  DataTable.Visible = False
End If
```

Alternately, the .NET `System.Diagnostics` namespace has even more debugging and tracing options, should you want to gain even further control over the ASP.NET tracing capabilities.

It is important to note that many types of errors will trigger an error before the `pageOutput` gets a chance to run. An unhandled programming error, for example, will throw a 500 status code, which will not show the trace data. In this case, you must use the ASP.NET trace viewer to view the trace report or handle the error in a `Try...Catch` block so that it fails gracefully enough for the trace information to be displayed.

Troubleshooting Tips

Where would a chapter on diagnostics be without some general purpose troubleshooting tips? A great troubleshooter can often solve complex issues even if it is a new technology to them, simply from mastering troubleshooting skills. Excellent troubleshooting can take years to master, but here are some tips that can be used in almost any situation. This method of troubleshooting takes four steps, which you can memorize by using the acronym *RIFT*, or "Reproduce, Isolate, Fix, and Test."

Before you start, it's important to back up your site and settings and to document all changes that you make. It's too easy, when something needs to be fixed "yesterday," to try random changes. But by the end, you're not sure what fixed the issue or how to get back to where you were before. These troubleshooting steps will help you make troubleshooting a deliberate and controlled methodology, but nothing replaces the importance of clear documentation. Be sure to take notes throughout the process and not depend on your memory alone to keep track of the changes that you made.

Reproduce

Reproduce, reproduce, reproduce!

Before making any changes, be sure to *reproduce* the issue. Without properly seeing the issue for yourself, you will be "troubleshooting by mistake," which is a poor practice. When you see in advance exactly what the issue is, you are able to confirm that your fix did, indeed, resolve the issue. Too often programmers and system administrators receive a report that something doesn't work, and instead of reproducing the issue to confirm that it is, indeed, broken, they make a quick change and ask the user to test again. The best troubleshooters always test before and after to confirm that they know exactly what their change fixed.

The ability to reproduce an issue is 50 percent of the battle. If you are able to quickly and easily reproduce the issue, you are well on your way to a complete solution.

Among the most difficult issues to resolve are those that do not happen often or on demand. In such cases, collect whatever information that you are able to, and use all the tools at your disposal until you are able to set up a test method of recreating the issue.

Some examples of troubleshooting that you might perform include:

❑ Fixing a failed web site that is throwing a 500 status code.

❑ Resolving a password prompt on a page that should not have one.

❑ Finding why an IIS worker process continues to fail prematurely.

❑ Determining high CPU or memory usage.

❑ Troubleshooting a failed connection from the web server to the database server.

In preparation for the Isolate stage, you should set up a test environment where you can reproduce the issue quickly, and where you can make modifications without affecting a production site or application. The easier that you can reproduce the issue and make modifications, the quicker you will be able to carry out the full RIFT process.

Isolate

Once you have reproduced the issue, it is time to find out the exact cause. Sometimes reproducing will not give any clues except at a very high level. The *Isolate* phase will drill down to the exact cause. The goal with the Isolate phase is to determine the single thing that is causing the failure. In some cases, there are compound issues, which makes it more difficult, but the principles are the same.

The following sections describe the five tricks that you should use to isolate the issue to its smallest factor.

Reproduce Trick

Reproduce, reproduce, reproduce! This may seem like a repeat of the first step, and it partially is, but reproducing the issue is something that you will do over and over again. Make sure that you can reproduce before you start, and then do it over and over again throughout the troubleshooting. This seems obvious, but it is amazing how often this is not done.

Fail Trick

This is a fun trick. Sometimes you may believe that you are addressing the correct issue, but you find out later that you were making a change to the wrong section, or even wrong site. This can sometimes be called a "Double Fail trick," because your goal is to break the broken site to determine positively that you are changing what you intend to.

Consider an example of a web site throwing a 500 error code on a web server with 100 web sites that use host headers. You believe that you are modifying the correct content, but you aren't quite sure. Assuming that the rest of the site can spare a few seconds of downtime, a simple test is to stop the web site and see if the error message changes. If it does, your change has confirmed that you are working with the correct web site. If the error message does not change, you might be making changes to something unrelated.

The Fail trick can apply to almost anything — file permissions on disk, web site or application pools, IIS settings, code settings, or even network or database connectivity.

Only 1 Trick

The Only 1 trick is a way to get *something* working, even if it is very simple. Again, this trick determines that you are considering the correct factors. If you have a web site that continues to fail and you are unsure if it is related to the code or the server configuration, it is helpful to run a simple test.

The goal is to get the site or issue working in its simplest form. It may be a static HTML page or a basic ASP.NET page, or you may create a new web site on an unstable server so that you can see if that bare-bones web site is also unstable. At first, you might completely ignore the issue itself and try to get a similar, but less complex, version of the site working.

Another way to consider this trick is as a "Hello World" test. The expression "Hello World" has been used for years to describe creating the first text output in a program. Many tutorials exist for creating a Hello World for COBOL, Java, JavaScript, Classic ASP, PHP, ASP.NET, or almost any programming language. Here, we share that term for any type of programming or administrative task where you get the most basic test working.

Once you have a basic test working, even if it is a long way from isolating the issue, you have the foundation in place for the Binary Halves Isolation trick, which can quickly take a complex failure and isolate it to its smallest factor.

Binary Halves Isolation Trick

Sometimes an issue is obvious; for example, you have an exact line number from which to work. But sometimes you do not have that luxury, for example, on a web page that fails without any error message. If you do not have any solid clue what is causing the issue, you may need to follow the Only 1 trick and then use the Binary Halves Isolation trick.

The Binary Halves Isolation trick involves breaking the issue into halves, and then halves again until you have determined the exact issue. To do this, you must be able to reproduce the failure and must have successfully carried out the Only 1 trick. Then pull out about half of the factors to see if it is still broken. From this, you can determine which half of the factors is causing the issue. Now repeat with about half of the remaining factors repeatedly until you have isolated the issue to the single item that is causing the failure.

As an IIS administrator, you will commonly be required to prove to a developer (even if that is also yourself) that the code is the problem. Even without extensive programming knowledge, it is possible to pull out parts of the code until you have proven the issue. A good troubleshooter can jump into almost any situation and isolate the issue, without being an expert in the technology or syntax of a programming language.

Another example would be to test a static HTML page on a server, or to temporarily remove or rename `web.config` and the ASP.NET application folders to determine if they are causing the failure.

Binary Halves Isolation Real-World Example

I recently found myself in a situation in which a web developer claimed that his web site worked in his test environment but would not work on the server that I provisioned. I was confident in the server but had to help the developer solve his issue and to prove and build confidence in the web server.

Continued

My first step was to find out how to reproduce the issue. During the troubleshooting process, I set up a copy of the web site on another server with a completely different configuration, and because the issue reoccurred there, I was quite confident that the issue wasn't caused by the server.

The web site existed in a subfolder that was marked as an application, so on the test web site I temporarily removed the web.config file at the site level to make sure that it was not the cause. The failure continued.

Then, I temporarily removed the web.config file at the subfolder level to see if any HTTP modules or other references were causing the issue. The failure continued.

I then temporarily removed all the app_* folders, at which point the issue stopped. Obviously, the rest of the web site didn't work as it should, but a simple "Hello World" proved that the cause of the issue existed in the app_* folders.

I added back half of the app_* folders and determined that the issue did not reoccur. I then added App_Browsers, one of the last two folders, and the issue reoccurred.

Now that I knew the exact folder, I carried out the Binary Halves Isolation trick on the files in the App_Browsers folder until I knew exactly which file was at fault.

Finally, I did the same thing with the sections of the file until I knew exactly what caused the issue.

It turned out that a login/membership module existed in the App_Browsers folder but it required a matching DLL file to be placed in the /bin folder. The developer had placed it in the root /bin folder, but not in the /application/bin folder.

Without any awareness of the application, I was able to use these standard troubleshooting tricks to prove to the developer that he had improperly placed the module, causing his application to fail.

There are times when breaking the issue into parts is difficult — for example, if there are interwoven dependencies. This makes things more difficult, but the same principles still apply. Break the issue down to the smallest part, and then add back about half of the issue. It may mean creating some tests or making some modifications to the situation, but it can be done using the same methodology.

All but 1 Trick

Finally, when you believe that you have the exact issue determined, it is wise to do a final fail test with the single factor that you believe caused the issue. This determines with absolute confidence what the issue is. Remember, don't troubleshoot by mistake. Be certain of the issue.

To do this, pull out, or add in, the single factor that caused the issue, and watch the error reverse. There are many examples, but consider a file system permission issue. If you added three or four Windows users to the NTFS permissions and tweaked a few other settings during your troubleshooting and the issue was resolved, you may have opened up a security hole by not fully understanding the exact permission requirement. It would be wise to remove the NTFS permission that you believe was the cause so that it fails again, which proves the exact issue.

Again, it is possible that there are compounded issues — keep that possibility in mind during all your troubleshooting.

Fix

Once you have determined the exact cause, the obvious next step in the RIFT process is to fix it. This may be something that you have control over, or it may be something that you have to refer back to someone else to take over. Not much needs to be said about this step since the fix is dependent on isolating the issue. Often more work is done in the Isolation step than in the Fix step.

Test

Finally, it is important to test to ensure that everything is back to normal and working. There are three parts to the Test step.

1. Reproduce, reproduce, reproduce! Don't walk away after fixing the issue without confirming that the change you made really works. It is amazing how often developers and system administrators will repair a bug or failure but not test it. It is also amazing how often it was not fixed even when the developer or administrator claimed that it was. Be sure to test that it is working afterward.

2. Ensure a clean environment when you are done. Be sure to clean up behind yourself. Remove any temporary users, files, folders, and notes that are floating around.

3. If there were specific lessons learned, be sure to document them in such a way that you and anyone else who requires it can benefit from them afterward. This can be done by updating company procedures or writing an article or blog or sending a memo to the applicable people.

Good troubleshooting skills transcend IIS 7.0 or even your areas of expertise. If you can master a few basic skills, troubleshooting can be a joy and sometimes a welcome challenge. Set yourself up for success in any type of issue that arises. Let the tools in this chapter enable you to walk through the RIFT steps to tackle the most challenging situations.

Additional Built-in Tools

Windows Server 2008 has several built-in tools that complement IIS troubleshooting. These tools are essential to isolating and solving the many types of issues that the system administrator is faced with. Many of these have been around since previous versions of Windows, some for many years, but their longevity just demonstrates their value all the more. This section includes tools that are either available out of the box or as a separate install.

Task Manager

Task Manager is an old-time favorite that most administrators are familiar with. There is no quicker way to get a good handle on the current state of a server than to fire up Task Manager. Needless to say, it should be one of the first tools to look at during any troubleshooting, often before IIS Manager is started. You can access it quickly by right-clicking on the taskbar and selecting Task Manager.

Task Manager gives a quick overview of the system resources of the server. With Windows Server 2008, you can not only see the CPU and running applications, you can also see the disk usage, the network usage, and the resources used by Windows services.

The Processes and Performance tabs are often the most useful, but there is important information in each of the tabs. The *Processes* tab shows detailed information for the worker processes running on the server. The *Performance* tab shows two real-time graphs: one of the CPU and the other of the memory usage. You can also see a summary of the physical and kernel memory usage, some key system information like the number of handles, threads, and processes, and the uptime of this server.

In the Processes tab, two columns that are worth adding that are not there by default are:

❑ **PID** — The Process ID can help link the process in Task Manager with the one seen in IIS or other tools.

❑ **Commit Size** — Commit Size is the corresponding column that lines up with the Private Bytes in IIS. If you set the application pool Private Bytes limit, then the Commit Size in Task Manager is important to monitor to see how the w3wp.exe process runs compared to the application pool limit.

Another change worth making in the Processes tab is to check the checkbox at the bottom to "Show processes from all users." When troubleshooting IIS, the background processes running under different users are often most important, but they are not displayed unless this checkbox is selected.

These changes are required only once per server, per user. After the change is made, Task Manager will retain that setting even after logging out and in again.

Event Viewer

Event Viewer has received a facelift in Windows Server 2008 and Vista, but the underlying concept is still the same. Information ranging from errors to warnings to informational notices is recorded in this extensive log storage source.

Virtually all Microsoft Windows programs will write errors and warnings to Event Viewer, and many third-party programs do the same. This makes Event Viewer the "go-to place" to gain details on any type of failure.

IIS is no exception. In fact, many production servers have more IIS- and ASP.NET-related entries than any other type of entry. Whether it is an application pool shutting down because of inactivity, or a worker process failing, Event Viewer offers a lot of clues to the issue at hand. In addition to failures and warnings, there are many informational messages such as the system update, reboot information, and new program installation data.

The information provided in Event Viewer is fairly detailed, but there are some errors that do not provide very useful information. An excellent web site to bookmark and visit regularly is www.eventid.net. It allows you to enter the Event ID and Source of any event, and there are thousands of events, event sources, and user contributions about almost every Event ID. Many will offer the exact clue that you may require to solve a particularly difficult issue.

The data format of Event Viewer is now a standardized XML format that all programs must conform to. This makes it easier to tap into, extend, and to import and export.

To access Event Viewer, go to Start ➪ Search box, type **Event Viewer**, and press **[Enter]**. The new GUI has been redesigned from previous versions of Windows, but it still has the categories on the left, details in the middle, and now has Actions on the right-hand side as seen in Figure 20-19. There are some note-worthy points of interest with the latest version.

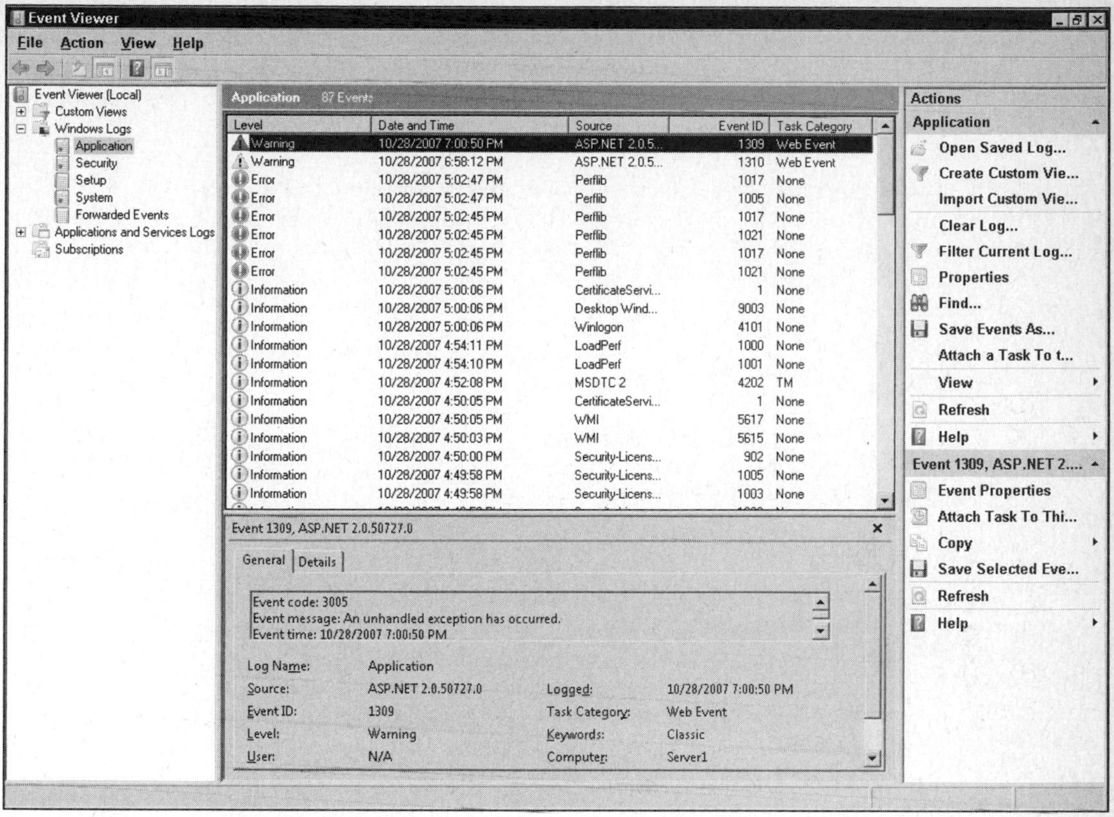

Figure 20-19

Attach Task to This Event

The IIS team has documented an extensive list of Event ID information that you will find valuable in your troubleshooting efforts. The starting page is at `http://technet2.microsoft.com/Windows Server2008/en/library/b19873a2-9f72-40c8-b73d-89f39cda62781033.mspx`. Using the navigation on the left, you can drill down into any of the managed entities until you find the information that you need. If this link expires, start at this page `http://technet2.microsoft.com/windows server2008/en/library` and drill down to Troubleshooting and then Internet Information Services (IIS) 7.0.

Among the best new features of Event Viewer is the "Attach Task to This Event" option. By right-clicking on an event or a category and selecting this option, you can schedule a task that will be triggered if the event happens. This allows you to pop up a message, send an e-mail, or trigger an application when a particular event happens. Rather than Event Viewer being a reactive tool, it is now a proactive tool and can push critical information to you in whatever method that you specify.

Applications and Services Logs

Another new feature in Event Viewer is the Applications and Services Logs section, which offers a wealth of information that was not previously available. These logs are for specific applications or services, rather than the system-wide logs in the Windows Logs section. A fresh install of Windows Server 2008 will already have dozens of categorized logs, and as more applications and services are installed, this list will grow. As you will quickly see, Windows Server 2008 has much better logging than any previous version of Windows.

By default, Analytic and Debug logs are hidden. You can enable them from the View menu at the top by selecting "Show Analytic and Debug Logs." This will add a few major categories and subcategories under the Applications and Services Logs category, which in turn will have one or more logs. The Analytic and Debug information is more detailed and not as easy to read casually, which is why it is disabled by default. When doing advanced troubleshooting, however, it is important to know of its existence and to enable it if desired.

Additionally, many of the logs are disabled by default; otherwise, it would quickly fill up your disk space; so, if there are any that you will need when troubleshooting a particular issue, be sure to confirm that they are enabled. You can enable a log by right-clicking on it and selecting Enable Log. If your only choice is Disable Log, then that category has been enabled already or was enabled by default. The default is different for each log; some are enabled already, but many are disabled out of the box.

Subscriptions

The new *Subscriptions section* allows you to centralize events from multiple servers. Once a subscription is active and events have been collected, you can view and manipulate these events as if they were locally stored events.

Forwarding uses the Windows Remote Management (WinRM) service and the Windows Event Collector (Wecsvc) service for this process.

Custom Views

In the past, filters were available to narrow a large set of Event Logs. Now there is a new category and tool called *Custom Views*. This allows you to set up a custom view that is always available to you for quick access.

You can create, import, view, or manage custom views from the Custom Views section on the left-hand pane. Another way to create a new custom view is to right-click on an existing folder (for example, Windows Logs ➪ System) and select Create Custom View. This new custom view will be saved in the Custom Views section. Once you set up a custom view, it is always available to you unless you purposefully delete it.

Additionally, you can write your own XPath query in the XML tab of the Create Custom View dialog box. This allows you to use XML, if you so desire, to customize the filter even further, or to reuse a filter from one that you previously created.

Reliability and Performance Monitor

The Reliability and Performance Monitor, also known as *perfmon*, is one of the most valuable tools in the Windows arsenal. To open Performance Monitor, select Reliability and Performance Monitor from Administration Tools or type **perfmon** from the Start ➪ Search box.

Under previous versions of Windows, perfmon only included what is currently the Performance Monitor section, but it has been expanded to include several new tools in Windows Server 2008. It is not quite as quick and easy to use as Task Manager or Ping, but with a bit of practice, it is easy to master and is very powerful.

There are hundreds and hundreds of counters, continuously exposing information on virtually every application and every part of the operating system. Perfmon makes all this information available in real time or by logging the data to be reviewed later.

In addition to counters, perfmon allows you to log and report on tracing information; system configuration information; and pre-packaged statistics, lists, and summaries. One example is a top 10 list of the most disk-intensive applications.

For an IIS administrator, this information is valuable to get into the heart of IIS, system resources, ASP.NET databases, and many other important applications necessary to troubleshooting IIS. Many issues that an IIS administrator faces are related to the performance of the web site. Issues can occur from hardware being underpowered, or a runaway script, to a particular resource bottleneck on the server. The trick is to find this information, understand it, and then deal with it accordingly.

Resource Overview

The Resource Overview screen, shown in Figure 20-20, is new to Vista and Windows Server 2008 and provides a wealth of information on four main resources: CPU, Disk, Network, and Memory. This information is available in real time and includes both a live graph and detailed charts. You can see the Resource Overview section by clicking on the top level; the Reliability and Performance heading. All the categories can be expanded to show a breakdown of every active worker process on the system and how much of that particular resource it is using.

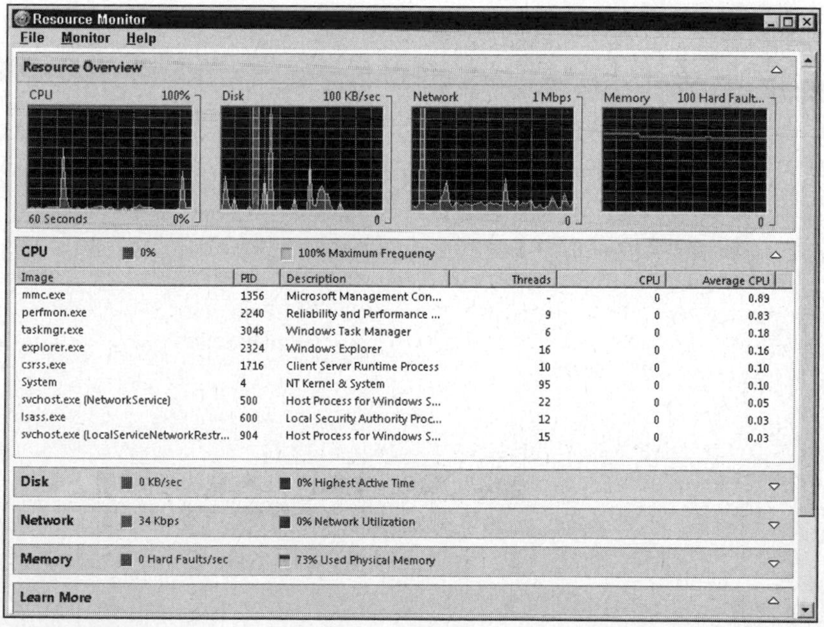

Figure 20-20

Performance Monitor

Within Reliability and Performance Monitor, the sub-tool that administrators of previous Windows operating systems are most used to is *Performance Monitor*. Performance Monitor has two purposes:

❑ To view the performance data on the system in real time

❑ To view historical data that was previously logged to disk

To view real-time counter data, select the Performance Monitor link from the left-hand pane, and follow these steps:

1. Click the green plus (+) button from the row of buttons at the top.

2. The Local computer will be selected by default, but you can point to a remote server if you desire.

3. In the middle left, you can select a counter. If there are multiple instances (for example, multiple disk volumes for PhysicalDisk), you can select _Total, <All instances>, or each individual instance.

4. When you have the counter(s) selected, click the Add > > button, which will move those counters to the right-hand pane.

5. Once you have all of the counters selected, press OK.

You will notice that the counters have been added to the list at the bottom, and more graph lines will start at the time that you add the counters.

<All instances> will add a counter for every instance, while _Total will add a single counter that is a sum of all the instances. When there is only one instance, they may appear to do the same thing, but they are really different.

A convenient option is the Highlight feature. When you click the icon that looks like a highlighter, the currently selected counter will be highlighted and stand out. This makes it much easier to find a particular line in the graph when there are many lines fighting to be viewed.

There are several features that you will appreciate about which we will not go into detail here — for example, the ability to pause, change graph types, copy data to the clipboard, graph properties, and many more. Take a few moments to familiarize yourself with these various features.

Reliability Monitor

Reliability Monitor is an impressive new sub-tool within Reliability and Performance Monitor. It has a daily timeline that shows five categories of events: Software (Un)Installs, Application Failures, Hardware Failures, Windows Failures, and Miscellaneous Failures. Using these categories of events, it graphs them in a visual chart and assigns your server an Index rating.

This information is extra-valuable when seen in a timeline like this. For example, if you notice that your system is less stable starting on a particular date, you can check to see if there was a software installation that was performed just prior to the new pattern of failures. Or, you may find that there is a hardware failure that first occurred during that timeframe.

For each day that no failures have occurred, the Index will climb back up toward 10. Each type of error is weighted differently, and the length of time since the error and between errors also affects the Index.

Software installations do not affect the Index but are useful for comparing installations to system stability to see if there is any correlation.

With Reliability Monitor, it is possible to see at a glance the current stability of the system and to potentially forecast future issues and resolve them in advance. It is also easier than in the past to associate hardware failures or installations with other hardware or software failures, to find out the root cause of an issue.

Logging Historical Data to Disk

One of the powerful features of Reliability and Performance Monitor is the ability to log data to disk for retrieval at a later time. For example, you can record performance information to disk before an issue occurs, so that when it does occur, you can review the saved data to help isolate the cause of an issue. The logging feature has received some major improvements over previous versions. Several logging and recording features are covered here.

User Defined Data Collector Sets

Data Collector Sets can be created to record and report on counters, events, and system configuration information. These Data Collector Sets can be customized to include specific information to provide an extensive report exactly to your specifications. They can also contain lists, summaries, tracing data, and customized wording and titles.

Figure 20-21 shows Reliability and Performance Monitor with two User Defined Data Collector Sets.

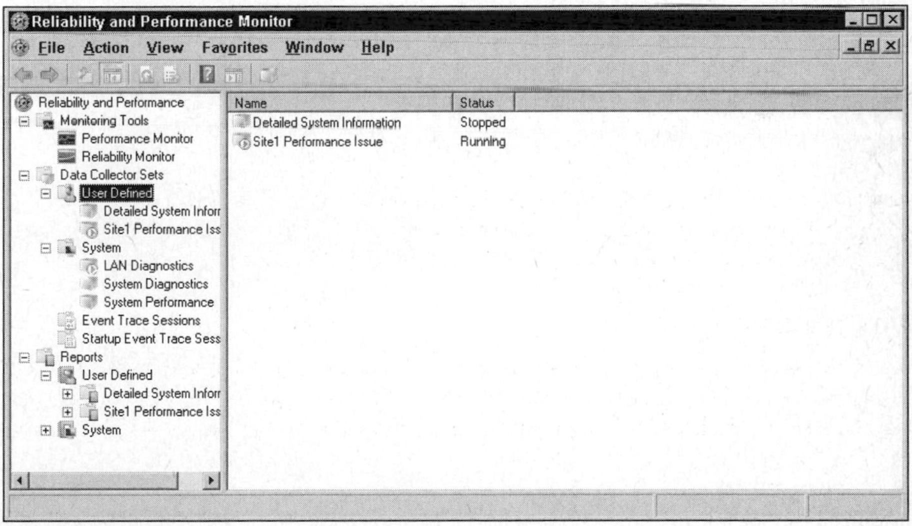

Figure 20-21

To create a new Data Collector Set, perform the following steps:

1. Start Reliability and Performance Monitor by going to Start ⇨ Search box, typing **perfmon**, and pressing Enter.

2. Expand Data Collector Sets.

3. Right-click on the *User Defined* folder, select New ⇨ Data Collector Set.

4. Give the Data Collector Set a name and select either "Create from a template" or "Create manually." Choosing "Create from a template" allows you to choose from one of three preexisting Template Data Collector Sets, or to browse for one that you may have obtained elsewhere. "Create manually" allows you to create your own Data Collector Set from scratch. You will be able to add your own *Performance counters*, *Event trace data*, and *System configuration information* counters, or, in the wizard, you can choose to set a *Performance Counter Alert* instead.

5. After choosing whether to create from a template or manually create a new set, complete the wizard with your preferred settings.

6. On the last step of the wizard, you have the options to "Open properties for this data collector set," "Start this data collector set now," or "Save and close" (see Figure 20-22). If you choose "Open properties for this data collector set" and click Finish, the properties window for the new Data Collector Set will appear, allowing you to customize it further. If you choose "Start this data collector set now" and click Finish, the wizard will complete and the new Data Collector Set will automatically start. The third option to "Save and close" will complete the wizard but will not start the Data Collector Set.

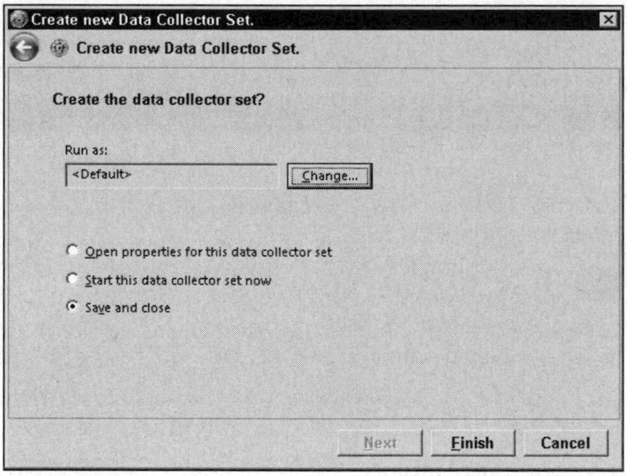

Figure 20-22

Once the Data Collector Set is created, you can edit its properties and change various information, ranging from the folder where the data is saved to the schedule and stop conditions. You can also add new Data Collectors to an existing Data Collector Set. A Data Collector can be performance counter data, event trace data, configuration data or performance counter alerts.

You can save a Data Collector Set as an XML template by right-clicking on the Data Collector Set and clicking on "Save Template". This offers a tremendous amount of control behind the scenes by allowing you to edit the XML file directly and create a new Data Collector Set from this template.

System Data Collector Sets

There are three Data Collector Sets already in place. They are *LAN Diagnostics*, *System Diagnostics*, and *System Performance*. You can start these at any time, collect data for as long as you need and then have a report generated for that data. These perform in the same way as the User Defined Data Collector Sets except that Microsoft has put together three recommended collectors to make your job easier.

Creating a Template from Real-Time Counters

If you have already added several real-time counters to Performance Monitor, you can save those as a template and log them to disk. This is convenient because you can visually tweak your list of counters before you begin logging, and then you can save it to a template when you are ready.

To save the real-time data as a template, perform the following steps:

1. Create the mix of counters that you are looking for in Performance Monitor.
2. In the right-hand pane, right-click Performance Monitor.
3. Select New ➪ Data Collector Set.
4. Follow the wizard through the steps as you would to create a User Defined Data Collection Set (see above).

This will add a new user-defined data collector set. If you did not start it during the creation wizard, then start it when you are ready. Alternately, you can have it started automatically based on an alert or a timed event. This will be covered shortly.

Reports

There is a new *Reports section* that keeps a report for each time a Data Collector Set instance is run. In past versions of Performance Monitor, it was necessary to maintain .log files on disk. With this version, however, all reports are neatly organized for easy retrieval and take on a whole new look from previous versions. The report names are placed in a folder in the Reports section that matches the Data Collector Set names. The filenames are named with the date when they were run.

Perfmon /Report

Possibly one of the most convenient means of getting a snapshot of the current state of a server is the perfmon /report option. From the command prompt or the Start ➪ Search box, type **perfmon /report**. This will start the System Diagnostics data collector for 60 seconds, after which it will display a detailed report of many of the server resources and settings. This is an invaluable tool to see the current state of the system resources.

Alerts and Threshold Starts

It is often desirable to have perfmon begin logging data as soon as a certain threshold is reached, rather than run it continuously. For example, let's say that once per week the CPU on the server runs wild, but you are unable to catch it before it recovers. You do not necessarily want detailed information logging around the clock until the issue occurs.

What you can do is set up an alert condition that starts the logging when the threshold is reached. This threshold can be set on any other performance counter, for example, when the CPU percentage is greater than a set value.

This can be set up with these steps:

1. Right-click Data Collector Sets/User Defined.
2. Select New ⇨ Data Collector Set.
3. Enter an applicable name for the collector set.
4. Select the "Create manually" radio button, and click Next.
5. Select the Performance Counter Alert radio button, and click Next.
6. Add one or more counters, set their threshold(s), and click Next.
7. Select the appropriate radio button — depending on if you desire to start the data collector set now or later.
8. Click Finish.

This does not specify an action for the alert yet. That takes another set of steps:

1. In the left-hand pane, select the new User Defined Data Collector Set that you just created.
2. In the main center pane, right-click the Data Collector that you want to set an alert action on and click Properties.
3. Select the Alert Action or Alert Task tab. The Alert Action tab allows you to specify that an entry will be added to the application event log in Event Viewer. In this tab, you can also specify a Data Collector Set. It must be a user-defined set, but you can create a user-defined set based on a predefined set. The Alert Task tab allows you to run specific tasks when the alert condition is run.
4. Click OK when finished.

The one disadvantage of the Alert mechanism is that it checks the threshold at regular intervals, and, if after a single failure it hits the threshold, it will trip the alert. The problem is that many thresholds are frequently hit during normal healthy usage, and it is actually sustained usage that system administrators are most concerned about. For example, you may not be concerned about high CPU unless it remains high for several seconds. Opening Task Manager is an example of a task that can spike the CPU for a brief instant, potentially causing the CPU alert threshold to be reached, even though there was not a real concern. Therefore, be aware that there may be false positives, causing more logging than you may have planned.

Viewing Logged Data

In addition to real-time data and Reports, the Performance Monitor view is also used to view performance counter data that was previously saved to disk. To do so, press *Ctrl+L* or click the second icon from the left, which looks like an ice cube but actually represents a cube of data. Click the "Log files" radio button, and click Add. Locate the file from disk, and click Open and then OK.

This view is the same as the real-time view except that the data is static. In the properties of this view, you can narrow the time to a specific range.

Overlaying Multiple Servers

Have you ever wanted to view perfmon graphical data from multiple servers at the same time? In the past, it would require adding all the server counters together into one large Performance Monitor session.

With Windows Server 2008, you can now overlay multiple windows to see them on top of each other. This is especially useful when you create a template with several counters and run them on multiple servers at the same time. It makes it convenient to compare several counters between servers.

The overlay option is available only in the standalone mode of Performance Monitor. You can open it by typing **perfmon/sys** from the Start ⇨ search box or from the command line.

In standalone mode, there is a new menu called *Compare* that allows you to set the transparency of the current window and to snap to another window (see Figure 20-23).

The Snap to Compare option will automatically resize and reposition the currently selected window so that it is the same size and is positioned exactly on top of the previously selected window.

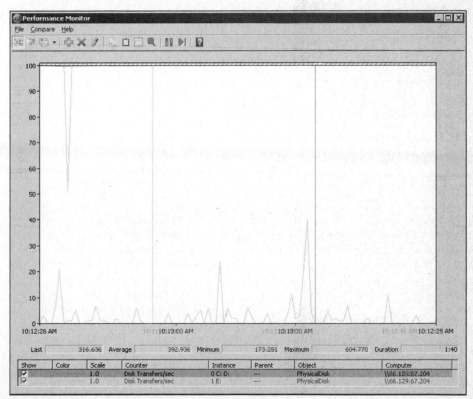

Figure 20-23

If you have multiple Performance Monitor windows open, click the one that is already positioned and sized correctly, then select the one that you want to resize and reposition and click Compare, Snap to Compare. The currently selected window will adjust to match the most recently "touched" window.

Logging NTFS Failures to Disk

A little-known trick that is available in Windows Server 2008, and previous operating systems, is to log all NTFS disk failures to Event Viewer. This can be very helpful when troubleshooting disk failures after they happen since it records them while you sleep, even if you were not anticipating a failure. It is helpful in finding incorrect permissions on files or folders.

This is accomplished by making two changes. First, the local group policy should be set to record failed objects, and then each disk volume should have Auditing enabled to record all failures.

Obviously, disk successes should not be recorded all the time because it would quickly fill your Event Viewer with useless information, but failures are not as common and are worth recording continuously.

The group policy change can be made by completing these steps:

1. Click Start ⇨ Run, and then enter **gpedit.msc**.
2. Under Computer Configuration, expand out to Windows Settings\Security Settings\Local Policies\Audit Policy.
3. Right-click the "Audit object access" Item, and click Properties.
4. Check the Failure checkbox and click OK.

Additionally, this can be set at the domain level in a group policy. In fact, if there is a domain-based policy in play, it will override this setting.

Once the group policy is set to record all object failures, the disk volumes need also to be set for auditing. They can be set by completing these steps:

1. Using Windows Explorer, navigate to the Computer section so that the disk volumes are visible.
2. Right-click on the first disk volume and select Properties.
3. Select the Security Tab and click Advanced.
4. Select the Auditing Tab and click the Edit button.
5. Click the Add button and add Everyone.
6. In the Failed column, click the Full Control checkbox, which will select all Failed options.
7. Click OK until everything has been acknowledged.

Now if there is a failure while attempting to access something on disk, the failed access will be logged to the Security section of Event Viewer. To view it, go to Event Viewer, Windows Logs and Security. Look for any Audit Failure errors, Event ID 4656, at the time of the failed attempt (see Figure 20-24).

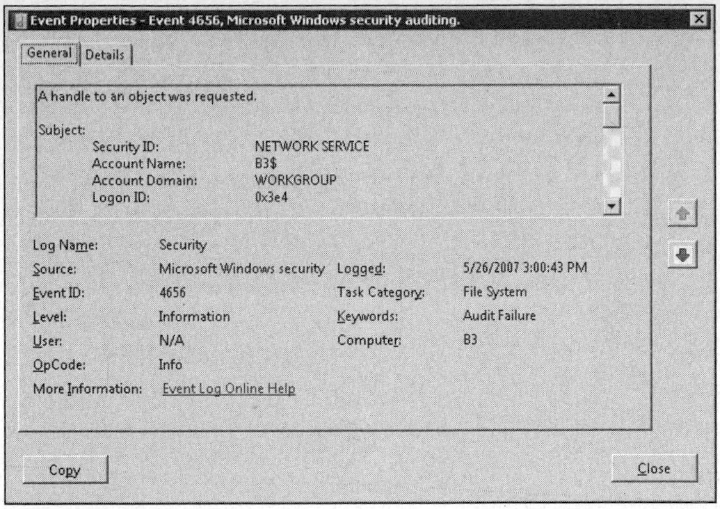

Figure 20-24

Figure 20-24 shows a partial view of the information available. By scrolling down, you can see the file that was denied access and the permission that it required.

The disk failure auditing described in this section is worth adding as part of the server build process since it does not fill up the logs too much under normal usage, and it is useful information to have after the fact.

Ping/Tracert/Pingpath

Ping and Tracert have been around for many years and are probably common knowledge to most readers of this book, but it is still worth being reminded of their value in troubleshooting IIS and web applications. Pingpath is a somewhat newer tool for Windows and is available from the command line.

It is worth giving a brief summary of each tool. All three are available from the command prompt as command-line tools. Many third-party tools exist to enhance these or to provide similar functionality from a graphical user interface, but these basic tools still live on in all their simple glory. They are quick and easy to access on all Windows Server 2008 servers.

Ping

Ping sends a packet of data to measure the time, in milliseconds, that it takes to do a round trip to a destination server or device. It sends an ICMP "echo request" packet to the destination server and waits for a reply. If it doesn't receive a reply within the time-out period, it will report it as a time-out.

Ping will also resolve a DNS name to an IP address before it begins the ICMP round trip, which doubles as another useful feature of this convenient tool (see Figure 20-25). There are about a dozen additional parameters to Ping, but the one most worth keeping track of is –t, which will send a ping test continuously.

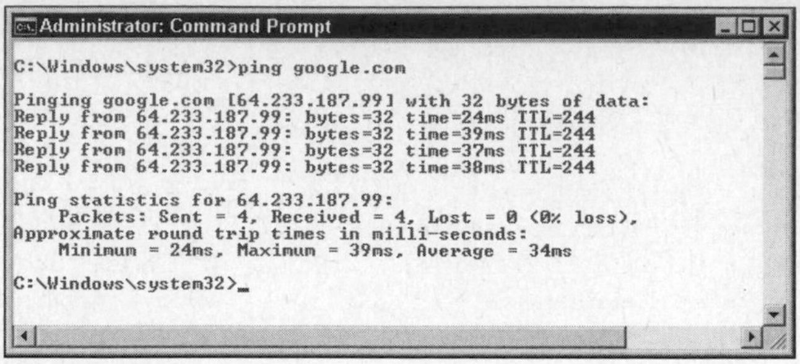

Figure 20-25

Ping is useful to confirm that there is network connectivity between the client and server and that the connection is stable and fast. If the ping time is consistent and within a healthy range, it will confirm that the network is not the cause of an issue. A healthy ping time varies tremendously according to the location of the server relative to the client, and the network in between. Times can range from just a few milliseconds to hundreds of milliseconds.

If you receive a report of a failure while viewing a web-based application, a ping test can quickly confirm that the network is not at fault. If the ping times are not consistent, it would be worth running a few ping tests with the -t parameter to compare connectivity to the server and possibly some other key Internet locations.

It's important to note that not all Internet devices will respond to a ping. Some will purposely run in stealth mode to reduce their attack surface. So, even if a device does not respond to a ping, it may still be performing normally.

A ping to www.google.com will often give one of the best times on the Internet because of their impressive infrastructure. An example of a site that will not respond to a ping is www.cnn.com.

Tracert

Like the Ping tool, the Tracert tool tests basic network connectivity, but it will also find the full route, or path, between the client and server. Then it will perform a ping test on each step. If there are network issues, a Tracert can show where the network breakdown is occurring. There are usually several hops across the Internet to a web site or server. If there is an issue, it is often easy to spot where it occurred by performing a Tracert test.

PathPing

PathPing is really a combination of the Ping tool and the Tracert tool, with some extra statistics included. It is particularly useful when looking at the network path between two computers to discover what is causing slowness or failures.

PathPing is available out of the box and installed by default. For detailed help, type **pathping /?** to list the nine possible parameters. A basic test of **pathping google.com** will show the network connectivity between the client server and the www.google.com data center that you are routed to.

Telnet

Telnet is a great tool for testing connectivity on a particular port and confirming access through a firewall. Just as Ping is used to check network connectivity, *Telnet* can be used to check port availability.

Telnet has several other uses, but the one that we'll describe here is specifically for port testing. Interestingly enough, the Telnet Client is not installed by default with Windows Server 2008. To enable it the first time, go to the Control Panel, Programs, "Turn Windows features on or off," click Add Features in the Features Summary section, then select "Telnet Client," and finish the wizard. Note that "Telnet *Server*" is a separate tool.

To test a particular port, from the command line, type:

```
Telnet {ServerName} {PortNumber}
```

For example:

```
Telnet Microsoft.com 80
```

This will test that you have access to port 80 for the domain called Microsoft.com. You can test by IP as well. The result will be a blank Telnet screen in this case, which is to be expected. If you know how to talk HTTP, you could talk to the Microsoft.com web server at this point. In this case, let's do a very simple test and type **GET http://www.microsoft.com/en/us/default.aspx**. Make sure that GET is in all capital letters. This will get the default homepage.

Some applications will give different information. Some start with a blank screen, whereas others will display some information right away. The key thing to note is that you don't get a time-out error. To compare this to a failed port, test by typing **Telnet Microsoft.com 81**. It will show "Connecting To microsoft.com..." for a while and eventually time out.

This underutilized trick makes a great port availability test using the built-in tools within Windows Server 2008.

Installable Tools

In addition to built-in tools that enhance IIS 7.0 troubleshooting, there are some other Microsoft and third-party installable tools that should be a part of your toolkit. All these are production-server-ready and can either be manually installed or have a well-tested installer. Some will require IIS to be reset so they can listen to the active traffic. Just be sure that you understand each of the additional tools that you decide to install.

IIS 6.0 Resource Kit Tools

Yes, that's the IIS 6.0 Resource Kit Tools. Chances are good that Microsoft will be releasing IIS 7.0 Resource Kit tools in the future, but there aren't any plans to release any updated IIS 7.0 Resource Kit Tools by the time that Windows Server 2008 ships. Not to worry — many of the tools in the IIS 6.0 Resource Kit still work and are valuable for troubleshooting IIS 7.0.

Some of the tools obviously aren't compatible with IIS 7.0 — for example, the IIS 6.0 Migration Tool, Metabase Explorer, and Apache to IIS 6.0 Migration Tool.

Many of the others still work, and some of them will be covered in more depth below. It is well worth being aware of the IIS 6.0 Resource Kit and the tools that it contains.

The complete list of tools in the IIS 6 Resource Kit are: Apache to IIS 6.0 Migration Tool, CustomAuth, IISCertDeploy.vbs, IIS Host Helper Service, IISState, Log Parser, Metabase Explorer, Permissions Verifier, RemapUrl, SelfSSL, TinyGet, Web Capacity Analysis Tool and WFetch. The following subsections don't cover all of the IIS 6.0 Resource Kit tools, but they cover tools that work well in IIS 7.0 and pertain to troubleshooting and diagnostics.

IISState

IISState, a debugging tool built specifically for IIS, was released after Windows Server 2003 shipped. It enables you to do a memory dump of relevant process information. The tool is run from the command line, but it is straightforward and easy to obtain the dump, although reading it can be overwhelming the first time you attempt to do so.

IISState, version 3.0 is available from the IIS Resource Kit, but the latest version is available at www. iisfaq.com/default.aspx?view=P197. To install IISState, you can run the iisstate.msi file or do a manual installation. A manual installation requires adding the debugger pack from Microsoft, which is unique for each build of the operating system. Windows debugger packs can be obtained from www.microsoft.com/whdc/devtools/debugging/symbolpkg.mspx.

Since the MSI installation doesn't add any registry keys or DLLs to the server, it is a safe install on a production server. During the install, specify the folder you want the install to be placed in. Take note of this folder because the output folder will be under the IISState installation folder. The Readme file will explain the manual install in depth, should you decide to go that way.

The command-line options are:

```
IISState –p <PID> [-d] [-hc] [-sc]
```

❑   The PID is the process identifier, which can be found in Task Manager. Running iisstate –p <PID> will do a memory dump of that one process and save to the <install dir>\output folder.

❑   -d will perform a full dump. Be careful posting this information publicly because it could contain sensitive information, like a credit card that was being processed at the time of the memory dump.

❑   -hc will tell IISState to wait until there is a Hard Crash (Dr. Watson) before it performs the memory dump.

❑   -sc will tell IISState to wait until there is a soft crash, which will typically be a Soft Crash (ASP0115) type failure. Since IIS will continue running after the soft crash, you can stop IISState by hitting *Ctrl+C*.

The memory dump will cause the process to pause while it is obtaining the dump. After it is finished, it will continue as it was, without killing the process. Only IIS-related processes can be used — for example, InetInfo.exe, dllhost.exe, or w3wp.exe.

Once a memory dump is performed, the output will either be in a text file or a dump file, if you used the -d command. The text file can be opened in Notepad or any other text editor. The dump file can be read in a debugger like WinDbg. Detailed instructions for configuring IISState can be found at www.adopenstatic.com/faq/IISConfigureIISState.aspx.

Microsoft does not formally support this product, but they assist on the IIS newsgroup (microsoft.public.inetserver.iis). If you send the log file to the newsgroup, they will point you in the right direction. Before doing that, take a look through the file to see if there is anything that you can pick up from the file. Each thread will be saved to the log file, and IISState will attempt to fill in key information, for example, if there are Jet (Microsoft Access) failures or if it knows the path to the file that the thread is running.

Here is an example of one thread from the log file:

```
Thread ID: 19
System Thread ID: 23ac
Kernel Time: 0:0:0.0
User Time: 0:0:0.0
Thread Status: Thread is in a WAIT state.
Other information: Thread is waiting for a lock to be released.  Looking for lock
owner.
Owning thread System ID: 208c
Thread Type: ASP
Executing Page: Unable to locate ASP page

 # ChildEBP RetAddr
00 02f5faf0 7c822124 ntdll!KiFastSystemCallRet
01 02f5faf4 7c83970f ntdll!NtWaitForSingleObject+0xc
02 02f5fb30 7c839620 ntdll!RtlpWaitOnCriticalSection+0x19c
03 02f5fb50 709ec965 ntdll!RtlEnterCriticalSection+0xa8
04 02f5fb98 709e271a asp!CHitObj::ViperAsyncCallback+0x101
05 02f5fbb4 75bd72a5 asp!CViperAsyncRequest::OnCall+0x92
06 02f5fbd0 7770f0eb comsvcs!CSTAActivityWork::STAActivityWorkHelper+0x32
07 02f5fc1c 7770fb38 ole32!EnterForCallback+0xc4
08 02f5fd7c 77710042 ole32!SwitchForCallback+0x1a3
09 02f5fda8 77694098 ole32!PerformCallback+0x54
0a 02f5fe40 777127fd ole32!CObjectContext::InternalContextCallback+0x159
0b 02f5fe60 75bd7649 ole32!CObjectContext::DoCallback+0x1c
0c 02f5fecc 75bd79a5 comsvcs!CSTAActivityWork::DoWork+0x12d
0d 02f5fee4 75bd833e comsvcs!CSTAThread::DoWork+0x18
0e 02f5ff04 75bd878a comsvcs!CSTAThread::ProcessQueueWork+0x37
0f 02f5ff84 77bcb530 comsvcs!CSTAThread::WorkerLoop+0x17c
10 02f5ffb8 77e66063 msvcrt!_endthreadex+0xa3
11 02f5ffec 00000000 kernel32!BaseThreadStart+0x34
```

This may seem cryptic at first but there is some information that can be easily gleaned from it. Notice that the Kernel Time and User Time are very low — actually it's zero in this case. This means that this thread did not cause high CPU. Those are two numbers to watch for in other cases since they can show the threads that are hogging the CPU. The difficulty is that because the Kernel and User Time are from when the process first started, they may have a high value even if that thread is not currently being used. Just the same, it gives a good clue, especially if you get two dumps back-to-back and compare the difference.

Back to this example. Notice that this thread is waiting for a lock to be released in a different thread — Thread ID: 208c. Let's look in the same log file for Thread 208c:

```
Thread ID: 18
System Thread ID: 208c
Kernel Time: 0:0:0.46
User Time: 0:0:1.312
*** WARNING: Unable to verify checksum for D:\com\ASPPop3\pop3svg.dll
*** ERROR: Symbol file could not be found.  Defaulted to export symbols for
D:\com\ASPPop3\pop3svg.dll -
Thread Type: ASP
Executing Page: ?

 # ChildEBP RetAddr
00 02f1f0dc 7c821364 ntdll!KiFastSystemCallRet
01 02f1f0e0 77e42439 ntdll!NtDelayExecution+0xc
02 02f1f148 77e424b7 kernel32!SleepEx+0x68
03 02f1f158 0331aa5a kernel32!Sleep+0xf
```

Now we are getting somewhere. Notice that pop3svg.dll is being used by this thread, and the bottom line shows that it is sleeping, waiting on something else. We can make a safe assumption that the code is using ASPPOP3, which is a COM+ component that can check POP3 accounts. Possibly the mail server is down, or there is a network connectivity issue between this server and the mail server.

Without digging deep into debugging steps, and without being an expert in reading memory dump information, we can use some common sense and trace the issue back to the ASPPOP3 component.

Not all memory dumps have information this obvious, and some of them don't give any clues, but IISState is a great tool to help in many situations because of the detailed information that it does make available.

> Process Explorer will also give this information in real time, including the Thread CPU usage. IISState is useful if you require a memory dump quickly so that you can research it later, or ask for help reading the memory information. Process Explorer offers value by allowing you to dig into the issue in real time as it is happening, and offers even more information than IISState does.

WFetch

WFetch is a simple but powerful tool to listen to all web traffic and see everything included in the communication between IIS and the web client, including the request, response, headers, body, content length, status codes and more (see Figure 20-26). It is excellent for troubleshooting the actual web traffic between a web browser and the IIS server, since it allows you to see the entire conversation between the two sides.

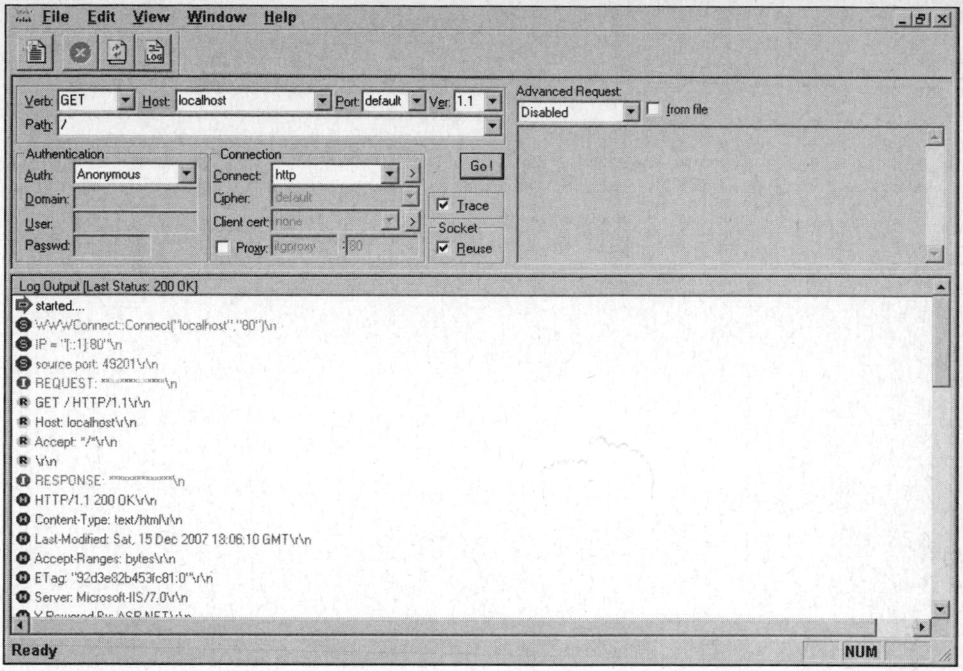

Figure 20-26

Web Capacity Analysis Tool (WCAT)

WCAT is a command-line tool that can be controlled using configuration files or from the command line directly. The output can be saved to a .log file or to an .xml file. There is a wealth of flexibility to create almost any type of test. This tool allows you to stress test a web site to know how it will perform under load, by simulating a large number of visitors to the web site.

Multiple WCAT client servers can be running at the same time to generate even greater load. You can greatly increase the value of WCAT by using it in conjunction with other tools mentioned in this chapter. For example, Performance Monitor will allow you to watch how the web server performs during the simulated traffic. The output can be saved to a .log file or to an .xml file, depending on which you prefer.

Be careful about running this against a production server, or running across a network where the cost of bandwidth is a concern. It can appear that a hacker is attacking the site and can bring a production site to its knees.

Log Parser

Log Parser is a dream come true for anyone wanting to dig into IIS logs, event viewer, registry, syslogs, XML data — you name it. Typically, it is used as a command-line tool, but there is a COM API included with it. Many third-party tools have sprung up to add GUI wrappers for it, making it not only extremely powerful, but quite easy. Log Parser isn't necessarily for the faint of heart because of its power and flexibility in using SQL-like syntax, but it is easy enough for anyone to pick up after spending a bit of time with it. The time invested will pay back with great rewards.

Gabriele Giuseppini, a software design engineer at Microsoft, was the primary developer and is also fairly active in the newsgroups answering questions. At the time of this writing, version 2.2 is the latest release and is available at www.microsoft.com/downloads/details.aspx?displaylang= en&FamilyID=890cd06b-abf8-4c25-91b2-f8d975cf8c07.

To run Log Parser, simply extract the zipped files in the download onto any computer, and either run across the network or copy logparser.exe to the computer you want to work on. No install is necessary. This is production-server-ready, very stable, and extremely fast.

As entire books and web sites exist to support Log Parser, this small space won't do justice to the options available. However, let's consider three examples:

Example 1 — To search Event Viewer for all Error entries in the System log:

The EventType value of 1 refers to Errors. You can specify the input format and output format, but Log Parser will take an educated guess if you leave it off. In the following example it will correctly guess the formats as –i:EVT for Event Viewer and –o:NAT for native format.

```
LogParser.exe "SELECT * FROM System WHERE EventType = 1 ORDER BY TimeWritten DESC"
```

You'll notice that the syntax is very much like what SQL used for database queries. That is intentional, and if you are familiar with SQL, writing Log Parser queries won't take long to figure out. This example executes LogParser.exe and passes in a single parameter, which is the Log Parser query. The query selects all (*) fields from the Event Viewer system log where the EventType is 1 (errors), and then sorts by the timestamp (TimeWritten) of the event entry, in descending order. The "System" keyword is a reserved word which tells Log Parser to query the system log of Event Viewer. It also allows Log Parser to know the input type without requiring you to specifically set it.

Example 2 — To get the registry values of the run key for HKEY Local Machine and HKEY Current User:

```
LogParser.exe "SELECT ValueName, Value FROM
\HKLM\Software\Microsoft\Windows\CurrentVersion\Run,
\HKCU\Software\Microsoft\Windows\CurrentVersion\Run" -i:REG
```

This example is pretty straightforward, but notice that there are two Run keys, the HKEY Local Machine and HKEY Current User, separated by a comma. You can add as many Registry keys as you want, separated by commas. The –i:REG means that the input is from the Windows Registry. That is optional since Log Parser is smart enough to figure that out based on the other information provided, but for the sake of the example it's good to see that the input type can be set if necessary.

Example 3 — To search the "Default Web Site" in IIS and retrieve a count of hits for each web page extension:

```
LogParser.exe "SELECT TOP 20 EXTRACT_EXTENSION(cs-uri-stem), COUNT(*) AS Hits FROM
<Default Web Site> GROUP BY EXTRACT_EXTENSION(cs-uri-stem) ORDER BY Hits DESC"
```

In this example, extract_extension will pull out the page extension from the web filename (for example, aspx, gif, html), group by extension, and provide a count of how many visits were made to each of the top 20 visited extensions. Notice that <Default Web Site> causes Log Parser to automatically query all of the log files for that web site, simply by referencing the web site's name. Log Parser will go into IIS, find the path to the log file and then query the log files for you. In this particular query example, the input type isn't set since Log Parser is smart enough to figure that out.

Note that Log Parser may take significant system resources to read through very large data stores, but other than that, it is safe to run on a production server.

DelegConfig

DelegConfig is a web application that helps to troubleshoot authentication issues on a server. It shows the Kerberos and delegating credentials, including Service Principal Names (SPNs), delegation settings, and the authentication method that is being used. This is particularly useful for Kerberos in a local domain environment since Kerberos is not used across the Internet.

To install DelegConfig, download it from the `www.iis.net` web site, extract it, and copy it to a sub-folder of a web site. Then mark the Kerberos folder as an application.

> *If you are running in Integrated mode in IIS 7, the included* `web.config` *setting of* `Impersonate="true"` *is invalid. Edit the* `web.config` *file, and change to* `impersonate="false"`, *or delete the line completely for DelegConfig to work.*

To run DelegConfig, browse to the Kerberos folder on the web site. The page has excellent explanations and gives a status beside each section with different icons depending on whether it passes or fails the test.

Process Explorer

Process Explorer is like Task Manager on steroids (see Figure 20-27). Where Task Manager stops, Process Explorer takes over in an impressive way. Process Explorer allows you to dig into the processes and even into the threads of all running processes, in real time. You can see what is in memory for each thread, find out what is locking a file, find out how much CPU each process or thread is using, and see DLL dependencies.

Process Explorer was written by Mark Russinovich and is available on `www.sysinternals.com`. In July 2006, Microsoft acquired Sysinternals, so this is now a Microsoft tool, but the `www.sysinternals.com` web-site is still valid.

Process Explorer is particularly useful to the IIS Administrator when isolating high CPU within a `w3wp.exe` worker process. It enables you to find out the CPU on each thread, and then see the contents of the thread itself. It also allows you, the system administrator, to see what is locking a file, and, if necessary, to release the lock. See Figure 20-28 to see the System Information view of Process Explorer.

Simply running Process Explorer and reading the information can be done safely on a production server without any installation necessary and without any impact on the operation of the server. Download it from the web site to any computer, and then copy `procexp.exe` to the server. Double-click on the file to start it.

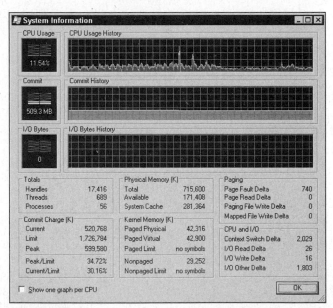

Figure 20-27

Figure 20-28

Be careful with Process Explorer. It is powerful enough to kill critical system processes. If you kill the wrong process, you can take down the operating system. This gives all the power you need, so use it wisely.

IIS Diagnostics Toolkit

The IIS Diagnostics Toolkit includes several valuable tools which you can install individually or as a whole. These tools enable you to dig deep into certifications, authentication, SMTP, web traffic, log file reporting, and more. Since some of them have been updated since the toolkit was released, it is worth searching for them individually to ensure that you have the latest version. The toolkit can be downloaded from www.iis.net.

At the time of this writing, the toolkit has not been updated for IIS 7.0 and Windows Server 2008; we are unable to confirm that there are plans to update it in the near future, but most of the tools continue to work well on Windows Server 2008.

SSLDiag

SSL Diagnostics is used for troubleshooting Secure Socket Layer (SSL) and certificates. Working with certificates can be reasonably straightforward if everything works as expected, but when something is wrong, it can be very difficult to find out what is happening. SSLDiag gives insight into the inner workings of IIS and SSL certificates in real time.

SSLDiag can be run from the command line or using the graphical interface. It can be set to listen to all traffic, or set to narrow down to just one site. On a busy server, it is often useful to narrow the scope to the smallest area possible that includes the issue.

Running SSLDiag in real time requires you to restart IIS, so be sure to implement this during a maintenance window or at a time when you can accept the interruption of your web sites.

At the time of this writing, SSL Diagnostics Tool v1.1 does not fully work in IIS 7.0; watch for future versions to offer full capability.

DebugDiag

Most of the features of the Debug Diagnostics Tool (DebugDiag) are now included within IIS 7.0 and are described above in this chapter, but it is worth taking note of this powerful tool since it is still supported on Windows Server 2008 and IIS 7.0.

DebugDiag is used for troubleshooting hangs, slow performance, memory leaks, and crashes. It is not just limited to IIS-related processes, although there are extra debugging scripts that target IIS and COM+ debugging.

DebugDiag was originally released as version 1.0 in the IIS Diagnostic Toolkit, but updated versions can be downloaded directly from www.microsoft.com.

It runs as a GUI tool and allows the administrator to listen to a particular URL and watch for a Crash, IIS Hang, or Memory and Handle Leak. When those occur, a memory dump will be generated, and then the Debug Diagnostic tool can be used to generate a report of the dump information. This information is valuable in finding out what is happening inside IIS and the IIS worker processes. It will report detailed information on the processes, threads, and the memory.

TraceDiag

Windows 2003 SP1 released some powerful tracing capabilities. TraceDiag is a toolkit aimed at making tracing easier to use and to give access to a wealth of information. As with DebugDiag, because of RSCA, FREB, and the other tools in IIS 7.0, TraceDiag will not be required as often. The new tools in IIS 7.0 are much more user-friendly. That being said, TraceDiag does still have its uses, and it is good to be aware of its existence.

It is a separate download, which can be found on Microsoft's web site. After it is installed, it will exist in the Start menu, and is run from the command line.

ELMAH

Above in this chapter, we looked at tracing to be able to output key information on a page or to the ASP.NET trace viewer. Atif Aziz has written an HTTP module that can be quickly added to your `bin` folder and referenced from your `web.config` file to log all errors to disk, or send an e-mail when the errors occur. The advantage of this is that the history can be kept as long as you want — to troubleshoot a failure after the fact or to be e-mailed to you as it occurs.

ELMAH stands for "Error Logging Modules and Handlers" and uses ASP.NET HTTP modules and HTTP handlers to extend any web site. Although this is not new to IIS 7.0, it applies just as much now as it does to ASP.NET on previous operating systems.

This is not a Microsoft tool, but it is used by many Microsoft folks, and there are several MSDN articles about it. A good place to start is with an MSDN article by Scott Mitchell and Atif Aziz, located at `http://msdn2.microsoft.com/en-us/library/aa479332.aspx`.

Configuration is straightforward, and after you have set up one or two of these, you can implement it within a couple of minutes. The module itself can be saved to the GAC or in the `/bin` folder, and then a few `web.config` additions are required. A reference to the HTTP Module and another reference to an HTTP Handler are required if you want to view the data online. You can configure settings like the logging database or e-mail address. In concept, it works very similar to Tracing, but with the added functions already described. The error log can be viewed by accessing the path set in the HTTP handler in `web.config`. By default, this is elmah/default.aspx. Figure 20-29 shows the error log with a couple of failures.

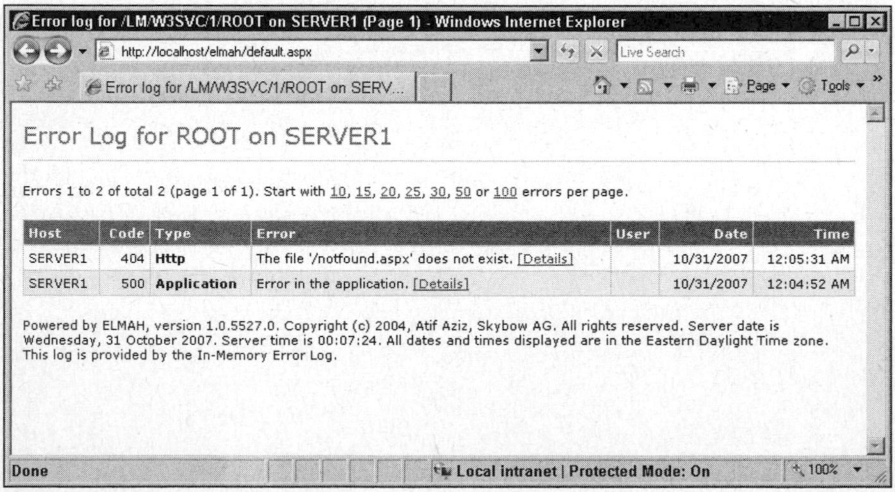

Figure 20-29

Some developers find it worthwhile to set this on every web site they develop or manage. This enables them to receive detailed error reporting as it occurs and be proactive to resolve any bugs in their software. The information provided is quite extensive, with plenty of information to aid in reproducing and resolving the issue.

Whether you implement this as a developer to be proactive, or require it to improve a buggy web-site ELHAM is a welcome tool to add to your toolkit.

Where to Go Next

The tools listed in this chapter are by no means an exhaustive list of the tools that are available for IIS 7.0 and Windows Server 2008 troubleshooting. It is important to always be on the lookout for new tools and to experiment with the various tools that are available. Microsoft's web site www.iis.net has become the fully supported web site that Microsoft and even the Product Support Services (PSS) team regularly use to get the latest tools and information. This is a site that should be at your fingertips to keep up-to-date on the latest tools.

Summary

Windows Server 2008 and IIS 7.0 offer a wealth of tools, many that are new and many that have been around for a while. With the right tools and the desire to work through any issue, a system administrator has at his or her disposal everything required to solve the most complex problem. In addition to the tools available for IIS 7.0 troubleshooting, it's important to know some general troubleshooting practices.

Troubleshooting is one of the areas where the most improvements have been made to IIS 7.0. Using the new Runtime Status and Control, it is now possible to see not only the currently running worker processes but also the currently running pages and the length of time that they have been running. This can be done from IIS Manager, AppCmd.exe, and from code.

Custom errors have also been greatly improved in IIS 7.0, giving you more insight into the real issue. In addition to a cleaner look, many error pages provide detailed suggestions and links to help you resolve the issue. Microsoft has taken great pains to make this information readily available to you.

Another new feature in IIS 7.0 is the Failed Request Tracing, which gives you the ability to save information to disk about particular pages that you want to track, whether they are failed or long-running pages. This gives you the ability to dig deep into the lifecycle of the page request and narrow down the issue at hand without purchasing expensive third-party tools or requiring you to learn cryptic tracing commands.

In addition to the tools provided within IIS 7.0, there are scores of additional Microsoft tools and third-party tools that provide you with even more powerful troubleshooting options. Familiarizing yourself with these tools and some troubleshooting principles in advance will allow you to quickly solve almost any issue when it occurs. With a bit of practice, any administrator can become proficient at IIS 7.0 troubleshooting and ready to tackle even the most difficult situations.

Module Reference

The following modules, from Microsoft's IIS 7.0 module reference (www.iis.net/articles/ view.aspx/IIS7/Managing-IIS7/Configuring-the-IIS7-Runtime/Configuring-Modules/ IIS7-Modules-Overview), ship with Windows Server 2008. Chapter 12 discusses extending IIS 7.0 by adding custom modules.

Utility Modules

These modules do not provide request services, but instead assist the server engine with its internal operation.

Module Name	UriCacheModule
Description	Implements a generic cache for URL-specific server state, such as configuration. With this module, the server will only read configuration for the first request for a particular URL, and reuse it on subsequent requests until it changes.
Configuration Sections	None.
Dependencies	None.
Potential Issues When Removing This Module	Performance loss due to state cached for each URL being retrieved for every request.

Module Name	FileCacheModule
Description	Caches file handles for files opened by the server engine and modules.
Configuration Sections	None.
Dependencies	None.
Potential Issues When Removing This Module	Performance loss. If file handles are not cached the files have to be opened for every request.

Module Name	TokenCacheModule
Description	Caches windows security tokens for password based authentication schemes (anonymous authentication, basic authentication, IIS client certificate authentication).
Configuration Sections	None.
Dependencies	None.
Potential Issues When Removing This Module	Performance loss. The user has to be logged on for every request if the token is not cached. This might be a major performance impact, e.g. if a password protected html page references 50 images that are also protected. This would result in 51 logonUser calls to the local account database or, even worse, to an off-box domain controller.

Managed Engine: ASP.NET Integration

Module Name	ManagedEngine
Description	Managed Engine has a special place within all the other modules. It is responsible for providing the IIS integration with hooking up the ASP.NET runtime.
Configuration Sections	
Dependencies	None.
Potential Issues When Removing This Module	ASP.NET integration will be disabled. None of the managed modules declared in the <modules> or ASP.NET handlers declared in the <handlers> section will be called when the Application Pool runs in Integrated Mode.

IIS 7.0 Native Modules

Module Name	HttpCacheModule
Description	The HttpCacheModule implements the IIS 7.0 output cache and also the logic for caching items in the http.sys cache. Cache size, output cache profiles etc. can be set via configuration after enabling this module.
Configuration Sections	System.webServer/caching
Dependencies	None.
Potential Issues When Removing This Module	Content won't be cached in kernel mode anymore. Cache profiles will also be ignored. Removing the HttpCacheModule will probably have adverse effects on performance and resource usage.

Module Name	DynamicCompressionModule
Description	Implements in-memory compression of dynamic content
Configuration Sections	system.webServer/httpCompression and system.webServer/urlCompression
Dependencies	There shouldn't be any dependencies because Dynamic compression is turned off by default.

Module Name	StaticCompressionModule
Description	Implements compression (in memory as well as persistent in the file system) of static content
Configuration Sections	system.webServer/httpCompression and system.webServer/urlCompression
Dependencies	None.
Potential Issues When Removing This Module	Potential Bandwidth saturation due to uncompressed content being sent back to the client.

Module Name	DefaultDocumentModule
Description	Implements default document functionality, i.e. requests that come in with a trailing / will be rerouted to a document in the default document list
Configuration Sections	system.webServer/defaultDocument
Dependencies	None.
Potential Issues When Removing This Module	Requests to /, e.g. http://localhost, will return a 404 error. A directory listing will be generated if directoryBrowsing is enabled.

Module Name	DirectoryListingModule
Description	Implements directory browsing functionality
Configuration Sections	system.webServer/directoryBrowse
Dependencies	None.
Potential Issues When Removing This Module	If neither the default document module nor the directoryListing Module handle a request for a / (folder with no page specified) then an empty response will be returned.

Module Name	ProtocolSupportModule
Description	Implements custom and redirect response headers. Implements the trace and Options Http verbs. Implements the supports for allowing or turning off keep-alive support via configuration.
Configuration Sections	system.webServer/httpProtocol
Dependencies	None.
Potential Issues When Removing This Module	TRACE or OPTIONS requests will return a "405 Method not allowed" error message.

Module Name	HttpRedirectionModule
Description	Implements redirect functionality
Configuration Sections	system.webServer/httpRedirect
Dependencies	None.
Potential Issues When Removing This Module	Potential security issue if resources were protected by redirection. When the Redirection module is removed the content becomes accessible again.

Module Name	ServerSideIncludeModule
Description	Implements server side includes. This module is mapped as a handler. This means it is only executed for requests ending in .stm, .shtm and .shtml
Configuration Sections	system.webServer/serverSideInclude
Dependencies	None.
Potential Issues When Removing This Module	.stm, .shtm and .shtml files will be handled by the static file module. If this module has a mimeMap for these extensions the files get served as text. This is not the default though.

Module Name	StaticFileModule
Description	Sends out static files with the file extension .html, .jpg and many others. The list of file extensions is determined by the staticContent/mimeMap configuration collection.
Configuration Sections	system.webServer/staticContent
Dependencies	None.
Potential Issues When Removing This Module	Static files don't get served anymore. Requests for files return a 200 OK with an empty entity body.

Module Name	AnonymousAuthenticationModule
Description	Implements anonymous authentication, i.e. this module would generate the HttpUser object if a URL is configured to allow anonymous authentication.
Configuration Sections	system.webServer/security/authentication/anonymousAuthentication
Dependencies	None.
Potential Issues When Removing This Module	At least one authentication module has to be configured. The IIS server core checks after the authentication phase if the HttpUser object is populated. The HttpUser object is an IIS data structure. A 401.2 error is generated without an authentication populating the HttpUser object.

Module Name	CertificateMappingAuthenticationModule
Description	Maps SSL client certificates to an Active Directory account (Active Directory Certificate Mapping).
Configuration Sections	system.webServer/security/authentication/clientCertificateMapping Authentication
Dependencies	SSL has to be configured for this module to work. The IIS machine has also to be a member of an Active Directory domain.
Potential Issues When Removing This Module	Requests would be allowed if Active Directory Certificate Mapping is used to protect a directory but the module is removed!

Module Name	BasicAuthenticationModule
Description	Implements HTTP Basic authentication described in RFC 2617.
Configuration Sections	system.webServer/security/authentication/basicAuthentication
Dependencies	None.
Potential Issues When Removing This Module	At least one authentication module has to be configured. The IIS server core checks after the authentication phase if the HttpUser object is populated. The HttpUser object is an IIS data structure. A 401.2 error is generated without an authentication populating the HttpUser object.

Module Name	**WindowsAuthenticationModule**
Description	Implements Windows authentication (NTLM or Negotiate (Kerberos)).
Configuration Sections	system.webServer/security/authentication/windowsAuthentication
Dependencies	None.
Potential Issues When Removing This Module	At least one authentication module has to be configured. The IIS server core checks after the authentication phase if the HttpUser object is populated. The HttpUser object is an IIS data structure. A 401.2 error is generated without an authentication populating the HttpUser object.

Module Name	**DigestAuthenticationModule**
Description	Implements digest authentication described in RFC 2617.
Configuration Sections	system.webServer/security/authentication/digestAuthentication
Dependencies	IIS server needs to be part of an Active Directory domain.
Potential Issues When Removing This Module	At least one authentication module has to be configured. The IIS server core checks after the authentication phase if the HttpUser object is populated. The HttpUser object is an IIS data structure. A 401.2 error is generated without an authentication populating the HttpUser object.

Module Name	**IISCertificateMappingAuthenticationModule**
Description	Implements IIS certificate mapping. Maps SSL client certificates to a Windows account. User credentials and mapping rules are stored within the IIS configuration store contrary to Active Directory Certificate mapping
Configuration Sections	system.webServer/iisClientCertificateMappingAuthentication
Dependencies	SSL with the requirement to receive client certificates has to be configured for this module to work.
Potential Issues When Removing This Module	At least one authentication module has to be configured. The IIS server core checks after the authentication phase if the HttpUser object is populated. The HttpUser object is an IIS data structure. A 401.2 error is generated without an authentication populating the HttpUser object.

Module Name	UrlAuthorizationModule
Description	Implements authorization based on configuration rules
Configuration Sections	system.webServer/security/authorization
Dependencies	None.
Potential Issues When Removing This Module	Authorization rules that protect content are not evaluated anymore. Content that was supposed to be protected might be served.

Module Name	IsapiModule
Description	Implements Isapi Extension functionality.
Configuration Sections	system.webServer/isapiCgiRestriction
Dependencies	None.
Potential Issues When Removing This Module	ISAPI Extensions mapped in the <handlers> section (modules= "IsapiModule") or explicitely called Isapi Extensions won't work anymore.

Module Name	IsapiFilterModule
Description	Implements Isapi filter functionality.
Configuration Sections	system.webServer/isapiFilters
Dependencies	None.
Potential Issues When Removing This Module	ISAPI filters often implement functionality applications rely on. Examples are ASP.NET or SharePoint. ASP.NET for example needs the aspnet_filter.dll to protect sensitive content and to rewrite URLs. Removing this module will prevent IIS from loading ISAPI filters and applications might stop working or might expose sensitive content.

Module Name	IpRestrictionModule
Description	Implements an authorization scheme which is based on the IPv4 address of the client request.
Configuration Sections	system.webServer/security/ipSecurity
Dependencies	IPv4 stack has to be installed.
Potential Issues When Removing This Module	Clients with IP addresses which are on the ipSecurity list will be allowed.

Module Name	RequestFilteringModule
Description	Implements a powerful set of security rules to reject suspicious request at a very early stage. This module is the successor of the ISAPI filter UrlScan.DLL that was shipped for IIS 5 and 6.
Configuration Sections	system.webServer/security/requestFiltering
Dependencies	None.
Potential Issues When Removing This Module	If this module gets removed, the rules specified in the requestFiltering section are not applied anymore. Potential security issues might be the result.

Module Name	CustomLoggingModule
Description	Implements the ILogPlugin interface on top of IIS 7.0. ILogPlugin is an old COM implmentation that allowed customers to extend IIS logging. It is not recommended to extend IIS7 using this interface. Customers are recommended to write a module and subscribe to the RQ_LOG_REQUEST notification.
Configuration Sections	system.webServer/httpLogging and system.applicationhost/sites/site/logFile/customLogPluginClsid
Dependencies	None.
Potential Issues When Removing This Module	A custom log plugin won't be called anymore. Example: ODBC Logging is implemented as ILogPlugin.

Module Name	CustomErrorModule
Description	Implements custom errors and the new IIS7 detailed error feature.
Configuration Sections	system.webServer/httpErrors
Dependencies	None.
Potential Issues When Removing This Module	IIS7 will return blank pages with minimal information when errors within the core server occur.

Module Name	HttpLoggingModule
Description	Implements standard IIS logging by Telling HTTP.SYS what to log.
Configuration Sections	system.applicationHost/log and system.webServer/httpLogging
Dependencies	None.
Potential Issues When Removing This Module	Standard IIS logging won't work anymore.

Module Name	FailedRequestsTracingModule
Description	Implements tracing of failed requests. The definition and rules of what a failed request is can be done via configuration.
Configuration Sections	system.webServer/tracing and system.webServer/httpTracing
Dependencies	None.
Potential Issues When Removing This Module	Tracing HTTP requests won't work anymore.

Module Name	RequestMonitorModule
Description	Implements the IIS 7.0 Run-time State and Control Interface (RSCA). RSCA allows its consumers to query for run-time information like currently executing request, start/stop state of a web-site or currently executing application domains.
Configuration Sections	None.
Dependencies	None.
Potential Issues When Removing This Module	RSCA interface stops working.

Module Name	CgiModule
Description	Implements CGI on top of IIS 7.0
Configuration Sections	system.webServer/cgi and system.webServer/isapiCgiRestriction
Dependencies	None.
Potential Issues When Removing This Module	CGI programs will stop working.

Module Name	TracingModule
Description	Implements ETW tracing.
Configuration Sections	system.webServer/httpTracing
Dependencies	None.
Potential Issues When Removing This Module	ETW tracing won't work if this module is removed.

Module Name	ConfigurationValidationModule
Description	Validates configuration files
Configuration Sections	system.webServer/Validation
Dependencies	None.
Potential Issues When Removing This Module	Implements configuration validation, e.g. if an application runs in integrated mode but has handlers or modules declared in the system.web section.

Managed Modules

Module Name	global.asax
Description	This module ensures that global.asax is executed when an application is started.
Configuration Sections	None.
Dependencies	ManagedEngine module has to be installed.
Potential Issues When Removing This Module	global.asax won't be executed in integrated mode.

Module Name	OutputCache
Description	See ASP.NET 2.0 documentation for details. The native HttpCacheModule implements the OutputCache functionality in native code. This provides a scalable and fast native alternative for the managed output cache.
Configuration Sections	system.web/caching/outputCache
Dependencies	ManagedEngine module has to be installed.
Potential Issues When Removing This Module	Managed content can't store content in the managed output cache anymore.

Module Name	Session
Description	See ASP.NET 2.0 documentation for details.
Configuration Sections	system.web/sessionState
Dependencies	ManagedEngine module has to be installed.
Potential Issues When Removing This Module	Managed session state is not available.

Module Name	WindowsAuthentication
Description	See ASP.NET 2.0 documentation for details.
Configuration Sections	system.web/authentication
Dependencies	ManagedEngine module has to be installed
Potential Issues When Removing This Module	

Module Name	FormsAuthentication
Description	See ASP.NET 2.0 documentation for details.
Configuration Sections	system.web/authentication
Dependencies	ManagedEngine module has to be installed.
Potential Issues When Removing This Module	

Module Name	DefaultAuthentication
Description	See ASP.NET 2.0 documentation for details.
Configuration Sections	system.web/authentication
Dependencies	ManagedEngine module has to be installed/
Potential Issues When Removing This Module	

Module Name	RoleManager
Description	See ASP.NET 2.0 documentation for details.
Configuration Sections	None.
Dependencies	ManagedEngine module has to be installed.
Potential Issues When Removing This Module	Role Manager functionality not available.

Module Name	UrlAuthorization
Description	See ASP.NET 2.0 documentation for details. The native UrlAuthorization module implements URL authorization functionality in native code. This provides a scalable and fast native alternative for the managed URL authorization module.
Configuration Sections	system.web/authorization
Dependencies	ManagedEngine module has to be installed.
Potential Issues When Removing This Module	

Module Name	AnonymousIdentification
Description	See ASP.NET 2.0 documentation for details.
Configuration Sections	
Dependencies	ManagedEngine module has to be installed.
Potential Issues When Removing This Module	

Module Name	Profile
Description	See ASP.NET 2.0 documentation for details.
Configuration Sections	
Dependencies	ManagedEngine module has to be installed.
Potential Issues When Removing This Module	

Module Name	UrlMappingsModule
Description	See ASP.NET 2.0 documentation for details.
Configuration Sections	
Dependencies	ManagedEngine module has to be installed.
Potential Issues When Removing This Module	

B

IIS Status Codes

This Appendix contains the HTTP and FTP status codes, as listed at
http://support.microsoft.com/kb/318380.

HTTP

1xx — Informational

These status codes indicate a provisional response. The client should be prepared to receive one or
more 1xx responses before receiving a regular response.

- ❑   100 — Continue.
- ❑   101 — Switching protocols.

2xx — Success

This class of status codes indicates that the server successfully accepted the client request.

- ❑   200 — OK. The client request has succeeded.
- ❑   201 — Created.
- ❑   202 — Accepted.
- ❑   203 — Non-authoritative information.
- ❑   204 — No content.
- ❑   205 — Reset content.
- ❑   206 — Partial content.

3xx — Redirection

The client browser must take more action to fulfill the request. For example, the browser may have to request a different page on the server or repeat the request by using a proxy server.

- ❏ 301 — Moved permanently.
- ❏ 302 — Object moved.
- ❏ 304 — Not modified.
- ❏ 307 — Temporary redirect.

4xx — Client Error

An error occurs, and the client appears to be at fault. For example, the client may request a page that does not exist, or the client may not provide valid authentication information.

- ❏ 400 — Bad request.
- ❏ 401 — Access denied. IIS defines a number of different 401 errors that indicate a more specific cause of the error. These specific error codes are displayed in the browser but are not displayed in the IIS log:
  - ❏ 401.1 — Logon failed.
  - ❏ 401.2 — Logon failed due to server configuration.
  - ❏ 401.3 — Unauthorized due to ACL on resource.
  - ❏ 401.4 — Authorization failed by filter.
  - ❏ 401.5 — Authorization failed by ISAPI/CGI application.
  - ❏ 401.7 — Access denied by URL authorization policy on the Web server. This error code is specific to IIS 6.0.
- ❏ 403 — Forbidden. IIS defines a number of different 403 errors that indicate a more specific cause of the error.
  - ❏ 403.1 — Execute access forbidden.
  - ❏ 403.2 — Read access forbidden.
  - ❏ 403.3 — Write access forbidden.
  - ❏ 403.4 — SSL required.
  - ❏ 403.5 — SSL 128 required.
  - ❏ 403.6 — IP address rejected.
  - ❏ 403.7 — Client certificate required.
  - ❏ 403.8 — Site access denied.
  - ❏ 403.9 — Too many users.
  - ❏ 403.10 — Invalid configuration.
  - ❏ 403.11 — Password change.

❑   403.12 — Mapper denied access.

❑   403.13 — Client certificate revoked.

❑   403.14 — Directory listing denied.

❑   403.15 — Client Access Licenses exceeded.

❑   403.16 — Client certificate is untrusted or invalid.

❑   403.17 — Client certificate has expired or is not yet valid.

❑   403.18 — Cannot execute requested URL in the current application pool. This error code is specific to IIS 6.0.

❑   403.19 — Cannot execute CGIs for the client in this application pool. This error code is specific to IIS 6.0.

❑   403.20 — Passport logon failed. This error code is specific to IIS 6.0.

❑   404 — Not found.

    ❑   404.0 — (None) — File or directory not found.

    ❑   404.1 — Web site not accessible on the requested port.

    ❑   404.2 — Web service extension lockdown policy prevents this request.

    ❑   404.3 — MIME map policy prevents this request.

❑   405 — HTTP verb used to access this page is not allowed (method not allowed).

❑   406 — Client browser does not accept the MIME type of the requested page.

❑   407 — Proxy authentication required.

❑   412 — Precondition failed.

❑   413 — Request entity too large.

❑   414 — Request-URI too long.

❑   415 — Unsupported media type.

❑   416 — Requested range not satisfiable.

❑   417 — Execution failed.

❑   423 — Locked error.

5xx — Server Error

The server cannot complete the request because it encounters an error.

❑   500 — Internal server error.

    ❑   500.12 — Application is busy restarting on the Web server.

    ❑   500.13 — Web server is too busy.

    ❑   500.15 — Direct requests for Global.asa are not allowed.

❑ 500.16 — UNC authorization credentials incorrect. This error code is specific to IIS 6.0.

❑ 500.18 — URL authorization store cannot be opened. This error code is specific to IIS 6.0.

❑ 500.100 — Internal ASP error.

❑ 501 — Header values specify a configuration that is not implemented.

❑ 502 — Web server received an invalid response while acting as a gateway or proxy.

❑ 502.1 — CGI application timeout.

❑ 502.2 — Error in CGI application.

❑ 503 — Service unavailable. This error code is specific to IIS 6.0.

❑ 504 — Gateway timeout.

❑ 505 — HTTP version not supported.

FTP

1xx — Positive Preliminary Reply

These status codes indicate that an action has started successfully, but the client expects another reply before it continues with a new command.

❑ 110 — Restart marker reply.

❑ 120 — Service ready in nnn minutes.

❑ 125 — Data connection already open; transfer starting.

❑ 150 — File status okay; about to open data connection.

2xx — Positive Completion Reply

An action has successfully completed. The client can execute a new command.

❑ 200 — Command okay.

❑ 202 — Command not implemented, superfluous at this site.

❑ 211 — System status, or system help reply.

❑ 212 — Directory status.

❑ 213 — File status.

❑ 214 — Help message.

❑ 215 — NAME system type, where NAME is an official system name from the list in the Assigned Numbers document.

❑ 220 — Service ready for new user.

❑ 221 — Service closing control connection. Logged out if appropriate.

❑ 225 — Data connection open; no transfer in progress.

❑ 226 — Closing data connection. Requested file action successful (for example, file transfer or file abort).

❑ 227 — Entering passive mode (h1,h2,h3,h4,p1,p2).

❑ 230 — User logged in, proceed.

❑ 250 — Requested file action okay, completed.

❑ 257 — "PATHNAME" created.

3xx — Positive Intermediate Reply

The command was successful, but the server needs additional information from the client to complete processing the request.

❑ 331 — User name okay, need password.

❑ 332 — Need account for login.

❑ 350 — Requested file action pending further information.

4xx — Transient Negative Completion Reply

The command was not successful, but the error is temporary. If the client retries the command, it may succeed.

❑ 421 — Service not available, closing control connection. This may be a reply to any command if the service knows it must shut down.

❑ 425 — Cannot open data connection.

❑ 426 — Connection closed; transfer aborted.

❑ 450 — Requested file action not taken. File unavailable (for example, file busy).

❑ 451 — Requested action aborted: Local error in processing.

❑ 452 — Requested action not taken. Insufficient storage space in system.

5xx — Permanent Negative Completion Reply

The command was not successful, and the error is permanent. If the client retries the command, it receives the same error.

❑ 500 — Syntax error, command unrecognized. This may include errors such as command line too long.

❑ 501 — Syntax error in parameters or arguments.

❑ 502 — Command not implemented.

❑ 503 — Bad sequence of commands.

❑   504 — Command not implemented for that parameter.

❑   530 — Not logged in.

❑   532 — Need account for storing files.

❑   550 — Requested action not taken. File unavailable (for example, file not found, no access).

❑   551 — Requested action aborted: Page type unknown.

❑   552 — Requested file action aborted. Exceeded storage allocation
       (for current directory or dataset).

❑   553 — Requested action not taken. File name not allowed.

C

WCF Primer

This short primer introduces you to the fundamentals of Windows Communication Foundation (WCF), Microsoft's new, unified programming model for service-oriented applications. WCF first shipped with Microsoft .NET Framework v3 and is included with Windows Server 2008. It shares several components with IIS 7.0, including the ability to be hosted by IIS 7.0, though not necessarily exposed over HTTP.

Service-Oriented Applications

Traditionally, applications have been object-oriented (see Figure C-1). In this model, a set of classes provides a template for objects. An application creates instances of these classes (known as *object instances*) at run time. These objects expose interfaces, methods, and properties that allow other objects to manipulate them. A program written in such a way is generally said to be "tightly coupled" because each object (whether running on a single machine or across multiple machines) needs to understand the "types" (for example, strings, integers, and other object types) that are being passed to it. Implementing such a consistent type system can be difficult across multiple platforms and technologies.

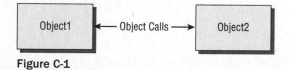

Figure C-1

In contrast, service-oriented programming involves a set of discrete services that interact with each other via messages (see Figure C-2). The services do not need to share a common type system. Instead, each service shares a schema that describes the data that it accepts, and a contract that defines its behaviors. Web Services (ASP.NET or otherwise) are an example of service-oriented programming.

Figure C-2

Service-oriented programming is not designed to replace object-oriented programming entirely. Instead, it's designed to allow for loosely coupled services that can be flexibly deployed in a distributed environment, regardless of the underlying platform hosting the service. Object-oriented programming can be used to write or program the actual services themselves.

The four central tenets of service-oriented programming are

- ❏ **Boundaries Are Explicit** — Service boundaries are formally and explicitly defined, and a service makes no assumptions about what lies beyond its own boundaries. This allows for flexible deployment of services that need to interact with each other, but requires discipline on the part of architects and developers, as service calls can be expensive if they cross geographic regions or trust domains. In contrast, object-oriented programming generally tries to abstract the notion of remote (distributed) or local objects from the developer, thus it's not always obvious what costs or assumptions are made when calling another object.

- ❏ **Services Are Autonomous** — A service should not depend on a called service being available or even located in a specific location. There is no central authority responsible for the management or versioning of services. In contrast, object-oriented programming typically requires an entire application to be redeployed, or clients to be updated, if a component within that application is changed.

- ❏ **Services Share Schemata and Contacts** — Services share the data they will exchange via schemata and the behaviors they expose via contracts. The internal implementation of how a service operates is hidden from outside view. In contract, object-oriented programming typically involves the passing of objects and types, leading to a tightly coupled environment.

- ❏ **Compatibility Is Policy-Based** — Services use policies to determine what they share in common and how they can interact with each other. Changing a service's access right does not involve changing any internal service configuration, but, rather, updating a machine readable policy.

WCF and ASP.NET Web Services

WCF can be thought of as the successor to ASP.NET Web Services. ASP.NET Web Services is tightly coupled to the HTTP protocol as a transport, and a verbose, text-based binary message format.

In many applications, requirements dictate the use of alternate communication mechanisms — for example, the use of .NET Remoting when application responsiveness and performance are paramount. WCF brings these disparate pieces together, allowing service-oriented development across a range of protocols and services.

WCF supports service calls to be routed across HTTP, named pipes, MSMQ, and TCP.

WAS and WCF

In addition to supporting additional protocol transports, WCF services can also be hosted outside IIS. WCF services can be hosted:

- ❑   In a client-managed application (that is, a stand-alone .exe .NET application).

- ❑   In a managed service (that is, a Windows NT service written using .NET).

- ❑   In IIS 6.0 (Windows Server 2003 and Windows XP x64) or IIS 5.1 (Windows XP x86), in a similar way to ASP.NET Web Services.

- ❑   In IIS 7.0 with Windows Process Activation Services.

In IIS 6.0, the Web Activation Service (WAS) was responsible for reading the IIS metabase and activating new worker processes (w3wp.exe) when incoming HTTP requests were received by the system. In Windows Server 2008, the Windows Process Activation Service has been separated out from the W3SVC service into its own discrete service. Both W3SVC and WAS live in a shared svchost.exe process (but can be independently started and stopped). W3SVC is still responsible for incoming HTTP requests, but WAS is now available system-wide for process activation and handling (recycling, monitoring, and so forth).

One of the main reasons to separate out the Windows Process Activation Service was to support WCF. As WCF supports several underlying transports, incoming requests routed across those transports can be received by transport listener adapters. If the WCF service is hosted by IIS 7.0, then WAS will examine the destination of the request and, if required, activate a new process (w3wp.exe) to host the service. WCF services hosted this way gain the benefits of process management by WAS (on-demand activation, inactivity timeout deactivation, recycling, and so forth). The W3SVC service is still responsible for receiving incoming HTTP requests (from Http.sys), but it communicates with WAS using the same adapter interface that WCF listener adapters use, as shown in Figure C-3.

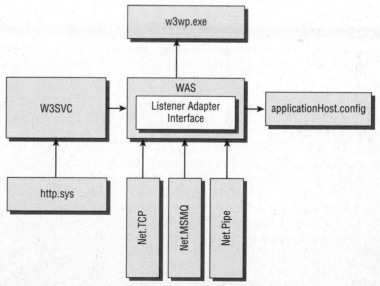

Figure C-3

applicationHost.config isn't called webServer.config (or similar) because it is read by WAS in order to determine how processes should be managed, both on behalf of IIS and WCF, and any other platform that chooses to utilize WAS.

In this way, IIS 7.0 can host applications such as WCF services without necessarily exposing them over HTTP, while still deriving benefits from the IIS 7.0 infrastructure (such as on-demand creation of w3wp.exe processes, process recycling, and so forth).

Configuring a WCF Application

Developing and deploying a WCF service are beyond the scope of this primer. However, as an IIS Administrator, you might be called upon to deploy WCF services on IIS 7.0 in a similar way to deploying other applications. A brief summary of configuration items is presented here. For more information on WCF, see *Professional WCF Programming: .NET Development with the Windows Communication Foundation*.

Initially, you will need to install WCF HTTP and/or non-HTTP Activation features. This can be done by installing the Application Server Role or by specifically installing the WCF HTTP and/or WCF non-HTTP Activation Features (located under .NET Framework v3) via Server Manager. For more information on installing roles and features, see Chapter 4, "Installing IIS 7.0."

To configure a web site to support non-HTTP-based activation, the web site's bindings need to be updated to support the additional protocols. In a similar way to adding additional HTTP or FTP bindings, you can use AppCmd.exe or the GUI. To use the IIS Manager Administrative Tool, see Chapter 6, "Web-Site Administration." To use AppCmd to add an additional binding, run the following code:

```
appcmd.exe set site "Default Web Site"
-+bindings.[protocol='net.tcp',bindingInformation='8080:*']
```

This adds an additional Net.TCP binding for port 8080 to the Default Web Site.

Beyond the additional binding, the web application that will be hosting the WCF service needs to have the NET.TCP protocol enabled. By default, web applications are HTTP-enabled. You can add an additional protocol using the IIS Manager Administrative Tool, or by using AppCmd, as follows:

```
appcmd.exe set app "Default Web Site/Application1" /enabledProtocols:http,net.tcp
```

Each web application in IIS 7.0 is assigned to a web application pool. This assignment determines which applications run in which w3wp.exe worker processes. Assigning a WCF application to a web application pool is no different from assigning any other HTTP-based application to a web application pool. Again, this can be done using the GUI or via AppCmd. For more information on web application pools and assigning web applications to them, see Chapter 8, "Web Application Pool Administration."

Finally, each WCF service may have configuration in its own configuration file. These settings are stored in the web.config file located in the application's root folder. Just as IIS 7.0 settings are stored in the <system.webServer></system.webServer> configuration container, and ASP.NET settings are stored in the <system.web></system.web>, WCF settings are stored in the <system.serviceModel> </system.serviceModel> section.

Just as there are innumerable settings for ASP.NET and IIS 7.0 that can be configured, there are many WCF settings that can be set. However, the endpoint attributes are generally configured in this configuration file, as this gives flexibility when deploying the application to different environments. Other attributes can be configured declaratively in the file or programmatically within the code of the service itself. The following configuration enables NET.TCP endpoints.

```
<system.serviceModel>
    <services>
        <service name="Application1">
            <!-- exposes the endpoint
net.tcp://servername:8080/Application1/service.svc -->
            <endpoint address="" binding="netTCPBinding" />
        </service>
    </services>
</system.serviceModel>
```

Generally, these configurations would be done by the developer of the application, and the configuration file then simply placed into the root folder of the WCF service.

As an IIS Administrator, you may be called on to deploy a WCF service or application in a similar way to deploying an ASP.NET application or web service. Deploying a WCF service that is hosted by IIS 7.0 involves making changes to configuration that are stored in the same configuration files that IIS 7.0 stores its own configuration in. This configuration information is read by WAS and used to initialize and manage worker processes in a similar way that worker processes for traditional web applications are managed.

D

Resources

This appendix lists several useful resources and links that can serve as additional reading and reference material for IIS Administrators.

IIS Product Group Resources

The IIS Product Group maintains the `www.iis.net` web site as a central repository for IIS-related resources, including downloads, walkthroughs, team blogs, and support forums. Readers may find the following sections particularly helpful:

❏ `http://forums.iis.net` hosts a set of forums for IIS issues, with members of the IIS Product Group, Microsoft MVPs, and Microsoft PSS staff assisting posters with issues and questions.

❏ `http://blogs.iis.net` hosts blogs of team members from the IIS Product Group.

❏ `www.iis.net/downloads/default.aspx?tabid=3` provides a set of downloads and add-ons for IIS 7.0 (and also for previous versions), from the IIS Product Group, from Microsoft, and from third parties. The major add-ons mentioned in this book (such as FTP 7) can be downloaded from here.

IIS Public Newsgroups

Microsoft also maintains an extensive set of newsgroups covering many products (including IIS). Various Microsoft personnel and MVPs can be found in these groups. Newsgroups can be accessed using a news reader (such as Vista's Windows Mail or Windows XP's Outlook Express). The following are some of the more popular IIS-related newsgroups:

❏ `news://news.microsoft.com/microsoft.public.inetserver.iis`

❑ `news://news.microsoft.com/microsoft.public.inetserver.iis.security`

These newsgroups are also accessible via a Web interface on the Microsoft Communities web site, located at `www.microsoft.com/communities/newsgroups/default.mspx`.

Standards Documents

Throughout the book, we have referred to various standards. For many protocols and applications, these standards are contained in RFC (Request for Comments) documents lodged with the Internet Society (ISOC). Some of these RFCs are subsequently adopted by the Internet Engineering Task Force (IETF) as Internet Standards.

There are several RFC repositories available on the Web. One of the more popular is `www.rfcs.org`, which allows you to retrieve any RFC by number or by searching text.

Some of the RFCs mentioned in this book include

❑ **HTTP v1,1** — RFC 2616.

❑ **SMTP and ESTMP** — RFCs 1123 and 2821, respectively.

❑ **MIME** — RFCs 2045 through 2049 and RFC 1521.

❑ **Digest Authentication** — RFC 2617.

❑ **Kerberos v5** — RFC 4120.

❑ **FTPS** — RFC 4217.

Blogs

In addition to the IIS Product Group team blogs mentioned earlier, many Microsoft staff members maintain blogs at either `http://blogs.msdn.com` (for developers) or `http://blogs.technet.com` (for administrators).

The following third-party IIS blogs maintained by MVPs may also be of interest:

❑ **Scott Forsyth** — `http://weblogs.asp.net/owscott/`

❑ **Bernard Cheah** — `http://msmvps.com/bernard/`

❑ **Paul Lynch** — `http://www.iisadmin.co.uk/`

❑ **Ken Schaefer** — `http://adopenstatic.com/blog`

❑ **Chris Crowe** — `http://blog.crowe.co.nz/`

Microsoft Documentation

As of this writing, documentation on the Microsoft site was still in beta, thus the links below may change when Windows Server 2008 and .NET v3.5 are released.

❑ **IIS 7.0 Technical Reference (Beta)** — `http://technet2.microsoft.com/windowsserver2008/en/servermanager/webserver.mspx`.

❑ **IIS 7.0 Native Code Core Reference (Beta)** — `http://msdn2.microsoft.com/en-us/library/ms692081.aspx`

❑ **IIS 7.0 Managed Code reference (Beta)** — `http://msdn2.microsoft.com/en-us/library/aa347649.aspx`

❑ **ISAPI reference (IIS 6.0)** — `http://msdn2.microsoft.com/en-us/library/ms524911.aspx`

Third-Party Products and Tools

The following are links to the third-party tools or products mentioned in this book:

❑ **Symantec i^3 for Web Applications** — `www.symantec.com/enterprise/products/overview.jsp?pcid=2246&pvid=i3_webapps_1`.

❑ **Microsoft Windows Server 2003 Performance Advisor** — `www.microsoft.com/downloads`.

❑ **Mercury SiteScope** — `www.mercury.com/us/products/business-availability-center/sitescope/features.html`.

❑ **WebTrends** — `www.webtrends.com/`.

❑ **Tivoli Monitoring for Web Infrastructure** — `www-306.ibm.com/software/tivoli/products/monitor-web/`.

Security Documentation

A number of security papers were referenced in the main body of the book, and are listed here:

❑ **Eric Glass' NTLM Whitepaper** — `http://davenport.sourceforge.net/ntlm.html`

❑ **Configuring URL Authorization walkthrough** — `http://www.iis.net/articles/onepagearticle.ashx/IIS7/Managing-IIS7/Configuring-Security/URL-Authorization/Understanding-IIS7-URL-Authorization`

❑ **Brian Tung's the Moron's Guide to Kerberos** — `http://www.isi.edu/~brian/security/kerberos.html`

Index